Tonal Harmony
in Concept
and Practice

Tonal Harmony in Concept and Practice

Third Edition

Allen Forte

Yale University

Holt, Rinehart and Winston
New York   Chicago   San Francisco
Atlanta   Dallas   Montreal   Toronto

Copyright © 1979, 1974, 1962 by Holt, Rinehart and Winston

Library of Congress Cataloging in Publication Data

Forte, Allen

Tonal Harmony in Concept and Practice, Third Edition

  Includes indexes.
  1. Harmony. I. Title,
MT50.F713T7   1979   781.3   78-12229

ISBN: 0-03-020756-8

Printed in the United States of America

9 0 1 2 3   XXX   9 8 7 6 5 4 3 2 1

Preface

This third edition of *Tonal Harmony in Concept and Practice* introduces certain changes in emphasis, notably the early inclusion of the four-voice exercise in chorale style, which parallels the keyboard-style exercise of the earlier editions. It is believed that this will enhance the treatment of voice-leading situations, providing the student with additional practice in finding interesting (and correct) solutions.

The new edition also includes a number of small but nonetheless important corrections and elaborations intended to clarify certain important points throughout.

Changes of larger scale are the addition of a Summary of Figured Bass and a Summary of Voice-Leading Guidelines and Rules. Both should be useful to student and teacher alike.

As every teacher knows, the successful completion of exercises is of the utmost importance to the study of harmony. Accordingly, the third edition of *Tonal Harmony in Concept and Practice* has added a number of exercises throughout the text in order to give the teacher a wider choice and to provide the student with additional materials. These added exercises, like most of the exercises in the previous editions, are based on actual music.

The educational purpose of this edition remains the same as that of the previous two editions: to prepare the student for the advanced study of tonal music through a thorough study of tonal harmony. It is hoped that the prose explanations and the large number of musical examples and exercises will provide for a broad background in basic aspects of tonal music.

The author is very grateful to David Smith for his many valuable suggestions and to Steven E. Gilbert, who also made significant recommendations that have been carried out in the third edition.

A.F.

Hamden, Connecticut
January, 1978

42 81

Contents

Tonal Harmony in Concept and Practice

1

Structural Characteristics of the Fundamental Materials

Composition *consists in two things only. The first is the ordering and disposing of several sounds . . . in such a manner that their succession pleases the ear. This is what the Ancients called* melody. *The second is the rendering audible of two or more simultaneous sounds in such a manner that their combination is pleasant. This is what we call* harmony, *and it alone merits the name of composition.*

Jean Benjamin de Laborde, 1780

By tradition, harmony study has been closely associated with the study of composition, with the study of the way in which tonal materials are organized to become music. This is not without justification, for the concepts of harmony are both basic and comprehensive. They stand at the very foundation of the art and reach forth to include its most elaborate expressions. The purpose of this book is to unfold those concepts and at the same time to present techniques that will enable the student to compose coherent and effective tonal music. To this end specific experiences are provided in the form of carefully planned exercises, exercises which contribute toward the ultimate goal: increased understanding of the art form. Without question this is the most important result of genuine technical training in music.

The primary aim of serious music study is to illuminate the subject, not to surround it with trivia and bury it beneath detail. At the same time one must realize that a technical approach to music, like a technical approach to any subject,

1

involves specific tasks that are often detailed. These include the learning of a new terminology, the memorizing of certain facts, and the intelligent working out of exercises in order to achieve basic skills. Without these one cannot hope to approach the general concepts essential to the art, nor can one attain the level of minimal ability that will enable him to enjoy the rewards of creative activity.

Let us begin by considering important characteristics of the fundamental materials.

1. Scale and Key

A scale is more than an exercise for fingers or vocal cords; it can also take the shape of a musical theme:

example 1. BEETHOVEN: *Piano Trio in B♭ major, Op. 97* ("Archduke")

This theme contains the seven different notes that belong to the key of B♭ major: B♭, C, D, E♭, F, G, and A. Thus it is not only an ascending scale but also a complete melodic statement of the key of B♭ major. By "key" we refer not in this instance to the key signature of two flats but to the collection of notes listed above, the scale. These scale degrees, as they are called, relate to one another in certain ways that are of the utmost significance for harmony. Accordingly, we are far more interested in the relationships between the scale degrees than in their letter names.

2. Chord and Interval

If we consider the Beethoven theme in Example 1 more carefully we see that certain scale degrees are stressed, while others are passed over without emphasis. The accented notes are marked by asterisks in the next example.

example 2.

If these accented notes are extracted from the theme and arranged vertically we obtain a harmony or *chord,* a group of notes which sound simultaneously.

example 3.

The notes of the chord are separated by spaces, spaces that before were filled by the *scale degrees.* These spaces, called *intervals,* are of fundamental importance to harmony, for they are used to measure and describe chord structure and succession.

Intervals are named according to the number of scale degrees they encompass. The intervals of the chord extracted from the Beethoven theme will serve well to illustrate this:

example 4.

In Example 4 the lowest note of the chord has been paired with each of the other chord notes in succession to form intervals of three different sizes. The first of these intervals encompasses three scale degrees: Bb, C, and D. Therefore it is called a *third* (written as 3rd). The next interval, from Bb to F, encompasses five scale degrees: Bb, C, D, Eb, and F, and therefore is called a *fifth* (written as 5th). The last interval, from Bb to Bb, spans eight scale degrees: Bb, C, D, Eb, F, G, A, and Bb; accordingly it is called an *octave* (written in musical notation as 8ve).

The smallest interval in tonal music is the *second* (2nd), an interval that encompasses only two notes. This is the interval we find between one scale degree and the next—for example, from Bb to C in the Bb major scale. The 2nd has two sizes, a fact easily verified by looking at a piano keyboard. We see that within the 2nd from Bb to C lies a third key, notated either as B♮ or as Cb. Moving up to the next 2nd in the Bb scale, from C to D, we also find a third key in the middle, notated as C♯ or Db. However, the 2nd just above, from D to Eb, contains no extra key; it is smaller than the two 2nds below it. This small 2nd, the 2nd which encompasses two scale degrees with no note between (D to Eb), is called a *minor 2nd.* The large 2nd, which encompasses two scale notes with one note between (Bb to C), is called a *major 2nd.* Thus the scale consists of the fixed succession of major and minor 2nds shown in the next example.

example 5.

One can easily remember the structure of the *major scale* by noting that the minor 2nd occurs twice: between scale degrees 3 and 4 and again between scale degrees 7 and 8. All other 2nds in the scale are major.

The major scale degrees require no sharps or flats (*accidentals*) other than those in the key signature. However, if we wish to represent the notes that lie within the major 2nds we must use accidentals. Such notes which do not belong to the key are called *chromatic* notes. When all five chromatic notes are combined with the unaltered scale degrees we have a scale called the *chromatic scale*. Example 6 shows the unaltered scale, or *diatonic* scale, at (*a*). The five chromatic notes are shown at (*b*), and the combined scale or chromatic scale is shown at (*c*).

example 6.

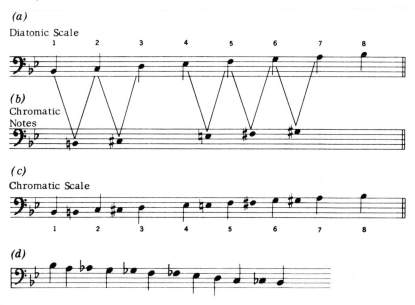

The minor 2nd is often called a *half step* or, by some writers, a *semitone*. The major 2nd is frequently called a *whole step* or *whole tone*. The terms half step and whole step are very convenient, and we shall use them a great deal. For example, in the naming of intervals the diatonic scale provides the measurement of general size

(2nd, 3rd, and so on) while the specific size of the interval is described in terms of half steps. Thus, we say that the minor 2nd is one half step smaller than the major 2nd, or that the major 2nd contains two half steps. The *chromatic scale* therefore is a series of half steps which comprises all the pitches of our equal-tempered system. From the standpoint of tonal music it is not an independent scale, but derives from the diatonic scale, as shown by Example 6.

In Example 6 at (d) the descending form of the chromatic scale is shown. Notice that the spelling of the non-diatonic notes has changed, compared with Example 6 (c). For example, in the descending form C♭ stands between C and B♭ whereas B occupies the corresponding position in the ascending form of the scale. In this case C♭ is said to be *enharmonically equivalent* to B. The two notes have the same sound on the keyboard, but C♭ descends to B♭, whereas B ascends to C.

3. Key Signatures and Diatonic Scale Structure

The sharps and flats in the various key signatures serve to fix the half steps between scale degrees 3 and 4 and 7 and 8. Thus, in the key of C no accidentals are required for the half steps. They occur naturally without accidentals.

example 7.

However, if we construct a scale upward from another note, say G, without accidentals we discover that a whole step occurs between scale degrees 7 and 8 instead of the required half step:

example 8.

This makes clear the relation between key signature and scale structure. The one sharp in the key signature of G major raises scale degree 7 to create the required half step, the leading note progression.

example 9.

If we proceed from the key of one sharp to the key of two sharps, of three sharps . . ., we discover that each added sharp applies to scale degree 7:

example 10.

Similarly, the single flat in the key of F major creates a half step between scale degrees 3 and 4.

example 11.

And each added flat applies to scale degree 4.

example 12.

4. The Minor Scale and Chord

Like the major scale, the minor scale can also be expressed as a theme. We quote from the opening of a Bach work:

example 13. J. S. BACH: *Concerto for Solo Harpsichord and Orchestra in D minor*

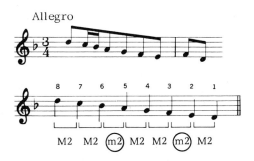

Directly below the theme is represented in equal note values the scale upon which it is based. Like the major scale this minor scale contains two minor 2nds (half steps). However, in the natural or unaltered minor scale they occur between scale degrees 2 and 3 and scale degrees 5 and 6.

If we extract the accented notes of the Bach theme in Example 13 and arrange them in vertical order as we did those of the Beethoven theme in Example 3 the chord shown in Example 14(*a*) is obtained.

example 14.

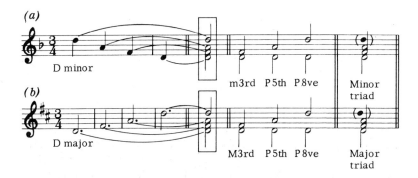

Directly below Example 14a we again present the Beethoven chord from Example 3, transposed to D major for easier comparison with the minor example. The intervals of each chord have been sorted out, as in Example 4, for identification and comparison. The lowest chordal interval in the minor key (Example 14a) is a' small 3rd, encompassing three half steps. This is commonly known as a *minor 3rd*

(m3rd). In contrast, the lowest chordal interval in the major key (Example 14b) is a large 3rd, or *major 3rd* (M3) encompassing four half steps.

The next chordal interval is the same in both minor and major. It encompasses seven half steps and is known as the *perfect 5th* (P5th). Lastly we find the *perfect 8ve*, which is also the same in both minor and major keys. It spans the entire array of twelve half steps and plays a special role in tonal harmony which is explained in the next section.

5. Octave Equivalence

The notes which form the 8ve always have the same letter name. One of the most fundamental axioms of tonal music is that notes which bear the same name are equivalent. We call this the axiom of *8ve equivalence*. It reads: A note which stands at the interval of an 8ve from another note and which has the same letter name is regarded as a duplication or 8ve *doubling* of that note, not as an additional and different chordal element. For this reason only three different notes are counted in the chords shown in Example 14. These three-note chords are called *triads*.

6. The Triad

Defined more precisely, a triad is a three-note chord that contains the intervals of a 3rd and a 5th, measured upward from the lowest note, called the *fundamental* or *root*. The last part of the definition is of the utmost importance since in tonal music we measure chordal intervals from the bottom up, not from the top down or from the inside out. Thus the difference between major and minor triads is a difference in the size of the first interval above the fundamental: the minor triad contains a minor 3rd, the major triad contains a major 3rd. Both triads contain perfect 5ths.

7. Arpeggiation of the Triad; Parallel Major and Minor Keys

The following examples present two themes, one based upon the major triad and one upon the minor triad.

example 15. BEETHOVEN: *Fifth Symphony*

example 16. BEETHOVEN: *Piano Concerto in C minor, Op. 37*

The theme in Example 15 opened with a horizontal statement of the major triad on C. A horizontal chord statement of this kind is also known as an *arpeggiation* of the chord. The theme shown in Example 16 opens in a strikingly similar way, but with an arpeggiation of the C minor triad.

When a major and minor scale both begin with the same note, as in the case of C major and C minor in the themes above, they are called *parallel.* Thus we say that the parallel major key of C minor is C major, the parallel minor of C major is C minor. The key which shares the same key signature but not the same first degree with another scale is called *relative.* Thus, the relative minor of C major is A minor (no sharps or flats in either key signature); the relative major of A minor is C major. The relative minor scale always begins a minor 3rd below a major scale.

We often speak of the major or minor *mode.* The term mode is held over from the pretonal period, during which it had more precise meanings. In tonal music it designates only the general character of the major scale as distinct from the minor scale, and vice versa. Thus we say "the minor mode," referring to the general characteristics of the minor scale, but "the key of C minor," meaning both the specific pitches which comprise that key as well as their relationships.

8. The Auxiliary Note and the Passing Note

The Beethoven themes above also illustrate two melodic events of fundamental significance to the study of harmony. First, in Example 15 attention is drawn to the note marked *aux.*

This abbreviation stands for *auxiliary note,* a note that stands at the interval of a 2nd above or below two occurrences of a more important harmonic note. In this instance the auxiliary note D stands between two C's, C being the more important note since it belongs to the C major triad, the *tonic* triad. The second melodic event of fundamental significance is marked *pn* in Example 16. This abbreviation stands for *passing note,* a note that passes between or connects two more important harmonic notes. Here D, the passing note, stands between E♭ and C, which belong to the C minor triad, the tonic triad in the key of C minor. The passing note differs radically from the auxiliary note. The auxiliary note departs from and returns to the same note. The passing note connects two different notes.

Auxiliary notes and passing notes are often chromatic. In such cases spelling depends upon the function of the note. For instance, in the Haydn theme below we find a chromatic passing note which connects scale degrees 1 and 2. Since the passing note ascends, it is spelled G♯, not A♭. The latter would be the correct spelling for a descending passing note.

example 17. HAYDN: *Symphony in G major, No. 94*

In the passage quoted in Example 18 the chromatic auxiliary note is spelled F♯, not G♭, since it ascends to the main note.

example 18. HAYDN: *Symphony in C minor, No. 95*

It will be observed that the auxiliary note F♯ here is not preceded by the main note, G. This is an example of one form of the *incomplete* auxiliary note. (See section 224.)

9. The Triadic Division of the Diatonic Major and Minor Scales

We have seen that both the diatonic major and the diatonic minor scales contain a triad, a triad whose fundamental note is scale degree 1. Because of its position in the scale this triad, the tonic triad, divides the scale into two parts. The largest interval of the triad, the 5th, delimits the first part of the scale, leaving the upper part of the scale within the interval of a 4th. The resultant *triadic* or *harmonic* division of the scale is illustrated in the following example.

example 19.

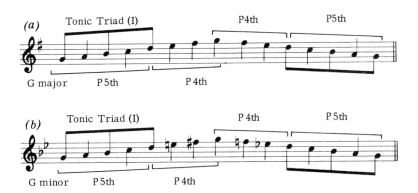

Example 19 shows the diatonic scales both in ascending and descending directions. The division of the scale into 5th and 4th is marked by brackets. The stems of the triadic notes are beamed together.

10.   The Leading Note and the Law of the Half Step

In the upper 4th of the harmonically divided scale we find two passing notes side by side: scale degrees 6 and 7. Of these two passing notes, scale degree 7 is most important since it completes the 8ve scale. It stands at the interval of a half step from the last note of the scale (the 8ve) and has a particularly strong attraction to that note. This can be verified empirically.

example 20.

If one plays or sings the incomplete scale shown in Example 20 he will remark the tendency of scale degree 7 to lead upward to the 8ve and thus to complete the scale. Because it has this strong tendency scale degree 7 is known as the *leading note* (or *leading tone*).

The leading note is only one instance of the operation of an important melodic law, the *law of the half step.* According to this law the strongest, most binding progression from one note to another is the half-step progression. If both whole-step and half-step progressions are available from a given note the half-step progression will always be preferred.

The law of the half step does not mean that, given the choice between a melodic progression involving a half step and a progression involving a whole step, one cannot take the whole step. As with every law there are exceptions, and the exceptions are interesting. For example, it is possible to have a progression over scale degrees 8 7 6 instead of 8 7 8, the latter being in accord with the law of the half step. Similarly, the progression 3 4 5, instead of 3 4 3, is possible. In both cases the harmonies supporting the progressions are of crucial importance. The topic of harmonization, which is central here, will be taken up in Chapter 7.

11. Alteration of Scale Degrees 6 and 7 in Minor

The law of the half step enables us to understand a modification which is normally made in the minor scale. Whenever a melody ascends through the upper 4th, scale degree 7 is raised one half step so as to convert it into a leading note like that of the major scale. At the same time the 6th degree is also raised, for if it were not raised it would tend to descend to scale degree 5 in accord with the law of the half step rather than progress upward as an ascending passing note. Example 21 shows the descending direction of the unaltered passing notes and their ascending direction when altered.

example 21.

half step   whole steps

These alterations of scale degrees 6 and 7 are so common that we do not regard them as genuine chromatic alterations. They have been assimilated as part of the diatonic minor scale. Thus the form of the diatonic minor scale depends upon the direction of melodic progression. In both directions the lower division of the scale, the 5th, remains the same. However, with ascending motion through the upper division, the 4th, scale degrees 6 and 7 must be raised. An example follows.

example 22.   VIVALDI: *Concerto grosso in G minor, Op. 3/2*

The descending scale in the first part of the theme requires no accidentals. It is part of the *natural minor* scale. However, when the scale ascends, the 6th and 7th degrees are raised so that they may serve effectively as ascending passing notes, as explained above. In this form the upper 4th of the minor scale is identical to that of its parallel major. The total minor scale pattern in Example 22, including the descending natural pattern and the ascending altered pattern, is called the *melodic minor scale.*

When the 7th degree is raised but not the 6th, the result is a third form of the minor scale, the *harmonic minor scale.* The following theme is based upon that form.

example 23.   SCHUMANN: *First Symphony*

In accord with the law of the half step, scale degree 6 functions as upper auxiliary note to scale degree 5. Its implicit progression is shown in parentheses in Example 23.

The harmonic minor scale occurs infrequently in melodic statements such as that in Example 23. Its importance lies with harmonic progression, as we shall see in Chapter 4.

The diatonic minor scale therefore has three forms: natural, melodic, and harmonic. They are summarized in Example 24 below.

example 24.

12. The Law of the Half Step as Applied to Scale Degree 4 in Major

The tendency of certain diatonic notes to move by half step has been illustrated in the cases of the leading note and the variable 6th degree of the minor scale. Another special case is scale degree 4 in the major mode, which by virtue of its diatonic position tends to descend to scale degree 3 by half step rather than ascend to scale degree 5 by whole step. Thus, 4 often serves as an upper auxiliary note to 3, as in the next example.

example 25. BRAHMS: *Variations on a Theme by Haydn, Op. 56*

Scale degree 4 serves as auxiliary note to scale degree 3 twice in this short melodic figure. It occurs first in a submetrical, then in a metrical value.

Because of its strong tendency to descend, scale degree 4 is a unidirectional passing note as well as an auxiliary note. Special harmonic conditions are required to make it serve as an ascending passing note.

13. The Inversion of Intervals

We have already mentioned the fact that notes which have the same letter name are regarded as equivalent. This is evident in the following theme.

example 26. MOZART: *Symphony in D major, K.385* ("Haffner")

The half note D in the second measure is not different from the first note of the theme, but merely another occurrence of the same note in a different octave. Both notes are called D. Similarly, all the notes in the third measure are C♯'s and both the notes in the final measure are A's. This reflects the operation of the principle of 8ve equivalence previously described. *Inversion*, a primary technique of chord generation, is dependent upon the principle of 8ve equivalence. We shall consider chord inversion in subsequent chapters; here discussion is limited to interval inversion. This is shown below.

Example 27.

Unison = 8ve

At (a) we have two voices or instruments sounding D at the same pitch level. They form the interval called the *unison*. (Actually, no "interval" is involved since the pitches are exactly the same, but the unison is commonly classed as an interval.) When one note of the unison is placed an 8ve higher, as shown at (b), the unison becomes an 8ve and the two intervals, unison and 8ve, are regarded as interchangeable. Thus interval inversion means the placement of the lower note an 8ve higher or the placement of the higher note an 8ve lower. Example 28 provides another illustration.

example 28. Interval Inversion

(a) lower note   *(b)* higher note
    placed 8ve higher   placed 8ve lower

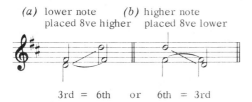

3rd = 6th   or   6th = 3rd

Example 28 shows that when the lower note of a 3rd is placed an 8ve higher the interval of a 6th results (*a*). Similarly, if the upper note of a 6th is placed an 8ve lower the interval of a 3rd results (*b*). We will examine inversions of other intervals after we have considered the dual classification of intervals into consonances and dissonances.

14. Consonant and Dissonant Intervals

In music the terms consonant and dissonant have nothing whatsoever to do with the pleasant or unpleasant quality of a sound. They are technical terms applied to phenomena of motion. The adjective *consonant* is applied to stable intervals, intervals which tend to remain stationary, in contrast to more active intervals called *dissonant* intervals. The intervals that make up the tonic triad are consonant, as is the 8ve which doubles the fundamental note of the triad:

example 29.

Triad   3rd   5th   8ve   6th   4th   unison

Example 29 shows that the triadic intervals and their inversions are consonant with but one exception: the 4th. This interval, the inversion of the consonant 5th, is consonant only under special conditions. (See section 20.)

All diatonic intervals other than the triadic intervals and their inversions are dissonant intervals. Leaving aside the question of the perfect 4th for the moment, we find only three types of dissonant diatonic intervals: the 2nd, the 7th, and the tritone. The first two are shown below.

example 30.

2nd   7th

Example 30 shows that the 2nd inverts to become the 7th. The 7th plays a major role in the generation of dissonant chords, as explained in Chapter 5.

Between scale degrees 6 and 7 in the harmonic minor scale there occurs a 2nd which is larger than the major 2nd by one half step. This is called the *augmented 2nd.* When inverted it becomes a small 7th called a *diminished* 7th:

example 31.

aug. 2nd   dim. 7th

The remaining dissonant diatonic interval occurs between scale degree 4 and the leading note:

example 32.

aug. 4th   dim. 5th

In comparison with other diatonic 4ths the 4th between scale degree 4 and the leading note is oversize by one half step. Whereas the others contain five half steps this one contains six. Therefore it is called an *augmented* 4th. When the augmented 4th is inverted it becomes an undersized 5th—in comparison with the other diatonic 5ths. This small 5th is called *diminished.* Both the augmented 4th and its inversion, the diminished 5th, span six half steps; therefore inversion does not affect the actual size of the augmented 4th, as it does all other intervals. In view of this fact the interval is often called a *tritone,* whether notated as an augmented 4th or as a diminished 5th. The term *tritone* refers to the fact that the interval spans three whole steps (= six half steps).

15. Perfect and Imperfect Consonances

Traditionally the consonant intervals are divided into two types: perfect and imperfect. There are four intervals of each type. Shown in Example 33 are the perfect consonances: the unison and its inversion the 8ve, the 5th and its inversion the 4th, the consonance or dissonance of which is dependent upon its context.

example 33.

unis. 8ve   5th   4th

Diatonic 3rds and 6ths are the imperfect consonances. They are shown below.

example 34.

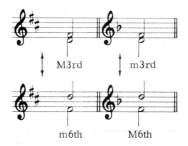

M3rd   m3rd

m6th   M6th

Example 34 shows that the major 3rd inverts to become the small or minor 6th, while the minor 3rd inverts to become the large or major 6th. Like the major and minor 2nds and major and minor 3rds, the two 6ths differ in size by only one half step.

16.   Compound Intervals

In the theme of Mozart's "Haffner" *Symphony,* Example 26, we saw that the principle of 8ve equivalence was not affected by the number of 8ves involved. That is, D above middle C has the same harmonic meaning as D one 8ve higher, two 8ves higher, three 8ves higher, . . . From this we can derive the following rule: the addition of an 8ve to an interval does not change the function of the notes involved. A melodic example follows.

example 35.   BACH: *Fugue in B♭ minor, WTC I*

9th

aux

Here an auxiliary note has been placed an 8ve higher so that it stands at the distance of a 9th, not a 2nd, from the main note. The addition of an 8ve does not affect the function of the note.

Example 36 shows three common compound intervals.

example 36.

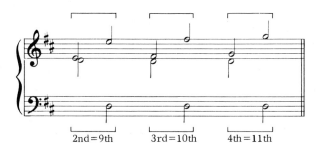

Regardless of the number of 8ves involved only one 8ve is added to the simple interval in naming the compound interval. The compound form of the 2nd therefore is the 9th, of the 3rd the 10th, of the 4th the 11th. The notes of the simple interval do not cross to form the compound interval. Therefore the process differs fundamentally from inversion. As a matter of convention compound intervals larger than a 10th are often expressed in terms of their equivalent simple forms.

17. Chromatic Intervals as Altered Diatonic Intervals

When one note of an interval is chromatic or when both notes are chromatic, the entire interval is called chromatic. Chromatic intervals arise by raising or lowering one or both notes of a diatonic interval, so that the interval is made larger or smaller by the interval of a half step. The rules of terminology, beginning with the smallest interval, are as follows:

> If it is made larger by one half step:
> > a minor interval is called major,
> > a major interval is called augmented,
> > a perfect interval is called augmented,
> > an augmented interval is called doubly augmented.
> If it is made smaller by one half step:
> > a minor interval is called diminished,
> > a major interval is called minor,
> > a perfect interval is called diminished,
> > a diminished interval is called doubly diminished.

Some of these *chromatic alterations* are illustrated in Example 37.

example 37.

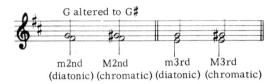

m2nd	M2nd	m3rd	M3rd
(diatonic)	(chromatic)	(diatonic)	(chromatic)

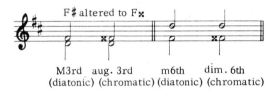

M3rd	aug. 3rd	m6th	dim. 6th
(diatonic)	(chromatic)	(diatonic)	(chromatic)

When naming such altered intervals one must ask two questions. First, what is the name of the interval in its unaltered form? (2nd, 3rd, . . .) Second, does the chromatic alteration make the interval larger or smaller? In connection with the first question we emphasize that chromatic alteration of a diatonic interval does not change the letter names of the notes involved but only adds an accidental to one or both notes. If a letter name is changed we do not have an altered interval, but an entirely different interval. For example, D to F✕ is an augmented 3rd, but D to G, which has the same appearance on the keyboard as D to F✕, is a perfect 4th. Since chromatic alterations always reflect the operation of melodic forces, it is important that they be accurately represented in notation.

18. Summary of Interval Types

Example 38 summarizes the interval types explained in preceding sections. It includes only representatives of each type, not all the available intervals. The keys of C major and C minor are used to give the intervals a diatonic context. The brackets indicate intervals related by inversion. Compound intervals are not shown separately since they are entirely dependent upon the simple intervals from which they derive.

example 38.

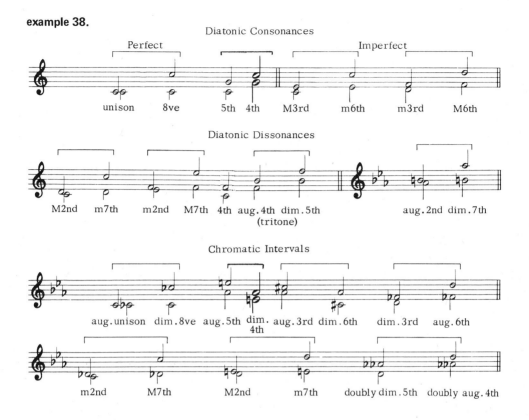

19. Summary of Inversion Nomenclature

With inversion, consonant intervals remain consonant, except for the consonant 5th which becomes a dissonant 4th. Likewise dissonances remain dissonances with inversion. The details of nomenclature are summarized below.

> When inverted,
>> perfect consonances remain perfect, but
>> imperfect consonances change as follows:
>>> major intervals become minor,
>>> minor intervals become major.
> When inverted,
>> minor dissonances become major,
>> major dissonances become minor;
>> augmented intervals become diminished,
>> diminished intervals become augmented.

20. Absolute Interval Values and the Influence of Context

An interval is like a word in that it takes on specific meaning only when it occurs in context with other intervals. Thus, if we open the dictionary and look up the word "land," we find that it is defined as "the solid part of the earth's surface: distinguished from sea." However, this is only one of its meanings. In all, ten definitions are given for the nominal form of the word "land" and ten more for the verbal form. The choice of a particular meaning depends upon the context in which the word occurs. Alone it is ambiguous. Similarly, a musical interval alone is ambiguous. Its precise meaning is revealed only when it is placed in a particular musical context. For the most part, consonant intervals behave like consonances, dissonant intervals like dissonances. However, under certain conditions a consonant interval may behave like a dissonance, a dissonant interval like a consonance. Thus the qualities of consonance and dissonance are not fixed, absolute values, but are subject to the ever-present influence of other elements, other organizing forces. Two of the most important of these are meter and rhythm.

21. Meter and Rhythm

Music is often described as the temporal art, for the dimension of time is crucial to music. In tonal music time is organized and measured out in two ways: by *meter* and by *rhythm*. Both, in turn, serve to organize and articulate melody and harmony. The functions of meter and rhythm are shown in the next example, which again uses the theme quoted at the beginning of this chapter.

example 39.

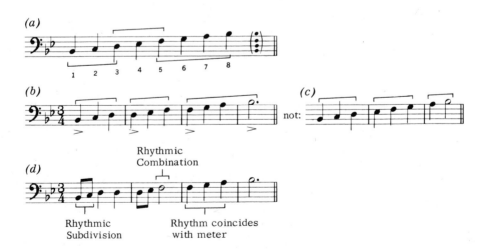

It will be recalled that the Beethoven theme in Example 1 was based upon the ascending B♭ major scale. Example 39(*a*) now shows that scale in equal note values. In connection with Example 1 we demonstrated that the ascending scale contained the B♭ tonic triad. In Example 39(*a*) the intervals of that triad are bracketed and the complete triad is represented in parentheses. However, the triad is not made evident by the succession of quarter notes shown in Example 39(*c*). These notes could group in several ways which would not reveal the underlying triad. But when the scale is measured out in groups of three quarter notes as at (*b*) the triadic intervals become distinct. This, then, is a metrical pattern. It exhibits the two fundamental characteristics of meter: (1) it is based upon a succession of notes of equal duration, and (2) the notes of equal duration are grouped in a regular and repeated pattern by accent. Both characteristics are represented in the notation. The meter signature shows the value which represents one of the equal notes, called the *metrical* unit, and also the number of those notes which form a group or measure. For example, the signature $\frac{3}{4}$ should be read as: "three quarter notes to each measure (group)." The bar line indicates the placement of metrical accent, the accent which marks off each group, or measure. This accent falls on the first note of the group. Secondary metrical accents often occur, but are standardized by tradition and not indicated in the notation.

Repetition is an important factor in the metrical organization of the Beethoven theme in Example 39. Scale degrees 3 and 5 are repeated so that the first note of each triadic interval falls on the accented first beat, or down-beat, of the measure. This repetition is essential, for if the ascending scale were to be measured out in $\frac{3}{4}$ without repetition and follow exactly the metrical succession of quarter notes the pattern shown at (*c*) would result. Clearly this pattern does not reveal the intervals of the tonic triad.

We have discussed the function of meter. Example 39(*d*) shows the function of rhythm in the articulation of the tonic triad that characterizes the Beethoven theme. In contrast to metrical pattern, which is a succession of notes of equal value grouped by regular accent, *rhythmic pattern* often consists of notes of different values, notes which are grouped in various ways, often by irregular accent. Thus, if we regard metrical pattern as the constant, underlying, repetitive pattern, rhythmic pattern is the varied and flexible pattern that is superimposed on the metrical pattern. Rhythmic pattern may act upon metrical pattern in four ways: (1) it may divide the metrical unit into notes of shorter duration; (2) it may combine metrical units into notes of longer duration; (3) it may shift or displace the metrical accent; (4) it may coincide exactly with the metrical pattern. In the Beethoven theme shown in Example 39(*d*) the rhythmic pattern relates to the underlying metrical pattern in three of these ways. In the first measure the rhythmic pattern subdivides the first quarter note, the metrical unit, into two shorter notes, eighth notes. In the second measure the rhythmic pattern combines two quarter notes into a longer note, the half note. In the third measure the rhythmic pattern coincides exactly with the metrical pattern. Thus each measure has a different pattern and each interval of the unfolding triad is expressed in a different way; yet the phrase as a whole is unified by the underlying metrical pattern. This careful adjustment of metrical and rhythmic pattern is not a matter of happenstance. Beethoven's sketches offer abundant evidence of the care he gave to just such details as these.

The only rhythmic operation not included in the Beethoven theme is shift or displacement. This can be seen in the following theme.

example 40. MOZART: *Symphony in D major, K.504* ("Prague")

At (a) we see the theme as it would be without rhythmic displacement; at (b), the theme as the composer wrote it. We find a rhythmic displacement of the metrical pattern in the third and fourth measures. A displacement of this kind is often called a *syncopation.*

Of most significance to harmonic and melodic development are shift of metrical accent and division of the metrical unit. Division, in particular, is so important that when we describe the function of melodic notes we must distinguish carefully between *metrical* durations—notes that have the value of the metrical unit or larger—and *submetrical* durations—notes of lesser duration than the metrical unit. Thus in the example below we describe the melody at (a) as a metrical arpeggiation, while we describe the passing eighth notes at (b) as submetrical passing notes.

example 41.

22. Simple and Compound Meter

Before we leave the topic of meter we must review certain essential terms and classifications. Meters are simple or compound. The simple meters either have two units per measure with the primary metrical accent falling on the first ($\frac{2}{8}$, $\frac{2}{4}$, $\frac{2}{2}$ or ¢), three units per measure with the primary metrical accent falling on the first ($\frac{3}{8}$, $\frac{3}{4}$, $\frac{3}{2}$), or four units per measure with a primary accent on the first and a secondary accent on the third ($\frac{4}{8}$, $\frac{4}{4}$ or C, $\frac{4}{2}$). The two-unit meter is called *duple* meter, the three-unit meter *triple* meter, the four-unit meter *quadruple* meter.

Often the rhythmic pattern divides each metrical unit into three equal durations, as in the following excerpt.

example 42. BRAHMS: *Intermezzo in A major, Op. 76/6*

Each group of three notes is called a *triplet.* When such a triplet pattern is continued throughout a composition it becomes in effect a new metrical pattern and is usually notated as a *compound meter:* a triplet subdivision superimposed upon a simple meter. In the excerpt below, the compound meter signature $\frac{6}{8}$ represents a continuous subdivision of this kind.

example 43. BRAHMS: *Intermezzo in E♭ major, Op. 117/1*

Compound meters retain the unit and the accent pattern of the simple meter from which they derive. Thus in $\frac{6}{8}$ the unit is the dotted quarter note and the metrical pattern remains duple in essence.

Example 44 (below) shows the common metrical patterns and illustrates the three primary rhythmic operations. In each case meter and rhythm combine to form a metric-rhythmic pattern which organizes the notes of the ascending major scale.

Example 44 also makes clear the basic similarity of all the metrical patterns of a particular type. For instance, the duple meters are essentially the same whether the unit is the eighth, the quarter, or the half note.

example 44. Common Metric-Rhythmic Patterns

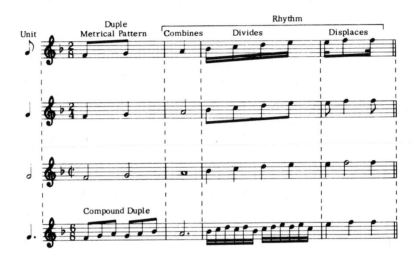

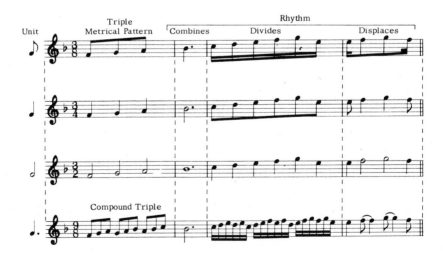

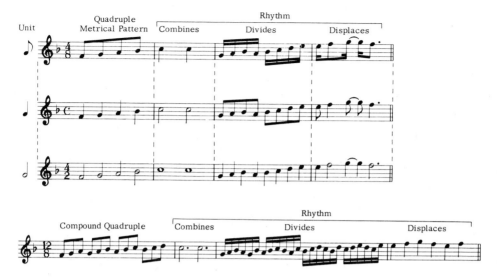

23. The Circle of 5ths

In the pages to follow we shall on many occasions refer to the entire spectrum of diatonic keys. These keys, fifteen major and fifteen minor, are customarily arranged by successive 5ths, a procedure which yields an orderly and easily memorized progression of key signatures. The arrangement is known as the *circle of 5ths* because its originator, Heinichen, represented it in the form of a circle. Here we have relinquished the circle, but retained the succession of 5ths.

example 45.

Sharp keys by ascending 5ths

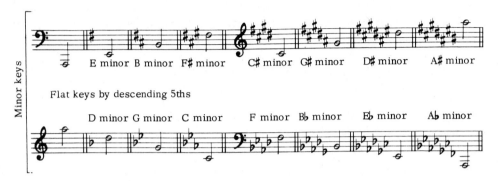

Minor keys

Flat keys by descending 5ths

Beginning from the major tonality without key signature, C major, the keys are arranged by ascending 5ths. This produces a series of "sharp" keys in which one sharp is added to each successive key. The "flat" keys are arranged by descending 5ths beginning from C again, and there too we see a series in which one flat is added to each successive key. The minor keys begin from the minor tonality without key signature, A minor. As in the major mode, the sharp keys arrange themselves by ascending 5ths, adding one sharp with each successive key, while the flat keys arrange themselves by descending 5ths, adding one flat with each successive key.

It should be emphasized here that the circle of 5ths is a visual convenience, a mnemonic device, nothing more. It does not represent fully any important structural aspect of tonal music, as we shall see in Chapter 7 which deals with harmonic progression.

24. Harmony and the Training of the Musical Ear

The musician cannot be content simply to hear; he must know what he hears and be able to communicate that knowledge. The systematic study of harmony provides an excellent opportunity to develop those skills.

Memorization plays an important role in hearing music. We remember melodies, harmonies, and rhythms just as we remember faces. And as one's acquaintance with tonal music widens, he must also learn the names of the various events which become familiar, for in that way both the sound and its structural meaning in the musical composition are fixed in mind.

To direct and encourage the development of the musical ear specific exercises are given at the end of each chapter. These begin with basic keyboard and aural exercises in the material newly introduced. If he consistently practices these exercises the student will find that his aural capacities will develop simultaneously with other musical skills.

25. Chapter Summary

It has been seen that the diatonic scale represents a key. It also serves as a map for locating notes and chords. Thus we refer to "scale degree 3" and "tonic chord" (I).

The diatonic and chromatic scales are used to measure intervals. Intervals, in turn, are used to measure and describe chords. We classify intervals first according to the number of diatonic degrees they span ("2nds," "3rds," . . .), then according to the number of half steps they contain ("minor 2nds," "major 3rds," . . .), and finally as consonances or dissonances. The intervals that can be extracted from the major and minor triads—3rd, 5th, unison, and 8ve—and the inversions of these intervals (with the frequent exception of the 4th) are the only consonant intervals. All other intervals are dissonant.

The triad divides the diatonic scale into two unequal parts. The lower division spans the 5th, the upper spans the 4th. We explained the melodic function of certain diatonic notes within these divisions as passing notes and auxiliary notes. Particular emphasis was given to the melodic function of scale degree 7 as leading note and to the variable 6th and 7th degrees of the minor scale. In all these cases we emphasized that the half step exerts the strongest melodic attraction (law of the half step).

The principle of 8ve equivalence underlies interval inversion, which is an extremely important procedure in tonal harmony since it produces chord inversion, as we shall see. Inversion is entirely different from the shift of 8ve that produces the compound interval. A simple arithmetical formula can always be used to determine whether two intervals are related on the basis of inversion: The sum of an interval and its inversion equals 9. Thus, the 3rd is the inversion of the 6th $(3 + 6 = 9)$. But, for example, the 9th is not the inversion of the 2nd $(9 + 2 = 11)$. The 9th is a compound interval, a 2nd plus an 8ve.

We have given a brief introduction to the function of meter and rhythm. Their interaction is of vital importance to harmony.

EXERCISES

A. List of Some Important Terms to Define and Memorize

Scale degree
Chord
Chromatic scale
Triad
Relative minor
Passing note
Auxiliary note
Half step
Leading note
Melodic minor scale
Inversion

Octave equivalence
Consonant interval
Dissonant interval
Tritone
Compound interval
Augmented 2nd
Diminished 5th
Compound meter
Submetrical
Rhythm

B. Sample Diatonic Intervals

INSTRUCTIONS
Each of the following melodic fragments features a particular diatonic interval.
Many perhaps are already familiar. All should be memorized without delay to provide a basis for interval recognition and for the singing of melodies and harmonies
required for subsequent exercises.

exercise 1. Ascending minor 2nd. (BEETHOVEN: *Ninth Symphony*)

exercise 2. Descending minor 2nd. (Chorale: *Ach Gott und Herr*)

exercise 3. Ascending major 2nd. (Chorale: *Freu dich sehr, o meine Seele*)

exercise 4. Descending major 2nd. (SCHUMANN: *Third Symphony*)

Allegro

exercise 5.   Ascending minor 3rd. (BRAHMS: *Lullaby*)

exercise 6.   Descending minor 3rd. (BERLIOZ: *Harold in Italy*)

Adagio

exercise 7.   Ascending major 3rd. (Chorale: *Es ist gewisslich an der Zeit*)

exercise 8.   Descending major 3rd. (BEETHOVEN: *Piano Sonata in E major, Opus 109*)

Adagio

exercise 9.   Ascending perfect 4th. (MENDELSSOHN: *Nocturne*)

Andante

exercise 10.   Descending perfect 4th. (SCHUBERT: *Unfinished Symphony*)

Allegro

exercise 11.   Ascending perfect 5th. (BACH: *Fugue in D♯ minor, WTC I*)

exercise 12.   Descending perfect 5th. (Chorale: *Aus tiefer Not*)

exercise 13.   Ascending minor 6th. (BRAHMS: *Fourth Symphony*)

exercise 14.   Descending minor 6th. (BACH: *Italian Concerto*)

exercise 15.   Ascending major 6th. (HAYDN: *Symphony in D major, No. 99*)

exercise 16.   Descending major 6th. (WAGNER: *Die Meistersinger*)

exercise 17. Ascending minor 7th. (BRAHMS: *Fourth Symphony*)

exercise 18. Descending minor 7th. (BACH: *Sixth Brandenburg Concerto in B♭ major*)

exercise 19. Ascending major 7th. (BRAHMS: *First Symphony*)

Animato

exercise 20. Descending major 7th and diminished 7th. (BACH: *Harpsichord Concerto in D minor*)

Adagio

exercise 21. Ascending perfect 8ve. (MOZART: *Piano Concerto in D minor, K.466*)

Allegro

exercise 22. **Descending perfect 8ve.** (MOZART: *Symphony in G major, K.444*)

Allegro

exercise 23. **Tritone.** (MOZART: *Symphony in C major, K.551*)

Andante

exercise 24. **Augmented 2nd.** (SCHUMANN: *First Symphony*)

Allegro

exercise 25. **Diminished 7th.** (BACH: *Fugue in A minor, WTC II*)

C. Structure and Notation of the Diatonic Scales

The purpose of this exercise is to make certain that the reader has a basic familiarity with the whole- and half-step patterns in the major and minor scales and that he understands notation, including key signatures.

INSTRUCTIONS

A single note is given. The numeral below the note indicates its position in the diatonic major or minor scale. Supply the correct key signature and write out the complete scale, marking the position of the half steps. The procedure is demonstrated below.

Given:
Major

Completed:

exercise 26. Major scales

exercise 27. Minor scales (melodic form)

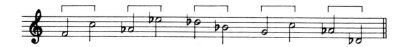

D. Intervals to Identify

INSTRUCTIONS

Each exercise contains intervals extracted from a single diatonic scale. Identify the key from the accidentals, then sing the intervals by scale degree numbers and letter names, identifying each interval by class (consonance or dissonance) and size.

exercise 28.

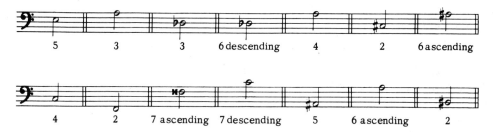

exercise 29.

exercise 30.

exercise 31.

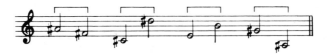

exercise 32.

exercise 33.

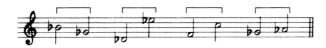

exercise 34.

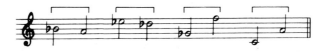

exercise 35.

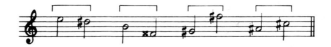

E. Familiar Melodies

INSTRUCTIONS
Portions of familiar melodies are notated below without key signature and without metric-rhythmic pattern. Identify the melody and supply the missing elements. Also label all intervals between successive notes.

exercise 36.

exercise 37.

exercise 38.

exercise 39.

exercise 40.

exercise 41.

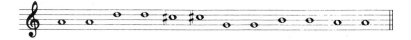

exercise 42.

exercise 43.

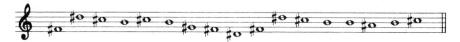

exercise 44.

exercise 45.

exercise 46.

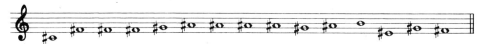

exercise 47.

2

The Triad: The Harmonic Basis of Tonal Music

Harmony differs from chord as whole differs from part.

Friedrich Wilhelm Marpurg, 1755

26.   How Chord Structure Is Described

The first focus in harmony study is the structure of chords. As indicated in Chapter 1, a chord is a group of three or more different notes that sound simultaneously. A chord has at least the value of a full metrical pulse. It may even extend over several measures, as in the following passage.

example 46.   BEETHOVEN: *Piano Sonata in E♭, Op. 7*

Each measure of this excerpt contains the same chord, a chord that consists of the notes E♭, G, and B♭. A description of a chord in terms of letter names is, however, of little general significance, and therefore chord structure is described by listing the intervals which make up the chord. In this way we represent not merely the notes of the particular chord, but the general class to which it belongs. As a result, we immediately know a great deal about its probable behavior in a particular context.

The intervals which comprise a chord are always reckoned from the bass upward. Thus, in Example 46 although the distribution of the notes above the bass changes from measure to measure the *intervals* which those notes form with the bass remain the same and we say that a single chord governs the entire passage. Since the chord contains the intervals of a perfect 5th and a major 3rd above the bass it is recognized as a major triad.

27. The Triad as Basic Consonant Chord

In Chapter 1 consonant intervals were emphasized as the stable and foundational elements of tonal music. We can now extend that statement to include consonant chords. When all the notes of a chord form consonant intervals with the bass and with one another, the chord is called consonant. If either of these two conditions is not met, the chord is dissonant. Therefore, the triad whose fundamental note is scale degree 1 is a consonant chord, since it contains the consonant intervals of a perfect 5th and a major 3rd measured upward from the bass and since the third interval (between the two upper notes) is also consonant. The triad on scale degree 7, however, is dissonant because it contains the dissonant interval of a diminished 5th.

example 47.

28. The Triads in the Diatonic Major Mode

As has been indicated triads can be constructed on each note of the scale. Example 48 summarizes the seven diatonic triads in the major mode.

example 48.

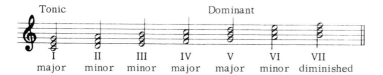

Each diatonic triad is designated by a Roman numeral which shows the diatonic position of its fundamental note. In addition, each triad has a name. For the time being we will use only two of these, those that refer to the most important triads. The triad on scale degree 1 (I) is called the *tonic* triad, and the triad on scale degree 5 (V) is called the *dominant* triad.

In the major mode all triads are consonant except one, the leading note triad, VII, which is called diminished after the size of its dissonant interval. Of the six remaining triads three are major (I, IV, and V) and three are minor (II, III, and VI).

29. The Triads in the Diatonic Minor Mode

The diatonic triads in minor are constructed both from the natural and the harmonic forms of the scale. As shown in Example 49 this means that V and VII both have two different forms, depending upon the scale from which they are drawn.

example 49.

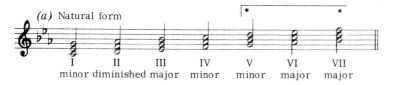

If drawn from the natural minor scale V is a minor triad, often called the *minor dominant.* If drawn from the harmonic minor scale V includes raised scale degree

7, the leading note, and therefore has the same notes as V in the parallel major mode. Similarly, if drawn from the harmonic minor scale, VII is a diminished triad, like VII in the parallel major, whereas if drawn from the natural minor scale, it is a major triad.

In connection with the harmonic minor scale as a source of diatonic chords it is important to realize that the leading note is not included as a chord note in chords whose fundamental notes lie below scale degree 5. Thus only V and VII contain the leading note. The following triad is not a functional diatonic triad:

example 50.

III ♮5

Occasionally one diatonic triad is drawn from the melodic minor scale: a major triad on scale degree IV. The major 3rd of this normally minor triad is raised scale degree 6 which characterizes the melodic minor scale.

example 51.

IV ♮

30. Harmony in Four Voices; Doubling

Although the three-note chord, the triad, is fundamental to tonal music, compositional practice features four-note chords. One reason for this is that the lowest note or bass was initially regarded as the foundation which supported the chord, as an independent element upon which the triad was constructed. Thus we have the familiar expression "bass and chord," meaning the bass note plus the three notes of the triad. Often, however, it is more convenient to regard the bass note simply as another chord note. In that case we see that the triad becomes a four-note chord when one of its notes is duplicated, or doubled, at the interval of the unison or the 8ve. In the following distribution each chord has one note doubled, with the exception of the next to last.

example 52. CHOPIN: *Nocturne in G minor, Op. 37/1*

We can describe the distribution of chord notes here more accurately by saying that the bass of each chord is doubled at the 8ve.

By tradition, each note of a four-note chord is designated according to the normative arrangement of two male and two female voices in choral music, whether or not the chord is actually intended for vocal performance. Thus, the highest voice in Example 52 is called the soprano, the voice below it the alto. The voice immediately above the bass is called the tenor. A typical vocal arrangement is shown in the following composition. As is customary in the four-voice vocal composition, the stems of the notes sung by the soprano point upward, those of the alto point downward. Similarly, the tenor stems point upward, while those of the bass point downward.

example 53. ALBRECHTSBERGER: *Miserere*

Soprano and bass are often referred to as the *outer voices,* alto and tenor as the *inner voices,* for obvious reasons. This pairing of voices is evident in the notation of many of the instrumental examples and exercises in the present volume: soprano and bass notes of the chord are each given separate stems, while the inner voices (alto and tenor) are attached to a single stem.

Voices are also called *parts.* Therefore we speak either of "four voice" or "four-part" harmony. The terms are identical in meaning. Since four-part harmony is the norm in triadic music, harmony in fewer than four parts may be regarded as incomplete, while harmony in more than four parts results from the doubling of more than one chord note or the tripling, quadrupling, and so on of one or more chord notes.

31. Positions of the Soprano Voice

The highest voice of the chord plays a primary role in harmonic and melodic progression. Therefore there is a special terminology to describe its position in relation to the bass of the chord. When the soprano doubles the bass we speak of the *position of the octave* (Example 54a). When the soprano carries the 3rd we have the *position of the 3rd* (Example 54b). When the 5th of the chord is in the soprano we speak of the *position of the 5th* (Example 54c).

Changes in soprano position do not affect the interval content of the chord. This is evident in the following excerpt, where only the soprano position changes in each successive statement of the chord (see Example 46).

example 54. MOZART: *The Magic Flute* (*Der dreimalige Akkord*)

When the three soprano positions of the triad are considered, one of the special advantages of four-voice harmony becomes clear. With only three voices one could not obtain a complete chord in the soprano position of the 8ve. Either 3rd or 5th would have to be omitted, as shown below.

example 55.

32. Chord Spacing

When the notes of the triad lie as closely together as possible the triad is said to be in *close position.* When the notes do not lie as closely together as possible the triad is said to be in *open position.* When the triad is distributed conveniently for the keyboard so that soprano, alto, and tenor are as close as possible the chord is said to be *in close position below the soprano.* Only the bass lies apart from the other notes in this spacing, which will be used extensively in the exercises in the present volume. This spacing, which is termed four-voice keyboard spacing, is shown in the following excerpt.

example 56. BRAHMS: *Vergangen ist mir Glück und Heil, Op. 48/6*

33. Figured Bass*

It has been emphasized that the bass is the foundation of harmonic structure. Its role as the bearer of harmony is evident in the system of musical notation known as *figured bass* which developed as an integral part of tonal music throughout the seventeenth and eighteenth centuries.

A figured bass consists of a series of bass notes with symbols above and below that indicate how the chords are to be completed and connected. For example, this is a fragment of an eighteenth-century bass:

example 57. MARCELLO: *Psalms*

At first this system was used only as a kind of musical shorthand which enabled composers to give minimal instructions to keyboard accompanists without the necessity of writing out all the notes. The performers, specially trained for their task, would then transform the figured bass into full-fledged accompaniments, often adding embellishments of various kinds.

*A Summary of Figured Bass is given in Appendix 1.

Gradually the figured bass, or *thorough bass* as it was known in England, came to be used by composer-performers to notate improvisations, actually compositional sketches. From this it was only a short step to the direct use of figured bass in the teaching of composition, and thus in the eighteenth century it became one of the fundamental means by which composers learned their craft. Bach, his sons, Haydn, Mozart, Beethoven—all were introduced to music via figured bass. The following excerpt from J. S. Bach's short treatise on figured bass indicates the close connection between figured bass and composition. It also demonstrates the importance of the consonant triad in his musical thought.

> The harmonic triad belongs properly to the subject of composition, but since a figured bass is the beginning of a composition, and . . . may even be called an extemporaneous composition, made by the person who plays the figured bass, the subject of the triad may be fitly mentioned in this place.

This clearly shows Bach's regard for the figured bass, a regard shared by many. In addition to its historical validity the figured bass has to recommend it this primary educational advantage: it provides the beginner with absolutely essential experience in the construction and connection of chords. Moreover, he can obtain this experience before learning about chord relations and chord progression. These come later, after a period of systematic, guided work with the basic materials and techniques of harmony. At this elementary stage he need only follow certain simple instructions and perform certain operations. Gradually, against an accumulated background of experience with the basic materials, concepts of tonal organization will be introduced which afford a deeper understanding of triadic music. In this way conceptual knowledge increases simultaneously with skill in performing the basic operations required by the art. We now present the first of these operations, the reading of figured bass.

The figures tell the musician which intervals make up the chord above the bass: Thus, if the chord is a diatonic triad the figures would be $\frac{5}{3}$, indicating that a 5th and a 3rd above the bass combine to form that particular chord. In actual practice, since the triad is the fundamental harmony in tonal music it usually is not figured at all. Therefore any bass note without an accompanying figure means that a diatonic triad ($\frac{5}{3}$) is to be constructed above that note.

example 58.

$\binom{5}{3}$

Thus for the accompaniment of the familiar French folk song, *Au clair de la lune,* one need only notate the bass and upper voice as shown in the next example. The melody is notated separately on the top staff.

example 59. *Au clair de la lune*

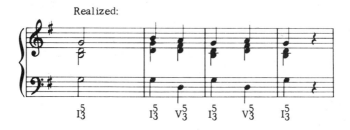

If each chord is played in close position below the soprano, that is, in four-voice keyboard spacing, an adequate accompaniment is obtained. The second part of Example 59 shows the accompaniment as it should be played or, to use the traditional term, "realized."

The figures do not indicate the soprano position or spacing of the chord. For the time being, the reader will not be concerned with these problems since the soprano will be given in all figured bass exercises and, unless otherwise stated, he will use the four-voice keyboard spacing as illustrated in Example 56 above.

Whenever a diatonic note is raised or lowered the alteration is indicated by the signs ♯, ♭, or ♮, as in regular notation. For example, in the accompaniment for the following song the bass note D is supplied with a ♯. This sign transforms the minor dominant triad into the dominant triad with the leading note. As a bass figure an accidental alone always refers to the 3rd above the bass and only to the 3rd. The numeral 3 is not required. In all other cases the accidental precedes the figure for the interval, for example ♭5.

example 60. *English Folk Song*

Realized:

Here, as in Example 59, the first task of the performer is to read the figured bass correctly and supply the indicated chord notes in close position below the soprano. He must then connect the chords in a coherent and effective way. The description of this procedure follows.

34. Chord Connection (Voice Leading)*

The figured bass system provides an excellent means for learning to construct chords. It also provides an excellent means for learning to connect them. These two operations, chord construction and chord connection, are fundamental to harmony study. They must be learned before more demanding tasks are undertaken.

Influenced by the two-dimensional notation of music, we often speak of chord construction as occurring in the *vertical* dimension, whereas chord connection occurs in the *horizontal* dimension. This distinction pervades musical terminology. Thus, the techniques of chord connection are commonly called *voice leading* techniques, referring to the progression of the individual chord notes which form "voices" in the horizontal dimension.

*A Summary of Voice-Leading Rules and Guidelines is given in Appendix 2.

The two basic techniques for connecting consonant chords are illustrated by the opening of a familiar song:

example 61. *America*

Here we see that when connecting one chord with another, notes common to both chords are kept in the same voice, while notes that have no counterpart in the subsequent chord move to the nearest note in that chord, preferably by stepwise motion. Sometimes there will be more than one possible stepwise progression, in which case the best choice is determined by rhythm, meter, distribution, register, and other factors which will be explained and illustrated as we proceed.

Voice leading is often described in terms of pairs of voices, for example, soprano and bass, or alto and tenor. When the voices move in the same direction and maintain the same interval we say that they are in *parallel motion.* When they move in the same direction but do not maintain the same interval they are in *similar motion.* When they move in opposite directions they are in *contrary motion.* And when one voice moves while the other remains stationary they are in *oblique motion.* These patterns are illustrated below.

example 62.

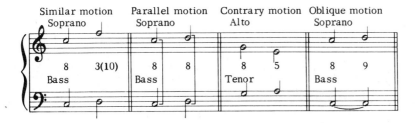

Example 62 shows soprano and bass moving in similar and parallel motion, alto and tenor in contrary motion, and soprano and bass in oblique motion. Also important are the intervals which the voices form. These are figured in Example 62.

Whenever two voices are in parallel motion particular attention must be paid to the intervals they form, lest they violate one of the most important principles of voice leading, a principle that exerts a large measure of control over melodic progression, the prohibition of parallel 5ths and parallel 8ves. By this is meant that two voices are not permitted to move from one chord to another in such a way that they form a succession of two perfect 5ths or two perfect 8ves in parallel motion. Therefore the following succession is incorrect:

example 63.

Parallel 8ves, as shown here, reduce the number of voices to three since the voice that doubles at the 8ve is not an independent voice but merely a duplication. Parallel 8ves may also confuse the functions of the voices, as here. If the upper voice succession G A is merely a duplication of the bass, then the actual soprano must be D E, the alto voice. This interpretation of course makes no sense, for it turns the texture inside out.

    Such duplication of voice leading is not, however, the only function of 8ve doubling. In many compositions we find that voices are doubled at the 8ve for reinforcement. For example, the bass of the classical period symphonic movement is ordinarily played by cellos and contrabasses, instruments which sound an 8ve apart. This kind of doubling for reinforcement is not at all the same as the doubling of an essential voice in the register of another voice, as in Example 63.

    Parallel 5ths are avoided because the 5th, formed by scale degrees 1 and 5, is the primary harmonic interval, the interval that divides the scale and thus defines the key. The direct succession of two 5ths raises doubt concerning the key. Example 64 illustrates.

example 64.

The prohibition of parallel 5ths is more than a pedantic dictum. It is an important negative principle that is responsible for many harmonic and melodic features of tonal music—for example, the use of inverted consonances explained in the next chapter. Without the limitation placed upon parallel 5ths and 8ves the art of tonal music would not have developed the elaborate and intricate forms which have given it such a unique position.

The problem of parallel 5ths and 8ves usually involves only two chords in succession, chords that are apt to be closely associated as a pair. Chords are often grouped in this way and we may regard the chord pair as the smallest unit of harmonic motion, the smallest harmonic context. Pairs of consonant chords are connected by stepwise voice leading as a general rule. However, nonstepwise motions ("skips") may be required in order to avoid parallel 5ths, or they may be desired in order to gain or maintain a particular register. In such cases skips are made freely and the rule of stepwise voice leading is disregarded. Different conditions obtain when dissonant chords are involved. There certain stepwise voice leadings are obligatory.

In subsequent sections closer attention will be given to the intervallic patterns formed by moving voices—in particular, to the patterns formed by the outer voices—since such patterns have very significant implications not only for the detail of tonal compositions but also for structures of longer span. (See, for instance, section 220.)

35. The Basic Cadence

Perhaps the most important chord pair in tonal music is the closing succession V I (dominant-tonic). When it occurs at the end of a composition or at the end of a longer harmonic unit this kind of succession is called a *cadence.*

example 65.

Scale
degree 2

V   I

Example 65 shows the basic cadence, sometimes called "authentic." The soprano progression from scale degree 2 to scale degree 1 is supported by the cadential harmonies V I. When the soprano comes to rest on scale degree 1, as in Example 65, the effect of completion or closure is stronger than when the soprano ends on scale degree 3, as below.

example 66.

This succession closes harmonically but not melodically. (See section 137.)

In example 66 notice that the leading note skips away to G instead of resolving to C in accordance with the law of the half step. This is done in order to obtain a complete chord of I. If the leading note had resolved to C, the final chord would not have contained a 5th. This exception to the law of the half step is often encountered at the cadence, and other instances will be seen as we proceed.

36. Temporary Shift to Five Voices

In certain situations one can add a fifth to the normative four-voice texture in order to obtain both stepwise leading and complete chords. Example 67 illustrates this, using the cadential succession V I.

example 67.

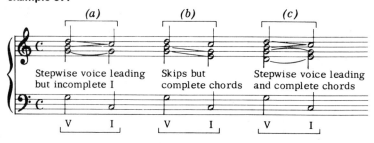

At (a) the voice leading is stepwise but the final chord lacks a 3rd. At (b) the inner voices must skip in order to achieve a complete statement of the final chord. This is the normal procedure in four voices. At (c) a fifth voice, D, is added to the V. This provides both stepwise voice leading and a complete final chord.

The temporary shift to five voices is a valuable technique that solves many voice-leading problems. However, it should be used sparingly since one must also learn to manipulate four voices in situations where a fifth voice would not be available, for example, in writing for a quartet of brass instruments.

EXERCISES

Notes on the Exercises

Beginning with this chapter the exercises are divided into various types: basic keyboard and aural exercises (including basic chord patterns), figured bass exercises (including figured outer voices), and exercises that have directly to do with the material presented in the chapter, such as the harmonization of given melodies, which is introduced at the end of chapter 7.

The Four-Voice Chorale Exercises

Many of the exercises are based upon traditional chorale materials, initially the outer voices (figured) of chorales and, later on (after Chapter 7), chorale melodies to be harmonized and elaborated. The main purpose of these exercises is to provide experience with voice leading and with selection of appropriate harmonic progressions.

   The chorale exercises may be notated in two ways: (1) in keyboard spacing (section 32); (2) in the traditional four-voice chorale setting for performance by male and female voices. This section is concerned mainly with the latter.

   Many composers have contributed their talents to the enrichment of the chorale genre. Of all chorale settings those by J.S. Bach are not only the best known but are also universally regarded as the finest. However, they are so highly developed melodically and harmonically that they do not function well as introductory examples. Therefore we use a less complex setting to demonstrate the procedure, one by Bach's contemporary, J.H. Graun.

Chorale: *O Haupt voll Blut und Wunden.*
Harmonization by J. H. Graun.

   Since the four-voice chorale setting is intended to be sung (and, indeed, should be sung in the class if at all possible), it is essential to take into consideration the normal voice range of each part. Effective ranges for an average group of mixed, untrained voices are as follows:

The small notes indicate practical limits, while the large notes show the limits for comfortable singing.

In the example the individual voices are indicated by stem direction. This is the traditional notation, as indicated in section 30. In the four-voice chorale the soprano is always notated with upward pointing stems, the alto with downward pointing stems, the tenor with upward pointing stems, and the bass with downward pointing stems. This notational convention makes clear the progression of each voice and also serves to show the various combinations and oppositions of voices.

In the four-voice chorale setting, as distinct from keyboard spacing (section 32), there is often a good deal of variation in the spacing between individual voices. In the Graun excerpt above, the first chord is in close position below the soprano; the next two, however, are not. There are guidelines for the spacing of voices. Of these, the most important for the beginner involves the interval between tenor and bass; this should not, in general, be smaller than a 5th when the bass is in its lower register (below the C below middle C). A very wide interval between tenor and alto causes the male and female timbres to be correspondingly separated and to lose the blended quality that is so characteristic of good music for mixed voices. In general, the vertical interval between two adjacent voices should not exceed an 8ve. An exception to this rule is the interval between tenor and bass, which often necessarily exceeds the 8ve limit.

Voices may cross if that is advantageous to the shape of the individual line.

J.S. Bach: *Meine Seele erhebt den Herren*

In the example above, Bach placed the bass above the tenor on the third beat of the first measure. The crossing occupies only one metrical pulse, however, and this is an instance of a general rule: a crossing may not exceed in duration two metrical pulses. The reason for this is obvious: with a more extended crossing the voices would tend to lose their structural identity and characteristic registers. In addition, the soprano is almost never crossed over. The student should regard crossing of voices as the exception rather than the rule. In most simple settings of the type to be found in the next few chapters, there should rarely be a need for crossing.

With respect to the intervals formed between successive notes in the same part, called *linear intervals*, the following guidelines apply:

1   Stepwise (conjunct) motion is preferred over non-stepwise (disjunct) motion, except in the bass, which characteristically skips a good deal.

2   Only consonant intervals are allowed as linear intervals. (The perfect 4th is a consonance in this instance.)

3   All dissonant intervals and intervals formed by chromatic alteration, such as the diminished 4th, which sounds like a major 3rd if taken out of context, are not permitted.

Examples of worked-out exercises are given below to demonstrate correct and incorrect solutions. In the first, at (*a*), are the given outer voices, figured. (Recall that the absence of a figure means $\frac{5}{3}$.) These given outer voices are not to be changed.

(*a*) After J.S. BACH

In two instances chords have been realized, since the particular type they represent has not yet been introduced in the text. At (*b*) is a correct solution.

(*b*)

Notice how often the two basic rules of voice leading (hold common tones and progress to the nearest note by step if possible) are observed. Also notice the doubling at the unison of bass and tenor on the first beat of measure 2. This is a type of doubling with which the student should familiarize himself as soon as possible, for it is extremely valuable in solving many voice-leading problems. At (c) are shown six flaws.

(c)

1   The wide skips in tenor (bracketed) and the skip in alto are unnecessary and can easily be obviated by the close spacing used at (b).

2   The tenor has a wrong note. It should be B.

3   Parallel 8ves between soprano and tenor.

4   Parallel 5ths between bass and tenor.

5   The chord is incomplete (no 5th).

6   Again, an incomplete chord (no 3rd).

Another chorale phrase is presented below in the form of figured outer voices to be completed in chorale style (a).

(a) After J.S. BACH

At (*b*) is a correct solution (by J.S. Bach, except for the final bass note, which is out of bass range in his setting).

(*b*)

At (*c*) is a realization that is fraught with errors. The comments below are keyed to the numbers above the exercise, as before.

(*c*)

1	The skip in tenor is unnecessarily large, making that voice more prominent than it should be at the beginning of the chorale.
2	Parallel 8ves between tenor and soprano.
3	Parallel 8ves continue, between tenor and soprano again.
4	Once again, parallel 8ves between tenor and soprano.
5	Parallel 8ves between tenor and bass. An unnecessary (and incorrect) skip of a tritone in the alto as well. Notice that the tenor has crossed above the alto at this point.
6	Here the tenor has crossed over the soprano and is the highest sounding voice. Quite unacceptable, in general, especially at the cadence.

Another chorale phrase is given below at (*a*).

(*a*) After J.S. BACH

At (*b*) is shown a correct solution to the exercise.

(*b*)

The shapes and interactions of the individual voices are worthy of attention. The bass moves by skip except for the closing motion A♯-B. The tenor is paired with the soprano in parallel 10ths until the last measure, while the alto descends in a step-wise formation. Thus, each line has an individuality, an aesthetically and structurally desirable feature. The solution at (*c*), on the other hand, contains a number of flaws and errors.

(*c*)

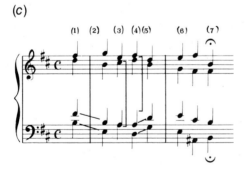

| 1 | The tenor is almost out of range. |
| 2 | Parallel 5ths between tenor and bass. |

3   The interval between alto and tenor is too large: a 10th.

4   Again, the interval between alto and tenor is too large: an 11th this time.

5   Parallel 5ths between tenor and bass.

6   The chord lacks a 5th.

7   The chord lacks a 3rd.

A final example of a figured outer-voice exercise is given below. Notice the parallel 5ths between soprano and bass over the second barline. The second of these is a diminished 5th, however, and the succession is not incorrect. Following C.P.E. Bach, we do not allow the reverse: a diminished 5th followed by a perfect 5th. (See Summary of Voice-Leading Rules and Guidelines, Appendix 2.)

(a) After J.S. BACH

The beginning of the correct solution (b) deserves comment.

(b)

Whenever the same chord harmonizes the opening two soprano notes, as here, the bass skips either up or down an 8ve. This provides for a strong motion, whereas simply repeating the same bass note would negate the impression of upbeat followed by downbeat.

(c)

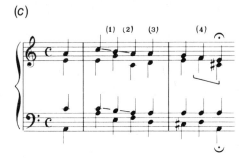

The solution at *(c)* contains errors:

1   Parallel 8ves between soprano and tenor.
2   Continuation of the parallel 8ves between soprano and tenor.
3   The chord lacks a 3rd.
4   The error here is not the 3rd doubled at the unison, which is possible, but the consequence of that doubling, the dissonant skip of the augmented 4th in the alto, F-C♯.

Four-voice chorale settings provide an excellent way in which to develop a mastery of voice leading and a sense of the function of the individual line in the musical continuum, but keyboard spacing enables the student to realize more quickly and fluently a given outer-voice exercise (or figured bass) and to gain an immediate aural experience. For these reasons we advocate both four-voice chorale and keyboard styles for the exercises, at the option of the instructor, of course.

In keyboard spacing, as defined in section 32, all the voices are in close position below the soprano. The left hand plays only the bass, the right hand the remaining notes. However, in freer keyboard style it is occasionally advantageous, even necessary, to change to an open spacing. This is called *divided accompaniment*. In divided accompaniment the left hand plays two notes (tenor and bass) and the right hand plays the other two (alto and tenor). Restrictions of register on the individual voices do not apply in keyboard style. Also, in keyboard style, unlike the four-voice chorale, it is possible to shift to five voices (section 36) or to three voices, as will be shown in section 40.

A final note before proceeding to the exercises. Parallel 5ths and 8ves are a source of concern and annoyance to student and instructor alike in beginning exercises in chorale style (and even later). There is a simple way to correct these: Once the exercise is completed check the six possible pairs of voices to see whether there are any residual parallel 5ths or 8ves. If there are, make the appropriate adjustments.

EXERCISES

A. List of Some Important Terms to Define and Memorize

Dissonant chord

Doubling

Outer voices

Position of the 8ve

Position of the 5th

Four-voice keyboard spacing

Alto voice

Figured bass

Voice leading

Similar motion

Cadence

Skip

B. Basic Keyboard and Aural Exercises

INSTRUCTIONS

Play each exercise at the keyboard. Then before going on to the next sing the exercise in the following ways, using the keyboard to check for accuracy not to accompany the voice.

1 Sing the entire bass.

2 Sing the entire soprano.

3 Beginning from the soprano note, sing all the notes of each chord in descending order, close position. Use the neutral syllable "la."

4 Beginning from the bass note, sing all the notes of each chord in ascending order, close position.

These four steps are illustrated below.

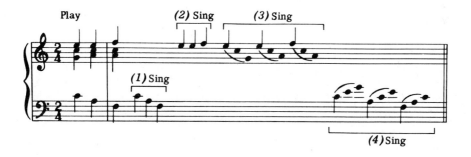

The exercises should be repeated until a certain degree of fluency is attained. With each repetition transpose the patterns to a different key and provide a different metric-rhythmic pattern. For singing, letter names should replace the neutral syllable, "la," when the exercises are repeated.

exercise 48. Triads in all three soprano positions. Continue until all keys have been included.

The following two exercises will be used again in subsequent chapters. For convenience, they are identified as Basic Chord Patterns 1 and 2. Both contain only diatonic triads.

exercise 49. **Basic Chord Pattern 1**

exercise 50. **Basic Chord Pattern 2**

Minor

I IV VII III VI II V I IV V I

C. Figured Bass Exercises

INSTRUCTIONS

The exercises consisting of given figured outer voices only can be realized either in keyboard style or in four-voice chorale style (or in both). The rules of voice leading—especially the prohibition of parallel 5ths, 8ves, and unisons—are to be observed, as well as the requirement that the chord be complete.

The exercises that consist of an outer voice accompaniment to a soprano line (for example, Exercise 55) are to be realized in keyboard style, again, in accordance with all the rules given in the chapter. In Exercise 63 the topmost accompanying voice is to be added as well, from the note given, moving by step wherever possible.

In some of the exercises (Exercises 55, 56, 58, 59, 61, 62, and 63) certain chords are given in full because they represent types that have not yet been introduced in the text. Since it was not possible to give all spacings for these, the simplest keyboard spacing has been used. If the exercise is realized in four-voice chorale style, a spacing different from that given may be advantageous. For instance, the fourth beat of the first measure of Exercise 56 is best spaced from the bass upward as B♭-G-G-D when the exercise is carried out in four-voice chorale style. This instruction applies to corresponding situations in all subsequent exercises and will not be repeated.

When the exercise is realized in four-voice chorale style it will be necessary to change the stem direction of the bass line so that all stems point downward.

exercise 51. **C. P. E. BACH**

exercise 52. **C. P. E. BACH**

exercise 53.   C.P.E. BACH

exercise 54.   Chorale: *Wenn wir in höchsten Nöten sein*

exercise 55.   Folk song: *Flow Gently, Sweet Afton*

exercise 56.   Chorale: *Wir Christenleut' hab'n jetzo Freud*

exercise 57.   *The Apprentice's Farewell* (German folk song)

exercise 58.   Chorale: *Was Gott tut, das ist wohlgetan*

exercise 59. *Dame d'esprit* (La Folie d'Espagne)

exercise 60. Chorale: *Durch Adams Fall ist ganz verderbt*

*The 3rd of this triad is doubled at the unison (by alto and tenor voices). There-
fore, on the piano only three voices sound. With other instruments or voices the
full four parts would be heard.

INSTRUCTIONS
1 Play each exercise at the keyboard in close position below the soprano.
2 Write the inner voices, grouping them together on a single stem in the treble clef.

exercise 61. SCHÜTZ: *Psalm 3*

exercise 62. *Old English Song*

exercise 63. JEREMIAH CLARKE: *Psalm 121*

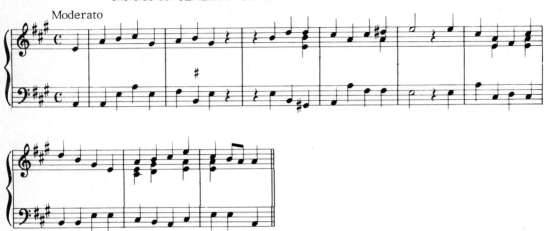

D. Exercises in Locating and Identifying the Diatonic Triads

The exercises in this group provide essential practice in the important skill of locating triads within the diatonic tonality and identifying them quickly by Roman numeral, type, and letter name.

INSTRUCTIONS

Each exercise below is made up of triads extracted from a single tonality. Identify the tonality, supply its key signature, and label each triad by Roman numeral. Also indicate the type of triad (major, minor, or diminished) and write out the letter names of its notes.

exercise 64.

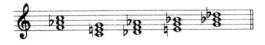

exercise 65.

exercise 66.

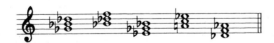

exercise 67.

exercise 68.

exercise 69.

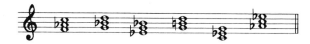

INSTRUCTIONS

The next group of exercises is somewhat more demanding. A series of bass notes is given. (1) Identify the key from the accidentals and supply the key signature. (2) Label each triad by Roman numeral. (3) Write out the letter names of the notes above each bass note. (4) Notate the upper voices in full, beginning from the soprano position indicated. The rules of voice leading should be observed, with special attention given to the stepwise progression of the soprano voice. The four steps are demonstrated below.

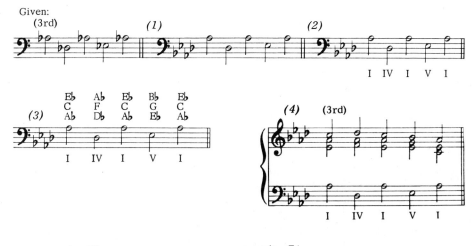

exercise 70.   exercise 71.

exercise 72.

exercise 73.

exercise 74.

exercise 75.

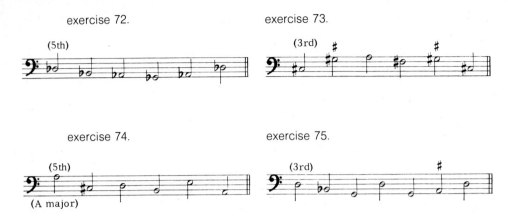

3

The Harmonic Process of Chord Generation: Sixth Chords

This principle of inversion is the core of all the diversity that characterizes harmony.

Jean Phillipe Rameau, 1722

37. The Generative Role of the Consonant Triad

Because the consonant triad is the basic harmonic element in tonal music one might well expect to find only chords of that structure in compositions. Of course we know that this is not the case. The harmonic vocabulary of tonal music is highly diversified. Yet the influence of the triad pervades the tonal universe, for all chords are generated from it by three processes—harmonic, melodic, and rhythmic. In the present chapter the first of these, the harmonic process, is introduced.

38. Inversion of the Bass: the Harmonic Process of Chord Generation

In section 13, Chapter 1, the inversion of intervals was explained. It was stated that the inversion of an interval is possible because notes an 8ve apart are regarded as equivalent. When this harmonic principle is extended to the triad the result is *chord inversion.* By chord inversion is meant the placement of the bass an 8ve higher (or two 8ves, three 8ves, . . .), so that the chord note which was immediately above the bass becomes the new bass note. The next example illustrates the relation between interval inversion and chord inversion.

example 68.

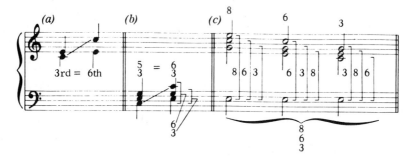

At (*a*) the lower note of the 3rd is inverted (placed an 8ve higher) so that a new interval is generated: the 3rd becomes a 6th. The two intervals are regarded as equivalent. At (*b*) the bass of a triad is inverted, leaving the former 3rd as a new bass note. By this means a new chord is generated which contains the same notes as the parent chord but in a different arrangement. This new chord comprises the intervals of a 6th and a 3rd above the bass and is called the chord of the 6th, or more simply the *6th chord,* after the interval that distinguishes it from its parent triad. Accordingly, it is figured 6, not $\frac{6}{3}$, the 3rd being understood in all cases. Example 68(*c*) shows the 6th chord in its three possible soprano positions: the position of the 8ve, the position of the 6th, and the position of the 3rd. As in all cases, the distribution of the upper parts does not affect the interval content of the chord. This is affected only by change of bass.

The 6th chord is regarded as equivalent to the $\frac{5}{3}$ from which it is generated. Under certain circumstances, however, it is not the harmonic equivalent of the parent triad, but has a melodic origin and function—circumstances that will be considered in subsequent chapters. For the present we shall regard the 6th chord as the counterpart of its parent triad and examine its various functions in relation to that chord.

39. The 6th Chord as Extension of the Parent Triad

The equivalence of the parent $\frac{5}{3}$ and its inversion, the $\frac{6}{3}$, is most evident when the two chords form a pair. This is illustrated in the next example.

example 69.

At (*a*) is shown a succession of four diatonic triads: I IV V I. At (*b*) the first three of these triads are followed by their 6th chords.

Example 69 illustrates an important function of inversion: an inverted chord often prevents or corrects parallel 5ths and 8ves without changing the harmony. The 5ths and 8ves marked by diagonal lines at (*a*) are corrected by the 6th chord inserted at (*b*). Here and elsewhere the prohibition of parallel 5ths and 8ves serves indirectly to create a more elaborate melodic and rhythmic texture.

Example 69 shows the 6th chord as a suffix that extends the parent triad. The 6th chord may also extend the parent triad by serving as a prefix. Example 70 illustrates.

example 70.

40. Doubling of the Notes of the Consonant 6th Chord

The 3rd of the triad usually moves stepwise to a note of the next chord. When the triad is inverted, the 3rd becomes the bass note of the 6th chord. Therefore if the bass is doubled at the 8ve, parallel 8ves often will result. This relationship is illustrated at (a) and (b) in Example 71.

example 71.

The two other possible doublings are shown at (c) and (d). Both are satisfactory and the selection of one or the other depends upon the melodic and rhythmic details of a particular context.

Doubling of the bass of the 6th chord does not always result in parallel 8ves. In the passage below, the doubling notes are led in contrary stepwise motion to the next chord.

example 72.

A four-voice succession of 6th chords in parallel motion (called *parallel 6th chords*) requires a different doubling for each chord if stepwise voice leading without parallel 5ths and 8ves is to be obtained. This technique of *alternate doubling* is illustrated at (a) in the next example.

example 73.

(a) alternate doubling

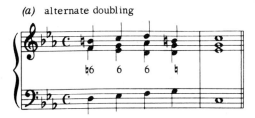

(b) 3 voices only – 6th in soprano

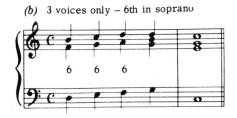

(c) 3rd in soprano creates parallel 5ths

If it is not essential to maintain four voices and if the 6th is in the soprano of each chord, one can shift to three voices temporarily, as shown at *(b)*—that is, in keyboard style only, of course. This can be done only if the 6th is in the soprano. If the 3rd is in the soprano parallel 5ths are created between the two upper voices, and if the 8ve is in the soprano parallel 8ves between bass and soprano result.

41. The 6th Chord as Representative of Its Parent Triad

The 6th chord often occurs without its parent chord, and serves not as an extension but as a representative. In this capacity it fulfills much the same function as would the parent chord in the same context. The next example offers a comparison between parent $\frac{5}{3}$ and 6th chord in the same contexts.

example 74. Chorale: *Herr Jesu Christ, dich zu uns wend*

At (*a*) the melody is harmonized by $\frac{5}{3}$'s. This creates two problems: the repetitious bass in the first and third measures and the parallel 8ves between soprano and bass in the second measure. At (*b*), 6th chords are substituted for $\frac{5}{3}$'s at the three problematic points and the defects are thereby removed.

42. The 6th Chord as First Inversion of the Triad

Each of the three notes of the triad can serve as bass note. The triad as a $\frac{5}{3}$ is said to be in *fundamental position,* or *root position.* The 6th chord is often called the *first inversion* of the triad and symbolized by combining a Roman numeral with the Arabic figure 6, as in the following excerpt.

example 75. HAYDN: *Variations in F minor*

The Roman numerals in Example 75 indicate the fundamental notes of the parent triads. The Arabic figure 6 means that the chord is the first inversion of the triad whose fundamental note or root is designated by the Roman numeral. Thus the symbol for the second chord in the excerpt is read as "the first inversion of the triad on scale degree 5." Similarly, the symbol I^6 does not indicate a 6th chord constructed above scale degree 1, but rather the first inversion of the triad whose fundamental note is scale degree 1.

To sum up, Arabic figures show the vertical structure of the chord and indicate its voice leading requirements (especially in the case of dissonant chords, as will be shown); the Roman numerals show chord relations and harmonic progression in terms of the diatonic triads.

A word of warning is in order here: Not all 6th chords are inversions of some parent triad. This distinction is amplified in section 208.

43. Dissonant Diatonic-6th Chords

The three dissonant diatonic triads, VII in major and minor and II in minor rarely occur in fundamental position in four voices. Usually they are represented by their 6th chords. In both modes the VII^6 often connects I with I^6 as shown below.

example 76.

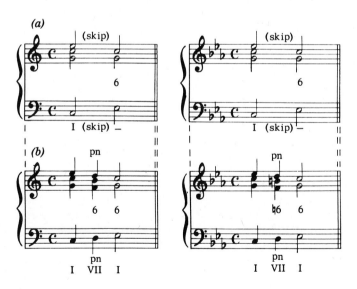

At (*a*) we see the chord pair I I^6 in both major and minor. At (*b*) bass and soprano add a passing note which fills in the skip at (*a*), while the inner voices complete the chord, VII⁶. Characteristically, the voice leading is stepwise and the bass of the dissonant-6th chord is doubled at the 8ve. The 6th is not doubled. Since it is the leading note and has a fixed progression, doubling would result automatically in parallel 8ves or unisons.

In Example 76 it is important to notice that the final 6th chord in each case serves as an extension of its parent triad since it is connected to the parent triad by the intervening dissonant-6th chord. This is a simple instance of a basic aspect of tonal music: the formation of a larger unit through the coherent interaction of its components. In Example 76, each group of three chords serves to extend the tonic triad.

The II⁶ in minor often prepares the cadential V. The chord is shown in the same context but with different doublings in Example 77 below.

example 77.

At (a) the bass is doubled. At (b) the 6th is doubled. The 3rd of this chord should not be doubled. Since it is scale degree 6 in minor it has a fixed progression downward by half step, and doubling would result automatically in parallel 8ves or unisons as in the case of the doubled leading note of VII⁶ remarked above.

44. Second Inversion of the Triad ($^6_4$) as a Dissonance

It has been seen that inversion of the bass of the fundamental triad produces a 6th chord, called the first inversion. Unless the fundamental triad is a diminished triad, the 6th chord thus generated is a consonant chord which can either extend its parent chord, as shown in section 39, or represent it, as shown in section 41. In both instances the 6th chord is a consonant chord equivalent to the parent chord. However, when the inversion process is extended beyond the first inversion a chord equivalent to the parent chord is not produced. The reason for this is shown in the following illustration.

example 78.

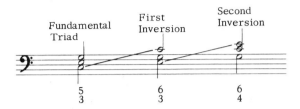

Example 78 shows that inversion of the bass of the 6th chord produces a chord that contains the intervals of a 6th and a 4th. Since the 4th is a dissonant interval this second inversion of the triad is a dissonant chord and therefore cannot be regarded as the extension or representative of the parent triad.

Unlike the parent triad and its first inversion, the $^6_4$ is a dependent, unstable chord which depends for its meaning upon a triad other than the parent chord. This dependence is clearly evident in the case of the $^6_4$ chord which often precedes V at the cadence, the *cadential* $^6_4$.

example 79. Chorale: *Wer weiss wie nahe*

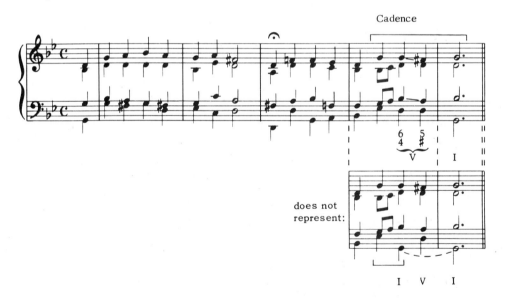

In Example 79 the cadential V is preceded by a $^6_4$. The 6th and the 4th descend together stepwise to the 5th and 3rd of the V, as indicated by the figures and by the diagonal lines in the example. The $^6_4$ embellishes and delays the V$^5_3$ upon which it depends for its meaning. It does not represent the parent triad, I. This fact can be demonstrated by substituting the parent I for the $^6_4$ as shown in Example 79. The effect of the parent triad is not at all the same as that of the $^6_4$. It creates a discontinuity in the bass line (indicated by the bracket) and anticipates in an undesirable way the final I (indicated by the dotted line).

Only in one special instance does the $^6_4$ represent its theoretical parent chord: in the case of the "consonant" $^6_4$. This form of the $^6_4$ as well as other variants of the dependent or dissonant $^6_4$ are explained and illustrated in Chapter 11.

EXERCISES

A. List of Some Important Terms to Define and Memorize

Harmonic process
6th chord as extension
6th chord as representative
Dissonant diatonic-6th chords
Parent triad

Parallel 6th chords
Fundamental position
First inversion
Second inversion

B. Basic Keyboard and Aural Exercises

INSTRUCTIONS
These are the same as the instructions given for the preliminary exercises in Chapter 2:
Play each exercise at the keyboard. Then, before going on to the next, sing the exercise in the following ways, using the keyboard to check for accuracy not to accompany the voice.
1   Sing the entire bass.
2   Sing the entire soprano.
3   Beginning from the soprano note sing all the notes of each chord in descending order, close position. Use the neutral syllable "la."
4   Beginning from the bass note sing all the notes of each chord in ascending order, close position.
The exercises should be repeated until a certain degree of fluency is attained. With each repetition transpose the patterns to a different key and provide a different metric-rhythmic pattern. For singing, letter names should replace the neutral syllable, "la," when the exercises are repeated.

exercise 76.   **Basic Chord Pattern 1 (see Exercise 49)**

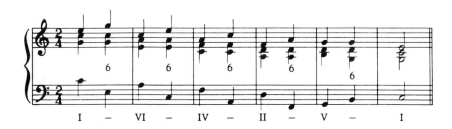

I   —   VI   —   IV   —   II   —   V   —   I

I   —   VI   —   IV   —   II   —   V   —   I

Here each chord of the basic pattern is followed by its first inversion. This greatly expands the basic succession. Arabic figures are shown between the staves, while Roman numerals which designate the position of the fundamental note in the diatonic scale are shown below the bass staff. The dash means that the preceding numeral still applies.

exercise 77. **Basic Chord Pattern 2 (see Exercise 50)**

In the preceding exercise the 6th chords served to extend the parent triad. Here they represent the parent triad: IV^6 stands in place of IV, III^6 stands in place of III, and so on.

At this point we add to the basic keyboard and aural exercises common cadential successions in which the cadential dominant is prepared by II or IV or by the first inversions of those triads. All should be committed to memory and, following the order of the circle of 5ths, played in every key.

exercise 78. **Cadential V prepared by II or II^6**

exercise 79. **Cadential V prepared by IV or IV⁶**

C. **Figured Bass Exercises**

INSTRUCTIONS

These are to be played at the keyboard, notated in full, and sung according to the instructions given for the basic keyboard and aural exercises. In addition, each 6th chord marked by an asterisk should be labeled either as extension or representative of its parent triad.

exercise 80. **Chorale:** *Schmücke dich, o liebe Seele*

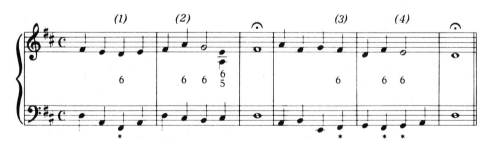

comments

1   The 6th (soprano), should be doubled here in order to avoid parallel 8ves in the connection to the following chord.
2   Impending parallel 8ves can be avoided by correct doubling of the first 6th chord.
3   Were the parent triad to be substituted for the 6th chord here, parallel 8ves and 5ths would automatically result in the connection from the preceding chord. Thus, the 6th chord serves as a voice leading corrective.
4   Change of harmony is required on the last beat.

exercise 81. **TELEMANN:** *Money*

comments

1   The figures $\begin{smallmatrix}6\\4\end{smallmatrix}$ $\begin{smallmatrix}5\\\#\end{smallmatrix}$ indicate the exact horizontal succession of voices. The $\begin{smallmatrix}6\\4\end{smallmatrix}$ is discussed in section 44.

2   Each bass note in this measure and the two following is embellished by an auxiliary eighth note that does not belong to the harmony. These notes develop the harmony rhythmically and melodically but have no effect either upon the structure of the chords or upon their connection.

exercise 82. **Chorale:** *Ich dank' dir, lieber Herre*

comments

1   The second eighth note belongs to the following harmony. This kind of embellishment is known therefore as an ***anticipation.***

2   The chord $\binom{5}{3}$ harmonizes the first of the two eighth notes. The second eighth note in soprano and bass is an unharmonized, unaccented passing note.

3   The figures here indicate the exact linear succession: the 4th above the bass moves to the raised 3rd above the bass.

exercise 83. Chorale: *Singen wir aus Herzensgrund*

comments

1   Whenever the bass of a 6th chord moves to the bass of a $\frac{5}{3}$ by step, as here, one
    must take care to double a note other than the bass, otherwise parallel 8ves
    may result. Here it is best to double the 3rd at the unison.
2   The figures indicate the exact horizontal succession: the 5th above the bass
    moves to the 6th above the bass.

exercise 84. Chorale: *Herr, ich habe misgehandelt*

exercise 85. **Chorale:** *Lobet den Herren*

exercise 86. **Chorale:** *Gottes Sohn ist kommen*

exercise 87.   BASSANI: *Harmonia festiva*

exercise 88. Chorale: *Vater unser im Himmelreich*

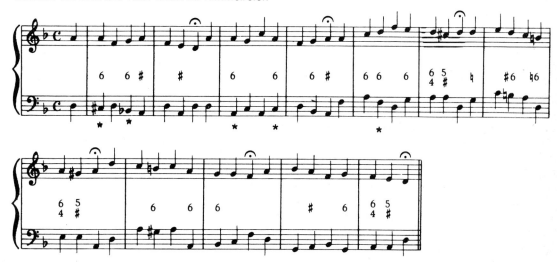

4

The Progression of Diatonic Triads

As I advance in the science of harmony I become convinced that its absolute principle resides in the relations between its sounds, relations of tonality. These result from a certain necessary order from which the sounds derive their functions, their attractions, their antipathies, and ultimately their laws of combination and succesion.

François Joseph Fétis, 1849

45. The Purpose of This Chapter

One writer, the early nineteenth-century theorist Gottfried Weber, has asserted that there are precisely 6888 possible harmonic progressions. Fortunately there is no need to study that many in order to understand tonal music. They can be dealt with in terms of general principles and applied in music of various styles.

By harmonic progression we do not refer to the voice leading techniques for moving from one chord to another. Rather, we mean the selecting and ordering of harmonies in such a way that they form coherent and effective units of several chords. In a still larger context harmonic progression means the progression of harmonies and harmonic units over the span of an entire composition. The reader should remember that the same principles apply to both small and large contexts.

46. Harmonic Progression and Tonality

The notion of harmonic progression is very closely bound up with the concept of *tonality* which emerged with fully developed tonal music. This concept embraces the main structural components of the tonal composition; within it are expressed the highly diversified events and multiple relationships which form a totality, a musical unity. This is not to say that all events within the tonal composition have harmonic significance. In subsequent chapters, notably 11 and 13, consideration will be given to those linear (contrapuntal) aspects of structure that do not have immediate harmonic significance.

The concept of harmonic progression can be approached directly from familiar and elemental materials, the scale and the triad. We begin with the triad.

47. The Tonic Triad as Source of the First Principle of Chord Relation

Diatonic consonant chords form the harmonic basis of all tonal compositions. Among these chords the tonic triad is of primary importance. It contains the first principle of chord relation and progression, a principle based upon the triadic interval of the 5th. The 5th is of fundamental importance because it, and it alone, identifies the triad. This primary role is illustrated below.

example 80.

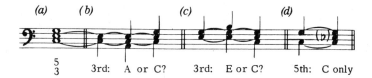

From the complete triad shown at (a) we extract the lower 3rd (b). As shown, this 3rd may associate itself either with the A minor triad or the C triad. It does not belong to either one exclusively. At (c) we extract the upper 3rd of the C major triad. Here again we see that it may belong to either one of two triads. However, at (d) we extract the 5th of the triad and see immediately that it is not ambiguous as is the 3rd. It belongs to one and only one triad the C triad, and identifies, or delimits that triad. The significance of the tonic and dominant triads now becomes clearer.

48. Tonic and Dominant Triads: Primary Triads That Delimit the Key

Just as the 5th delimits the triad, so the cadential succession V I delimits the key. Example 81 summarizes, showing first the vertical 5th as it delimits the triad, then the horizontal bass and harmonic progression V I as it delimits the key.

example 81.

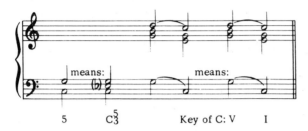

The triads I and V are called *primary triads* to indicate their primary function described above. Those on the remaining scale degrees are called *secondary triads.* Example 82 shows the two classes.

example 82.

The remainder of this chapter is devoted to the ways in which these two classes of triads are related and to the ways in which they combine to form chord progressions.

49. Diatonic Position and Progression by Bass 5th

The term progression suggests an orderly motion from one point to another. Thus, to describe a harmonic progression we must be able to give the positions of its beginning and ending chords. It also would be desirable to have a way of measuring harmonic distance. The primary triads and the 5th by which they relate to one another provide the initial means for fulfilling those requirements.

First, the location of each diatonic triad is described in terms of its distance from I as measured by the bass interval of the descending 5th. If we begin with the triad nearest to I by the interval of a 5th, namely V, we can easily determine the position of the remaining triads by continuing the process, that is, by adding the nearest triad to V by 5th, and so on. Example 83 illustrates.

example 83.

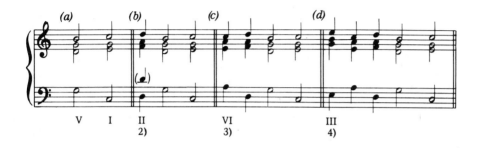

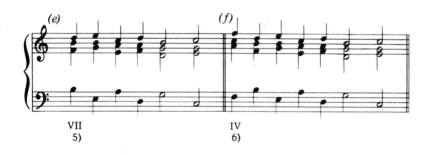

At (a) are the primary triads. V progresses to I by 5th. At (b) the triad which lies a 5th above V is added: II. (In order to keep the progression within the range of the bass clef we represent every other descending 5th by its inversion, the ascending 4th.) At (c) the triad which lies a 5th above II is added to the progression: VI. And so the process continues until all seven diatonic triads are combined in a harmonic progression, a progression which moves by successive bass 5ths. The number in parentheses below each secondary triad indicates the number of 5ths by which it is distant from I.

In Example 84 the same progression is given a metrical setting, with I serving as initial upbeat. This has the advantage of revealing the way in which the chords form a succession of pairs that culminate in the cadential pair, V I.

example 84.

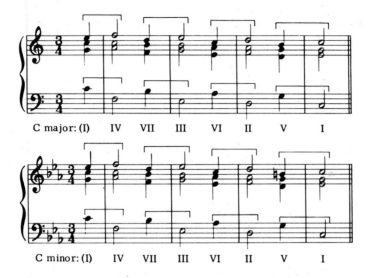

C major: (I) IV VII III VI II V I

C minor: (I) IV VII III VI II V I

50. The 2nd as Melodic Interval of Chord (Bass) Relationship

The 5th relationship, as explained above, is the most important for harmonic progression. All other intervals of progression are subordinate to it. Next in importance is the 2nd relationship exemplified by the chord pair IV V. The 5th relationship is exemplified by the chord pairs I IV and V I.

example 85.

I IV V I

Example 85 shows IV as a prefix to V. The interval of bass progression from chord to chord is the 2nd. We will characterize this stepwise interval of bass progression as melodic. We can then describe such stepwise progressions more specifically as auxiliary note or passing note formations. For instance, the bass of IV (F) here serves as a lower auxiliary note to the bass of V.

When the triad on IV serves as a stepwise preparation of V as shown in Example 85 we will call it a *dominant preparation.* Similarly, VI often serves as a stepwise dominant preparation. An illustration follows.

example 86. BEETHOVEN: *Quartet in F major, Op. 59/1* (registers simplified)

51. The 3rd Relationship

Bass 3rd relationships between chords are always subordinate to other, stronger, relationships, either the 5th or the 2nd relationship. Example 87 demonstrates this.

example 87.

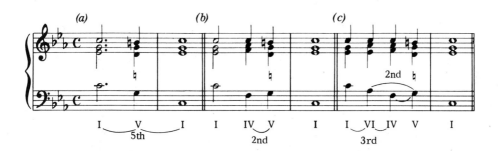

At (*a*) we see the 5th relationship I V I. At (*b*) V is prepared by IV, a second relationship. At (*c*) VI is added to the chord succession, forming 3rd relationships with both I and IV.

Of first importance, however, is the 2nd relationship of VI to V as stepwise preparation. Thus, read from left to right Example 87 illustrates the relative values of the intervals of chord progression. The 5th is first in importance; next comes the 2nd; and finally the 3rd, which is always subordinate either to the 5th or to the 2nd, rhythmic and other conditions being equal.

Example 88 provides another short illustration of the three intervals of progression in combination.

example 88.

At (*a*) the interval of progression is the 5th. At (*b*) the dominant preparation VI adds the two other intervals of progression, forming a 3rd relationship with I and a 2nd relationship with V. In the complete progression the 5th remains as the main interval, with the 2nd next in importance, and the 3rd last. Thus VI and V form a chord pair, not VI and I. Similarly, at (*c*) III and VI form a pair related by the 5th, while the 3rd between III and I is of secondary importance.

52. Inversion of the Interval of Progression

In connection with Example 83 we remarked that the 5th relationship was represented by the inversion of the 5th, the 4th. Inversion does not alter the interval of progression. The inverted equivalents of 5th, 2nd, and 3rd relationships are summarized in Example 89.

example 89.

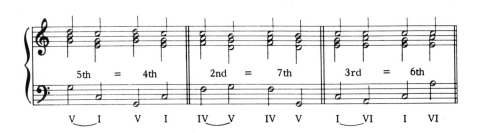

Example 89 also shows that the three intervals of progression (5th, 2nd, and 3rd) plus their inversions (4th, 7th, and 6th) comprise all the diatonic intervals except the 8ve and unison. The 8ve is an interval of progression only insofar as it is involved in the inversion process. Therefore, in order to complete our examination of consonant chord relationships and progression we must consider the function of 6th chords, which are produced by the inversion process.

53. The Function of 6th Chords in Consonant Chord Progression

In Chapter 3 we examined the function of 6th chords as extensions or representatives of the parent triad. In longer harmonic units composed of several chords, such as those we are considering in the present chapter, 6th chords pose no new problems. In fact, only the representative 6th chord requires comment. Often the bass of the representative 6th chord moves by 2nd, whereas the bass of the parent chord would move by 5th in the same context.

The 6th chord thus combines the 2nd and 5th relationships. The 2nd relationship is actually given; the 5th relationship is implicit. Example 90 illustrates.

example 90.

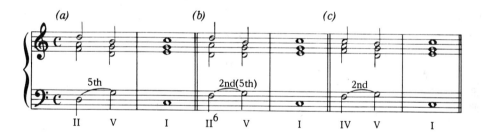

At (a) we see the progression II V I, which is based entirely on the 5th relationship. At (b) II6 is inserted to represent the parent II. The bass now moves by 2nd and the chord serves as a stepwise dominant preparation similar to IV(c). Yet the underlying harmonic relationship is the 5th relationship indicated by the Roman numerals. In all cases these show the progression of the fundamental note of the triad.

In working out chord progressions one must often consider both relationships, the explicit 2nd of the bass and the implicit 5th of the fundamental.

Example 91 provides another illustration of II⁶ as dominant preparation.

example 91. HAYDN: *Symphony in G major* ("Oxford")

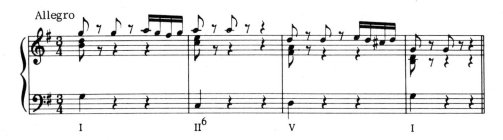

In this context 2nd and 5th relationships are balanced. There are, however, instances in which the melodic function of the first inversion far outweighs its relation to the parent chord. An example follows.

example 92. SCHUMANN: *Carnaval*

Clearly the melodic value of the I⁶ as upbeat to IV is primary here. Note that the bass moves in parallel 10ths with the upper voice toward the accented IV. If the parent I were substituted for I⁶, as at (b), the effect would not be at all the same. The parallel 10ths here provide an instance of the importance of linear intervallic patterns. (See section 220.)

54. The Functions of the Dissonant Diatonic Triads

In section 43 it was stated that the dissonant diatonic triads rarely occur in fundamental position. Most often they are represented by their first inversions. These
chords, VII in major and minor and II in minor, are used to connect consonant
chords, and although essential from the melodic standpoint they are secondary to
the consonant triads with regard to harmonic progression. This is perhaps most
convincingly demonstrated by the fact that a dissonant triad is never a goal of a
harmonic progression. (See section 58.)

55. Harmonization of Scale Degree 6 in Minor as Ascending Passing Note

Like the dissonant diatonic triads, the chord which usually harmonizes scale degree
6 in minor is only of local significance. Since it is essential for melodic reasons we
include it here as a diatonic consonance, but with the qualification that its use is
restricted to the harmonization of scale degree 6 in minor as an ascending passing
note. Example 93 shows that scale degree first in the soprano, then in the bass.
In both cases the chord which harmonizes the altered 6th degree is IV♮. The
Roman numeral is enclosed in parentheses to indicate that the chord is not equivalent to the regular IV in harmonic value. In this context it serves a linear function
to make consonant the first of the two passing notes that fill out the interval of
the 4th from G to C.

example 93.

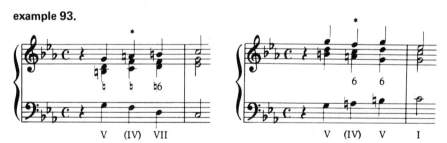

56. The Secondary Dominant Triad as Chromatic Extension of V—I Relation

Thus far discussion and examples have been restricted to diatonic triads. There is,
however, a consonant chromatic triad of such common occurrence even in pre-
dominantly diatonic contexts that it should be considered at this point. This is the
secondary dominant triad. The following series of examples illustrates the structure
and function of this chord.

example 94.

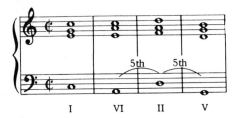

$$\text{I} \qquad \text{VI} \qquad \text{II} \qquad \text{V}$$

Example 94 shows a progression of four chords terminating on V. The last three chords are related by 5th. In the next example the bass remains the same, but the 3rd of the second chord has been raised, creating a chromatic passing note in the soprano.

example 95.

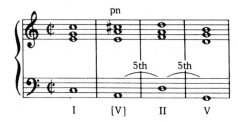

$$\text{I} \qquad \text{[V]} \qquad \text{II} \qquad \text{V}$$

This altered, or chromatic, triad now relates to the following chord exactly as does dominant to tonic in minor. The chromatic passing note may be regarded as a transitory leading note, exemplifying the law of the half step (section 10). For these reasons it is called a secondary dominant triad and symbolized by [V]. It does not usurp the role of the main dominant triad in the key, the primary triad, but merely imitates its structure and function, and thus enhances the progression to the triad which it precedes—II in this instance. Example 96 presents the passage upon which Examples 94 and 95 are based.

example 96. BEETHOVEN: *Prometheus Overture*

Allegro molto

$$\text{I} \qquad \text{[V]} \qquad \text{II} \qquad \text{V}$$

Any consonant diatonic triad can be preceded by a secondary dominant triad. Below is an example of secondary dominant triads drawn from a seventeenth-century composition. The original is without bar lines. Brackets have been supplied to indicate the harmonic groups; key signature and accidentals have been modified to conform with modern practice.

example 97. HEINRICH SCHÜTZ: *Kleines Geistliches Konzert IX*

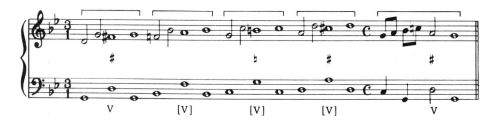

V   [V]   [V]   [V]   V

example 98. Chorale: *Das walt' Gott Vater und Gott Sohn*

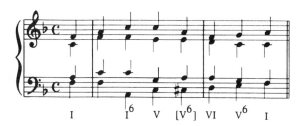

I   I⁶   V   [V⁶]   VI   V⁶   I

Here VI is preceded by the first inversion of a secondary dominant triad, [V⁶], whose bass is a chromatic passing note that serves as a transitory leading note.

Secondary dominants (sometimes called "applied dominants") are so common in tonal music—and will be encountered so often in subsequent examples—that further illustrations at this point seem unnecessary. It is, however, necessary to point out that although secondary dominants are most often chromatic triads, there are two common instances in which they are diatonic triads. These are the secondary dominant of IV (I) in the major mode and, in the minor mode, the secondary dominant of III (VII).

57. Harmonic Direction

We have seen that consonant triads form chord pairs related by one of three intervals, the 5th, the 2nd, or the 3rd. In harmonic progression the most important of these three intervals is the 5th. Example 83 has illustrated how the position of each consonant triad in the key is measured in terms of 5ths distant from I. From these concepts of chord relationship, harmonic position, and chord progression, we derive the concept of harmonic direction: the orderly progression from one chord toward another chord—the harmonic goal. The factor of direction distinguishes harmonic progression from mere harmonic change. Progression toward a specific goal may involve several chords which form subgroups consisting of chord pairs, threes . . ., but the main elements of the progression are, first, the harmony which serves as point of departure and, second, the harmonic goal. The following example illustrates those two elements:

example 99. BEETHOVEN: *Piano Sonata in G major, Op. 31/1*

The point of departure for the progression is I. The harmonic goal of the progression, V, is indicated here and elsewhere in the present volume by an arrow. After the statement of I in the first measure the composition unfolds only in the melodic dimension—through changes of soprano position—until the point marked by an asterisk. There VI serves as a cue to the direction of the progression toward V, the harmonic goal.

58. Direction and the Harmonic Axis I V I

Essentially there are two harmonic directions: toward I and toward V. These primary diatonic triads form the *harmonic axis* of tonal music. Two models are presented below (one in major, one in minor) which show how the consonant diatonic triads function with respect to this axis. These models are designed to show the norms of diatonic progression succinctly so that they can be learned easily. They have many practical applications, for example, in selecting chords to harmonize melodies, in harmonizing basses, and of course in analyzing and composing chord successions.

example 100. Model of Consonant Diatonic-Chord Progression in the Major Mode

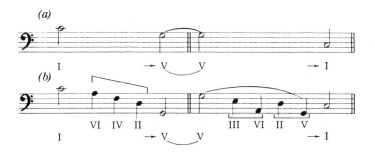

At (a) we see the harmonic axis formed by the progression I V I; at (b) the consonant diatonic triads (secondary triads) in relation to this axis. The first part of (b) shows VI, IV, and II, as they carry the progression from I to V. With the exception of VI none of these triads relates closely to I. Instead, they direct the progression toward V, and therefore are called *dominant preparations*. Each may move to V separately—VI and IV by 2nd, II by 5th—or all three may occur in the order shown.

The second part of Example 100 shows the progression from V to I. Here the secondary triads III, VI, and II implement the progression. In contrast to the secondary triads within the progression I V, which form a group of three chords, the triads here form chord pairs, as indicated by the brackets.

The model of progression in the minor mode follows.

example 101. Model of Consonant Diatonic-Chord Progression in Minor Mode

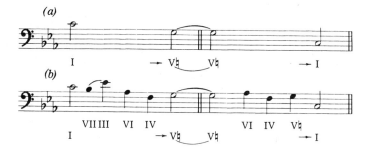

As noted earlier, the triad on the leading note is dissonant in both major and minor modes. Therefore it is excluded from the models. In the minor mode II is also dissonant and therefore excluded. The remaining triads arrange themselves with respect to the harmonic axis as shown in Example 101. This model is similar to that of the major mode except for the more prominent role of III in the progression from I to V. And, since II is excluded, the progression from V to I in minor is shorter than that in major.

59. Circular Progression

There are three main types of harmonic progression, all illustrated in the models: (1) *circular* progression; (2) *opening* progression; (3) *closing* progression. The first of these, circular progression, departs from a chord and has as its goal the same chord—for example, I I, or V V.

example 102. SCHUBERT: *Waltz in E major, Op. 18a/1*

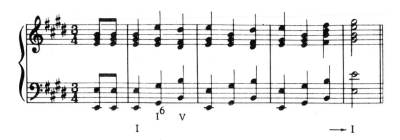

Here the harmony unfolds between two soprano positions of the tonic triad. At the beginning of the progression I is in the soprano position of the 5th; at the end of the progression it is in the soprano position of the 3rd. The I is both point of departure and goal. There is no other harmonic goal, since the I^6 serves as an extension of I and the V has a subsidiary function, as indicated by its position in the metric-rhythmic pattern. From the standpoint of harmony therefore the progression is circular, self-contained.

60. Circular Progression by Sequence

A special type of circular progression is illustrated by the example below, a somewhat shortened version of Basic Chord Pattern 2.

example 103.

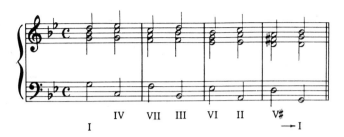

The progression begins and ends on the tonic triad and includes every diatonic triad but one, the dissonant VII. The triads are so arranged that their bass notes form an unbroken succession of descending 5ths. (Every other descending 5th is represented by its inversion, the ascending 4th.) A progression of this kind, which involves the repetition of a bass and chord pattern is called a *sequence.* (In Chapter 11, section 220 the intervals formed by the outer voices of such patterns are discussed.) (See also Chapter 7, section 140.)

Handel has used the sequence shown in Example 103 in a short keyboard composition:

example 104. Based on HANDEL's *Passacaglia* from *Keyboard Suite in G minor*

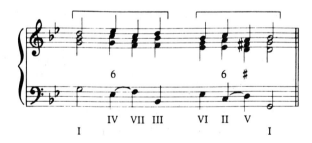

Here the sequence is slightly modified. Both IV and II are inverted, so that in place of the uninterrupted bass progression of alternating 5ths and 4ths we hear the two groups marked by brackets. This division is made even clearer by the melodic pattern in the upper voice, which repeats after two measures:

example 105. HANDEL: *Passacaglia* from *Keyboard Suite in G minor*

61. Opening Progression

In contrast to a circular progression, an opening progression departs from one chord and has as its goal a different chord. The prime example of this type of progression is I V, the progression shown in Example 99 (Beethoven's *Op. 31/1*). A shorter illustration follows.

example 106. SCHUMANN: *Folk Song* (*Album for the Young*)

The first change, from I to V⁶, forecasts the goal, but the progression is completed only with the final V (in fundamental position). A longer example of opening progression follows.

example 107. BRAHMS: *Waldesnacht, Op. 62/3*

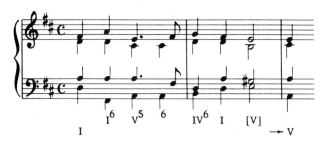

The harmonic goal of this progression, V, is approached via its secondary dominant triad. This serves to establish V firmly as the goal.

Opening and circular progressions combine in the next example.

example 108. Based on Chorale: *Auf meinen lieben Gott*

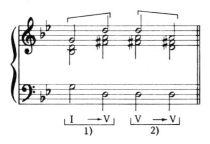

This passage consists of two progressions, only the main harmonies of which are shown in Example 108. The first moves from I to V, an opening progression. The second moves from V to V, a circular progression. Example 109 presents the two progressions in their entirety.

example 109. Chorale: *Auf meinen lieben Gott*

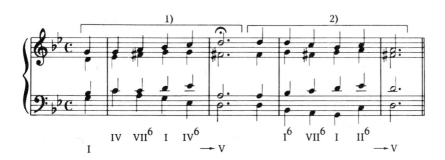

Single progressions of this kind are often called *phrases.* In the present volume the term progression or harmonic unit usually is used instead of phrase because the latter term often is confusing to those who are accustomed to associate it with the vocal or instrumental phrase, a musical unit which may or may not correspond to the harmonic phrase.

62. Closing Progression

By closing progression is meant a progression that returns to I, usually from V. Two examples are given below.

example 110. Chorale: *O Ewigkeit, du Donnerwort* (reduction)

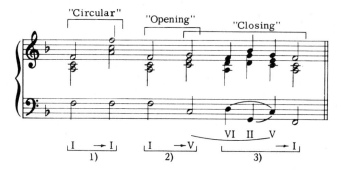

Example 110 is a synopsis of the full chorale setting. It contains three harmonic units, the first a circular progression, the second an opening progression, the third a closing progression from V to I. Thus all three types of progression are represented. In the closing progression the triads on VI and II behave as indicated in the model, Example 100: as dominant preparations they direct the progression toward the cadential V.

Progressions based on consonant chords can be expanded to any length. The three basic progressions shown in Example 110 above are greatly expanded in the complete setting of the chorale presented below.

example 111. Chorale: *O Ewigkeit, du Donnerwort*

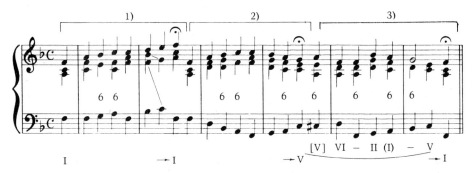

We draw attention particularly to the chords within the third unit, the closing progression. The basic progression is VI II V I. Here, in the expanded progression, VI is introduced by its secondary dominant triad and followed by its first inversion. The II is also followed by its first inversion—but not immediately. Inserted between II and II[6] is the bass passing note A. This A supports a I[6]. Since the I[6]

here neither extends nor represents the tonic triad, but has only a subordinate melodic function as a connection between the II and II⁶, the Roman numeral I is enclosed in parentheses.

The next excerpt is more symmetrical than the chorale above. Again, a synopsis of the harmonic progression is given first.

example 112.

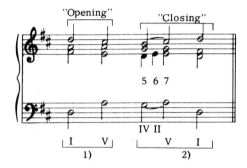

The first harmonic unit is an opening progression I V. The second is a closing progression, in which II^6 prepares the cadential V. The complete passage is given in the next example.

example 113. MOZART: *Symphony in D major, K.385* ("Haffner")

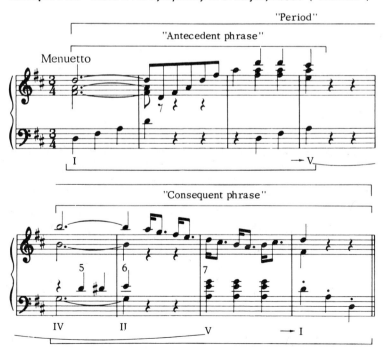

The complete closing progression includes IV as well as II. Observe that the change from IV to II involves a change of only one note: D to E, or in figures, 5 to 6.

A succession of two phrases such as that illustrated by Example 113 is often called a *period.* The first phrase of the period opens to the dominant and is called the *antecedent phrase,* while the following phrase is called the *consequent.* (These terms are used infrequently in the present volume.)

63. Harmonic Goals Other Than I or V

In the foregoing sections we have concentrated on harmonic progression as it is controlled by the harmonic axis I V I. Only I and V have been shown as harmonic goals. A consonant secondary triad can occur as a harmonic goal under one of the conditions described below:

1   When the secondary triad is an intermediate goal. For example, the dominant preparations II and IV are often intermediate harmonic goals of progressions which then continue toward V. An instance of this is quoted in Example 116 below.

2   When the secondary triad has been established as a *quasi-tonic.* Under this condition it then has its own secondary triads and controls a harmonic domain in the same way as the main tonic triad. This usually involves the process of modulation—the subject of Chapter 9.

3   When the secondary triad substitutes—as in the case of the substitution of VI for I. (See section 65.)

64. Harmonic Function

We have seen that the harmonic function of a chord is described in terms of its direction in relation to the two triads, I and V, that form the harmonic axis. For example, if it is preceded by I the function of VI is to direct the progression toward V. If VI then forms a chord pair with IV the direction toward the dominant is further confirmed. The normative harmonic function of a triad is not always confirmed, but the exceptions can easily be understood with the aid of the models of progression presented in Examples 100 and 101.

In harmonic progression, as in speech, there are often digressions, repetitions, interpolations, and ellipses. An understanding of these comes not from experience alone, but from experience combined with a sure knowledge of normative harmonic functions and the principles of chord relationship from which they derive.

Under certain circumstances linear intervallic patterns take precedence over harmonic functions, and, indeed, in these cases attempts to read harmonic progressions will lead to peculiar results. (See section 220.)

65. Substitution

An important aspect of harmonic function is the technique of *substitution.* By substitution is meant the exchange of one diatonic triad for another which has the same direction in relation to the harmonic axis. For example, the dominant preparations II, IV, and VI are interchangeable.

Substitution is not the same as the representation of a triad by its first inversion, although the two techniques are related. Substitution involves two different triads, for example, II and IV, whereas representation involves the same triad in two different forms, such as I and I^6. An inversion may of course substitute for a triad other than its parent triad, as when II^6 substitutes for IV at the cadence.

example 114.

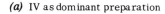 *(a)* IV as dominant preparation
 *(b)* II^6 substitutes for IV

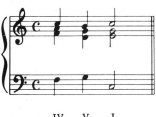

IV   V   I

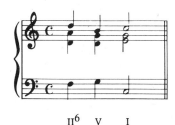

II^6 V   I

Although certain triads are interchangeable from the harmonic standpoint they may differ markedly from the melodic standpoint. Thus in Example 114 the soprano in the case of II^6 is quite different from the soprano in the case of IV. Melodic and rhythmic requirements therefore determine the choice of chord when more than one is available for a particular harmonic function.

The general information on progression given above is applied below in brief descriptions of the normative functions of each diatonic triad. In each case differences between major and minor modes are considered. This summary also affords an opportunity to review the names customarily given to the diatonic triads. Although the present volume uses only a few of these the remaining terms are widely used and therefore the student should know them.

HARMONIC FUNCTIONS of the INDIVIDUAL DIATONIC TRIADS

66. I (Tonic)

The tonic triad has two principal harmonic functions. It serves as the point of departure for progression, notably at the beginning of the composition, and it serves as the ultimate goal of harmonic progression.

The equivalence of the tonic triads in major and minor is illustrated by the chromatic alteration of the cadential I in minor which forms the *tierce de Picardie*. An example follows.

example 115. Chorale: *Von Gott will ich nicht lassen*

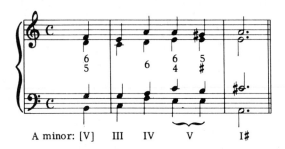

Tierce de Picardie is the traditional name given to the raised 3rd of the minor triad at the final cadence, as in the example above.

Occasionally there occurs a chord which has the structure of I but not its function. An instance of this was remarked in connection with Example 111. In such cases the Roman numeral is enclosed in parentheses.

67. II (Supertonic) in the Major Mode

The term supertonic indicates the position of this triad *above* the tonic. Functionally, however, the supertonic triad has little relation to the tonic triad. By virtue of the 5th relationship II always functions as a dominant preparation.

In some cases II serves as an intermediate harmonic goal (see section 63). An example is given below.

example 116. MOZART: *Symphony in D major, K.504* ("Prague")

68. II in the Minor Mode

In minor the supertonic triad is diminished, a dissonant triad. We will see later that dissonant intervals require progression by 2nd. For this reason the II in minor rarely occurs in fundamental position as a $\frac{5}{3}$ progressing to V by 5th, as does II in major, unless it is part of a sequence as in Basic Chord Pattern 2. Usually it occurs in the first inversion.

II functions in minor just as it does in major: as a dominant preparation. A short example is provided below:

example 117. SCHUMANN: *Anfangs wollt' ich*

Because it is a dissonant triad and entirely dependent upon a consonant chord for its structural meaning, the supertonic triad in minor cannot be a harmonic goal as can the supertonic in major.

Indeed, the harmonic function of II is so firmly determined by the rules of harmonic syntax that, as shown in Example 118 at (a), it cannot serve as a passing chord between I and I⁶, although the voice-leading is perfectly correct, without implying a progression to V. In the pretonal music of the Renaissance, of course, one finds successions such as those at (a), but in tonal music the dissonant 6th chord (or its equivalent) is the rule.

example 118.

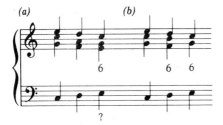

69. III (Mediant) in the Major Mode

The normative function of the mediant triad in major is indicated in the model, Example 100: it progresses to VI by 5th. It is important to notice that III does not serve as a dominant preparation. On the contrary, it occurs as a suffix to V. It also occurs as a suffix to I. Thus III is quite distant from both elements of the harmonic axis, and is related to them only through VI.

The mediant triad often occurs in a subordinate melodic role as a connective between I and IV:

example 119. Chorale: *Nun lob', mein Seel', den Herren*

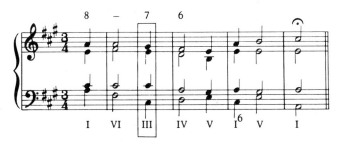

In this role III supports the soprano progression 8 7 6 (scale degrees), as shown here. Every consonant triad may have subordinate melodic functions of this kind, a fact that will become even more evident in the sections devoted to melodic structure, Chapter 7.

70. III in the Minor Mode

The function of III in minor differs significantly from that of III in major. Whereas in major the mediant is relatively unimportant, in minor it is a quasi-primary triad. Its importance has already been indicated both in the model, Example 101, and also in the Handel *Passacaglia,* Example 104. The structural reasons for this more important role are to be found in the relationships which two other triads bear to III, relationships which derive from the structure of the natural minor scale. Example 120 illustrates these.

example 120.

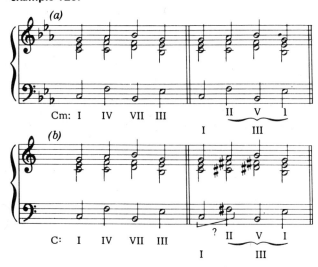

At (*a*) we see the diatonic progression I IV VII III in minor. The last three chords easily group themselves in relation to III as a tonic—without chromatic alteration—so that III is heard as a harmonic goal. In short, IV in relation to C minor (I) becomes II in relation to III (E♭ major), while VII in relation to C minor (I) becomes V in relation to III (E♭ major). We see at (*b*) that an analogous situation is impossible in the major mode without extensive and disruptive chromatic alterations.

A short excerpt will illustrate the function of III in minor as a quasi-primary triad.

example 121. Chorale: *Ach wie nichtig*

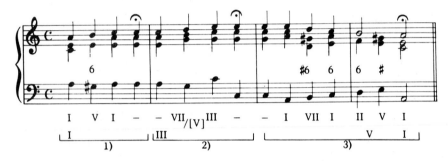

The first unit contains a circular progression; the second a progression to III via VII which serves as [V] of III. (The dual function of VII is indicated by the slant.) The third unit contains a progression from III back to I via V. Example 122 below summarizes the passage in terms of harmonic goals.

example 122.

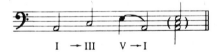

Here we see that the bass line arpeggiates the notes of the tonic triad, another indication of the control which the tonic triad maintains over the longer span of harmonic progression.

71. IV (Subdominant) in Major and Minor

The triad on IV is called the subdominant because it occupies a position *below* the tonic triad analogous to that occupied by the dominant above:

example 123.

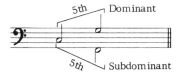

Its symmetrical position in relation to I and V led Rameau and many subsequent writers to rank the subdominant triad with the tonic and dominant triads. Thus one often reads of the *three* primary triads, I, IV, and V. This is a fallacious viewpoint since the IV usually functions as a dominant preparation, one of three such chords.

Sometimes the IV assumes a more independent role, as in the excerpt below.

example 124. SCHUBERT: *Death and the Maiden*

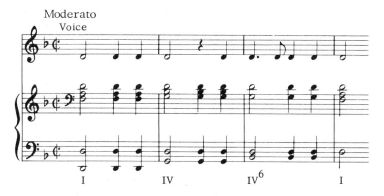

Here the IV and its first inversion stand between two statements of I. When the IV occurs apart from the V, as in this excerpt, its function is primarily melodic.

The IV sometimes occurs at the close of a composition, forming a cadential pair with I.

example 125. BRAHMS: *First Symphony*

In this context the IV I succession is called a *plagal* cadence. Actually, the plagal cadence rarely closes the composition, for it is usually preceded by a basic dominant-tonic ("authentic") cadence.

Earlier we saw the idiomatic use of the altered IV in minor to harmonize scale degree 6 as an ascending passing note (section 55). Still another subdominant idiom, this one in major, is illustrated below.

example 126. WOLF: *Benedeit die sel'ge Mutter*

Moderato

Here IV^6 stands between two statements of V^6. It serves two functions here: its bass note embellishes the bass of V^6 and the chord as a whole substitutes for the tonic triad.

72. V (Dominant) in Major

V serves to establish the tonic triad. This function is particularly evident at the cadence. Apart from this cadential function, which is a local matter, V forms with I the harmonic axis that controls harmonic progression over the entire span of the composition. The full meaning of this will become apparent as we proceed. However, even in the present chapter we have found that a progression to V as harmonic goal, an "opening" progression, literally does open the way for further harmonic expansion. It is in this role that V is most cogently expressed as part of the harmonic axis. The cadential function, as we have said, is a purely local matter. There has been much confusion regarding these two distinct functions of V because many writers have not recognized that one has to do with detail, the other with harmonic development over the longer span of the composition. This confusion is evident in the persistent use of the term "half cadence" to describe the function of V as a harmonic goal. For instance, the V which stands at the end of the first harmonic unit of the Mozart passage quoted earlier (Example 113) would be described as a "half cadence" by many writers, and presumably, so would the V in the second, fourth, and sixth measure of the following excerpt.

example 127. MOZART: *Quintet for Clarinet and Strings in A major, K.581*

Actually, the passage above is composed of four harmonic units, marked by brackets. The first three have V as goal; the fourth terminates on I. Thus, the passage consists of three statements of the opening progression I V, followed by the expected closing progression to I. There is only one cadence—in the final measure.

73. V in the Minor Mode

As explained earlier (section 29) the dominant triad has two forms in the minor mode. When it is the major triad which contains the leading note it functions just like the dominant triad in the major mode. However, when it is the minor triad which contains the natural 7th scale degree it is more independent of I, and often controls a large harmonic domain as a quasi-tonic.

As mentioned in section 69, every triad may have subordinate melodic functions. In the case of V in the minor mode, a characteristic subordinate melodic function is exemplified by the situation shown in Example 128.

example 128.

Here, although one might label the second chord V, it clearly has no harmonic function, but is the result of a descending passing note (scale degree 7) in the bass, paralleling the melodic descent in the soprano. (Compare Example 229.)

74. VI (Submediant)

The triad on VI is called the *submediant* because it occupies a position *below* the tonic triad analogous to that occupied by the mediant above the tonic triad. (See dominant and subdominant, Example 123.)

example 129.

We have seen that VI serves as a dominant preparation both in major and in minor. Often it follows I immediately, providing the first cue to progression toward V. This is shown in the model, Example 100. In addition to this main function, VI has other roles. Of these the most important is its role as substitute for the tonic triad. An illustration follows.

example 130. Chorale: *Meine Seele erhebet den Herrn*

for:

One would expect the tonic triad at the opening of the chorale. Instead, the VI is found in its place.

VI plays a prominent role altogether in this progression. In the second measure ,it is extended by means of its secondary dominant and in the third measure assumes its normative function as dominant preparation.

A special case of VI as substitute for I is the *deceptive cadence.* This is illustrated below.

example 131. MOZART: *Quintet for Clarinet and Strings in A major, K.581*

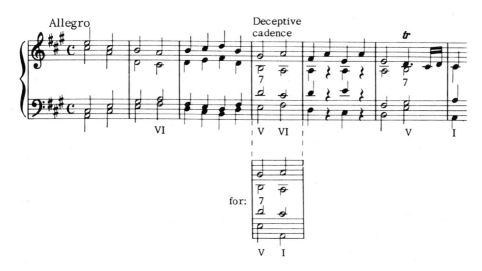

In the fourth measure one expects an authentic cadence which would close the first harmonic unit. Instead V progresses to VI, a motion called a deceptive cadence. This permits further extension of the dominant harmony. The cadential V occurs again after one measure, this time closing to I. By deceptive cadences progressions are not only extended but often are redirected toward a harmony other than I (or V).

75.   VII (Leading-Note Triad) in Major

The VII is a dissonant triad both in major and in minor. Like II in minor, it occurs rarely in fundamental position. When represented by its first inversion it often stands between I and I⁶, as shown below.

example 132.   Chorale: *Wer in dem Schutz des Hochsten*

$$I \quad VII^6 \quad I^6$$

The exclusively melodic function of VII⁶ is evident here. It connects two forms of the primary harmony. The same melodic function is illustrated in the next example.

example 133.   Chorale: *Gott der Vater, wohn' uns bei*

$$I \qquad IV \quad VII^6 \quad I \quad [VII] \quad V$$

In Example 133 the VII⁶ stands between IV in the first measure and I. It harmonizes scale degree 7, the leading note, serving as a substitute for V. The second measure contains a chord of the same structure which functions as VII⁶ in relation to the goal harmony, V. In this context the chromatic VII⁶ substitutes for an inverted secondary dominant-7th chord (see section 109).

76. VII in the Natural Minor

As a major triad on unaltered or natural scale degree 7 in minor the VII functions as a secondary dominant triad in relation to the mediant. This was shown in Example 121. A further instance is quoted here:

example 134. BRAHMS: *Intermezzo in A minor, Op. 76/7*

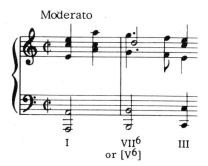

77. Summary of Functions of Diatonic Triads

In both large and small contexts the normative functions of the secondary diatonic triads and their first inversions are as follows:

DIATONIC LOCATION OF FUNDAMENTAL NOTE	NAME	FUNCTION(S) IN RELATION TO I AND V
II	Supertonic	Dominant preparation.
III (in major)	Mediant	Leads to dominant preparations IV, II⁶, or VI.
III (in minor)		Independent triad that often usurps role of tonic.
IV	Subdominant	Dominant preparation or melodic embellishment of tonic.
VI (in major)	Submediant	Dominant preparation or tonic substitute.
VI (in minor)		Dominant preparation.
VII (in major and harmonic minor)	Leading-note triad	Dominant substitute or melodic embellishment of tonic.
VII (in natural minor)	Natural VII	Secondary dominant in relation to the mediant triad.

EXERCISES

A. Some Important Terms to Define and Memorize

Harmonic progression
Interval of progression
Diatonic location (position)
Primary triads
Secondary triads
Dominant preparation
3rd relationship
Secondary dominant triad
Harmonic direction
Harmonic axis

Circular progression
Opening progression
Closing progression
Harmonic sequence
Phrase
Period
Harmonic function
Substitution
Subdominant
Submediant

B. Analysis

INSTRUCTIONS

1. Play each passage at the keyboard.
2. Place appropriate figured bass symbols above the bass staff to show chord structure.
3. Place appropriate Roman numerals below the bass staff to show the positions of the chords in the key.
4. Be sure to understand the harmonic function of each chord in relation to the harmonic axis, I V.

exercise 89. SCHÜTZ: *Christmas Story*

exercise 90. BRAHMS: Ach lieber Herre Jesu Christ

Con moto

Figured
bass
symbols:

Roman
numerals:

C. Basic Keyboard and Aural Exercises

Before undertaking these exercises review those at the end of the previous chapter. The same procedure applies to these exercises, with additional instructions given below.

exercise 91. **Basic Chord Pattern 1**

Here the pattern is expanded by diatonic triads which serve as stepwise prefixes. It is interesting to observe that both I and V thus serve as embellishing chords.

INSTRUCTIONS
Fill in the inner voices and add the bass where missing.

I   (V)   VI   III   IV   (I)   II   V   I

exercise 92.

By means of the 6th chords the preceding pattern is expanded still further.

exercise 93. **Basic Chord Pattern 2**

Here the 5ths' progression of the pattern is expanded by means of arpeggiation, which creates a succession of 3rds in each measure. In accord with the norms of progression the 3rds are secondary to the main progression which proceeds by 5ths.

D. Figured Bass Exercises

These exercises provide additional and essential practice in locating and connecting chords. For the most part they contain only chords explained thus far. All unfamiliar chords as well as certain unfamiliar rhythmic situations are realized. The figured-bass exercises also provide excellent material for analysis. After playing and writing out the exercises in the usual manner identify each chord by Roman and Arabic numerals. Then determine the extent of each harmonic unit. Finally, characterize each progression as circular, opening, or closing.

exercise 94. **Chorale:** *Was ist mein Stand, mein Glück*

comments

1   If the 3rd of the preceding 6th chord is doubled, a correct connection to this chord may be achieved by dividing the chord between the hands, that is, open spacing. In that case the left hand takes a B♭ 8ve, while the right hand takes F and D. In continuo playing this technique is called **divided accompaniment.**

exercise 95. **LOEILLET:** *Solo for Flute and Continuo*

Allegro

comments

1   The 6th chord arises naturally here from the upward skip of the bass. It does not require a figure.

2   The dash here and elsewhere in the present volume indicates that the previous harmony remains in effect. That is, the voices above the bass do not change.

3   The harmonic unit which begins here contains a progression toward II as harmonic goal.

4   Here the situation is the reverse of that in measure 1: the $\frac{5}{3}$ arises as a result of the descending skip from the bass of the 6th chord. In order to have full harmony on the second beat an inner voice must replace the C♯ temporarily lost in the bass.

exercise 96.   **Chorale:** *Ach Gott, wie manches Herzeleid*

comments

1   The first progression is an opening progression. Its goal is the secondary dominant triad, [V] of V. In accord with the logic of harmonic progression, the harmonic goal of the subsequent unit is the V itself.

exercise 97. **HASSE:** *Solo for Flute or Violin*

comments

1   Shift to three voices for these two 6th chords. Since one of the parallel 5ths
which will result is not perfect they are not objectionable. If four-voice harmony is maintained, the notes must be divided equally between the hands.

E. Unfigured Outer Voices

At this point we introduce a new type of exercise: the realization of unfigured outer voices. The purpose of these exercises is to provide practice in the selection of appropriate chords under conditions of limited choice. These exercises constitute an important step toward the independent harmonization of upper voices and basses (Chapter 7).

INSTRUCTIONS

1 Sing the upper voice. If the exercise consists of solo part and accompaniment sing both the solo line and the upper voice of the accompaniment.
2 Sing the bass line.
3 Play the outer voices. If the exercise consists of accompaniment and solo, play only the outer voices of the accompaniment.
4 Supply Roman numerals and figure bass indicating your selection of chord. Only chords explained thus far may be used; diatonic triads—both consonant and dissonant—and secondary dominant triads and 6th chords.
5 Play and write the exercise as you would a figured-bass exercise.
6 Analyze the progressions from the standpoint of chord function, harmonic goals, as well as the harmonic function of the individual chord, the interval relationships which group the chords together, the harmonic direction of each group or larger unit, and the type of progression represented by each unit.

exercise 98. *Welsh Air*

exercise 99. JOHN WILSON: *From the fair Lavinian Shore*

exercise 100. **Chorale:** *Von Himmel kam der Engel*

exercise 101. **PURCELL:** "Ah, How Pleasant 'Tis to Love" (solo voice and bass combined)

comments

1 Unharmonized bass passing note. Retain harmony from previous beat.
2 Unharmonized passing note in upper voice. Retain previous harmony.
3 The change of bass should fall on the second beat. Instead it is delayed by one eighth note, creating an unusual rhythm.

exercise 102. Chorale: *Gott lebet noch*

exercise 103. PURCELL: "I Attempt from Love's Sickness"

comments

1   This is a bass suspension chord, figured $\frac{5}{2}$. See section 184.

exercise 104.   **WILLIAM CROFT: "I Love the Lord"**

comments

1   The meter signature is to be interpreted as $\frac{4}{2}$.
2   The quarter note requires a chord.

exercise 105.   **Gemiani:** *Sonata for Violin and Continuo in E Minor*

Largo

5

The Melodic Process of Chord Generation: Seventh Chords

When we consider musical works we find that the triad is ever-present and that the interpolated dissonances have no other purpose than to effect the continuous variation of the triad.

Lorenz Mizler, 1739

78. Melodic Process Compared to the Harmonic

In tonal music all chords are generated from the triad by one of three processes, the harmonic, the melodic, and the rhythmic processes. The harmonic process, inversion, is applied to all triads, beginning with the tonic triad:

example 135.

I   I⁶

Melodic (stepwise) progression of voices is not a factor in the harmonic process. The bass alone shifts to a higher 8ve, leaving the original 3rd of the chord as the new bass note.

In contrast to this, the melodic process of chord generation is characterized by stepwise progression, as its name indicates. Further, the harmonic process involves only one triad, whereas the melodic process involves two, I and V:

example 136.

Example 136 shows the chord pair V I. Stepwise and common-tone progression occurs in all voices above the bass except the soprano, which skips from scale degree 5 to scale degree 3. Stepwise progression in all voices above the bass is achieved when the skip is filled by scale degree 4 as a passing note:

example 137.

Earlier we defined a chord as a group of three or more notes which have the duration of a full metrical unit. Since the passing note, scale degree 4, in this case has the value of a full metrical unit it must be counted as a chord note. And since the interval which it forms with the bass is a 7th, a dissonant interval, it has also created a new kind of chord, called a *7th chord.*

This, then, is the melodic process by which the 7th chord was introduced into tonal music: the triad assimilated a passing dissonance. Since the triad involved is the dominant triad this particular kind of 7th chord (there are others) is called the *dominant 7th,* symbolized V^7. Let us examine its interval structure.

example 138.

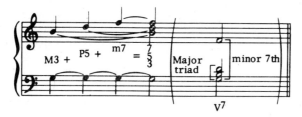

As illustrated in Example 138 above, the dominant 7th chord contains a major 3rd, a perfect 5th, and a minor 7th. In short, it consists of a major triad plus a minor 7th.

The full figuring of 7th chords is not used in figured bass. The figure 7 alone implies the 3rd and usually the 5th as well. Both 3rd and 5th are represented if chromatically altered, however. And in certain cases where the 5th is obligatory the chord is figured $\frac{7}{5}$.

79. The V⁷ as Representative of a Class of Dissonant Chords

All chords that contain a dissonant interval are called *dissonant chords.* All dissonant chords that contain the intervals of a 7th, a 5th, and a 3rd are called 7th chords. Since 7th chords are derived directly from triads, the basic harmonies, they constitute the first and most important class of dissonant chords. And since the dominant 7th chord is derived from a primary triad it is the most important representative of the entire class of 7th chords. As we shall see, its behavior is characteristic of 7th chords in general.

80. Melodic Function: the V⁷ as Passing Chord

In section 64 harmonic function was explained. We now introduce the concept of melodic function. The melodic function of its soprano note determines the melodic function of the V⁷. If a passing note is in the soprano the chord is called a *passing chord.* If an auxiliary note is in the soprano the chord is called an *auxiliary chord.* Not all chords have strong melodic functions; some are stable consonant chords which have primarily harmonic significance. The 7th chord, however, always has a melodic function. If the 8ve is in the soprano—the only stationary note of the chord—we describe melodic function in terms of the motion of the dissonant note, wherever it may lie.

The V⁷ in the next example is a passing chord.

example 139. BEETHOVEN: *First Symphony, Minuet and Trio*

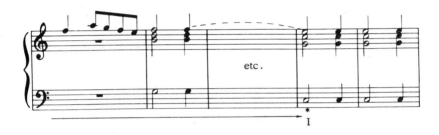

The first part of the trio ends on V in the soprano position of the 8ve. The next part begins with the passing 7th in the upper voice. This 7th is retained, with embellishments, for a total of eighteen measures before descending to the 3rd of the tonic triad. *Duration never alters chord function.* Example 139 is essentially the same melodic and harmonic pattern as that shown in Example 137.

81. Resolution of Dissonant Notes

When the dissonant note in Example 139, the 7th, finally progresses to the consonant 3rd of the tonic triad, we say that the dissonance is *resolved.* By resolution we mean therefore the obligatory progression of dissonant intervals to consonant intervals. Three rules govern the resolution of dissonance. They are illustrated by the V^7:

1   The dissonant note must resolve. The direction of resolution is determined by the second rule:

2   The dissonant note always resolves by step (usually in descending direction) to the nearest consonant note. The law of the half step explained in section 10 applies here with particular force.

3   The dissonant note is not doubled.

82. Resolution of the Tritone

The V^7 contains scale degrees 4 and 7, the two notes that form the dissonant diatonic interval of a tritone:

example 140.

Since both notes are governed by the law of the half step (in major) they resolve in contrary motion as shown in Example 140, either expanding to resolve on the 6th or contracting to resolve on the 3rd. In the minor mode, resolution of the tritone is the same as in major but it depends more upon the leading note since there is no half step between scale degrees 3 and 4.

It is important to recognize that scale degree 7 is not the same as the 7th of V^7. It is for this reason that we say "7th" when we refer to the interval, and "scale degree 7" when we refer to the diatonic position of a note.

83. The V^7 as Auxiliary Chord

The next example illustrates the evolution of a V^7 chord from an auxiliary note embellishment. Rhythm plays an important role in this case.

example 141.

Here a submetrical eighth note dissonance (a) is enlarged and assimilated as a chordal element (b).

Example 142 shows the same chord arising from an auxiliary note approached by skip.

example 142.

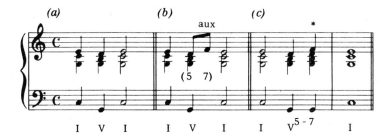

The figures 5-7 represent the change from the triad V to the dissonant-7th chord.

The melodic role of the 7th is clearly illustrated in the following excerpt.

example 143. CHOPIN: *Berceuse*

At the beginning of the composition the repeated auxiliary note figure in the accompaniment (F-Gb) prepares for the entrance of the soprano melody on F in the third measure. The reduction at (*b*) shows the relationship more directly.

The next excerpt illustrates the V⁷ as passing chord (twice) and as auxiliary chord.

example 144.   BEETHOVEN: *Fifth Symphony,* Last Movement

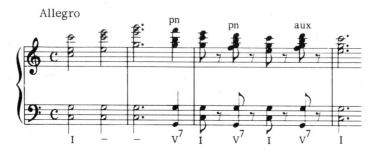

Before we examine the V⁷ in other characteristic contexts we must consider certain important additional aspects of its structure and progression.

84.   Soprano Positions of the V⁷

The most active soprano positions are those of the 7th and the 3rd. These are the notes which form the tritone, a dissonant, active interval that seeks resolution. The 8ve position occurs seldom since it is the least active melodic note, being simply a doubling of the bass.

85.   Doubling of the Notes of the V⁷

Since the resolution of the 7th is fixed—it must descend by step—it cannot be doubled. Parallel 8ves would result:

example 145.

This rule applies to all dissonant notes. They cannot be doubled, except in unusual circumstances.

In four-part harmony the 5th of the V^7 often is omitted and the bass is doubled. This doubling permits stepwise resolution to a complete tonic triad (Example 146*a*), whereas if no note is doubled, the chord resolves stepwise to an incomplete triad, a triad that lacks a 5th (Example 146*b*).

example 146.

The 3rd of V^7 is almost never omitted, for it is essential to the dissonant interval of the tritone which characterizes the chord.

86. Apparent Exceptions to the Rule That the 7th Always Descends

The 7th always resolves downward. Under certain conditions, however, it seems to ascend stepwise at the point of resolution. Three such situations are illustrated and explained in the next examples.

example 147.

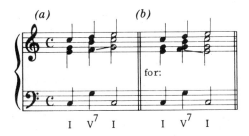

In the succession shown at (*a*) the 7th ascends to make the final triad complete. If it were to descend the final triad would lack a 5th. When the V^7 is in five parts as at (*b*) both conditions are satisfied: the final triad is complete and the 7th resolves as it should. Another common apparent exception to the rule of descending resolution is illustrated by the following passages.

example 148.   J. S. BACH (?): *Prelude for Organ*

$$\text{V}^{7(8)} \qquad \text{I}$$

example 149.   BEETHOVEN: *Six Bagatelles for Piano, Op. 126/1*

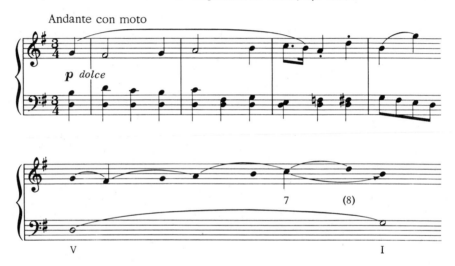

Andante con moto

p dolce

Here in both cases the 7th is embellished by its upper auxiliary note. This embellishment forms an 8ve against the bass and may momentarily give the effect of having resolved the 7th. Actually it only temporarily displaces the 7th, which remains in effect to resolve downward as indicated by the arrow.

Still another melodic technique creates the illusion of ascending resolution in the next example.

example 150.

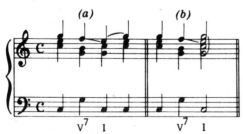

At (*a*) the 7th resolves downward normally to the 3rd of the tonic triad. The upper voice then changes to a different position, to the position of the 5th, as indicated by the slur. At (*b*) the resolution of the 7th and the shift of soprano position occur simultaneously: as the 7th resolves downward G replaces E as soprano note. This telescoping of two motions is indicated by the arrows. The technique illustrated here is called *overlapping* (after Schenker). A somewhat complicated instance is shown in Example 151. Notice that the left-hand part clarifies the underlying voice-leading.

example 151.   MOZART: *Piano Concerto in D minor, K.466,* Second Movement

87.   V⁷ at the Cadence

Very often V⁷ represents V at the cadence. The difference between the two chords lies in the fact that the 7th of V⁷ tends to emphasize the 3rd of the final tonic triad. This is evident in the following example, where the resolving tritone points up both the 8ve and the 3rd of the I, and the 5th of I is omitted.

example 152.   BEETHOVEN: *Piano Sonata in B♭ major, Op. 22*

88. The Skip Away from the Leading Note at the Cadence

The 3rd of V^7 is the leading note. Normally it resolves upward. However, if all the following conditions exist, the leading note does not resolve upward but may instead skip down to the 5th of the I: (1) if the texture is limited to four parts; (2) if the V^7 is in the soprano position of the 5th; (3) if a complete final tonic triad is required. Example 153 illustrates this situation.

example 153.

Since the 5th is in the soprano and therefore cannot be omitted the leading note (3rd of the V^7) must skip down to take the 5th of the final I, while its normal note of resolution is taken by the upper voice.

89. Secondary Dominant-7th Chord [V^7]

In section 56 the secondary dominant triad was introduced as a chromatic extension of V. The chromatic extension of V^7 is the secondary dominant-7th chord. This chord, symbolized [V^7], serves the same function as the secondary dominant triad. The following excerpt contains two of these chords.

example 154. BEETHOVEN: *Third Symphony*

The first [V^7] serves as prefix to II. The second [V^7] serves as prefix to IV. Any consonant diatonic triad may be embellished by a chord of this type.

90. The Minor-7th Chord (m^7)

In all, there are five types of 7th chord. The first type is the dominant 7th explained previously. The second type is the minor 7th. II^7 in the major mode is the diatonic model for this chord. Its origin, illustrated below, resembles that of the dominant-7th chord.

example 155.

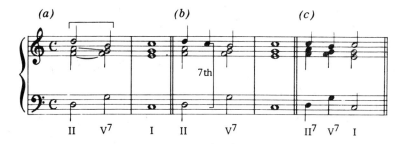

At (*a*) we see the triadic succession II V^7. Alto and tenor move by step while the soprano skips. At (*b*) the skip of a 3rd in the soprano is filled by a metrical passing note which creates a 7th that is assimilated by the II. As in the case of the V^7, the addition of the 7th does not alter the direction of the II. Indeed, the dissonant 7th only makes the direction toward V more explicit. We can extend this observation to formulate a general principle that applies to all 7th chords: Harmonically they function exactly as the diatonic triads from which they derive.

Like the V^7 explained in section 83 the II^7 can also originate from the auxiliary note embellishment.

The intervals of the II^7 are compared with those of the V^7 in the next example.

example 156.

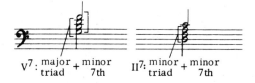

The V^7 consists of a major triad plus a minor 7th, while the II^7 consists of both a minor triad and a minor 7th. Hence the name minor 7th is given to the latter type. Note also that the minor-7th chord does not contain a tritone, as does the V^7, but like the 7th of V^7, the 7th of II^7 requires descending resolution.

91. IV⁷ in Minor

The only minor-7th chord in the diatonic minor mode (harmonic form) is IV⁷.
Like the diatonic triad from which it is derived, IV⁷ is often a dominant prepara-
tion. In that capacity every voice of the chord, including the bass, moves stepwise.
Example 157 provides an illustration.

example 157. SCHUMANN: *Auf einer Burg* (piano accompaniment only)

92. The Half-Diminished-7th Chord

This third type of 7th chord is exemplified by II⁷ in the minor mode. Like II⁷
in major, it also serves as a dominant preparation. Example 158 shows that the
half-diminished-7th chord originates from a passing metrical dissonance just as do
the dominant-7th and minor-7th chords.

example 158.

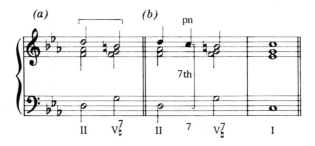

As we shall see, the *full diminished-7th chord* (°7) consists of a diminished triad
plus a diminished 7th. The half-diminished 7th, symbolized ⌀7, also is based
upon a diminished triad but its 7th is minor, not diminished. Hence the name of
the chord. Example 159 shows the II⁷ at the beginning of an art song.

example 159. SCHUMANN: *Ich will meine Seele tauchen*

The harmonic synopsis at (*b*) shows the chord succession without the arpeggiation. It is based upon the triadic progression II V I.

A detailed picture of the typical resolution of II^7 is provided by Example 160.

example 160.

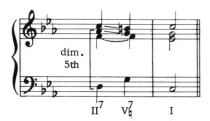

As in all 7th chords, the dissonant 7th of the half-diminished chord resolves downward by step. The 3rd of the half-diminished usually remains to become the 7th of the V^7, as shown here. A peculiarity of the half-diminished-7th chord, however, is the progression of the dissonant interval of the diminished 5th, the tritone. This interval does not behave as does the tritone of the dominant-7th-type chord. Instead, the 5th descends stepwise in parallel 3rds with the 7th, as shown in Example 160. Thus, in the half-diminished-7th chord the tritone does not operate as a dissonant interval.

The half-diminished-7th chord occurs in the major mode on scale step VII. The chord is not often an independent 7th chord, however, as is explained in section 112.

93. The Major-7th Chord (M^7)

The fourth type of 7th chord is exemplified by IV^7 in the major mode. Its melodic origin is shown below.

example 161.

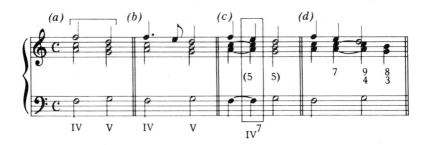

The dominant preparation IV becomes IV^7 when the submetrical passing note is enlarged and assimilated into the chord. This chord consists of a major triad plus a major 7th—hence its name.

In Example 161(c) it may be observed that when the major-7th chord resolves to V parallel 5ths occur between two of the upper voices. These can be prevented in several ways, one of which is shown at (d) where the 7th resolves but the progression of the parallel voice is delayed until the following beat. This technique forms a suspension chord (see Chapter 10).

94. 7th Chords in Sequence

A combination of melodic and rhythmic processes may affect a series of triads in such a way that a sequence of 7th chords is created, as shown by the series below.

example 162.

(a)

III   VI   II   V   I

(b)

8 7 8 7 8 7 8 7

(c)

7   7   7   7

At (*a*) is seen the progression III VI II V I. Eighth passing notes at (*b*) increase the melodic content. At (*c*) the passing notes are enlarged and assimilated as chord elements, thus producing an uninterrupted series of 7th chords. An example of this, accompanied by a harmonic synopsis, is given below.

example 163.   J.S. BACH: *Prelude in A♭ major, WTC I*

(a)

(b)

VI   II   V   I

In such sequences of 7th chords the dissonant 7th resolves to an interval consonant with the bass. However, the chord of which the interval is a part is no longer a consonant chord.

95. Summary of the Diatonic-7th Chords

The diatonic-7th chords are summarized in Example 164. Of the five main types four have been explained, namely the dominant 7th (V^7), the minor 7th (m^7), the major 7th (M^7), and the half-diminished 7th ($\phi7$).

example 164.

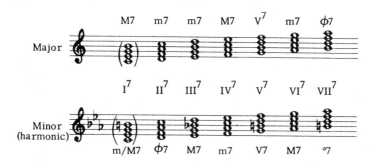

The fifth type of 7th chord, the diminished 7th, has a different structural origin and therefore is explained elsewhere (section 111). Since 7th chords based upon I in both major and minor are not independent 7th chords they are enclosed in parentheses in Example 164. (See section 174.) In these and in many other cases one must consider not only the vertical structure of the chord in isolation but also its linear or melodic context.

96. Summary of the Harmonic Functions of 7th Chords

Much more important than the distribution of the various 7th chords in the diatonic tonalities are their functions. The 7th chords, and indeed all dissonant chords, have two general harmonic functions: (1) they expand the harmonic content of a progression; (2) they make harmonic direction more specific. The 7th chords never replace the diatonic chords upon which progression is based. They make the direction of those basic harmonies more explicit and, in Mizler's words, "effect the continuous variation of the triad." Thus the progression of the 7th chord is always the same as that of the diatonic triad from which it derives. II is a dominant preparation; therefore, II^7 is also a dominant preparation. The cadential V progresses to I; therefore the cadential V^7 also progresses to I, and so on.

97. Summary of the Melodic Functions of 7th Chords

The 7th chords also serve the soprano or other melodic voice. The 7th itself is always either a passing note or an auxiliary note. It is never a stable note, no matter how long it may be prolonged.

98. Comparison of 7th Chords

The 7th chords resemble one another since they originate from the same melodic-rhythmic process. Their common origin is reflected in the fact that the dissonant note, the 7th, resolves downward by step in each case. However, the 7th chords differ in function, just as do the diatonic triads from which they derive. They also differ with respect to interval structure. Only the V^7 (and the diminished 7th, which is explained in Chapter 6) contain an operative tritone. The half-diminished 7th contains the tritone but the interval does not necessarily resolve like a dissonance.

EXERCISES

A. List of Some Important Terms to Define and Memorize

Melodic function (of a chord)
Resolution
Secondary dominant-7th chord
Minor-7th chord

Half-diminished-7th chord
Major-7th chord
Dominant-7th chord
Overlapping

B. Keyboard Exercises

exercise 106. Basic Chord Pattern 1
Expanded by secondary dominant-7th chords.

exercise 107. Basic Chord Pattern 2
Progression expanded by 7th chords.

I IV – VII III – VI II – V I – IV – V I

154

C. Figured Outer Voices

INSTRUCTIONS

These exercises should be carried out in the same way as those at the end of the previous chapter. They should be realized at the keyboard and on paper, chord structure and function should be indicated, and the harmonic units and goals should be designated.

exercise 108. **Chorale:** *Alle Menschen müssen sterben*

[VII]

exercise 109. Chorale: *O Welt, ich muss dich lassen*

exercise 110. Chorale: *Werde munter mein gemüte*

exercise 111. PEPUSCH: *English Cantata* *

*The exercise is excerpted.

D. Unfigured Outer Voices

exercise 112. **Folk Song:** *Barbara Allen*

exercise 113. **Chorale:** *In dulci jubilo*

exercise 114. HANDEL: *Sonata in G minor for Flute and Continuo*

This is an interlude between two fast movements. The harmonies should be read in G minor, in terms of their direction toward V. Thus, the interlude begins with VI and the first unit cadences on that harmony. The next unit is directed toward IV, which like VI is a preparation for the dominant triad. This appears in the final measure of the excerpt, and leads to the tonic triad which begins the subsequent Allegro (not shown).

6

The Inversions of the Seventh Chords

*There is within every chord a funda-
mental and natural order . . ., but the
circumstances of a particular progression, of taste, of expression, of beautiful
melody, of variety, of* rapprochement
*with the harmony, often cause the com-
poser to change that order by inverting
the chords, and in consequence to
change the disposition of the parts.*

Jean Jacques Rousseau, 1768

99. General

There are three major classes of dissonant chord: 7th chords, suspension chords, and linear chords. Of these only the 7th chords are inverted.

Inversion of a 7th chord raises two important questions: (1) In what way does it relate to the parent 7th chord; that is, how does it represent the function of the parent chord? (2) Each inversion has what individual characteristics that render it particularly appropriate for a certain context? Both questions will be answered in the present chapter as we discuss the inversions of the main types of 7th chord, beginning with the inverted dominant 7th.

THE INVERSIONS OF V⁷

100. Structure and Function of Inversions in Relation to Parent Chord

By successive inversion of the bass (shown by the arrows in Example 165) each note of the 7th chord serves in turn as bass note.

example 165.

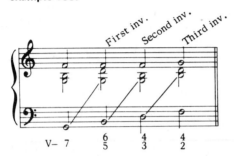

The first inversion has the original 3rd as bass note, the second the original 5th, the third the original 7th. Although the arrangement of the notes and thus the intervals of each inversion differ from those of the parent 7th chord, the inversions nevertheless have the same harmonic function as the chord from which they originate. This is shown in the next example.

example 166.

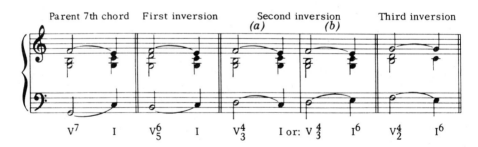

Example 166 shows that each inversion resolves either to I, as does the parent 7th chord, or to I⁶. Since an inversion usually has the same harmonic function as the parent 7th chord it often serves as an extension of that parent chord in much the same way that a 6th chord serves as an extension of its parent triad. Chord pairs formed in this way do not represent a change of harmony but, rather, different forms of the same harmony.

Despite the strong harmonic similarity between the parent 7th chord and its inversions the latter have individual melodic characteristics, and in some cases do not follow the pattern of resolution established by the parent chord. Before examining individual inversions let us consider two major aspects of their relationship to the parent chord.

First, the dissonant elements of the parent 7th chord not only are represented in each inversion, but they also resolve in the same way in each inversion. In the case of V^7 and its inversions the dissonant elements are the notes that form the tritone, that is, the 3rd and the 7th above the bass of the fundamental 7th. The 7th is dissonant against the bass, while the 3rd is dissonant against the 7th, an internal dissonance.

example 167.

Example 168 shows the resolution of the tritone in each inversion of the dominant-7th chord.

example 168.

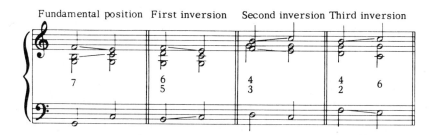

In each case the tritone resolves stepwise to the same notes of the tonic triad or its first inversion, in accord with the law of the half step.

The second major aspect of the relationship between the inversions and their parent 7th chord is this: All the notes of the inversion progress by step, whereas the parent chord normally combines stepwise progression in the upper voices with a skip in the bass.

We turn attention now to the individual characteristics of each inversion of the dominant-7th chord.

101. The First Inversion (V_5^6)

The complete figuring of the first inversion is $_5^6\!\!\!_3$.

example 169.

As indicated by the parentheses, only the figures $_5^6$ are used unless the 3rd is altered chromatically. These figures refer to the two notes which represent the interval of the 7th in the parent chord. In Example 169 the note which represents the original 7th is shown as a black note.

The dissonant notes of the V_5^6 are the bass and the 5th. These form the tritone, as shown above. Accordingly, the bass resolves upward by half step; the 5th resolves downward by half step. Because of its characteristic stepwise progression an inverted 7th chord can be described most effectively with respect to the melodic roles of its outer voices. In the case of the V_5^6 the bass plays the most active melodic role, serving either as auxiliary or as passing note. Both functions are illustrated below.

102. The V_5^6 as Auxiliary Chord

The following example shows the V_5^6 between two consonant chords, I^6 and I. Since the bass note of the V_5^6 here is an incomplete lower auxiliary note (the leading note in the key) the chord is called an auxiliary V_5^6.

example 170. BEETHOVEN: *Fifth Symphony*

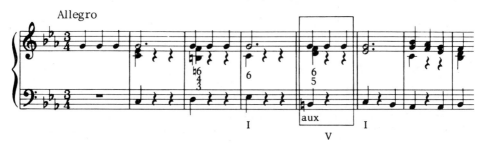

103. The V$^6_5$ as Passing Chord

When the V$^6_5$ features the bass as a passing note, it is called a passing V$^6_5$.

example 171. HAYDN: *Symphony in F♯ minor* ("Farewell")

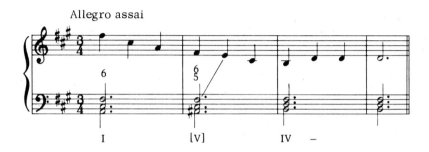

Here the bass is a chromatic passing note which supports a [V$^6_5$]. Moreover, the dissonant fifth enters as a passing note on the second quarter of the measure, as indicated by the diagonal line in Example 171 and as shown in the representation of the underlying voice-leading in Example 172.

example 172.

104. The Diminished Triad as Part of V$^6_5$

Very often the 5th of the $^6_5$ is stated horizontally, as in Example 171. In figured bass this kind of statement of the $^6_5$ may be represented by the linear figures 6 5, as demonstrated below.

example 173.

The figures 6 5 indicate the exact linear succession in the upper voice. In addition, they imply that the 6th is to be held over to form a $\frac{6}{5}$. They do not mean that the 6th chord progresses to $\frac{5}{3}$, a diminished triad. In figured bass practice this retention of the 6th was understood. Thus both 5 and ♭5 in the following excerpt would be realized as $\frac{6}{5}$'s.

example 174. BUXTEHUDE: *Trio Sonata in C minor*

105. An Apparent Exception to the Rule about Tritone Resolution

Occasionally one finds the following progression of the $\frac{6}{5}$.

example 175.

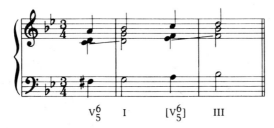

$$V_5^6 \qquad I \qquad [V_5^6] \qquad III$$

Here the dissonant 5th resolves upward instead of downward both in the V_5^6 and in the $[V_5^6]$. By this means, stepwise voice leading is obtained from strong to weak beat. If the dissonant note resolves normally there results a skip from strong to weak beat, which brings with it an undesirable accent on the weak beat:

example 176.

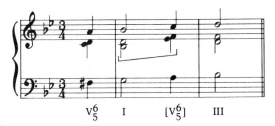

$$\text{V}_5^6 \qquad \text{I} \qquad [\text{V}_5^6] \qquad \text{III}$$

The irregular progression of the dissonant 5th in Example 175 also may be explained as a transferred resolution: The note to which the dissonant 5th would normally resolve, B♭, is taken by another and more prominent voice (the soprano in this case) so that the stepwise resolution of the dissonance becomes superfluous. Clearly the doubling of B♭ in Example 176 lacks point and only disturbs the metric-rhythmic pattern, as suggested above.

106. The Second Inversion (V$_3^4$)

The complete figuring of the second inversion is $_4^6$. Example 177 shows this chord in relation to the parent V^7 and the V$_5^6$.

example 177.

$$7 \qquad \begin{matrix}6\\5\end{matrix} \qquad \begin{matrix}6\\4\\3\end{matrix}$$

As in the case of the first inversion, the complete figuring is not used. Only the figures $_3^4$, which represent the interval of the 7th in the parent chord, are required. The 6th is understood and always included, but is not figured unless altered chromatically.

The dissonant notes of the $_3^4$ are the 6th and the 3rd. These notes form the tritone and resolve accordingly, the 6th upward by half step, the 3rd downward by half step. It may seem strange that two notes both consonant with the bass should behave like dissonances and require resolution. This is because they form the dissonant internal interval of the tritone which resolves in the inversions just as it does in the parent 7th chord.

107.   The V$_3^4$ as Auxiliary Chord

Like the $_5^6$ the $_3^4$ can serve as an auxiliary chord. Example 178 provides an opportunity to compare these two chords in a similar structural role.

example 178.   SCHUMANN: *Ich wandel'te unter den Bäumen*

Here we see the bass of the V$_3^4$ as upper auxiliary note to the bass of the tonic triad. The bass note of the V$_5^6$ which follows serves as lower auxiliary note to the bass of the same triad. Example 179 summarizes this relationship.

example 179.

Notice that the eighth-note B shown in Example 179 is a passing note in both outer voices; it does not constitute a return to B of the tonic triad. The latter occurs only on the downbeat of m. 3.

108. The Passing V$_3^4$

The second inversion of the dominant-7th chord often has the passing function illustrated in the following excerpt.

example 180. BEETHOVEN: *Sixth Symphony*

The bass of the V$_3^4$ here serves as descending passing note which connects I⁶ with I. The tritone resolves normally.

In contrast, when the bass note of the V$_3^4$ is an ascending passing note the tritone may not resolve normally. Instead, the 3rd above the bass, which should descend (since it represents the 7th of the parent 7th chord) ascends, as shown in Example 181.

example 181. German Folk Song: *Freut euch des Lebens*

This is an instance of transferred resolution (see section 92). Example 182 illustrates the technique by comparing the auxiliary $_3^4$ with the passing $_3^4$.

example 182.

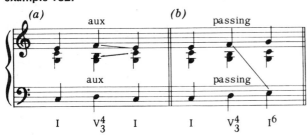

At (*a*) we see the auxiliary V_3^4. Both soprano and bass are auxiliary notes. The tritone resolves normally. At (*b*) both soprano and bass of the V_3^4 are passing notes. The resolution of the dissonant 3rd in the soprano is transferred to the bass.

Observe also that the outer voices of the passing $_3^4$ move in a pattern of ascending parallel 10ths. These fluent intervals carry the progression upward, over-riding the tendency of the dissonant 3rd to resolve downward.

109.   VII⁶ as a Substitute for V_3^4

The dissonant diatonic-6th chord, VII⁶, closely resembles the V_3^4, and in fact is often substituted for it. Example 183 illustrates their association.

example 183.

Here the two chords are shown in the same context. The VII⁶ differs from the V_3^4 by only one note. It lacks the 4th.

In a strict four-voice texture, if the bass is doubled by the soprano, the VII⁶ is required as a substitute for the V_3^4. (In order to have the V_3^4 another part would have to be added, making a total of five voices.)

example 184.

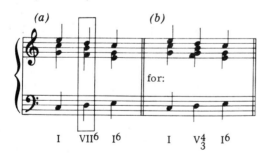

An illustration of the VII⁶ in its role as obligatory substitute for V_3^4 is provided by Example 185.

example 185. BEETHOVEN: *Piano Sonata in C major, Op. 2/3*

F major: VII$^6_\flat$

Before leaving the VII^6 we note that it has a chromatic counterpart, just as V has as its chromatic counterpart the secondary dominant chord. This chord is marked [VII^6]. In figured basses it is easily recognized by the alterations which the 6th and sometimes the 3rd require. Example 186 shows [VII^6] of V in comparison with [V$\frac{4}{3}$] of the same triad.

example 186.

110. The Third Inversion (V$\frac{4}{2}$)

The complete figuring of the third inversion is $\begin{smallmatrix}6\\4\\2\end{smallmatrix}$.

example 187.

Unless, however, the 6th is altered only the figures $\frac{4}{2}$ are used. Actually, only the figure 2 is necessary, but when speaking of this chord we say $\frac{4}{2}$ in order to avoid confusion with the Roman numeral II.

The bass itself is now dissonant and must resolve downward, normally to I^6, as shown in Example 187. The descending resolution tendency of the bass of this inversion is so strong that it can overcome even the descending resolution tendency of the 7th of the parent V^7. An instance is quoted below.

example 188. BEETHOVEN: *Piano Sonata in E major, Op. 109*

An example of the usual resolution of V^4_2 and $[V^4_2]$ follows:

example 189. HANDEL: *Concerto grosso in G minor*

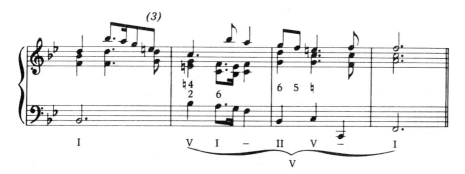

This excerpt is presented in some detail in order to demonstrate the functions of an inverted dominant-7th chord in relation to the basic consonant structure.

1   At this point IV, a dominant preparation, is introduced by its secondary dominant 7th in the third inversion. What appear to be parallel 5ths between two of the upper voices actually are not. At this point the soprano suddenly skips down to an inner voice, and the inner voice, in turn, takes the note to which the soprano would have moved in the normative stepwise voice leading shown below the example.

2   The V^4_2 chord here is somewhat concealed by the submetrical passing notes in the soprano. The eighth note which falls on the beat does not belong to the harmony at all, but is an accented passing note, as shown by the reduction.

3   The E♮ here belongs to the following harmony. The entire passage consists of two harmonic units. The first contains an opening progression from I to V. The second unit contains another opening progression which moves even more strongly to the dominant. The last part of this progression is a modulation, a special kind of progression which is the subject of Chapter 9. Thus all the chords within the last three measures are shown in relation to V as a quasi-tonic.

The function of the three inverted dominant-7th chords is constant. In each case they serve as stepwise prefixes to more essential diatonic harmonies.

THE DIMINISHED-7th CHORD

111.   The Diminished-7th Chord: an Altered Inversion of V⁷

In Chapter 5, section 90, it was stated that there are five types of 7th chords. Only four of these were explained in that chapter. We come now to the fifth type.

Consonant chords are often connected by dissonant chords called *diminished-7th chords* (°7). Unlike the 7th chords explained in Chapter 5, which are independent 7th chords derived from triads, the diminished-7th chord is an entirely dependent chord derived from an inverted dominant-7th chord. Its origin in the diatonic minor mode is illustrated below.

example 190.

At (*a*) we see V$^6_5$, whose bass note is the leading note. At (*b*) the 6th in the soprano is embellished by a metrical auxiliary note which forms a diminished 7th with the bass. The chord thus created takes its name from that characteristic interval.

Sometimes we regard the chord as a 7th chord on the leading-note triad, as shown at (*c*). This may be convenient if it occurs without preparation by V$^6_5$ as at (*c*), but one should bear in mind that the leading-note triad usually occurs in fundamental position only in sequences and therefore is not apt to have generated the diminished-7th chord.

Inversions of the diminished-7th chord derive from the second and third inversions of the dominant-7th chord:

example 191.

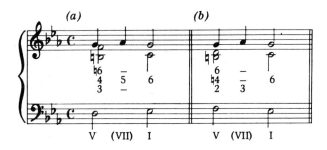

Example 191 points up another important characteristic of the diminished-7th chord: It differs from the inverted dominant-7th chord by only one note. This difference is reflected in the figures. The figures for the diminished-7th chord are always one inversion lower than those of the chord from which it derives. Thus in Example 191 the diminished-7th chord at (a) is figured $\frac{6}{5}$, while the preceding dominant-7th chord is figured $\frac{4}{3}$.

For purposes of practical application it is important to remember that the diminished-7th chord is derived from an inverted dominant-7th chord by a change of only one note. Two other characteristics are important for the same reason. First, the diminished 7th shares no notes with the chord of resolution. Second, every note of the diminished 7th resolves stepwise. These characteristics guide us if we wish to convert an inverted secondary dominant-7th chord into a diminished-7th chord. The two may be regarded as interchangeable; a consonant chord or chord pair may be embellished by either one.

To illustrate, let us assume we wish to provide a IV⁶ chord with a diminished-7th chord (°7) as prefix. We begin by considering the possible secondary dominant-7ths, as shown in Example 192.

example 192.

G major: [V]   IV   [V]   IV

Either [V$\frac{4}{3}$] or [V$\frac{4}{2}$] serves as prefix to IV⁶. Next, we apply our knowledge of the special voice-leading characteristic of the °7: stepwise resolution of all voices. Since only one note (G) in each inverted secondary dominant-7th chord does not progress by step, if we raise that note by a half step we derive the diminished-7th chords shown in Example 193.

example 193.

°7   IV   °7   IV

The lack of common tones between the °7 and the chord of resolution also provides a rule for correct notation: The °7 shares no notes of the same letter name with the chord to which it resolves. Thus in Example 193 it would be incorrect to notate the A♭ as G♯, since the note G is in the chord of resolution.

We emphasize that the °7 derives only from inverted dominant-7th chords. The parent V⁷ cannot be replaced by a °7 without changing its direction entirely.

The reader may have observed that in Example 193 neither diminished-7th chord actually contains the interval of a diminished 7th. Only the diminished-7th chord derived from the dominant $\frac{6}{5}$ contains that characteristic interval. Quite apart from the spelling of the notes, however, every diminished-7th chord consists of a series of minor thirds above the bass note. Therefore, because the notes of the °7 chord are equidistant and because each is a four-note chord there are only three °7 chords:

example 194.

In four-part harmony all notes of the °7 must be present. No note is doubled. This, as well as other characteristics of the °7 described above, can be seen in the following examples.

example 195.   BEETHOVEN: *Piano Sonata in C minor, Op. 13*

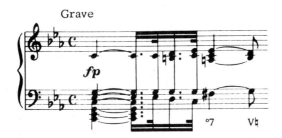

In Example 195 we find the V prepared by a diminished-7th chord. To appreciate the special effect of the latter chord, consider how the passage would sound if a secondary dominant-7th chord replaced it, as in Example 196.

example 196.

We have come to associate the diminished-7th chord with a feeling of greater intensity. The following excerpt shows even more clearly the difference between its effect and that of the secondary dominant-7th chord.

example 197. BEETHOVEN: *Piano Sonata in C minor, Op. 10/1*

Here we see that the passing V_3^4 in measure 4 becomes a diminished-7th chord (VII_5^6) in the following measure. This involves a change of only one note: G is replaced by A♭. The diminished-7th chord is prolonged for almost four measures, finally resolving to I^6 at the end of the passage, as indicated by the arrow.

The diminished-7th chord can also occur as a linear chord without dominant implications. This mode of occurrence is explained in Chapter 11, section 219.

112. The Half-Diminished-7th Chord in Major (VII⁷)

Like the VII^7 in minor, VII^7 in major is derived from V^6_5.

example 198.

Example 198 shows first the succession V^6_5 I. The metrical auxiliary note is included at (b), forming a minor 7th with the bass. At (c) the 7th chord is shown without preparation by V^6_5. This chord is sometimes identified as VII^7, a half-diminished chord which resolves to I and which substitutes (rarely) for V^6_5. Actually it is used sparingly in compositions, although it does occur often in the idiom shown below.

example 199.

Here the half-diminished-7th chord connects IV and V. Its passing function resembles that of a secondary dominant-7th chord and therefore the Roman numeral VII is enclosed in brackets. Another example of the same idiom follows.

example 200. BRAHMS: *Variations on a Theme by Haydn, Op. 56b*

In this excerpt the VII⁷ stands between II⁶ and the cadential $^6_4$, again serving as a passing chord much like a [V$^6_5$].

Like the triad VII, the VII⁷ progresses by 5th only in sequences.

THE INVERSIONS OF THE MINOR-7th CHORD

113. General

Again we take as model of the minor-7th chord the II⁷ in the major mode. Successive inversion of the bass of this chord produces the following array of four chords:

example 201.

The figures for inverted 7th chords are the same regardless of the type of parent 7th chord from which the inversions derive. As in all cases, figures indicate only the general interval content of the chord. The exact size of each interval is determined by the chord's position in the diatonic tonality or by chromatic alterations if they occur.

The resolutions of the three inversions of the II⁷ are summarized in Example 202:

example 202.

The parent chord, II⁷, progresses to V or to V⁷. Each of the first two inversions also resolves to V or V⁷. The third inversion resolves to V⁶.

Unlike V⁷, II⁷ does not contain the tritone. This is a major difference between the two types. As a consequence the only note which requires resolution is the 7th of the parent chord and the note that represents the 7th in each inversion. As indicated by the diagonal lines in Example 202, the 7th descends in parallel motion with the 5th. This pattern is continued in each inversion. We now survey the typical behavior of each inversion.

114. The First Inversion (II$_5^6$)

Measured upward from the bass the II$_5^6$ contains only consonant intervals. The chord does not function as a consonance, however, for it still contains the 7th of the parent chord, and therefore requires resolution. The 5th is the dissonant note in this inversion.

The following excerpt illustrates the two most common functions of II$_5^6$.

example 203. MOZART: *The Magic Flute* (First Quintet)

The first harmonic unit contains a progression directed toward I. The cadence, however, is deceptive: VI replaces the expected tonic triad. The second harmonic unit begins in the same way as the first, but this time the progression to I is completed. Within the first unit II$^6_5$ serves as a combination passing-auxiliary chord between I^6 and V: the bass of II$^6_5$ is a passing note, its upper voice an auxiliary note. At the deceptive cadence II prepares the dominant. Its bass functions as a lower auxiliary note to the bass of V. Within the second four-measure unit the first II$^6_5$ again serves as a passing-auxiliary chord. It also prepares the V, replacing the II used in the cadence of the first unit. In this connection, note that the first cadence contains only consonant chords. The composer reserves the dissonant equivalents of these consonant chords for the heightened effect of the second cadence.

When II^7 progresses to V^7 the 3rd of II^7 is retained as a common tone which becomes the 7th of V^7.

example 204.

The 3rd of the parent chord becomes the bass of the first inversion. Thus, when the common tone is retained, as shown in Example 204, the succession II$^6_5$ V$^4_2$ results.

example 205.

The next example illustrates the II$^6_5$ as an intermediate harmonic goal.

example 206. BEETHOVEN: *Minuet in E♭ major*

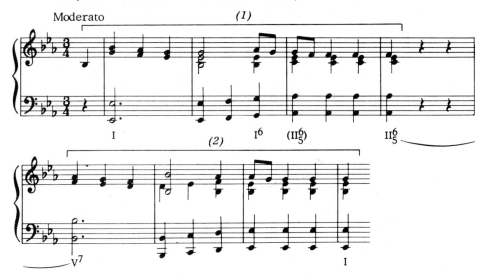

Here II$^6_5$ stands at the end of the first harmonic unit. Its dissonant character suggests that it is only an intermediate goal, however, and this is confirmed by the subsequent unit, which begins on V^7. Thus the function of II$^6_5$ is the usual one: it prepares the V^7. In melodic terms the bass note of the II$^6_5$ here is an ascending passing note which connects I^6 with V^7, just as in Example 203.

115. The Second Inversion (II$^4_3$)

The II$^4_3$ occurs infrequently. As a passing chord leading to V it is usually replaced by [V$^4_3$]:

example 207.

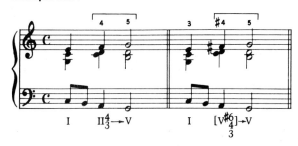

The reason for this substitution is melodic: The [V$^4_3$] contains the raised scale degree 4 (♯4) which carries the melodic progression upward more effectively than does the natural scale degree 4. This again is an instance of the law of the half step.

When the bass of the II$_3^4$ is an ascending passing note, as in the following example, the 3rd (which represents the 7th of the parent chord) must progress irregularly.

example 208.

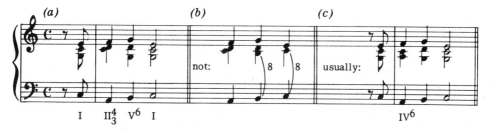

At (*a*) the dissonant note (the 3rd) must skip down rather than resolve downward by step, for if it were to resolve stepwise the bass of V^6 would be doubled, as shown at (*b*), and parallel 8ves would result between V^6 and the I. The bass progression shown here (scale degrees 6-7-8) is more often harmonized by IV^6 V^6 I (*c*). This succession permits stepwise voice leading without impending parallels.

116. The Third Inversion (II$_2^4$)

Like V$_2^4$ the progression of the II$_2^4$ is fixed since the dissonant note is in the bass. Thus the third inversion prepares V^6 or V$_5^6$, as shown in the next example.

example 209. MENDELSSOHN: *An die Entfernte* (voice and accompaniment combined)

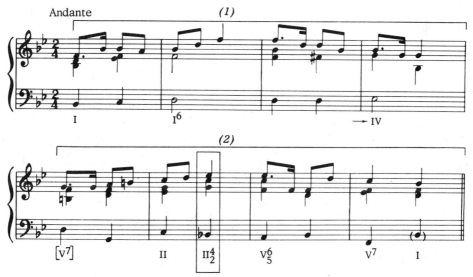

THE INVERSIONS OF THE HALF-DIMINISHED-7th (II⁷) CHORD

117. General

The half-diminished-7th chord and its inversions function in much the same way as do the minor-7th chord and its inversions. Indeed, if we compare the II⁷ in a major key with the II⁷ in its parallel minor key, we find that they differ by only one note. The inversions of the half-diminished are summarized below.

example 210.

Like the minor 7th, the half-diminished 7th contains two voices which descend in parallel motion: the dissonant 7th and the 5th. The resolutions of the half-diminished 7th and its inversions are easily remembered if this fact is borne in mind.

118. The First Inversion (II⁶₅)

Example 211 illustrates the normative function of II⁶₅ as a dominant preparation.

example 211. CHOPIN: *Nocturne in C minor, Op. 48/1*

This progression is made up of two chord groups. The first comprises the first two measures, centering upon I. The second group begins with the two dominant preparations, VI and II$\frac{6}{5}$, then leads through the V⁷ to the final I, closing the progression.

119.   The Second Inversion (II$\frac{4}{3}$)

In section 115, we explained certain of the difficulties involved in the use of the minor $\frac{4}{3}$. The half-diminished $\frac{4}{3}$ is even more restricted, although it does occur more frequently than the minor $\frac{4}{3}$. The bass of the half-diminished $\frac{4}{3}$ can only descend.

example 212.

The bass never ascends, as shown in Example 212. This is because the interval of the augmented 2nd is formed between the bass notes of II$\frac{4}{3}$ and V$\frac{6}{5}$, an interval that requires special treatment in order to be accommodated to a melodic progression, whether in the bass or in the upper voice.

120.   The Third Inversion (II$\frac{4}{2}$)

The opening of Haydn's "Farewell" Symphony illustrates the II$\frac{4}{2}$.

example 213.   HAYDN: *Symphony in F♯ minor* ("Farewell")

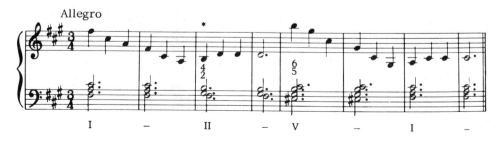

Observe the way in which the dissonant bass of the II_2^4 propels the harmony toward V_5^6. The passage quoted consists of a circular progression, the first statement of the tonic triad at the beginning of the movement.

121. Inversions of the Major-7th Chord (IV⁷)

Apart from sequences, the major-7th chord with descending resolution occurs infrequently. Its function as a dominant preparation is limited by the law of the half step which applies to the 7th of the chord itself in this case and dictates the ascending resolution of the 7th shown at (*a*) below rather than the descending resolution shown at (*b*) which is required for progression to the dominant.

example 214.

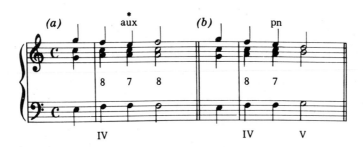

For this reason the idiomatic use of the half-diminished-7th chord [VII⁷] explained in section 112 is preferred over IV⁷ in such melodic contexts.

Although the fundamental position of the IV⁷ is not often used the first and third inversions occur frequently. Example 215 illustrates a typical context for the first inversion:

example 215.

The following excerpt contains IV$^6_5$ in a somewhat more elaborate setting.

example 216. CHOPIN: *Fantaisie in F minor, Op. 49*

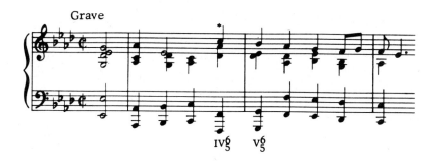

The third inversion of the major-7th chord, IV$^4_2$, commonly arises as the result of a passing note in the bass.

example 217.

Neither the major-7th chord nor its inversions have the same binding harmonic effect as do the other 7th chords. In many cases the functions of this chord are most efficiently and correctly explained entirely in melodic terms. For this reason we exclude it from the following summary.

122. Summary of the 7th Chords and Their Inversions

Example 218 summarizes the four main types of 7th chords.

example 218.

Dominant 7th
V⁷ – I

Diminished 7th
(°7)
Substitute for
inversions of
V⁷ or [V⁷]

Minor 7th
(m7)
II⁷ – V⁷

Half-
diminished 7th
(ᶲ7)
II⁷ – V⁷

EXERCISES

A. List of Some Important Terms to Define and Memorize

Transferred resolution

Passing $\frac{4}{3}$

Exchange of voices

Diminished-7th chord

Internal dissonance

Obligatory VII⁶

B. Analysis

INSTRUCTIONS
1 Play each passage at the keyboard.
2 Place appropriate figured bass symbols above the bass staff, showing chord structure.
3 Place appropriate Roman numerals below the bass staff, showing the position of the chord in the key.
4 Analyze for harmonic groups, harmonic direction (goals), and individual chord functions.

exercise 115. GLUCK: *Iphigénie en Aulide*

exercise 116. MOZART: "Smanie implacabili" *(Cosi fan tutte)*
(details of accompaniment not shown)

C. Basic Keyboard Exercises

Each inverted 7th chord is played and sung in close position as the first chord of a pair. The chord is then played in the various soprano positions and the outer voices are sung as shown. The chords may also be arpeggiated from the soprano downward, as before, but this of course does not indicate the inversion. Here the main effort should be directed toward recognition of the inverted 7th chords and their contexts. Arpeggiation from the bass upward reveals the inversion, while singing of the outer voices shows the soprano position. Only the inversions of the V^7 are shown here. They provide a model for the inversions of the other 7th chords, which should be worked out fully in the same way.

exercise 117. **Basic Chord Pattern 1 in major**

(b)

(c)

In the exercises at the end of the previous chapter, secondary dominant-7th chords were inserted before every other chord of this pattern in order to expand the progression. Here inverted secondary dominant-7th chords are inserted for the same purpose. They differ from the parent 7th chords in that they create a far more active bass line.

exercise 118. **Basic Chord Pattern 1 in minor**

(a)

(b)

(c)

exercise 119. **Basic Chord Pattern 2 in major**

At the end of the previous chapter the triads of the basic pattern were changed
into 7th chords. Here those 7th chords are replaced by their inversions.

(a)

(b)

(c)

exercise 120. **Basic Chord Pattern 2 in minor**

exercise 121. **Cadences which include II$\frac{6}{5}$**

exercise 122.

D. Figured Basses

INSTRUCTIONS
The exercises should be utilized fully, as follows:
1   *Sing* soprano and bass lines from beginning to end before realizing the figures. After realization sing the chords in arpeggiation both from the bass upward and from the soprano downward.
2   *Play* the realization both as it is being made and when it is completed. Those with limited ability at the keyboard should strive to achieve a steady tempo, no matter how slow. Try to think ahead and prepare for the next chord. Anticipate the change of harmony. If possible perform the accompanied vocal or instrumental pieces. In cases where there are no words the line can be sung on the neutral syllables "la" or "loo."
3   *Write out* the realization in all cases. With further experience it should be possible to write the exercises away from the keyboard, always trying to imagine the sound as completely as possible. The keyboard can then be used to check. The singing of soprano and bass and the arpeggiation from bass and from soprano are valuable aids towards the development of this skill.
4   Describe the structure of each chord and its harmonic and melodic functions.
The inversions of the 7th chords can be located easily at the keyboard by using the following procedure:
1   In close position, left hand, the $\frac{6}{5}$ is a triad plus a 2nd on top:

2   In close position, left hand, the $\frac{4}{3}$ is a 6th chord plus a 2nd above the middle note:

3   In close position, left hand, the $\frac{4}{2}$ is a triad added one step above the bass note:

exercise 123. Chorale: *Herzlich tut mich verlangen*

exercise 124. **Chorale:** *Herr, ich habe misgehandelt*

exercise 125. **Chorale:** *O Gott, du frommer Gott*

exercise 126. **Chorale:** *Schwing dich auf zu deinem Gott*

exercise 127. BASSANI: *Harmonia festiva (Lucida aurora)*

exercise 128. Chorale: *Du, o schöness Weltgebäude*

exercise 129. VIVALDI: *Sonata for Violin and Continuo in D major*

Realize a four-voice accompaniment to the given melody, moving the soprano by step wherever possible.

E. Unfigured Outer Voices

exercise 130. **LOEILLET:** *Sonata for Flute and Continuo*

exercise 131. Chorale: *O Welt, sieh hier dein Leben*

exercise 132. **JEREMIAH CLARKE: "An Hymn for Good Friday"**

exercise 133. **JEREMIAH CLARKE: "An Hymn for Christmas Day"**

exercise 134. GRAUN: Harmonization of *Ich werde dir zu Ehren*

exercise 135. TELEMANN: *Fantaisie*

E. Four-Voice Chorale Settings

exercise 136. **Chorale:** *Nun ruhen alle Wälder.* Figures by J. C. Kühnau

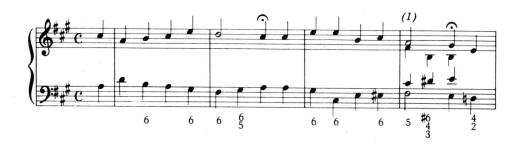

comments

1 The alto skips to another note of the harmony in order to avoid impending 8ves with the bass.
2 Compare the harmonization of this phrase with that of the second phrase.

exercise 137. Chorale: *Ach, lass dich jetzt finden komm*
Author of figures unknown (from Rinck Manuscript Collection, Yale Music Library).

comments

1   The $\frac{4}{2}$ serves here as a lower auxiliary note chord. It is not an authentic 7th chord but a chord which is entirely linear in origin. Therefore it belongs to the class of dissonant chords explained in Chapter 11.

The entire chorale consists of three phrases. The harmonic plan is symmetrical: the two outer phrases contain circular progressions, while the central phrase opens to V.

These four-voice chorale exercises represent an important step toward original composition. Their advantages are many. They reveal more clearly than do the keyboard arrangements the motion of the individual voices and consequently enable us to see the possibilities for developing voices separately and in combination. In Chapter 14 those possibilities are examined more systematically.

7

The Soprano Voice and Harmonic Progression

The true goal of music–its proper enterprise–is melody. All the parts of harmony have as their ultimate purpose only beautiful melody. Therefore the question of which is the more signific- ant, melody or harmony, is futile. Be- yond doubt, the means is subordinate to the end.

Johann Philipp Kirnberger, 1771

123. The Special Importance of the Soprano

Of the three voices above the bass the uppermost, the soprano, is most important. There are two main reasons for this: (1) the succession of intervals which the soprano forms with the bass outlines and delimits the harmonic progression, and (2) the soprano voice almost always carries the themes and motives that charac- terize a particular composition and that serve both to unify and diversify it.

124. The Technical Meaning of the Term "Voice"

By "voice" we mean the succession of notes performed by a single human voice or single-line instrument. This voice may be quite complex. It may even carry several melodic elements simultaneously. The next two sections present certain fundamental facts about the structure of the soprano voice in tonal music. While these facts also apply to the other voices, they are most clearly evident in the soprano. Many will seem familiar from Chapter 1, for in a sense this is a review and extension of material presented there.

125.   Basic Melodic Progression

Every tonal melody contains stepwise motions and may also contain skips. Stepwise progression, however, is primary. It characterizes many simple melodies, for example, the chorale tune given below.

example 219.   Chorale: *Jesu, Leiden, Pein, und Tod*

Basic melodic progression therefore is defined as progression by 2nd. To be sure, we often use the term melodic somewhat loosely to designate any succession of notes, regardless of the intervals they form. Nonetheless, in the technical sense basic melodic progression is identical with stepwise progression. The term "line," or "melodic line," refers specifically to the stepwise characteristic of melody. This definition of melody is implicit in earlier sections of the present volume, especially in Chapter 4 (section 50 and elsewhere) and in Chapter 5, where the two fundamental melodic functions, the auxiliary note and the passing note, were shown as chord-generating elements in the evolution of the harmonic language.

126.   Scale and Triad: Melody and Harmony

In Chapter 1 the scale was described as a complete stepwise ordering of the notes of the diatonic key. Accordingly, the diatonic scale can be regarded as a kind of ideal melody. The tonic triad, on the other hand, represents harmony and the harmonic intervals, 3rd, 5th, and 8ve.

It is sometimes said that melody exists in the horizontal succession of notes, while harmony exists in the vertical simultaneity of notes (chords). This is false. Vertical and horizontal dimensions constantly interact. We have seen that an entire class of chords, the 7th chords, emerges when melodic elements, passing or auxiliary notes, are incorporated into the vertical grouping we call a chord. Further, we have found that the harmonic (triadic) intervals often are stated in the horizontal dimension. Thus, we distinguish between melody and harmony solely on the basis of intervals. The 2nd and its inversion, the 7th, are the melodic intervals. All other simple intervals are harmonic.

127. Metrical and Submetrical Elements

Like the ideal melody, the diatonic scale, the basic stepwise melodic line is made up of notes which form harmonic intervals and notes which connect and extend those intervals. For instance, the first phrase of the chorale tune quoted above consists of the intervals of the tonic triad filled in by passing notes. An analysis of that fragment is shown below. The harmonic intervals are extracted and shown at (b).

example 220. Chorale: *Jesu, Leiden, Pein und Tod*

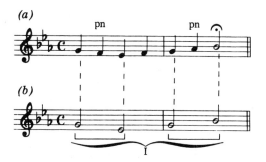

In this case the passing notes have the duration of the metrical unit, the quarter note, and therefore are called metrical passing notes. More complicated melodies may contain submetrical as well as metrical durations. Example 221 below illustrates the combination.

example 221. BACH: *Chorale Variations* on *Sei gegrüsset, Jesu gütig*

The original form of the melody is given at (a). In the variation shown at (b) the second note is embellished by submetrical notes. Chapter 12 is devoted in part to a detailed consideration of such submetrical notes. Their use comprises a highly important aspect of compositional technique. The present chapter, however, is concerned only with metrical melodic notes since they alone normally have harmonic value.

The metrical auxiliary note and passing note have just been illustrated. The *metrical arpeggiation,* which characterizes many melodies, is a special case which requires more detailed explanation.

128. Metrical Arpeggiation

Many soprano voices contain skips in addition to stepwise progression. Example 222 illustrates the meaning of the metrical skip, of arpeggiation, in relation to the basic stepwise pattern.

example 222.   Chorale: *Wie schön leuchtet der Morgenstern*

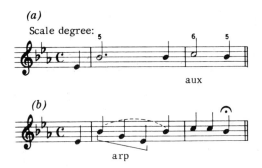

At (a) following the initial skip we see the basic stepwise pattern: scale degree 5 followed by a metrical auxiliary note, scale degree 6. At (b) scale degree 5 is embellished further by an arpeggiation which descends through the tonic triad. This arpeggiation is subordinate to the main stepwise progression, and therefore the dotted line shows that scale degree 5 continues, after having been interrupted by the arpeggiation.

The concept of basic stepwise progression is a traditional part of music theory, although many late nineteenth-century and early twentieth-century theorists apparently were unaware of it. In the eighteenth century J. D. Heinichen provided a very clear illustration which deserves to be quoted here.

example 223. HEINICHEN: Analysis of a recitative passage. From *Der General-bass in der Composition* (1728)

(a)

(b)

Heinichen first presents the recitative as shown at (*a*). He then demonstrates the correctness of its voice leading by showing the underlying continuity of the soprano voice (*b*). The combination of stepwise succession in the soprano with bass line he calls the "fundamental notes." Reductions such as those shown at (*b*) were first used extensively and systematically by Heinrich Schenker, the eminent twentieth-century theorist, to illuminate complicated and sophisticated processes in art music of the tonal period. Some of the basic aspects of those processes are dealt with in Chapter 13 of the present volume.

129. Arpeggiation as Compound Melody

If the individual melodic strands of an arpeggiation are developed in such a way that each has its own continuity and rhythmic identity the result is *compound melody.* This type of melodic development is illustrated in the next excerpt. The example shows step by step how the compound melody of the final version arises.

example 224. TELEMANN: *Fantasy*

At (*a*) we find the familiar harmonic progression I II$^4_2$ V$^6_5$ I. Over this the soprano line descends from scale degree 5 to scale degree 3. Scale degree 5 is expanded by a metrical auxiliary note, scale degree 6.

At (*b*) the two upper lines are inverted: the alto is placed above the soprano. At (*c*) (the complete version as Telemann wrote it) these two lines are activated rhythmically and expressed as a single voice. This, then, is compound melody: the expression by a single voice of more than one melodic progression.

It is extremely important to note that each melodic line at (*c*) progresses just as it did at (*a*) and (*b*). That is, scale degree 5 in the soprano moves via scale degree 6 to scale degree 4, while the alto progresses from scale degree 1 to 2 and back again. Because these connections are expressed by a single voice in the final version (*c*) they are not continuous as shown at (*a*) and (*b*). The dotted lines at (*c*) show the actual progression, which is temporarily interrupted by the skips from one line to another. Note that the melody in the second measure of (*c*) does not contain G♯. The melodic focus is on the lower of the two lines. However, it is present in the accompaniment and returns as an active melodic note in the third measure.

Harmonically controlled melodic progression, as illustrated here, is a traditional concept in music theory, although the degree to which melody possesses independence from harmony or actually influences harmony has been debated extensively. J. P. Rameau represents one extreme position when he writes: ". . . melody is only a consequence of harmony." J. Mattheson represents the other extreme position when he writes: "In opposition to [Rameau's concept] I place melody at the very foundation of the entire art of composition." To a great extent both men were confused by the definitions of harmony and melody as isolated aspects of structure. It is in order to avoid this that we focus upon the coordination of melody and harmony, upon their combined role in tonal composition.

The concept of compound melody is of the utmost importance to analysis and composition. It enables one to understand more complicated melodic structures and to compose melodies of greater subtlety and interest. In the past, major teachers of composition have been aware of this fact. For example, Kirnberger took great care to explain the concept. He described what we have called compound melody as a "single voice which is constructed in such a way that it carries its own harmony with it and sounds like a two- or three-part composition . . ." He illustrates as follows:

example 225. KIRNBERGER: *Die Kunst des reinen Satzes* (1771)

Kirnberger says that the voice shown at (*a*) sounds almost like the two-line setting at (*b*). In this way he demonstrates the continuity of each voice which "to the untutored" may not be readily apparent at (*a*) alone. He goes on to illustrate what we might call a three-line melody:

example 226. KIRNBERGER: *Die Kunst des reinen Satzes in der Musik*

Again he provides a vertical condensation (*b*) to show the continuity of each individual line and its course within the harmonic progression.

Compound melody is not restricted to any style within the tonal period. Every developed tonal composition utilizes the technique. In some cases it is more evident than in others, as in the following two excerpts.

example 227. MOZART: *Piano Sonata in A minor, K.310*

Here the compound structure is made apparent when the component lines suggested in the first measure are notated in full in the second. Similar verification of compound structure is provided by the next excerpt.

example 228. BRAHMS: *Intermezzo in B♭ major, Op. 76/4*

The opening "melody" of the piece is shown at (*a*). Clearly Brahms regards this as a compound structure, for when the same melody returns later in the piece (*b*) the upper of the two lines is actually sustained.

Extreme instances of compound melodic structure are provided by Bach's compositions for solo cello and solo violin. In the excerpt shown in Example 229 the melody (*a*) is actually a complete three-voice texture, as shown at (*b*).

example 229. BACH: *Suite in G major for Solo Cello, Menuet II*

130. The Transient Skip

Not every arpeggiation or partial arpeggiation represents compound melody. Very often it may be entirely a local event, a skip from one line to another and an immediate return. This kind of arpeggiation, which we have called a *transient skip,* does not influence melodic structure over a longer span, as does compound melody. An example follows.

example 230. Chorale: *Meine Seele erhebet den Herrn*

The soprano of this phrase is essentially a stepwise progression. The skip to E (bracketed) does not establish compound melody but is merely a temporary motion to another harmony note.

The transient skip is sometimes filled in by a passing note, as here:

example 231. BACH: *Chorale Variations* on *Sei gegrüsset, Jesu gütig*

(a)

(b)

At (*a*) is the basic chorale melody. When this is compared with (*b*), an embellished version, we see that scale degree 3 in the second measure is followed by a transient skip down to scale degree 1. This skip is filled in by a passing eighth note.

131. Nonconsecutive Melodic Relations

In the previous examples we have seen that melodic notes need not be in immediate succession in order to be related. In the Telemann *Fantasy* (Example 224c) the notes of each stepwise line in the soprano voice were not always in immediate succession, yet their relation was made clear by the voice leading within the harmonic progression. This fact is of great importance to melodic structure and has practical value in the harmonizing of a given melody, the composing of a soprano voice, and many other musical tasks.

132.   Displacement of a Line from Its Normal Position

Before leaving these general characteristics of melodic structure to deal with specific types of melodic progression we should observe the frequent displacement of a main line of compound melody from its normal position above the other line or lines. This was shown in the Telemann *Fantasy* (Example 224c), where the main line, which descends from scale degree 5 to scale degree 3 over the span of the entire phrase, lies below a static, secondary line.

HARMONIZATION OF COMMON TYPES OF STEPWISE SOPRANO PROGRESSION

133.   Melodic Groups and Melodic Goals

A discussion of melodic progression presupposes the existence of melodic goals and melodic groups. Therefore let us begin by considering the factors that delimit a melodic group. A melodic group is defined by the metric-rhythmic pattern and by harmonic progression. When a harmonic goal is reached the melodic goal coincides with it. However, the harmonic goal may differ from the melodic goal in an important respect. For example, the harmonic goal may represent closure, while the melodic goal may be such that the melody remains "open," active, demanding further progression. Our next example illustrates this.

example 232.   Chorale: *Allein Gott in der Höh' sei Ehr*

Here the bass and harmony execute a circular progression which closes on the tonic triad. The soprano, however, ends on an active note, the 3rd of the triad. This means that the composition is not completed, for although the harmony closes, the melody does not.

134. Types of Melodic Progression

The ultimate goal of a melodic line is always one of the stable notes of the diatonic scale (1, 3, 5, or 8), just as the ultimate harmonic goal is always one of the chords of the harmonic axis. Melodic progressions to, from, and around these stable notes may be characterized as "opening," "closing," and "circular," just as we characterize harmonic progressions with respect to the harmonic axis. In addition, we find a general type of melodic progression which traverses a triadic interval in descending direction. Each type is taken up separately in the following sections.

135. Circular Melodic Progression

The auxiliary-note embellishment is typical of circular progression, although intervals larger than the 2nd may also be traversed in a circular pattern. Standard harmonizations of the diatonic upper-auxiliary notes are summarized in the next example.

example 233.

The standard harmonizations of the upper auxiliary note are the same in major and minor. At the end of Example 233(*b*) is a reminder that raised scale degree 6 is only a passing note, never an auxiliary note. Examples which illustrate two of the above patterns are given below.

example 234. HAYDN: *Chorale St. Antoni*

example 235. SCHUMANN: *Viennese Carnival Jest*

Standard harmonizations of the diatonic lower-auxiliary note are summarized in the next example.

example 236.

In the major there are only two diatonic lower-auxiliary note formations: 8-7-8 and 3-2-3. By the law of the half step, scale degree 4 is bound to scale degree 3 and does not serve well as lower auxiliary note to 5. (In the rare instances when 4 does serve as lower auxiliary to 5 it is harmonized by IV⁶.)

In the minor each note of the tonic triad has available a lower auxiliary note. This is because scale degree 4 is a whole step away from both 3 and 5 and thus is not bound to either one by the law of the half step.

136. Opening Melodic Progression

The ascending progression from scale degree 1 to scale degree 3 typifies the opening progression: The line ascends from a stable note through a passing note to the active scale degree 3, thus opening a melodic interval (the 3rd) for further progression. A model chorale tune is presented in Example 237.

example 237. Chorale: *Wer Gott vertraut*

The standard harmonization of the melodic progression 1 2 3 is shown in the next example.

example 238.

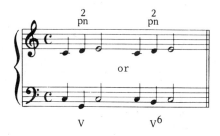

The passing note, scale degree 2, is harmonized by V (as in Example 237) or by V⁶. A more elaborate setting, using V⁶, is shown below.

example 239. LOEILLET: *Solo Sonata for Flute and Thorough-Bass*

The basic stepwise progression of the soprano voice is indicated both by the stems pointing upward and by the scale degree numbers above the staff. The remaining notes in the soprano voice are submetrical embellishments: auxiliary notes and arpeggiations. The bass is embellished by transient skips.

The passing note, scale degree 4, in the ascending progression 3 4 5 in major is harmonized either by V_3^4 or by IV^6.

example 240.

The V_3^4 in this situation has been described as the "passing" $_3^4$ (see section 108). It enables scale degree 4 to escape the law of the half step by moving the outer voices in parallel 10ths. The IV^6 achieves the same result by providing a "neutral" consonant setting for scale degree 4. An illustration of the latter harmonization is provided below.

example 241. BACH: *Concerto in C major for 2 Harpsichords* (reduction)

It is important to note that IV⁶ does not lead to V in this context, but to I⁶. When V harmonizes scale degree 5 as melodic goal, the passing scale degree 4 is raised chromatically and harmonized by a [VII⁶] of V, as shown below.

example 242.

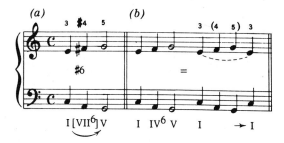

By raising scale degree 4 the half step occurs between ♯4 and 5, and in accord with the law of the half step ♯4 ascends. Without this chromatic alteration of scale degree 4 neither the melodic not the harmonic goal is reached in an effective way. V may not sound like a harmonic goal. Instead, the progression may sound as though it should continue toward scale degree 3 over I, as shown at Example 242(*b*).

In the minor mode scale degree 4 presents no special problem since, as remarked earlier, it stands equidistant from both 3 and 5. The following is a characteristic opening progression in the minor mode.

example 243. Chorale: *Auf meinen lieben Gott*

Here the soprano ascends directly to scale degree 5 while the bass carries an opening harmonic progression, I V. Often the melodic opening from 1 to 5 in minor is coordinated with a harmonic progression from I to III, as shown in our next example.

example 244. Chorale: *Ach wie nichtig*

The ascent to scale degree 5 is achieved in two groups. Scale degrees 1 2 3 are under the direct control of I. In the second group, however, passing scale degree 4 is harmonized by [V] of III so that at the end of the group the melodic goal, scale degree 5, coincides with the harmonic goal, III.

137.   Descending Melodic Progressions within Triadic Intervals

Thus far we have considered two types of melodic progression: (1) circular progressions involving auxiliary note embellishments of stable diatonic notes and (2) opening progressions, progressions which ascend through the triadic intervals of 3rd and 5th to the active notes of the triad.

There is a third type of progression, which descends through a triadic interval or its inversion but does not close on scale degrees 2 or 1. Two examples are given below.

example 245. Chorale: *Ach Gott und Herr*

Here the soprano traverses the upper 4th of the major scale.

Another common descending progression of this type is shown in Example 246:

example 246.

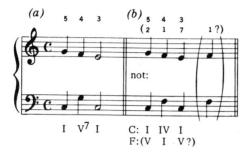

This progression descends from scale degree 5 to scale degree 3. The passing note, scale degree 4, is harmonized by V^7. In major keys it is rarely harmonized by IV, as shown at (b), because of the ambiguous 5th relation between I and IV, indicated in parentheses. This limitation applies only when scale degree 3 is the end of the melodic motion, as here.

Observe that neither of the above progressions has the effect of an opening progression, such as one finds at the beginning of a composition. Rather, they suggest progression toward closure. The next section deals with that type of progression.

138. Closing Progressions

Lines that end on scale degree 1 are called closing progressions. Usually such lines descend from the 5th or 3rd of the scale, as below:

example 247. Chorale: *Jesu, meine Freude*

Closure to scale degree 1 is effected either by the soprano progression 2 1 (as in Example 247) or by the progression 7 8, shown below.

example 248.

V   I

Over the cadential succession V I the soprano progresses from 7 to 8 while the inner voice descends from 2 to 1. The typical closing soprano progression descends. Much less often does the line ascend to the final degree progression 7 8, as in Example 248 and below.

example 249. Chorale: *Valet will ich dir geben*

139. Partial Closure

When a line descends to scale degree 2 over V we say that the progression is a partial closure. Both melody and harmony are directed strongly toward a cadence, yet the progression is not fulfilled. This partial closure is similar to a semicolon in effect. To illustrate we use the second phrase of the chorale whose first phrase served earlier to demonstrate opening progression (Example 243).

example 250. Chorale: *Auf meinen lieben Gott*

The next example shows a partial closure followed by a closing progression, the normal sequence of progressions.

example 251.   Chorale: *Mach's mit mir, Gott, nach deiner Güt'*

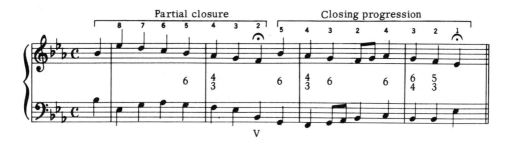

The partial closure should not be confused with the more general descending progression within a triadic interval as described in section 137. None of the latter type end on scale degree 2 and therefore do not suggest closure.

140.   Melodic Sequence

A melody that features immediate repetition of a pattern at different pitch levels is called *sequential.* An example of such a melody is quoted below.

example 252.   MARCELLO: *Concerto for Oboe*

To say that a melody is sequential does not indicate the type of progression it represents. This can be done only after one has determined its direction, the interval it traverses, and its melodic goal. In Example 252 the sequential melody of the oboe is a series of ascending arpeggiations, each ending on the note which represents the basic stepwise line. This line, which is carried more obviously by the soprano of the continuo, contains two progressions: first, a circular progression that centers upon scale degree 5, then a progression which descends from scale degree 5 to scale degree 3. The two are summarized in Example 253.

example 253.

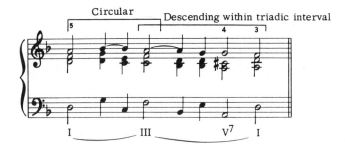

Example 253 also shows that the melodic progressions coordinate with two distinct harmonic progressions, the first an opening progression from I to III, the second a closing progression from III through V⁷ to I.

A more comprehensive treatment of sequences is given in section 220, Linear Intervallic Patterns.

141. Harmonization of the Diatonic Major Scale

Several of the types of progression explained above are represented in the harmonization of the diatonic scales. The scale harmonizations provide valuable guides to harmonization in general and should be memorized.

example 254. Harmonization of the Diatonic Major Scale

example 255. Harmonization of the Diatonic Minor Scale (melodic)

THE HARMONIZATION PROCEDURE

142. The Principle of Harmonic Definition

When we supply chords for a given soprano voice, it is recognized that a soprano voice alone can have several meanings, depending upon the way it is harmonized or "set." A demonstration of this fact follows.

example 256. SCHUBERT: *Die Nebensonnen*

Example 256 presents the melody without its chordal support. Assuming from the signature that the key is A major we read the upper voice as the degree succession 3-2-(3)-4-3-2-1. The 3 in parentheses is a passing note which connects scale degree 2 with scale degree 4, an upper auxiliary note. Schubert's first setting of the melody is in accord with this reading.

example 257.

However, the second setting, which occurs a few measures later in the song, gives quite a different structural meaning to the upper voice.

example 258.

F♯ minor: I   IV⁶ [V⁶₄] IV   I   V⁶   I
(VI)

Here the soprano is set as the degree succession 5-4-(5)-6-5-4-3 in the key of the relative minor or submediant (VI). The two different interpretations of the same soprano voice are summarized in Example 259:

example 259.

I or VI

The 3rd is shown first as a linear succession C♯-B-A, then as the vertical 3rd A-C♯. Schubert first interprets this 3rd as the lower 3rd of the A major triad (I), then as the upper 3rd of the F♯ minor triad (VI).

These two different interpretations of the same melody reflect the operation of a fundamental harmonic principle, *the principle of harmonic definition,* which is stated as follows: The structural meaning of the soprano voice is always defined by the bass and harmony. An additional demonstration of this principle is given below.

example 260. Chorale: *Nun ruhen alle Wälder*

We assume from the key signature that the key of this melody is B♭ major and therefore read the succession as scale degrees 3-1-2-3-5-4-3. The melodic progression is circular, focusing upon scale degree 3. The harmonic setting shown in Example 261 confirms this reading of the soprano voice.

example 261. Chorale: *Nun ruhen alle Wälder.* Bach's setting

Bb major: I   IV VII⁶I   V⁶ IV⁶V⁶₅ I

Like the melodic progression, the harmonic progression is circular, beginning and ending on I. Further on in the chorale Bach has set the same soprano line in a different way:

example 262.

G minor: V⁶   I [V⁶]III [V⁶₅] IV   [V♮]
(VI)

There the line is heard in terms of the "relative minor" (VI) as the degree succession 5-3-4-5-7-6-5. This is essentially the same harmonic reinterpretation as that used by Schubert above where the soprano line was heard first in relation to I, then in relation to VI. Both instances demonstrate the principle of harmonic definition. From this fundamental principle we can derive two criteria for the selection of appropriate chords to harmonize a given soprano voice:

1   The chord succession must support the melodic function of each note of the melodic succession and make clear its direction.

2   At the same time, each chord must have a specific and logical function in the harmonic progression. This applies to the main consonant chords which underlie the progression as well as to those chords which have secondary functions. Consider, for example, the following settings of scale degree 2 as a passing note.

example 263.

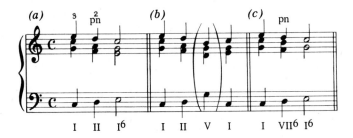

At (*a*) II has been selected to support the descending passing note D. This chord is incorrect because it suggests the further harmonic progression shown at (*b*). In a specific sense it is too strong harmonically to serve as a passing chord in this small context. It functions as a dominant preparation but is not followed by a dominant.

An appropriate passing chord for this situation is shown at (*c*): VII⁶, the dissonant 6th chord which so often has that melodic function.

The second criterion listed above is based upon harmonic function. This criterion may sometimes take precedence over the first, which has to do with the melodic functions of the soprano notes. In such cases the standard harmonization patterns must yield to the requirements of harmonic progression. As an instance of this, consider the standard setting of the circular progression 3-2-3-4-3 as shown at Example 264(*a*):

example 264.

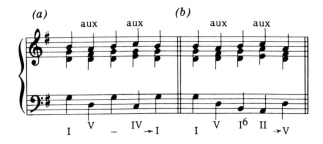

When the harmonic progression is directed toward V, as at (*b*) the standard harmonization is forsaken for one which prepares the goal more effectively. At (*b*) the deviation from the standard progression occurs with the I⁶, the chord which introduces the dominant preparation II. Example 265 presents the passage from which this progression was drawn.

example 265. BEETHOVEN: *Concerto for Piano and Orchestra in G major, Op. 58*

We turn now to the step-by-step procedure for harmonizing a soprano voice.

143. The Six Steps in Soprano Harmonization

The main purpose of the harmonization procedure outlined below is to provide for organized and intelligent applications of the principles of harmonic progression as they relate to the progression of the soprano voice. The ear and aural intuition are to be used at all times, of course, but the "picking out" of chords at the piano will teach nothing. True, this method may occasionally yield passable results with elementary material, but eventually it will lead only to frustration. The procedure outlined below is designed to guide the student toward logical and productive method that will prove effective regardless of the complexity of the material. To demonstrate the procedure we begin with the initial phrase of a familiar chorale melody:

example 266. Chorale: *Herr, wie du willst*

STEP 1. Analyze the melody for:

a. degree succession (basic stepwise line).

example 267.

b. metrical embellishments (submetrical embellishments are harmonized only in special circumstances).

example 268.

c. types of melodic progression.

example 269.

opening progression   closing progression

d. subgroups within the progression, particularly sequences.

example 270.

sequential subgroups

STEP 2. Sketch in the bass and symbols for the *minimal harmonization.*

example 271.

I V I V – I V I IV I V I I V I

The minimal harmonization employs only diatonic triads in fundamental position, plus V[7], and VII[6]. Wherever possible use the standard harmonizations. At this stage we are not concerned about 5ths and 8ves, but only about chord selection in terms of harmonic function.

The importance of the minimal harmonization cannot be overestimated. From this firm basic structure one can proceed in an orderly fashion to construct more elaborate settings. Often the minimal harmonization will contain parallel 5ths and 8ves and sound somewhat dull. Nevertheless, it is of great value in achieving an effective final harmonization. Kirnberger has stressed the value of such a basic harmonization in the following words: "A complete composition must be constructed in such a way that when all dissonances are eliminated the remainder is harmonically coherent. Therefore as an essential part of the art of composition one must know how to support a melody with consonant harmonies alone."

STEP 3. Invert the minimal harmonies in order to correct parallel 5ths and 8ves, improve the melodic structure of the bass, achieve a better counterpoint between the outer voices, and in order to render the metric-rhythmic pattern more coherent and effective.

example 272.

Inversions: 6 6 6

STEP 4. Use secondary triads as substitutes for primary triads if they improve the progression.

example 273.

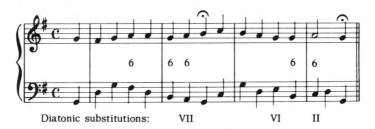

Diatonic substitutions: VII   VI   II

In Example 273 three substitutions have been made. The first and last fulfill the need for stepwise bass progression indicated in Example 272 by asterisks. The second substitution (VI for I) prevents the tonic chord from arriving in an accented position too early and thus arresting the forward motion of the progression.

STEP 5. Where the context is appropriate replace triads with 7th chords and inverted 7th chords. [V] and [V⁷] may also be introduced.

example 274.

STEP 6. Complete the harmonization sketched out at Step 5 by working out all the details of voice leading, just as in a figured bass with given soprano.

example 275.

The procedure thus consists of the six steps summarized below. The student should memorize them and follow them consistently until he has gained sufficient experience to enable him to condense the procedure.

SUMMARY OF STEPS IN THE HARMONIZATION PROCEDURE

1 Analyze the melody.
2 Minimal harmonization (triads in fundamental position, V^7, VII^6).
3 Invert minimal harmonies.
4 Substitute triads.
5 Add 7th and inverted 7th chords.
6 Notate in full.

In Chapters 10 and 11 two new classes of chords will be presented, completing the vocabulary. In the outline above, these may be introduced quite naturally at Step 5.

144. Sample Harmonizations

We now apply the procedure to several soprano voices, each of which features a different type of metrical embellishment. The first features a form of the auxiliary note.

example 276. Given soprano: *Austrian Folk Song*

example 277. Step 1: Analysis

example 278. Step 2: Minimal harmonization

I   IV   V   I   I   V   V   I

Our minimal harmonization here is defective at two points (marked by brackets) where the bass and harmony are repeated across the bar line. A repetition of this kind has an adverse effect upon the metric-rhythmic pattern, since change of measure should be marked by change of harmony. Inversion of the chords involved is not a satisfactory solution since they remain closely related to the parent chords they follow. A satisfactory solution can be obtained by introducing one substitute and by supplying one primary triad with a prefix. However, we have delayed this until Step 4, where it belongs. Thus at Step 3 (Example 279) we use only two inversions. Although not essential to the harmonization these render the bass line more fluent melodically.

example 279. Step 3: Invert minimal harmonies

Inversions: 6   6

Observe particularly the effect of IV⁶ in the first measure of Example 279 as compared with the parent IV in the first measure of Example 278. The parent chord provides too much harmonic accent for the incomplete upper auxiliary note. It tends to hinder the unfolding of the soprano voice. In large part this is due to the counterpoint of the outer voices, which emphasizes the 8ve B♭.

example 280. Step 4: Substitute triads

6   6   6

Diatonic substitutions: VI   II

By substituting VI for I and preparing V by II⁶ we have removed the repetition over the bar line mentioned above.

example 281. Step 5: Add 7th and inverted 7th chords

7ths and secondary dominants: [V]   VI

The only 7th chord introduced here is the cadential V⁷. However, the secondary dominant triad is used to good advantage in the second measure. It serves to link the two melodic groups together strongly and, in addition, corrects the impending parallelisms between I and VI which are evident in Example 280.

example 282. Step 6: Notate in full

I   IV   V   [V]   VI   II   V   I

Another step-by-step harmonization follows. Here the given soprano combines passing and auxiliary notes.

example 283. Given soprano: Chorale, *Schmücke dich, o liebe Seele*

example 284. Step 1: Analysis

example 285. Step 2: Minimal harmonization

Two aspects of the minimal harmonization should be noted. First, the bass line is extremely repetitious and greatly restricted by the tonic and dominant harmonies. This defect can be remedied easily in the subsequent steps. Second, we use the V^7 here in the minimal harmonization for the first time. (The V^7 and VII^6 are the only dissonant chords admitted to the minimal harmonization.) As shown above in Example 246, IV is unsatisfactory as a harmonic setting for scale degree 4 when that degree serves as a descending passing note. V^7, V^6_5, or V^4_3 are standard.

example 286. Step 3: Invert minimal harmonies

Inversion improves the bass line but does not remove all the other defects. With the aid of substitute harmonies and prefixes the static points indicated by brackets in Example 286 can be corrected at the next step.

example 287. Step 4: Substitute triads

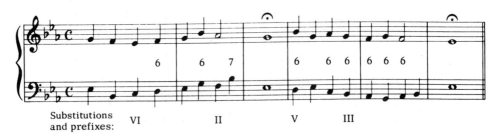

In the second measure II serves as prefix to V^7 so that the soprano note A♭ is harmonized by two chords. III^6 has been substituted for I in the fourth measure. The substitute chord does not progress in the same way as the original. This can be tested by playing the succession III^6-V^6 and noting the effect of discontinuity. The bass succession which follows logically from III^6 forms a counterpoint of parallel 6ths with the soprano (with only one exception), a very fluent progression of imperfect consonances which leads to the two perfect cadential intervals, 5th and 8ve.

example 288. Steps 5 and 6: Add 7th and inverted 7th chords. Notate in full

The next soprano features an ascending arpeggiation.

example 289. Given soprano: Chorale: *Sollt ich meinem Gott nicht singen*

example 290. Step·1: Analysis

Arpeggiation, especially complete arpeggiation as in this case, provides the most obvious clue to harmonization. Here is seen the complete tonic triad unfolded in an ascending arpeggiation. The melodic progression as a whole is circular, beginning and ending on scale degree 1. Within the over-all progression are two subgroups, the first the arpeggiation, the second the auxiliary note pattern 8 ♯7 8.

example 291.   Step 2: Minimal harmonization

$$I \quad - \quad - \quad - \quad \quad V \quad I \quad -$$

example 292.   Step 3: Invert minimal harmonies

The single inversion here improves the bass progression somewhat. But again, substitutes and prefixes are required to provide harmonic development (Step 4).

example 293.   Step 4: Substitute triads

Only the dominant preparation IV is added here. This improves the bass of the second measure, but the first measure remains static since it is bound to the tonic triad and its first inversion.

example 294.   Steps 5 and 6: Add 7th and inverted 7th chords. Notate in full

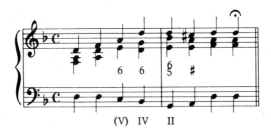

Here II$_5^6$ replaces IV as dominant preparation. In consequence, IV can be used one beat sooner. We continue "thinking backwards" and fill in the bass 3rd, D-B♭, with the passing note C. This C forms a 6th with the soprano A, suggesting a passing 6th chord or possibly a $\frac{4}{2}$. We choose the 6th chord since it effects a stronger change to correspond with the secondary metrical accent. Now the bass and harmony of the first measure have a feeling of movement which matches to some extent the strong ascending arpeggiation of the soprano.

The next soprano, the English song *Thou soft flowing Avon*, also features arpeggiation, both complete and partial.

example 295. Step 1: Analysis

Example 295 shows that the basic stepwise line is interrupted often by skips down to a lower voice, the voice which is stated on the initial upbeat. The short group which begins in the fourth measure and which centers on scale degree 1 actually belongs in the lower register, as shown by the noteheads in parentheses.

example 296. Step 2: Minimal harmonization

The minimal harmonization presents no special problems since the analysis showed clearly the melodic function of each note in the given soprano. It made clear, for example, that the A♭ in the third measure is a descending passing note, not an auxiliary note, and therefore is to be harmonized by V^7.

example 297. Step 3: Invert minimal harmonies

Compare the counterpoint of the outer voices in the third measure here with that in the third measure of Example 296. VII[6] here is a substitute for a passing V^4_3

This particular melody does not lend itself to substitute triads; therefore we omit Step 4 and proceed to the final stage of the harmonization, combining Steps 5 and 6 as before.

example 298. Steps 5 and 6: Add 7th and inverted 7th chords. Notate in full

145. Common Mistakes in Harmonizing Melodies

Before proceeding to the exercises in harmonization, it may be helpful to list some of the pitfalls. As remarked above, chords "sound wrong" for specific reasons. Of course it is important to know that a particular chord is incorrect, but that alone is insufficient. One must understand why. The reason often has to do with a conflict between harmonic and melodic function. An instance of this has already been seen in the II which was used as a passing chord (Example 263). As a general rule one should take special care when using chords which have a strong harmonic direction, particularly when they are in fundamental position: for example, the triads which form the harmonic axis, I and V, and V^7. These chords must be distributed strategically in the total progression. They should not be made to serve secondary melodic functions which other harmonies could serve more effectively.

A summary of the main requirements for correct harmonization follows:

1 *Chord selection.* The chord must be selected with regard to its function in the harmonic progression as a whole and with regard to its definition of the soprano note as a point of departure, melodic goal or metrical embellishment. Some chords quite correctly have a purely local effect; others form the basic progression of the passage. Some chords are essentially passing chords, others auxiliary chords. Confuse the two and the harmony sounds wrong.

If selected with regard to the requirements of the particular progression, substitute chords can serve many valuable melodic and rhythmic functions. One must remember, however, that a substitute chord, especially a triad, may have a direction which differs greatly from that of the original chord. For example, if VI is substituted for I it is apt to direct the progression toward V, which may or may not be desirable in a given context.

Both inversions and substitute chords must be used with restraint. If they serve no purpose they should not replace the original chord.

In no event are chords to be selected for each melodic note as though it existed in isolation. This inevitably leads to poor harmony. If the harmonization procedure outlined above is followed this will not occur.

2 *Chord structure.* The triad must be complete in four parts. In the case of 7th chords (but not their inversions) the 5th may be omitted and the 8ve doubled.

3 *Chord connection* (voice leading). Parallel 5ths and 8ves are to be avoided. All dissonant notes must be correctly resolved. Stepwise voice leading is the norm.

Several of the common types of mistake are collected together in Example 299. The mistakes are lettered to correspond to the observations that follow.

example 299. Chorale: *Ach Gott vom Himmel sieh darin*

(a) Chord incomplete. Here the I also gives a feeling of cadence. A substitute, VI, would be far better. (Also parallel 8ves between outer voices.)

(b) Repetition over the bar line obscures metrical pattern.

(c) Parallel 8ves between outer voices.

(d) Wrong harmonic goal. From this point on the harmonic progression lacks specific direction. There is a tendency, though not well defined, to progress to III, but this is contradicted by the final cadence.

(e) Either this chord should be a D$\frac{5}{3}$ or the preceding chord should be a ♯6. As they are they do not form a pair.

(f) Again the chords do not form a pair. The dissonant-6th chord should serve as a passing chord or auxiliary chord and lead to a B-minor triad in first or second inversion, not to the G-major triad as here.

(g) This chord does not follow from the preceding chord at all. The problem here is one of coherent harmonic progression.

(h) The function of the D$\frac{5}{3}$ here on the downbeat is quite unclear.

(i) The sudden occurrence of the V of B minor is jarring. There is no preparation whatsoever for this important harmony. Also note that the 3rd has not been raised, which makes it impossible for the chord to function properly as a dominant.

A correct setting of this chorale, by Kirnberger, is given in Example 300.

example 300. Chorale: *Ach Gott vom Himmel, sieh darin.* Setting by Kirnberger

Observe particularly the way in which closure is avoided at the fourth note in the melody—by substitution of VI for I. Also observe the way in which the final two melodic groups, which are identical, are set. The first is not permitted to anticipate the cadential progression of the second.

EXERCISES

A. List of Some Important Terms to Define and Memorize

Voice

Basic melodic progression

Metrical arpeggiation

Compound melody

Transient skip

Circular melodic progression

Partial closure

Melodic sequence

Harmonization procedure

Minimal harmonization

Principle of harmonic definition

B. Basic Keyboard and Aural Exercises

INSTRUCTIONS

These alternate scale harmonizations should be played and sung following the usual procedure. In addition, they are to be transposed to at least three major and minor keys with a change of metric-rhythmic pattern for each new key.

exercise 138.

exercise 139.

C. Soprano Voices to Be Harmonized

INSTRUCTIONS

Harmonize, showing fully each step of the harmonization procedure.

exercise 140. **Chorale:** *Herr, straf' mich nicht in deinem Zorn*

exercise 141. Chorale: *Wie nach einer Wasserquelle*

exercise 142. Chorale: *Warum sollt' ich mich nicht grämen*

exercise 143. Chorale: *Eins ist Not!*

exercise 144. Chorale: *Singen wir aus Herzens Grund*

INSTRUCTIONS
Analyze these harmonizations in terms of the harmonization procedure. Realize for vocal performance.

exercise 145. Chorale: *Gleich wie ein Hirsch eilt*

exercise 146. Chorale: *Ach Herr mein Gott straf mich doch nicht*

exercise 147.   **French Folk Song:** *Le Jeune Berger qui m'engage*

Moderato

exercise 148.   **German Folk Song:** *Winters Abschied*

Quietly

exercise 149.   **French Folk Song:** *Laire lan, laire lan laire*

Allegro

exercise 150.   **Chorale:** *Nun sich der Tag geendet hat*

exercise 151. Chorale: *Seelenbräutigam*

exercise 152. *French Air*

Not too slow

exercise 153. French Song: *Margot sur la brune*

exercise 154. **J.B. SENAILLÉ**: *Sonata for Violin and Continuo in G minor*

Allegro

exercise 155. Chorale: *In allen meinen Taten*

exercise 156. Chorale: *Als der gütige Gott*

exercise 157. **J. CHURCH**: *Psalm 14*

8

Composing A Soprano Voice and Harmonizing A Bass

Thorough bass teaches us to reduce to its simple, original, natural, and derived chords, every composition—for whatever instrument it may be written, and however florid the melody, accompaniment, or embellishments. It reveals the whole wonderful construction of a work of art. . . .

Johann Georg Albrechtsberger, 1790

The preceding chapter dealt with harmonic structure from the standpoint of the soprano voice and its harmonic implications. Part of the present chapter is given over to the complementary procedure: the realization of the harmonic and melodic implications of a bass. Essential to this compositional technique is the ability to construct a coherent and effective soprano voice. Therefore the first part of the chapter is devoted to explaining a procedure by which one may develop that ability.

There are two methods of composing a soprano. First, it may be composed before the harmony but with careful consideration of its harmonic implications. This is the method often employed by the gifted and experienced composer. Second, the soprano may be derived from a given harmonic succession. In this case it is controlled by the bass and harmony from the outset. That is to say, the course of the soprano is limited by the voice leading of the harmonic progression. The first method, for all its virtues, presupposes a background of experience which the

246

reader of these pages may not possess. The second method, outlined below, offers him a secure approach to the multiple problems of melodic structure.

146. The Procedure for Composing a Soprano Voice

We begin with the harmonic progression given in Example 301.

example 301. After HANDEL: *Chaconne for Clavier*

Since the soprano voice is to be based upon a stepwise progression, controlled by voice leading, we must decide which of the harmonic strands will serve most effectively. Therefore we proceed systematically to construct a stepwise progression beginning with each soprano position of the initial chord in turn (Step 1).

example 302. Stepwise line from the 8ve Position

Here the soprano begins in the position of the 8ve and is led stepwise note against note of the bass. When there is a choice of stepwise progression the line is led to the active rather than to the static melodic note, since the soprano carries the sensitive notes of the harmony, those notes that provide melodic impetus in the progression. The active quality of a note therefore is determined by the interval which it forms with the bass and by its function in the chord. In general, the accented 8ve with the bass is avoided during the course of the phrase, especially when the 8ve is to be the goal. And in general the line takes the dissonant note of the harmony in preference to the consonant note. If the line does not follow these precepts it soon will begin to move along a more static strand of the harmony and consequently will not give the effect of direction and impetus which one expects of tonal melody. The first melodic group in Example 302 is good in these respects. It opens without interruption to scale degree 5. At the beginning of the third measure, where two stepwise progressions are possible, the progression to the active scale degree 3 is chosen rather than the progression back to scale degree 1, which would form an 8ve with the bass. The second melodic group in Example 302 is less satisfactory. It is circular, centering upon scale degree 5, and appears to resist all efforts of the harmonic progression to move it toward a closure. We may discover a better line for this group as we consider the other possibilities.

example 303. Stepwise line from the Soprano Position of the 3rd

Example 303 is included here only for the sake of systematic procedure. It is evident that with the exception of the first note the line is the same as that in the previous example, Example 302, but since the line here does not open from scale degree 1, as in Example 302, its effect is somewhat different. Let us examine the next possibility.

example 304. Stepwise line from the Soprano Position of the 5th

In an effort to break away from scale degree 5 the line has been led to E in the third measure. E, in turn, moves stepwise to scale degree 7 (the leading note) as the melodic goal of the first group. The leading note then resolves to scale degree 8, which dominates the second group. Taken as a unit, the two groups execute a closing progression which ascends from scale degree 5 to scale degree 1. Between the groups there is no contrast of progression nor is there much activity within either group. We have now completed Step 1. Step 2 is described below.

STEP 2: Select the best stepwise line. If no suitable stepwise line is available apply the technique of compound melody.

Since in each instance above, the stepwise line of the second group was very static we must apply the technique of compound melody to that part if we are to maintain an active and interesting progression. Example 305 illustrates an effective solution for the total line.

example 305.

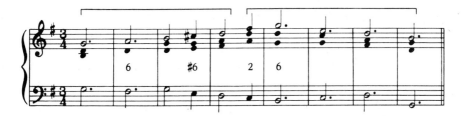

The first group carries the ascent to scale degree 5 as in Example 302. This is a very satisfactory progression. The second group begins with the skip to F♯ in the fourth measure. From G the voice then ceases to progress entirely stepwise, and moves instead by a series of descending skips and steps. If we compare these skips with the stepwise progressions examined above we see that in each case the skip avoids a repetition. Thus in the sixth measure the soprano skips to E rather than retain G, the common note. Repetition is not necessarily "bad." However, in this short group it seems to be disadvantageous, since in every instance it leads to a circular progression which is at odds with the harmonic progression.

Often the basic stepwise progression must be abandoned, as in the second melodic group above. Indeed, this is highly advantageous in many situations—for example, if the stepwise line has become centered upon a single note, as above, or if it begins to descend toward closure before the harmonic progression has completed itself. A situation of this kind is demonstrated below.

example 306.   BACH: *Sieben geistliche Oden*

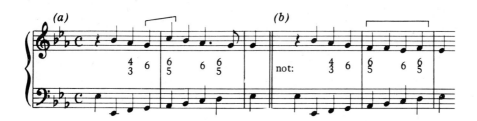

The composer does not follow stepwise progression all the way to the end in the upper voice here, but skips away at the point indicated by the bracket. The reason for this skip becomes clear when we consider the consequence of continued stepwise progression shown at (b). There the stepwise soprano line descends to scale degree 2 (F) and centers upon that note until the close on scale degree 1. This very dull line sounds like an inner voice. It does not interact in an effective way with the ascending bass line, as does Bach's line at (a).

Adherence to stepwise progression is obligatory under only one condition, a familiar one: A voice cannot skip away from a dissonant note, leaving it unresolved. Thus, the skip bracketed in the next example is incorrect.

example 307.

The F♯ in the fourth measure should have resolved upward to G in accord with its function as leading note in the scale and its tritone relation to the bass and harmony. Although certain other kinds of skips are not "forbidden" they may be considered poor from the standpoint of melodic coherence and orderly development. Faulty skips are indicated by asterisks in the next example.

example 308.

In the third measure a skip is made to an inactive note of the harmony whereas the voice should have followed the stepwise progression through the altered note C♯. The notes of the second group lack coherence, mainly because the skip from E to A destroys stepwise continuity and has no clear purpose at that point.

On the other hand, skips properly used are essential to good melody. No amount of metrical or submetrical embellishment will improve the following step-wise succession!

example 309.

We continue now to Step 3.

STEP 3: Add metrical arpeggiations wherever they enhance the progression of the basic line.

Example 310 illustrates two embellishments by metrical arpeggiation. Observe that the skips do not displace the basic progression selected in Example 310. The small notes above the bass may be played by the left hand while the right hand plays the soprano alone—a more convenient arrangement for the keyboard.

example 310.

The soprano voice shown at (a) is the basic structure selected earlier (Example 305). At (b) this basic structure is expanded by means of skips within the harmony. With the exception of the skip in the third measure these are descending skips. In every measure of (b) the note which represents the basic structure occurs in the same metrical position as it did in (a). Example 310(c) offers a more refined treatment of metrical arpeggiation. There, more weight is given to the embellishment. For example, in the second measure the arpeggiated note D takes two beats of the three-beat measure. It is important to realize that this in no way affects the basic structure. D remains an embellishment; it does not usurp the function of the note A, which carries the main stepwise progression. Observe that the skip in the seventh measure ascends, in contrast to the preceding skips, and that it also reverses the rhythmic pattern of the preceding measures. By such means the melody achieves variety and interest.

Although submetrical embellishments are reserved for special treatment in a later chapter, two have been introduced in the fourth measure of Example 310(c): the passing note E and the skip D.

147. Common Mistakes in Metrical Arpeggiations

Arpeggiations are activated chordal intervals; they obey the laws of voice leading. One cannot introduce as an arpeggiated note a note which would be incorrect in an unembellished chord succession. The doubling and voice leading expressed by an arpeggiation must conform precisely to that of the underlying chord succession in its pristine state. This principle was set forth in section 129 in the explanation of compound melody. It is illustrated again here using the fourth and fifth measures of the progression studied in the previous section.

example 311.

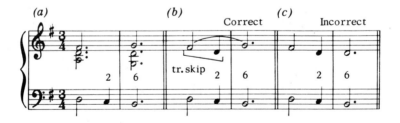

At (a) the chords are shown in full four parts; the voice leading is fully expressed. At (b) the soprano skips down over the change of bass. However, the previous note, F♯, remains in effect since it is still in the harmony. Moreover, it still requires resolution in the line where it originally occurred. Accordingly, the treatment of the skip as shown at (*b*) is absolutely correct, whereas that shown at (*c*) is entirely incorrect. In the latter case the F♯ is abandoned; it remains unresolved in the line where it originally occurred. The effect is one of discontinuity, for a melodic progression was prepared but unfulfilled. In sum, the techniques of arpeggiation do not permit lines to skip about haphazardly within the harmony. They must be applied with regard for the requirements of voice leading. If those requirements are disregarded, skips may also express parallel 5ths and 8ves as in the following example which is based upon the second part of our progression above.

example 312.

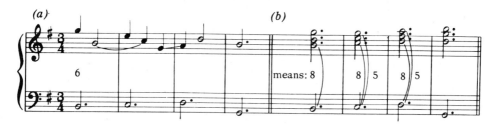

In the first measure the doubling of the bass (B) is incorrect since it inevitably gives rise to parallel 8ves. The succession G A from the second to the third measure likewise is incorrect, since it creates even a more obvious parallelism.

HARMONIZING A BASS

As the counterpart of harmonizing a soprano, harmonizing a bass is an important part of compositional technique. The unfigured outer voices in previous chapters provide a background of experience for the more detailed explanation of procedure which follows. The purpose of the exercises in unfigured outer voices was mainly practice in recognizing contexts for particular chords. The unfigured basses at the end of this chapter go beyond this. They afford valuable practice in constructing harmonic progressions and in composing the fundamental soprano voice which is indispensable to effective tonal music.

Like the standard harmonization of the soprano scales given in Chapter 7 the following standard harmonizations of the bass scales serve as guides. They are subject to modification depending upon metric-rhythmic pattern and other factors in specific contexts.

148. Standard Harmonizations of the Diatonic Scales in the Bass

Bass-scale harmonizations are not to be confused with the norms of harmonic progression given in Examples 100 and 101. The latter represent more general principles not shown in the bass-scale harmonizations. The bass-scale harmonizations afford a guide to the treatment of short successions within a larger progression. For example, if one were about to realize an unfigured bass consisting of scale degrees 1-2-3, the standard harmonization would show how this succession is often treated in tonal compositions. Whether the standard harmonization is in fact suitable for the particular passage would depend upon the nature of the progression as a whole, its point of departure, goal, metric-rhythmic pattern, and so on.

example 313. Harmonization of the Major Scale in the Bass

The standard scale harmonization thus provides a convenient repertoire of patterns. It is particularly useful in relationship to the problematic upper 4th of the scale, both in major and minor. Almost invariably this is harmonized as shown in Example 313. The following excerpt is typical.

example 314. MOZART: *Die Zauberflöte*

I

The ascending minor scale resembles that of the ascending major scale.

example 315. Harmonization of the minor scale in the bass

S.D.	1	2	3	4	5	6	7	8	8	7	6	5	4	3	2	1
	I	V	I	IV	V	IV	V	I	I	V	IV	V	V	I	VII	I

Note, however, that the descending fourth of the minor scale requires a somewhat different harmonization than that of the major—for reasons of voice-leading parallelisms.

149. Procedure for Harmonizing an Unfigured Bass

A specimen unfigured bass is given in Example 316:

example 316. HAYDN

Adagio

As in the procedure for harmonizing a given soprano voice we shall now consider the step-by-step transformation of this given part into a complete musical setting.

example 317. Step 1: Identify the harmonic groups and goals

We bring to bear on this task the principles of progression as summarized in Examples 100 and 101, the standard bass-scale harmonizations given above, and the various exercises carried out thus far. It is often helpful, though not absolutely essential, to number the scale-degree succession first, as in Example 317. One should then bracket the harmonic groups, label the type of progression, and supply Roman numerals to indicate the basic consonant chords. With the goals and types of progression clearly defined, attention can be given to the details of the harmony, to secondary harmonic and melodic functions.

example 318. Step 2: Identify secondary harmonic and melodic functions and select appropriate chords

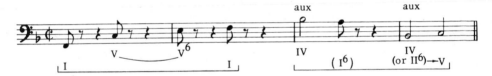

Here we read scale degree 5 in the first measure as the bass note of V connecting two statements of I. In relation to the soprano voice, which will be worked out below, this V probably serves as a passing or auxiliary chord. In the second measure, E (scale degree 7) is interpreted as an extension of the dominant harmony and labeled, accordingly, V⁶. In both the third and fourth measures B♭ is an auxiliary note to scale degree 5, harmonized by V. In the third measure it is important to notice that the bass note A serves as an auxiliary note between the two B♭s and is harmonized by the consonant 6th chord (I⁶).

example 319. Step 3: Write out the harmony in full, taking care to construct a good basic soprano line

The actual melody of the composition from which this bass was extracted is quite elaborate and contains a number of submetrical embellishments. What we have here in Example 319, although relatively complete, is still only an outline of the actual work. Beyond this point substitute chords and 7th chords could be introduced, the melody could be supplied with metrical embellishments, and so on. However, the bass has served its purpose and we move on to apply the same procedure to two additional basses. As before, the steps are illustrated fully in musical notation and verbal explanation is minimized.

example 320. HANDEL. Step 1: Identify the harmonic groups and goals

In completing the next step the standard scale harmonization will be helpful.

example 321. Step 2: Identify secondary harmonic and melodic functions and select appropriate chords

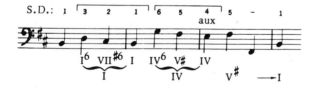

The first descending pattern (bracketed) can be harmonized with the standard chords shown in the descending minor-scale harmonization (Example 315). The standard setting can also be used for the second stepwise descending pattern, with the exception of the last note, scale degree 4. In the descending harmonization, scale degree 4 is obviously a descending passing note and is harmonized by V_2^4. Here, however, scale degree 4 is an auxiliary note to scale degree 5. This suggests that it is the bass of one of the dominant preparations; the most obvious choice is IV. The two descending patterns thus center upon I and IV respectively, and the over-all progression is the familiar I IV V I.

example 322. Step 3: Write out the harmony in full, taking care to construct a good basic soprano line

The last bass for demonstration of the procedure is given below.

example 323. CORELLI. Step 1: Identify the harmonic groups and goals

example 324. Step 2: Identify secondary harmonic and melodic functions and select appropriate chords

The secondary bass notes here could be harmonized entirely in the standard way, except for scale degree 6 in the third measure, which represents a deceptive cadence on VI. For the sake of melodic variation II⁶ and II$^6_5$ have been substituted for IV in the fourth and sixth measures.

example 325. Step 3: Write out the harmony in full, taking care to construct a good soprano line

EXERCISES

A. Memorization of Basic Materials

Memorize the standard harmonizations of the diatonic scales in the bass, Examples 313 and 315. Play in all keys, following order of the circle of 5ths.

Memorize the step-by-step procedure for composing a soprano voice over a given harmonic progression.

Memorize the step-by-step procedure for realizing an unfigured bass.

B. Basic Keyboard and Aural Exercises

INSTRUCTIONS
Play and sing in the usual manner. Compare these harmonizations with the standard harmonizations. Compose different sopranos for the first two exercises.

exercise 158. **The major scale in the bass harmonized by diatonic consonances plus VII^6 and passing $^6_4$**

exercise 159. **The minor scale in the bass harmonized by diatonic consonances plus VII^6 and II^6**

C. Figured Basses

INSTRUCTIONS
To be realized in four voices, with special attention to the soprano.

exercise 160. **HANDEL**

exercise 161. **BOYCE**

exercise 162. **MATTEI**

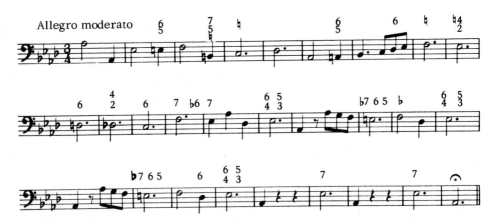

exercise 163. **PERGOLESI**

exercise 164. BOYCE: *Trio Sonata in G minor*

exercise 165. HANDEL: *Rodelinda*

D. Unfigured Basses

INSTRUCTIONS
To be realized in four voices, with special attention to the soprano. Show all steps in the solution of the exercise.

exercise 166. **PERGOLESI**

Adagio

exercise 167. **CORELLI**

Grave

exercise 168. **PURCELL**

Moderato

exercise 169.   HAYDN

exercise 170. BUXTEHUDE: *Cantate Domino*

exercise 171. HANDEL: *Sorge nel petto*

exercise 172. PERGOLESI: *Trio Sonata in F major*

Menuetto

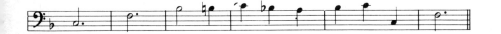

9

Modulatory Progression

Modulation is the essential part of the art. Without it there is little effect, consequently little music, for a piece derives its true beauty not from the large number of fixed modes which it embraces but rather from the subtle fabric of its modulation.

Charles-Henri Blainville, 1767

150. Modulation as a Primary Means of Harmonic Extension

In earlier chapters two important means of harmonic development were examined: the harmonic, and the melodic processes of chord generation. By these fundamental means the harmonic content of tonal music was greatly expanded. The present chapter explores still another technique, one that permits extension beyond the harmonic unit controlled directly by the tonic triad. This technique is called modulation, or better, modulatory progression. So important is modulatory progression to tonal music that without the development and refinement of this technique it is doubtful whether such extended and unified tonal works as Beethoven's *Eroica Symphony* would have come into existence.

The essentials of the technique are shown in the following chorale setting.

example 326. Chorale: *Ach was soll ich Sünder machen.* (Setting after J. S. Bach)

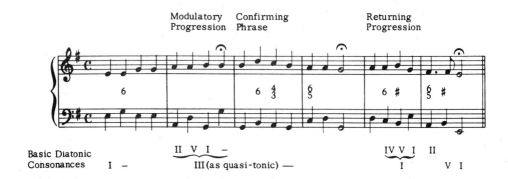

The first measure presents the tonic harmony. In the second it may be observed that the progression is directed very strongly toward III. As shown by the Roman numerals and brace the harmonies of that measure group themselves around III as though it were a tonic. When a triad begins to function like a tonic, as in this case, we shall call it a *quasi-tonic.* The function of III as a quasi-tonic triad is confirmed by the circular progression of the next harmonic unit. The temporary nature of this quasi-tonic then becomes evident, for the progression of the third phrase is directed back to the main tonic once more. When, as here, a diatonic triad becomes a quasi-tonic, the progression which establishes it in this semi-autonomous role is called a *modulatory* progression.

By means of modulatory progression a diatonic consonance is stabilized so that it assumes a degree of independence from the tonic. The process of modulation thus affords a means of harmonic development, a way of extending beyond the direct control of the tonic triad to create longer musical statements which are unified and coherent despite apparent diversity.

The basis of unity and coherence is this: A triad temporarily stabilized by modulation (quasi-tonic) nevertheless retains its characteristic function in relation to the harmonic axis. That is, it behaves in exactly the same way as when it occurs in a small context under the direct control of I. Neither duration nor quasi-tonic function affect the identity and ultimate direction of a diatonic triad. This is evident in Example 326, where the succession of basic consonances I III I V I over the span of the three phrases is exactly the kind of succession one might also find as a brief circular progression within a single unit. It is in this sense that we understand harmony in the larger dimension indicated by F. W. Marpurg when he wrote: "Harmony differs from chord as whole differs from part." In subsequent sections we will see that longer tonal compositions are nothing more nor less than stretched-out successions of consonant triads which behave according to the norms described in Chapter 4. Modulation therefore should be regarded as ordered harmonic extension, not as "change of key for the sake of variety," as some authors would have us believe.

The process of modulation is a remarkable part of the tonal system. Its logic is an extension of the logic of tonality. For this reason "free" modulation, or arbitrary modulation does not exist in art music. Modulation of this kind occurs only in music patched together for commercial purposes and in other poorly composed music. In fine music modulatory techniques operate entirely within the concept of tonality as the sum of harmonic, melodic, and rhythmic events regulated by a single tonic-dominant relationship: the harmonic axis of triadic music.

Modulations are of two general types: diatonic and chromatic. When the modulatory progression has as its goal a diatonic triad in the main tonality we say that the modulation is diatonic. When the goal of a modulatory progression is a triad which does not belong to the diatonic tonality, but which is based upon a chromatic degree, the modulation is called chromatic. This chapter is concerned only with diatonic modulation. The resources of chromatic modulation are discussed in Chapter 16.

151. Minimal Conditions Required for Modulation

Modulatory progression requires certain minimal harmonic, melodic, and metric-rhythmic conditions. These are outlined below, beginning with the harmonic conditions.

The minimal chords required for modulation are three in number: (1) the *quasi-tonic triad,* a consonant diatonic triad (2) the *modulating dominant,* which defines the goal harmony as a quasi-tonic (3) the *pivot chord,* the chord that prepares the modulating dominant and that serves as a link with the main tonality. In the following example the three chords are numbered to correspond with the above order.

example 327. Chorale: *Ach was soll ich Sünder machen*

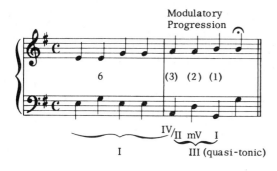

The functions of the modulating dominant and the quasi-tonic are familiar: They imitate the main dominant and tonic. The pivot chord, however, requires explanation. In Example 327, the pivot chord serves both as IV in relation to the main tonic (E minor) and as II in relation to the quasi-tonic (III, or G major). It thus serves as a chord of transition, as a signal for a change of harmonic focus. Its double function is indicated by the slanted line, so that we read the symbol IV/II as "IV becoming II."

To point up the special role of the pivot chord, Example 328 illustrates the direction which the pivot chord in question might have taken had it not served as a modulatory agent.

example 328.

Here IV serves as dominant preparation of V. No modulation occurs since V is not preceded by chords which establish it as a quasi-tonic.

Before leaving the subject of the pivot chord an important fact must be noted: The pivot chord is always a dominant preparation, always either II, IV, or VI in relation to the quasi-tonic.

Minimal melodic conditions for modulation are as follows: the modulating melody either must contain a recognizable segment of the scale which belongs to the quasi-tonic or it must contain the leading note in a strategic position. Consider the following example:

example 329.   Chorale: *Das neugeborne Kindelein*

The second phrase indicates a modulation to the minor dominant triad. Two clues are provided by the melody: the progression D E F, which suggests scale degrees 1 2 3 in the key of the minor dominant (D minor) and the chromatic note, C♯, which is the leading note in that key.

With regard to metrical-rhythmic pattern the modulatory progression is the same as any other progression. The quasi-tonic triad falls on a metrically accented beat. The modulating dominant receives a metrical accent, and the pivot chord is almost always given a prominent position in the pattern, either by metrical or by rhythmical accent. Especially crucial is the case of modulation to V. In that case the modulating dominant, not the quasi-tonic, must be accented if V is to be maximally stabilized (section 158).

152. The Logic of Modulation

As we stated before, the logic of modulation is an extension of the logic of tonality. Many books on harmony give the impression that all modulations are equally feasible. This is erroneous. The selection of a particular diatonic triad as a goal of modulatory progression is made in accord with the norms of diatonic progression (Examples 100 and 101). Thus, V is the most frequent goal of modulation. In minor, III also is a common goal. And in a series of modulations from one secondary triad to another, the order and direction of the goal harmonies also is that given in the schematic norms. A modulation to IV is followed by a modulation to II, a modulation to VI followed by a modulation to II or to IV, and so on. In short, progression in the larger dimension is still controlled by the main harmonic axis despite the local control exerted by the quasi-tonics.

In accord with the logic of tonality certain diatonic modulations appear to be more "natural" than others. Natural modulations are those for which all or some of the minimal harmonic elements are available without chromatic alteration. A prime example is the modulation from I to III in minor, in which the modulating dominant and the three dominant preparations (VI, IV, and II) are available without alteration. This is the only completely natural modulation.

example 330.

$I/_{VI}$ $VI/_{IV}$ $IV/_{II}$

153. The Returning Progression

Thus far modulation has been discussed in terms of progression away from I toward another triad. Once this triad has been established as a quasi-tonic it may be extended for some time. Ultimately, however, the harmonic focus returns to the main harmonic axis. The passage that effects the return will be referred to here as the *returning progression.* Invariably the returning progression is directed toward V of the main tonality, or toward a dominant preparation, but not toward I. Once V is reached I follows naturally.

154. Limitations upon Diatonic Modulation

The main limitation placed upon diatonic modulation is imposed by the very foundation of the tonal system: the harmonic axis. Modulatory progression must be carried out in such a way that the harmonic axis remains intact, for if its identity is destroyed or weakened the entire tonal structure becomes incoherent in terms of the system's premises. Specifically, this means that in instances where either the pivot chord or the modulating dominant are altered versions of either I or V, the particular modulation is less advantageous structurally, less accessible. And one case in which the primal function of the tonic itself is threatened—the modulation from I to IV in major—must be regarded as highly problematic.

An additional limitation is placed upon certain modulations if the essential pivot chord is not a diatonic triad in the main tonality. This means that the pivot chord, itself a dominant preparation, must be prepared in some way. Further difficulties arise when chromatic conflicts occur at the point of transition or when parallelisms are impending. The operation of these limiting factors is clearly evident in highly developed tonal music, and accordingly a number of examples will be cited as we survey modulation from I to each of the other diatonic triads. Since the structural differences between major and minor are especially pronounced with respect to modulation the modes will be examined separately, beginning with the major.

MODULATIONS IN MAJOR

155. Modulation from I to II in Major

The harmonies involved in the modulation from I to II and in the return are represented in Example 331.

example 331.

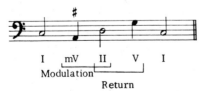

This modulation occurs rarely, probably because it is very difficult to stabilize II. It will be recalled that this chord relates by 5th to the V and therefore tends strongly to return to the harmonic axis rather than to pursue an independent career. In addition, none of the three possible pivotal chords is diatonic. These are summarized in the next example.

example 332.

An instance of modulation from I to II in major is quoted below.

example 333.   SCHUBERT: *Das Wirtshaus* (Voice and accompaniment condensed)

Although the modulatory progression is complete, the II is not confirmed by the subsequent phrase. Instead, there is an immediate return to I. Example 334 is a synopsis of the passage, showing the main harmonic changes.

example 334.

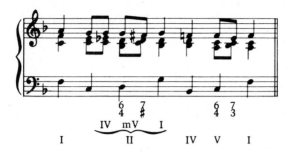

Schubert uses the altered V (C minor triad) in place of a diatonic pivot in the modulation to II (see section 264). The return to V is made via IV.

156. Modulation from I to III in Major

With the exception of the pivot chord the minimal chords for this modulation and for the return are shown below.

example 335.

The three pivot chords are shown in the next example.

example 336.

Modulation from I to III in major occurs less frequently in compositions. Although III is accessible by diatonic pivot chord it is remote from V of the harmonic axis and therefore two or more harmonic steps are required for the return. In an instance of this modulation, Brahms circumvents the problem of return by abandoning III and beginning again on I without dominant progression:

example 337. BRAHMS: *Waltz in B major, Op. 39/1*

157. Modulation from I to IV in Major

Of all diatonic modulations the modulation from I to IV in major is the most problematic (cf. section 71).

example 338.

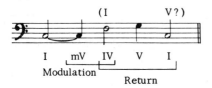

The reason for this is that when the tonic triad itself serves as modulating dominant the IV assumes the primal role and the tonality shifts to a different axis. In no other modulation is the functional identity of the tonic triad threatened in this way. For this reason the IV is rarely stabilized by modulation. True, IV often is used in opposition to I, for example in the trios of many minuets and in rondo forms, where marked harmonic contrast is desired. However, in such cases IV is stated directly; the change of harmonic focus is not prepared by modulatory progression.

Let us consider the pivot chord possibilities.

example 339.

/II   mV   /IV   mV   II/VI   mV

We note here that II is a poor pivot chord since it is an altered form of V in the main tonality.

An instance of modulation from I to IV is quoted below.

example 340.   BEETHOVEN: *Eighth Symphony* (*Minuet and Trio*)

I   mV⁷

IV as quasi-tonic

II   V⁷   I

By no means is this a strong modulation to IV. Indeed, since there is no pivot chord and since the metrical accent is given to the 7th chord the entire passage might well be regarded as an extension of the chord pair [V⁷] IV. Observe that II and V⁷ effect the return to I. A more convincing modulation to IV is contained in the following chorale opening.

example 341. Chorale: *Nun preiset alle.* (Setting after Bach)

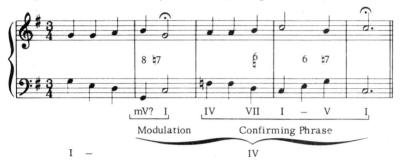

In this instance not the modulation but the confirming phrase establishes the IV as a quasi-tonic. The modulatory progression is too brief and also lacks a pivot chord.

158. Modulation from I to V in Major

Since V is part of the harmonic axis it is only natural for it to be the most frequent goal of modulatory progression. Yet, in the major mode V is not easily stabilized as a quasi-tonic since it retains its tendency to yield to the gravitational pull of the tonic itself. This is evident in the following chorale setting.

example 342. Chorale: *Valet will ich dir geben* (Bach's setting)

In the third phrase there occurs a modulation to V. However, even the subsequent confirming phrase does not erase the persistent tendency of V to sound like the dominant of E♭. It lacks the independence of a quasi-tonic such as III in minor.

The following summary shows that V is very accessible by diatonic pivot chords.

example 343.

159. Modulation from I to VI in Major

Here the modulating dominant does not conflict in any way with the harmonic axis, and the return to V is easily accomplished, often via II in order to avoid impending parallelisms between VI and V in direct succession or to reinforce the returning progression by the 5th relation, II V. The harmonic plan of the modulation and return is shown below.

example 344.

Example 345 summarizes the pivot chords:

example 345.

In this modulation all the pivot chords are diatonic. Since the dissonant triad VII is so restricted, it rarely serves as a pivot chord; consequently only two of these are practicable.

An example of a returning progression from VI to I follows.

example 346. BEETHOVEN: *Rondo for Piano, Op. 51/2*

Here VI progresses directly to the returning dominant, which is represented by its first inversion in order to avoid the parallelisms inherent in the succession.

A more radical and abrupt return from VI is made in the following composition.

example 347. SCHUBERT: *Waltz, Op. 27/12*

This excerpt begins with a cadence on VI which confirms that triad as a quasi-tonic. Still under the control of VI there follows the succession IV V$_3^4$ I^6 V. Then instead of returning to the quasi-tonic VI the next phrase begins on the returning V^7 and closes on I.

MODULATIONS IN MINOR

160. Modulation from I to III in Minor

Since in addition to I there are only four consonant diatonic triads in minor there are only that many diatonic modulations. We begin with the modulation from I to III, which is the only completely natural modulation, since both modulating dominant and all three pivot chords are diatonic. Example 348 summarizes the latter:

example 348.

Here in one instance the tonic chord itself serves as pivot (I/VI). Observe its use in the following modulatory progression.

example 349.   Chorale: *Was sorgst du ängstlich für dein Leben*

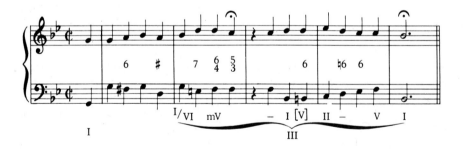

This modulatory progression spans two phrases. The first phrase carries the progression as far as the modulating dominant; the second completes the motion to III.

The following modulation to III uses the pivot IV/II. In this case the IV is replaced by the seventh chord, IV$_5^6$.

example 350. MOZART: *Symphony in G minor, K.550*

Like III in major, III in minor is remote from V of the harmonic axis. It must return to V via one of the dominant preparations. The chorale harmonization below demonstrates one way in which this can be done.

example 351. Chorale: *Herr, ich habe misgehandelt*

Observe that the pivot II/IV is preceded ~~~~~~ ~~ominant. This suggests the possibility that modulations may ~~ ~~~~~~~ ~~ged by embellishing the pivot, which is indeed the case in many extended compositions.

161. Modulation from I to IV in Minor

In the modulation from I to IV in minor no diatonic pivot chords are available. Further, the modulating dominant is an altered version of I. Although the problem of shifting the harmonic axis does not exist here to the same extent as it does in major (see section 157), since the minor I does not contain the leading note, composers intuitively have been cautious about this modulation.

example 352.

Thus, IV is approached often from V or from VI by modulation but it is rarely approached from I directly. Beethoven preferred to avoid the altered tonic triad altogether in a famous passage from the *Eroica Symphony.* There in the modulatory introduction to the fugato, which centers on IV, he approaches IV via three diminished-7th chords, as shown in the following reduction:

example 353.

The dominant equivalents of the °7's are represented below the staff in Example 353. This shows more clearly that the modulating V_5^6 is preceded by its secondary dominant-7th chord, in the first inversion. (The unusual succession of two inverted 7th chords has to do with melodic development of the bass.) The passage is quoted in full below.

example 354. BEETHOVEN: *Eroica Symphony,* Second Movement

162. Modulation from I to V in Minor

In the minor mode the dominant triad as quasi-tonic is almost invariably the minor dominant, not the dominant which contains the leading note. Example 355 summarizes the pivot chords for this modulation.

example 355.

The first pivot is not diatonic (/II). The last, although diatonic, is apt to function like III, the quasi-primary triad which tends to be a goal of modulatory progression itself. Therefore the most effective pivot is I/IV. An example follows.

example 356. CHOPIN: *Mazurka in A minor, Op. 7/2*

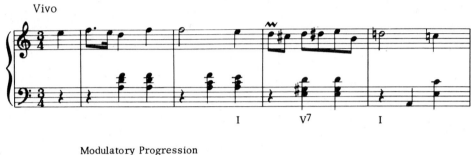

Vivo

I   V7   I

Modulatory Progression

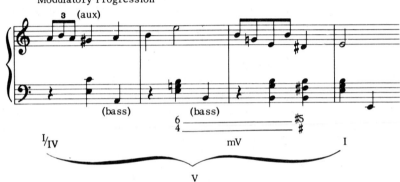

(aux)

(bass)   (bass)

$^I/_{IV}$ mV   I

V

Since the minor dominant does not contain the leading note and therefore does not suggest immediate return to the tonic it is far more stable as a quasi-tonic than is the dominant in major.

The return from the minor dominant requires only the raising of the 3rd of that triad so as to gain the leading note. Often this chromatic change is made simultaneously with arrival at the goal, as in the following excerpt.

example 357. HANDEL: *Courante in E minor*

V♯   —

163. Modulation from I to VI in Minor

VI in minor is difficult to stabilize. There are two reasons for this. First, it has a subdominant relationship to III and therefore tends to be drawn into the domain of that quasi-primary triad. Second, it affords direct access to V by half step and therefore even more strongly tends to fulfill its role as dominant preparation. These relationships are shown in Example 358:

example 358.

Examination of the pivot possibilities reveals further difficulties in the modulation from I to VI in minor.

example 359.

Of the three possible pivot chords, two relate strongly to quasi-tonics other than VI (VII relates to III as dominant; IV relates to V as dominant preparation). For all these reasons modulatory progression to VI occurs infrequently in the minor mode.

   We may find that VI often controls a large section or movement of a work, but like IV in major, it is rarely established as a quasi-tonic by modulation in that role. Example 360 proves the rule by an exception drawn from the works of a composer famous for unorthodox techniques.

example 360. SCHUBERT: *Piano Sonata in A minor, Op. 164,* First Movement

The chromatic harmonies preceding the establishment of VI as a quasi-tonic are not labeled since they represent techniques of harmonic development discussed in a later chapter (Chapter 16). Their general effect here is to completely dissolve the harmonic axis so that by the time VI is reached it assumes a stability which it would not otherwise have in a more normative diatonic context.

We have now examined all the diatonic modulations in both modes, indicating their special problems and advantages in harmonic extension. The following sections are devoted to other aspects of modulation.

164. Modulation by Sequence

The sequence is often used as a modulatory means for achieving a rapid change of tonal focus. The basic elements of the modulation remain—pivot chord and modulating dominant—but they are embedded in the sequential progression. Consider the following.

example 361.

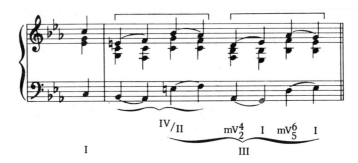

The next example presents the complete passage from which this sequence is drawn.

example 362. BEETHOVEN: *Piano Sonata in C minor, Op. 13*

In the following example, a reduction of a more elaborate passage, the soprano voice clearly belongs to the scale of the goal triad, A minor (V), and thus prepares the change of harmony.

example 363. BACH: *Fugue in D minor* (reduction)

(The symbol ¼ means scale degree 1 becomes scale degree 4.) A sequence is very flexible. It can be bent in several directions. For instance, the sequence in Example 363 could be returned to the tonic if only the soprano of the fifth chord were changed to Bb, as here:

example 364.

A sequence can be used for a returning progression also. In this capacity it often avoids parallelisms or other structural problems. An instance of sequence used for returning progression is quoted below.

example 365. BACH: *Prelude in E minor*

A full four-part version of the foregoing passage is given in Example 366. Sub-metrical embellishments and metrical passing notes have been eliminated in order to show the underlying sequential progression clearly.

example 366.

The harmonies in this modulatory sequence appear to have no functional relation to the harmonic goal. Indeed, they seem to be directed toward a G-major triad (III), which, indeed, the progression would reach if it were continued through one more chord pair. The basis of progression here is imitation. Each chord pair (bracketed) prepares each subsequent chord pair, until the final chord pair is defined as the cadential succession in the main tonality.

Although sequences are very flexible and often useful, particularly when a change must be made quickly—as in fugal expositions—they are at the same time quite weak from the standpoint of clear harmonic direction. A more general discussion of such sequences is given in section 220.

165. Modulatory Series

Modulations often occur in series. In the following example the modulatory series is based upon the chord succession I III IV V⁷ I. Both III and IV are goals of modulatory progressions.

example 367. CHOPIN: *Ballade in F minor, Op. 52* (harmonic structure and basic voice leading only)

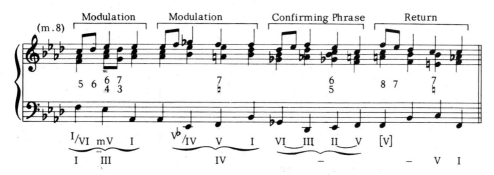

166. Interlocking Modulations

Interlocking occurs when the modulatory phrase ends on the modulating dominant and when the quasi-tonic which follows at the beginning of the next phrase is also a pivot chord in a new modulation.

example 368. Chorale: *Ach, bleib mit deiner Gnade*

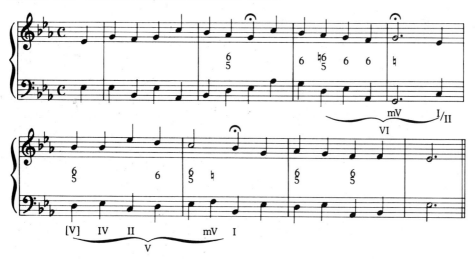

With interlocking modulation the goal harmony is not strongly stated and the effect is one of accelerated progression. Quite a different effect is achieved by the technique of *incomplete* modulation explained below.

167. Incomplete Modulation

Although C. P. E. Bach, Mozart, and Haydn used it, the technique of incomplete, or implied, modulation belongs primarily to nineteenth-century music after Beethoven. Abundant examples are found in the works of Chopin and Brahms, and almost any page of a Wagner score provides at least one illustration. An excerpt from Brahms is quoted here.

example 369. BRAHMS: *Waltz, Op. 39/9*

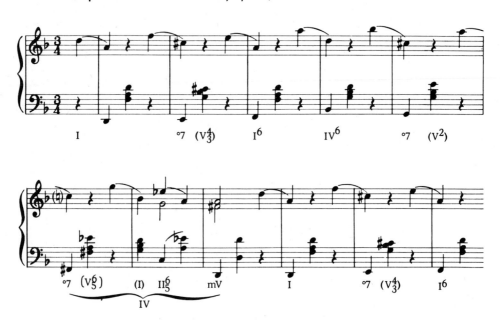

The progression is directed strongly toward IV. The modulating dominant stands at the end of the unit and IV is expected on the downbeat of the next measure. Instead, there is a return to the main tonic and the progression begins anew. The implied harmonic goal, IV, is never reached, despite the convincing preparation.

An instance of incomplete modulation to a more remote triad is the following.

example 370. CHOPIN: *Nocturne in F major, Op. 15/1*

In this case III is prepared as the goal of a modulatory progression. The modulating dominant stands at the end of the phrase, as in the Brahms example above. However, the goal harmony is never stated. Instead, there is a return to I via V^7. Observe that the modulatory progression does not contain a pivot chord, although the VI in the fourth measure suggests that at that point the harmony is moving in the direction of III.

168. Harmonic Extension without Modulation

Before closing this chapter on modulation it is essential to point out again that harmony often is extended compositionally without modulation. Many works, particularly shorter and more stylized forms (waltzes, minuets, scherzi, . . .) contain sections controlled by secondary triads which are not stabilized by modulation. An example follows.

example 371. BEETHOVEN: *Piano Sonata, Op. 10/3,* Menuetto (reduction)

Example 371 summarizes the harmonic structure of this movement which comprises eighty-one measures. The Minuet consists of three harmonic units. The first of these is controlled by I. The second contains a modulatory sequence directed toward V. The third restates I. The Trio is approached directly, without modulation. Its controlling harmony is IV. Near the end of the Trio there occurs a progression that returns to V⁷. This in turn leads back to I and the repetition of the Minuet. The important thing to observe here is that the subdominant harmony of the Trio was not defined as a quasi-tonic by modulation. In this case and in a great many others we witness harmonic extension away from the harmonic axis, but extension that does not involve the process of modulation. These harmonies, which control long sections of compositions but are not stabilized by modulation, are often the very harmonies that are problematic with respect to the harmonic axis, as in the case of IV above, or which for other reasons are difficult to stabilize. Another instance is VI in minor (section 163). It is featured in the Mozart work represented below, a work which is remarkable for harmonic development, both in large dimension and in detail.

example 372. MOZART: *Rondo in A minor for Piano, K.511* (reduction)

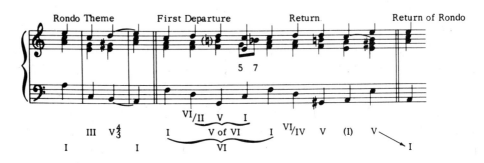

As indicated, Example 372 is a reduction. Certain important features have been omitted altogether, such as the elaborate chromatic section following the modulation to V of VI in the First Departure. However, the outline does have the advantage of showing the large-scale harmonic organization of the piece and the function of VI. This harmony is approached directly, without modulation. It then stabilizes its own dominant by modulation before returning to the main dominant.

Still another means of extension is illustrated in the next example, a harmonic sketch of the complete piece.

example 373. HANDEL: *Courante from Suite in F minor*

The statement of I is followed by a modulatory progression which prepares the natural V as harmonic goal. Simultaneously with arrival at V the 3rd of the triad is raised, enabling V to return immediately to I. However, V does not resolve; the next harmonic unit begins directly with III. After III has been stated and confirmed by its dominant the progression is directed back to V once more. This chord arrives at the end of the unit, after the progression has bypassed I (in parentheses). The completion of the connection V I occurs at the beginning of the third unit, a repetition of the first unit. Harmonic excursions of this kind are not unusual. They constitute important means of compositional extension along with modulation.

EXERCISES

A. List of Some Important Terms to Define and Memorize

Modulation

Quasi-tonic

Modulating dominant

Pivot chord

Natural modulation

Returning progression

Modulating sequence

Modulatory series

Interlocking modulations

Incomplete modulation

B. Analysis

INSTRUCTIONS

Label all modulations, using the proper symbols.

exercise 173. BUXTEHUDE: *Gott fähret auf mit Jauchzen*

C. Basic Keyboard and Aural Exercises

INSTRUCTIONS
Play and sing the following modulations in the usual way. Transpose each one to a different key, following the order of the circle of 5ths. In each case the best initial soprano position is indicated in parentheses.

Major mode (after Mattei):

exercise 174. **From I to II in major**

exercise 175. **From I to III in major**

exercise 176. **From I to IV in major**

exercise 177. **From I to V in major**

exercise 178. From I to VI in major

Minor mode (after Albrechtsberger):

exercise 179. From I to III in minor

exercise 180. From I to IV in minor

exercise 181. From I to V in minor

exercise 182. From I to VI in minor

D. Unfigured Outer Voices

INSTRUCTIONS
Realize in four parts at the keyboard and on paper. Identify all chords by Roman numeral. Label all modulations, using the symbols introduced in this chapter.

exercise 183. **Chorale**

exercise 184. **LULLY:** *Alceste*

exercise 185. Chorale

E. Soprano Voices to Harmonize

The soprano usually contains clues to the goal of modulation. It may unfold the scale or a portion of the scale that belongs to the quasi-tonic, for example the descending 5th from scale degree 5 to scale degree 1, or the ascending 4th from scale degree 5 to scale degree 8—both strong indicators of the new quasi-tonic note. In the ascending motion just mentioned the soprano incorporates the new leading note. Consider the following chorale melody.

Here shortly after the beginning of the second phrase the F♯ provides a strong clue to the modulatory progression toward V. If the subsequent notes are read as scale degrees in the G major scale, the scale of V, we find that they form a pattern which closes on scale degree 1. Observe particularly the pivotal melodic note 3/6. This corresponds to the pivot chord in the harmonic progression. A minimal harmonization for this chorale melody is sketched out below.

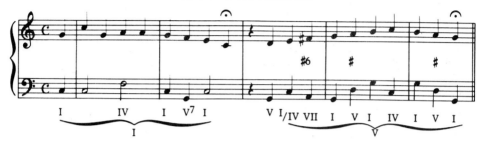

Once the pivotal harmonic and melodic points have been identified the remainder of the progression can be harmonized with the aid of the standard harmonization patterns, bearing in mind that these are now applied to the scale of the quasi-tonic. For example, A in the fourth measure is not scale degree 6 in relation to the C major triad (I), but scale degree 2 in relation to the G major triad (V). The minimal harmonization's faults are corrected in the next version:

*Corrections.

The soprano voice sometimes does not carry obvious clues to the direction of the modulation. In this case the entire melody must be analyzed carefully to determine the over-all progression and the function of each individual phrase. In this way the harmonic implications of the melody will reveal themselves. The natural modulation from I to III in minor often has this noncommittal characteristic. An example follows.

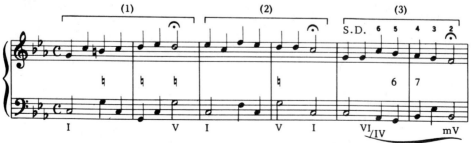

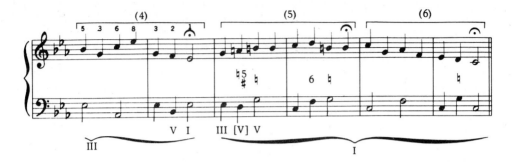

Phrase 3 is somewhat ambiguous if considered alone. But when grouped with Phrase 4 it is seen to be the first phrase of a modulatory period whose goal is III. The chorale as a whole thus has the following harmonic design:

I	III	I
2 phrases	2 phrases	2 phrases

When ascertaining the goal of a modulatory progression one must follow the same principle as when selecting an individual chord: context determines appropriateness. The harmonization exercises follow.

exercise 186. *Franklin is fled away.* **Modulation from I to II in major**

Moderato

exercise 187. **Chorale. Modulation from I to III in major. For keyboard**

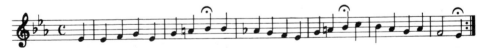

exercise 188. **Chorale. Modulation from I to IV in major. For keyboard**

exercise 189. **Chorale. Modulation from I to V in major. For SATB**

exercise 190. *The Baffled Knight.* **Modulation from I to VI in major. For solo voice with keyboard accompaniment**

exercise 191. *John Anderson, my Jo.* **Modulation from I to III in minor. For solo voice with keyboard accompaniment**

(mV)

exercise 192. Chorale. Modulation from I to IV and from I to VI in minor.
For SATB

exercise 193. Chorale. Modulation from I to V in minor. For keyboard

F. Unfigured Basses, Soprano Given

INSTRUCTIONS
In all cases the soprano is to be regarded as a solo voice and the bass is to be set out as a four-part accompaniment.
The soprano line of the accompaniment should follow the simplest and most direct succession as determined by the voice leading, yet in accord with good melodic structure. It may often double the solo line, although this is not essential. Doubling of this kind is actually reinforcement, not doubling of the voice leading; therefore it does not constitute parallel unisons or 8ves. Once completed the realizations should be analyzed for modulations and for specific modulatory techniques.

exercise 194. HANDEL: *Flute Sonata in E minor*

exercise 195. RAMEAU: *Diane et Acteon*

G. Unfigured Basses, Soprano to Be Composed

INSTRUCTIONS
Realize the bass in four parts, paying special attention to the progression of the soprano voice. Supply figures where none are given and in all cases indicate modulatory progressions, using the symbols presented in this chapter.

exercise 196. BONONCINI: *Sonata for Two Violoncelli*
Some figures are given at problematic points.

exercise 197. CORELLI: *Corrente* from *Trio Sonata in G minor*

exercise 198. CORELLI: *Trio Sonata in B♭ major*

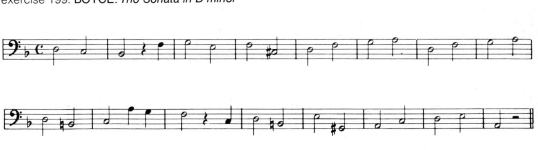

exercise 199. BOYCE: *Trio Sonata in D minor*

10

The Rhythmic Process of Chord Generation: Suspension Chords

Thus far the development of the harmonic vocabulary has been examined in terms of two fundamental processes: the harmonic (inversion), which yields inverted triads, and the melodic, which produces 7th chords. The latter are also invertible.

The resources of harmony are further extended by still a third process, one that is essentially rhythmic. When applied to triads, 7th chords, and their inversions, this process creates a large and important class of dissonant harmonies. We can see the process at work even within a single composition. Consider the following excerpt.

example 374. GLUCK: *Orfeo*

The bracket in Example 374 indicates a note that is repeated over the bar line. The note marked by an asterisk is a dissonance which momentarily displaces the chord note from its normal metrical position above the bass. This submetrical embellishment does not affect the structure of the chord, however. The chord remains a passing $\frac{4}{3}$ as figured. In a subsequent repetition of this passage we find that the submetrical embellishment has been greatly expanded in duration:

example 375.

Now that the note repeated over the bar line has the value of the metrical unit it is more than a momentary displacement of the expected chord note and therefore must be regarded as a chordal element. Accordingly its interval relation to the bass is figured as shown. The figures reveal the structure of this new chord: it is a second inversion of a 7th chord, except for the 7 which displaces the 6. A note held over in this way from a previous harmony so that it displaces a note of the prevailing harmony is called a *suspension.** And the transient chord which is formed by this rhythmic process is called a *suspension chord.*

---

*The suspended note may or may not be tied over from the previous chord. With or without tie the suspension is the same rhythmic and harmonic event.

Another example of the suspension process at work within a single composition is provided in Example 376.

example 376.   BEETHOVEN: *Piano Sonata in C♯ minor, Op. 27/2*

Here the second eight-measure group repeats the first eight-measure group. The second group differs from the first only in that it has a suspension chord on the downbeat of each measure. Otherwise the progression remains the same. These and all other suspension chords are totally dependent for their existence upon the chords which they temporarily displace.

Thus, although suspension chords constitute a resource of great beauty they do not affect harmonic direction, order, function, or any other aspect of progression. Their purpose is to develop and intensify the rhythmic texture. Therefore they should be examined together with the more fundamental chords they displace, the triads, 6th chords, 7th chords and their inversions—the chords which were presented in Chapters 3, 5, and 6. We shall make a systematic survey of suspension chords in that way after having considered the basic conditions under which they occur.

169. The Three Chords of the Suspension Formation

The suspension process always involves three chords: (1) the *chord of preparation,* a chord which contains the note or notes about to be suspended, (2) the suspension chord itself, which falls on a metrical accent, and (3) the *chord of resolution,* on an unaccented beat.

example 377. GLUCK: *Orfeo*

Three important rules regarding the suspension formation are outlined below. All are illustrated in Example 377.

1 The suspended note must resolve stepwise to the note it has displaced.
2 The note of resolution should not be present in the suspension chord, otherwise the purpose of the suspension is negated.
3 Since the suspended note is always a dissonance, the general rule that dissonance cannot be doubled without causing parallel octaves must be observed.

DISPLACEMENT OF THE TRIAD

170. Single Suspension Chords That Displace Notes of the $\frac{5}{3}$

All the notes that can be suspended to displace notes of the triad are shown as quarter notes in Example 378.

example 378.

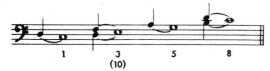

The bass can be displaced by the note above it, the 2nd. The 3rd can be displaced by the 4th. When the 3rd is expressed in its compound form, as a 10th, it can also be displaced from below by the 9th. The 5th may be displaced by the 6th. Finally, the 8ve can be displaced both by the 7th and by the 9th. We shall now examine these suspensions individually.

171.   Displacement of the 3rd of the Triad (4 3)

A typical suspension of this type, called a "four to three" suspension is shown in Example 379.

example 379.

The figure 5 is sometimes placed above 4 in order to prevent one from assuming the double suspension $\frac{6}{4}$ (see Example 379). This precaution applies particularly to a figured bass alone. Another important detail: the dash above 3 means that the preceding 5th is still present. This saves writing out the 5 again and is standard practice in figured basses. An illustration follows.

example 380.   MOZART: *Don Giovanni*

Both in Example 377 and in Example 380 the chord of preparation is a dissonant chord. We find that the chord of preparation can be either a consonant chord or a dissonant chord of any type except a suspension chord.

172.   Displacement of the 5th of the Triad (6 5)

Although normally a consonant interval, in this situation the 6th resolves to the 5th which it displaces and thus functions like a dissonant interval.

example 381.

This transformation of interval values is characteristic of suspension chords. Often such chords create illusory effects, as explained in the next section.

173.   Illusory Effects of Suspension Chords

It is extremely important to recognize that the structural meaning of the 6th chord by suspension differs altogether from that of the 6th chord by inversion. If the 6th chord in the previous example is incorrectly regarded as a first inversion which represents a parent triad (VI in that case) the harmonic direction of the passage make little sense. Here the supposed VI^6 would have no harmonic function either as a tonic substitute or as a dominant preparation. Correctly regarded, the progression consists of the chord pair IV I; the suspension merely delays the appearance of the full tonic harmony.

Suspension chords often simulate triads or 7th chords with independent harmonic functions, misleading the untrained ear. We shall call such illusory harmonies false triads, or false 6th chords, false 7th chords, and so on.

Harmonic progression depends primarily upon consonant triads and their inversions, and secondarily upon the 7th chords that derive from triads. If the illusory harmonies sometimes created by the suspension process are taken to be those fundamental chords, the logical system of harmonic values and functions characteristic of tonal music is distorted beyond recognition.

We continue now with the suspensions that displace the triad.

174.   Displacement of the 8ve by the 7th (7 8)

This suspension chord simulates the major-7th chord presented earlier (section 93). However, the two chords differ basically. The 7th of the true major-7th chord resolves downward over a change of bass. The major-7th chord by displacement of the 8ve, a false 7th chord, resolves upward over the same bass. The first has some degree of independence; the second is entirely dependent upon the chord of resolution. Example 382 shows the major-7th chord by suspension in a typical context. In order to make clear the harmonic structure of the passage we present first its chordal succession without displacement by suspension (a), then with displacement (b), and finally the complete passage with all its rhythmic activity and melodic embellishment (c).

example 382.   CHOPIN: *Prelude in F♯ major*

175.   Displacement of the 8ve by the 9th (9 8)

A typical context for the suspension chord of the 9th is shown in Example 383.

example 383.

The bass note of the suspension chord is C, the note to which the suspended 9th subsequently resolves. This appears to contradict the rule given in section 169 which says that the note of resolution should not be present in the suspension chord. The bass, however, is always a special voice. And in this instance it carries the fundamental note of the triad, which cannot be omitted without changing the harmony altogether.

176. Ascending Resolution of the 9th (9 10)

The 9th also serves to displace the 10th. It should be borne in mind that the 10th is a compound interval which represents the 3rd of the triad.

example 384.

The suspended 9th chords are completely dependent upon the chord of resolution. They differ fundamentally from the quasi-independent 9th chord explained in section 199.

177. Double Suspension Chords

Thus far we have dealt only with the suspension of the single note. When more than one chord note is displaced by suspension we speak of double, triple, and quadruple suspension chords, depending upon the number of suspended notes.

Each note of the multiple suspension chord resolves exactly as it would if it were a single suspension.

The notes of a multiple suspension may resolve one at a time, providing an additional means of rhythmic elaboration. For the sake of uniformity only simultaneous resolutions will be shown here.

A familiar chord, the $\frac{6}{4}$, often occurs as a double suspension chord:

example 385.

Here both 5th and 3rd of the cadential dominant are displaced. Compare this with the single suspension $\frac{5}{4}$ shown in Example 379.

Another typical double suspension is shown in Example 386 below.

example 386.

In this cadential succession the notes that form the tritone of the V^7 are suspended over the bar line to displace the 8ve and the 3rd of I.

The double suspension that follows consists of the 9th and 4th. These notes resolve to the 8ve and 3rd of a triad, forming a succession of parallel 6ths marked by brackets.

example 387.

In the case of suspended 9ths, as here, the figure 2 is never used in place of 9 since the complete figuring would then read $\frac{4}{2}$ and the suspension chord might be mistaken for the third inversion of a 7th chord.

178. Triple and Quadruple Suspension Chords

A representative triple suspension chord is the $\frac{9}{7}$, which combines the suspensions illustrated in the two preceding examples.

example 388.

Since each suspended note resolves to the triadic note which it displaces, both 7 and 9 resolve to the 8ve, leaving the final tonic triad without a 5th.

The quadruple suspension chord shown below is a five-note chord which combines all the intervals that displace notes of the triad: 9, 7, 6, and 4. Figures for triple and quadruple suspensions are always one digit higher than those of the chord they replace, unless the note must ascend in accord with the law of the half step, as 7 in Example 389.

example 389.

In Example 389 only the bass of the triad is not displaced. The reverse situation often occurs: the bass is suspended while all the other voices progress as expected.

179. Displacement of the Bass

When the bass of the triad is displaced by suspension a chord is formed which contains the intervals of a 7th, 4th, and 2nd.

example 390.

Bass suspension figures are easily remembered since they are always one digit lower than those of the chord they displace.

DISPLACEMENT OF THE SIXTH CHORD

180. The Available Suspensions

The available displacements of the notes of the consonant-6th chord are summarized in Example 391.

example 391.

Observe that only the 6th can be displaced both from above and from below. Each of the other notes can be displaced only by the note that lies directly above it.

181. Displacement of the 6th by the 5th (5 6)

This suspension formation is of particular interest since here the suspended 5th, normally a consonant interval, behaves like a dissonance. The suspension chord in this case is a false triad. Compare the false 6th chord in Example 381.

example 392.

182. Displacement of the 6th by the 7th (7 6)

A series of 7 6 suspensions is shown in Example 393 at (*a*).

example 393.

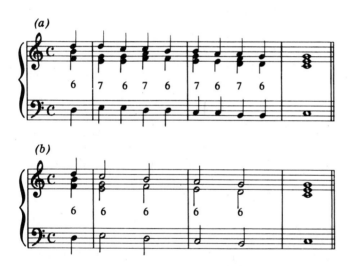

Example 393(*b*) shows the series of descending 6th chords that are displaced by the suspension chords.

The suspended 7th chords shown above in Example 393 are entirely dependent upon the 6th chords to which they resolve over a stationary bass. They are false 7th chords. In contrast, the authentic 7th chords shown in Example 394 are far more independent since they are derived from a succession of $\frac{5}{3}$'s at (*b*) by the enlargement and assimilation of descending passing notes.

example 394.

183. Triple Suspension Displacing the 6th Chord

Every note of the triple suspension chord shown in Example 395 is dissonant against the bass.

example 395.

184. Displacement of the Bass of the 6th Chord ($\frac{5}{2}$)

When the bass itself is suspended while every note above it moves to a note of the 6th chord we have an instance of the $\frac{5}{2}$ chord. Albrechtsberger has supplied the following illustration.

example 396. ALBRECHTSBERGER

C. P. E. Bach explains the $\frac{5}{2}$ chord in this way: "This chord consists of the 2nd and the 5th. One of these two notes is doubled to become the fourth voice [in four-part harmony]. The $\frac{5}{2}$ chord always sounds empty, whether it be in four parts or in three. The resolution makes it full." To this we may add the reminder that the bass is never doubled, since it is dissonant. The figures for this suspension chord are easily remembered if we observe that like all bass suspension figures they are one digit lower than those of the chord of resolution: $\frac{5}{2}$ $\frac{6}{3}$.

DISPLACEMENT OF THE 7th CHORDS AND THEIR INVERSIONS

185. An Important Limitation

Suspension chords displace not only consonant chords but also the first class of dissonant chords, 7th chords. However, an important limitation is placed upon such suspension chords: neither the 7th of the parent chord nor the note which represents the 7th in the inversion can be displaced by a suspended note. A moment's reflection will indicate why this is so. Displacement of the dissonant note reverses the dissonance-consonance succession which characterizes the suspension formation. The effect of this is illustrated in Example 397.

example 397.

Here the 7th is displaced by the 6th. As shown, this has the harmonic meaning I III^6 I, not I V^7 I, and the effect is ambiguous. The 7th appears to be only a dissonant upper-auxiliary note to the 6th of the consonant-6th chord, III^6, as shown. From this demonstration we can understand the following general rule for suspension chords which displace 7th chords: only the consonant notes of the 7th chord or its inversions can be displaced by suspension.

Nor can the bass note of the parent 7th chord be suspended. This is because displacement by the second above creates a $\frac{4}{2}$, which has a different progressional tendency. Displacement by the second below doubles and thus conflicts with the 7th of the chord.

186. Displacement of the 5th of the 7th Chord

In the passage quoted below, the suspension is prepared by a dissonance, by the 7th of a major-7th chord.

example 398. CHOPIN: *Scherzo in D♭ major (B♭ minor), Op. 31*

This suspension formation is entirely dependent upon the chord of resolution, the V^7, for its structural meaning. It is not the fictitious "13th chord" which stems from the erroneous theory of chord generation by successive superposition of 3rds (see Example 417).

187. Displacement of the 3rd of the 7th Chord

Here the suspended 4th resolves exactly as it would within a triad. The following passage permits us to compare the two.

example 399. BRAHMS: *Sonata for Violin and Piano in G major, Op. 78*

188. Displacement of the 6th of the $\frac{6}{5}$

An example of the suspended 7th displacing the 6th of the $\frac{6}{5}$ is provided below in a reduction that shows succinctly the context in which the suspension arises.

example 400. SCHUMANN: *Schöne Fremde* (reduction)

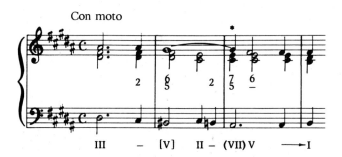

Two aspects of this passage should be remarked. First, the progression from III to I by modified sequence is unusual, especially here at the beginning of the composition (see section 262). Second, we have here an instance of the half-diminished-7th chord, VII[7], as a 7th chord by suspension, a false 7th chord.

Sometimes the true 7th chord is incorrectly regarded as a suspension chord. This is apt to occur if the 7th is prepared as a suspension, for example in the sequence $\frac{4}{2}$ 6 $\frac{4}{2}$ 6, . . . Consider the following situation, in which the 7th of the II[7] is prepared in the preceding chord.

example 401.   PERGOLESI: *Trio Sonata in E minor* (continuo part only)

Here and elsewhere one can easily test the authenticity of the 7th chord by determining whether or not it can be omitted without affecting the progression in some marked way. If it cannot be omitted, as is the case here, it is authentic. If it can be omitted it is a transient suspension chord, a false 7th chord. As explained above, the distinction between the two kinds of chord is crucial since it reflects the difference between fundamental harmony, as derived from the triad, and various degrees of orderly harmonic development by melodic and rhythmic means.

189.   Displacement of the 6th of the $\frac{4}{3}$

The 3rd is always the dissonant note in the second inversion of the 7th chord since it represents the 7th of the parent chord. Therefore, this note cannot be displaced by suspension. Example 402 presents one of the possible suspensions that displace the $\frac{4}{3}$.

example 402.   WOLF: *Schlafendes Jesuskind*

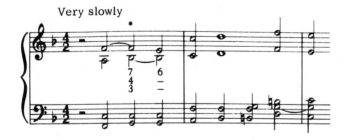

The parallel 8ves in the upper part of the second measure are not voice-leading 8ves. They come about with a shift to three voices, one of which is doubled at the 8ve for reinforcement.

190. Triple Suspension Chord Which Displaces the $\frac{4}{2}$

When the bass of the $\frac{4}{2}$ progresses in accord with the strict metrical pattern while the other notes of the chord are suspended the following formation results.

example 403.

The false major-7th chord here is easily recognized.

191. Displacement of the Bass Note of the Inversions

It has been seen that neither the bass note of the parent 7th chord nor the bass note of the third inversion can be displaced by suspension. This leaves two forms of the 7th chord, the first and second inversions, whose bass notes can be displaced. They are both illustrated in the next example.

example 404.

Of the two, the displacement of the bass of the first inversion occurs more frequently. As in the case of the $\frac{5}{2}$, above, the seemingly complicated figuring is easily memorized if one observes that each numeral of the suspension chord is one less than the subsequent numeral in the chord of resolution.

192. Change of Harmony at the Point of Resolution

Sometimes a suspension is formed, but because of the requirements of the metric-rhythmic pattern or the harmonic progression the harmony changes at the point of resolution. This does not affect the actual suspension. It resolves as usual. However, the chord of resolution is not the expected one.

example 405. PERGOLESI: *Trio Sonata in G major* (continuo part only)

In the third measure the suspended 7th itself resolves as usual. However, the expected chord, 6, is not heard. Instead, the harmony changes to a $\frac{6}{4}$. (Actually this chord is a $\frac{4}{2}$, but the 2nd is omitted from the three-voice realization.) A similar occurrence is the change of bass at the point of resolution, explained in the next section.

193. Change of Bass and Harmony at the Point of Resolution

Occasionally the bass as well as the harmony may change just as the suspension chord resolves. Two examples of this follow.

example 406. MOZART: *Quintet for Clarinet and Strings in A major, K.581*

In this instance the suspension chord is prolonged for an additional beat so that it resolves over the bass of the succeeding chord. The normative resolution is shown at (*b*). A more complicated instance is shown below.

example 407.   BRAHMS: *Sonata for Violin and Piano in A major, Op. 100*

The second measure carries a double suspension. The suspended 4th is more prominent than the 9th, which appears only in the accompaniment. Just as the 4th resolves (arrow) the bass ascends instead of remaining stationary as expected. The 4 3 suspension in the last measure of the excerpt is normal except that the resolution occurs one eighth note sooner.

194. Interrupted (Embellished) Resolution

Direct stepwise connection from suspended note to resolution may be interrupted by submetrical embellishments. In the following case, the direct progression from the suspended 4th to its resolution is interrupted by a submetrical auxiliary note.

example 408. Chorale: *Lobt Gott, ihr Christen allzugleich.* Setting by Bach

A more intricate embellishment is shown below.

example 409. SCHUMANN: *Winterszeit (Jugendalbum)*

This excerpt contains two suspension formations. The first, a 7 6, resolves in the usual way. The second, a triple suspension, is embellished.

195. Abbreviated Resolution

Normally the suspension is resolved by a note at least equivalent to itself in duration. If the note following the suspension is shorter than the suspension it may well be an embellishment of the resolution, not the resolution itself, as illustrated in the foregoing section.

However, it sometimes happens that the resolution takes place on an isolated short note which stands in place of a longer note. In such a case, illustrated below by an excerpt from Schumann, the suspension is effectively resolved.

example 410. SCHUMANN: *Bunte Blätter, Op. 99/2*

The resolution of the suspended 9th (asterisk) is modified in two ways. First, the note of resolution is shorter than the suspension, as explained above. Second, the bass changes at the point of resolution, so that the 9 8 is represented by 9 6.

196. Anticipation Chords

Like the suspension chord, the anticipation chord is purely rhythmic in origin. We have seen that suspension chords arise when the full change of harmony is delayed. Anticipation chords arise in precisely the opposite circumstance, that is, when a partial change of harmony occurs before it is expected. Such chords occur very rarely in actual composition. Kirnberger's illustration is quoted below.

example 411. KIRNBERGER

EXERCISES

A. List of Some Important Terms to Define and Memorize

Suspension chord   Triple suspension chord
Chord of preparation   Interrupted resolution
Chord of resolution   Abbreviated resolution
Bass suspension   Anticipation chord
False 6th chord

B. Analysis

INSTRUCTIONS
Figure each suspension chord and indicate by Roman numeral the chord which is temporarily displaced.

exercise 200. BUXTEHUDE: *Man fragt nach Gott*

exercise 201. BUXTEHUDE: *Bedenke Mensch das Ende*

exercise 202. **BRAHMS:** *Der Frühling*

C. Basic Keyboard and Aural Exercises

exercise 203. **Basic Chord Pattern 1**

We have expanded and elaborated the basic chord patterns in several ways: by introducing 6th chords, 7th chords, and inverted 7th chords. The basic chord patterns can be elaborated still further by suspension chords, as shown below. Only a few of the many possibilities are included here.

exercise 204. **Basic Chord Pattern 2**

D. Figured Basses, Soprano Given

INSTRUCTIONS
The first and second basses in this group are to be regarded as keyboard pieces. The third bass should be realized as a continuo accompaniment to the solo voice which is given.

exercise 205. **FÖRSTER: Exercise in suspension chords**

exercise 206. **After LOEILLET**

exercise 207. MARCELLO: *Sonata in B minor for Violin and Continuo*

exercise 208. KUFFERATH: Harmonization of *Ach wann doch, Jesu*

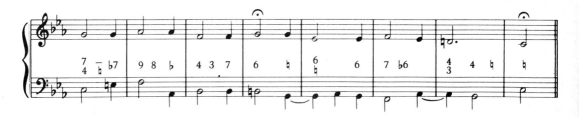

E. Figured Basses

INSTRUCTIONS

Realize in four parts. For maximum effect the suspensions should be placed in the upper voice wherever possible.

The basses by Albrechtsberger are to be supplied with a metric-rhythmic pattern, then transposed to all keys.

exercise 209. **ALBRECHTSBERGER: Diatonic Progressions in the Major Mode**

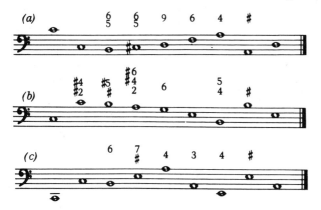

exercise 210. **ALBRECHTSBERGER: Diatonic Progressions in the Minor Mode**

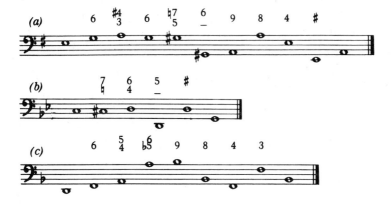

exercise 211. HANDEL: *Sonata for Violin and Continuo in G minor*

exercise 212. GLUCK: *Que d'attraits*

F. Unfigured Basses

INSTRUCTIONS
Realize in four parts as continuo accompaniments. Plan out main harmonic progressions first, then elaborate wherever possible by introducing suspensions, either in the soprano, in the inner voices, or in the bass itself.

exercise 213. **BACH:** *Trio Sonata in E♭ major*

Largo

exercise 214. **LULLY:** "Le héros que j'attends" (*Alceste*)

Andantino

exercise 215. **CORELLI:** *Trio Sonata in G minor*

Adagio

exercise 216. **TARTINI.**

Presto

G. Soprano Voices to Harmonize

INSTRUCTIONS

Three folk songs are given below to provide practice in identifying suspension con-texts from the soprano alone. The suspension is always either a prolonged auxiliary note or a prolonged passing note, generally the latter. It is prepared on a weak beat, dissonates on the following strong beat, and resolves on the next weak beat. Thus, the clue to suspension in a given melody is the passing or auxiliary note repeated from weak to strong beat. These are bracketed in the first two melodies below.

exercise 217. **Welsh**

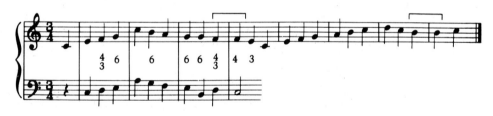

exercise 218. **Czech**

exercise 219. Welsh

Slowly

For the four exercises below only the soprano is given. The harmonizations are to be arranged for mixed voices (SATB). When working out the final harmonization suspensions should be introduced where appropriate. Any note that meets the melodic-rhythmic and harmonic requirements of the suspension formation may be suspended. To review these requirements:

1. The suspended note must be the repetition of a passing or auxiliary note. It must fall on a strong beat.
2. The chord it displaces must have a coherent harmonic function. The suspension must not destroy the identity of the chord of resolution.

exercise 220. Chorale: *Was ist mein Stand, mein Glück*

exercise 221.   Chorale: *Ach Gott, erhör mein Seufzenmund*

exercise 222.   Chorale: *Ach Gott vom Himmel sieh' darein*

exercise 223. German Folk Song: *Wann Morganröth'*

11

Linear
Chords
and
Intervallic
Patterns

*In addition, there are various chords
which are neither dependent upon a
fundamental chord, nor are they suspensions or anticipations. For the most
part they occur in passing, over a
stationary bass. Since these chords owe
their existence only to embellishment of
the melody and since they are not completely authentic chords in the harmonic sense they are called Deceptive
Chords.*

Daniel Gottlob Türk, 1791

197. Linear Chord Defined

We come now to the third and last class of dissonant harmonies. In the first class,
7th chords, the melodic process of chord generation was witnessed. In the second
class, suspension chords, we saw the formation of new harmonies by the displacement of consonant chords and 7th chords, a rhythmic process of chord generation.
The third class contains chords that do not fall into either of the two other categories. We shall call them *linear chords* since they are described most easily in
terms of the linear, or melodic, functions of their notes. To the linear chord,
horizontal context is of first importance. The vertical arrangement of its intervals
has secondary significance.

    Not all linear chords are dissonant from the standpoint of vertical structure
but since all are transient chords whose meanings are derived from more funda-

337

mental harmonies they function like transient dissonances with, for the most part, only local effect upon harmonic direction.

Linear chords are of two main types, diatonic and chromatic. We begin with a survey of representative diatonic linear chords.

DIATONIC LINEAR CHORDS

198. The Diatonic Linear Chord by Unaccented Passing Note

Examples have been seen of dissonant-7th chords and even of consonant chords that arise in the service of passing notes. The linear passing chord differs from both of these in that it is of a more transient nature. For example, it occurs often between two different forms of the same chord, as shown below.

example 412.

At (a) we see a 7th chord followed by its first inversion. At (b) the skips of a 3rd in both soprano and bass are filled by metrical passing notes, creating an additional chord. The vertical structure of this new chord would require a rather complicated figuring. However, we need not concern ourselves with describing the vertical intervals. We need only know that the chord is produced by passing notes.

The transient nature of the linear chord in Example 412 is further indicated by the dash after the 7. The chord does not represent harmonic change, nor does it influence harmonic direction. It serves only to increase the melodic content of the passage, which remains under the harmonic control of the dominant-7th chord.

Linear passing chords perform particularly valuable service in connecting dissonant chords, as in Example 412, where a consonant chord would be ineffective. Often linear chords are associated with dissonances in other ways. Example 413 contains a linear chord that serves to intensify the preparation of a dissonance.

example 413. MOZART: *Piano Sonata in F major, K.280*

Here in the third measure the harmony is seen changing from 8 to ♭7. The linear chord arises on the second beat of the measure as a combination of descending passing note in the soprano and ascending double passing notes in the lower voices. It should be emphasized again that the meaning of this chord resides entirely in its linear function.

The chord in the following example arises when an ascending passing note connects two different soprano positions of the dominant-7th chord. This linear-9th chord is not to be confused with the quasi-independent 9th chord explained in section 199. Here the "9th" chord is entirely dependent upon the two 7th chords that enclose it.

example 414. SCHUBERT: *German Dances, Op. 33/16*

The asterisk in the second measure marks another type of linear chord, an appoggiatura chord. This type is explained in section 201.

199. The Diatonic Linear Chord by Accented Passing Note

Our first example of this type is figured 9. Since the 9th in this instance resolves over a change of bass, it gains a degree of independence not shared by the suspended 9th chord in Example 384, and therefore may be termed a *quasi-independent 9th chord.*

example 415. SCHUBERT: *Waltz, Op. 50/2*

Very often 9th chords, whether suspension chords or linear chords, are created when the 7th is accompanied at the interval of a 3rd above, as here. Melodic parallelism of this kind is characteristic of waltzes and other forms of light music.

The accented passing note in the next example resolves to the 5th of a dominant-7th chord. The linear chord which it creates contains both a 7th and a 6th.

example 416. CHOPIN: *Sonata in B♭ minor, Op. 35*

In some treatises this chord would be regarded as a "chord of the 13th." This designation stems from the viewpoint that the vertical structure of the chord is its most important aspect, and consequently that all chords can be regarded in terms of successive superpositions of thirds. Thus, the 7th chord is regarded as a triad plus a 3rd, the 9th chord is regarded as a 7th chord plus a 3rd, and so on. This thesis is illustrated in the following example.

example 417.

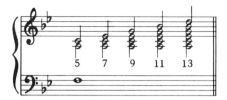

In contrast, we have taken the position that so-called 9th, 11th, and 13th chords are more adequately explained as suspension chords or as linear chords—chords that are always dependent upon triads or authentic 7th chords. Thus, with the exception of the quasi-independent 9th chord we do not recognize independent dissonant chords larger than the 7th. The so-called 11th is actually a 4th; the so-called 13th is actually a 6th. The use of compound intervals here is an unnecessary encumbrance.

Accented passing notes in the bass frequently create linear chords. Two types are illustrated in Example 418.

example 418.

In both instances the unaccented passing eighth note is enlarged in value to a quarter note, displacing the actual bass note from its metrical position. The figures for the linear chords thus produced are identical with certain bass suspension chords explained above. However, the context is quite different, as here. In the case of suspension chords the dissonant bass note is prepared. Here it occurs without preparation.

200. The Diatonic Linear Chord by Auxiliary Note

In addition to their harmonic functions triads, 6th chords, 7ths and inverted 7ths often serve auxiliary notes. Linear-auxiliary chords, to borrow Türk's words, "owe their existence only to embellishment of the melody." Two examples follow. First is a sequence of linear-9th chords created by accented upper auxiliary notes which embellish secondary dominant triads.

example 419. BRAHMS: *First Symphony*

Next, Example 420 shows an auxiliary note chord arising by parallel motion in the outer voices of a V_5^6.

example 420.

201. The Appoggiatura Chord

When an auxiliary note is not preceded by the note it embellishes it is called an incomplete auxiliary note. By tradition an incomplete auxiliary note that receives metrical or rhythmic accent is called an appoggiatura. Consequently a linear chord that features an appoggiatura is called an *appoggiatura chord.* Such chords always stand out in the musical texture, as in the following excerpt.

example 421. CHOPIN: *Mazurka in A♭ major, Op. 24/3*

Here the auxiliary note, F, is introduced in the melody without stepwise preparation. Since it receives the rhythmic accent characteristic of the mazurka we call both it and the entire chord an appoggiatura chord.

The following passage contains an instance of an appoggiatura chord brought about by the bass.

example 422. SCHUBERT: *Piano Sonata in B♭ major*

202. Diatonic Linear Chord by Combined Auxiliary and Passing Notes

Particularly in nineteenth-century music we find many unusual linear chords created by a combination of auxiliary and passing notes. A remarkable example from the works of Schubert is given below.

example 423. SCHUBERT: *Waltz, Op. 77/8*

203. The $\frac{6}{4}$ as a Linear Chord

From the preceding discussion of linear chords it is evident that many can be described most effectively in terms of their linear contexts. Certainly this is the case with the $\frac{6}{4}$. This chord is sometimes described as the second inversion of a triad. However, since the $\frac{6}{4}$ contains a dissonant interval, the 4th, it cannot represent the parent triad, which is a consonant chord. There is one apparent exception to this rule which will be explained now.

204. The Consonant $\frac{6}{4}$

The $\frac{6}{4}$ extends the parent chord and therefore is consonant whenever it is immediately preceded by the parent chord, as in the following example.

example 424. C. P. E. BACH: *Minuetto* from *Kurze* und *Leichte Klavierstücke*

Directly below the excerpt is the succession of basic harmonies that it represents. By comparing the two we realize that the bass of the $\frac{6}{4}$ is a result of arpeggiation. It does not represent an actual change of harmony but merely an extension of the parent harmony. Thus, it is not a dissonant $\frac{6}{4}$ since the 4th does not require resolution to the 3rd as in the other $\frac{6}{4}$ chords. This type of $\frac{6}{4}$ is called the consonant $\frac{6}{4}$ to distinguish it from the other types of $\frac{6}{4}$ described below, all of which are dissonant chords.

Another example of the consonant $\frac{6}{4}$ is quoted below.

example 425. WAGNER: *Die Meistersinger*

The $IV\frac{6}{4}$ here obviously represents the parent triad, with the bass skip to C providing melodic emphasis. Compare the $IV\frac{6}{4}$ in Example 429.

205. The Cadential $\begin{smallmatrix}8\\6\\4\end{smallmatrix}$

The cadential $\frac{6}{4}\ \frac{5}{3}$ progression is very familiar. However, we have not yet considered an important form of the cadential $\frac{6}{4}$, the $\begin{smallmatrix}8\\6\\4\end{smallmatrix}$. This figuring indicates that the octave is in the soprano.

example 426.

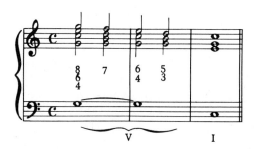

As is seen in Example 426, the octave position of the soprano serves to extend the cadential progression melodically. The $\begin{smallmatrix}8\\6\\4\end{smallmatrix}$ does not progress to the $V\frac{5}{3}$ as does the $\frac{6}{4}$ but moves through a dominant-7th passing chord to the actual cadential $\frac{6}{4}$.

206. The Passing $^6_4$

This chord often connects a sixth chord with its parent chord.

example 427. BEETHOVEN: *Piano Concerto in C major, Op. 15*

Compare this passing $^6_4$ chord (a "V^6_4") with the passing V^4_3 and the VII^6. To a certain extent these three chords are interchangeable. The choice of one or the other depends upon the harmonic direction of the particular chord succession.

The next example shows a passing $^6_4$ between two dissonant chords.

example 428.

207. The Auxiliary $^6_4$

This chord often occurs as a IV$^6_4$. We can accept the convention of inversion theory here as a convenience in labeling the chord, but we must bear in mind that the chord is actually a linear chord created by upper auxiliary notes moving in parallel motion. Its relation to the parent triad is tenuous.

example 429. MOZART: *Don Giovanni*

"IV"

In this instance submetrical auxiliary notes (asterisk) embellish the resolution of the $\frac{6}{4}$. As in the cadential $\frac{6}{4}$ the bass is doubled at the 8ve, while the 6th and 4th descend in parallel 3rds.

LINEAR CHORDS of the 6th

208.   The Linear 6th as Distinct from the 6th by Inversion

In Chapter 10 it was demonstrated that the 6th chord by suspension bears no relation to a parent $\frac{5}{3}$. It results from the rhythmic process alone, not from the harmonic process of inversion, and functions like a dissonance. A similar case is the linear 6th chord, the 6th chord which arises from the action of an auxiliary note or a passing note. Like the 6th chord by suspension this chord is not derived from a parent $\frac{5}{3}$. Example 430 illustrates.

example 430.

In order to demonstrate the lack of relation between the linear 6th and a hypothetical parent chord Example 430(*b*) substitutes the hypothetical chord for the

6th chord. This proves to be VI, a dominant preparation, and is clearly not appropriate in this context. An example of the linear 6th chord is given below.

example 431. SCHUBERT: *Du bist die Ruh'*

The first 6th chord (asterisk) arises by the action of an incomplete auxiliary note symbolized by the familiar figures 5 6. The second 6th chord is a 6th chord by inversion. It represents the parent $\frac{5}{3}$, a tonic chord. Again, we can test the derivation of the linear 6th chord by substituting the hypothetical parent chord:

example 432.

As shown in Example 432 the supposed parent chord tends to fulfill its normative function as dominant preparation and leads quickly to the cadential succession II$\frac{6}{5}$ V[7] I. The effect of the entire progression thus differs radically from the original, which extends the tonic triad, referring only briefly to the dominant at the end of the phrase.

When a chord can be read as a functional part of a harmonic progression it may be said to have *harmonic value.* When it is solely the result of linear processes, as in the case of the linear 6th chord, it does not have harmonic value, and it is incorrect to interpret it as a harmonic event. In section 220 the notion of harmonic value will be used to interpret an important feature of tonal compositions, linear intervallic patterns.

209. Linear-6th Chords in Parallel Motion

Thus far only the single 6th chord has been considered. When linear-6th chords occur in direct succession and in parallel motion, they serve one of two purposes: (1) they neutralize an otherwise dissonant passage; (2) they expand a single harmony or a harmonic connection in a highly fluent way. The first of these functions is illustrated below.

example 433. CHORALE: *Straf' mich nicht in deinem Zorn*

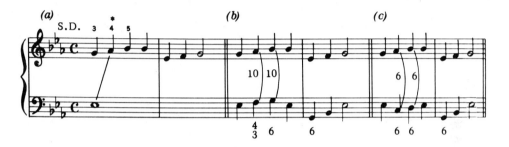

At (*a*) we see the familiar ascending scale degree 4, which requires harmonization in order to overcome the descending attraction of the half step. A common dissonant harmonization is shown at (*b*). A common consonant harmonization is shown at (*c*). There the parallel 6th chords effectively neutralize the dissonant 4th. Another example follows.

example 434. Chorale: *Lobet den Herren*

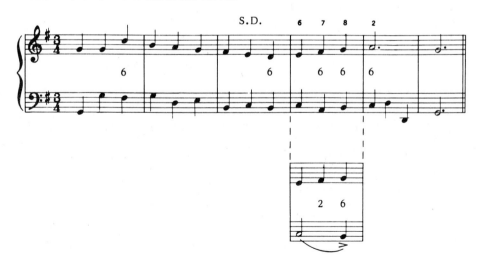

This example shows the function of a succession of three linear-6th chords in carrying the soprano fluently to the point of melodic emphasis, scale degree 2. The alternative harmonization sketched in below the fourth measure is unsatisfactory because it places harmonic emphasis upon the last beat and thus interferes with the forward motion of the soprano line.

The second function of parallel 6th chords—the extension of a single harmony or harmonic connection—is illustrated by the following extracts.

example 435. LOEILLET: *Sonata in C major for Flute and Continuo*

Here the bracket marks the linear 6th chord as an embellishment of the first inversion of the dominant triad. In this context and in many others the 6th chord is realized in three parts only. In four parts alternate doublings would be required in order to avoid parallel 8ves.

The asterisk in Example 435 draws attention to the dissonant bass note. The harmony on this beat is V, supporting ascending scale degree 2 in the soprano. However, the bass line is imitating the soprano in canonic fashion so that the contrapuntal device takes precedence over the harmonic progression at this point.

Our final example in this section shows a series of parallel 6th chords which connects one main harmony to another.

example 436. HAYDN: *Fantasy in C major for Piano*

This entire succession (bracketed) lies within the control of the dominant triad. The large connection, as illustrated below, is from V^6 to V at the end of the phrase.

example 437.

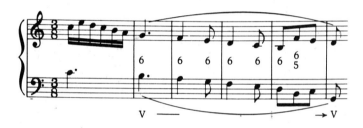

An alternative harmonization of the same soprano line is offered below.

example 438.

The rhythmic-harmonic effect of this harmonization is entirely different from the original. Here the long line achieved by the 6th chords of the original has been broken up into three smaller segments, indicated by slurs in Example 438. And whereas the original line began on G, this line begins on F, since G is defined harmonically here as the end of the first group, not as the beginning of the second.

CHROMATIC LINEAR CHORDS

210. Chromatic Linear Chord Defined

By chromatic linear chord is meant simply a chord entirely of linear origin which contains one or more chromatic notes. A great many of these chords are to be found in the literature. Here we shall cover only certain representative types which, by virtue of their association with the primary triads, have become sufficiently universal to have attained an identity. In each instance we shall demonstrate how these chords derive by linear motion from more familiar diatonic chords.

The various chromatic linear chords all share one characteristic: They exploit half-step melodic progressions in one or more voices and thus intensify the motion of the diatonic chords from which they derive and which they often represent.

211. The Augmented Triad and the Altered 6th Chord

The augmented triad arises when a chromatic passing note ascends from the 5th of the triad, creating the interval of an augmented 5th with the bass, as here:

example 439. BEETHOVEN: *Third Symphony,* First Movement

A chord of similar sound arises when a chromatic passing note ascends from the 3rd of a 6th chord:

example 440. SCHUBERT: *Pause*

The augmented triad and the altered 6th chord occur in similar contexts and almost invariably follow the consonant chord from which they derive. Sometimes the augmented triad is classified with the major, minor, and diminished triads. Although this may be convenient for textbook authors it is extremely misleading regarding the origin and function of the augmented triad. This triad is entirely the result of chromatic linear motion; it is not an independent diatonic triad.

212. The Diatonic Origin of the Augmented-6th Chord

In the minor mode the chord pair formed by the dominant and one of the dominant preparations, II, IV, or VI, is sometimes expanded to a three-chord group by the inclusion of a chromatic passing chord, a special type of linear chord known as the *augmented-6th chord*. There are three varieties of this chord, all closely related. We shall consider each separately.

213. The Italian 6th (+6)

The form of the augmented-6th chord called the Italian 6th derives from the dominant preparation IV⁶ by the melodic process of chord generation. Its evolution is demonstrated in the following example.

example 441.

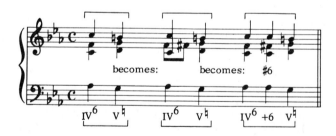

This example first shows the basic progression IV⁶ V. A chromatic passing eighth note then connects the 6th of the IV to the 8ve of the V. Finally, the passing note is enlarged metrically and assimilated by the harmony to form a new chord. This chord is characterized by the interval which the chromatic passing note forms with the bass, the interval of an augmented 6th. In all cases the two notes that form this dissonant chromatic interval expand outward to resolution on the 8ve. The chord is figured by indicating the alteration of the 6th, ♯6 in this case. We shall also find it convenient to indicate the augmented-6th chords in general by the sign +6.

The effect of all the augmented-6th chords is to intensify the progression to V. This is illustrated by the Italian 6th in the following passage.

example 442.   C. P. E. BACH: *Sonata in G major*

There are two important things to observe in this passage. First, observe that the +6 chord is not preceded by IV[6], as in the model progression (Example 441), but stands in place of that chord. The +6 can represent the chord of origin, as here, or it can follow it, as in the model. Second, notice that the 3rd of the +6 chord is doubled. This is the only doubling possible, for the resolution both of the bass and of the augmented 6th are bound by the law of the half step and thus a doubling of either one would give rise to parallel 8ves.

214.   The French 6th ($\begin{smallmatrix}6\\4\\3\end{smallmatrix}$)

The basis for the assignment of nationality to each augmented-6th chord remains obscure. Nevertheless, the terms have a certain usefulness in designating the somewhat different structure of each type. The so-called French 6th derives from $II\begin{smallmatrix}4\\3\end{smallmatrix}$, as shown below.

example 443.

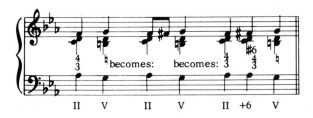

Again, as in the case of the Italian 6th, a chromatic passing note ascends from the 6th of the first chord to the 8ve of the second chord. The difference between the two chords is this: whereas the Italian 6th derives from a consonant chord, IV^6, the French 6th derives from a dissonant chord, II$\frac{4}{3}$. In the French 6th no notes are doubled, no notes are omitted. An example follows.

example 444. SCHUBERT: *Am Feirabend*

Here the French 6th stands between a suspension chord ($\frac{5}{4}$) and its resolution, illustrating again the unique role the linear chords play in connecting dissonant harmonies.

215. The German 6th ($\frac{6}{5}$)

This chord derives from IV$\frac{6}{5}$, as shown in the next example.

example 445.

Again the chromatic linear chord arises when a chromatic passing note is enlarged and assimilated by the harmony. A voice-leading peculiarity of this chord is indicated by the diagonal lines: parallel 5ths occur when the chord resolves to V. Often these 5ths are avoided by interpolation of the $\frac{6}{4}$ between the +6 and V:

example 446.

$$IV \quad - \quad V \quad -$$

Since the augmented-6th chords derive from dominant preparations they themselves serve as dominant preparations. And because the dissonant interval of the augmented 6th always expands outward to resolution on the 8ve of the dominant harmony, the augmented-6th chords are even more specific indicators of direction toward the dominant triad than are the diatonic dominant preparations from which they originate. Observe the effect of the German 6th chord in the following modulatory sequence. Here, typically, it is in a prominent, metrically accented position.

example 447. BEETHOVEN: *Piano Sonata in E♭ major, Op. 7*

Only with the augmented-6th chord does the direction of the sequential progression become specific.

The German 6th is sometimes prepared by the triad on VI, as shown below.

example 448.

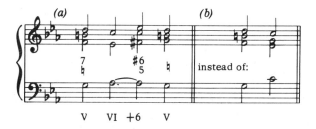

instead of:

V   VI   +6   V

The progression from V⁷ to VI here resembles a deceptive cadence. Its effect is to avoid the progression from V to I shown at (*b*) and to extend V instead. As part of that extension the VI is converted to a German 6th by the addition of an augmented 6th (F♯). A more elaborate illustration of the same technique is given in the next example.

example 449.   HAYDN: *Piano Sonata in G minor*

Like the Beethoven and C. P. E. Bach excerpts (Examples 442 and 447) this passage is part of a modulatory progression. Here the ultimate goal of the progression is III in minor (the B♭ major triad). Again we note that the augmented-6th chord occurs in a harmonic context that suggests the parallel minor mode (B♭ minor).

216. Summary of the Augmented-6th Chords

Any of the three forms of the +6 chord may be located easily in the following way. The bass of the chord is found a half step above the dominant note. Above the bass we place the augmented 6th and major 3rd. This is the Italian 6th. We can then easily locate the other two forms from the Italian 6th. The French 6th adds an augmented 4th above the bass; the German 6th adds a perfect 5th. The procedure is illustrated in Example 450.

example 450.

217. The Linear $\frac{4}{2}$

The linear $\frac{4}{2}$ is a chromatic dominant preparation that simulates the third inversion of a dominant-7th chord, a particularly striking harmonic effect. Two of the linear contexts in which it originates are shown in the following examples.

example 451.

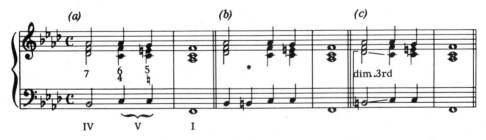

In Example 451 the linear $\frac{4}{2}$ comes into existence as a chromatic passing chord between IV[7] and the $\frac{6}{4}$ that precedes the dominant (*b*). At (*c*) the linear $\frac{4}{2}$ usurps the position of IV[7] and receives the full metrical accent.

The following example, in the major mode, shows the linear $\frac{4}{2}$ as it may arise from another dominant preparation, $II\frac{6}{5}$.

example 452.

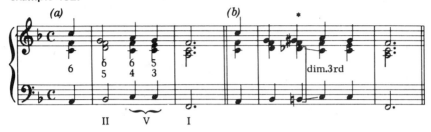

Here the linear $\frac{4}{2}$ results from the motion of three chromatic passing notes which connect $II\frac{6}{5}$ with the cadential $\frac{6}{4}$. Both here and in the previous example the linear $\frac{4}{2}$ is characterized by the diminished 3rd between the bass and one of the upper voices. This interval contracts to resolution on the 8ve, recalling the augmented 6th, which expands to resolution on the 8ve. Sometimes the linear $\frac{4}{2}$ is spelled like an authentic $\frac{4}{2}$, as in the following example:

example 453. CHOPIN: *Nocturne in B major, Op. 32/1*

The linear $\frac{4}{2}$ occurs where the final tonic is expected and introduces a long, recitativelike close, finally resolving to the cadential $\frac{6}{4}$. The bass note of the linear $\frac{4}{2}$ would normally have been spelled as E$\sharp$. In this case it is spelled as F$\natural$, possibly in order to simplify the notation of the upper parts, which feature E.

218. The Neapolitan Chord as Dominant Preparation Derived from IV

Like the augmented-6th chords this chromatic linear chord originates in the minor mode.

example 454.

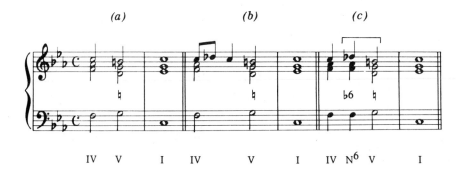

Example 454 illustrates its evolution from IV in three stages: (*a*) the basic progression IV V I. (*b*) the submetrical embellishment of the 5th of the IV by its chromatic upper auxiliary note. (*c*) the enlargement and assimilation of that note into the harmony, forming the chord of the lowered 6th known as the *Neapolitan 6th* (presumably because it was characteristic of music by the late Baroque Neapolitan composers).

This chord serves as a dominant preparation. Its hallmark is the horizontal interval of a diminished 3rd (bracketed in Example 454), a dissonant interval which comes about when the chromatic auxiliary note does not return to the main note (C in the present case), but instead progresses directly to the 3rd of the dominant triad. The Neapolitan 6th is also another instance of false consonance, for although it contains only consonant intervals it functions as a dissonance in the linear context. Here again, as in all linear chords, inversion theory does not apply. The Neapolitan chord is not the first inversion of a hypothetical triad on the lowered 2nd degree of the scale.

The example below contains both Neapolitan and its chord of origin, IV.

example 455. BEETHOVEN: *Bagatelle, Op. 119/5*

Risoluto

N⁶

219. Pedal Point Chords

When the bass note of either I or V is sustained below moving chromatic and diatonic harmonies we call it a pedal point and describe the harmonies as pedal-point chords. Since they do not influence progression these chords are regarded as linear chords within the control of a more fundamental chord, either I or V depending upon which is the pedal point.

example 456. RAMEAU: *Traité de L'Harmonie* (Rameau's figures)

In this instance the controlling harmony is I; its bass note remains stationary throughout the passage. The chords above the pedal point commence with the tonic itself and descend chromatically to measure 4 where, disregarding for a moment the stationary bass, we find a V$^4_2$. This chord resolves to I⁶, which is followed by a II$^6_5$ V$^4_2$ I⁶ succession. Thus, the pedal-point chords are not as unfamiliar as they might seem to be at first glance. Usually pedal-point chords are cadential chords, chords closely associated with I and V, as in this instance.

In the next excerpt a series of pedal-point chords is found at the beginning of a composition.

example 457. BACH: *Prelude in B♭ minor, WTCI*

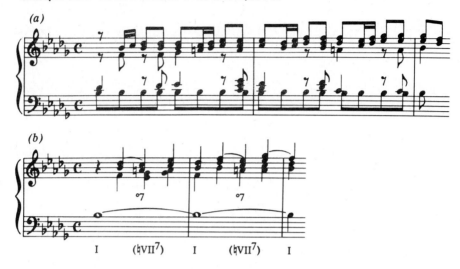

Example 458(*b*) is a harmonic sketch from which rhythmic and melodic detail has been eliminated. This reduction reveals the familiar chords that underlie the succession: I and VII[7].

In section 111 the diminished-7th chord was explained as an altered inversion of V[7]. Example 458 shows the diminished-7th chord formed by auxiliary notes above the sustained bass note, G. As indicated by the figures, this linear chord occurs in the context of the succession $\frac{6}{4}$ $\frac{5}{3}$.

example 458. MOZART: *Piano Sonata in C major, K.545,* Second Movement

(Compare Example 429 by the same composer.)

220. Linear Intervallic Patterns

Thus far, we have dealt with individual chords, the origins of which are linear, and with series of linear chords (the linear 6th chords and pedal-point chords). The final section of this chapter is concerned with linear formations of somewhat larger scope which will be called *linear intervallic patterns:* repetitive patterns formed by the outer voices. Characteristically, such formations contain chords without harmonic value (section 208). Example 459 will serve to introduce the concept.

example 459.   HAYDN: *Farewell Symphony,* First Movement

Shown at (*a*) is a reduction of the orchestral passage, a transition to the second theme of the exposition. At (*b*) is a representation of the underlying progression.

This begins with V in m. 49 and ends with the same harmony in m. 53, as indicated by the long slurs. The linear intervallic pattern in this instance consists of the succession 10-7*, the intervals formed by the outer voices. Although some components might be said to have harmonic value—in particular, the last three in the progression (II-V-I)—the linear intervallic pattern is the predominant bearer of motion, carrying the progression to its goal in m. 53. Within the pattern the succession of parallel 10ths is of primary importance, and, indeed, the linear intervallic pattern consisting of 10ths alone (10-10) is commonly found in tonal music of all periods.

Closely akin to the linear intervallic pattern 10-7 is the pattern 10-5. Example 460 provides an instance.

example 460. BACH: *Fugue in A minor, BWV 947*

*Patterns of this kind are sometimes called sequences (cf. section 140). The term linear intervallic pattern is preferred, however, since the melodic detail may change while the pattern remains constant. Example 461 provides a clear demonstration of this.

(b)

II   V   I

(c)

cf. 10   7   10   7   10   7   10

(d)

In this passage, the close of a fugue by Bach, the 10-5 pattern is used to effect the connection from I to V in the bass with a corresponding motion in the upper voice from scale degree 3 down to the leading note, G♯. Again, the underlying pattern of *(a)*, the complete notation, is shown at *(b)*. At *(c)* is shown the equivalent 10-7 pattern.

Example 460 permits a comparison of figured bass notation and the notation for linear intervallic patterns. Obviously, the figures represent the complete voice-leading, whereas the notation of the linear intervallic pattern extracts only the numerals that represent the outer voice intervals. The correspondence is spelled out at *(a)*, where the succession 3-5 matches the linear pattern 10-5 at *(b)*.

Finally, at *(d)* in Example 460 the correct analytical interpretation of the closing passage is given. This shows that the upper voice progression from C to G♯ is a motion from the outer to the inner voice. The return to the outer voice B is then supported by the bass motion C-D-E. Since this motion to B in the upper voice is not actually stated, but only implied by the bass, B is enclosed in parentheses in the representation at *(d)*.

Example 461 shows the 10-5 pattern over a still longer span of music. Again, from the full notation at *(a)* is extracted the basic pattern shown at *(b)*. An interesting feature of the pattern is the passing note in the bass in m. 26 and again in m. 28. With the acceleration of the pattern that begins in m. 29 the passing note is omitted.

Example 461 is a clear instance of change in melodic pattern (m. 29) of the upper voice, while the linear intervallic pattern 10-5 continues. For this reason the term *pattern* is preferred to "sequence."

Example 461 also illustrates what might be called a truncated linear intervallic pattern. As shown at (c), the continuation of the pattern after m. 31 would have led to the same melodic-harmonic goal. The braces at (c) enclose the part of the pattern that is truncated.

The main harmonic components of Example 461(a) are shown schematically at (d); they comprise a progression from VI to V, as indicated.

example 461.   BACH: *Prelude in E♭ major, WTC II, BWV 876*

(b)

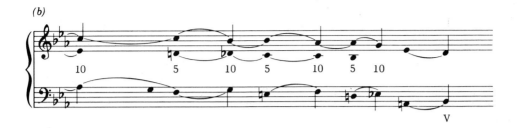

(c)

(d)

Example 462 presents one of the many beautiful instances of linear inter-vallic patterns to be found in the symphonic literature, the passage leading to the closing theme in the exposition of Schubert's *Unfinished Symphony.* Here the prominent motive of the second theme is carried by the bass and imitated by the upper part (m. 74), while the slower moving parts on the uppermost staff (wood-winds) carry the basic voice leading of the soprano and inner voice, with chromatic passing notes (A♭ and E♭) joining each occurrence of the pattern.

The linear intervallic pattern in this case is $\frac{6}{5}$-5, a more elaborate variant of the basic pattern 6-5. As shown at (c) the pattern as a whole effects a connection from secondary dominant to dominant within VI. The representation at (c) differs from that at (b) with respect to the upper voice beginning in m. 81. Whereas (b) shows E in the upper voice at that point, (c) gives C♯, which more directly represents the continuation of the upper voice of the linear intervallic pattern.

example 462. SCHUBERT: *Unfinished Symphony,* First Movement

(b)

(a)

(b)

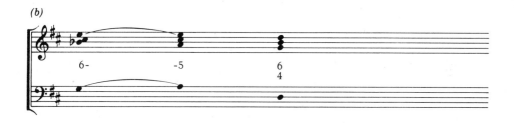

(c)

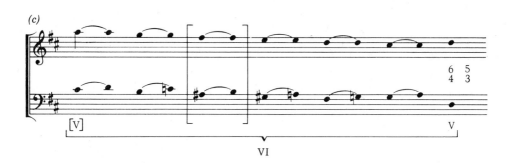

A more complicated instance of the linear intervallic pattern $\frac{6}{5}$-5 is provided by Example 463.

example 463. MOZART: *Piano Sonata in F major, K.280,* First Movement

(a) Allegro assai

(b)

(c)

For the sake of precision and clarity the analysis is shown in three stages. At (a) the notation is given in full. At (b) embellishing notes are systematically eliminated to show the descending lines and arpeggiations.* The voice leading underlying the latter is shown at (c). There the descending lines spanning the 6th are shown as inner voice 3rds (e. g., G down to B♭ becomes G up to B♭). Further, the arpeggiations are reduced as follows: the ascent to the octave is represented by a single note in the lower register in each case (e. g., A in the second space represents A on

---

*Although the treatment of embellishing notes is not undertaken until Chapter 12 it is hoped that the reader will be able to follow the analysis here.

the first leger line above the staff), while the second quarter note is shown in its correct voice-leading context as the 6th above the bass. As indicated at (*d*) the entire pattern is an elaboration of a succession of linear 6ths.

Example 464 presents an excerpt from the development section of the first movement of Beethoven's *Piano Sonata, Op. 78.* Here the linear intervallic pattern 6-5 is stretched out over some five measures.

example 464. BEETHOVEN: *Piano Sonata in F♯ major, Op. 78,* First Movement (Development)

Notice that in each case the outer voice 5th is embellished by inner voice auxiliary notes—perhaps most clearly shown at (c).

The over-all stepwise progression of both outer voices cannot be interpreted analytically without reference to the beginning of the development section (and, ultimately, to the exposition). Therefore, suffice it to say that the harmonic goal of the progression is IV, as indicated. It is especially evident in this example that any effort to assign harmonic value to the $\frac{5}{3}$'s over the span of the entire passage will lead to absurd results; the linear pattern is the predominant bearer of motion.

The detail of this excerpt warrants two additional comments. Notice, first, that the rhythmic figure of the left-hand part effects an obvious association with the theme. (If the music is unfamiliar to the reader he should consult the complete score.) Not so obvious is the descending thematic motive carried by the 16th-note diminution. The first occurrence of this is bracketed in m. 47 at (b).

example 465. BEETHOVEN: *Piano Sonata in D major, Op. 28,* Third Movement

Example 465 requires minimal explanation. As shown at (*c*), the underlying pattern is a series of linear 6ths. The upper voice of the pattern departs from C♯ in the inner voice (m. 32) and leads up to G (m. 47), which is the continuation of the upper voice A at m. 32. Both A and G are shown in a single register at (*c*) in order to make the connection evident graphically. The lower voice of the pattern follows the upper voice in parallel 6ths, and, in this sense, has a dependent function. Although this aspect of linear intervallic patterns is not insignificant for the general case, further discussion at this point is not appropriate to the introductory nature of this section.

example 466. F. COUPERIN: *Les Sylvains* (*from the Premier Ordre*)

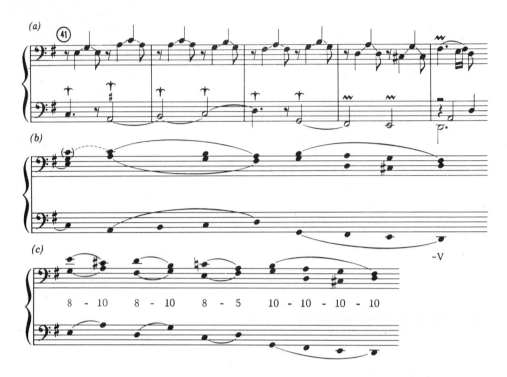

In the passage from a keyboard piece by Couperin shown in Example 466 we find a mixture of linear intervallic patterns. As shown at (*c*), the pattern 8-10 occurs at the beginning of the passage. This is supplanted by 8-5 beginning at m. 40, and the passage closes with the 10-10 succession indicated.

The underlying patterns shown at (*c*) are given an elaborate setting in the music, as indicated at (*b*). Each 8-10 pattern is filled out with pairs of voices moving in parallel 10ths. The ultimate harmonic goal of the entire linear complex is V (m. 44), which leads to the restatement of the first part of the music.

Perhaps no other situation in tonal music so strikingly dramatizes the inter-action of linear and harmonic processes as the linear intervallic patterns. Although the present section is only a brief introduction to this structural aspect, some general observations can be made.

To sum up, two situations can be distinguished with respect to passages that exhibit linear intervallic patterns: (1) The chordal components have no harmonic value, as can be demonstrated by attempting to read them as elements of a har-monic progression, and only the point of departure and the goal are harmonic; (2) Some of the chordal components have harmonic value—as is often the case in the 10-7 pattern, by virtue of the 5ths progression—but the over-all linear pattern formed by the outer voices is a significant aspect of the motion and may even take precedence over the harmonic; (3) In all cases the linear intervallic pattern either extends a single harmony or effects a connection between two harmonies, with modulation a special case of the latter.

EXERCISES

A. List of Some Important Terms to Define and Memorize

Linear chord	Italian 6th
9th chord	French 6th
Appoggiatura chord	German 6th
Consonant $^6_4$	Linear $^4_2$
Passing $^6_4$	Neapolitan chord
Linear-6th chord	Pedal point
Parallel 6th chords	Linear Intervallic Pattern

B. Basic Keyboard and Aural Exercises

Here the chords of the basic pattern are connected by inverted secondary dominant-7th chords. The latter, in turn, are connected by dissonant linear chords. As an exercise in analysis, to supplement those given later in this section, the basic chord patterns should be examined in terms of linear intervallic patterns.

exercise 224. **Basic Chord Pattern 1 in major**

exercise 225. **Basic Chord Pattern 1 in minor**

exercise 226. **Basic Chord Pattern 2 in major**

This version of the basic pattern features appoggiatura chords and a linear half-diminished chord which prepares the dominant.

exercise 227. **Basic Chord Pattern 2 in minor**

The minor version also features appoggiatura chords. However, the dominant here is prepared by an enharmonic $\frac{4}{2}$.

C. Chord Identification

INSTRUCTIONS
Identify all chords in the following excerpts. Linear chords made up of odd combinations of intervals should be labeled "lin." Those explained in the preceding sections should be identified by appropriate symbols. All excerpts are to be studied thoroughly for progression, especially modulatory progression, melodic structure, metric-rhythmic pattern, etc. After playing each as written, transpose to at least two other keys and sing the bass while playing only the upper parts.

D. Figured Bass, Soprano Given

INSTRUCTIONS

Realize in four parts. Identify all chords, paying particular attention to linear chords.

exercise 228. BACH: *Ihr Gestirn, ihr hohen Lüfte.* (Schemelli's *Gesangbuch*)

This soprano voice may be regarded as a solo line and the bass realized as a four-voice accompaniment.

exercise 229. BACH: *O Jesulein süss.* (Schemelli's *Gesangbuch*)

exercise 230. J.S. BACH: *Gib dich zufrieden*

E. Unfigured Basses, Soprano Given

INSTRUCTIONS
Realize in four parts. Identify all chords, paying particular attention to linear chords.

exercise 231. TELEMANN: *Fantasy* *

_____

*Occasional parallel 5ths and 8ves are unavoidable in these free compositions (for example, in the first and second measures).

exercise 232. BACH: *Bist du bei mir* (incomplete)

Realize the bass as an accompaniment for solo voice. Shift to three voices where advantageous.

exercise 233. SCHUBERT: *Ländler*

exercise 234. MENDELSSOHN: Harmonization of *Nun danket alle Gott*

F. Soprano Voices to Harmonize

INSTRUCTIONS
While constructing the minimal harmonization observe cues for linear chords, for example, appoggiaturas, accented passing notes, passing or auxiliary notes within a a dissonant harmony. Linear chords are required even for the harmonization of many familiar songs.

exercise 235. **German Folk Song. For SATB**

exercise 236. Italian Folk Song. For vocal solo with piano accompaniment

exercise 237. German Folk Song: *Es steht ein Lind'.* Transpose to A♭ for SATB

exercise 238. German Folk Song: *Mein Mädel hat einen Rosenmund.* Transpose to A for solo voice with piano accompaniment.

Fast

exercise 239. **German Folk Song:** *In Stiller Nacht*

Slowly

G. Passages to be Analyzed for Linear Intervallic Patterns

INSTRUCTIONS
Using notation indicate the intervallic pattern(s) for each excerpt.

exercise 240. **F. COUPERIN:** *La Diligente* (*Second Ordre*)

exercise 241. MAHLER: *Fourth Symphony,* Third Movement

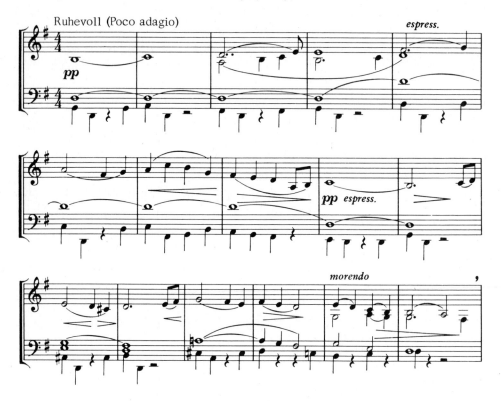

exercise 242. MOZART: *Symphony in E♭, K.543,* Second Movement

exercise 243. SCHUMANN: *Im Rhein, im heiligen Strome* (*Dichterliebe*)

Ziemlich langsam

exercise 244. BACH: *Air* from the *Orchestral Suite in D major*

As an additional exercise supply figures and realize the continuo part.

12

The Techniques of Melodic-Rhythmic Development

Certainly no one doubts the need for embellishments. . . . They are indeed indispensable, for consider their uses. They connect notes, animate them, lend them a special effect and weight when required, make them pleasing and thus arouse a particular attentiveness. Embellishments help to clarify the content of the notes-be is sad, joyful, or of other nature. . . .

C.P.E. Bach, 1753

221. The Structural Role of Submetrical Embellishment

Chapter 7 considered the structure of the soprano voice and its relation to the progression of the harmony. There the soprano voice was regarded as a special case of melodic progression, and it was observed that any voice, including the bass, can exhibit melodic characteristics. Let us review those characteristics here, giving special attention to the relation between metrical and submetrical embellishment.

A consonant harmony can be developed melodically in three ways: (1) by auxiliary note (2) by arpeggiation (skip) (3) by a passing note which fills in an arpeggiated harmonic interval. These three techniques are summarized in Example 467. Since the embellishments have full metrical value they require harmonization, as shown.

example 467.

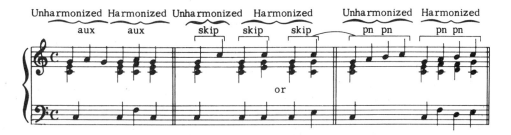

One of the most remarkable aspects of tonal music is that these basic techniques are applied both at the metrical and submetrical levels and over both short and long spans of music. An introduction to large-scale arpeggiations, passing and auxiliary notes is given in Chapter 13. Here we are concerned with the basic procedures as they apply to shorter spans of music.

The relation between metrical and submetrical embellishments is illustrated in the next example.

example 468.

At (a) we see the harmonized metrical auxiliary note pattern. At (b) this basic pattern is developed melodically by transient skips—submetrical embellishments. At (c) further development has taken place with the filling of one of the skips by a submetrical passing note.

From this illustration it can be seen that metrical embellishment provides a means of *extending* a harmony to include other harmonies, whereas submetrical embellishment serves to elaborate and activate a single harmony.

Example 468 illustrates still another significant fact: submetrical embellishment necessarily means rhythmic as well as melodic development. For this reason the title of the present chapter uses the composite expression melodic-rhythmic.

Submetrical embellishments are sometimes called "unessential" notes, a term which suggests that such embellishments are superfluous, that they have no significant function in the tonal composition. This is an erroneous notion. Sub-metrical embellishments are no more extraneous than flesh on bone. If, occasion-ally, we omit them from illustrations in the present chapter it is in order to provide a clear view of underlying harmonic relations, not because we consider them superfluous.

We have seen that there are only three basic techniques of melodic-rhythmic development. However, these occur in various forms, producing diverse textures. For example, arpeggiations are complete or incomplete, auxiliary notes are ac-cented or unaccented, and so on. One must be familiar with all these modes of occurrence and be able to recognize them immediately in order to achieve an ade-quate basis for the development of analytical as well as compositional technique.

The relevance of melodic-rhythmic embellishments to composing is readily apparent. In order to progress beyond the elementary level of note-against-note harmonization in close position one must exploit the resources offered by sub-metrical embellishment. In addition, an understanding of submetrical embellishing techniques is prerequisite to composition in two and three voices, and in free textures—all of which are introduced in Chapter 14.

222. Motive, Theme, and Figuration

These three terms are used frequently in connection with melodic structure and embellishment. We can draw illustrations of all from a single work.

example 469. BEETHOVEN: *Sixth Symphony* ("Pastorale")

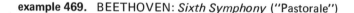
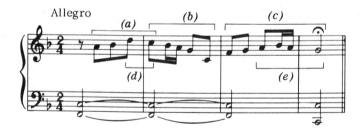

This opening melodic group consists of several segments marked off by brackets in Example 469. Each segment contains a distinct submetrical embellishment. When segments such as these are repeated during the course of a composition in such a way that they become characteristic features of its melodic structure they are called *motives*. Motives may recur in their original form or they may undergo transformations. For example, the identifying rhythmic pattern of the motive may be retained while its characteristic melodic shape is changed. Compare mo-tive (*b*) in the following example with its original form in Example 469.

example 470. (BEETHOVEN: *Sixth Symphony*)

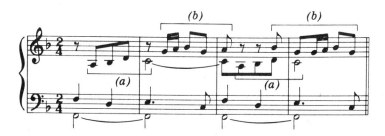

Here motive (*b*) has retained only the rhythmic shape of the original, whereas motive (*a*) recurs unchanged.

In contrast to the transformation of motive (*b*) just described, the characteristic melodic shape may be retained while the rhythm is changed, as in Example 471:

example 471. (BEETHOVEN: *Sixth Symphony*)

In this passage motive (*d*) has been expanded in duration so that it now occupies a complete measure. An expansion of this kind is known as an *augmentation.* Another example of augmentation is shown below.

example 472. (BEETHOVEN: *Sixth Symphony*)

As in the previous example the note values of the original motive have been doubled in this transformation. Observe also that there are two statements of the motive and that the second statement is extended.

The counterpart of augmentation is *diminution**** of the original form of the motive. With this manipulation the original form is made proportionally smaller.

When the melodic shape of the original is turned upside down the motive is said to be *inverted.* Example 473 shows motive (*a*) in its original form combined with its inversion.

example 473. (BEETHOVEN: *Sixth Symphony*)

Contour inversion of this kind has nothing whatsoever to do with harmonic inversion of intervals. Unfortunately, the same term has been applied to both.

Similar difficulty has beset the term *figuration.* If the term is used alone it usually refers to instrumental figurations such as those shown below.

example 474. (BEETHOVEN: *Sixth Symphony*)

Typical instrumental figurations are bracketed at (*f*) and (*g*). The first of these is a type of arpeggiation found in many pieces and sometimes called the Alberti Bass. The second (*g*) is a repeated submetrical auxiliary-note pattern, a measured trill. These patterns are not distinctive, nor are they characteristic of this composition, for they may be found in a wide variety of works.

---

*Although the term diminution is current, the term *contraction* might be better since diminution is the traditional designation for embellishment in general.

The term figuration is also used to describe the general process of melodic embellishment. Thus, we often read of "figurated" melody or of chorale "figuration." The latter in particular is widely used and will be found in the present volume. Figuration has nothing to do with figured bass, except insofar as numerals often designate embellishing notes.

Finally, we come to the term *theme*. A theme, as distinct from a motive, is a longer and more complex melody which executes a complete progression of one of the types explained in Chapter 7. Example 469 may be regarded as the first statement of a theme. Like most themes it comprises several motives.

Themes and motives serve to enhance melodic and harmonic progression by preparing changes, by unifying and contrasting various phases of a composition, by signaling and intensifying climaxes, and by performing many other essential tasks. In large part they achieve this by virtue of the particular combinations of submetrical embellishments which they contain. These are discussed below in some detail.

THE AUXILIARY NOTE

223. The Complete Auxiliary Note

The complete auxiliary-note pattern consists of the main note, the auxiliary note or notes, and the restatement of the main note—in that order. The complete auxiliary-note pattern thus has four possible forms, summarized in Example 475.

example 475.

At both (*a*) and (*b*) we see a single auxiliary note embellishing a main note. At (*c*) upper and lower auxiliaries are combined in a formation of five notes. At (*d*) both upper and lower auxiliaries precede the final main note. This form of the auxiliary note is often overlooked, although it occurs very frequently in compositions. Excerpts from the literature follow.

example 476. BACH: *Chorale-Prelude, Wir danken dir, Herr Jesu Christ* (for organ)

The complete lower-auxiliary-note motive occurs in every voice except the sopra-no, which carries the chorale melody.

Auxiliary notes are altered chromatically when required in order to support the prevailing harmony and voice leading. For example, when the V is reached as a harmonic goal in the example below, C♯, not C♮ is the lower auxiliary note. C♮ belongs to the inverted V⁷ which follows, whereas C♯ belongs to the consonant-goal harmony.

example 477. (BACH: *Chorale-Prelude, Wir danken dir*)

The following excerpt contains two auxiliary-note formations, the first metrical the second submetrical.

example 478. CHOPIN: *Prelude in F♯ major, Op. 28/13*

The first auxiliary-note formation is type (*d*) shown in Example 472. The second is type (*c*), the five note figure, here distributed evenly over the first full pulse of this compound metrical pattern.

The next example contains submetrical auxiliary notes of type (*d*) as well as metrical auxiliary notes.

example 479. BRAHMS: *Third Symphony*

The first submetrical auxiliary note in Example 479 falls directly on the beat and thus is relatively more accented than the auxiliary notes in Examples 476 and 477. Our next excerpt contains an even more strongly accented auxiliary-note pattern.

example 480. BEETHOVEN: *Piano Sonata in C major, Op. 2/3*

The motive indicated by brackets is a variant of type (*c*) in Example 475.

224. The Incomplete Auxiliary Note

The incomplete forms of the auxiliary note are two-note motives, with one exception. In all cases the main note occurs only once, either at the beginning or at the end, not in both positions as in the complete forms:

example 481.

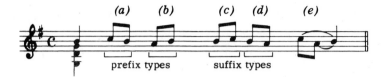

In types (*a*) and (*b*) the auxiliary note serves as a prefix to the main note, while in types (*c*) and (*d*) the auxiliary note is a suffix to the main note. Both auxiliary notes precede the main note in type (*e*).

When the prefix type receives the full metrical accent it is called an *appoggiatura* (section 201). An example follows.

example 482. C.P.E. BACH: *Sonata in C minor*

The asterisks mark auxiliaries of type (*b*), the appoggiatura. Example 482 also offers a comparison between these incomplete patterns and complete auxiliary-note patterns (bracketed). In both cases the auxiliary note is accented.

The suffix type is illustrated in the passage below.

example 483. BACH: *Chorale-Prelude, An Wasserflüssen Babylon*

Example 483(*a*), a reduction, contains only submetrical passing notes. Example 483(*b*), the complete version, contains incomplete auxiliary notes marked by asterisks. Thus, there are submetrical embellishments at two distinct rhythmic levels: passing eighth notes and their embellishments, the auxiliary sixteenth notes. The suffix type auxiliary note shown here is also characteristic of the embellished-suspension resolution (see section 194).

225. The Secondary Auxiliary Note

Occasionally in very elaborate figurations a submetrical auxiliary note will be supplied with a still smaller embellishing auxiliary note—generally for rhythmic reasons. This smaller auxiliary note is called *secondary* to indicate its subordinate function in the embellishment as a whole. Example 484 shows how such notes may fit into an intricately ornamented melody.

example 484. MOZART: *Symphony in C major, K.551* ("Jupiter")

The three stages of Example 484 show analytically the melodic-rhythmic development of a passage that serves to bring about a return to the tonic. At (a) may be seen a sequential progression of [V⁷]'s which leads to the final V⁷. At (*b*) the 7th of each chord is embellished by an upper auxiliary note. At (*c*), the complete version, the 7th of each chord is further embellished by a six-note group that contains a lower auxiliary note, the upper auxiliary note shown at (*b*) and a secondary auxiliary note marked by an asterisk. The reader will also recognize this passage as an instance of a familiar linear intervallic pattern (section 220).

ARPEGGIATION

226. Incomplete Arpeggiation (Skip)

Melodic lines are often embellished by submetrical skips above or below. Like metrical skips these may be purely of local effect, that is, transient skips, or they may represent the more elaborate technique of compound melody. An excerpt containing transient skips is quoted here:

example 485. SCHUBERT: *Ländler, Op. 67/2*

The submetrical transient skips are marked by asterisks. These skips are primarily of rhythmic significance. They do not represent compound melody as do the skips in the next example.

example 486. BACH: *Chorale-Prelude, In dir ist Freude*

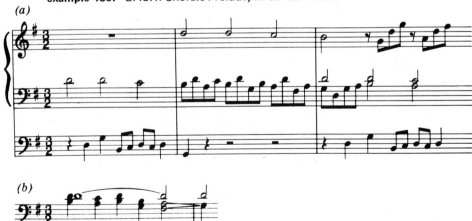

The submetrical skips in the second measure are activated harmonic intervals which can be represented as continuous lines moving in slower note values to form a succession of 3rds (*b*).

227. Complete Arpeggiation

A complete arpeggiation involves all the intervals of a chord. Like the incomplete arpeggiation this may be merely a local embellishment of a note in the main line, or it may be a more extended activation of the full harmony, that is, compound melody. Example 487 illustrates the complete arpeggiation in its more transient role.

example 487. BRAHMS: *Deutsche Volkslieder,* "Ich stand auf hohem Berge"

The submetrical arpeggiation bracketed in Example 487 serves as embellishment above and below the main note, D. The melody contains two other forms of the arpeggio. The first two measures contain a metrical arpeggiation of the tonic triad. The next to last measure contains another metrical arpeggiation of the tonic triad. This time the arpeggiation is filled in by accented passing notes, as shown by the supplementary sketch.

A familiar example of complete arpeggiation which represents the technique of compound melody is given below.

example 488. BACH: *Prelude in C major, WTC I*

In Example 489 the arpeggiation shown at (*b*), a reduction, is embellished by auxiliary notes in the complete music shown at (*a*).

example 489. CHOPIN: *Waltz in B minor, Op. 69/2*

THE PASSING NOTE

228. The Unaccented Passing Note

Passing notes fill arpeggiated chordal intervals. Therefore it is not only convenient but also structurally correct to regard passing notes as embellishments of skips. The meaning of a passing note depends, then, upon the structural function of the skip which it fills. Consider the passing note in the following passage.

example 490. MOZART: *Piano Sonata in F major, K.280*

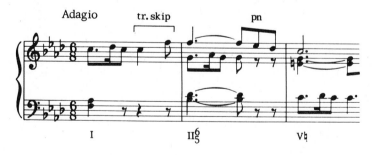

The soprano voice centers upon C in this excerpt. The transient skip away from C in the first measure is counterbalanced by the stepwise return in the second measure via the unaccented passing note, E♭.

In elaborate textures, passing notes may connect the notes of the harmony to form more complicated patterns such as those shown in Example 491:

example 491. BACH: *Chorale-Prelude, Heut' triumphiret Gottes Sohn*

The D in parentheses is understood from the harmony ($I\frac{5}{3}$). Thus C is a passing note. Actual statement of D would be out of keeping with the characteristic motive of this prelude, which is a descending or ascending eighth-note succession preceded by a rest. Three of these motives fill the interval of a 4th and therefore contain two passing notes. The first motive traverses the upper 4th of the minor scale and therefore the two passing notes are altered chromatically, in accord with the melodic minor scale.

Passing notes are often of greater harmonic significance when they fill the intervals formed by a compound melody. Consider the following variational example.

example 492. HANDEL: *Gavotte and Double (variation)* from *Suite in G major*

The soprano at (*a*) is a compound melody which, together with the bass, outlines a succession of triads at the outset. At (*b*) two of the original skips are filled by passing notes (bracketed). These passing notes bring into play a 7th in each case, thus enhancing the original harmonic progression.

229.   The Accented Passing Note

The accented passing note performs the same functions as the unaccented passing note and therefore does not require prolonged discussion. One aspect, however, does merit our special attention. The accented passing note displaces the main note from its metrical position. Several instances of this have already been seen. An additional example follows.

example 493.   BRAHMS: *Es war ein Markgraf über'm Rhein*

Accented embellishing notes must be used with care if they displace dissonant notes, lest they inadvertently destroy the identity of the harmony. As a general rule they should not be used in connection with dissonant notes unless they too are dissonant against the bass and unless the harmony is identified by context as well as structure.

Here and in all cases of accented embellishments the bass and harmony define the main structural elements. One further example will serve as a reminder of this important principle, the principle of harmonic definition (section 142).

example 494. HAYDN: *Symphony in D major, No. 104*

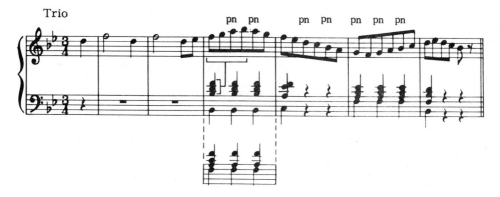

The bass and harmony of the third measure define F-B♭ as the chordal interval in the upper voice. Accordingly, A is an accented passing note within that interval. If, however, the bass and harmony were those shown in the sketch the harmonic interval in the upper voice would be F-A and B♭ would be an auxiliary note, not a passing note.

230. Submetrical Suspensions and Anticipations

Sometimes submetrical passing notes and auxiliary notes occur as suspensions in miniature. Since they do not retard the progression of the harmony and have only embellishing significance, they are not considered full-fledged suspensions. Three examples are quoted below. The first shows a submetrical suspension in combination with an actual suspension chord.

example 495. BRAHMS: *Intermezzo in E major, Op. 116/6*

The submetrical suspension in the second measure occurs directly below a suspended 4th. Observe that this submetrical suspension resembles an appoggiatura and could indeed be considered as such if the note were not present in the preceding chord.

In the next example the apparent submetrical suspension is better described as an accented auxiliary note embellishing A.

example 496. MOZART: *Don Giovanni*

Similarly, the submetrical suspensions in the next excerpt are perhaps better regarded as special cases of the accented passing note.

example 497. BEETHOVEN: *Piano Sonata in D minor, Op. 31/2*

The eighth notes form pairs, as indicated by the brackets. The second note of each pair is consonant, but is immediately repeated to become a dissonant, accented embellishing note. The two-note quasi-suspension motive prepares the suspension chord which displaces the dominant triad at the asterisk.

Submetrical anticipations occur quite often, especially in late eighteenth-century music. Example 498(*a*) shows a rhythmically simplified version of a passage which contains two anticipations. Example 498(*b*) presents the passage in full.

example 498. HAYDN: *Piano Sonata in E major*

The anticipations are marked by asterisks in Example 498(*b*). The first of these embellishes a metrical passing note. The second embellishes the suspension resolution.

231. Interrupted Passing Notes

As explained in section 131, melodic notes need not be in immediate succession in order to be closely related. Relations of this kind are called nonconsecutive relations. Submetrical as well as metrical embellishments may serve to interrupt consecutive notes and thus bring about nonconsecutive relations. Consider the following excerpt.

example 499. MOZART: *Piano Concerto in D major,* First Movement

Here the passing note E in the second measure is interrupted by the submetrical skips.

A more unusual situation is quoted below.

example 500. CHOPIN: *Mazurka in A minor, Op. 67/4*

At first glance D in the soprano of the second measure appears to be an auxiliary note standing between two C's. However, the bass and harmony assign it a different role. As the figures 8 7 indicate, the D is actually a passing note. Here the C on the second beat is somewhat misleading. Although it appears to be a main note, the harmony defines it as an accented-metrical passing note which effects a stepwise return to D after the descending skip away from E on the first beat.

The concept of nonconsecutive relations is essential to the understanding of progressions of larger scale. The latter will be introduced in the following chapter, Chapter 13.

232.   Obligatory Chromatic Passing and Auxiliary Notes

Chromatic passing and auxiliary notes perform valuable functions of many kinds. For instance, the submetrical F♯ in the following passage (asterisk) serves to repeat and intensify the previous metrical F♯, as indicated by the dotted line.

example 501. MOZART: *Quintet in C minor, K.406,* First Movement

The F♮ of the alternative embellishment sketched in below the fourth measure is "correct" from the standpoint of voice leading, but since it does not express the motivic relationship of the original F♯, it is defective from the standpoint of coherent melodic detail.

In certain instances such chromatically-altered auxiliary and passing notes are obligatory, for their diatonic counterparts would interfere with the melodic progression. Consider the following theme.

example 502. MOZART: *Symphony in D major, K.385*

Example 502(*b*) is a reduction of Example 502(*a*). The submetrical embellishments have been omitted in order to show the basic melodic progression more clearly and the necessity for the chromatics. The first four measures contain a repeated arpeggiation; the second four contain an ascending line which ends with a skip to scale degree 5. Every chromatic embellishment in the complete version is obligatory. The reason for this can be seen if we compare an alternative version which substitutes diatonic embellishments for chromatic.

example 503.

(a)

(b)

pn?

aux?   aux?

Example 503(*b*), a reduction of Example 503(*a*), reveals that this purely diatonic version is in conflict with the original at every point where the chromatic embellishment has been exchanged for a diatonic embellishment. Thus G♮ in the third measure sounds like an interrupted passing note here, whereas in the original version its chromatic form G♯ is an auxiliary note. Even more striking is the change which the diatonic substitutes bring about in the second part of the theme. The line no longer ascends in the sixth measure since E now sounds like an upper auxiliary note embellishing D, a reversal of the original relationship.

This demonstration of obligatory chromatic embellishments indicates the many ways in which embellishments of all kinds influence the more fundamental aspects of musical texture: harmonic progression, voice leading, and metric-rhythmic pattern. The following sections examine these influences in more detail.

THE EFFECTS OF MELODIC DEVELOPMENT UPON HARMONIC PROGRESSION, VOICE LEADING, AND METRIC—RHYTHMIC PATTERN

In general, submetrical embellishments may displace metrical elements from their normative positions, shorten them, delay them, or interrupt them. Embellishments

of this kind provide some of the most beautifully refined details in tonal compositions. At the same time they are often difficult to decipher because they tend to
conceal the more fundamental elements upon which their structural meaning
depends. Perhaps the most obvious instances of such concealment occur with extended embellishments of the bass.

233. Concealment of Bass Progression by Embellishment

The bass can be developed by arpeggiation to such a degree that it becomes a self-
contained compound melody, as in the following case.

example 504. PURCELL: *A New Ground*

Here the composer himself has deciphered the compound melody for us. At (*a*)
we see the first statement of the recurring bass theme or "ground," as it was called.
At (*b*) the second statement of the theme is seen. There the bass is sorted out
from the other lines in this compound melody and notated as a continuous,
uninterrupted line.

Sometimes a transient skip below the bass momentarily interrupts the
progression.

example 505. BACH: *Little Prelude in D minor* (Wilhelm Friedemann Bach
Büchlein)

The transient skips marked by asterisks here are not part of the bass progression. In this case the bass figure as a whole imitates the soprano of the first
two measures.

The accented passing note frequently conceals the actual progression since it momentarily displaces the bass note. An example follows.

example 506. BACH: *Chorale, Ihr Gestirn', ihr hohlen Lüfte*

Two forms of notation are used in Example 506 to indicate the accented passing notes. In the first measure the slant marks the accented passing note; the actual bass note which follows is figured. In the second measure the dash following 5 means that the notes above the bass remain unchanged. These are much simpler procedures than figuring the intervals upward from the accented submetrical passing note as though it were the real bass note. Only if an accented passing note in the bass has full metrical value are the intervals above it figured, for example, the linear passing chord $\frac{5}{2}$ which displaces a 6th chord. (See Appendix 1, Summary of Figured Bass.)

234. Embellished Suspension Resolutions

Section 194 examined resolutions that are interrupted by embellishments. More extended submetrical embellishments such as those under discussion in the present chapter sometimes delay the resolution to an even greater extent than those shown there. In the next example an arpeggiation intervenes between suspension and resolution. As a result both suspension and resolution are stated only as sixteenth notes. Of course they are implicit in the chords, as indicated by dotted lines in the illustration.

example 507. BACH: *Prelude in F minor, WTC II*

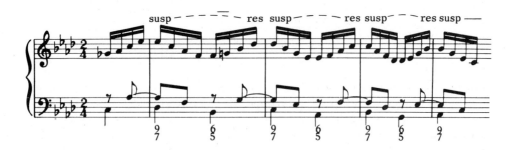

This passage contains a further complexity caused, in this case, by harmonic development. The $\frac{9}{7}$ suspension chord normally resolves to a 6th chord. Here both bass and harmony change before the upper voice resolves.

Another instance of delayed resolution is quoted below.

example 508. SCHUBERT: *Die liebe Farbe*

The suspended 9th in the third measure does not resolve immediately as do the submetrical suspensions in the second and fourth measures. Instead, the soprano skips down to an inner voice and returns to resolve the suspension only on the last sixteenth note in the measure.

235. Parallel 5ths Involving Submetrical Embellishments

The following example contains parallel 5ths between soprano and alto as marked.

example 509. Chorale: *Ach lieben Christen, seid getrost* (after Bach)

However, one of the notes involved is a submetrical auxiliary note and therefore the parallelism does not affect the harmonic succession. Such 5ths (or 8ves) are called *5ths by embellishment* to distinguish them from *voice-leading 5ths* which involve metrical notes essential to the progression.

Composers differ in the extent to which they tolerate parallelisms of this kind. One finds occasional examples even of parallelisms involving metrical embellishments, such as the two passages that follow.

example 510. MOZART: *Piano Sonata in C major, K.279*

The parallel 5ths between the outer voices here are not voice-leading 5ths. As indicated, F♯ is an auxiliary note which embellishes the actual harmony note, G.

In the next passage the parallel 5ths are the incidental result of transient skips below the actual bass progression E-F-G.

example 511. BEETHOVEN: *Piano Sonata in C major, Op. 2/3*

A rare case of voice-leading 5ths is quoted below

example 512. BACH: *Chorale, Herr, wie du willst*

EXERCISES

A. List of Some Important Terms to Define and Memorize

Motive

Theme

Figuration

Augmentation

Diminution

Inversion

Complete auxiliary-note pattern

Incomplete auxiliary-note pattern

Secondary auxiliary note

Concealed passing note

Obligatory chromatic auxiliary note

B. Preliminary Keyboard Exercises

These exercises are of two types: (1) sequential progressions and (2) short figured basses. In both cases the soprano is to be embellished and, if possible, the bass. The first exercise is worked out in some detail to demonstrate the procedure.

exercise 245.

(a) An unembellished realization, beginning from the soprano position of the 3rd, but incorporating the line which begins from the soprano position of the 5th:

(b) Passing notes fill the skips in the soprano:

413

(c) Passing notes fill bass skips in imitation of soprano:

(d) Soprano of chords on even beats embellished by submetrical skips:

(e) Auxiliary notes embellish submetrical skips and submetrical skips added to chords on odd beats:

(f) Auxiliary notes embellish submetrical skips on every beat:

(g) Passing notes fill skips on even beats while bass of odd beats is embellished by combination auxiliary and passing-note motive:

(h) Beginning from the soprano position of the 8ve a bilinear melody is created by ascending skips:

(i) On the odd beats passing notes connect the two lines; submetrical skips occur on the even beats:

(j) Compare this further embellishment with (e):

*Skip necessary to avoid impending 8ves brought about by the submetrical embellishment.

(k) Beginning from the position of the 5th we obtain the descending line which was incorporated in the melody at (a):

(l) Upper auxiliary notes embellish the soprano progression while the bass is embellished by the motive used at (g) and by a new motive which moves within a 3rd (filled transient skip):

exercise 246. **Sequential Progression in Major**

exercise 247. **Sequential Progression in Minor**

exercise 248. **Sequential Progression in Major**

exercise 249. **Sequential Progression in Minor**

exercise 250. **Sequential Progression in Major**

exercise 251. **Figured Bass. (Mattei)**

exercise 252. **Figured Bass. (Corelli)**

exercise 253. **Figured Bass. (Mattei)**

C. Embellished Melodies to Harmonize

INSTRUCTIONS

The first step in harmonizing an embellished melody is to analyze it carefully until the relation between the basic metrical soprano line and the submetrical embellishments is clear. Minimal harmonization of the metrical soprano is the next step. The usual procedure can be followed thereafter, except that one should consider possibilities for introducing submetrical harmonies—especially if the tempo is slow.

Other styles of accompaniment and figuration can be used now. In almost all cases specific styles have been suggested. Parallel 8ves sometimes occur between the accompaniment and the soprano in these freer styles. These are acceptable if the bass is not involved. Avoid parallel 5ths between any pairs of voices.

exercise 254. *German Folk Song*

exercise 255. *Italian Folk Song*

exercise 256. *Swedish Folk Song*

exercise 257. *Swedish Folk Song*

exercise 258. *English Folk Song*

exercise 259. HANDEL: *Andante*

Andante

Adagio

exercise 260. J.A. HILLER: *Du süsse schöne Rose*

Moderato

D. Longer Figured and Unfigured Basses

INSTRUCTIONS
Each bass is to be realized as an embellished solo melody for treble instrument or voice with four-part continuo accompaniment. Until one achieves fluency it is wise to limit the ratio of submetrical to metrical melodic notes. Embellishments which move 2:1 against the metrical unit should be worked out before attempting 3:1 or 4:1.

In all cases the motivic aspect of melodic development should be heeded so that the detail has both consistency and clarity. Motives and themes must articulate harmonic groups and coordinate with the metric-rhythmic pattern. If they establish independent patterns the result will be loss of coherence. Thus it is important to mark off the harmonic units, large and small, and take care that the melody does not run past or fall short of them.

Since compound melody is usually the most difficult to construct, it should not be attempted until a certain degree of facility with single lines has been attained.

A final admonition: However attractive its submetrical embellishments may be, the effectiveness of a melody ultimately depends upon its basic metrical structure. In this regard Kirnberger has written:

The true basis of beauty in an aria [embellished melody] always lies in the basic melody which remains when all notes which belong to the embellishment have been taken away. If this is incorrect with respect to declamation, progression, or harmony, the errors cannot be concealed by embellishment.

exercise 261. **Passacaglia bass (after Handel)**

At least five solo soprano voices should be written as variations upon this bass and harmony, beginning with slow note values and becoming progressively faster with each variation.

Bear in mind here and elsewhere that since the continuo carries the complete harmony the soprano will inevitably double one of the continuo voices at the 8ve. This is perfectly normal. The only doubling prohibited is 8ve doubling of the bass by the soprano.

exercise 262. **LOCATELLI**

After the fundamental version of the continuo has been worked out, embellishments can be introduced into its soprano voice. These may double the solo soprano at the 3rd or 6th, may imitate the embellishments of the solo soprano, or otherwise enhance the progression of the solo part.

exercise 263. BACH

The slants in this exercise, for example in the eighth measure, indicate accented passing notes in the bass. The chord which belongs to the next bass note is to be played over the accented passing note in such cases so that, in effect, the chord precedes its bass note. (See section 233.)

exercise 264. PURCELL: *Elegy on the Death of Queen Mary*

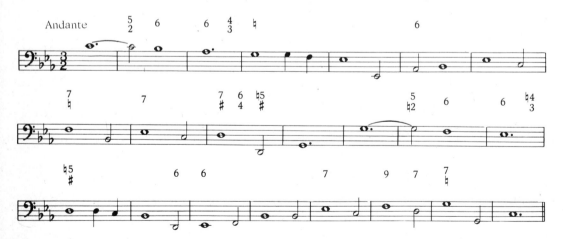

exercise 265. TELEMANN: *Partita in G major*

exercise 266. VIVALDI: *Sonata for Violin and Continuo in G major*

exercise 267. HANDEL: "arioso" (*Rodelinda*)

Largo

exercise 268. HANDEL: *Sonata for Violin and Continuo in A major*

13

Large-Scale Arpeggiations, Passing and Auxiliary Notes

The arpeggiation of a chord remains a harmonic event, despite its successive nature. The passing note, in contrast, is a melodic event, always dissonant, even though through transformation it may be expressed as a consonance. The same holds for the auxiliary note. . . .

Schenker (*Tonwille*)

236. Introduction

In Chapter 12 the various functions of arpeggiations, passing notes and auxiliary notes were discussed and illustrated. It was shown that these procedures serve to develop or expand musical content. This development of content occurs not only in short spans of music, such as those given in the examples of Chapter 12, but also—and more importantly—in larger musical contexts. The present chapter develops this basic concept.*

---

*Although the influence of Heinrich Schenker is apparent in other portions of the present volume, it is most explicitly evident in this chapter. The author's indebtedness, which extends over a period of many years, is gratefully acknowledged.

237. Arpeggiations of Longer Span

Of the three basic procedures, arpeggiation in the upper voice is perhaps the least common within the entire repertory of tonal music, with respect to occurrences of longer span. Two examples are given below.

example 513. CHOPIN: *Nocturne in C minor, Op. 48/1*

The full notation of the opening of a work by Chopin is shown in Example 513 at (*a*). The reduction at (*b*), which omits much of the detail, reveals a long arpeggio that descends from the opening melodic note, G. When the arpeggio reaches C, the bass and harmony change, bringing in the dominant preparation VI, followed by II^6, then V, as shown. Thus, with the unfolding arpeggio there is a corresponding development of the harmony as well. To sum up, the structure of this passage may be described as a *prolongation* (Schenker's term) of the tonic harmony, with G as the main structural note in the upper voice.

example 514. BACH: *Sinfonia 15, BWV 801*

(b)

(c)

Whereas Example 513 shows an arpeggiation of large scale, each component of which is supported by auxiliary notes or skips, Example 514, from the last of the so-called three-part inventions, shows arpeggiations over two different spans. Each beat (dotted eighth note) carries an arpeggio, while just below the surface of these obvious patterns (*a*) is projected an arpeggiation of longer span, as shown at (*b*). The observant reader will notice that this latter arpeggiation is brought about by the subdivision of the six-note pattern into groups of two—an instance of *hemiola*.

As in Example 513, the arpeggiation in Example 514 prolongs the tonic triad. In the latter instance, however, the main upper voice note is clearly the third of the triad, as shown in Example 514 at (*c*). (Compare Example 517.)

Although arpeggiation is only infrequently the underlying structure over longer spans in the upper voice, it is commonly found in the bass, where it serves to unify sections and even complete movements. Example 515 provides a typical instance from the rondo movement of Beethoven's *Pathetique* Sonata. The large-scale bass motion progresses from I (Theme 1) to III at m. 25. The mediant harmony is then prolonged through the statement of Theme 3, with the dominant returning before m. 62 to complete the arpeggiation and prepare the return to I at m. 62. The example also provides an illustration of a large-scale auxiliary note in the bass, corresponding to the prolonged VI that serves as dominant preparation.

example 515. BEETHOVEN: *Piano Sonata in C minor, Op. 13,* Third Movement

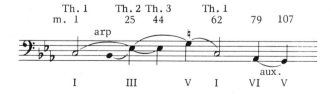

238.   The Passing Note over Longer Spans

It is probably safe to say that every well-constructed tonal composition employs the passing tone to create longer unified spans of music. It operates over the longer span just as it does in the detail of the music: connecting two "more important" notes. Another, and perhaps better, way of saying the same thing is that the passing note fills an intervallic space and performs a connective function. Example 516 illustrates.

example 516.   BEETHOVEN: *Piano Sonata in C minor, Op. 10/1,*
Second Movement

In the upper voice of the first two measures we see that A♭, scale degree 1, is prolonged by means of the descending third, C-A♭. (Compare (a) and (b).) In the next two measures the upper voice prolongs the large-scale passing note B♭, scale degree 2, again by means of a descending third. The ascending motion is concluded on the downbeat of m. 5, as the upper voice reaches C, scale degree 3, harmonized by the tonic triad. The essential motion is shown at (c): the entire first phrase consists of the ascent from scale degree 1 (A♭) through the passing note B♭ to scale degree 3 (C).

In the present chapter we shall concentrate on the passing note as a connector that fills out a consonant interval, as in Example 516. The passing note can also operate within a dissonant interval, but this type of motion involves a different level of structure, as will be evident in the discussion of Example 518.

Example 517 is similar, in its application to the motion of longer span, to the passage shown in Example 516.

example 517.   BACH: *Sinfonia 15, BWV 801*

Here the right-hand part consists of a compound melody, the upper voice of which carries a line that ascends from scale degree 1 (B) through the passing note C♯ (scale degree 2) to the melodic goal, scale degree 3. The lower component of the compound melody consists of the sustained F♯, embellished by its upper auxiliary note, G. The latter embellishing motion is shown in parentheses here to signify that it does not affect the melodic progression of longer range—the ascent from B to D. A condensed version of the basic structure is shown at (c). The melodic goal, D, in Example 517 is the note which is then prolonged by the arpeggiation, as shown in Example 514.

The two previous examples of passing notes involved an ascent to the main melodic note through a passing note that traversed the interval of a 3rd. In contrast, the next example, Example 518, shows a motion that prolongs the main melodic note, C, by a descent through the passing note B♭ to scale degree 3.

example 518. MOZART: *Piano Sonata in C major, K.279,* Second Movement

The summary of the over-all motion at (*c*) shows the simplest version of the basic progression, while the analytical representation at (*b*) provides more detailed information. Perhaps the most important aspect of (*b*) is the descent from B♭ to E (m. 2–3), indicated by notes with downward stems. This is a motion that traverses a dissonant interval, namely, the tritone formed by the 7th and the 3rd of the dominant-7th chord, a motion that serves to prolong the large-scale passing note B♭. Notice that, within the line that descends from B♭ to E, A is a passing note. Further, that A is supported by an F-major triad. This triad, however, is not a functional tonic; to label it as such would be incorrect in terms of harmonic progression, for the direction here is toward V⁷, through II⁶.

A secondary, but significant aspect is the exchange of voices indicated by the crossing lines in (b) at m. 3. (See section 241.) Here the exchange clearly supports the reading of an implied A, indicated by parentheses, in the soprano at the close of the passage.

Thus far, we have seen examples of passing notes filling out intervals of the 3rd and 5th. The next example, Example 519, shows the passing note within a still larger interval, the 6th.

example 519. CHOPIN: *Waltz in C♯ minor, Op. 64/2*

(c)

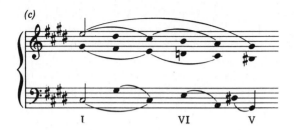

At this point the reader should be capable of reading a notational display of this kind. A few comments are perhaps in order, however. The prolongation of E in the upper voice through a descent of a 6th to G♯ traverses the corresponding descending minor-scale segment; at m. 6, however, the chromatic passing-note B♯ occurs in order to permit mm. 5 and 6 to replicate mm. 1 and 2. That is, only the chromatic note B♯ is available as a passing note connecting C♯ and B. The only interruption of this descending pattern occurs at mm. 3—4 and 7—8, and consists of the skip to the inner voice in each case. As shown at *(c)*, the harmonic progression corresponding to the descending 6th is a progression from I to V, and the latter is prepared by VI. More specifically, the first 3rd, from E to C♯, unfolds over the tonic triad, with V^7 as a passing chord. The next 3rd, from C♯ to A, corresponds to the progression to VI through its dominant. The final motion to G♯ coincides with the change of bass and harmony to V. At this point, as shown in *(b)*, the parallel octaves of the outer voices are broken up by the 5th which is formed by the bass skip to D♯, producing the outer voice pattern 8-5-8. One other detail should perhaps be pointed out: the elegant ascending passing motion from E to A in the inner voice mm. 5—8, which coincides with the upper-voice motion from C♯ to A.

A final instance of passing notes over a long span of music is provided in Example 520.

example 520.   BACH: *Twelve Short Preludes, No. 1, BWV 924*

(a)

(b)

(c)

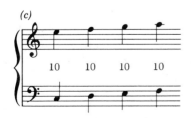

At (c) the fundamental progression is shown: an ascending line in the upper voice, accompanied by the bass moving in parallel 10ths. The connection from G to A in the upper voice is prolonged, as shown at (b), by a secondary prolongational line, the onset of which is signaled by the change in bass pattern in m. 3. This descending line brings in the final note of the pattern, A, an octave lower than the register established in the upper voice at the beginning of the piece—an instance of *transfer of register* (after Schenker).

Before proceeding to the next section, the reader should take time to convince himself that the detail shown in Example 520 at (a) reduces to the more fundamental structure shown at (b). This may also be regarded, in part, as a review exercise in suspensions (Chapter 10).

239. The Auxiliary Note over Longer Spans

In this section instances of prolonged auxiliary notes will be presented and discussed. First, however, let us consider an example of an unprolonged auxiliary note.

example 521. CHOPIN: *Waltz in F minor, Op. 70/2*

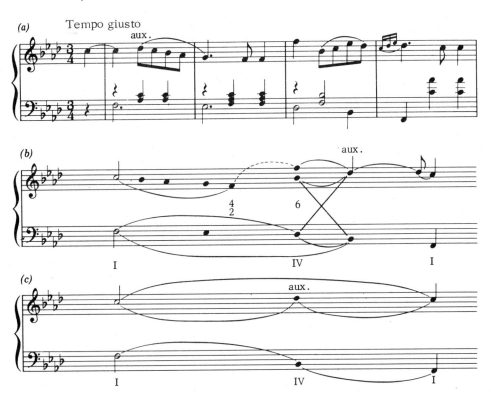

In the excerpt from the Chopin Waltz provided by Example 521 the auxiliary note is introduced in a somewhat complicated way. The analysis shown at (b) is intended to clarify the situation. Following the initial prolongation of C in the upper voice by means of a descent to F over $\frac{4}{2}$ there is an exchange between bass and soprano that brings the auxiliary note Db into the soprano voice. Although the exchange, as well as the transfer of register of F, may be regarded as prolonging the auxiliary note (in the manner of a preparation), once stated, the auxiliary note resolves immediately. The simplest version of the passage is shown at (c). It is important to notice that here, and in many such instances, the harmonically supported auxiliary note (m. 3) is an enlargement of shorter auxiliary notes (m. 1 and m. 4).

Subsequent examples all deal with prolonged as distinct from the unprolonged auxiliary note shown in Example 521.

example 522.   BRAHMS: *Variations on a Theme by Haydn, Op. 56*

The middle section of a well-known composition is given in full notation at (a) in Example 522. The analysis at (b) shows, first, an ascent from the inner voice F over V to the upper voice D over I. The auxiliary note Eb then enters and is prolonged through the descent to A. Here it is essential to realize that the upper voice D in m. 16 is a passing note in the descending prolongational motion and does not represent a resolution of the auxiliary note. The resolution occurs only with the return of D over the tonic harmony at the restatement of the main melodic theme in m. 19. As in the Chopin example (Example 521), the auxiliary note is an important motivic component of the music, and, indeed, is perhaps the most prominent melodic feature of the upper voice at the opening.

As a final example of the auxiliary note over a long span of music, Example 523 presents an analysis of the opening section of Bach's Two-Part Invention in D minor.

example 523. BACH: *Inventio 4, BWV 775*

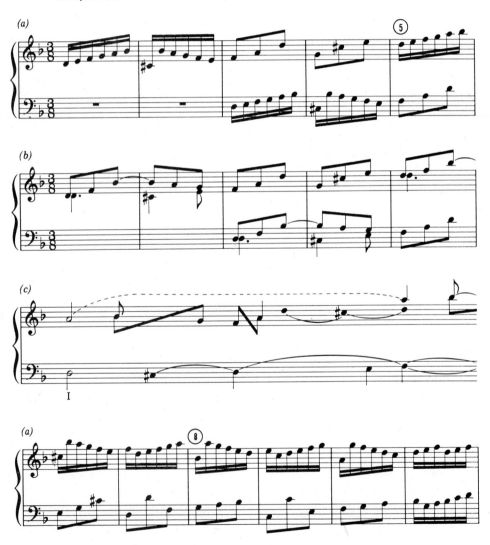

Because of the complexity of the music, the analysis is presented in four stages. At
(*b*) is shown a metrical reduction of (*a*). The reader's attention is directed to m. 8,
where the transfer of register of B♭ (*a*) is undone, so to speak, in (*b*). The same
analytical operation is performed at m. 12 and m. 14 in order to show the long-
range progression in the upper voice more directly.

The analysis at (*c*) interprets the structural relations. The music begins with
a prolongation of A in the upper voice through its upper auxiliary note, B . This is
a small-scale prolongation of the auxiliary note, subsequently to be repeated,
which prepares the long-span prolongation that begins in m. 8. The beams connecting B♭ to G and F to A here represent what Schenker calls an *unfolding:* a motion
to an inner voice and back out again.

The large-scale prolongation of the auxiliary note B♭ is shown in detail at (*c*)
beginning in m. 8. First, however, the reader's attention is directed to the condensed version of the melodic and harmonic progression as shown at (*d*). There
the auxiliary note is introduced over the progression from II to V^7 of III, so that
the return of the auxiliary note to the main note coincides with a change in harmony from I to III.

The details of the prolongation can now be read from (*b*). The prolongation
consists of the descending bass progression G (II^7) to C (V^7) and the linear intervallic pattern (section 220) 10-7-10, as a result of which the upper voice moves in
10ths with the stepwise bass until it reaches F (m. 14). At that point B♭ is brought
in in the upper voice once more and immediately becomes the 7th of V^7 (m. 15).
Once again there is an unfolding down to G and out to A, as in mm. 1—3 and
5—7, and the auxiliary note B♭ resolves to an implied A on the downbeat of m. 18.

EXERCISES

A. List of Some Important Terms

Prolongation   Transfer of register
Prolongational line   Unfolding

B. Analyses

The following excerpts from compositions are to be analysed for arpeggiations, passing notes, and auxiliary notes, with special attention to large-scale structures such as those illustrated in the foregoing chapter. The student should endeavor to show more than one stage (as in the chapter examples) in order to clarify his reading. In some cases either the beginning of the analytical representation is given to aid the student in starting out correctly or a hint is given in order to avoid a misreading of the structure.

exercise 269.   HANDEL: *Sonata for Flute and Continuo in E minor, Op. 1/1*

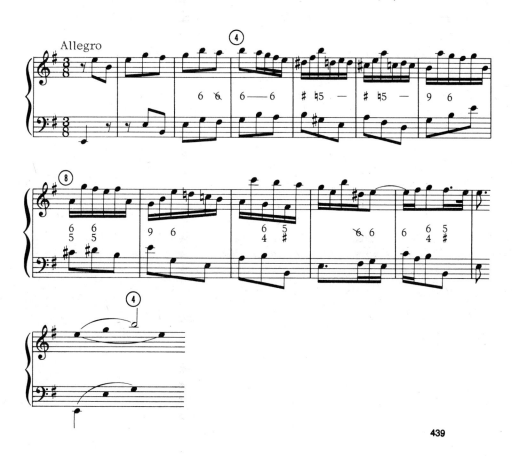

exercise 270. BEETHOVEN: *Piano Sonata in C major, Op. 53* ("Waldstein"), First Movement

exercise 271. MOZART: *Piano Sonata, K.282,* First Movement

Notice that the upper voice motion E♭-D (mm. 1–2) does not interfere with the basic progression of the upper voice. Those notes merely follow the bass progression C-B .

exercise 272. MOZART: *Eine kleine Nachtmusik, K.525,* First Movement

Be sure to take into account the fact that the F♯ in the upper voice at the cadence is a temporary displacement of E ($^6_4$), and that therefore the main note in the upper voice at that point is E.

exercise 273. HANDEL: *Air* from the *Suite in E major*
                   ("Harmonious Blacksmith")

This passage features a prolongational line (passing notes) as well as an auxiliary note.

exercise 274. **BACH:** *Brandenburg Concerto V, BWV 1050,* First Movement
(Soprano and continuo only)

This famous opening utilizes the passing note as well as arpeggiations. One obvious
occurrence of the latter is evident in the upper part.

exercise 275. **HAYDN:** *Piano Sonata in F major*

It is advisable to make a metrical reduction of this first—i. e., reduce to three
quarter notes in each measure. This excerpt contains arpeggiations over two different time spans, as well as an instance of transfer of register and a somewhat
concealed exchange of voices.

14

Multiple Melodic Development

For as so many men, so many minds, so their inventions will be divers and diversely inclined.

Thomas Morley, 1597

By *multiple melodic development* we refer to the simultaneous and extended embellishment of two or more voices. This kind of embellishment typifies many tonal compositions. Although we shall concentrate on one style of composition here, the figurated chorale of the Baroque period, the principles and techniques to be discussed are relevant to other styles as well, for they reflect a general concept of structural development that spans the entire tonal period.

240. Chorale Figuration

Chorale figuration is practiced at several levels of complexity. All involve orderly and sustained melodic development under the control of harmonic progression and in accord with the principles of voice leading. Clarity of rhythmic structure is the hallmark of the chorale figuration. Let us consider examples of two different levels of melodic development in that style—first the relatively uncomplicated chorale phrase below.

example 524.   BACH: *Chorale, Lobt Gott ihr Christen, allzugleich*

This excerpt illustrates well two characteristic features of chorale figuration. First, it contains a single motive which is used consistently throughout. In this instance the motive is derived from the chorale melody itself (brackets). Second, it exhibits perfect rhythmic clarity. The motive begins in the alto, passes to the tenor, which is then joined by the bass. The tenor then continues alone, to join with the soprano at the close of the phrase. Rhythmic continuity is provided by the overlapping of each motivic statement on the next.

A much more elaborate figuration of the same chorale phrase is given in Example 525.

example 525.   BACH: *Chorale-Prelude, Lobt Gott, ihr Christen*

This extract is typical of the short chorale-prelude. It features a distinctive embellishment carried in the inner voices. The soprano carries the melody, and the bass has its own figuration. With melodic elaboration of this kind, particularly the embellishment of the bass, the harmonies of the original chorale setting are modified to a considerable degree. Here almost every triad of the original is replaced by a 6th chord.

Some of the detailed problems in chorale figuration will be considered in connection with the exercises. At this point we turn to certain general aspects of multiple melodic development.

241. Representative Kinds of Linear Interaction

The embellished voices may combine in various ways. Often they move in parallel 3rds, 6ths, or 10ths. All three of these parallel patterns are illustrated in the following excerpt.

example 526. BACH: *Chorale-Prelude, Lob sei dem Allmächtigen Gott*

When two voices move in contrary motion traversing the same interval we call their interaction an *exchange of voices.* Three such exchanges occur in the following example.

example 527. BACH: *Chorale, Herzliebster Jesu, was hast du verbrochen*

The diagonal lines in Example 527 indicate the voices involved in the exchange. Since the voices traverse the same interval, but in opposite directions, they literally do exchange positions.

Exchange of voices is a valuable technique for obtaining melodic motion within a harmonic interval. It is found in many styles of composition, often disguised by embellishments, as in the passage quoted below.

example 528.   BRAHMS: *First Symphony*

If an exchange of voices occurs in the same register, the voices cross and momentarily exchange registral positions as well:

example 529.   BACH: *Fugue in G minor WTC I*

Immediately after the exchange here the soprano returns to the upper register, thus restoring the normative arrangement of the voices. A more elegant type of exchange is shown in Example 530. Here the voices interchange in successive measures, creating the intervallic pattern 6-6 10-10. This is by no means an isolated instance of this pattern, for it occurs throughout the instrumental and orchestral repertory.

example 530. MOZART: *Piano Sonata in A minor, K.310,* Third Movement

(a)   Presto

(b)

A special kind of chromatic interaction between two voices is called *cross relation.* This term refers to the successive statement in different 8ves of a diatonic note and its chromatically altered form. An example follows.

example 531. BACH: *Fugue in C minor, WTC I*

This passage contains a series of cross relations indicated by asterisks. Normally the diatonic note and its chromatic form would occur in the same voice. When they are distributed between two voices, as here, we still tend to regard the progression in terms of a single line, now expressed in two registers. This is particularly so in the passage quoted since the lower line does actually carry the complete chromatic succession (note dotted lines). In each instance, however, the chromatic note is stated first in the upper voice.

242. The Effects of Multiple Melodic Development On Basic Elements of the Structure

The changes brought about by multiple melodic development are of the same nature as those brought about by development of the single line, with one exception: multiple melodic development often creates submetrical harmonies.

Multiple melodic development may affect the resolution of dissonant chords. For example, the resolution of a bass suspension may coincide with an embellishing motion in another voice that normally would have remained stationary.

example 532. SCHRÖTER

More startling effects are obtained when one voice completes a motive at the expense of the harmony, as in the following passage.

example 533. BACH: *Chorale-Prelude, Wir danken dir, Herr Jesu Christ*

The asterisk in Example 533 marks the point at which the bass completes its motive, creating a 7th chord in place of the expected $\frac{5}{3}$ and carrying the progression through the cadence to the beginning of the next phrase.

EXERCISES

A. Analysis

INSTRUCTIONS
Analyze for the following features:
(a) Characteristic embellishments used
(b) Types of linear interaction
(c) Effects of multiple melodic development on basic elements of the structure
(d) Submetrical harmonies, if any

exercise 276. J.S. BACH: Two Chorale settings of *Wer nur den lieben Gott lässt walten*

The two settings are aligned for comparison. The first is relatively simple, whereas the second approaches in elaborateness the chorale-prelude technique.

B. Figured Chorales to Be Realized for Four-Part Vocal Performance

INSTRUCTIONS

These figured-outer-voice exercises provide preliminary experience in chorale embellishment (and multiple melodic development in general). Each exercise should be notated in full, played at the keyboard, and sung. Here and elsewhere the figures do not indicate the voice that is to contain the embellishment. This will depend upon the disposition of the inner parts in each case. The figures also do not indicate the rhythm of the embellishment, but usually this can be determined without difficulty.

exercise 277. **Chorale:** *Mach's mit mir, Gott* (setting by Rinck)

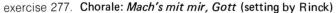

exercise 278. J.S. BACH: Setting of *Gott, wie gross ist deine Güte*

exercise 279. Chorale: *Wie soll ich dich empfangen* (setting by Kühmstedt)

C. Exercises in Chorale Figuration

INSTRUCTIONS

These exercises in multiple melodic development may be notated for performance on a single keyboard, for two-manual organ with pedals, for piano duet, or for an instrumental ensemble of one bass and three treble instruments.

As long as the embellished single line follows the voice leading and satisfies the essential conditions of progression, it can move without restriction. Similarly, two voices can be embellished simultaneously provided each remains clearly under the control of the melodic and harmonic progression.

The only additional limitations apply to the interval succession formed by the embellishments. These are set forth below. When the embellishing voices move together note for note in parallel motion the familiar prohibition of 5ths and 8ves is effective. For example, this sequence should not be embellished in the following way:

And successions of parallel imperfect consonances often change the harmony, as below:

Here the voice in the treble staff moves in 10ths with the bass and brings into play a dissonant note, the 5th, which transforms the original 6th chord into a $\frac{6}{5}$. In this context the change is not incorrect; indeed it enhances the progression and therefore is a genuine development of the harmony. In other contexts a motion of this kind might very well confuse harmonic and melodic progression.

When three embellishing voices move simultaneously they create submetrical harmonies. These are difficult to control, particularly if they move in a ratio greater than 2:1 against the metrical unit since they then obscure the constant underlying harmonic pulse. Consider the effect of the following multiple embellishment:

To demonstrate the procedure for working out the exercises we begin with a four-voice setting of the first phrase of a famous chorale melody: *Alle Menschen müssen sterben*:

It is of the utmost importance that the basic setting be uncomplicated harmonically, as it is here. Minimal use of dissonances should be the rule since they are the products of melodic motion. If we begin with a partially developed setting there are that many less opportunities for active development by submetrical embellishment. If a 7th is already present in a chord it cannot be unfolded melodically. In contrast, consonant settings are "open" and lend themselves to development.

Our first step, then, is to study the setting for specific opportunities to embellish. The skips in alto and bass at the outset and again at the beginning of the second measure suggest the passing note as a basic motive. We begin by embellishing the alto alone:

Merely filling in the available intervals in this way proves unsatisfactory. There is motion, but no distinctive melodic direction. The embellishment is enclosed within a single interval at the very outset and does not suggest a continuation. This brings us to a fundamental principle of chorale figuration and of melodic development in general: In order to exploit more fully the possibilities for figuration one must provide effective interval contexts. This means that a four-voice setting cannot be embellished effectively and yet retain its original form in all respects. One must rearrange intervals or, if necessary, substitute other chords. In the present case we can extend the passing note motive and give it a more interesting progression by changing the doubling of the third chord so as to open another 3rd between alto and soprano:

We must now consider how to continue the figuration. Since it is based upon the passing eighth note which fills the interval of a 3rd, that interval must either be available in the basic setting or it must be made available. A glance at the basic setting, below at (a), tells us that a 3rd is not available in any voice. All voices move stepwise from the third to the fourth chord. The doubling of the third chord cannot be changed without sacrificing the alto figuration, and a change in the doubling of the fourth chord offers no advantage.

At (b), however, we see a solution that maintains the passing eighth-note motion: by submetrical skip the tenor opens a 3rd which is then filled in. With the tenor skip the chord lacks one note, D, on the second half of the beat. This is corrected by the bass, which skips down to D, exchanging voices with the tenor as marked. Beginning on the fourth chord the alto moves in parallel 10ths with the tenor, and the exchange on the first beat of the second measure enables both voices to continue the passing note figuration.

    This somewhat detailed explanation was intended to demonstrate that chorale figuration (and melodic development in general) involves not merely the application of embellishments to given chords wherever they happen to fit, but rather the manipulation of intervals and voice leading so as to *create* contexts for the continuation and development of figuration.

    The following example contains a 4:1 figuration in the alto of the chorale setting discussed above. Compare this with the 2:1 figuration above and observe the changes in voice leading which are required to accommodate this more elaborate embellishment and yet maintain complete harmony.

The asterisk calls attention to a skip in the bass which serves to break impending 5ths between bass and alto. The dissonant F♯ in the alto above it also helps to conceal the 5ths.

Given below are chorale melodies to be figurated. Following these, more difficult figurations are suggested for chorale melodies which are given in full.

exercise 280. **Chorale:** *Dies ist der Tag, zum Segen eingeweihet*

exercise 281. **Chorale:** *Der Himmel jetzt . . . .*

exercise 282. **Chorale:** *Cum luce*

exercise 283. **Chorale:** *Meinen Jesum lass ich nicht* (after Bach)

Remainder of chorale melody:

exercise 284. **Chorale:** *Straf' mich nicht in deinem Zorn* (from Rinck manuscript collection, anonymous)

Since the chorale melody is somewhat concealed by the embellishment in the upper voice, it is given in its entirety below.

exercise 285. Chorale: *Herr Jesu Christ, du höchstes Gut*

exercise 286. Chorale: *Christus ist erstanden*

15

Introduction To Composition in Two and Three Voices

It is far easier to create a harmony in four voices than to condense it into two. . . . and the ability to say much with little does not become completely one's own until he has developed—nor can wine be made until the grapes are mature.

Abt Vogler, 1803

243. Preliminary: Interval and Triad

Before the advent of tonality the interval was the basic structural element in composition; harmonies were formed by combining intervals. For example, the 3rd and the 5th combined to form what we recognize as a triad:

example 534.

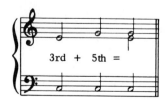

3rd + 5th =

It is important to understand that at that period each of these intervals was regarded as complete in itself, implying no other interval.

During the tonal period the triad, not the interval, became the basic structural element in compositions. Thus, in tonal music an interval does not stand alone; it always implies at least one other interval. For example, the 3rd alone may imply the 5th which completes the $\frac{5}{3}$ or the 6th which completes the $\frac{6}{3}$.

example 535.

$$3 \quad \text{implies} \quad \frac{5}{3} \quad \text{or} \quad \frac{6}{3}$$

Thus the two voices in Example 535 may imply a third note to complete a consonant harmony, as indicated. Obviously, to avoid ambiguity in this instance it would be preferable actually to state the third note. With four-voice harmony there is no difficulty of this kind since complete harmonies can be stated at any point in a progression.

It is possible, however, as indicated in Example 536, to express the complete harmony, either implicitly or explicitly, in fewer than four voices. The present chapter explains how this is done and also indicates the extensive compositional resources which the techniques of two and three voice composition afford. Here will be considered also the special characteristics of compositions in one voice and in five voices, as well as combinations of various kinds, which we will call free textures.

THREE-VOICE COMPOSITION

244. Complete and Incomplete Chords in Three Voices

Let us examine first the ways in which a single consonant chord can be expressed in three voices. These are summarized in Example 536.

example 536.

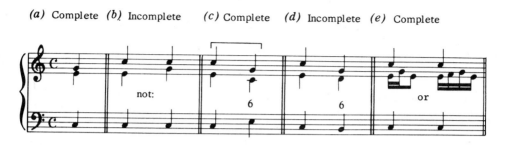

(a) Complete *(b)* Incomplete *(c)* Complete *(d)* Incomplete *(e)* Complete

At (*a*) is the complete triad in three voices. At (*b*) the triad is in the soprano position of the 8ve; therefore it cannot be complete in three voices. Either the 3rd or the 5th must be omitted. Here and in all three-voice consonant triads in the soprano position of the 8ve, the 3rd is included and the 5th omitted. In such cases the 5th must be implied by harmonic context.

The complete statements shown at (*c*) and (*e*) are of most importance to us here. Example 536(*c*) shows that the triad can be stated completely in three voices by metrical arpeggiation. The complete statement therefore requires two metrical units. In an actual composition it may be impossible to retain the same harmony for that duration and a change of harmony may occur, as shown at (*d*). In that situation the missing 5th is clearly implied by the harmonic context.

And finally, turning to Example 536(*e*), we see that a complete statement can be obtained within the metrical unit by submetrical arpeggiation. There the inner voice skips up to add the missing 5th to the harmony.

The foregoing explanation can be summarized as follows:

1   If three voices move metrically (note against note) those notes are extracted from the complete chord which most effectively represent the harmonic progression. Often the progression of the soprano or the progression of the bass may render impossible the statement of the complete chord on each metrical pulse. In that event the missing notes should be implied by the context.
2   If it is desirable or necessary to state the complete harmony this can be done in two ways: by metrical arpeggiation or by submetrical arpeggiation.

Let us now apply this information to the composing of a three-voice chorale setting. Example 537 shows first the four-voice setting which serves as a guide, then three ways in which the three-voice setting may be composed.

example 537.

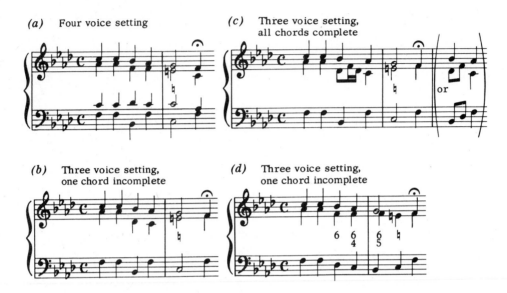

(a) Four voice setting

(b) Three voice setting, one chord incomplete

(c) Three voice setting, all chords complete

(d) Three voice setting, one chord incomplete

Examples 537(a) and 537(b) require no explanation. At (c) the third chord is stated completely by means of submetrical skip. If the bass skips also, as shown in parentheses, the rhythmic pattern of the inner voice is simplified since it need not return to the 3rd (Db) before progressing to C. Example 537(d) shows still another setting. This one uses inversions but no submetrical embellishments. All chords are complete except the $\frac{6}{5}$.

At this point it is evident that three-voice composition always requires careful consideration of the relation between metrical and submetrical notes as they state or imply the harmonic progression. The following sections examine this relation in more detail.

245. Single and Multiple Melodic Development in Three Voices

As in four-voice compositions, submetrical melodic development can occur in a single voice while the others progress metrically, or it can occur in more than one voice simultaneously. The excerpts quoted below in Example 538 illustrate some of the possibilities.

example 538. HANDEL: *Variations on Air in D minor*

(*a*) Four-voice realization of the *Air:*

(*b*) First variation (submetrical embellishment of soprano only):

(*c*) Second variation (embellishment of bass only):

Observe the changes here that the bass embellishment brings about in the original harmony.

(*d*) Third variation (embellishment of inner voice and bass):

In the Baroque trio sonata, which in many respects is an apex of three-voice composition, all voices may develop simultaneously in different rhythms, creating a complex texture such as that illustrated here:

example 539. BACH: *Trio Sonata* from *The Musical Offering*

In this passage, which confirms the modulation to the dominant, may be seen extended and elaborate development in all voices. The underlying four-voice harmonic succession is carried in full by the continuo, as shown by the realization below.

example 540.

246. Bass Arpeggiation to Complete the Harmony

Submetrical arpeggiation of the bass often has the specific purpose of completing the harmony. Instances of this are marked by asterisks in the following passage:

example 541. MARCELLO: *Psalms*

Of particular interest here is the overlapping of the thematic statements in the fourth measure, so that they form a 5th. The bass arpeggiation then completes the triad, adding the 3rd. Note that in every case the 3rd is introduced as quickly as possible—always on the second beat, not on the last.

247.   Dissonant Chords in Three Voices

If it is limited to a single metrical unit and not embellished, the dissonant four-note chord is necessarily incomplete in three voices. The question then arises: which notes should be selected to represent the chord most effectively? Since the bass is essential it cannot be omitted. Therefore only two notes may be selected. The general rule is this: always select the dissonant note or notes in preference to the consonant notes unless special melodic progressions make this impossible (section 248). Consider the II_5^6 at the cadence in the following passage. A four-voice version is supplied at (b) for comparison.

example 542.   PERGOLESI: *Trio Sonata in C minor*

The dissonant note of the II_5^6 is the 5th, which represents the 7th of the parent chord. The note against which it dissonates is the 6th. These two notes together with the bass identify the chord. Other combinations are ambiguous:

example 543.

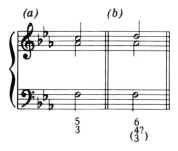

At (*a*) the 3rd is included instead of the 6th. The result is not the $\frac{6}{5}$ but a $\frac{5}{3}$. Similarly, omission of the 5th at (*b*) produces a 6th chord which might imply a $\frac{4}{3}$ as well as the $\frac{6}{5}$. The same principle applies to all the 7th chords.

Three-note suspension chords which displace triads and 6th chords present no new problems since their vertical structures are dependent upon chords of resolution discussed above. For example, the passage below contains a bass suspension which displaces a $\frac{5}{3}$.

example 544. MARCELLO: *Psalms*

In addition to the three-voice suspension chord marked by the asterisk this excerpt contains incomplete diminished-7th chords. The diminished-7th chord can be represented in three voices by bass, 7th, and either 5th or 3rd depending upon the melodic progressions of the voices involved. In this respect the diminished 7th is far more flexible than the other 7th chords, a characteristic discussed earlier.

In three voices suspension chords of four notes are expressed by omitting the note which is not required in the chord of resolution. In the next example the 5th is omitted.

example 545. MOZART: *Piano Sonata in A minor, K.310*

When the duration of the four-note chord is more than one beat it can be stated completely by metrical embellishment or by an inversion which extends the parent chord. In the following example the required dissonant note is brought in by the inner voice just before the change of harmony.

example 546. HAYDN: *Piano Sonata in A major*

(b)

The four-voice version of the passage, shown at *(b)*, reveals more clearly the interaction of the various lines. In the 5 $\frac{6}{5}$ sequence, with which we are mainly concerned here, the tenor introduces the 6th on the last beat of each measure. At the same time the soprano replaces the 5th which the tenor was carrying (note diagonal line). In the actual composition the soprano is displaced by syncopation so that it occurs one half beat later than the tenor, just before the change of harmony in each case.

We have already seen one instance in which the full dissonant harmony was stated by means of submetrical embellishment: Example 538*(b)*, the $\frac{6}{5}$ at the end of the first measure. Another example is given below.

example 547. BACH: *Prelude in D major*

Complete four-note dissonances obtained by submetrical skips are bracketed and figured in Example 547. In each case the essential dissonant note is marked by an asterisk. The + marks a note which belongs to the chords on both beats in each measure and which would still be present on the second beat if the soprano did not suddenly skip away (transient skip) on the last eighth note before the change of harmony.

As an instance of the free treatment of dissonance in elaborate three-voice compositions another passage from Bach's works follows:

example 548. BACH: *Trio Sonata* from *The Musical Offering*

The complete realization of the continuo at (*b*) shows the 7 6 resolution in its normal form, whereas in the violin part the 7th is stated without preparation as part of an ascending arpeggiation and resolved in another register. Both points are marked by asterisks in the illustration.

248. The Influence of Parallel Melodic Lines on Chord Structure in Three Voices

It is a mistake to assume that complete vertical statement of the harmony is the only requirement of three-voice composition. Linear forces also influence the structure of individual chords. We have already seen an instance where the overlapping statement of a motive left the harmony incomplete (Example 530).

Other melodic factors cause similar deviations. Foremost among these are the parallel lines in 3rds, 6ths, and 10ths which are commonly found in three-voice compositions. For example, the best vertical arrangement of the dominant 7th chord retains the 3rd and 7th and omits the 5th. Yet, if the 5th is the main soprano note and if the 7th doubles it at the interval of a 6th below, the preferred vertical arrangement cannot be maintained. An instance of this is shown in the passage below.

example 549.   BRAHMS: *Liebeslieder, Op. 52/9*

The succession of parallel 6ths bracketed in Example 549 clearly represents a linear technique that takes precedence over the vertical structure of the individual chords. A similar situation occurs in the next example.

example 550.   BACH: *Trio Sonata in G major*

Here the $\frac{6}{5}$ of the full harmony (Bach's figures) is represented by a $\frac{5}{3}$ in three voices. If vertical structure were the only consideration this chord should consist of the 6th and the 5th above the bass. Here again the parallel 6ths between the two upper voices take precedence over the vertical structure of the individual chord.

To close this section a familiar example is quoted—a linear chord which results from parallel 10ths in the outer voices.

example 551. MOZART: *Piano Sonata in A major, K.331*

The bass and soprano move in parallel 10ths throughout. Mozart retains this parallel succession even in the third measure where it creates a linear chord, a false 7th chord in this case.

249. The Selection of Appropriate Passing Notes

Submetrical and metrical arpeggiations in three-voice settings are often filled by passing notes. The selection of passing notes is particularly crucial here since an unwanted change of harmony may be implied by the wrong passing note. (See section 232.)

The general rule for passing notes is as follows: they must fill the intervals of the chord without changing its structure and function. Thus the prevailing diatonic scale may serve as a guide to appropriate passing notes—unless a particular diatonic passing note might be assimilated as a note that would change the harmony. This situation is illustrated below.

example 552. HANDEL: *Chaconne with 64 Variations*

(a)

(b)

The C♯ is required in the second measure since the diatonic note C♮ would be assimilated as a chord note and thus change the structure and function of the chord as shown at (b).

Passing notes of course must not contradict dissonant chord-notes and therefore again C♯, not the diatonic C♮, is required in the third measure.

When a minor triad is involved special care must be taken with ascending passing notes. These must follow the pattern of the melodic minor scale, otherwise an unwanted change of harmony will be effected. Consider the situation illustrated in the next example.

example 553.

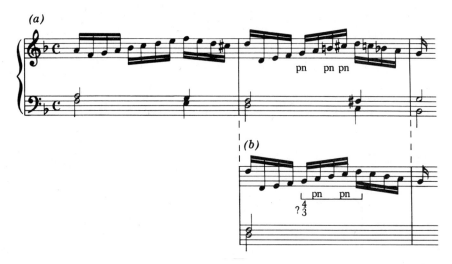

The chromatically altered passing notes at (*a*) belong to the melodic minor scale of D, the chord that is being embellished. If these alterations are not made, there is a strong conflict between harmony and embellishment since the unaltered passing notes imply the change of harmony shown at (*b*).

TWO-VOICE COMPOSITION

The principles of three-voice composition apply to two-voice composition as well. However, the two-voice composition must depend even more upon submetrical arpeggiation (and filled arpeggiation) to state or imply the harmonic progression. In general this means that two-voice compositions are more active rhythmically. Both voices, bass and upper voice (usually soprano), need not be active. Often the upper voice moves slowly against a faster pattern in the bass which fills out the harmony. Or if the bass is unembellished the soprano moves quickly and is usually a compound melody. Examples of three rhythmic relationships between soprano and bass are provided below.

250. Submetrical Bass Arpeggiation against Metrical Soprano

In the example following, the soprano moves almost entirely in metrical durations or larger, while the bass arpeggiates and fills in the harmonic intervals.

example 554. MENDELSSOHN: *Italian Symphony*

(a) Andante

(b)

Example 554(*b*) presents a portion of the repetition of the thematic statement shown at (*a*). The repetition harmonizes fully the two-voice outline of (*b*), even including several submetrical harmonies.

In the following example the lower voice figuration of the chord succession (the familiar Alberti bass) achieves full statement of the harmony.

example 555. MOZART: *Piano Sonata in G major, K.283*

Allegro

The harmony can also be fully stated if the relationship above is reversed so that the soprano is active rhythmically while the bass moves more slowly. This relationship is illustrated in the following section.

251. Compound Soprano against Metrical Bass

Just as a three-voice composition can state four-voice harmony by means of submetrical embellishment so a two-voice composition can state three- and even four-voice harmony by the same means. Kirnberger has provided us with a clear illustration of this.

example 556. KIRNBERGER

At (a) is a two-voice passage in which the bass moves metrically against submetrical arpeggiations in the soprano. Kirnberger tells us that this two-voice passage sounds like the three-voice passage at (b). One of the chords, the $\frac{6}{5}$, is a four-note chord whose 3rd has been omitted. The first chord lacks a 3rd, but is stated fully over two beats.

    Complete statements of four-note chords are achieved by means of elaborate submetrical arpeggiations such as those shown in the following example.

example 557. BACH: *Short Prelude in C minor*

The compound soprano voice at (*a*) states the complete succession shown at (*b*). Only the V⁷ is not given in its entirety. All the other harmonic strands are woven into the melody. In contrast to this a soprano voice may be very active and yet only hint at the changes of harmony, as in the passage below.

example 558. BEETHOVEN: *Fifth Symphony*

Arpeggiation in the soprano voice may occasionally conceal the basic line. For example, the basic line of the following upper voice centers upon the 3rd of the tonic triad. This line is covered by two harmony notes arpeggiated above it. The sketch at (b) reveals the line by rearranging the voices so that the basic line is uppermost.

example 559.   BACH: *French Suite in B minor*

252.   Arpeggiation in Bass and Soprano Simultaneously

If both voices are arpeggiated, each usually has its own rhythm. In the following example the soprano moves in a ratio of 2:1 against the bass.

example 560.   HANDEL: *Suite in F major*

In the second measure of this excerpt the compound soprano includes a suspension. Here and elsewhere the suspension is treated like any other chord note. It may be approached or left by skip but its function in the voice-leading pattern must be fulfilled.

253. Parallel 5ths and 8ves in Compositions of Fewer than Four Voices

There is a venerable rule that says: "The fewer the parts, the stricter the voice leading." It is true that parallel 5ths and 8ves are more exposed in three- and two-voice compositions than in four voices. This is particularly the case if they progress metrically. And since submetrical embellishments may also carry important notes of the harmony, as has been seen, one must take care to see that they do not form parallelisms. This is easily done if compound melodies are consistently regarded in terms of vertical harmonies, in the way demonstrated by Kirnberger (Example 556). The distinction between voice-leading parallelisms and parallelisms by embellishment remains the same as in four-voice composition (section 235).

254. One-Voice Compositions

The term one-voice composition does not include short unison or 8ve passages such as those illustrated in Example 561:

example 561. MOZART: *Symphony in C major, K.551* ("Jupiter")

Passages of this kind are unharmonized lines.

The true one-voice composition is a single voice of compound structure which, harmonically as well as melodically, is self-contained. Seldom is this texture used throughout an entire work. The Chopin *Prelude* quoted below is an exception, for the entire composition consists of a single voice in one hand doubled at the 8ve by the other for reinforcement.

example 562. CHOPIN: *Prelude in E♭ minor, Op. 28/14*

The triple subdivision of each beat here permits a complete statement of the harmony in three voices.

Perhaps the most remarkable one-voice compositions in the musical literature are those for solo violin by J. S. Bach. An excerpt follows.

example 563. BACH: *Sarabande and Double in B minor for Solo Violin*

Example 563(*a*), the *Sarabande,* is played in chordal fashion—insofar as the technique of the violin permits. Example 563(*b*), the *Double,* is an arpeggiated version of the *Sarabande* progression. Like the Chopin example above it is a compound melody which expresses a three-voice structure.

255. Composition in Five Voices

It is important to distinguish between a temporary shift to five voices and extended composition in five voices. For the purposes of reinforcement voices are sometimes added to the normal four-voice texture. Doubling of this kind is the rule rather than the exception in orchestral works, but we find it often in other media also. Here is an example drawn from a keyboard work:

example 564. HANDEL: *Suite in D minor*

The extra voices in this passage have nothing to do with voice leading. Both harmonic progression and voice leading can be fully expressed in four voices as shown at (*b*). Neither have the added voices individual melodic structures; they are merely 8ve duplications of other lines.

Only when the added voices affect voice leading and when they have an independent function do we speak of harmony in more than four voices. Let us confine our discussion here to harmony in five voices since this is the most frequently used number of voices beyond four and since the principles governing larger numbers of voices remain the same as those governing the single additional voice.

Harmony in five voices occurs temporarily in four-voice settings when it is required in order to complete a chord or in order to satisfy the requirements of voice leading and complete harmony at the same time. In Example 565 below, the 8ve soprano position of the $\frac{4}{3}$ requires that an extra voice be added in order to complete the chord and assure stepwise voice leading. In such situations the temporary addition of another part is a valuable technique.

example 565.

The actual composing of five individual voices, called "real" voices, requires constant shifts, alternate doubling, and crossings, in order to avoid parallelisms. This is shown in the following example, which offers a comparison of two almost identical harmonic successions drawn from the same work.

example 566. MOZART: *Quintet in C minor, K.406*
(Last movement: variations)

The four-voice passage (*a*) and the five-voice passage (*b*) are shown in condensed score rather than in the customary open score in order to show more clearly the arrangement of the voices. Slight rhythmic simplifications have been made for the same reason.

The specific instrumental registers are not shown, but doubling and voice leading are exact. The four-voice passage does not require comment. It serves here merely as a basis for examining the five-voice version.

The diagonal lines in the five-voice passage indicate skips that the fifth voice must make in order to avoid parallel 8ves (represented here as unisons). The numbered comments below refer to the numbers between the staves at (*b*).

1   Here the doubling is in the outer voices. Consequently the bass cannot resolve stepwise, in accord with the stepwise resolution of the diminished-7th chord, but must skip down to G. Compare (*a*) at this point.

2   Here the fifth voice skips away from the unison but returns to it immediately.

3   The five voices permit full statement of the cadential succession as well as stepwise voice leading.

256. Variable Texture

A great many compositions consist of what may be called *variable textures,* that is, combinations of four-voice, three-voice, two-voice, and unison passages, with occasional excursions into five voices. Voice-leading principles still apply to these textures but the continuity of individual voices may occasionally be interrupted. Voices are dropped out and added depending upon a number of compositional factors: register, instruments or voices involved, type of progression, position in the progression, and so on. There is one primary restriction upon the abandonment of a voice, however. A voice is never abandoned on a dissonant note, so that the dissonance is left unresolved, nor is it abandoned before it has completed its function in the harmonic progression. Examples of typical variable textures follow.

example 567.   BEETHOVEN: *Second Symphony*

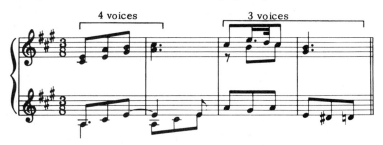

example 568.   BRAHMS: *Intermezzo, Op. 76/6*

example 569.   C. P. E. BACH: *La Stahl*

Often the texture of a work changes by abandoning the bass temporarily. An example follows.

example 570. SCARLATTI: *Sonata in A major*

In many cases the bass may be abandoned for even longer periods while attention is focused on the melodic or rhythmic development of the upper voices. However, the bass is always implicit in such cases.

EXERCISES

A. Melodies to Set in Two or Three Voices with Figuration

INSTRUCTIONS
Beginnings of the figurations are given. Complete the setting in the same style.

exercise 287. **Chorale melody and figurated bass (from Rinck manuscript collection—anonymous)**

exercise 288. Chorale: *Meinem Jesu lass ich nicht* (from Rinck manuscript collection—anonymous)

485

exercise 289.   Chorale: *Jesu, Leiden, Pein und Tod* (from Rinck manuscript collection—anonymous)

exercise 290.   HUMMEL (in classical period style). Extend to a sixteen-measure variation theme, including a modulation to V and return. Write three variations.

exercise 291. HUMMEL (in classical period style). To be used as a basis for a set of three variations.

Each of the following chorale melodies may be set in one of three ways:
1 as a three-voice composition with embellished bass and inner voice
2 as a two-voice composition with embellished bass
3 as a two- or three-voice composition with embellishment in all voices either singly or in combination.

The latter possibility is particularly attractive since by this means the chorale can be transformed into a number of freer forms. The excerpt below indicates the wide variety of styles one can obtain without forsaking the basic harmonic and melodic progression.

First phrase of *Jesu, meine Freude:*

Walther's variation on this phrase:

exercise 292. Chorale: *Dein Heil, o Christ*

exercise 293. Chorale: *Vater unser im Himmelreich*

exercise 294.   **Chorale:** *Wie gross ist des Allmächt'gen Güte*

The folk songs that follow may be arranged for voices in various combinations, for example, tenor and bass, or two tenors and bass (if the melody is transposed to fit the tenor range), soprano-alto-baritone. Embellishment may occur in any voice except the upper.

exercise 295.   **English song:** *All in the Downs*

exercise 296. **Scotch song:** *On a Bank of Flowers*

exercise 297. **English song:** *Thou soft flowing Avon*

B. Basses to Realize as Two- and Three-Voice Compositions

INSTRUCTIONS
These basses are to be realized as instrumental compositions in two or three voices. In addition, one or two may be realized as solo voices with two- or three-voice accompaniment.

SPECIAL ADDITIONAL INSTRUCTIONS FOR THE TRIO SONATA
Those who are more advanced may realize a bass as a trio-sonata movement. It is important to bear in mind that the trio-sonata movement is actually two compositions in one. The two solo voices form a three-voice composition with the bass, and the continuo accompaniment is also complete in itself, usually in four, but possibly in three or in two voices. The solo voices can double any note in the harmony, except the bass, at the 8ve.

exercise 298. BOYCE

Realize as a duet for violoncello and violin

exercise 299. MATTEI

Realize as a trio sonata movement

exercise 300. TÜRK

exercise 301. **LOCATELLI**

exercise 302. **HANDEL**

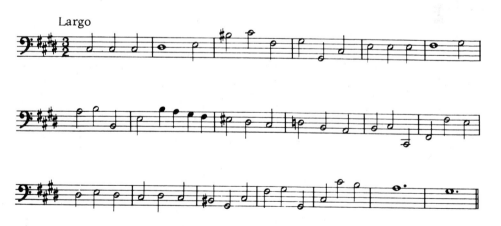

exercise 303.   MARCELLO

exercise 304. C.P.E. BACH

16

Further Techniques of Harmonic Development

Little by little, human reason has suc-
ceeded in understanding all conceivable
harmonic combinations. . . , The entire
harmonic fabric of the composition as
well as the individual parts.

Heinrich Koch, 1802

We may not share Heinrich Koch's confidence in the capability of human reason to understand the artistic products of the human mind, particularly because we are in a position to survey a vast and complex musical development which Koch in 1802 could hardly have foreseen—the period that begins with the mature works of Beethoven and extends through the late works of Brahms.

Nevertheless, in this final chapter we shall examine some of the techniques that characterize the music of that period as well as certain extended practices in earlier periods. All these are techniques which in some way deviate from the normative harmonic and melodic procedures discussed in previous chapters. Although we shall examine both diatonic and chromatic techniques, the latter are of particular interest since they enable us to understand many aspects of the music composed during the last part of the tonal period. For although the resources of chromaticism were sampled earlier, only with Beethoven and his successors were they exploited to achieve harmonic extension on a large scale in ways consistent with the logic of tonality.

496

The techniques to be discussed apply not only to small contexts of a few chords but also to larger contexts, including complete sections of compositions. Accordingly, the chapter is divided into two parts: the first deals with small, the second with larger contexts.

TECHNIQUES COMMONLY APPLIED TO SMALLER CONTEXTS

257. Chromatic Substitution

The chromatic expansion of tonality which characterizes much of nineteenth century music is illustrated in miniature by the substitution of a chromatic harmony for an expected diatonic harmony. This technique resembles the deceptive cadence, which involves the substitution of another diatonic chord for the expected diatonic goal harmony. The following passage contains a clear instance of chromatic substitution.

example 571. WOLF: *Zur Ruh, zur Ruh*

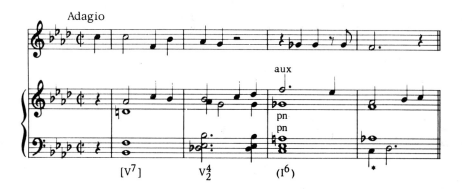

Here a chromatic-appoggiatura chord replaces I⁶, as indicated. In all other respects the passage is normative, with the possible exception of the bass suspension marked by the asterisk (see section 173). Substitution of a single chromatic chord like this of course cannot be regarded as large-scale harmonic extension. In represents linear development which affects only the local context. Of far more importance to the longer span is the substitution of a chromatic consonance, since it may be established as a quasi-tonic and thus extend indefinitely. We shall discuss this harmonic resource in a later section. Here let us consider the substitution of chromatic consonances in small contexts. In the major mode a substitute chromatic consonance often proves to be a triad which has been taken from the parallel minor mode. This process, described below, is called *mixture of mode* or simply *mixture.*

258. Mixture of Mode: a Special Case of Chromatic Substitution

Example 572 surveys the possibilities for the assimilation by the major mode of consonant triads from the parallel minor mode.

example 572.

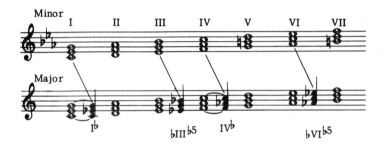

Example 572 shows that four consonant triads from the minor mode may replace their counterparts in the major mode. These we call *chromatic triads by mixture.* The amount of harmonic change wrought by a particular mixture depends upon the extent to which the borrowed triad differs from the triad it replaces. Example 572 shows that in two cases, I♭ and IV♭, only the 3rd of the borrowed triad differs from that of the diatonic triad, while in the other two cases both the fundamental and the 5th differ. (The alteration of the fundamental note is indicated before the Roman numeral.) In the latter cases the harmonic change is far more marked.

Two examples of mixture of mode follow.

example 573. BRAHMS: *Third Symphony*

In the first measure of Example 573 is seen the diatonic upper-auxiliary-note figure, G A G. In the third measure this is replaced by the chromatic figure, G A♭ G and the chromatic auxiliary note is harmonized by the VI from the parallel minor mode. The other chromatic triad in this passage, IV♭, is also taken from the parallel minor mode and also harmonizes the chromatic auxiliary-note A♭.

The second example of mixture in a small context offers a comparison between a diatonic chord and its chromatic substitute, as did Example 573.

example 574. LISZT: *Der du von dem Himmel bist*

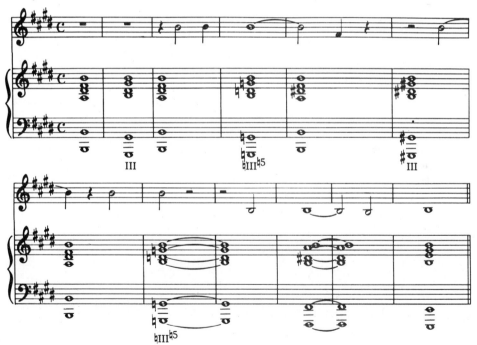

This excerpt contains the III from the parallel minor mode in alternation with the diatonic III. The chromatic substitute finally serves as preparation for the cadential V$^4_3$.

TECHNIQUES COMMONLY APPLIED TO LARGER CONTEXTS

259. Multiple Chromatic Substitution

We have considered examples of chromatic substitution in small contexts. The remarkable effect of extended or multiple substitution is illustrated in the composition below. For study purposes the diatonic harmonies of the variation theme are placed above the chromatic substitutions.

example 575. C. P. E. BACH: *Variation* on *La Folie d'Espagne*

Aligned are: (*a*) variation theme, and (*b*) variation.

Two relations between theme and variation are obvious immediately: (1) the melody of the theme is retained almost intact in the variation; (2) chromatic dissonances are present in addition to the chromatic substitutes. Of most interest to us here are the latter. These mainly involve the primary triads I and III. In

order to preserve the basic tonal outline no substitution was made for V throughout or for I when it occurred at the close of the harmonic unit. Perhaps the most
remarkable aspect of this variation is that, despite the elaborate chromaticism, the
basic harmonic direction of the original is retained. Without exception the substituted chromatic chords or chord pairs have the same direction as the I or the
III they replace. However, in three instances the progression of the substitute is
not completed. At the last moment an irregular resolution of dissonance occurs.
Thus, the $\frac{4}{2}$ in the second measure should resolve to a 6 over bass E; the $\frac{4}{2}$ in the
fifth measure should resolve to a 6 over bass F; and the 7 in the seventh measure
should resolve to a $\frac{5}{3}$ over bass C. Nevertheless, of these three instances only the
first radically affects the harmonic direction of the progression.

260.   Extension from a Diatonic or Chromatic Substitute

The reader is familiar with the substitution of a diatonic chord for an expected
diatonic chord in the case of the deceptive cadence. A more elaborate example
of diatonic substitution occurs in the next example.

example 576.   MOZART: *Symphony in C major, K.551* ("Jupiter")

The two asterisks in Example 576 mark substitutions. At the first asterisk IV substitutes for the expected II⁶, both being dominant preparations. At the second asterisk, VI (prepared by its secondary dominant) substitutes for the expected I. By means of these two substitutions the passage is greatly extended. After Beethoven not only diatonic chords but also chromatic chords were frequently used in this way. A striking example from Brahms is quoted below.

example 577.   BRAHMS: *Sonata for Violin and Piano in A major, Op. 100*

At the asterisk the substitution of the chromatic 6 over E for the expected diatonic 6 serves as point of departure for a long extension, only part of which is shown in Example 577. The relation of the chromatic substitutes to the harmonic axis cannot be demonstrated without quoting a much longer segment of the composition. Over a longer span the main chromatic harmony shown here, the G major triad, proves to be IV of the diatonic IV (D major triad)—an unusual extension of the subdominant relationship.

In the next example the relationship between diatonic and chromatic harmonies is much more easily grasped since both the initial substitution and the chords that follow it are chromatic triads by mixture with the parallel minor mode (E♭ minor).

example 578. BEETHOVEN: *Piano Sonata in E♭ major, Op. 81a*

Still another type of chromatic substitution is illustrated in the next example. In this case the III with a raised 3rd replaces the expected I.

example 579. WOLF: *Bedeckt mich mit Blumen*

The common note G serves as a link between the V⁷ and the substituted chord, III♮, and compensates for the abruptness of the change.

The relation between a chromatic chord and the harmonic axis may not be immediately apparent, as remarked earlier. In this instance we note that chromatic alteration of the 3rd alone, as in Example 579, does not affect the diatonic position or function of a consonant triad (unless the triad then serves as a secondary dominant). We must also distinguish clearly between this kind of chromatic chord (Example 579) and a chromatic chord by mixture. The technique of mixture is not used in Example 579.

261. Elision and Incomplete Progression

Elision affects larger contexts when it occurs where one expects a harmonic goal. Two examples of such elision are contained in the following passage.

example 580. WOLF: *Mignon* (*Kennst du das Land*)

Example 580(*b*) summarizes Example 580(*a*). It shows that the first part of the passage centers harmonically around the F minor triad (VII in the tonality of the song). Resolution to this triad is prepared by the V_2^4 and again by the linear $_2^4$. In both cases the expected chord of resolution is elided. The linear $_2^4$ then proves to be a returning dominant.

262. Nontonic Beginnings

Compositions normally begin with a statement of the tonic triad. Harmonic extension and melodic development follow from that primary element. But particularly in the nineteenth century we find many compositions that begin *in medias res* with chords other than the tonic. Often quite a long passage precedes the statement of the tonic triad, serving as a kind of extended harmonic upbeat. An example from Chopin is quoted below.

example 581. CHOPIN: *Waltz in A♭ major, Op. 69/1*

Again, the harmonic sketch at (b) summarizes. The composition begins with the dominant preparation IV⁶. This chord progresses to another dominant preparation, II⁶, via a linear-6th chord and a passing diminished-7th chord. With the [V⁶₅] the direction toward V becomes even more specific. The V⁷ then arrives (preceded by ⁶₄) and finally the progression reaches its ultimate destination, I, after a harmonic prefix that has spanned seven measures. No sooner is I reached, however, than the prefix begins anew, as can be seen in Example 581(a).

In the example below, the tonic triad receives its definitive statement at the very end of the progression, but occurs in secondary roles earlier. The final chord has two functions. It serves as tonic and simultaneously as V leading back to IV at the beginning of the progression. The augmented-6th chord also has a unique dual role. It stands in place of V and at the same time serves as preparation for the [V].

example 582. BRAHMS: *Fourth Symphony*

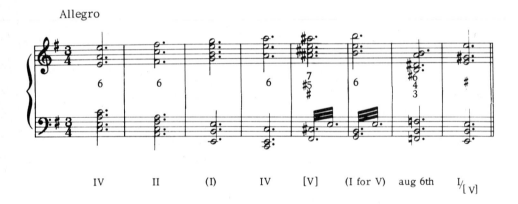

Since its end is simultaneously its beginning this ingenious progression is particularly appropriate to the passacaglia form, which is based upon successive variations of the same harmonic or bass pattern. Each variation carries forward to the next, creating a chain of repetitions. A comparison with the variation theme in C minor by Beethoven (*Thirty-two Variations*) sheds further light on Brahms' unique progression.

example 583.

For easier comparison we have transposed Beethoven's theme to E minor and represented only the most essential harmonic and melodic elements. In many ways it is remarkably similar to that of Brahms. Both span eight measures in $\frac{3}{4}$ meter; both sopranos ascend by step to scale degree 5, and both have the same harmonic goal. Yet no two measures correspond harmonically. The Brahms progression turns on the axis of the dominant preparation IV, while the Beethoven progression unfolds within the more normative succession I V I.

263. Modulation to Chromatic Triads

In Chapter 9 it was seen that any consonant diatonic triad could be established as a quasi-tonic and maintained for a long period without losing its relation to the main harmonic axis I V. Beginning with Beethoven chromatic triads also came to be treated as goals of modulatory progression and established firmly as quasi-tonics. This process, which greatly increased the resources of tonality, was utilized more and more by composers during the last part of the nineteenth century, mainly in longer works but also in short compositions such as songs. In these shorter works such modulations are often incomplete; the goal is prepared but never stated, as in the case of incomplete diatonic modulation (section 167). Similarly, the returning progression may be very brief or absent altogether.

A summary of the modulations to chromatic triads follows. Like the diatonic modulations, certain chromatic modulations offer harmonic and melodic advantages and therefore were favored by tonal composers. Others contain inherent structural problems and were rarely used. So that the chromatic triads may be more easily surveyed we have divided them into three classes, depending upon their relation to the diatonic scale. Each class contains two triads. In the first are two of the four triads by mixture. Included here are only the two triads with both chromatic fundamental and 5th.

We do not include in this summary the two triads with chromatic 3rd alone since as goals of modulation they do not differ significantly from their unaltered counterparts. The harmonic conditions essential for modulation are the same in both cases. In the second class we place the two remaining triads on chromatic scale degrees, ♭II and ♯IV. And finally we include in a special class the dissonant diatonic triads in both modes which become consonant chords by chromatic alteration of the fundamental or the 5th.

example 584. Summary of Consonant Chromatic Triads Available as Goals of Modulation

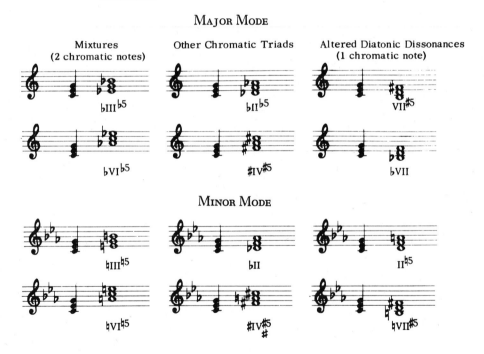

Examples of some of these modulations are given below. We begin with the first class, modulation to chromatic triads by mixture.

example 585. BEETHOVEN: *Piano Sonata in C minor, Op. 13*

With lowering of the 3rd the tonic triad becomes identical in structure to III of the goal harmony, VI from the parallel minor mode. To make the notation more accessible, Beethoven has spelled the VI enharmonically. In A♭ minor, the parallel minor, it would be an F♭ triad. Here he has spelled it as an E major triad to avoid double flats in the other chords that make up the progression. From the standpoint of technique the modulation is conventional. Only the goal harmony is unusual.

The most direct return from ♭VI to I is achieved by converting the ♭VI into an augmented-6th chord. However, for the movement illustrated in Example 585, Beethoven composed the more elaborate returning passage summarized in Example 586 below.

example 586.

The returning V is preceded by a II$\frac{4}{3}$ which belongs to the parallel minor mode, A♭ minor. This chord, in turn, is introduced by a diminished-7th chord which stands in place of a [V$\frac{4}{3}$].

The next two examples show modulations to the chromatic consonance on the tritone, ♯IV. Of all chromatic triads this lies the greatest distance from the tonic, measured in terms of the 5th relation. The problem of effective and coherent returning progression therefore is acute. A different solution is shown in each example.

example 587. BRAHMS: *Requiem* (harmonic reduction, rhythmic pattern not represented)

There is no pivot chord in this modulation to ♮IV. The modulating dominant is related to the preceding chord only by two notes which they hold in common. The returning progression is based on the same connection (asterisk).

This passage is particularly interesting because of its symmetrical harmonic design. It divides into two parts, each of which contains the progression I VI IV V I. The bass descends by 3rds in each part and the over-all progression ends as it began, with the ♮IV standing exactly in the middle.

The modulation to the tritone takes place in two stages in the next example.

example 588. BEETHOVEN: *Piano Sonata in A♭ major, Op. 26* (harmonic reduction, rhythmic pattern not represented)

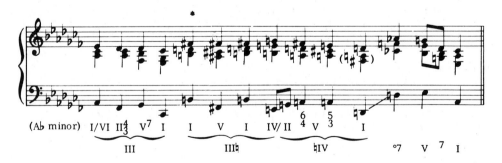

The passage begins with a modulation to the diatonic triad on III, carried out in the conventional way. The 3rd of III is then lowered and the triad is notated enharmonically as a B minor triad. This triad is then extended until its IV is reinterpreted as II, signaling the modulation to ♮IV, as shown by the symbols in Example 584. The return to I is effected by the diminished-7th chord, which represents a [V⁶₅] leading to the V⁷ of A♭ minor, the main tonic.

In Example 588 the altered 3rd of III (asterisk) is the key to the unusual extension, for it provides the pivot chord IV/II. This pivot is not available within the diatonic III, C♭ major.

We come now to two examples of modulation in the third class of chromatic triad, the diatonic dissonance made consonant by chromatic alteration. The goal is the same in both instances, but the techniques of progression differ. First, an excerpt from a work by Hector Berlioz.

example 589. BERLIOZ: *Harold in Italy*

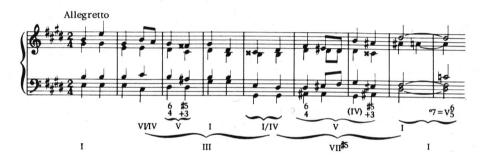

Like the Beethoven example above, this passage contains two modulations. The first is a conventional diatonic progression from I to III, in which VI serves as pivot. The second, which is of most concern to us here, is the modulation to the altered VII. The modulatory technique itself is familiar: the quasi-tonic chord, III, serves as pivot, becoming IV in relation to the new quasi-tonic. The goal of the progression, however, is unusual: the normally diminished triad on scale degree VII which is converted into a minor triad by a change of only one note. The altered note is of course the 5th of the triad. It is raised to change the diminished 5th into a perfect 5th. In Example 589 the return to the main tonic is effected by restoring the diatonic and dissonant form of VII and then adding a 7th. As shown in the example, the resulting °7 serves as a substitute for the returning V⁶₅.

This excerpt demonstrates clearly that no consonant triad, diatonic or chromatic, is far removed from the harmonic axis. If it is distant when measured in terms of the 5th relation, as is the altered VII in Example 589, it is close melodically, when measured in terms of the 2nd relation. We will call this *the principle of proximity.*

The next example of chromatic modulation also provides a convincing demonstration of that principle. In this case the dominant triad itself is the pivot chord, becoming the dominant preparation, VI, in relation to the modulating dominant. The return reverses the relationship: VI becomes the returning dominant.

example 590. SCHUBERT: *Auf dem Flusse*

264. Modulatory Progression without Diatonic Pivot Chord

We come now to another process of development which differs from the norm. As has been seen, diatonic modulations almost always utilize a pivot chord. The present section illustrates three other techniques by which the modulating dominant is prepared.

example 591. Preparation of the modulating V by chromatically altered chord.

SCHUBERT: *Mein!* (accompaniment only)

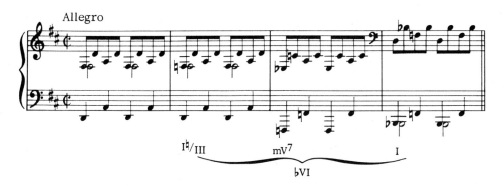

Here the 3rd of the tonic triad is lowered so that it becomes III of ♭VI.

example 592. Preparation of the modulating V by enharmonic reinterpretation of a dissonant embellishing chord.

BEETHOVEN: *Fifth Symphony*

The dominant-7th chord in the third measure at first seems to be an embellishment of a forthcoming IV. Subsequently, however, it is reinterpreted as a German 6th which resolves to the modulating dominant of III♮.

example 593. Preparation of the modulating V by linear chords.

WAGNER: *Parsifal* (orchestral reduction only)

Because of the large number of chromatic embellishments in this passage we have represented the basic harmonic elements in the simplest possible terms. Both the modulating dominant and its preceding secondary dominant are embellished and prepared by complex linear chords.

265. Linear Chords That Assume Harmonic Stability

Linear chords are normally only transient, dependent chords which lack stability and consequently harmonic significance. Occasionally, however, we find that they have been invested with harmonic meaning and that they play important roles in directing progressions. The Mozart passage below contains a linear chord which is reinterpreted as a quasi-tonic chord and extended for many measures.

example 594.   MOZART: *Piano Concerto in A major, K.488*

From the outset the progression is directed toward VI. But at the cadence a linear 6th chord (asterisk) replaces the expected VI. This proves to be more than a temporary delay of the cadence. As can be seen in Example 594 the linear chord is redefined as a quasi-tonic by its own dominant and serves as point of departure for a new section of the piece.

Although the two linear 6th chords marked by asterisks in the following excerpt do not assume as much harmonic significance as the 6th chord in the Mozart passage, Example 594, they do assist in directing the progression, contrary to expectations when they first appear.

example 595.   BRAHMS: *Requiem*

The familiar linear chord, the Neapolitan 6th, is temporarily stabilized by its own dominant in the passage quoted below.

example 596.   BEETHOVEN: *Bagatelle, Op. 126/3*

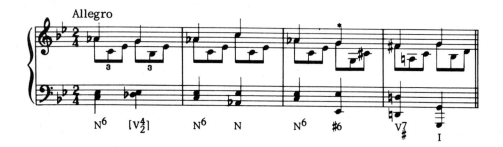

This excerpt also illustrates the quasi-diatonic relationship which can be established between two transient chromatic chords. In this case the $[V^7]$ of N^6 is associated enharmonically with the augmented 6th chord which prepares the main V^7 (asterisk)

266.   Progression by Chromatic Sequence

In the music of Chopin and his successors we often find passages that move chromatically by intervallic pattern, the pattern itself being their sole rationale. Such progressions are essentially nonharmonic in that they do not depend upon the harmonic axis for coherence. (Compare section 220.) A famous instance is quoted below.

example 597.   WAGNER: *Tristan und Isolde*

The second pattern is an exact duplication of the first, pitched a minor 3rd higher. Although the key signature as well as the harmony of the first measure indicate

A♭ major, the chords in the sequence do not express that tonality. The coherence and direction of the progression depend upon the establishment of pattern by repetition, not upon the harmonic axis of tonality.

Another sequence from Wagner is given in Example 598.

example 598.   WAGNER: *Parsifal*

Here again the sequence as well as the chords within each pattern do not contain recognizable harmonic connections. Rather, their meanings lie entirely within the melodic and rhythmic figures and are established by repetition alone without reference to the harmonic axis which controls tonal music.

Procedures such as this foreshadow the abandonment of tonality and the consequent efforts to develop other ways of organizing musical elements, efforts which characterize the whole of music history. Thus in closing let us recall Riepel's words, which perhaps are the best possible final words for a technical book devoted to introducing a single phase of music:

> *Die Musik ist ein unerschöpfliches Meer.*
> (Music is an inexhaustible sea.)

EXERCISES

A. Some Important Terms to Define and Memorize

Chromatic substitution

Mixture of mode

Elision

Multiple chromatic substitution

Incomplete progression

Nontonic beginning

Chromatic modulation

Principle of proximity

Chromatic sequence

B. Analysis

INSTRUCTIONS
1 Label all harmonies and progressions.
2 Identify the technique or techniques exemplified by the passage.

exercise 305. BEETHOVEN: *String Quartet, Op. 18/2*

(The key is G major.)

exercise 306. LISZT: *Credo*

exercise 307. STRAUSS: *Tod und Verklärung*

(Meter, rhythm, and details of voice leading have been omitted in order to present this long excerpt.)

C. Short Chromatic Modulations

INSTRUCTIONS

All these short chromatic modulations have been notated as figured basses. They should be realized in four voices or in free texture at the keyboard, transposed, and supplied with various metric-rhythmic patterns. After the progressions have been analyzed and compared, one from each group should be memorized. In each instance it is assumed that the initial tonic chord has been established by a previous progression. Therefore, only the modulatory progression is shown in full.

The progressions by Mattei are shown in their original form. Both C. P. E. Bach and Albrechtsberger notated their progressions without rhythm, and they are presented in that way here. As a visual aid only, we have notated the point of departure and the goal as half notes, while the modulatory harmonies are shown as quarter notes. These need not be the actual durations, of course.

exercise 308. **Modulation from I to ♭III**

C. P. E. BACH

ALBRECHTSBERGER

MATTEI

exercise 309. **Modulations from I to ♭VI**

ALBRECHTSBERGER

C. P. BACH

MATTEI

exercise 310. Modulations from I to ♭II

MATTEI

ALBRECHTSBERGER

C. P. E. BACH

exercise 311. Modulations from I to ♯IV

C. P. E. BACH

ALBRECHTSBERGER

MATTEI

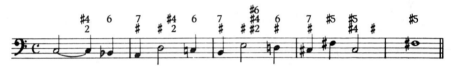

exercise 312. Modulations from I to VII♯5

MATTEI

C. P. E. BACH

ALBRECHTSBERGER

D. Completion Exercises

INSTRUCTIONS

In each case part of a progression is given. You are then asked to complete the progression, following specific instructions. The initial task is analysis of the given part. The extension should then be sketched out over as large a span as possible. This can be done in several ways: by notating the essential harmonies in the form of bass and figures, by Roman numerals, by projecting the outer voices, or by sketching in the soprano voice alone. Working out of the voice-leading details then follows, as in a harmonization exercise.

exercise 313. **From a composition by Wolf, adapted**

Fill in the upper voices in the blank measures and extend approximately eight measures to a close on I; use techniques consistent with those in the given part.

Adagio

exercise 314. **From a composition by Brahms, adapted**

Complete the bass and harmony in the blank measures and extend approximately eight measures to a close on I; use chromatic techniques.

exercise 315. **From a composition by Wolf, adapted**

Beginning with the final chord given here write a passage at least eight measures in length that returns to I by means of chromatic sequence.

exercise 316. From a composition by Chopin, adapted

The metric-rhythmic pattern is not given, although general proportional relations are indicated by the notation. This passage is to be provided with a metric-rhythmic pattern, embellished, and extended harmonically at several points.

exercise 317. From a composition by Schubert, adapted

This composition is in the key of C minor. Metric-rhythmic pattern is to be supplied. Elaborate the given succession melodically and harmonically, then extend it approximately ten measures, using techniques consistent with those given.

(VI)

exercise 318. HUMMEL

Using multiple chromatic substitutes, write at least one variation on this theme.

D. Melodies to Harmonize

exercise 319. LISZT (adapted)

Con moto

exercise 320. **WOLF** (adapted)

exercise 321. **LISZT** (adapted)

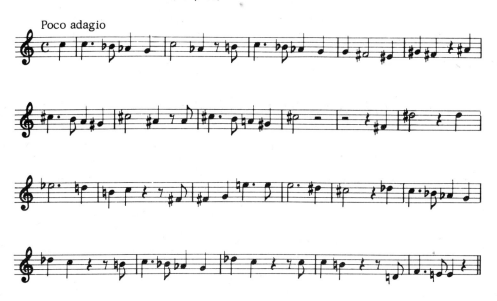

Appendix 1

Summary of Figured Bass

Figured bass symbols indicate precisely the intervals of chords measured upward from the actual bass notes (not from a theoretical "root" of some kind). These symbols consist of numerals, accidentals (either alone or attached to numerals), and a few special signs, such as the dash and the slash.

The conventions of figured bass notation varied from time to time, from country to country, and even from composer to composer within the same country. All the symbols used in this text, however, are to be interpreted consistently as explained in this section. Not all possible figures are included in this summary, but only those that represent types appearing in the examples and exercises.

Before the figures are explained, two important points must be stressed. First, unless an accidental is given as part of the figure, the intervals designated by the numerals in the figure are diatonic. Second, the signature does not indicate how the notes above the bass are to be distributed. To locate the required notes it is convenient to think first of the chord as it would be if sounded in close position above the bass—that is, with the notes of the chord as close together as possible directly above the bass. This arrangement is shown in all the examples that follow, together with a distribution for four voices. The actual distribution in a particular musical setting will of course depend upon the voice-leading context.

Converting a figured bass into a (normally) four-voice musical setting is known as "realizing" the bass. The realization may take the form of a keyboard accompaniment for a solo vocal or instrumental line, a four-voice chorale setting, an instrumental composition, and so on.

When a bass note of metrical value appears without a figure, the figure $\frac{5}{3}$ is understood. That is, the figure specifies notes that lie a 5th and a 3rd, respectively, above the bass: a triad of some kind (Example A).

example A.

When an accidental occurs alone above a bass note with no numeral attached to the accidental, the accidental always refers to the note that lies a 3rd above the bass. It specifies the way in which the note is to be altered.

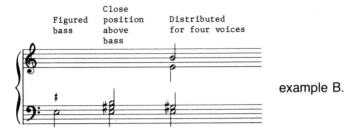

example B.

In Example B the sharp above the bass note E indicates that G, the note that lies a 3rd above E, is to be raised.

When an accidental stands before a numeral, the note designated by the numeral is altered accordingly. Thus, in Example C the sharp before 5 instructs the person who is realizing the bass to raise by one half step the note a 5th above the bass. The natural sign standing alone below the numeral 5 in Example C further specifies that the note a 3rd above the bass is to have that accidental applied to it.

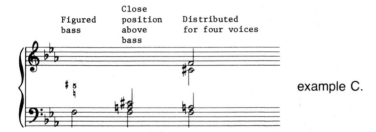

example C.

In a number of cases notes are understood and are to be realized even though they are not figured. (The most extreme case, of course, is the $\frac{5}{3}$ as shown in Example A.) The most common of these are presented below.

The figure 6 implies that the note a 3rd above the bass is to be taken along with the note a 6th above.

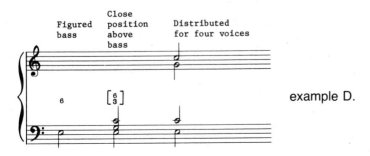

example D.

Notice that here as elsewhere the figures do not provide any information on doubling, just as they do not indicate how the notes of the chord are to be distributed. In Example D the 6th is doubled; however, any of the other notes, including the bass, could be doubled, depending upon the voice-leading context.

The figure $\frac{6}{5}$ also implies the addition of a note a 3rd above the bass. In Example E a chromatic alteration is specified for the note a 6th above the bass, in addition.

example E.

The figure $\frac{4}{3}$ implies the inclusion of the 6th above the bass as well.

example F.

If the 6th above the bass is altered, so that the figure 6 must be included, then the complete figure $\frac{6}{4}_3$ must be given.

example G.

Otherwise the figure would be $\frac{6}{3}$ or $\frac{6}{4}$ and the chords other than the $\frac{6}{4}$ would be specified (incorrectly).

The figure 2 implies that the notes a 6th and a 4th above the bass are also required.

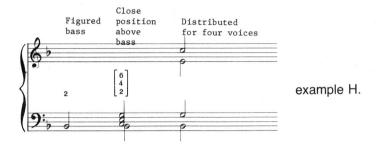

example H.

If the 4th is altered, it must of course be represented as a modified numeral in the figure. And if the 6th above the bass of a $\frac{6}{4}$ chord is altered, then all the numerals must appear, since otherwise the chord would appear to be a ^{6} or $\frac{6}{2}$, both quite different from the intended sonority.

example I.

Notice that the bass note in Example I is itself a chromatically altered note; however, there is no way in which that alteration can or should be indicated in the figures, which always represent intervals *above* the given bass note.

The figure 7 always means that the 3rd above the bass should be included as well.

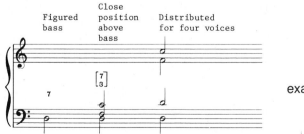

example J.

The figure 7 may imply that the 5th above the bass is to be included along with the 3rd. In Example K it is evident that the 7th chord is associated with the triad on scale degree 7, hence the 5th should be included.

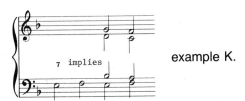

example K.

However, in Example L the 7th has arisen as a suspension displacing the 6th of the subsequent 6th chord. Here the 5th would be redundant and even misleading with respect to the progression, as shown in Example M.

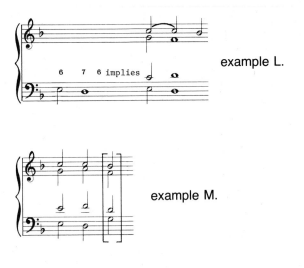

example L.

example M.

That is, in Example M the triad-associated 7th chord over bass D suggests a sequential continuation to a triad-associated 7th chord over bass G.

The figured-bass representation of diminished-7th chords may require multiple chromatic alterations of figures associated with the $\frac{7}{5}$ chord and its inversions. (See section 111, where the relation between the diminished-7th chord and the dominant-7th chord is explained.) Example N will suffice to illustrate.

example N.

If an attempt were made to interpret the figured bass here in terms of Roman numerals, it would appear that a 7th chord was in operation. However, this apparent 7th chord is an elaboration of a $\frac{6}{5}$, as explained in section 111. This voice-leading situation can serve as an effective reminder of the limitations of figured-bass representations. The figured bass symbols give the intervals formed above the bass and, in some cases, information about linear succession. They usually do not provide a correct interpretation of harmonic function and, in fact, may be misleading with respect to chord classification, as in the present instance.

The successive figures 7 6 in Example L are illustrative of a number of common figures that represent actual linear successions in some part above the bass (often the soprano). Other instances are shown in Examples O through R.

Example O shows the way in which the 6 5 succession may be realized. Notice that the 6th (C) is doubled. Since the 6th is consonant, one of the doubled C's can skip away, thus avoiding parallel 8ves. (cf. Summary of Voice-Leading Rules and Guidelines, Appendix 2.)

example O.

The reverse of the 6 5 pattern, 5 6, is shown in Example P.

example P.

When the 5 6 pattern occurs repeatedly over an ascending bass and when the realization must be in four independent voices, alternate doubling must be used in order to avoid either parallel 8ves (unisons) or accented 8ves (unisons). (See Summary of Voice-Leading Rules and Guidelines, Appendix 2.)

The familiar figures 8 7 are shown in Example Q. Notice that the 7th is chromatically altered there.

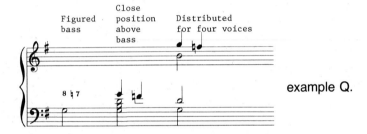

example Q.

The figure 9 8 usually arises in the context of a suspension and, accordingly, belongs in the main discussion of suspension figures below. However, it is introduced at this point in order to explain the peculiar linear succession 9 6. Example R presents a typical occurrence of 9 8.

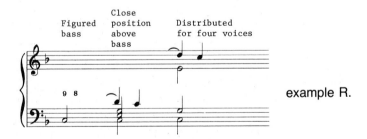

example R.

The linear succession 9 6 (Example S) sometimes causes confusion, since it suggests that a voice skips from a dissonant 9th to a consonant note of resolution, the 6th above the bass. The actual resolution is shown in Example S: as the 9th resolves, the bass ascends a 3rd. Thus, the resolution of the 9th occurs over a chord of the 6th.

example S.

In the following passage, examples of figures that can result from suspensions are given. As will be shown, some of these figures can arise in other ways as well. Since Chapter 10 of the text covers suspensions exhaustively, no attempt will be made here to review all the possibilities. Only representative formations resulting from multiple displacements of notes of the $\frac{5}{3}$, 6, 7, $\frac{6}{5}$, and $\frac{4}{3}$ will be presented together with displacements of the bass notes of those chords by metrical suspensions or by submetrical passing or auxiliary notes.

The following general situation will be recalled. First, when voices other than the bass are suspended, the figures of the resolution are always exactly 1 less than the figures at the point of suspension; for example:

9 8
4 3

Of course, notes that belong both to the suspension and to the resolution are represented by the same figure in both cases. The dash notation, explained below, is used in such situations; for example:

5 —
4 3

(In the case of upward resolving suspensions such as 7 8 or 9 10 the rule is reversed, of course.)

example T.

Second, when the bass itself is suspended, the figures of the resolution are greater by exactly 1 than the figures at the point of suspension; for example:

7 8
4 5
2 3

In Example U three consecutive sets of figures are given, representing the preparation of the suspension, the suspension, and the resolution. Example U presents a triple suspension: the 8ve is displaced by the 9th and the 7th.

example U.

Every note of the suspension is dissonant against the bass. Because both the 9th and the 7th resolve to the 8ve, the chord of resolution lacks a 5th.

The reverse of the situation shown in Example U is presented by Example V. In the latter every component above the bass either moves to its note of resolution or holds a common note (A), while the bass alone is suspended.

example V.

The figure $\frac{5}{2}$ represents a very common bass suspension, as shown in Example W. It always resolves to $\frac{6}{3}$. The numeral 2 here is not to be confused with the numeral 9. The latter is used for an upper-voice suspension exclusively.

example W.

Although figures such as $\frac{4}{2}$ and $\frac{5}{2}$ are usually associated with suspension formations, they abound in music in which the bass is extensively elaborated by submetrical notes. In such music the bass note that supports basic voice-leading changes is often displaced, creating the kind of formation at the submetrical level that one finds in the suspension. Example X illustrates.

J.S. BACH: *Von der Rechtfertigung* (Schemelli's Gesangbuch)

example X.

Here Bach has figured the metrical beats (quarter notes), as shown at (*a*). Thus the bass F in the first measure is an auxiliary note that displaces the structurally more basic note, E, which supports the chord of the 6th. Similarly, the D in the bass of the first measure is an accented passing note that displaces the more fundamental bass note, C, which supports the $\frac{5}{3}$. At (*b*) is shown a realization of the continuo accompaniment implied by the figured bass of (*a*).

The convention of figuring metrically accented bass notes (as in Example X) may be interpreted as an extension of the standard practice of figuring bass notes of full metrical value. As an alternative to figuring the metrically accented bass notes, which gives rise to figures such as $\frac{7}{2}$ the diagonal line (slash) is used over the accented bass auxiliary or passing note. This slash indicates that the main bass note follows immediately. Consequently, the person realizing the bass knows that over the note designated by the slash he is to take the notes that belong to the next figured note. Example Y illustrates.

example Y.

In Example Y the slash above the bass note E informs the realizer that the upper-voice notes at that point are those that belong to the following 6th chord over bass note D. Alternatively, if the accented passing note E were figured here, the figure would be $\begin{smallmatrix}7\\5\\2\end{smallmatrix}$.

Notes of 7th chords and inversions of 7th chords may also be displaced by suspensions (with the important limitations explained in Chapter 10). This gives rise to figures which may at first seem strange but which are not difficult to interpret.

example Z.

In Example Z the 6th of the $\begin{smallmatrix}6\\5\end{smallmatrix}$ is displaced by a 7th above the bass. The dash notation used here is explained below.

Example AA is similar to Example Z. Here again, the 6th above the bass is displaced by a 7th. The basic chord, however, is a $\begin{smallmatrix}4\\3\end{smallmatrix}$.

example AA.

Only two inversions of the 7th chords may have their bass notes displaced by suspension. These are shown in Examples BB and CC.

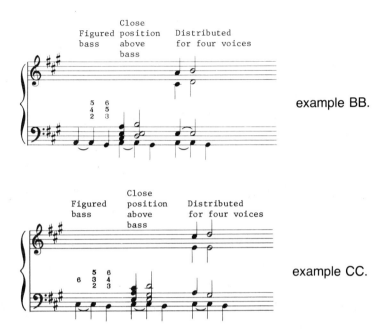

example BB.

example CC.

Again, as stated above, the figures of the resolution are greater by exactly 1 than the figures of the suspension. In Example CC notice that the bass of the 6th chord that prepares the suspension is doubled. Both bass and 8ve doubling have different and correct stepwise resolutions. (See Summary of Voice-Leading Rules and Guidelines, Appendix 2.)

In figured bass the dash essentially indicates that the harmony above the bass is to be held unchanged. Two different circumstances may be distinguished. First, the bass changes, but the dash indicates that the harmony of the previous bass note is to be applied to the current bass note. Second, the bass does not change, and the dash indicates that the notes above the previous bass note are to be maintained.

example DD.

Both circumstances are shown in Example DD. At (*a*) the dash prevents one from changing the harmony over the metrical passing note (for example, to 6). At (*b*) the dash prevents a change over the repeated bass note (for example, to $\frac{5}{3}$).

As suggested at the beginning of this summary, the full repertory of figured bass symbols is much larger than the collection presented here. This summary is intended to cover the main types of figures encountered in the body of the text, particularly in the exercises. It does not pretend to be exhaustive.

Appendix 2

Summary of Voice-Leading Rules and Guidelines

Before proceeding to the main summary, we give here an overview of the main interval types and their treatment. In Example 38 (Chapter 1) the main interval types found in tonal music are presented. Of the three types presented there—diatonic consonances, diatonic dissonances, and chromatic intervals—only the latter two types are of interest with respect to voice leading in the sense of rules of resolution, since diatonic consonances are not bound to any particular intervals of resolution, but are free. For the diatonic consonant intervals, successions of intervals of the same size require special consideration. Successive (parallel) unisons, 8ves, and perfect 5ths are prohibited, while diatonic 3rds (10ths) and 6ths can be, and are, used freely in succession.

Rules for figured-bass voice leading involving 5ths and 8ves (unisons) differ in a number of respects from rules of species counterpoint, which is the study of pure counterpoint according to the system of Fux. The most important of these are discussed below.

The case of parallel 5ths in which one 5th is diminished requires special attention. In figured-bass voice leading such successions occur. There is, however, a traditional rule that permits the succession from perfect 5th to diminished 5th, but prohibits the reverse. The probable reason for this rule is illustrated by Example A.

example A.

P 5th/dim.5th   dim.5th/P 5th

At (a) the diminished 5th can be properly resolved to a 3rd (10th). At (b), however, there is no possibility for resolution: the diminished 5th progresses directly to the perfect 5th.

Parallel 5ths and 8ves are of course prohibited between notes of submetrical value as well as metrical value. They are also prohibited (usually) when one note of the pair is submetrical. Example B illustrates. (See also section 235.)

example B.

Accented 5ths and 8ves, that is, 5ths and 8ves formed on successive accented beats, are not treated as strictly in figured-bass voice leading as in species counterpoint. The progression shown in Example C at (a) is allowed. Similarly, hidden 5ths, the situation in which a perfect 5th is approached in similar motion in two voices, suggesting a parallelism, are not regarded as seriously in figured-bass voice leading as in species counterpoint (Example C at (b)).

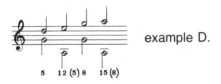

example C.

So-called antiparallel 5ths and 8ves are, however, just as nefarious in figured-bass voice leading as in species counterpoint. These are 5ths and 8ves formed by voices moving in contrary motion. The contrary motion, however, does not change the situation, since a 15th is equivalent to an 8ve and a 12th is equivalent to a 5th by the axiom of 8ve equivalence (Example D).

example D.

The normative resolutions of diatonic dissonances are summarized in Example E.

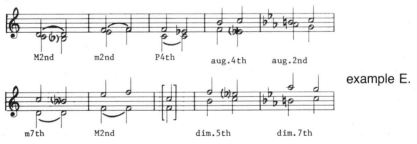

example E.

Notice in Example E that the intervals of resolution are inversionally related for each vertically aligned interval pair. For example, the major 2nd resolves to the minor 3rd, and the minor 7th resolves to the major 6th, the inversion of the minor 2nd.

The perfect 4th as a dissonance resolves to the 3rd. The inversion of the perfect 4th, the perfect 5th is of course always a consonance. Thus, when the diminished 7th resolves to a 5th, its inversion resolves to a 4th; in this case the 4th is regarded as a consonance.

Whereas in the major and minor dissonances one note of the interval remains fixed in the normative resolution, in the augmented and diminished intervals both notes move stepwise to resolution. The augmented 4th expands outward to a 6th; the diminished 5th collapses into a 3rd. Similarly, the augmented 2nd expands outward to a perfect (consonant) 4th, and the diminished 7th collapses into a perfect 5th.

The chromatic intervals are much more difficult to present systematically with respect to normative resolutions, since the resolutions depend upon linear context.

example F.

However, in Example F an effort is made to show normative resolutions for the main chromatic intervals, excluding intervals formed by doubly altered notes. In general, these resolutions are to consonant intervals (except for the augmented unison and the diminished 8ve). The motions of the individual notes are usually suggested by the accidental with respect to the nearest diatonic degree.

Of the chromatic intervals listed in Example F, the most common are the augmented 5th, the augmented 3rd, and the augmented 6th, in all of which the chromatic note is typically a passing note. The augmented 6th, of course, is the hallmark of the several varieties of augmented 6th chords (summarized in section 216).

We now proceed to the main rules and guidelines of voice leading. These are organized for the convenience of the student, approximately according to the order of presentation of chord-types in the text. Many of the rules have exceptions under extraordinary circumstances, circumstances that the student is unlikely to encounter in the course of working out the exercises in the text. Closely associated with voice-leading rules are rules and guidelines for doubling. Such rules and guidelines cannot be considered apart from specific contexts, that is, apart from successions of two or more harmonies.

In the present summary all the rules presented in the text have been reassembled, together with guidelines and important observations made in the exercises. In addition, certain more sophisticated situations not covered in the text have been included (several inspired by C.P.E. Bach).

The four basic guidelines for voice leading that involve motion from one chord to another are: (1) maintain common tones in the same voice; (2) move by step when possible; (3) if motion by step is not possible, move by consonant skip; dissonant linear intervals or intervals involving chromatic notes, such as the augmented 2nd, are usually inadvisable because they suggest a disconnected compound melodic structure; (4) maintain all the notes specified or implied by the figured bass. (See Summary of Figured Bass, Appendix 1.)

The two basic rules of voice leading are:

Rule 1: parallel 5ths or 8ves (unisons) are prohibited;
Rule 2: the law of the half step (section 10) effectively governs the progression of individual voices, with the following proviso: a note may be doubled whenever it is bound to a voice leading by half step, provided that there is also a different stepwise voice leading available to its counterpart.

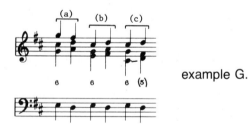

example G.

Example G at (a) and (b) presents typical cases of the application of this rule. The leading note is the extreme case in which the proviso does not apply, since there is only one stepwise progression available to the leading note in the progression V I (or VII I), and that is the progression to the tonic note. A doubling of the leading note accordingly produces parallel 8ves or unisons, as in Ex. G at (c). (It is of course possible to skip away from the leading note in order to obtain a complete chord of resolution, especially at the cadence.)

Rules for Consonant Triads

Example H illustrates the application of rules of voice leading to a succession of consonant triads.

C.P.E. BACH

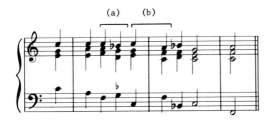

example H.

The two basic rules (Rule 1 and Rule 2) are observed in all but one case, indicated as (*b*) in the example. Because the upper voice does not maintain the common tone C from the one chord to the next (*b*¹), the voice leading becomes disjunct.

  The succession labelled (*a*) in Example H exemplifies an important rule, one that prevents parallel 5ths and 8ves:

Rule 3: when the bass ascends or descends by major 2nd and the specified harmonies are ⅗'s, all the upper voices must move in contrary motion to the bass.

Alternatively, as shown at (*a*¹) of Example H, the 3rd of the first chord can be led in parallel 3rds (10ths) to the 3rd of the second chord, with the result that the 3rd of the second chord is doubled.

  Example H at (*a*¹) also reminds us of a fallacious rule that is sometimes put forth: "Do not double the 3rd of a triad." In fact, any note of a triad may be doubled, depending upon the voice-leading context. Indeed, there is one very common situation in which the 3rd of the triad *must* be doubled, as discussed below in connection with Example I.

C.P.E. BACH

example I.

Example I, like Example H, shows normative voice leading in a short passage. Rule 3, concerning triadic succession over bass notes a major 2nd apart, is applied at (*a*) to effect correct voice leading. At (*b*) another rule must be applied:

Rule 4: *when a bass succession that supports two triads ascends by half a step and both triads have major 3rds, the 3rd of the second triad must be doubled.*

Contrary motion, as in the case of the rule involving bass progression by major 2nd (Rule 3), will produce an unwanted augmented 2nd, as shown in Example I at (*b'*). Doubling of the 3rd is also obligatory in the succession labelled (*c*) in Example I. The outer voices move in 10ths, the tenor remains on D, while the alto moves by step to G.

Rules for 6th Chords

Doubling is of crucial importance in the correct treatment of 6th chords. All the rules except one, given below, involve the selection of an appropriate doubling.

Rule 5: *when the 6th and 3rd are major, either may be doubled.*

Example J illustrates.

example J.

When the 6th is doubled, as at (*a*), each of the doubled notes has a stepwise and different resolution. When the 3rd is doubled, however, as at (*b*), one of the doubled notes (here the doubling is at the unison) must skip away. In this situation, according to the guidelines, the doubled 6th is preferred.

Rule 6: when the 6th and 3rd of the chord are both minor, either may be doubled.

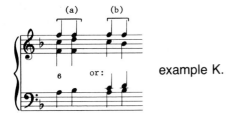

example K.

Both (*a*) and (*b*) are correct, according to Rule 6. At (*a*) the doubled notes are retained as common tones in the second chord, while at (*b*) the doubled notes proceed in contrary motion to the second chord. Preference for the one or the other would depend upon the individual configurations of the lines over a longer span than that shown in the example.

Rule 7: when the 6th is major, but the 3rd is minor, do not double the 6th.

Example L illustrates.

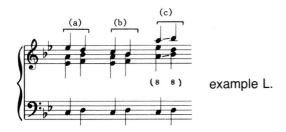

example L.

At (*a*) the 3rd is doubled; both voices have correct stepwise resolutions. At (*b*) the bass is doubled, and again both voices have correct stepwise resolutions. At (*c*), however, both A's are bound to resolve to Bb's, hence progress in parallel 8ves. Furthermore, the second chord at (*b*) lacks a 3rd.

Rule 8: when the bass functions as a leading note and is bound by the law of the half step to a single note of resolution, with no other stepwise possibility, it cannot be doubled.

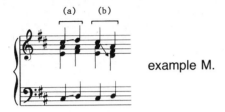

example M.

This situation is very similar to that shown in Example L. Both stem from the same basic rule (Rule 2). Example M at (a) shows the parallel 8ves that result from doubling the bass in this situation. In Example M at (b) is an attempt to correct the parallel 8ves by moving the doubled bass in the soprano to A. The correction is illusory, however; the common-tone A is maintained, E moves to F♯ in parallel 10ths with the bass, and C♯ *still* moves to D, but to D a 7th down instead of a 2nd up. The latter situation (b) is commonly found on student papers, and should be regarded as a serious and easily avoided violation of correct voice leading.

Rule 9: The bass may be doubled without consequent difficulty in any situation in which both notes have different stepwise progressions.

Example N shows a common voice leading of this type.

example N.

Both the first and second chords in Example N have doubled bass notes, and in both instances a different stepwise continuation is available to the doubled notes. Notice that an exchange of voices occurs between soprano and bass over the entire succession.

We come now to the two general cases in which the bass of the 6th chord *must* be doubled (after C.P.E. Bach).

Rule 10: The bass of a 6th chord must be doubled whenever it prepares or resolves a dissonance.

After C.P.E. BACH

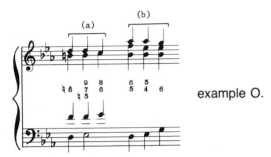

example O.

At (a) in Example O the doubled bass (in the soprano) prepares the suspended 9th. At (b) in Example O the bass of the 6th chord is necessarily doubled by the resolution of the 4th over bass E♭.

Rule 11: If four independent voices are to be maintained over a succession of 6th chords where the bass moves by 2nd (parallel 6th chords), as would be obligatory in four-voice chorale style, the technique of alternate doubling must be employed.

Example P illustrates this procedure.

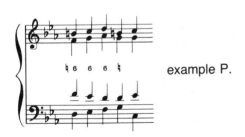

example P.

The succession of parallel 6th chords in Example P is typical of alternate doubling. On the first chord the 3rd is doubled (by alto and tenor at the unison), on the second the bass is doubled (by tenor), and on the third, the 6th is doubled (by soprano and tenor). The voice leading is completely stepwise, and there are no illegal parallels.

If it is not essential to retain four independent voices in parallel 6th chords, the reduced three-voice texture (keyboard style) cannot have the 3rd in the soprano; otherwise parallel 5ths will ensue (Example Q).

example Q.

The only possible soprano position is that of the 6th for parallel 6th chords in three voices.

Rules for the $\frac{6}{4}$

Voice leading of the $\frac{6}{4}$ presents no particular problems, since the typical $\frac{6}{4}$ is followed by $\frac{5}{3}$, and the exact linear succession is indicated by the pair of figures $\frac{6}{4}$ $\frac{5}{3}$: the 6th moves to the 5th and the 4th moves to the 3rd.

Doubling in the typical dissonant $\frac{6}{4}$ is also unproblematic. Example R shows three types of $\frac{6}{4}$'s and their doublings.

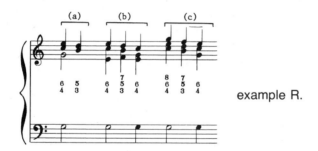

example R.

At (a) in Example R we see the usual $\frac{6}{4}$ and the application of *Rule 12: double the bass of the $\frac{6}{4}$*. The reason for this is that both the 6th and the 4th are committed to a stepwise descent. If either is doubled, parallel 8ves (unisons) result. The 8ve-doubled bass, however, remains stationary.

At (b) in Example R, however, is shown a situation in which the 6th can profitably be doubled. There the doubled notes have different stepwise progressions available, since the second figure is $\frac{7}{5}$. One 6th proceeds to the 5th, as usual, while the other brings in the 7th. Finally, at (c) in Example R, the $\frac{8}{6}$ is shown. The top figure, 8, specifies that the doubled bass (the 8ve) is to be in the soprano. As a consequence, the $\frac{8}{6}$ almost always implies the progression shown, a motion through a passing 7th to another soprano position (the position of the 6th) of the $\frac{6}{4}$. In both $\frac{6}{4}$'s the bass is doubled (Rule 12).

Rules for 7th Chords

Rule 13: the 7th of the true 7th chord always descends stepwise to resolution.
Since the 7th chord contains four notes, there are no problems of doubling (in four voices) if all are represented. Example S at (*a*) shows this situation.

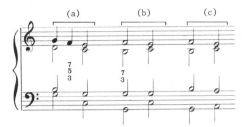

example S.

Notice at (*a*) that the leading-tone B in the tenor, normally bound by the law of the half step to ascend to the tonic note C, skips away to the 5th of the tonic triad. It does this in order to satisfy a guideline; a complete triad is specified over the bass C. If B were to progress to C the final chord would have a tripled bass, a 3rd, and no 5th. A complete stepwise resolution *and* a complete final chord are obtained, however, by adopting the doubling shown at (b) in Example S. There the bass is doubled by the tenor and the 5th is omitted. The guideline regarding complete harmony is violated for the 7th chord in order to obtain stepwise voice leading and a complete final chord.

It is even possible to double the 3rd and omit the 5th of a 7th chord, as shown at (*c*) in Example S. There the 3rd is doubled at the unison by tenor and alto. Both, however, have different stepwise resolutions. Notice that here the soprano and tenor first form a diminished 5th and then a perfect 5th, violating a guideline that that succession should not be used. However, as pointed out earlier, the prohibition applies most strongly to the outer voices.

Rule 14: since the 7th of the 7th chord is bound to descending stepwise resolution (Rule 13), the 7th may never be doubled; otherwise, parallel 8ves or unisons would ensue.

Rules for Suspension Chords

Voice leading for suspension chords is governed by three main rules (Rules 15, 16, and 17).

Rule 15: do not include the note of resolution in the suspension chord unless it is in the bass.

example T.

The exception stated in rule 15 is shown in Example T at (*a*). There the note to which the 9th resolves, C, is a member of the suspension chord itself; however, it is in the bass and hence has a special and necessary function. It could not be omitted.

Rule 16: do not double the suspended note.

Since the suspended note has a fixed resolution—namely, to the note which it is displacing— any note that doubled it would also have the same note of resolution; hence parallel 8ves or unisons would result.

Rule 17: any note of a 7th chord or an inversion of a 7th chord can be displaced by suspension except the 7th (or the note representing the 7th in an inversion).

The reason for this is shown in Example T at (*b*). There the 6th, E, presumably displaces the 7th, F. The F, however, functions as a dissonant upper auxiliary note to E. Thus the succession is reducible to that shown at (*b¹*): I III⁶ I. There is, therefore, no suspension.

Linear Chords and Intervallic Patterns

Since linear chords are contextually determined, as passing or auxiliary chords between regular consonant or dissonant harmonies, their doubling and voice leading are fully determined and there are no particular voice-leading problems.

In linear intervallic patterns, doublings are of the utmost importance. It is not possible to form simple general rules, since a number of factors come into play, for example, the position of the soprano voice.

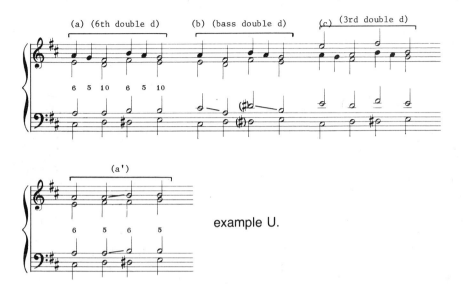

example U.

Example U illustrates the case of the linear intervallic pattern 6 5 10. At (a) the 6th is doubled, resulting in a stepwise leading of all the voices. At (b) the bass is doubled; the doubling voice, tenor, skips away to the 5th. If the continuation of the pattern remains diatonic (that is, without the change to bass C♯), this doubling scheme works well. With the change to C♯ in the bass, however, a leading-tone effect is created and the skip in tenor from C♯ to A sounds like a violation of the law of the half step (Rule 2). At (c) in Example U the 3rd is doubled and the voice leading is quite acceptable. Of the doubling pair, one proceeds by step (tenor) and the other skips a consonant interval (soprano). Notice that the stepwise progression is by whole step, not by half step.

Example (a¹) illustrates a general and undesirable situation. It is nearly the same as (a), except that the soprano remains on G, so that the 5th is doubled in the $\frac{5}{3}$, causing the alto to take the 3rd. As a result, parallel 8ves are created between tenor and soprano.

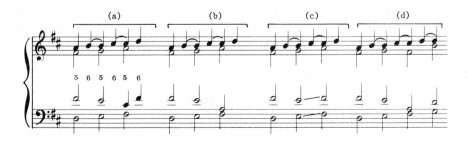

example V.

Finally, in Example V the reverse of the 6 5 pattern, 5 6, is illustrated, with various solutions that involve decisions concerning doubling. At (a) the optimal solution is given: 5 6 is the pattern of the outer voices, and alternate doubling is used to prevent parallelisms and to maintain correct spacing. In the first $\frac{5}{3}$ the 3rd is doubled, in the second the 8ve, and in the third the 5th. At (b) the choice of a doubled 3rd for the third $\frac{5}{3}$ introduces a wide spacing between the adjacent voices alto and tenor. At (c) the doubling of the bass of the second $\frac{5}{3}$ sets up the conditions for parallel 8ves. At (d) the pattern begins auspiciously, but disjunct motion in two voices is required in the progression from the third chord to the fourth. Although this is not fatal, it does not compare well with the voice leading of the optimal solution (a).

This final example may serve to illustrate a general point about voice leading. There may be many possible solutions in a particular situation. Some of them will violate traditional rules or guidelines or both. It is not always easy to find the elegant and correct solution.

Index of Musical Examples

Subject Index

THE ROOTS OF EVIL

BEING A TREATISE ON THE METHODS OF
DEALING WITH CRIME AND THE CRIMINAL
DURING THE EIGHTEENTH AND NINETEENTH
CENTURIES IN RELATION TO THOSE OF A
MORE ENLIGHTENED AGE

BY THE HON.
EDWARD CADOGAN
C.B.

LONDON
JOHN MURRAY, ALBEMARLE STREET, W.

First Edition . . . *1937*

Made and Printed in Great Britain by Butler & Tanner Ltd., Frome and London

CONTENTS

v

LIST OF ILLUSTRATIONS

Except for the last item, these illustrations are reproduced by courtesy of the British Museum.

PREFACE

SEEING that the appetite of the reading public for the consumption of books dealing with the detection of crime appears to be insatiable it occurred to the author of this volume that, if the catching of the thief is a subject which makes so wide an appeal, possibly also the making of the thief, his treatment and even his reformation—kindred subjects which in their importance should have a far more serious claim upon the attention of the ordinary citizen—might prove a not unprofitable study.

It is noteworthy for how long in our domestic history these vital matters were neglected, not only by the general public, but by those whose duty and whose obligation it was to devote their attention to them. Only in quite recent times has the treatment of the malefactor become rational and humane. The subject should make a compelling appeal to the present generation that seems to have been born with a far keener sense of its responsibilities and its mutual obligations than any of its predecessors.

I readily admit that an author who is bold enough to select a theme which is both historical and technical and who in addition has sufficient confidence to express thereon his own views, which may or may not be in conflict with those of the accredited experts, is under some obligation to his readers to offer an excuse or at any rate an explanation for his temerity.

Inadequate as my qualifications may be for the task

I have set myself, it concerns a problem in which I have for long taken the keenest personal interest. When I was first elected to Parliament I had intended to regard the welfare of the youth of this country as one of my preoccupations. As I explain in the text that follows, I have always held the view that the treatment of the young offender is one of the most important matters under this heading. But my ambition was to a considerable extent frustrated. For nearly five years out of the twelve that I was a Member of the House of Commons it was my fate to devote time and industry to the question of the reform of the Indian Constitution, during three years on the Royal Statutory Commission (commonly known as the " Simon Commission "), and during eighteen months on the Joint Select Committee of both Houses of Parliament dealing with the same question, and, although I hope my contribution to the final result was not negligible, it proved a long and serious interruption to the work I had planned to make my especial province. Nevertheless, I was able, to the extent of my vote and my part in debate, to make myself responsible on various occasions for legislation on those Home Office and Educational questions which in minor official capacities, I have since been responsible for administering.

For the rest I must leave the reader to judge whether I have yet sufficiently graduated in the subject to have any claim upon his attention.

For the history with which I deal in the following pages I have drawn in varying degrees and extent, amongst others, upon the following authoritative works and State Papers :

Sir Evelyn Ruggles-Brise—*The English Prison System*.
Arthur Griffiths—*Chronicles of Newgate*. 1812.
Vilette's *Annals of Newgate*.

Muralt's *Letters on the English*.

Andrew's *Eighteenth Century*.

John Howard's *On the State of Prisons*, with Appendix thereto.

Colquhoun—*Works on Prisons and Police*.

Fielding—*Late Increase of Robbers*.

Malcolm's *Manners and Customs of London*.
   Anecdotes of London in the Eighteenth Century.

Miller's *Eighteenth Century*.

Aitken's *Life of John Howard*.

J. B. Brown's *Life of John Howard*.

Rev. T. Field's *Life of John Howard*.

Mrs. Fry's *Journal*, by her two daughters.

Mark's *Tyburn Tree*.

Sir T. Fowell Buxton—*An Inquiry whether Crime and Misery are
   produced or prevented by our present System of Prison Discipline*.
   1818.
   Account of Prisons at Ilchester and Bristol. 1818.

Melville Lee—*A History of Police in England*.

F. W. Maitland—*Justice and Police*.

E. Carpenter—*Prisons, Police and Punishment*.

Pike's *History of Crime*.

Laurie's *Newgate Calendar*.

Lecky's *History of the Eighteenth Century*.

Charles Hitchin—*On the Discovery of the Conduct of Receivers
   and Thief Takers*. 1818.

James Neild—*On the State of Prisons in England, Scotland and
   Wales*. 1812.

Stow's *Surveys of London*.

Sir J. Jebb—*Life of W. Crawford*.

William Forster's *Life of Sir G. Grey*.

Mrs. Creswell's *Life of Elizabeth Fry*. 1845.

Susannah Corder's *Life of Elizabeth Fry*. 1853.

Mrs. Fry's *Observations on Family Prisoners*. 1827.

Eden Hooper—*Newgate and the Old Bailey*.

Sir E. Du Cane—*Punishment and Prevention of Crime*.

Wright's *Memoirs of Oglethorpe*.

Beccaria—*On Crimes and Punishments*.

Historical Register, 1729.

Misson's *French Traveller.*

Sir J. Stephen's *History of Criminal Law.*

Andrew's *Highwaymen.*

B. de Mandeville's *Enquiry into the Causes of Frequent Executions, etc.*

C. Oake's *Life of Sir Samuel Romilly.*

Defoe's and Fielding's *Life of Jonathan Wild.*

" Chronicon Newquissimus," *Life of Jonathan Wild.*

Life of Jonathan Wild, Anonymous. 1830.

Fletcher's *Account of the Police of the Metropolis.*

Eden's *State of the Poor.*

Edward Gibbon Wakefield—*On Prisons.*

William Smith—*On the State of the Gaols in 1776.*

B.L. of Twickenham's *Description of Newgate.*

Mrs. Le Mesurier—*Boys in Trouble.*

David Collins—*Account of the English Colony in New South Wales.*

A. Phillip—*Voyage of Governor Phillip to Botany Bay, 1790.*

James Bonwick—*First Twenty Years in Australia.*

Merivale's *Lectures on Colonisation.* 1861 Edition.

J. O'Hara—*History of New South Wales.* 1817.

J. Oxley—*Historical Account of the Colony of New South Wales.* 1821.

Archbishop Whately—*Thoughts on Secondary Punishment.* 1832.

Howell's *State Trials.*

Parliamentary History, Vol. VIII.

Marion Phillips—*A Colonial Autocracy.*

Extracts from letters of James Backhouse—*Visit to Van Dieman's Land and New South Wales.* 1838.

Thomas Reid—*Two Voyages to New South Wales and Van Dieman's Land.* 1822.

H. Montgomery Martin—*Secondary Punishments Discussed.* 1835.

Report of the Association for Improvement of Prison Discipline in 1815.

Committee of Inquiry into London Prisons, *Journals* of House of Commons, Col. 21 (1728–9).

Parliamentary Inquiry into the State of Newgate, 1814.

Select Committee on the State of the Police of the Metropolis, 1816.

Select Committee of the House of Commons on Secondary Punishment, 1831.

Select Committee of the House of Lords on the State of Gaols and Houses of Correction in England and Wales, 1835.

Report from Committee of House of Commons on the King's Bench, Fleet and Marshalsea Prisons, 1813.

Select Committees on Transportation, 1831 and 1837.

The Departmental Committee, 1894. Inquiry into the Prison Systems.

EDWARD CADOGAN.

14 EDWARDES SQUARE,
   KENSINGTON,
      LONDON.

INTRODUCTION

TOWARDS the end of the eighteenth century there lived in the neighbourhood of Red Lion Street, Whitechapel, a worthy young couple of the not very distinctive name of Jones. The husband was making a competence in a small line of business adequate to meet their domestic obligations, which included the upbringing of two infant children. His wife, Mary, was a model of all the domestic virtues. Exceedingly attractive in appearance, with a wealth of auburn hair and of a countenance so frank and pleasing as in itself to proclaim her virtue, she was occupied in nursing a newly-born child when the felicity of this modest but contented household was disturbed by the forcible entry of the Press Gang, one of the vilest institutions of an iniquitous age.

It would be difficult to overestimate the devastation which so rough and ready a form of conscription inflicted upon the family life of England at this period, by forcing industrious labourers and thrifty tradesmen into the two services against their inclination and, after jeopardizing whatever prospects were held out to them in their normal avocations, by turning them adrift as soon as the ship to which they were consigned was out of commission, or the regiment in which they had been compelled to enlist had no further need of their services. It is one of the enigmas of history that such an outrage against the liberty of the subject obtained so long, especially in view of the fact that it failed to provide either the requisite numbers or the appropriate quality for the fighting forces of the Crown. Indeed, so unsatisfactory was the result that men impressed into the army were often encouraged by their officers to desert.

This infamous system was no doubt responsible for many a young wife, robbed by the State of her husband, discarding the obligations of the marriage vow. In the case of Mary Jones the impressment of her husband produced results far more distressing than conjugal infidelity.

In vain she pleaded in an anguish of tears with the inexorable myrmidons of the law. In vain she protested her circumstances. Hardened by the vicious system of which they were the agents they turned a deaf ear to her supplications. Even had they been of a more considerate disposition, the exigencies of the political situation rendered a drastic conscription essential. The Government at this psychological moment had taken alarm at the Spanish claims to the Falkland Islands which seemed to make war inevitable and required reinforcement for the Navy at whatever cost to individual convenience.

The young wife found herself bereft of all means to support her infant family, completely destitute and neglected. So long as the activities of the Press Gang endured there was never at any time the smallest effort made by the State to compensate wives for the loss of the breadwinner thus forcibly abducted from the domestic hearth. Moreover, there were in those days few, if any, privately organized benevolent institutions which could have proffered a helping hand to the victims of such contingencies. Mary Jones had to face the future alone with the responsibility of rearing two immature children without any visible means of subsistence. Before long she found herself in need of bedding, clothing, fuel and food. The house was bare of the very first necessities of life. But with commendable self-restraint she resisted all temptation to barter what she prized as much as the lives of the children—the faith which she had plighted to her husband.

One luckless morning, half-starved and in the depths of despair, staggering forth into the street she entered a milliner's shop. A few small pieces of worked muslin were displayed upon the counter. Her hand, stretched forth in a fit of aberration, to take these trifles, was seized by the shop assistant. Before her offence, crime it could hardly be called under the circumstances, was even completed, the minions of the law were summoned and proceeded forthwith to arrest the culprit. That evening Mary Jones was incarcerated in Newgate. There in a noisome dungeon she found herself in the companionship, night and day, of women in every stage of profligacy and degradation. In due course she was brought to her trial. The pathetic story was recounted to an audience hardened by the constant repetition of such experiences, and to a tribunal that operated on the system that all criminals were much alike and that the gallows was the most efficacious cure for crime. She herself was being tried upon a capital charge. One hundred and fifty years ago, incredible as it may now seem, the punishment for a woman purloining a small piece of muslin, whatever might be the extenuating circumstances, was hanging upon Tyburn Tree.

When asked what she had to say in her self-defence she replied: "I have been a very honest woman in my lifetime. I have two children. I have worked very hard to maintain them since my husband was pressed. I have lived in credit and wanted for nothing until the press gang came and stole my husband from me, but since then I have had no bed to lie upon. I might have

done something wrong for I hardly knew what I did."
Her defence was fully corroborated. The Jury, no
doubt wearied of an oft-told tale, with little hesitation
brought in a verdict of guilty. Thereupon the wretched
girl, actuated by pent-up feelings which all the misery
she had undergone induced, with the cries of her starving children ringing in her ears, beside herself, as well
she might be under the circumstances, broke through
the bonds of her natural modesty. Springing to the
front of the dock, oblivious of the consequences, she
apostrophized the Judge with opprobrious names, which
the subsequent proceedings testified that he richly
deserved. This loss of self-control sealed her fate.
Such an affront to the dignity of the law, embodied as
it was in the person of a Judge who rated it higher
than the quality of mercy, belonged in his eyes to the
class of offence impossible to be forgiven. It was
doubtless in his power that she should be reprieved.
It was her first offence. But all chance of escaping
the supreme penalty of the law had evaporated in that
wild cry of hers from the dock at the conclusion of her
trial. She was re-conveyed to the place from whence
she had come, the place in all the world least appropriate for those who would spend their last hours in
prayer and meditation. Amid scenes of indescribable
debauchery, the stone walls of the condemned cell
echoing to the unrestrained language and ribald laughter
of murderers, thieves and prostitutes, suffering terror
and torment to body and soul, this innocent victim
of a ferocious law endeavoured with what success
she could command to concentrate upon her awful
fate, to prepare herself for the inevitable end, and to
entreat for that mercy in the next world which she had
failed to find in this.

Her neighbours in Whitechapel raised a petition on

her behalf, but the Judge, a fit agent to dispense such a travesty of justice, nursing the affront to his dignity, declined to relent. Upon the appointed day, the 16th October, 1771, Mary Jones set out towards her calvary in a wretched cart along those dread three miles, through an avenue of the lewdest of mankind influenced by an unnatural craving to gloat upon the predicament of a less fortunate fellow-creature. It is recorded that she displayed amazing fortitude throughout the indescribable tribulation which was the common lot in those days of the malefactor condemned to public execution, until the very moment when the cart was withdrawn, leaving her body swinging lifeless upon the triple tree.

In the same month twenty-two years later another woman, born in a very different station of life from that to which Mary Jones belonged, was conveyed in a tumbril through streets swarming with as lewd a crowd as execrated Mary Jones, to the place of her execution.

The fate of Marie Antoinette is responsible for one of the most oft-quoted phrases of the most oft-quoted writings in English literature. " I thought ten thousand swords must have leaped from their scabbards to avenge even a look that threatened her with insult. But the age of chivalry is gone." So Edmund Burke wrote of the French Queen. He was a Member of Parliament when Mary Jones was executed, and when hundreds of English men and women were suffering the extreme penalty for equally trivial offences, but there is no evidence that her piteous fate evoked any remonstrance from so influential a source. Surely he might have spared some of his rhapsodical outbursts which he voiced for an alien queen, martyred in the name of Revolution, for a wretched fellow-citizen martyred in the name of our statute law. It is quite true that Edmund Burke denounced the criminal code as abominable, and made jokes about the multiplication of capital offences. It is quite true that he did on one occasion casually mention the subject of our prisons to his constituents, but that was exclusively upon the abuse of imprisonment for debt. " As we grow enlightened," he said, " the public will not bear for any length of time, to pay for the maintenance of whole armies of prisoners, nor, at their expense to keep jails as a sort of garrisons." He was a false prophet. For at least another half-century of " enlightenment" the public bore the burden of this wasteful expenditure.

Historians may differ as to what extent the royal house of France deserved its fate—but through all the ages there can be only one opinion on what was correctly described in Parliament by one of Mary Jones's contemporaries. " I do not believe," said Sir William Meredith, " that a fouler murder was ever committed against the law than the murder of this woman by the law."

We who live in an age of clemency may well pause to inquire how it came about that the reform of our criminal code and the purging of the ghastly dungeons, which served as prisons both in London and the provincial towns, found few if any champions in the Legislature during the eighteenth century. The first part of the answer may very well be that it was only in the nineteenth century that Parliament began to concern itself with social and domestic reform. In the eighteenth century the illustrious statesmen who are held up by historians to posterity as models of all the virtues, for the most part concerned themselves with and achieved renown in the waging of dynastic wars, and the sustaining of diplomatic struggles with their opposite numbers on the Continent. If a list of Prime Ministers and Secretaries of State from the Premiership of Sir Robert Walpole until the Premiership of Earl Grey were examined, few names will be found that can be associated with any conspicuous measures of social reform. Even in the reign of Queen Victoria her first Prime Minister is recorded to have exclaimed : " Oh if you would only have the goodness to leave the factory children alone." Lecky, the historian *par excellence* of England in the eighteenth century, finds social reform so little character-istic of the epoch, that he devotes to the subject but an exiguous space out of a total of four thousand eight hundred pages, and is careful to explain that William Pitt the Younger showed very little real superiority outside the Parliamentary arena. " The great social problems arising from the sudden development of the factory system which began in his time, never appear to have for a moment occupied his thoughts."

Their deeds and accomplishments recorded upon sumptuous cenotaphs which obliterate the graceful lines of Westminster Abbey, and throw out of balance the majestic proportions of St. Paul's, bear testimony to the fact that the statesmen and diplomatists of the eigh-teenth century made England feared among the nations of the world, but afford no evidence that they supplied any contribution to the moral or physical welfare of their fellow-citizens.

One of the most remarkable phenomena which must impress itself upon the student of the history of England in the eighteenth century, is the position of power and influence which Britain had come to occupy in the councils of Europe, combined with the complete and utter blindness of her statesmen to the detestable con-ditions in which the poor lived and the flagrant abuses of laws which they were competent to alter but with which they in no way concerned themselves. We are left to judge these distinguished administrators exclusively by the successful conduct of their foreign policy. If their worth was to be assessed by the standard of their domestic policy our glorious fanes might have been spared some of the clumsy memorials that congest their aisles and transepts.

Again, the politician of the eighteenth century was more solicitous to surpass a rival upon his own side or to confound in debate his opponent on the other, than to leave his country better than he found it, idiosyncrasies which are not imperceptible in politicians of a later age. Education, sanitation, the treatment and reform of the criminal, the welfare of the young, were matters with which members of the legislature displayed no inclination to occupy themselves. Arthur Griffiths, in his *Chronicles of Newgate*, attempts to exonerate the legislature : " The neglect of prison reform in those days," he writes, " was not to be visited upon the legislature," but the fact that through all the intervening years ceaseless committees of both Legislatures sat and reported, and that ultimately various measures of amelioration were placed on the Statute Book gives the lie to any such extenuation of this national crime. Both the Executive and the Legislature were to blame. If these reforms could have been sanctioned in 1837 by Parliament they could equally well have been effected a hundred years before by the same agency.

During the preoccupations of continental politics the statesmen who guided the destinies of England found neither time nor indeed evinced any inclination to deal with the glaring abuses that cried out for redress nearer home. But if it was not the fashion of English statesmen of the eighteenth century to indulge in introspection there was no diffidence displayed by them in animadverting upon the shortcomings of other countries.

In the year 1756 the news of an atrocity committed by an Indian satrap caused a thrill of horror to run through the length and breadth of the land which has its reverberations even to this day. Siraj-ud-Dowlah, the young Nawab of Bengal, having captured the fort of the East India Company in Calcutta, confined his English prisoners in a dungeon eighteen feet square, with the result that only twenty-three survived until the following morning. At the moment that his unfortunate victims were fighting over the prone bodies of the dying for a breath of air the Duke of Newcastle was nominally Prime Minister, but William Pitt the Elder, although ostensibly in the subordinate situation of the Secretary of State, was the controlling genius of the Cabinet. It is hardly to be supposed that Pitt could have known or indeed, if he had known, recked anything of the conditions of Newgate and of the provincial gaols, or he and his colleagues might not have been quite so solicitous to condemn Siraj-ud-Dowlah. He had only to explore beneath that famous nose of his to discover barbarities in this country which would have given him little enough sanction to criticize the abuses of less-enlightened governments. After all, the young Bengalee Nawab was, according to our own standards, little more than a savage, educated upon the principle that when you have your enemy in your hands you must crush him. But such was not the ostensible principle upon which the treatment of the delinquent in England was founded, although in effect it was indistinguishable.

The epoch from the dawn of the eighteenth century, to the initiation of domestic social reform in the middle of the nineteenth century, was undeniably an era of great men and of great events in English history. But the superficial reader is apt to be led away by the glamour of foreign conquests and the sparkle of an intellectual society which has had no equal. A reviewer, criticizing a recent publication, wrote : " Probably there never was a more brilliant society in London than that of the period covered by Lord Chesterfield's long life from 1694 to 1773." Far too many biographies and histories dwell exclusively upon the glamorous side of that period and ignore the deplorable social conditions under which the majority of our people suffered. The information upon which the author bases the contents of the following pages, drawn from the most reliable sources, will reveal to the reader how little justification there is for regretting the vanished glories of a sumptuous age. The social history of England of those times serves to bring out into sharper contrast the hideous evils that degraded the lives of all save the aristocratic few who supplied so much material for the cultured student of art and of literature.

There was not even the excuse that these vile things were hid from the public gaze. Not even ignorance explained the phenomenon. On the contrary they were made as public as the plays of Gay and Cibber, while they drew a much larger and more varied audience.

The social conditions which were mainly responsible for corrupting the young and making criminals out of material which was worthy of a better use, the inefficient system of preventing and detecting crime, the ferocity of the law and its administration, the ghastly condition of our prisons and the treatment of its victims, and the ultimate efforts of the reformers to redress these evils, provide the subject-matter of the following pages.

CHAPTER I

THE UNTILLED SOIL

IT is not an easy task for the historian to draw any very definite conclusions from the fragmentary sources of information available, as to whether the conditions under which the working classes lived during the greater part of the eighteenth century were generally prejudicial to their physical well-being. But although so many different factors have to be taken into consideration, and so difficult is it to compare the standard of values at different stages of national development, yet it may be argued legitimately that before the industrial revolution brought upon the towns the evils of overcrowding, overworking, and under-nourishment, the urban working classes, as far as creature necessities, creature comforts and general conduct of domestic life were concerned, had the advantage over those of a later generation of industrial history, although James Malcolm informs us that "very confined residences destroyed the health of parents and their offspring."

The sources from which reliable information on this particular phase of the national life can be drawn are exiguous for the very sufficient reason that there was not the same solicitude in responsible quarters for the moral and physical health of the working classes as there is to-day. Investigation by royal commissions and committees, the system of inspectorates, had hardly commenced their operation. There is, however, sufficient evidence to indicate that the eighteenth century for the most part was a period of almost uninterrupted and ever-increasing prosperity. Not even the American War of Independence could permanently prejudice the well-being of the people. The universal rise in prices accrued to the benefit of the productive classes. Even the agricultural labourer shared in the general amelioration until the wars of the French Revolution dislocated the whole framework of European commerce. We may conclude then that the standard of living was on the whole comparatively high.

But in one respect all the most authentic accounts are agreed—and there is certainly more than sufficient official testimony to vindicate this view—that a general depravity, with hardly any parallel in any other epoch, in any other country, characterized all ranks of English society during the eighteenth century. The attempts to control the evil propensities of the populace by legislation were rare. Although a now happily obsolete school of morals once advanced the view that the endeavour to make people virtuous by legislation is not within the sphere of practical politics, the student of the history of the eighteenth and nineteenth centuries cannot on the evidence accept that thesis. Whenever the attempt has been made by the State to deal drastically with contemporary abuses, the effort has been proved conspicuously successful. It is safe to assert that there was not one of the social evils recounted in the following chapter that could not have been obviated by remedial legislation. Henry Fielding subscribed to this view when he wrote: "The gentlest method I know, and at the same time perhaps one of the most effectual of stopping the progress of vice is by removing the temptation." That is a proposition that no one can gainsay, but the power to remove temptation from the people resides more effectively in government than in the private individual, or in any association of private individuals.

The blame for such a condition of things, as is revealed in the chronicles of the eighteenth century, must attach to the government no less than to the so-called governing classes. In its opening phases and for many years to come a Prime Minister whose influence upon public morality was highly questionable and whose influence upon private morality was deplorable, held in his hands the destinies of the people. Of dissolute personal conduct himself, Robert Walpole was hardly qualified to affect for good the general moral standards of his time. It might be argued that, at a period of history when few among the lower classes could read, when there were no newspapers for universal consumption, when that devastating publicity in which those who occupy responsible positions move to-day was comparatively unknown, the importance of those in authority setting an example in their own private lives, so long as their conduct of public affairs was unexceptionable, was not so obvious as it afterwards became. The workers and the apprentices in the industrial districts of the eighteenth century, for example, may not have been aware that King George II kept mistresses with the approval, if not with the connivance of his Queen, and that the Prime Minister, himself living in open adultery and indulging in every sort of excess, regarded the domestic arrangements of this remarkable royal *ménage* with complacency. The influence of the governing class upon the morals of the governed may not have been so direct as it was in the Victorian era, but for good or ill—and during the eighteenth century it was undoubtedly for ill—the influence of those in authority inevitably filtered through the various strata of human society, tainting each as it percolated downwards, corrupting the whole soil, which as a consequence yielded more tares than wholesome grain.

Walpole, sceptical and unemotional as he was by nature, appears to have entertained a cynical contempt for his own generation, but in that memorable indictment of his of the society in which he moved, " I always talk bawdy at meals as that is a subject in which all can join," he was unconsciously condemning himself and the baneful influence he exercised upon society in general. It never occurred to him that the reason his guests so readily assimilated themselves to such talk was that they were aware that this was the subject most congenial to their host. He never concerned himself to reflect that had he endeavoured to raise the general level of the public taste, all classes would have readily responded to one whose influence over his own generation was unquestioned.

His influence was corrupting in two respects. By his personal conduct he lowered the level of private morality, and in his administration of public affairs he deliberately set himself against all attempts to raise its level. He sneered at any junior Member in the House of Commons who evinced an ambition to set higher standards of political integrity, or who strove to initiate a campaign of social reform.

His influence upon young men [writes Lecky] appears to have been peculiarly pernicious. If we may believe Chesterfield, he was accustomed to ask them in a tone of irony, upon their entrance into Parliament, whether they too were going to be saints or Romans, and he employed all the weight of his position to make them regard purity and patriotism as ridiculous and unmanly.

In these efforts he was quite remarkably successful. Through the greater part of the century there hardly emerged one Member of Parliament who could, by any contortion of the term, be designated a social reformer. The baneful influence of Walpole's cynicism long survived him. For many a decade after he had ceased to be Prime Minister it was not possible to indicate any measure that was calculated to make a substantial contribution towards ameliorating the debased moral condition of the country, or to the remedying of the defective machinery employed in the treatment of delinquents, for whose delinquency that defective machinery was in the main responsible.

The justification for Walpole's claim upon the gratitude of his contemporaries was that he achieved a well-earned reputation as a great Peace Minister. But by his success in seeking peace and ensuing it he deprived himself of the one excuse he might have pleaded for his neglect of social reform, an excuse which can at least be advanced in some measure to exonerate the younger Pitt of similar negligence on his part. Walpole might have employed the years of peace and plenty, for which he must have full credit, as an opportunity to concern himself with an endeavour to improve the deplorable moral condition into which the country had sunk. The premierships of Walpole and the two Pitts covered a period of little less than fifty years. They were years in which those who governed England interpreted patriotism as meaning love of country rather than love of fellow countrymen, and who, although they were possessed of an ambition to make British arms victorious by land and sea, were of no ambition to raise up the oppressed or to strengthen the moral fibre of the nation.

It is true that the elder Pitt and his illustrious son were both men of unblemished private character, but we search in vain through the records of their administration of public affairs for any effectual attempt to remedy the vile abuses corrupting the morals of all classes. The baffling social problems arising from the sudden development of the factory system, which began in the lifetime of the younger Pitt, never appear to have occupied his thoughts. He left the abuse of child labour unrestricted by law while he even urged the propriety of turning the industry of children to commercial profit.

The fashion that the governing classes set during these stagnant years was deplorable. If we have any doubt of how far it was responsible for the increase of crime and debauchery in all classes inferior in the social scale, we have only to consult the writings of those contemporaries who had sufficient patriotism to protest. Of these, the two brothers, John and Henry Fielding, and James Colquhoun stand out pre-eminent. They are, of all the authorities on the moral conditions of the eighteenth century, the most frequently and the most confidently drawn upon by historians in arriving at their conclusions, and the one definite conclusion which all reliable historians arrive at is that the Legislature and the governing classes were to blame for the low state of public morals.

To obtain the correct background to the picture of the social life of England during this period, particularly in the large industrial towns, it must be realized that scarcely any provision except of the most pernicious character—and of this there was an abundant supply—was made for the leisure hours of the industrial classes.

What an immense variety of places [exclaims Henry Fielding] have this town and its neighbourhood set apart for the amusement of the lowest order of the people where the master of the house, or wells, or gardens may be said to angle only in the *kennels* [1] where baiting with the vilest materials, he catches

---

[1] Kennel in this connection means "gutter."

only the thoughtless and tasteless rabble . . . The necessary consequence must be ruin to many . . . I would be understood to aim at the retrenchment only not at the extirpation of diversions.

But Fielding's suggestion as to the appropriate remedy proved that even he was incapable of getting down to fundamentals. He would allow the upper classes to have their fun, but adds " the business of the politician is only to prevent the contagion from spreading to the useful part of mankind." Ranelagh and Vauxhall he would tolerate, but " such a fashion should not be allowed to spread amongst those in town and country who cannot afford it." In other words, diversions are for the rich, who come to little harm by indulgence in them, but are to be denied to the poor, who can only afford those of the most injurious description.

If there be any who doubt that education has been of the value which is claimed for it, let us bear in mind that the greater part of the wholesome amenities that now fill the lives of the working classes derive their origin from education and are only congenial to those who have at least a modicum of intellectual endowment. It is by education too that men are given a distaste of those occupations which to the ignorant are the only solace in their vacant lives. " The want of a due provision for education," said Lord Hale in one of his discourses, " and relief of the poor in the way of industry, is that which fills the gaols with malefactors."

But Colquhoun passes a still harsher judgment upon those responsible for such a universal state of ignorance :

To suffer the lower orders of the people to be ill educated, to be totally inattentive to those wise regulations of State policy which is to guard and improve their morals and then to punish them with a severity unexampled in the history of the world either ancient or modern, for crimes which have originated in evil habits has too much the appearance of creating delinquents for the purpose of putting them to death.

It is quite certain that whatever the intention may have been, this was the ultimate effect of the attitude of government towards social reform in the eighteenth century. There was no attempt made to better the condition and the circumstances of the poor, in order to obviate the particular temptations which are at all times so overwhelming to the destitute. Still worse, when the criminal had been made either by the neglect or almost by the acquiescence of government, there was no attempt to effect his reformation. Small wonder then that the gravest aspect of the social life of the century was an ever-increasing epidemic of crime and immorality in every rank of human society.

Although it is not always easy to determine cause and effect there is no question that this great increase of crime, synchronized with an excess of drinking and gambling in the first half of the century. In this the educated classes set the worst possible example. Robert Walpole's father encouraged his son to drink with him more than he drank himself, in order that he should not have the shame of bearing witness to his father's insobriety. Dr. Johnson spoke of a time that he could recollect when all the decent people of Lichfield became drunk every night and were none the worse thought of for that. These particular tastes, unwholesome enough even for those who could afford them, and whose gaming and drinking took place under comparatively decent circumstances, were a thousand times worse for the morale of a class who had not the margin of income to justify the risk of the one or the cost of the other, and whose habits could only be gratified in the worst haunts of vice and crime in the Metropolis.

Until the introduction of gin-drinking into England

in 1735, which Lecky describes as an event incomparably more momentous than any event in the purely political or military annals of the country, beer was the comparatively innocuous beverage of the working classes. The constituents of beer, while much less inebriating than the coarse spirits favoured by the working man, are more nutritious.   While the home-brewed beverage was certainly consumed in vast quantities there is no very definite evidence that the habit produced an appreciable effect upon the morals or the prosperity of the community at large.   But the craze induced by the first importations of the Dutch distilled spirit into England, it is agreed by all historians, wellnigh altered the course of the social history of the country.   It sensibly checked the increase of the population.   It materially affected the efficiency and therefore the output of our industries.

So great was the demand for and the consumption of gin, that even in the first year of its introduction into this country nearly five and a half million gallons of the spirit were distilled in England, a figure which rose to eleven million gallons in 1750.   The account of how retailers of gin were in the habit of hanging out painted boards announcing that their customers could be made drunk for a penny, dead drunk for twopence, and have straw to lie upon for nothing, is a commonplace of every school history book.   Gin is described in a contemporary satirical publication as

the kind companion of the neglected wife, the infuser of courage in the standing army, the source of the thief's resolution, the support of pawn-brokers tally men, receivers of stolen goods, and a long etcetera of other honest fraternities alike useful and glorious to the commonwealth.

But the evil quickly assumed proportions which rendered joking thereon inappropriate.   The Grand Jury of Middlesex protested that much the greater part of the poverty, the murders, and robberies of London might be traced to the single cause of gin-drinking. Bishop Benson in a letter written from London in the middle of the century wrote :

There is not only no safety of living in this town but scarcely any in the country now ; robbery and murder have grown so frequent. Our people have become what they never were before, cruel and inhuman. Those accursed spirituous liquors which to the shame of our Government are so easily to be had and in such quantities drunk, have changed the very nature of our people, and will, if continued to be drunk, destroy the very race.

That this was not the exaggeration of a narrow-minded divine, obsessed by the virtue of abstinence, is amply attested by all the most reliable contemporary writers. In 1750 the London physicians stated that there were in and about the Metropolis 14,000 cases of illness, most of them beyond the reach of medicine, directly attributable to this newly-acquired habit of gin-drinking.

Fielding entirely corroborates Benson in ascribing the increase of crime to this baneful habit, and estimated that it formed the principal diet of more than 100,000 people in the Metropolis, adding the comment that

should the drinking of this poison be continued at its present height during the next 20 years there would be very few of the common people left to drink it. . . . The intoxicating draught itself disqualifies them from any honest means to acquire it, at the same time as it removes any sense of fear and shame and emboldens them to commit any wicked and desperate enterprise. . . . What must become of the infant who is conceived in gin with the poisonous distillations of which it is nourished both in the womb and at the breast. Are these wretched infants (if such can be supposed capable of

The Lamentable Fall of Madame Geneva   *From a satirical print published by E. Foster*

arriving at the age of maturity) to become our future sailors and our future grenadiers ? Is it by the labours of such as these that all the emoluments of peace are to be procured us and the dangers of war averted from us ?

When this vice had attained proportions that threatened the very life of the State, it was inevitable that Government had to take cognizance of the danger. By the irony of fate the destinies of the country were at this moment in the hands of one whose bacchanalian orgies in his Norfolk home had so disturbed the peace of the countryside that his neighbours had fled from their domestic hearths in dismay. Periodically when England evinced any symptoms of anxiety to be saved from itself, Robert Walpole would leave Houghton for the Metropolis and lumber along the quagmires which did duty for turnpike roads, at the risk of a hold-up by footpads and highwaymen, whose activities his Government was incompetent to suppress. But even Walpole, whose own tastes and inclinations would naturally foster a cynical disregard for the morals of the people, and who was too busy employing the resources of Government solely with a view to strengthening his political influence, was compelled to acknowledge the necessity of taking some steps to obviate the evil. Corpulent in mind and body, he was slow to commit himself on these troublesome occasions, to any definite line of executive action. What he regarded as premature and precipitate decisions were abhorrent to him.

In 1736 he consented with some reluctance to the imposition of a duty of twenty shillings a gallon upon all spirituous liquors. This indirect attempt to make England sober by legislation yielded little result but the encouragement of a clandestine retail trade that defied with success every attempt to suppress it, and the exasperation of the mob which paraded the streets with the disconcerting slogan, "No gin no King." Moreover, apothecaries retailed the liquor under the specious label of medicine or cordial. In 1749 more than 4,000 persons were convicted of selling spirituous liquors without a licence, while the number of private gin-shops was estimated at 17,000, statistics which give some measure of the failure of Walpole's one modest effort at social reform, and which perhaps also go to prove that even a Prime Minister is hardly qualified to cure the defect in others which he has neglected to cure in himself.

But if this indulgence in spirituous liquors was a grave menace to the national well-being, the character of the depositories where it was sold and consumed was even a greater social evil and even more immediately responsible for the alarming prevalence and increase of crime. We who are accustomed to look upon the public house as a well-regulated pleasant social place of gathering, where cheerful guests assemble under the auspices of a no less cheerful host, where well-to-do and poor alike can obtain warmth and refreshment under decent and reputable surroundings, must banish from our minds any such pleasing picture if we would reconstruct a faithful likeness of the original.

Both individual reformers and public inquiries in various published reports make it perfectly clear that the gin-shops and drinking-dens which jostled each other in every street in the industrial districts of great towns were almost without exception hotbeds of vice and the very nurseries of young criminals. It was in such an environment that the young novice underwent his apprenticeship in depravity under the able tuition of the habitual malefactor. It was here that the harlot made assignation with her employer; it was here that the worst of all miscreants, the receiver of stolen goods, wove the net about his victim; it was here that thieves planned their next enterprise; it was here that apprentices and boys and girls of tender years were to be found taking their part in scenes of lewdness and debauchery.

The police system, or indeed any system of control that existed, was so defective and incompetent, that every form of moral prostitution flourished without let or hindrance in these dens of iniquity.

It is not to be supposed that, where a system of licensing, if such it could be called, was so inoperative, the type of publican who presided over these houses was calculated to raise their tone. Instead of entrusting licences, as the intention is to-day, exclusively to men of unimpeachable moral conduct, the justices assigned them so indiscriminately that the keepers of the ale-houses and gin-shops were for the most part those disposed rather to promote drunkenness, gambling and every description of immorality which could be the means of fostering their trade, while not a few of them were associated with highwaymen, prostitutes, common thieves and utterers of base money with the object of supplementing whatever more legitimate earnings they could claim.

That the drinking and gambling houses of the Metropolis continued to be a standing reproach to Government and a perpetual menace to the welfare of the youthful population throughout the whole of the eighteenth century, is amply attested by the evidence produced before the Select Committee on the Police of the Metropolis, which reported in July, 1816. It is a long stride forward for the student of history from the age of Walpole to this date, but nowhere on his journey will he find any evidence that these particular evils suffered the slightest check from remedial legislation. The conditions that were revealed before this tribunal had persisted without interruption for over a hundred years. This evidence therefore is as appropriate a description of what obtained in any part of the eighteenth century as in the early days of the nineteenth, when the Committee reported. It is the most reliable evidence to be found, and it is therefore from its pages that the following paragraphs dealing with this particular social evil are mainly drawn. The evidence is given and corroborated by a long procession of witnesses with monotonous and unvarying precision.

A very great number of the public-houses in the gin-drinking days were disorderly both in the legal and in the customary sense of that description. Many of them, the habitual resort of thieves and bad characters, were known as "flash-houses." They were mainly supported by disorderly persons of both sexes, because forsooth they could not be otherwise supported with any prospect of remuneration. The type of harlot that frequented them was one calculated to invest them with a particularly sinister repute. In his evidence before the Select Committee of the House of Commons Colquhoun expressed the following view upon this unsavoury subject :

It appears to me that in addition to the increase of prostitution, there is also a great increase of profligacy of manners among that class of unfortunate females. In addition to this the major part of them derive a considerable portion of their subsistence by the robbery of those who come in contact with them of their watches and money ; a vast proportion of them are associated with thieves, who actually live with them, and who follow them in the streets, not only to tutor them in the way they are to commit robberies, by pulling out watches, money, etc., but also are near at hand, ready to attend them when they commit those robberies, in order to receive the booty and run off.

The extent to which liquor was consumed in these drinking-dens can be estimated from the evidence given by Thomas Spring, a victualler: "I last week sent a man to watch the door of a gin-shop on Holborn Hill . . . between the hours of 7 and 10 in the evening there went in and came out 1,411 persons excluding children." He knew of a gin-shop which served 1,000 to 1,500 on a Sunday before Divine Service:

I am shocked at seeing . . . the indecency and profligacy and even children intoxicated, with their fathers and mothers, children of from 7 to 14 years of age, with their parents on a Sunday morning in the dirt and rags they have been in all night.

Little or no attempt was made to suppress them, and often enough when information had been tendered it was overruled, the majority of the magistrates displaying a curious reluctance to convict. It was of rare occurrence that these houses were closed down. The usual course adopted was to change the licensee. But the facility with which licences were granted and renewed to persons of bad character and reputation rendered such a proceeding futile, while honest magistrates despaired of effecting any improvement where brewers and distillers were making fortunes out of these infamous haunts, profits being their one concern.

Some of the worst-conducted houses in London were the most lucrative. From the words of a contemporary we derive the following description of them:

There almost every practice prevails that is calculated to inflame the criminal propensities of youth. Boys and girls met there, the most daring enjoying the hero worship of their fellows, divided themselves into gangs, elected a captain, "worked" certain districts in shifts by day and night in small parties of two or three, meeting again at a set time to divide the plunder. One party divided £400 in one night. This was the usual system at most "flash-houses." Boys and girls kept late hours with cards and dice, the landlord gambling with his customers.

A list of these favourite haunts of the underworld showed that there were two hundred of them situated in St. Giles, Drury Lane, Chick Lane, Saffron Hill, the Borough, and Ratcliffe Highway, frequented by 6,000 boys and girls, some no older than twelve years of age, who lived solely by dishonest courses and were the associates of thieves. During the daytime they were occupied alternately with stealing and gambling, indulged in without let or hindrance in the open streets.

The Committee ruled that the long immunity which these vile dens enjoyed had contributed perhaps more than any other cause to that early depravity and extent of juvenile delinquency which every magistrate acknowledged to prevail. An attempt was even made to justify their continuance on the specious plea that they offered a facility for the apprehension of offenders. One police officer giving evidence stated that " flash-houses " were certainly a necessary evil; alleging that if these houses were done away with " we should have the thieves resort to private houses and holes of their own, and we should never find them." The answer to such an apology for their existence was painfully obvious. Though criminals might be apprehended in their habitual resorts, crimes were planned there. In these schools and academies for vice, adapted to both sexes and to all ages, where one thief was seized one hundred were trained in the science of thieving, in which a large proportion might never have graduated had it not been for the facilities afforded by these legalized haunts of prostitutes and felons. Furthermore, the publicans favoured the worst offenders as their best customers, and were therefore more likely to offer them protection than to secure their apprehension.

The public-houses were so numerous and competition in the trade of the publican so severe that it would not have been an easy task for them to have cleared profits solely by honest means. It is impossible therefore to resist the conclusion that they found their main support in disorderly persons of both sexes, because failing such co-operation they could not be otherwise sufficiently lucrative to continue to exist.

The findings of the Committee were that the chief causes of juvenile delinquency were the existence of " flash-houses," brothels almost exclusively set apart for children of both sexes, and the bad management of prisons, which instead of correcting the criminal delinquents by discipline were nothing better than schools of crime.

Colquhoun was convinced that young offenders became earlier initiated into the systems of crime by frequenting these houses than in any other way.

There are various streets in Westminster [he said in his evidence] where there are a number of those houses which lodge prostitutes . . . Facilities for an illicit intercourse with the sexes at an early age prevail, I believe, in every quarter of the town more or less . . . It is the first stage of corruption of morals, young men getting connected with these women.

A great number of the juvenile depredators cohabited with girls of their own age. This early association of the sexes prevailed to an alarming extent. There were houses exclusively for the reception of boys and girls— one at St. Giles had accommodation for four hundred. Money for this form of indulgence in vice was obtained by the proceeds of thefts. The girls were allowed to visit their young lovers in prison. It is on record that

27

one boy of fourteen asked the girl with whom he had cohabited to keep their lodging going during the three months of his imprisonment.

The most detestable feature, therefore, of the " flash-house " system was the facility for debauchery among children. The Ordinary of Newgate stated that the boys in his school freely confessed to having had intimate relations with girls at a very early age, that persons had repeatedly presented themselves at Newgate calling themselves sisters and relations of the boys, but were the common prostitutes kept by them.

One other feature of the " flash-houses " calls for notice. Clubs of apprentice boys were harboured in them for the purpose of supporting any of their ilk who had run away from their masters, and of affording them every opportunity to indulge themselves easily amid scenes of lewdness and drunkenness, the cost of which they reimbursed themselves by pilfering their masters' property and disposing of it at the old-iron shops. In this process, from being once industrious and honest apprentices to a lawful trade, they became the apprentices of thieves who frequented these houses with the deliberate intention of discovering boys fit for their purpose.

Andrews tells of a house in the neighbourhood of Smithfield which, when demolished, was discovered to be a hiding-place of highwaymen and assassins, with secret spouts for the conveyance of stolen property from floor to floor in case of search, and its subterranean passages. Many of a similar description probably existed in the eighteenth century. One of these cellars in Chick Lane, Smithfield, was so notorious for almost daily murders that it was called the Blood Bowl House.

In enumerating the haunts of malefactors, mention must be made of the sanctuary offered by the Old Mint in Southwark. Here unruly ruffians preserved it sacred

28

from the officers of the law in spite of the Statute of William III. A regular organization gave security in this area for the thief and the murderer. A Master of the Mint with his bodyguard was appointed for the internal discipline and government of the sanctuary. Scouts and sentries were posted at all the outlets until ultimately a statute of George I abolished its immunities.

So much for the "flash-houses" and their excrescencies as causes of the prevailing conditions of depravity. But there was another, equally potent, carried on both within the "flash-houses" and almost everywhere outside in every walk of life. Gambling, which is invariably the twin evil of drunkenness, reached unprecedented proportions in the first part of the century, having its outward historical expression in the South Sea Bubble. The subscriptions to every form of wild enterprise were innumerable, from trading in the South Seas to breeding silkworms in Chelsea Park. So eager was everyone high and low to speculate that the general cry was "For God's sake let us but subscribe to something, we do not care what it is." Facilities for play were everywhere to suit the taste and fashion of all classes. Houses were opened under the sanction of aristocratic names, where an indiscriminate mixture of all ranks of society was to be found, from the finished sharper to the raw inexperienced youth.

The idle rarity [writes Colquhoun] of being introduced into what is supposed to be genteel society where a fashionable name announces an intention of seeing company has been productive of much domestic misery.

Lotteries, with all their attendant abuses of "agents" and their friends, who monopolized the tickets by the use of false names, assisted to whet the appetite of the public for getting something without working for it.

In 1770 there were no less than 400 lottery offices in London and its neighbourhood. The newspapers of the day teemed with proposals issued by every ravenous adventurer who could collect a few valuable articles to raffle.

Another institution selected by most historians as being at the deepest root of all evil was the receiver of stolen goods, who from earliest times until our own has been the bane of human society. If capital punishment could have been reserved for any other crimes than murder and treason, the selection could surely have been made with some justification to include in its operation this type of miscreant most easily dispensed with, and without whom the world would be a better place to inhabit.

There is no question that young boys were taught and encouraged to be thieves by this product of the underworld, mostly of foreign importation. The repulsive figure of Fagin which Charles Dickens has portrayed upon his imperishable canvas is not overdrawn, and faithfully reproduces a character that for hundreds of years has been more responsible for the corruption of youth than any other agency, direct or indirect, that can be adduced to account for it.

At the time Colquhoun wrote his treatise upon crime there were estimated to be three thousand of these human birds of prey in the purlieus of the Metropolis alone.

It is a melancholy reflection [he exclaims] to consider how many individuals, young and old, not of the class or description of common thieves, who are implicated in this system of depredation, who would have probably remained honest and industrious had it not been for the easy and safe mode of raising money which these numerous receivers of stolen goods hold out in every by-street and lane in London, where although a beggarly allowance of old iron, old rags or second-hand clothes is only exhibited, the back apartments are often filled with the most valuable articles purchased from artificers, labourers in the docks, humpers, glutmen, menial servants, journeyman porters, chimney sweepers, itinerant Jews and others. Thus it is that the moral principle is totally destroyed among a vast body of the lower ranks of the people, for whenever prodigality, dissipation, or a want of economy, or gaming, whether in the Lottery or otherwise, occasions a pressure for money, they avail themselves of every opportunity to purloin public or private property, and recourse is had to all those tricks and devices by which even children are enticed to steal before they know that it is a crime, and to raise money at the pawnbrokers or the old iron and rag shops to supply the wants of profligate parents.

Colquhoun also describes what he terms

latent receivers who do not keep open shops, but secretly support the professed robbers and burglars by purchasing their plunder the moment it is acquired, of which class there are some who are said to be extraordinarily opulent.

One whom he refers to as " a considerable dealer in rags and old iron," informed him that there were two varieties of receiver, wholesale and retail. The retail were those who purchased in the first instance from the thieves or agents, and as soon as they had collected a sufficient supply, parted with it to a larger dealer for ready money. Many of these rogues employed subordinates to delete the government mark from iron and metal stores, by which device they were able to sell them back to the government repeatedly.

Considerable difficulty was experienced in detecting these hidden agents of crime and in bringing them to justice, owing to the disorganized condition of London's administration, which comprised a number of separate jurisdictions that so clashed with one another as to impair any effective co-operation in vigilance and energy of pursuit.

There were regular markets in various London public and private houses held by the principal dealers in stolen goods, where hawkers, pedlars, fraudulent horse-dealers, unlicensed lottery-office keepers, the riff-raff of the fairs, Irish labourers, hackney-coach owners, and many others who would not be suspected, were regularly supplied with counterfeit copper and silver. Scarce a wagon or coach departed from the Metropolis that did not carry boxes and parcels of base coin to the camps, seaports and manufacturing towns, so that the country was deluged with counterfeit money.

Lowest in the scale of villainy that made the thief can be classified the atrocious scandal of the houses set apart for the accommodation of vagabonds. There is on record a particularly lurid description of one of these night shelters provided by the contemporary High Constable of Holborn.

In the parish of St. Giles there are great numbers of houses set apart for the reception of idle persons and vagabonds, who have their lodgings there for twopence. In the above parish and in St. George's, Bloomsbury, one woman alone controls several of these houses, all accommodated with miserable beds from the cellar to the garret for such twopenny lodgers. In these beds, several of which are in the same room, men and women, often strangers to each other, lie promiscuously, the price of a double bed being no more than threepence, as an encouragement to lie together; but as these places are thus adapted to whoredom, so are they no less provided for drunkenness, gin being sold in them all at a penny a quartern, so that the smallest sum of money serves for intoxication. In the execution of search warrants Mr. Welch, the Constable, rarely finds less than twenty of these houses open for the receipt of all comers at the latest hours. In one of these houses, and that not a large one, he numbers 58 persons of both sexes, the stench of whom was so intolerable that it compelled him in a short time to quit the place.

Fielding supplements the foregoing account with one of his own experience in Shoreditch, where he saw two little houses of this description emptied of nearly seventy men and women, amongst whom was a young and pretty bride with her newly-married husband. Such was their poverty that the money on all of them did not amount to one shilling, with the exception of the bride, who, he learned, had robbed her mistress. "Among other mischiefs," he adds, "attending this nuisance is the great increase of thieves."

From all the available evidence it is an obvious conclusion to draw that one of the most indefensible features of this period of moral stagnation was the callous neglect of youths of tender years by the State, or indeed by any controlling authority. Even at the close of the century there were not less than three thousand of them under twenty years of age in the London prisons; nearly half this number were under seventeen years of age, and a thousand of the latter were convicted of felony. Many of those sent to prison were barely nine or ten years of age. Incredible as it may seem there were even cases of children of six years old charged with crimes.

The extreme poverty and misery of the lowest stratum of society and the absence of any attempt at legislation which might have alleviated the lot of the poorer classes may serve to account for this phenomenal state of infantile depravity.

Herds of very young children were driven famished into the streets every morning by indigent or profligate parents who neither could find employment for them, nor had the means of binding them out as apprentices to trades, and were dared to return home without plunder

under a penalty of flogging, while a number of orphans with no friends of any kind joined with them in their illicit pursuits. They would sleep in sheds, the streets, the market-places. No one would employ them. Corporal chastisement and prison only served to degrade them the more. Sheer necessity drove them to crime, for in reality prison was their only home.

The Clerk of Bridewell Hospital, giving evidence before the Police Committee upon this subject, observed :

> So far from theft being discouraged by their parents it is too frequently the principal source of their support, and in many instances the unnatural father is himself found to be the instructor of his children in crime as well as the participator in their plunder. The fate of female children in such families is still more deplorable, and it is only too well ascertained that the ruin of multitudes of females for life takes place at so early an age is perfectly shocking to humanity ; in most of such cases I have found the parents the tempters and destroyers of their own children ; indeed it is almost impossible that without their connivance and consent their children could become abandoned and depraved at so early an age.

The booths of Covent Garden Market were stated to have been the nightly resort and shelter of hundreds of such youths, and it was here that they consorted with women of the basest description. The police were in the habit of trying to scatter them instead of taking them into custody. In Covent Garden or in the purlieus of St. Giles and Whitechapel these indigent young boys and girls took up their nightly abode in a state of promiscuous depravity. They were rarely reclaimed. It was not a long stride from this life of mendicancy to the "flash-houses" where every facility was afforded them to qualify for the gallows.

Of other evil influences upon the general moral tone of society in the eighteenth century most contemporaries make special mention of the Fairs which, although they may be associated in our minds with " Merrie England " and much that is picturesque and attractive in fiction, in reality were the favourite resorts of all the worst scoundrels who preyed upon their fellows, and were the forcing-house of every conceivable kind of vice and evil practice. Evidence was given before the Select Committee on the State of the Police in 1816 to the effect that these fairs tended

to the corruption of the morals of females and ultimately to their seduction ; that there were some 80 annually held within 10 miles of London at which assembled some of the worst characters in the Metropolis.

It was at the London fairs that booths were erected for the purpose of staging plays, the majority of which appear to have been of the most demoralizing description. The drama must certainly be responsible for an even lower tone than would have obtained without its influence. Swift placed its degraded condition among the foremost causes of the general depravity of the age. The matter even came before the notice of the House of Commons in the year 1735.

Inferior masquerades are also included by Fielding in his general indictment of this form of public amenity. " These are no other than the temples of drunkenness, lewdness and all kinds of debauchery."

Among the influences which cannot be ignored in estimating what were the factors which made for conditions of universal degeneracy must be reckoned the looseness of the marriage tie, and indeed the easy custom of men and women living together, dispensing with its restrictions altogether. Colquhoun animadverts upon this aspect of social life in no unmeasured terms.

The total ignorance of moral and religious duties among the

lower ranks of people in the Metropolis is manifested by the vast numbers who cohabit together without marriage, from which connections a numerous progeny arises reared up (where want of care and disease does not shorten their days) under the example of parents whose conduct exhibits nothing but the vilest profligacy.

Reference to this subject necessitates allusion to the extraordinary abuse of the so-called Fleet marriages, which were not abolished by law until the year 1753. Clergymen confined for debt in the Fleet prison previous to this Act were allowed the lucrative privilege of marrying couples within its precincts. It is on record that one of these improvident parsons married monthly on an average 150 couples. Women who were in debt could be married to a husband regularly attached to the establishment for this purpose, and as soon as married separate from him, the husband content for a gratuity, to be liable for the debts of his wife, who was thus able to laugh at her former creditors and open fresh credit elsewhere. No questions being asked, unsuspecting minors were entrapped and married, and even some united forcibly against their will to men whom they had never seen before. Smollett bears witness to the prevalence of this social evil:

There was a band of profligate miscreants, the refuse of the clergy, dead to every sentiment of virtue, abandoned to all sense of decency and decorum, for the most part prisoners for debt or delinquency, and indeed the very outcasts of human society who hovered about the verge of the Fleet prison to intercept customers, plying like porters for employment, and performed the ceremony of marriage, without licence or question, in cellars, garrets or ale-houses, to the scandal of religion and the disgrace of that order which they professed. The ease with which this ecclesiastical sanction was obtained, and the vicious disposition of these wretches open to the practices of fraud and corruption were productive of polygamy, indigence, conjugal infidelity, prostitution and every curse that could embitter the married state.

At one time these marriages took place at the rate of 8,000 per annum. The evil was ultimately put a stop to by the Marriage Act, which rendered it punishable by death to give a false certificate or make a false registry.

Most writers who analyse the causes of depravity in the eighteenth century include in their strictures the bad influence exercised upon the behaviour in towns by gentlemen's servants, a very numerous class in those times. There were, as to-day, various grades of servants, commencing with the link-bearer, a wretched class composed of the very poorest and worst clad, many of whom according to Gay were in league with the thief bands. Higher in the social scale were the footmen and male house servants, who were usually idle and dissolute. From among them the ranks of the highwaymen were commonly recruited. Indeed a large proportion of the most famous of that brotherhood had been in domestic service. Hawkins, James, Maclean (Horace Walpole's assailant), John Rann and Page, to mention a few of the more renowned, had all been aforetime in livery.

The deplorable condition of the streets, particularly by night, which ensured to the highwayman in the country and the footpad in the towns complete immunity, and held out to the apprentice in crime an easy and safe means of obtaining an illicit livelihood, was not the least remarkable example of the Government's impotence to terminate abuses from which the public suffered.

So great were the dangers by which the roads were beset that many used barges on the Thames by preference, but even here there were risks to be encountered from the evil practices of the boatmen. Highwaymen infested Hampstead Heath, Bagshot, Finchley Common, Epping Forest, Hounslow Heath, Shooter's Hill and Blackheath. In the Metropolis itself, Whitechapel, Holborn, the Strand and Shoreditch were their happy hunting-grounds. Even in Berkeley Square and St. James's Street members of the aristocracy were occasionally held up. Piccadilly was dangerous after dark, and Islington was secure for none but the law-breaker.

It is a curious circumstance that the so-called " knights of the road " were not always professional thieves. Distressed tradesmen sometimes took to the road in desperation as being an easy and comparatively safe method of obtaining a livelihood. It is said that instances were not rare of persons being stopped by men of their own acquaintance who although masked might be recognized by their voices, and who robbed travellers with a promise of returning the money at a certain place and hour on a pledge of secrecy, as they were in urgent need of ready cash for their business. But the majority of those who made the road unsafe by their depredations were professionals. So intolerable became their activities, so immune they seemed to be from apprehension and so perpetual a menace had they become to law-abiding citizens, that in 1744 the Lord Mayor and Aldermen of London conveyed an address to the King in which they indicated that evil persons of all sorts

commit the most daring outrages upon the persons of His Majesty's subjects whose affairs obliged them to pass through the streets, by terrifying, robbing and wounding them, and these acts were frequently perpetrated at such times as were heretofore deemed hours of security.

Fielding describes how some of the well-known highwaymen committed robberies in broad daylight in the sight of many people without molestation. Officers of justice confessed to him that they had passed such offenders in the streets with warrants in their pockets against them without daring to effect their arrest. If they had done so twenty or thirty armed villains would have come to the rescue of their comrades in arms.

Another authority describes how pickpockets made no scruple to knock people down with bludgeons in Fleet Street and the Strand, that they paraded Covent Garden in large bodies, armed, in sufficiently formidable numbers to assail whole parties of wayfarers. In Piccadilly a highwayman was known to have attacked a post-chaise and eluded capture. As late as 1780 it was customary for travellers coming to town to remain all night at the Angel in Islington, rather than push forward in the dark, as the road was bad and infested by robbers. Pedestrians in London preferred walking to riding in a hackney coach " on account that they are in a readier posture to defend themselves or call out for aid if attacked."

Evidence testifying not only to the insecurity of the King's highway, but also to the depths of depravity to which sections of the community had sunk also is afforded by the activities of the Society of Mohocks, which seemed to have been recruited for no other purpose but to commit crimes of the utmost barbarity in the streets at night. As if impelled thereto by some unwholesome complex, boys of quite good birth are said to have implicated themselves with the bestial enterprises of these youthful degenerates.

Andrews thus describes their nightly plan of campaign.

One party would sally forth for the purpose of " tipping the lion," violently flattening the noses of passengers who fell in their way, and gouging out their eyes ; another " tribe " would give pursuit to some trembling passer-by and on overtaking him they would prick him with their swords till they had exhausted his powers of endurance. Then there were the " tumblers," who devoted themselves especially to the diversion of turning females upon their heads, and the " dancing masters," who took their name from their skill in keeping their victim in constant motion by running their swords into his legs. One " tribe " delighted in thrusting females into barrels and then setting them rolling down hill; another derived its chief sport from beating and ill-using the watchman . . . they made a point of drinking till they were in a state of perfect frenzy before they sallied forth.

Fielding also makes a complaint of what we should term the defective town-planning of London, which served to give immunity to every description of lawbreaker.

Whoever considers the cities of London and Westminster with the late vast addition of their suburbs, the great irregularity of their buildings, the immense number of lanes, alleys, courts and by-places, must think that had they been intended for the very purpose of concealment they could scarce have been better contrived. Upon such a view the whole appears as a vast wood or forest in which a thief may harbour with as great security as wild beasts in the deserts of Africa or Arabia, for by wandering from one place to another and often stripping his quarters he may almost avoid the possibility of being discovered.

Finally, it cannot be forgotten that one of the contributory causes of the general demoralization was the atrocious condition of the Services, the appalling overcrowding of ships and barracks, and the habitual circumstances in which soldiers and sailors lived, all leading to vice and crime. Wars reacted unfavourably in two ways. While they were being waged the Government might plead the excuse that it could not attend to social reform, and when hostilities had ceased the returned troops had nothing to do and turned to the evil courses which Government, by its neglect, made so easy and so alluring.

The counteracting influences which to-day have so altered and improved the social conditions of the country were entirely lacking. The inability or the unwillingness of the Government to institute any social reforms resulted in free rein being given to the lowest of human impulses. Those who complain to-day of the expense and the interference in domestic lives of a vast army of officials and the doubtless irritating supervision of inspectors, have only to study the conditions which prevailed when liberty was synonymous with licence in order to revise their verdict.

The Churches throughout the greater part of the eighteenth century preached a cold and tolerant doctrine, deprecated enthusiasms and failed to make their influence felt against the prevalent scepticism or indifference, until the preaching of the Methodists and the Evangelical school kindled the dying embers of religious enthusiasm into a flame which their detractors protested gave more heat than light.

Education was deplorably deficient. It was not until the end of the eighteenth century that Lancaster opened his establishment in London and that Robert Raikes instituted the Sunday Schools. What little defective teaching was available was provided by the various religious denominations, the voluntary associations and the benevolence of private individuals, without government assistance. There was a number, by no means sufficient, of endowed schools dating from an earlier period which gave free education to children and there also existed the parochial charity schools. But for sixty years after the death of Queen Anne the Government did nothing whatever for education.

In England it was the prevailing doctrine that the education of the people was entirely foreign to the duties of Government and a common belief that it would unfit the poor for the state of life to which they had been called.

Gibbon complained that the greatest city of the world was still destitute of a public library. When it is estimated how much spare time is nowadays spent in profitable reading by the young which, if the facilities for such wholesome occupation were as lacking as in the eighteenth century, would be spent upon less edifying pursuits, the conclusion can be drawn that the want of provision for the intellectual tastes of the people was by no means a neglible origin of crime in England.

Added to all these potent causes there was no machinery by which public opinion in favour of amelioration might be organized and ventilated. It is difficult for us who live in an age when the Press is the rapid and convenient vehicle of public opinion on all affairs, imperial and domestic, to realize a condition of things where such a facility is not provided. But its absence accounted for the long continuance of the dire abuses recounted in these pages. The Press indeed existed, but it was prejudiced in its effectiveness by the rigorous laws of libel, by the primitiveness of the printing press, by the slowness of communications and by the illiteracy of the majority of the population, who would to-day be capable of forming an opinion against abuses and insisting on their redress, while the Courts held over the heads of distracted publishers the law of libel with pillories, fines, imprisonments and all the machinery of the law.

The House of Commons itself thoroughly resented any part of its proceedings being reported, so that there was no means of a public opinion being formed through a medium which to-day is the most efficacious for ventilating grievances. In 1738 a resolution was passed to the effect that it was a high indignity and a notorious breach of its privileges to publish any of its proceedings, and that the House would proceed with the utmost severity against offenders. Even had the public been sufficiently in touch with the proceedings in Parliament to influence its members, the Legislature was so unrepresentative that the County of Middlesex, including London and Westminster, returned only eight members in 1769, the year of the first serious effort at redistribution.

The party system as we understand it to-day was gradually evolving, but as yet no scheme of internal domestic reform had bound together an effective and critical opposition, the various elements of which might have voiced the grievances of the oppressed and given them definition.

Instead of ensuring the provision of wholesome counteracting influences, the only expedients adopted by government to cure these ills of state had the reverse effect of that which was intended. A parenthetic reference must be made to them in this chapter for completeness' sake as they were amongst the chief contributory causes to the great increase of crime in the eighteenth century, but a more thorough investigation of their ultimate effect is so important that a separate chapter has been devoted to their consideration. Nothing could have been so ill conceived as the publicity of these spectacles mistakenly supposed to act as a deterrent to the potential criminal, but which were in fact more calculated to demoralize than to convert. There can be no doubt whatever that public executions, the gibbet at the street corner, the pillory, the floggings and all other exhibitions of revolting cruelty merely served to harden and to demoralize. Add to these the law's ferocity which

43

defeated its own object and the hopeless inefficiency of the police, both of which subjects are separately treated in this work, and the degeneracy of the times is no longer a matter for surprise.

From the foregoing it can be gathered how easy it was in the eighteenth century for the young lad of apprentice age to abandon an honest calling in favour of less reputable methods of earning a livelihood. Under the conditions which prevailed in every town during the eighteenth century it is remarkable, not that so many youths went astray, but that there were any to keep to the narrow path of virtue. That many went wrong who might have kept straight had Government concerned itself with the welfare of the young, and had not the criminal code been put into operation in so brutal a fashion, there can be no doubt.

The probability that so many young men who fell by the wayside might have led decent and respectable careers but for the neglect of the State to realize its responsibility induces us to make a more generous estimate of the youth who had made a false start, rather through the fault of others than his own, and who, had he been given a chance, might have turned into a valuable citizen. At least one historical illustration of this particular type comes down to us based on fairly authentic records owing to the fact that contemporary public interest was aroused and has ever since been sustained by posterity in the extraordinary escapades of the individual concerned. It is not for that reason that reference is here made to his circumstances. Something of the history of this unfortunate youth is briefly recounted here by the author, not to emphasize the picturesque and romantic aspects of it, but rather to take as an exemplification a youth who, for all his notoriety, was of a very normal type, and one which nowadays is constantly submitted and reacts favourably to the cure which the State provides, and who probably might never have been heard of had he been given the opportunity and the incentive so many lads are afforded to-day of returning to the paths of virtue. It may strike the reader as inappropriate that the example of Jack Sheppard has been chosen to point the moral because, probably owing to the notoriety of his phenomenal escapades from prison, he is generally looked upon as a prince among thieves. A closer scrutiny of his circumstances and career should serve to dispel that illusion. He was born in Stepney in the year 1701. He came of a line of honest carpenters in Spitalfields. His father, unfortunately for him, died when the boy was a mere infant. His mother, although doting upon him, seems to have had little enough share in his education. He was brought up in the Bishopsgate workhouse, an institution typical of the abominable neglect which characterized the local government of those times. Everyone's hand was no doubt against the unfortunate boy, whose hand as a result was to be against that of everyone else. He seems to have begun life as a cane chair-mender, but being brutally ill-used he was high-spirited enough to desert his employer. He was not, however, without a friend. One of the name of Kneebone, a woollen draper who had employed his father, taught him to read and write, and apprenticed him to Owen Wood, a cabinet-maker of Wych Street, Drury Lane.

Sheppard was by no means an unattractive youth. He was short, standing about five feet four, very slender but robust and of great strength, with a pale complexion and fine dark eyes. He had an impediment in his speech. Like so many of his type he was of a vain disposition, and unfortunately for his vanity he appears to have possessed a fatal attraction for the fair sex. It is difficult to believe that one who afterwards proved himself to be so active and courageous could have faithfully represented the type of idle apprentice made familiar to us in a series of Hogarth's most famous canvases. His story is the ordinary story of a lad who had not too high a standard of virtue, who had nothing to do with his leisure hours, but found the need supplied by those least qualified to influence him for good. It is more than probable that he owed his downfall to an early acquaintance with one of the unsavoury "flash-houses" already described, to which it was so easy for the ordinary poor boy in those days to gain access and from which it was so difficult to dissociate himself. It is recorded that he frequented the Black Lion, a typical example of those establishments that provided every facility to debauch the youth of London. Before the period of his apprenticeship was up it was here that he coincidentally enough met one Elizabeth Lyon, known to the underworld as Edgeworth Bess, doubtless one of the lures of this particular haunt of vice, who commenced the tragic sequence of influences that led to his ruin. Sheppard's standards were in all probability not very exacting, but he had sufficient discrimination to describe this woman in appropriate terms : "There is not," he observed, in allusion to her, "a more wicked, deceitful, lascivious wretch living in England."

There can be little doubt that the boy found himself in the clutches of the infamous Jonathan Wild at an early stage of his short criminal career, the medium of his introduction to so undesirable an acquaintance being the detestable "flash-houses" which caused the ruin of so many of his contemporaries. Once in that thraldom there was no escape for the wretched youth.

It does not appear that he was particularly criminally

46

minded. His first offence was a theft of silver spoons from the Runner Tavern in Charing Cross. His subsequent crimes were not very mean nor very heinous. It was his amazing courage, strength and effrontery that enabled him to effect those almost miraculous escapes from gaol which sealed his ultimate fate and which gave him immortal fame in the annals of Newgate. After a further robbery in 1723 he discreetly removed himself, unfortunately in the company of Edgeworth Bess, to the seclusion of Parsons Green. At the end of the year he was brought up as a runaway apprentice on a warrant to St. Clement's Round House, but his former master, who evidently had conceived an attachment for the boy and hoped for something better on the evidence of his personal qualities, procured his release. But by this time he was too much corrupted by evil communications to mend his ways. He seems, however, still to have had sufficient discrimination, and to have been sufficiently fastidious, to be aware of the vileness of his comrades in crime. He described the famous Joseph Blake *alias* Blueskin, in whose company he pursued his evil course, either of his own volition or under some compulsion, as "a worthless companion, a sorry thief, and that nothing but his attempt on Jonathan Wild could have made him taken notice of."

The rest of his career consisted of a series of burglaries alternating with short sojourns in various prisons, from which he effected those sensational escapes that have made his name famous for all time and which have given a very exaggerated reputation of the youth as a criminal.

The detestable Jonathan Wild seems to have been from the first his evil genius and his sworn enemy. Possibly Jack Sheppard had offended one who never forgave an affront. It was Wild who effected his arrest in Rosemary Lane in the year 1724. By a coincidence his elder brother had been transported for stealing within a few months of his own capture. He was tried and sentenced to death, but by the aid of his two mistresses he managed to escape from the condemned hold, and after a short excursion into Northamptonshire he was bold enough to return to his erstwhile haunts and pursuits, where he renewed his intercourse with dissipated companions. Although he was well known to the habitués of Wych Street, no one either dared or had the inclination to inform against him. On the 31st of October, dressed like a gentleman, he went into the city and made merry at a public-house not far from the place of his old confinement. At four that same afternoon he passed under the walls of Newgate in a hackney coach, the windows drawn up. Eventually he was seized, probably again at the instance of Jonathan Wild, on Finchley Common, and once again thrown into Newgate, from which he effected his last and most sensational escape. But by this time life could have held out few attractions for him beyond frequenting those purlieus where his apprehension was sooner or later a certainty.

During his final wanderings as a marked man there is one point to be noticed in his favour. Ten days after his escape from Newgate he sent for his mother, for whom he appears through thick and thin to have entertained a touching filial affection. Whether or not she was the penitent Magdalen as she is portrayed in the famous novel she certainly returned his devotion. He met her in the Sheers Tavern, Maypole Alley, near Clare Market. It is said she went down on her knees and implored him to go abroad while it was yet possible. But her son was too reckless of his fate to heed her prayer. Instead he ordered three quarterns of brandy and drank himself silly, in which condition he was that night arrested.

Jack Sheppard on the way to execution

W. Clarke del.

In prison he managed to secrete a penknife upon his person with the object of severing the cords that bound his hands on the way to Tyburn and of jumping from the cart into the crowd and escaping through Little Turnstile, where the mounted officers could not follow him. Failing such an artifice he had arranged with his friends that they should obtain possession of his body as soon as cut down and place it in a warm bed in the hope of resuscitation. But every expedient failed and Jack Sheppard paid the penalty of his misdeeds on the 26th of October, 1724.

It is intriguing to speculate upon what might have been the fate of Jack Sheppard had he lived to-day. He certainly would not have suffered the disadvantage of being brought up in a squalid workhouse. He would have doubtless received his education not at the hands of a casual philanthropist but in one or other of the excellent elementary schools that now exist in the neighbourhood. So likely and attractive a youth would have been bound to draw to himself the special attention of a teacher well trained in the art of eliciting from such a character all that was best and suppressing all that was worst in his composition. After leaving school and entering a trade he would be given every opportunity of joining one of the voluntary organizations—boy scouts, boys' brigade, boys' clubs, and others—that would offer him every wholesome outlet for his superfluous energy. No vestige of the " flash-house " remains to-day to lure the hapless youth. There are, it is true, public-houses, strictly regulated as to hours and providing refreshment at such prices, thanks to licensing laws, that excessive indulgence in them by those whose means are exiguous is prohibitive. If he thereafter displayed a disposition towards unruliness he would inevitably come into contact with a vigilant policeman who, unlike the thief-taker of old, would be more solicitous to check this tendency than to encourage him to weigh his weight in crime, and would drop some kindly hints before taking stronger measures. When he had entered upon the difficult stage of adolescence he would no doubt be waylaid by a modified version of Edgeworth Bess. He might or might not come unscathed through this ordeal, but certain it is that he would have much less excuse to give way to evil courses of this nature which would thus be available to him, than he would in the eighteenth century. In our own times there are far more wholesome occupations and opportunities to assist the adolescent in sublimating his animal passions than in the days when poor Jack Sheppard succumbed to his evil circumstances. More than likely such a character would "take up" with a decent respectable female companion, with whom he would associate in his leisure hours until he had reached a position in his trade which would permit of his marrying her.

But let us return to the unlikely hypothesis that he has not taken advantage of the leniency of the law and its administration nor of the various good influences which are his to command. For sundry minor offences, nothing more reprehensible than those due rather to the exuberance of youth than to any vicious propensities, he will be had up before the children's court. For the benefit of the uninitiated it must be explained that in the eyes of the law a boy is a "child" until he reaches the age of seventeen. By that time a youth of his enterprise, energy and intrepidity is likely to have tasted the fruits of the tree of knowledge, and will probably resent being classified as a child, and will regard the proceedings as something of an affront to his dignity. All taint of the police court will be absent. Something of the atmosphere of the headmaster's study will take its place. As a result of this interview with superior authority our modern Jack Sheppard, after spending a few days in a remand home while his antecedents, general health and mental condition are being meticulously inquired into, will be placed on probation. The same process may be repeated many times before anything worse happens to him. A case of a boy being placed on probation eight times came to the notice of the author not long since. If he still refused to answer to treatment, and it is difficult to believe that by this time Jack Sheppard would prove unregenerate, he will at length find himself within a court of law, with all the panoply of state, with policemen, no longer disguised as civilians, standing over him. But prison is not yet in sight. He is sent to a Borstal Institution, where probably somewhat to his surprise he discovers that a generous impulse for his reformation is predominant over any anxiety for his punishment. His housemaster and his officers—the term warder is taboo—are his best friends, and it is brought home to him that the world forgives a boy however hard it may be with a man. Being of the self-reliant type, more easily moved than controlled, in all probability he would prove responsive to such a system and the wholesome self-restraint it teaches. On completing his term of detention he finds himself out on licence to the Borstal Association, which establishes him in some reputable trade and watches over him lest again he enters into temptation. If even after all these efforts on his behalf he discards the helping hand he will find that his licence is revoked and that he will be returned for further treatment. But is it likely, we can ask ourselves, that Jack Sheppard *redivivus* would have, under such favourable circumstances, tried authority so high? Is it not more likely that one of his courageous and generous disposition would have yielded to better influences and recovered his moral equilibrium long before the ultimate process described above was complete?

The reader may consider this digression fantastic and absurd, but all those who have made a conscientious study of juvenile delinquency, who have been connected officially or professionally with the institutions which endeavour to help young men to retrace their steps into the paths of virtue, and who have had personal acquaintance with them, cannot fail to agree that there is nothing either fantastic or absurd in the above speculation, and that if Jack Sheppard had had the advantages of the modern youth he would have passed into the ranks of the ordinary, decent, responsible citizens and would have cheated only the author who has immortalized him in the pages of the *Dictionary of National Biography*.

CHAPTER II

THE SOWING OF THE TARES

IF it is legitimate to conclude that by the most reprehensible neglect on the part of government the conditions which prevailed in the eighteenth century were such as to make thieves, there can be no doubt that the steps taken to apprehend the delinquent were of a nature well calculated to aggravate the evil conditions they were intended to abolish.

The police system, if it can be so called, had been inherited from mediæval times. The responsibility for securing honest citizens from the unwelcome attentions of the malefactor originally attached to each hundred and tithing, and the members of these administrative divisions were held jointly liable for any infraction of the law within the appropriate boundaries. " Frankpledge," as it was termed, incorporated in the Statute of Winchester, together with the institutions of " Watch and Ward " and " Hue and Cry " remained as the basis of the police system for at least three centuries.

The irrational idea of exacting hostages in this manner—punishing the innocent for the guilty—was the essence of such a system. The entire hundred was made to suffer for any offence against the law committed within its limits, and equally the tithing for offences committed by one of its members, a procedure sometimes adopted by less enlightened schoolmasters who lack sufficient good fortune or acumen for the successful detection of a delinquent pupil. The result of employing it in the apprehension of transgressors against the community was that when, as might often be the case, the thief was not apprehended everyone else suffered unjustly, to the general discomfiture of the community. Moreover, it afforded opportunity for the Sheriff to practise extortion of the most devastating kind.

The Justice gradually superseded the Sheriff and the Constable the tithing man in the maintenance of order. Hitherto there was no such institution as a separate body of police, but gradually a distinct order of watch-men came into existence.

In the eighteenth century the protection of the public was still the exclusive concern of parochial effort. The City of London with its various wards, each with its own local management and its own local jealousies, numbered amongst them less than a thousand constables, unpaid, and about 2,000 watchmen and patrols paid at the discretion of the persons in authority in each ward, parish, hamlet, liberty or precinct. In Westminster in every parish the watch was under the direction of a separate commission composed of persons who had served the offices of Churchwarden and Overseer. The Commissioners of the respective parishes appointed the beats of their watchmen without conferring together, leaving the frontiers of each parish indeterminate. These watch-men were appointed by the vestries and received the most inadequate pay of twelve shillings a week in summer and seventeen shillings and sixpence in winter, a remuneration for their services which they often supplemented by taking bribes from prostitutes or a share in a burglar's loot. Failing such adventitious accretion to their legitimate earnings they had recourse to the usurer. They were altogether insufficient in numbers and their duties were manifestly inappropriate to their age and physique. Moreover, their beats were too extensive to enable them to exercise a sufficient supervision.

The infirm and decrepit, who were unable to work and consequently compelled to apply to " the parish " for relief, were considered fit enough candidates for the duties of watchmen. It is related that a " sturdy strong fellow " was rebuked for applying for the situation as he was " capable of labour." Therefore it happened that they were often old and feeble and secured their appointment for no other reason than that in the alternative they would become a burden on public resources. They were served out with a rattle, a staff, and a treble-caped great-coat à la elder Mr. Weller. Thus equipped they were placed in a district and on a certain beat with the ostensible object of protecting the lives and property of the inhabitants. Aware no doubt of their incompetence to discharge these functions, they acquired the habit of forsaking their beat whenever so disposed in order to obtain refreshment at a local ale-house or for the purpose of adding to their inadequate pay by lighting wayfarers to their homes. As to affording any protection from thieves they were careful to warn the latter of their approach by striking the pavement resonantly with their staves. There was no other method of punishing them for neglect of duty than by dismissing them, " which in fact is not a punishment, for they find it difficult to get men to serve in that office." In order to shelter them from the weather during the inclement season of the year they were provided with a little wooden box against the wall, in which contrivance for their comfort they more often than not spent the greater portion of the night in peaceful oblivion. During their conscious moments, carrying a lantern, the candle of which they were called upon to provide out of their meagre stipend, they tottered around their respective beats announcing the hour and the state of the weather, the only check on their vigilance save the occasional rounds of the parish beadle.

This custom, irritating as it would be to a later generation which expects the constable to go about his just occasions in discreet silence, was no doubt a survival of that which Stow describes of the bellman of the ward, who, especially in the long nights, perambulated the streets and lanes ringing a bell, and " saluted his masters and mistresses with some rhymes suitable to the festivals and seasons of the year and bids them look to their lights." It is difficult to comprehend why these nocturnal activities brought any feelings of comfort or security to the inhabitants for whose benefit they were intended, in view of the fact that the watchman was equally incompetent for the purposes of protection whether awake or asleep.

After their rounds these venerable guardians of the peace retired to their lairs to slumber until the next hour called them forth again, provided their peace of mind was not rudely interrupted by the cry of help from a fellow-watchman set upon by a gang of roughs. In these conflicts the " Charlies," as they were scornfully named by the general public, seldom emerged victorious. " Let us go and tease the Charlies " was the frequent exclamation of the incorrigible young libertines who found time hanging heavy upon their hands. If the watchman was asleep his box was unceremoniously overturned and the wretched victim of this rude horse-play was submitted to every kind of indignity, against which he was incompetent to retaliate.

Until the middle of the eighteenth century London was probably behind every other European town in the matter of illumination. The fact that the streets were

The " Charlies "   *John A. Atkinson del.*

ill lit made the duties of the watch and ward still more hazardous. It is true that in 1716 a regulation was put into force by which every householder whose dwelling adjoined the street was obliged to hang out a lantern, and that this obligation rested also upon public buildings, schools and churches. But even with these precautions the cover of darkness was still one of the best aids to evil doing and the worst hindrance to the officers of the law's protection.

The parish constables were originally nominated by the court of burgesses or court leet. Although any householder was liable to discharge this onerous and unremunerative public duty, he was at liberty to avoid the responsibility by buying a substitute or purchasing what was known as a "Tyburn ticket," a transferable form of exemption from service in parish offices granted as a reward for the capture of a felon, the result being that their deputies in many instances were characters of the worst and lowest description. The fine they received from the person who appointed them varied from ten shillings to five pounds. Having certain definite expenses and no salary they were induced to live by extortion, by countenancing all species of vice, by an understanding with the keepers of brothels and disorderly ale-houses, by attending in courts of justice and bearing false witness to ensure a conviction, when their expenses were paid, or by any other means which might compensate them for the lack of a sufficient salary.

The inefficiency of the constable, whose duties were presumed to be in the nature of pursuit rather than protection or detection, necessitated the creation of an auxiliary force known afterwards as the Bow Street runners. These extra constables, whose co-operation with the watchmen was somewhat adventitious, at first took the name of the magistrate to whose office they

were attached—for example, " Justice Wright's people."
There were fifty paid men divided among the nine police
courts of the Metropolis, who may be regarded as the
forerunners of our modern detective, although falling
far short of him in enterprise and resource. They were
nominated from Whitehall by the Secretary of State.
The " runners " were paid £1 a week, with a special
recompense consisting of a share in the private reward
offered in the event of a successful apprehension, or in
the case of a conviction a portion of the public parliamentary recompense, £40, awarded on the authority of
the Bench.

Although the Bow Street runners were more energetic
and efficient than the watchmen, nothing could have
been more detrimental to the public interests than
this particular system of encouraging the activity of
the thief-taker. There can be no doubt that young
offenders were suffered to be trained on in their
career of crime from the first offence which made
them amenable to the law, while they were not yet
objects of profit from the point of view of the Government reward, until step by step they were seduced into
the commission of crimes for which on their conviction
the reward could be obtained. The infelicitous consequence of this ill-judged experiment in thief-taking was
incidentally an appreciable increase of juvenile crime.
Hapless boys, finding that their first offences went
unpunished, took fresh courage, and when in the next
stage of this rake's progress they were introduced to the
questionable amenities of the " flash-houses " they were
afforded every opportunity of observing thieves and
thief-takers sitting together and drinking on terms of
easy fellowship. Every new experience was calculated
to give them an impression that they might rob without
fear of retribution. The unsuspecting youth did not

pause to reflect that the leniency of the officers of the law would cease once they had committed a " £40 crime," when they should " weigh their weight," according to the current slang, and that they would then be sacrificed to the cupidity of their pursuers.

When conviction was doubtful the offender enjoyed long immunity from arrest, as the officers were unwilling to take decisive action until they were certain of the reward. It is said that in 1808 the value of property stolen without anybody being apprehended for its theft amounted to £15,000. With the same object in view some of the police officers were even led to forswear themselves, and were tempted to sell the lives of their fellow-creatures for gain. It is not surprising to learn that juries began to be chary of convicting on police evidence. Nothing, therefore, could have been more pernicious than this system of offering large rewards for the apprehension of a capital offence and no reward for the encouragement of discovering minor felonies, more especially as it was responsible for the emergence of a particularly revolting type of public enemy, the " thief-taker," who flourished upon this habit of concealing and encouraging budding thieves in their evil doing until their crimes made it worth his while to set the law in motion against his victims.

The official functionaries were so unsuccessful in the detection of crime that the administrators of the law were constrained to have recourse to the meanest and lowest of mankind to supply the information they required. No expedient could have been more disastrous as, although it led to the apprehension of criminals, it in all likelihood made as many as it took, and many of those who were taken might never have been criminals had it not been for the insidious methods employed by the thief-taker.

There was a pamphlet published in 1753 entitled *The Thief Catcher, or Villainy Detected* by one who concealed his identity under the description " A Lover of His Country." It purported to be written for the information of Members of Parliament in the hopes that it would be useful to them. The author must have been of a sanguine temperament, as this subject was not one which evoked the interest of his contemporaries at Westminster. In this work the thief-catcher is thus described, " One of the most wicked and dangerous set of felons yet taken notice of is the class of rogues commonly known and distinguished by the name of Thief Catchers." Their commission does not appear to have been of an official character. An example can be quoted of one William Norton, who, during the examination of a case of highway robbery, when asked how he got his living replied, " I keep a shop in Wych Street and sometimes I take a thief."

Of these thief-takers the infamous Jonathan Wild has come to personify the type. For the combination of malevolence and avarice there cannot have been one of his professional colleagues who could bear any comparison with him. But from the most reliable sources there emerges the conclusion that he was not a thief-taker in the sense that he was officially and regularly employed by Government to catch thieves or to prevent crime. The silver-mounted truncheon he was in the habit of carrying as the emblem of his office was in all probability a piece of impertinence on his own part. That he was used surreptitiously by authority there can be little doubt, but only on the principle of setting a thief, or in his case something much worse than a thief, to catch his ilk. Whether we can describe him correctly as an official under Government or not there is little doubt that government for a time connived at his

nefarious practices failing more legitimate methods for
the discovery of those who had broken the law.

But that such an institution as Jonathan Wild existed
at all, is in itself conspicuous proof of the incompetence
of our criminal administration in the eighteenth century.
Some account of the career of this prince of ruffians is
therefore not inappropriate to the purpose of this
chapter.

Wild was born in 1683 at Wolverhampton. For a
time he became an apprentice to a buckle-maker, but he
early afforded sufficient evidence to his employer that
he was of the idle variety. Finding honest toil not to
his taste he absconded to London where, consorting
with bad characters, he quickly found himself in debt,
a predicament which in those days entailed forfeiture of
liberty. He was in due course arrested and lodged in
the Wood Street Compter, where he made contact with
the thieves, pickpockets and low characters who, for
very sufficient reasons, constituted the society most
congenial to him. In this receptacle for the arrested
awaiting trial, he formed a liaison with one Mary
Milliner, a particularly disreputable prostitute, well
qualified to be his instructress in those very accomplishments in which he was destined to excel. From this
confederate in sin he learned the methods employed by
thieves in their nefarious occupation. As soon as he
was at large again he opened a miniature public-house
in Cock Alley, which through his own encouragement
became the resort of robbers of all denominations. It
was here that he first conceived the project of instituting
an agency for stolen property, in the management of
which he became the master and tyrant of those attracted
by its possibilities of a livelihood. The habitués of this
den of robbers brought him news of illicitly acquired
booty. He, on his part, offered to restore it to the

rightful owner in return for a recompense, sometimes as much as half the value of the stolen article. But he took every precaution to cover his own tracks. He would intimate to those who had been robbed that he knew of an " honest broker " into whose hands their purloined property had drifted, and in return for an extortionate reward he would arrange for the transfer of the property from the fictitious broker to the rightful owner. He was careful never to handle the goods himself, and meticulously avoided any of those hazards that beset either thief or receiver. He pursued this highly lucrative profession for fifteen years without incurring any public stigma upon his character, although he ultimately acknowledged having pocketed £10,000 as the price paid to him for the restoration of stolen property.

The evil influence of such as Wild was so comprehensive and so devastating that even Parliament took cognizance of it and placed upon the Statute Book a law providing that any person who should accept a reward in consequence of restoring stolen effects without prosecuting the thief was guilty of a capital offence. But this well-meant effort on the part of contemporary legislators failed to place any serious obstacle in Wild's pathway. With characteristic ingenuity he hit upon the device of arranging for the ransom money to be left at some appointed place and the stolen property to be returned on the same day. His own comment upon this ingenious procedure is worth quoting :

My acquaintance among thieves is very extensive, and when I receive information of a robbery I make inquiry of the suspected parties and leave word at proper places that if the goods are left where I appoint, the reward shall be paid and no questions asked. Surely no imputation of guilt can fall upon me for I hold no interview with robbers, nor are the goods given into my possession.

In other and plainer words, he ran no personal risks of being caught in taking the substantial proceeds and therefore he could not be classed as a criminal. The only crime he accepted as such was that of being found out, a crime which ultimately led him to the very gallows upon which hundreds of his victims had previously paid the penalty which he had so often and so richly merited in their stead.

In order to sustain his value as a thief-taker he was obliged occasionally to surrender one or two of his victims to the gallows as hostages for his own good name and to reserve to himself credit for his public-spirited action. When expediency urged such a course he provided a few additional victims in the form of those who had committed no offence whatsoever. The motive sometimes was that they were in possession of evidence against himself or it was sometimes merely that he knew a heavy reward had been offered for the conviction of anyone who might have perpetrated a crime, and it was quite as easy, with his gang in attendance, to prove the case against an innocent person if the guilty was not forthcoming. As for his value as a thief-*maker*, it was inestimable. He had easy enough material to work upon among the wretched, uneducated, un-housed youth of England. He would play his proselytes off one against the other, ever drawing tighter his stranglehold upon them all. It is said that he divided the town and country into districts, all under his supreme direction, with separate gangs allocated to each, detachments of whom he engaged upon particular tasks. For instance, there was a special corps for robbing a church, and another for pickpocketing at country fairs.

Eventually he became a man of means and status, even, it is said, commanding a certain measure of respect amongst his fellow-men. He set up an office for the business of recovering stolen property, where clients gave details of their losses, paid a fee of a crown for the making of inquiries. Pocket-books, documents of all kinds, apart from other valuables, came to hand. He made a speciality of stealing shopkeeper's ledgers and holding them to ransom against disclosures to other tradesmen. If the owner would not pay his price he would threaten blackmail.

He was careful to register the names of all who came within his power with particulars of their operations, and devised methods of his own for compelling fair dealing towards himself on the part of the gang of thieves who had come within his power. He kept them always on short commons the more easily to avoid any retaliation on their part. Once in his clutches the chances of salvation for the young delinquent were remote. There are sufficient grounds for believing that Jack Sheppard came under his influence, although not for the romantic reasons adduced by Harrison Ainsworth. It was said that Jonathan Wild never helped any man to business or to promotion without endeavouring to corrupt him, selecting as his victims the " down and outs," amongst whom he found the transportees who had succeeded in repatriating themselves, a very easy prey. Giving them food and lodging he could secure their blind obedience by threats to denounce them if they failed to come to heel. From among lonely and vagrant children left to wander the streets in destitution and beggary he also secured valuable instruments for the conduct of his nefarious trade. Often he apprehended mere boys, whom he had instructed in criminal habits, by the time they " weighed their weight" in reward. He would also draw his recruits from the Mint district of Southwark, a haunt of bad characters of every description and variety. It is recorded that in one instance he murdered a footpad who had deserted from his service, took all his money, and subsequently claimed the reward and the credit for having exterminated a highwayman. For his own purposes he would assist criminals in various ways provided they conformed to his scheme of things, but if they failed him he would trump up charges against them and in this way dispose of those likely to be inconvenient to himself. As a consequence, he was often called upon to identify persons in court, and would sometimes defend them if it suited his purpose to do so, thus establishing a reign of terror amongst the London thieves, who came to believe that he could save or hang them at his own discretion. All the while he paraded the Metropolis as a disinterested authority " controlling the enormities of the dissolute."

Wild associated occasionally with magistrates in city taverns. It may have been in one of these social haunts that he first met Charles Hitchin, a corrupt City Marshal. The two congenial spirits entered into alliance with each other, Wild posing as Hitchin's assistant. They visited and denounced the habitués of bawdy houses and apprehended them, invariably protecting those who paid sufficient hush money. They created a monopoly in this blackmailing business and fixed a tariff for the payment of thieves. They preyed particularly upon the more miserable type of harlot, forcing them to deliver into their hands articles stolen from clients instead of to the pimps who protected them, threatening them with Bridewell if they refused, and forbidding them to solicit in the streets unless they surrendered. Wild would sometimes arrest street walkers or abduct them from their usual haunts and then lodge them in a workhouse, where they were further corrupted by others of his creatures.

Pickpockets, mostly boys, some under twelve years of age, were brought under the " discipline " of these two vile confederates. The motive behind such tutoring of youth in crime was no doubt the fact that the laws were not rigidly executed in respect of juvenile delinquents. The thief-taker therefore traded on the well-known humanity of the law towards children. They would employ young lads to corrupt others. Detachments of these boys were to be found near St. Paul's and at Moorfields. Hitchin would hobnob with them, giving them cakes and ale. There is a case on record of two of these youngsters being taken to Newgate. But fortunately for them Hitchin had been by this time declared to be the occasion of their ruin and was suspended by the Lord Mayor, the boys being acquitted. At length, as thieves will do, Hitchin and Wild fell out. The former attacked the latter by means of a pamphlet, the most classic example of the pot calling the kettle black. But the pot retaliated, and it is safe to say that the most reliable material as to the respective characters of these two arch-villains is to be found in these two broadsides. But Hitchin's animadversions had little immediate effect upon Wild's fortunes, which continued for a while to flourish as the green bay-tree. He grew bolder in evil-doing, and even had the impertinence to open an office over against the Old Bailey itself. There he was resorted to by rich and poor alike. His schemes met with success. He embarked upon various lucrative " side lines." He became the owner of a sailing vessel in which he used to convey some of his surplus " stock " to Holland. This proved to be a not indefinitely prosperous venture. After two years of successful illicit trading the ship was impounded for smuggling. Another enterprise of his was to employ an adept staff to alter the settings of jewellery in order to prevent identification, and he even established a hiring department for furnishing burglars with the necessary tools of their trade.

But Wild ultimately tried fortune beyond endurance. It is obvious that he could not have maintained his authority had he not shown now and again what at first sight might seem a certain disposition towards chivalry, and that he was incurring risk for the good of the community over which he presided. But he made this gesture once too often. A highwayman was apprehended near Bow. Wild came to the rescue and aided him to escape from his captor. For this offence he was committed to Newgate. The fear with which he had hitherto been regarded faded away. Whereupon certain persons not well disposed towards him supplied information as to where a quantity of valuables which he had acquired by crooked means could be found. Wild begged to be tried at once on the original charge, but he was detained while information on the other charges upon his indictment poured in. Having failed to establish his innocence, he attempted to take poison in prison, but without succeeding in cheating the Tyburn gallows, whither, amid the execrations and jeers of a tumultuous mob, he was conveyed to pay the extreme penalty for his sins in May, 1725.

Jonathan Wild owed his long immunity and thousands of his victims their perdition to the fact that the Government was too preoccupied with foreign affairs to concern itself with the reform of the social conditions of England. He may have had his value in certain cases where he alone had the requisite information and facility to apprehend the particular enemy of society which the law required. But it is inconceivable that a civilized government should either directly or indirectly have employed an agent who was so vast a power for evil amongst the poorer citizens of the Metropolis. If it is true to say that Wild took thieves when it suited his purpose and his purse to do so, it is equally true to say that he made far more felons than he ever took.

Colquhoun has much to say on the subject of detection in the eighteenth century.

As the laws now stand no energy enters into the system of detection so as to give vigour and effect to that branch of the police which relates to the apprehension of persons charged with offences, and no sooner does a magistrate commit a hackneyed thief, a receiver of stolen goods, or a fraudulent person charged with any other offence, than recourse is immediately had to some disreputable attorney whose mind is made up and prepared to practise every trick and device which will defeat the ends of substantial justice. Depraved persons are hired to swear an alibi. Witnesses are cajoled, threatened or bribed either to mutilate their evidence or to speak doubtfully on the trial, although they spoke positively before the committing magistrate.

If bribes and persuasions will not do, the prosecutors are either intimidated by the expense or softened down by appeals to their humanity, and under such circumstances they neither employ counsel nor take the necessary steps to bring forward evidence, and the result is that the bill is either returned " ignoramus " by the Grand Jury, or if a trial takes place under all the disadvantages of a deficient evidence, without a counsel for the prosecution, an advocate is heard for the prisoner, availing himself of every trifling inaccuracy which may screen his client from the punishment of the law. The hardened villain is acquitted and escapes justice, while the novice in crime, unskilled in the deficiencies of the law, or unable from the want of criminal connections, or lacking that support which the professed thief receives from the buyer of stolen goods, to procure the aid of counsel to defend him, is often convicted. . . .

The registers of the Old Bailey afford a melancholy proof of the evils arising from the present mode of trying criminals without a public prosecutor for the Crown. . . .

Towards the end of the eighteenth century an agitation commenced for the better protection of society and for the surer detection of the thief, but with little effect. At the commencement of the nineteenth century it was estimated that there was one criminal for every twenty-two of the population and yet, to take an example fairly representative of prevailing conditions, in the district of Kensington, covering an area of some fifteen square miles, so little provision had been made to secure the general public against the activities of so undue a proportion of criminals in their midst that there were only three constables officiating in that area. Not until the year 1829 did government admit by its action the need of drastic reform. It was during Sir Robert Peel's ministry at the Home Office that at last a properly regulated and efficient police system came into being.

Disraeli was apt to sneer at Sir Robert Peel for lending too ready an ear to the latest reformer. He refers to the subject in a passage in his *Life of Lord George Bentinck* : " There was always some person representing some theory or system, exercising an influence over his (Sir Robert Peel's) mind. In his ' sallet days ' it was Mr. Horner or Sir Samuel Romilly." It is difficult to understand why Disraeli should have taken exception to Sir Robert Peel, during his occupation of the Home Office, coming under the influence of Sir Samuel Romilly. For any minister who had ambitions to reform the criminal code or the administration of the criminal law, there could have been no mentor more fully qualified.

In view of the deplorable conditions which had prevailed so long in the Metropolis it is very remarkable that when Sir Robert Peel introduced into Parliament his scheme for a Metropolitan Police Force he encountered a violent outburst of criticism. The scheme was denounced as an insidious attempt to enslave the people by arbitrary and tyrannical methods. This new semi-military force, as it was designated, was to be employed as the instrument of a new despotism. The force would serve the purpose of a standing army under a centralized authority, the terror of peaceable and law-abiding citizens. But these ill-informed views soon gave place to a more rational interpretation of the great reform with which Sir Robert Peel's name will be for all time honourably associated. Not only was the Metropolitan Police Force instituted with obvious success, but it served as a model which was quickly to be adopted by local authorities all over the country.

The Police Act of 1856 made the institution of a paid county force obligatory upon all local authorities, and the system which Sir Robert Peel is responsible for remains in broad general outline the system as we know it to-day.

CHAPTER III

THE SEARING OF THE LEAF

THE idea prevalent from earliest times and not yet eradicated in the eighteenth century was that the best deterrent to the criminal was a combination of a ferocious criminal code, ferociously administered, and a public demonstration of the retribution that awaits the malefactor. While it is true that innocence or guilt ceased to be tested by ordeals which depended upon the violation or suspension of the most elementary laws of nature, the odds were so heavily weighted against the man in the dock from the outset, that although there was a somewhat more civilized and rational method of elucidating the facts, the chances of his establishing his innocence were equally remote.

While it is generally accepted by historians that torture as a means of establishing the guilt of the arrested or eliciting evidence from that source was abolished before the dawn of the eighteenth century, this is not the whole truth. Apart from the fact that the ordinary day-to-day treatment of prisoners in the gaols of England amounted to torture of an aggravated kind, there obtained well into the eighteenth century the peculiar process of forcibly extracting information from them, known as the *peine forte et dure*, which was nothing but a mediæval torture worthy of the Spanish Inquisition. Primarily it was a drastic method of inducing the unfortunate victim to plead; like the rack, it was employed presumably for "the better bolting out the truth of the matter," although why the truth was more likely to come out of the mouth of the man enduring exquisite agonies only the judicial authorities of the eighteenth century would be competent to explain. If guilty, Beccaria wisely observed, torture was unnecessary and if not guilty the innocent are being tortured.

As an example of this anachronistic custom, in the year 1721 two men who were indicted for highway robberies refused to plead. The court thereupon gave orders to issue the following judgment, appointed to be executed on such as stand mute:

that the prisoner shall be sent to the prison from whence he came and put into a mean room, stopped from the light, and shall there be laid on the bare ground without any litter, straw or other covering and without any garment about him *except something about his middle*. He shall lie upon his back, his head shall be covered and his feet shall be bare. One of his arms shall be drawn with a cord to the side of the room and the other arm to the other side, and his legs shall be served in a like manner. Then there shall be laid upon his body as much iron or stone as he can bear and more. And the first day after he shall have three morsels of barley bread without any drink, and the second day he shall be allowed to drink as much as he can, at three times, of the water that is next to the prison door, except running water, without any bread, and this shall be his diet until he dies.

Incidentally it is difficult to understand why in a proceeding so vile in the company of such base persons any concession should have been made to the more exacting conventions by an official order that the prisoner's loins should be girt. It is extremely doubtful that the victim derived any consolation under the circumstances from such tender solicitude for his modesty.

In this particular case the men were carried back in

due course to Newgate. As soon as they entered the " press room " one of them consented to plead, the other remained obdurate. The latter was therefore subjected to the press. It is on record that he bore three hundred and fifty pounds weight for half an hour, then, fifty more being added, he begged that he might be carried back to plead, which " favour " was granted. After this diabolical treatment it is not altogether surprising to learn that he was very faint and almost speechless for two days. One of the reasons he gave to the Ordinary of Newgate for enduring the press with such fortitude was that none might reproach his children by telling them their father was hanged.

In 1726 one Burnworth, who was arraigned at Kingston for murder, stood mute and was placed under the weight. For an hour and three-quarters he endured the torture and sustained a pressure of nearly four hundredweight. At last he asked for mercy. He was brought to the Bar and pleaded guilty. He was subsequently committed and hanged. Sir Robert Walpole was Prime Minister in this particular year of grace.

There is a story of another highwayman, one of Jonathan Wild's victims, who refused to plead because his fine clothes had been taken away from him, and explained that he wished to die as he had lived, like a gentleman.

Beccaria exposed the fallacy of torture when he wrote that it is confounding all relations to expect that a man should be both accuser and accused and that pain should be the test of both, as if truth resided in the muscles and fibres of a wretch in torture. By this method the robust will escape, the feeble be condemned. But the *peine forte et dure* was not the only torture which survived from the Middle Ages until more enlightened times.

73

The most brutal form of corporal punishment, flagellation, survived in the case of men into the reign of Queen
Victoria, while women were flogged until the end of the
eighteenth century.

This punishment took various forms. One of the
most barbarous was the flogging of the victim through
the streets and the market-place. But perhaps it was
not so much in England as in our first penal settlements
overseas that this abominable practice was so prevalent.
It was carried out with such cruelty in Van Dieman's
Land that the transportees preferred the risk of almost
certain death in their efforts to abscond into the trackless
woods and wilderness of that inhospitable land. As
for its application in the Royal Services, it is very difficult
to believe that the victims could have survived the
reputed severity of its application. A case was brought
before the Privy Council in 1806 of a naval officer who
had flogged to death three seamen on board H.M.S.
Trident. Grey, the Secretary of State, with unconscious
candour intimated that it was undesirable to draw
attention to the matter.

There was an instance of a guardsman at the
Tower who for being absent twenty-four hours received 300 lashes. It was not until the year 1812
that the use of the lash was limited even to 300
strokes. Leigh Hunt was indicted for condemning
such barbarity in the Services, although thanks to the
advocacy of Brougham he was acquitted. In this
particular case, during the summing up, Lord Ellenborough, who still advocated the pillory as a reputable
form of punishment for civilians, asked the somewhat
irrelevant question : " On what occasion do you find
the soldiery of Great Britain unmanned by the effect of
our military code ? "

Nowhere was the ferocious administration of the law

better illustrated than in the court itself. Here the assumption was that the man in the dock was guilty unless proved innocent. Until the Treason Act of William III was placed upon the Statute Book the accused was not permitted to be supplied with a copy of the indictment before his trial, neither might he have witnesses sworn in his defence, nor counsel to advocate his cause. Until the reign of Queen Anne a prisoner put upon his trial for felonies short of treason could not insist as a right that the witnesses in his favour should be examined on oath. Indeed, it was not until the year 1836 (when the Prisoners' Counsel Act was passed) that a person accused of felony, although entitled to examine and cross-examine opposing witnesses, could enjoy the full benefit of counsel's aid in matters of law as well as of fact, and also the advantage of counsel's address to the jury.

The jurors, it is hardly necessary to observe, discharged an invidious duty under a system where the accused was assumed to be guilty, and although they were directed to form an unbiassed opinion, they were not only permitted but expected to decide by the light of their own knowledge of the facts as well as by the evidence given in court. They were sometimes deliberately chosen from the neighbourhood in which the crime had been committed for this very purpose. It was not until Lord Ellenborough's chancellorship in 1816 that the maxim was definitely laid down that a judge who should tell jurors to consider as evidence their own acquaintance with matters in dispute would misdirect them.

Jurors in those days might be described appropriately enough as witnesses for the prosecution. There is a passage in the columns of the *London Evening Post*, 2nd April, 1774, in which it is asserted that in all Crown cases Middlesex juries " are allowed an elegant dinner at Appleby's and five guineas a man if a verdict be given for the Crown," otherwise they paid their own expenses. If, however, they failed to respond to treatment they did so at their cost. In Penn's case the court actually fined the jurors forty marks " for going contrary to plain evidence," in other words, finding the accused innocent. The evidence of guilt was always quite clear to the Judge, whose object was to convict and who regarded himself as prosecutor for the Crown, especially in cases of high treason. The man in the dock was a criminal, there was an end of the matter, and very often of the victim. The sentence of death was pronounced in as imposing and as vindictive a form as could be conceived : " To be drawn on a hurdle to the place of execution and there to be hanged until you be dead ! dead ! ! dead ! ! ! "

Most of the judges who presided over criminal courts in the eighteenth century seem to have inherited the peculiar genius of the notorious Judge Jeffreys, whose memorable charge to his successor, Herbert, as Lord Chief Justice : " Be sure to execute the law to the utmost of its vengeance upon those who are now known by the name of Whigs," gives the measure of his impartiality as a dispenser of justice.

Sir Matthew Hale, Lord Chief Baron, at a trial at Bury St. Edmunds over which he presided, in his charge to the jury declared " that he made no doubt at all that there were such creatures as witches," and proceeded to pass sentence of death upon two unfortunate women convicted of witchcraft, which goes to prove that glaring as was the injustice of the criminal code in those days it became, when allied to ignorance on the Bench, a menace to the first rights and principles of citizenship.

If the proceedings in court were ferocious the ferocity of punishments meted out to the convicted were in proportion to the habitual conduct of a criminal trial. It is curious how obstinately judges of the eighteenth century adhered to the doctrine that the more ferociously you dealt with the criminal the fewer citizens would stray from the paths of virtue. The result of centuries of experience which taught the reverse seems to have had no influence whatever upon their methods of interpreting our statute law.

Moreover, not only was the administration of the law ferocious, but its ferocity was inequitable. For instance, for assaults of the most cruel and violent nature the offender was seldom punished in any other manner save by fine and imprisonment, but if a delinquent stole " privately " from his neighbour more than the value of twelve pence the law condemned him to death. The standard of values is well assessed by Beccaria as " a multitude of laws which contradict each other, which expose the best men to the severest punishment, which render the ideas of vice and virtue vague and fluctuating, and even their existence doubtful."

In the eighteenth century there were many abuses that survived from the Middle Ages. Not the least anomalous was that which was known as " benefit of clergy." While numerous offences entailed the death penalty, exemption was granted by this privilege to those who could read. Women with the exception of nuns were excluded from its protection. Certain modifications of such unaccountable leniency were introduced at various times, although benefit of clergy was not entirely abolished until 1827. But the worst inheritance from an unenlightened age was the anomalous law that privately stealing property up to the value of one shilling was a capital offence, while those who deprived their neighbours of the same openly, were merely liable to the lesser penalty of transportation.

Cruel as the criminal code was in the Middle Ages, it has been said that at the commencement of Henry VIII's reign there was some indication of a more merciful disposition. If so, the tendency was to be reversed by his two daughters. It was probably true of the conditions prevailing in both their reigns to say that "if a man held one opinion he would be hanged, and if the opposite he would be burnt." It was also said with some degree of truth that "you were burnt for refusing to say something which you believed to be untrue, or tortured in order that you should say something which you knew to be untrue." But harsh punishment neither in Tudor times, nor in any other period of history, seems to have acted as a deterrent. On the contrary, the original decision to incinerate heretics started a conflagration which burnt itself out only when men realized that this was not the most effective way to purge the world of heresy. Arson of such a nature was as stupid and as futile as the burning of a witch.

In the reign of Elizabeth it was even a capital offence " to be seen in any company or fellowship of vagabonds calling themselves Egyptians." Four yeomen of Medmenham, in Buckinghamshire, were accused of " counterfeiting, transforming, and altering themselves in dress, language and behaviour to such vagabonds called Egyptians and were hanged." It is true that this was anterior to the period with which this work deals, but until the reign of Queen Victoria men and women were hanged for offences little more reprehensible than consorting with " gypsies." In May, 1777, a child not fourteen years of age was sentenced to be burnt for having in her possession some farthings whitewashed to make them resemble shillings, which she secreted in her stays at the instigation of her master, who was incidentally hanged a few days previously. The sentence, it is said, would have been carried into effect had not the attention of Lord Weymouth been called to the case, with the result that on his urgent intercession the child was reprieved. On the 8th August, 1750, six malefactors were hanged for robbing their several prosecutors of no more than six shillings. Buxton quotes a case much later in date of a boy of respectable character sent to prison for non-payment of one penny, to which he had been sent for a month in default of paying a fine.   He was in the employ of a corn chandler and went into London with his master's cart and horse. Passing through the toll bar and not seeing anyone he went on his way rejoicing until he was arrested and thrown into Newgate.

Colquhoun, writing in 1776, says :

It will scarcely be credited that by the laws of England there are above 160 different offences which subject the parties who are guilty to the punishment of death without benefit of clergy . . .   Under such circumstances the injured through compassion will often forbear to prosecute, juries through compassion will sometimes forget their oaths and either acquit the guilty or mitigate the nature of the offence—and Judges through compassion will respite one half the convicts and recommend them to the Royal Mercy.

It should have been painfully obvious to those in authority that if death is the punishment for offences both grave and trivial, there will be two disastrous consequences of this anomaly—the first is that a considerable number of rogues will be returned upon society through the misguided compassion of the more humane amongst judges, and the second that, there being practically no gradation of crime when the stealing of a piece of muslin entails the same punishment as the murder of a wife, the tendency will be for the malefactor to regard the greater crime of no more flagitious a character than the lesser offence.

There can be no better illustration than the story, as told by Harrison Ainsworth, of the murder of Mrs. Wood, the wife of Jack Sheppard's benefactor, by his companion in crime, Blueskin. It must be said in justice to Jack Sheppard's memory that the story is purely apocryphal. There is no evidence in history that, whatever else he may have done, he was ever connected either directly or indirectly with a murder. But, fiction as it is, the story serves well as an admirable illustration of the argument.

One night, so runs the story, Jack Sheppard in company with his confederate set out for Dollis Hill, where they intended to plunder the house of Jack's former employer. Entering the house with burglarious intent they broke into the bedchamber, where Mr. and Mrs. Wood were sleeping. While they were occupied in withdrawing the good man's savings from a wooden chest Mrs. Wood woke up and gave the alarm. Whereupon Blueskin, with the aid of his knife, ensured that Mrs. Wood would for ever hold her peace. If there is any moral in this story it certainly concerns the subject of this chapter. Blueskin before the murder was committed had already rendered himself guilty of an offence for which he knew the punishment was death. If he was to avoid the penalty of his first crime he decided that his only chance of avoiding detection was to silence the garrulous old lady whose vociferation would in all likelihood lead to his detection by means of a crime for which the penalty was identical with that of the crime he had already committed. Although to the moralist there might be a steep gradation of crime as between burglary and murder, there was none measured by the test of punishment, the only standard that concerned Blueskin,

who consciously or unconsciously decided, that if worst
came to the worst, he might just as well be hanged for
a sheep as for a lamb.

And it was not only Blueskin who in fiction made the
decision. Numerous criminals in real life were actuated
by a similar process of logic, and thus for this reason
amongst many others there emerged the curious result
that hanging, being the punishment for so many offences,
far from acting as a deterrent, positively increased crime.
But despite the fact that by 1752 murder had increased
in proportion to the ferocity of the law, an Act was
passed providing for the execution of every criminal
one day after the passing of the sentence and ordering
that the body should be handed over for dissection at
the Barber Surgeons' Hall, Old Bailey.

While it is true to say that owing to the fact that there
were as many at one time as 200 capital offences during
the eighteenth century, a great many rogues who would
otherwise have met their fate, were thrown loose
upon society, nevertheless the statistics of the number
of persons condemned to death and actually suffering
the supreme penalty are truly appalling. Between the
years 1749 and 1756 in the London and Middlesex area
alone, no less than 306 were executed. One Townsend,
a veteran Bow Street runner, in his evidence before the
Parliamentary Committee in 1816, gave evidence that
between 1781 and 1787 as many as twelve, sixteen or
twenty were hanged at one execution. Twice he saw
forty hanged in one day.

In 1783 the Secretary of State, still unable to link up
cause and effect in these matters, advised the King to
punish with all severity. The number of offences of a
serious nature was so considerable and was so much on
the increase, that a letter was circulated among the Judges
and Recorders, to the effect that His Majesty would

dispense with the Recorders' reports and that the worst criminals should be picked out at once and ordered for execution. But this expedient failed in its effect. Nowhere in history can a better illustration be found of Montesquieu's theory that severity of punishment defeats its own object.

After the War of Independence the country was overrun with discharged soldiers and sailors out of work and in distress, with no assistance from a government which had employed them and on behalf of which they had risked their lives. It was inevitable that crime should increase from this if from no other cause. In 1783 at the September Old Bailey Sessions fifty-eight were convicted for capital offences. The Deputy Recorder in passing sentence said it gave him pain " to behold a bar so crowded with persons whose wickedness and impudence had induced them to commit such enormous crimes as the laws of their country justly and necessarily punish with death." It was presumably as much as his place was worth to pass strictures on a government that sent soldiers and sailors to a far country to fight and then on their return cast them adrift. This senseless ferocity merely increased the crimes it was intended to obviate. In 1785 the Lent Assizes all over England accounted for 242 capital sentences, of which 103 suffered execution. At one moment there were forty-nine persons lying in Newgate under sentence of death. Boys were convicted of highway robbery. Joseph Wood and Thomas Underwood, one fourteen years of age the other twelve, were convicted of highway robbery and duly hanged.

In the course of the Parliamentary Inquiry into Newgate in 1814 a witness gave evidence as to the extreme youth of many of the prisoners.

I have [he said] in my pocket an order for the removal of

fifty-two who are under sentence of transportation, many of whom are seven or eight years old, one nine years, and others not above twelve or thirteen . . . they are for transportation, but they go to the hulks in the first instance. There are girls of all ages in Newgate. There was a little girl tried at the last Session but one that was not above nine years old I think. She was privately whipped by order of the Court.

As late as 1833 a sentence of death was passed on a child of nine who had poked a stick through a pane of glass in a shop front and thrusting his hand through the aperture had stolen twopennyworth of paint. This was construed as housebreaking, the principal witness being another child of nine. The boy was not executed, but the picture of a youth of such tender years passing through the awful tribulation of a death sentence is not one which we of a more enlightened age can contemplate with equanimity.

Appalling as the death-roll of Tyburn Tree is to our generation, the fact that capital punishment was so easy to come by had the effect we have observed in a former paragraph of releasing without let or hindrance a great many who were the enemies of society. Clemency even in that cruel age was on this account often exercised. As Beccaria rightly adjudged, this frequent application of mercy amounted to a tacit disapprobation of the laws.

Colquhoun observes in commenting upon this peculiar consequence of a ferocious code that

no sooner does the punishment of the law attach to a criminal than humanity becomes his friend. Pardons are applied for. The King's clemency is abused by depraved agents who have recourse to every species of falsehood and forgery, plundering at the same time the friends and the relations of the prisoner as the wages of his villainy and misrepresentation.

Pardon in some cases was granted to convicted men

on joining the Services. But this concession was frequently abused by desertion or by obtaining discharge on the plea of some pretended physical incapacity which enabled them to return to their former evil practices.

It is said that banking gave rise to the crime of forgery, which was made a capital offence. The circulation of small notes and increase of wealth certainly provided favourable conditions and opportunities for the expert in this particular line of business. Few guilty of this practice, it is said, could hope to escape the gallows. Between 1805 and 1818 there were 207 executions for forgery. As many as seventy-two of these were the victims of proceedings instituted by the Bank of England. But had capital punishment for forgery been invariably carried into effect, there would have been an average of about four executions daily for that particular offence in Great Britain and Ireland alone. But the police, being many of them thieves turned thief-takers, either moved to compassion from a fellow feeling or a more substantial motive, connived at the escape of those they pretended to secure. Juries hesitated to convict and seized upon any pretext to be lenient, as indeed they often displayed themselves in cases of larceny for the very same reason. There is a typical case recorded in the year 1808 of a woman indicted on a charge of stealing privately from a dwelling-house a ten-pound note. On this occasion the jury deliberately assessed its worth at thirty-nine shillings. These violations of their oaths by jurymen, it was said, became so frequent that they occasioned no resentment and were overlooked as a pious fraud.

Even judges in the face of these circumstances displayed the quality of mercy. Respites and reprieves were often granted when cases of conviction were considered by the Privy Council. The punishment was so certain that humane persons refrained from prosecuting. Instances are recorded of bankers compromising with the delinquent rather than be responsible for his death. The prosecutor would sometimes pretend that his pockets had been picked of the forged instrument or that he himself had destroyed it. The aggrieved persons went so far as to meet forged bills of exchange rather than be responsible for the death of the forger. Some prosecutors forfeited their recognizances rather than appear in court.

So great were the efforts to prevent the law taking its course that one Gibson, who had been found guilty of forgery, was in Newgate eighteen months between conviction and execution, the jury having found a special verdict for the determination of twelve judges, who ultimately decided his crime came within the meaning of the law.

Thus crime continued steadily to increase in spite of the awful consequences of detection. It was probably forgery and its punishment that first led to an effectual agitation in influential quarters outside government against the ferocity of the law. Among other cases which brought the matter to a head was that of a young and hitherto guiltless woman of the name of Harriet Skelton, who was sentenced to death for forgery. Her behaviour in prison was unexceptionable. Some of her companions in guilt were heard to say that they supposed she was chosen for death because she was better prepared than the rest of them. Her circumstances evoked the most lively compassion, and as a result various distinguished persons came to visit her in the condemned cell. Mrs. Fry enlisted the sympathy of the Duke of Gloucester on her behalf. His Royal Highness, after visiting her himself, applied to Lord Sidmouth and the Bank of England directors, who had power under the

Act of Parliament to select such persons as they con sidered fit subjects to plead guilty to the minor count and so escape death.

In 1770 a Committee of the House of Commons had reported that for certain offences the penalty of death might with advantage be exchanged for some other reasonable punishment, but no effective action seems to have been taken.

In the report from the Select Committee on the State of the Police in the Metropolis, 1816, occurs the following comment upon the administration :

The severity of a criminal code which inflicts death on upwards of 200 offences acts very unfavourably on the mind of the juvenile delinquent, for while the humanity of the present age forbids the execution of the greater part of these laws, the uncertainty of their operation encourages the offenders to calculate, even if convicted, on a mitigated punishment ; but if the laws have no tendency to prevent crime, it is truly shocking to witness the direct facilities which the vicious inclinations of the delinquent receive from the system on which the police of the Metropolis is now conducted . . . The practice of holding out rewards for the apprehension of criminals in proportion to the enormity of their guilt, stimulates the officer to overlook the minor depredations of the incipient thief, and often might lead to an early arrest in his course but for the principle on which it becomes the interest of the officer that the young offender should continue in iniquity until he attains maturity in crime. The encouragement which the police officers give to those pestiferous haunts, termed " flash-houses," to which they themselves are accustomed to resort, is a very serious evil ; in these nurseries of crime are to be found the most experienced and notorious thieves ; boys and girls from nine years of age, women of the most profligate description, associating indiscriminately and mixing with the very men who are employed for the preservation of public morals. . . .

Dreadful therefore is the situation of the young offender, he becomes a victim of circumstances over which he has no control—the laws of his country operate not to restrain, but to punish him. The tendency of the police is to accelerate his career in crime.

Enough evidence has been reproduced already to convince the reader that the administration of the criminal law in the eighteenth century was utterly barbaric, but there remains one other subject which is most appropriate to this chapter. The treatment of debtors was perhaps the most conspicuous example of the unenlightenment of those times. Nothing could have exceeded the insensate savagery which characterized the attitude of the law towards these defaulters, the majority of whom were victims of circumstances. It is the case, no doubt, that there have always been two distinct categories of debtor—on the one hand the man who is merely insolvent, often as not through no fault of his own, but who has been guilty of neither felony nor misdemeanour; and on the other hand there is the fraudulent debtor, who has deliberately imposed upon his creditors. But in the eighteenth century there was no distinction made between insolvency and fraud.

It is true that no exception can be taken to a debtor who is guilty of a fraud being made to suffer for his offence, but to make the number of shillings in the pound which he may be able to pay the criterion of his guilt or innocence was anomalous in the last degree. To condemn as a crime what in nine cases out of ten was misfortune is one of the worst aspects of the ferocity of the law. The debtor, for whatever reason he may have been such, was treated without exception as a criminal, and the treatment he experienced in the debtors' prisons was as barbarous as that meted out to the worst felon in Newgate.

The debtors' prisons in the eighteenth century and the early years of the nineteenth were a byword. The inmates were allowed to surround themselves with their women and children, who were thus early brought into contact with the most evil influences. The filth and squalor of the buildings, the depredations upon the unfortunate debtors practised by those set in authority over them, the drunkenness and other vices allowed free vent, the promiscuous association between the sexes, the overcrowding, the want of necessities, much less comforts, all compose a picture which to the modern mind was as revolting as it was ineffectual.

In virtue of the fact that a somewhat detailed account of the conditions of the English gaols in the eighteenth century is given in a later chapter, and in order to avoid an unnecessary multiplication of these horrors that will merely serve to nauseate the reader, it is sufficient for the purpose to observe that the debtors' prisons and the sections of the ordinary gaols devoted to debtors were as vile as they could be, and that all the strictures which apply to other gaols are appropriate in double measure to both the prisons exclusively set apart for debtors and those sections of ordinary prisons devoted to their use. But in order to illustrate the great abuses of the administration of debtors' prisons during the first period of the eighteenth century reference must be made to the type of Warden into whose hands the fate and health of the debtors was entrusted. In the case of the evidence given before a Parliamentary Committee set up in 1729 to inquire into the London prisons, the following facts were elicited concerning one of the Wardens of the Fleet, Bainsbridge by name. Like most of his vile fraternity he charged exorbitant fees and abused his trust in every possible way in order to extract money from his wretched charges. He kept no account books. Among his malpractices was one of registering the prisoners as long as he thought fit on the Committal Book by issuing an escape warrant against them, and thus detaining them until he had extracted the uttermost farthing. On the other hand he aided escapes from prison for those who could pay for that privilege. Sometimes he refused to admit prisoners to the ordinary side of the gaol, insisting that they should occupy what was termed the spunging house at exorbitant fees. He would also force the inmates to call for liquor and to spend upon it more than they could afford. He treated each prisoner in accordance with his means, some being allowed a handsome room and bed to themselves, some being stowed away in garrets three in a bed, or even put in irons. There was an instance given in the course of evidence before the Committee of one man who finally revolted against the Warden's rapacity. This bolder spirit was returned to the spunging house, where small-pox was then raging. Even the Warden's creatures protested against such an outrage, but the man was sent there, where he contracted the smallpox of which he died, leaving all his affairs in the greatest confusion and a numerous family of small children in the utmost distress.

The Warden was in the habit of letting out Fleet tenements to victuallers for the reception of prisoners. He let one of these to a woman tenant. The rent was increased from £32 to £60 a year, with a promise of a certain number of prison clients, and the woman was compelled to make Bainsbridge in addition a present of £40 and a model silver ship he coveted " for which four score broad pieces had been offered her." It was even said of him

that it is not the only design of the said Thomas Bainsbridge to extort money from his prisoners, if they survived his inhuman treatment, but he seems to have a further view, in case it causes death, of possessing himself of their effects.

It is some consolation to reflect that this miscreant, as a result of the revelations before the Committee, was thrown into Newgate. But the fact that the Executive was so utterly careless of the administration in this country as to appoint such a man to a position of great responsibility is a measure of the corruption and the degeneracy of those days. When Bainsbridge was Warden of the Fleet Sir Robert Walpole was Prime Minister.

The Marshalsea, another of the prisons devoted exclusively to debtors, was as vile in its domestic economy as the Fleet. On the Common Side there were 320 prisoners at the time the Committee sat, most of them in the utmost need. Some were locked up thirty to fifty in a room of 16 feet square, although there was a large room kept empty and another let as a workroom for a tailor. Half the prisoners used hammocks, the rest the floor. They were locked up from 9 p.m. to 5 a.m. in summer, and in winter from 8 p.m. until 8 a.m. They were not allowed out for any purpose. The food rations were of the scantiest.

When the miserable wretch hath worn out the charity of his friends, and consumed the money which he hath raised upon his clothes and bedding, and hath eaten his last allowance of provisions he usually in a few days grows weak for want of food, with the symptoms of hectic fever, and when he is no longer able to stand, if he can raise 3*d*. to pay the fee of the common nurse of the prison, he obtains the liberty of being carried into the sick ward, and lingers on for about a month or two, by the assistance of the above-mentioned portion of Providence and then dies.

In the women's sick ward many lay on the floor with no bedding, perishing of extreme want. The men's

ward was overcrowded. The death-rate was appalling.
The proceeds of charities were grossly perverted by the
gaolers.

Benevolently disposed persons would come to the
prison and pay for the release of the inmates by settling
their debts. The gaoler and his friends would present
to them a number of " dummy " debtors, for whom they
received payment and employed them in this way over
and over again as a source of income.

Even the practice of sending out persons with begging
baskets for the debtors was turned to a source of profit
by their gaolers. The prisoners saw little of the food
and the money not at all.

Torture by thumbscrew and other methods was by no
means unknown. The gaolers acted as self-appointed
magistrates, and not only decreed punishment but
carried it out unmercifully. " Numberless are the instances of their immoderate beating poor debtors, at
their pleasure ; in so much that the very name of the
instrument, hanging up in the lodge, for beating the
prisoners, became a terror to them." Even this was not
enough, as " they found a way of making within this
prison a confinement more dreadful than the strong
room itself, by coupling the living with the dead." One
victim was kept in a yard with two dead bodies which
had been there for four days. Instances of the abominations which were discovered in these gaols are innumerable in the state papers which record them.

Although the Marshalsea prison was specially devoted
to debtors, there were debtors' sections in Newgate, the
Fleet, Ludgate, Giltspur Street and the Borough Comp-
ters. Neild, when he visited Newgate, found men and
women who had been there any period of time up to
thirteen years for debts of a few shillings.

It was not until the end of the eighteenth century that

there was any publicly expressed resentment against the atrocious legal abuses so utterly discreditable to government, and even then only a mere handful of Members of Parliament dared or cared to give it expression. Amongst these one stands out pre-eminent. No history of the reform of the ferocious penal code would be complete without mention of the remarkable part played by one of the greatest of English philanthropists, Sir Samuel Romilly. His name has been deservedly rescued from comparative oblivion by Mr. C. G. Oakes in an admirable biography of this " vastly amiable man." Born in 1757 of Huguenot extraction he had gradually built up a successful Chancery practice. Entering Parliament in 1802 he was appointed Solicitor-General in 1806, and thereafter devoted himself amongst other useful preoccupations to the reform and the mitigation of the criminal law. Drawing his inspiration from Montesquieu he believed that the first guiding principle of any such reform must be the certainty of punishment.

No man would steal [he observed] what he was sure that he would not keep; no man would by a voluntary act deprive himself of his liberty, though but for a few days. No man would expose himself to certain disgrace and infamy without the possibility of gain. It is the desire of a supposed good which is the incentive of every crime.

The second reform he suggested was that there should be some guiding principle for judges by which there might be uniformity as to the severity and the appropriateness of the punishment. Two men might be guilty of the same offence, one might be sentenced to two or three months' imprisonment, the other to transportation, and the latter might be still waiting for transportation to Botany Bay when his comrade in crime had already been released.

Samuel Romilly, from the moment that he found

himself in a position of authority and influence, set himself to procure reform of these glaring abuses by definite action, but during the whole of his public career he fought against overwhelming odds. Time after time he introduced bills into the House of Commons, mainly with the object of decreasing the number of capital offences. Either his bills were defeated in the first instance, or if they passed the Lower House they were defeated in the Upper. Always ranged against him in his philanthropic efforts was the powerful influence which both Lord Eldon and Lord Ellenborough brought to bear against any measure of progress or improvement. These two reactionary peers both owed their rise to the highest posts at the Bar, the one Lord Chancellor and the other Lord Chief Justice, to their great abilities, their untiring industry as students of law, but both are conspicuous examples of men of great knowledge and ability without any vision or human sympathy. Consistently and violently and successfully they opposed all reform. To Romilly's pleading they were completely deaf. Amongst Romilly's papers was found a prayer in his handwriting in which occurs the phrases: " I am indulging the hope that I may at some time prove an humble instrument in the divine work of enlarging the sphere of human happiness." It was apparently the mission in life of Lords Eldon and Ellenborough to keep it contracted. Certain it is that they foiled Romilly's ambition. When he died, however, he bequeathed his mantle to Sir James Mackintosh and Sir Thomas Fowell Buxton, who by their persistent efforts carried out his intention to mitigate the ferocity of our criminal code. The completion of the work devolved later upon Sir Robert Peel, but true history will always associate the eradication of ferocity from our criminal administration with the honoured name of Sir Samuel Romilly.

CHAPTER IV

THE FORCING HOUSE OF CRIME

THE inquisitive tourist who sets forth to discover any trace of Newgate Gaol upon the traditional site will be grievously disappointed. Even its exact position relative to the existing streets is not easy to determine, so fundamental a change has the whole neighbourhood and its environment undergone in recent years. Of the old building every vestige has vanished. On the wall of the palatial new Sessions House facing Newgate Street is affixed a blue enamel plaque recording the bare information that this was the site of the famous gaol. It is perhaps as well for the good repute of the Corporation of the City of London that no further detail is vouchsafed to the wayfarer of its history. But it is to be deplored that the architect of the new Old Bailey could not have seen fit to incorporate at least the famous gateway into his own design. Like others of his calling he seems to have been deficient in that sense of historical association which might have prompted him to preserve some trace of the original to assist our imaginations in conjuring up the past.

It is also conceivable that the Corporation of London was not over-anxious that the story of Newgate should be perpetuated in tablets of stone, and preferred to commence a new era with complete obliteration of the past. And yet if the glorious deeds of former generations of mankind are to be commemorated as an example to posterity it is legitimate to suggest that some memorial of our evil deeds should be perpetuated as a warning.

No two streets in London are more instinct with the history of its social life from earliest to contemporary times than the Old Bailey and Newgate Street. They present to-day an aggressively modern aspect. Vast garish structures, no doubt in themselves of some architectural merit, have taken the place of much that would, had they survived, been fascinating and instructive to the student of our domestic history. The houses in the modernized Newgate Street suffer from that lack of uniformity which renders so many of our thoroughfares in London hideous. But even deprived of any assistance to his imagination the least sentimental cannot fail to pause at the junction of these two famous streets to indulge in retrospect. Within an acre or so where he stands there has been concentrated for a thousand years more of human misery, torture and degradation, more of cruelty, lust, and oppression, than any other given space in the three kingdoms.

It is not the purpose of these pages to give a detailed history of Newgate Gaol from its first vague origin of a small lock-up in one of the ancient gates of the City, or to trace it through all its various evolutions, but rather to subject it to examination from the dawn of the eighteenth century, a period when England was presumed to be civilized.

For 800 years it served as the principal Metropolitan gaol. Throughout that period until 1903, the date of its final demolition, discounting various minor modifications, there were four different buildings upon approximately the identical site. The first was evolved out of one of the ancient City gates. The second, which was erected incongruously enough with the moneys bequeathed by Sir Richard Whittington to be employed for good works, was partially destroyed by the Great Fire in 1666. The third, constructed upon the ruins, endured until 1770, when it was rebuilt, the reconstruction being interrupted by the Gordon Riots. The fourth, which although encased in the same shell was completely reconditioned within, was commenced in 1857. It might be conceived, therefore, that an historical account of Newgate and its administration would naturally divide itself into four separate chapters, but the truth, attested to by John Howard himself, and by later reformers, is that, in spite of material reconstructions, the atrocious abuses of the seventeenth century were for the most inherited by the eighteenth century, and survived well on into the nineteenth century until Newgate became merely a place of detention for those awaiting trial. It might have been said of Newgate at any time during its existence: "Plus ça change, plus c'est la même chose."

The sources from which the necessary information can be drawn are meagre enough until Howard made his courageous investigations into its abuses, for the very sufficient reason that neither sheriff, magistrate, nor anyone else cared or dared to make a visit of inspection within the precincts. In fact, there can be no more perfect example of a vicious circle than that while gaol fever acted as a deterrent to the responsible authority to survey the domestic enonomy of Newgate, gaol fever might have been exterminated if only that same authority had inspected Newgate. Not until the year 1777, when John Howard, a layman, revealed the detestable condition of our gaols to the world was the public conscience aroused or the public authorities stirred into any kind of activity by which the scandal of the Metropolitan prisons could be terminated.

There was only one sound principle upon which

English prison administration of the eighteenth century was conducted, but its application was so brutal and cruel as to render nugatory much of its essential value. That principle can best be summed up by Howard's caustic comment, " the builders of Old Newgate seem to have regarded in their plan, nothing but the single article of keeping prisoners safe in custody." The security of the gaol and the durance of the prisoners was indeed so well provided for as to relegate to secondary importance both their physical and their moral welfare. The walls on this account were of colossal thickness. Apertures which might have permitted a modicum of light and air were few and far between. Until the construction of the last gaol the felons' side and the common debtors' side were so dark, thanks to the overriding consideration of obviating any means of escape, that it was necessary to use links and burners all day long. Except in what was called the Press Yard, artificial illumination was necessary both by day and night. The temperature of the interior was so frigid, owing to the fact that security precluded any firing for heating purposes, that the few apertures open to the air which existed were normally closed.

Nothing could have been more inappropriate from every point of view, and more especially from the point of view of sanitation, than the site itself of Newgate. The foundations of the new gaol were estimated in 1766 to cost £19,000, as it was necessary to sink them to a depth of 40 feet, the site being that of the ditch of the old London Wall.

But the health of the prisoners was of no account whatever to the Corporation of London or to anyone else. What primarily signified was that, whether the occupants of these foul dungeons lived or died, the fortress which contained them must be rendered impregnable from within and from without. It is true that in 1750 the Corporation of the City of London, moved by a letter from the Lord Chief Justice, appointed a Committee to suggest " the best means for procuring in Newgate such a purity of air as might prevent the rise of those infectious distempers." But in case it might be inferred that such a step was taken out of any tender solicitude for the health of the prisoners, it must be remembered that the famous gaol fever, probably a form of typhus, contracted from the lack of air and light which the security of the prison necessitated, had spread to an alarming extent outside the walls of the gaol itself. The distemper, in fact, was broadcast both in the courts, where the prisoners coming straight from this fever-laden atmosphere stood their trial, by visitors to the gaol who caught the infection, and by the discharged prisoners, mainly those drafted into the Services, who disseminated its ravages far and wide. At one period of our history the ex-prisoners carried the infection on board His Majesty's ships and imparted it to the Navy. It is recorded that the first English fleet sent to America lost by this means no less than 2,000 men. In the year 1750 at the Old Bailey Sessions Court, which was only 30 feet square, on the occasion of a particularly heavy gaol delivery the matter came to a head. There had been a severe outbreak of fever in the gaol itself. The court was in direct communication with the bail dock and the rooms beyond, whence an open window carried a draught poisoned with infection towards the occupants of the Judges' Bench. Of these, four were seized with the fever and died. Others, including under-sheriffs, bar and jury, to the number of forty, also succumbed. At the Lent Assizes in Taunton in 1730 prisoners infected the court with the result that the Lord Chief Baron Pengelly, the Sergeant (Sir James Sheppard) and the

Sheriff all died. In 1750 the Lord Mayor and some of the aldermen met with the same fate from an identical cause. It is not very surprising, therefore, that the Corporation, more solicitous for its own well-being than for that of those for whom it was responsible, took alarm and set up a Committee of investigation. But even so, the security of the gaol, the only sound principle upon which it was administered, must be their first concern. No drastic or fundamental reform of the prison was therefore effected, in spite of these disastrous occurrences. The net result of the Committee's deliberations was a pill for an earthquake. It was decided to reconstruct the ventilator. The unfortunate workmen who were employed for this purpose, in opening one of the tubes of the old ventilating system, were so overpowered by the excruciating stench which arose therefrom that they had to be removed to hospital.

One of the workmen, a lad of fifteen, who had been forced by his fellows to go down the shaft, on emerging into the open was immediately attacked by sickness. A peculiarity in his case was that he had been twice let down into the ventilator when the machine on the leads had been standing still, and he had suffered no ill effects, but the last time it was in motion the heavily laden atmosphere drawn up from below had wellnigh poisoned him and two others who had dragged him out of the shaft.

It was in this fœtid atmosphere that the prisoners down below lived and moved and died. But their security was all that mattered to the Corporation of London. Incidentally, the new ventilator was of so little practical value that in 1757 the unfortunate residents in the immediate neighbourhood of Newgate petitioned the Corporation, setting forth their apprehensions that the stenches proceeding from the gaol were prejudicial to the health of the vicinity. Again a Committee was set up, but as its recommendation was to the effect that nothing short of an expenditure of £40,000 would be of any avail, and as the Chancellor of the Exchequer hinted that no public money would be forthcoming for that purpose, the Corporation, unwilling to provide the necessary finance itself, did nothing. At any rate, the prisoners were secure.

But the bastioned walls and the heavy iron bars were not the only medium of security in Newgate. Upon the prisoners themselves were imposed fetters of iron. The precaution of ironing a felon had existed from times immemorial, but in spite of the fact that no less an authority than the Chief Justice, Coke, gave his opinion at the commencement of the seventeenth century against the legality of irons, all felons were ironed at Newgate and at other gaols for many years to come. The Prison Discipline Improvement Society reported that as late as the year 1823

prisoners at one county gaol are double ironed on first reception, and thus fettered are at night chained down in bed, the chain being fixed to the floor of the cell and fastened to the leg fetters of the prisoners. The chain is of sufficient length to enable the prisoners to raise themselves in bed. The cell is then locked, and he continues thus chained down from 7 o'clock in the evening until 6 o'clock the next morning. There were but two gaol deliveries in this county for the year— so a prisoner may continue to be thus treated for from six to eight months and then be acquitted as innocent.

Dr. Dodd, George III's unfortunate chaplain, and friend of Dr. Johnson, whose improvidence induced him ultimately to commit forgery, complained of the sound of the rattling chains which added so much to the horror he experienced in the grim cells and passages of Newgate.

Quite apart from the obvious reason for securing a prisoner hand and foot with irons, there was another excuse for the infliction upon him of this painful and degrading operation. Throughout the eighteenth century there was no prison uniform. Those who were thrown into Newgate, many of them in verminous rags, save for a small amount of clothing distributed as a charitable gift, doubtless on condition of a fee being extorted, continued in their forlorn condition with nothing to differentiate them from the motley crowd of visitors that swarmed day by day in the yards. It was necessary to set some distinguishing mark upon the permanent inhabitants of the gaol. Irons were considered therefore doubly appropriate. They confined the prisoner's movements and they prevented him from passing himself off, or indeed taking himself off in the guise of a visitor.

There is no doubt that the ironing of a prisoner was a terrible hardship. Apart from the fact that fetters of this sort degrade the human being to the level of the brute beast, such means of securing him are physically cruel. Irons weighing sometimes as much as eight pounds were imposed upon men and women, most of them in a weak condition of health, making walking or sleeping difficult. Moreover, there is little doubt that the evil custom known as " the choice of irons " was prevalent. In other words, the weight of the irons depended upon the amount of the bribe offered to the gaoler.

While the principle of security, upon which the administration of Newgate was conducted, had it been more humanely applied, would have been legitimate enough, there were many other principles of the most questionable kind which served as the basis of the day-to-day life in the prison. The most comprehensive and the most far-reaching in its evil effects was the principle of corruption, which penetrated the whole government of the gaol.

It is perhaps hardly surprising when we learn that in 1718 the Earl of Macclesfield, the then Lord Chancellor, practically admitted to having sold the office of Mastership in Chancery to presumably the highest bidder, to having connived at the fraudulent disposition of the property of suitors by men whom he had corruptly appointed on the grounds of ancient and uninterrupted usage, that far lesser luminaries in the administration of justice and its consequences should have indulged in the same lucrative process upon identically the same pretext. From the top to the bottom of the gaol administration during the eighteenth century, we discover the vilest system of corruption at the expense of the unfortunate prisoner in every department of its domestic economy. Turning gaols to profit underlay the whole system of prison management. While there may have been exceptions—very rare indeed—in the various grades of prison officials, a general accusation can be made with historical accuracy.

Of all the governors of Newgate during the last 200 years of its existence as an ordinary prison, Mr. Ackerman, to whose kindness and consideration James Boswell pays a tribute, stands out as the one most above reproach. It was he who submitted to John Howard a table of fees which was given to him for his direction when he commenced upon his official duties, as if the exaction of them were part of his legitimate functions. The taking of fees had thus become almost a matter of official routine. But corruption did not start with fees in gaol, it commenced with the worst abuse of all, the sale of office. In the history of Newgate £3,000 had been paid to the keeper for the purchase of his office, and as much as £5,000 was paid to Lord Clarendon by Jack Huggins, an infamous character, to obtain the keepership of the Fleet for himself and his son. Truly has it been said that " He that sells a gaoler's place sells the liberty, the estate, the person, nay the very lives of the prisoners under his jurisdiction."

How long this practice of auctioneering the Governorship of Newgate Gaol continued it is difficult to estimate, for these things are done in secret, but to judge by the type of man who was appointed to the office it must have been looked upon as fair game by the dispenser of patronage and the place-hunters during the whole of the eighteenth century. Although admittedly not entirely typical, we have the instance of the Governor Cope, who, if he did not owe his position to corruption, owed it to no other qualification.

The chief turn-key, the official warders, and those convicted promoted to a position of warder, day in and day out practised the most barefaced system of corruption.

An example of how both the Governor and the subordinate officials of Newgate were able to turn their offices to some account beyond the receipt of legitimate emoluments comes down to us from the pen of the author of the *History of the Press Yard*. In a graphic description of his experiences he relates how, after being mulcted for drink and " garnish " (to be hereafter explained), he was thrown into the condemned hold. Of a sudden he heard a voice from above coming through a trap-door in the ceiling :

Sir, I understand that your name is —— and that you are a gentleman too well educated to take up your abode in a vault set apart for thieves, parricides and murderers. From hence criminals after sentence of death are carried to the place of execution, and from hence you may be removed to a chamber equal to one in any private house where you may be furnished with the best conversation and entertainment, on a valuable consideration.

His deliverer informed him that he had once been in a similar situation, and that a fellow feeling, plus the opportunity for profit, accounted for this act of humanity on his part. At the lodge, the author continues, "we gave our service to one another in a glass of wine drawn by Dame Sparling, the fat hostess who kept the tap in the lodge." Terms were fixed for £20, and he soon found himself in the Governor's lodge taking a glass of arrack with Mr. Pitt, who saw to it that for a further consideration he was provided with clean sheets in a "somewhat barrack of a room" but better than any association with pickpockets "in a dark and stinking cellar."

Felons who could pay the price were permitted, irrespective of their character or offences to purchase the greater comfort of the master's side. The keeper naïvely declared that thanks to the parsimony of the Corporation he could not pay the salaries of the turn-keys and servants nor keep the prison going at all without these particular extortions. The occupants of this side, save for the ration of bread, supported themselves by paying fees for candles, coals, and other modest requisites. The best accommodation was reserved for the prisoners on the state side, from whom still higher fees were exacted to swell the revenue of the prison. Not the least pernicious feature of this abuse was that for this purpose unwarrantable demands were made upon the women's quarters. The luxury of the state side was open to all who could pay. Prisoners paid for four beds to secure the privilege of a private room. Sometimes the keeper would let out a portion of his own house, as much as £30 having been given for the concession. These facts, of course, deal with the less seamy side of gaol corruption and its less injurious aspect. Here we have an illustration of the rich man able to pay for superior quarters, and being all the better in mind and soul for such an advantage over his fellows. But a far worse consequence of the prevalent corruption was the plight of the indigent who were unable to afford the gaol fees. Witness is borne by the two first inspectors appointed in 1835 that in the middle yard, where the worst felons were accommodated, to this effect:

We have reason to fear that poverty, ragged clothes, and an inability to pay the ward dues, elsewhere exacted for better accommodation, consign many of the more petty and un-practised offenders to this place, where they inevitably meet with further contamination from the society of the most abandoned and incorrigible inmates of the gaol.

Every new-comer to the gaol, rich and poor alike, was called upon to pay a fee known as " garnish." The committing words were " pay or strip." Some who had no coin of the realm were obliged to forfeit part of their own clothing, and then if they had no bedding or straw, as might sometimes be the case, contracted chills and often died of the effects of such privation. It is interesting to note that in 1730 four prisoners were sentenced to death for this practice. The keeper had no control over the prisoners' garnish money. They used it to eke out the scanty supply of coal supplied by charities. Those not paying " garnish " would be driven away from the fires, such as they were, and would be denied the use of candles, pepper, salt, etc., which were bought with the proceeds from this nefarious practice, and would be made to wash and sweep the wards.

Below the turn-keys, who not only purchased their situations but supplemented their salaries with fees, there were unofficial guardians chosen from the prisoners themselves. Both on the felons' and on the debtors' sides a so-called steward, one of the prisoners, was elected by the whole body from a panel of six whom the keeper nominated. This steward was almost supreme in his special sphere of activity. All the allowances of food passed through his hands, he collected garnish and distributed charity grants. He had for his own consumption a double allowance of bread deducted from the too limited ration of the rest.

Nothing was more disgraceful in the domestic economy of Newgate than that, far from there being any system of rationing provisions by properly constituted authority, this function was left to convicted felons. The food, grossly inadequate from the start, was issued weekly in bulk. It was imperfectly cooked before a ward fire, scrambled for, and then gluttonously devoured by the half-starved inmates. Broken victuals were brought in from city shops, which barely preserved the indigent prisoners from starvation.

Under the stewards there were captains of wards, chosen in the same way and performing analogous duties. They bought office from one another. Cases are recorded of the place of wardsman being sold for considerable sums. So valuable were they deemed that as much as £50 was offered to the keeper for the post, which he was no doubt able to turn to substantial profit. These underlings measured food with fees, one of the methods by which they reimbursed themselves for the price they had paid for their authority in the first instance.

The first two inspectors, Mr. Crawford and Mr. Russell, have something to say of these wardsmen in their report. They found that prisoners had their places assigned to them by the inner gatesman, himself a convicted prisoner, and a wardsman, or responsible head of a room.

So great is the authority exercised by him and so numerous were his opportunities for showing favouritism that all the prisoners may be said to be in his power. If a man is poor or ragged, however inexperienced in crime, or however trifling may be the offence for which he has been committed, his place is assigned among the most depraved.

The wardsmen were on the most intimate and familiar terms with the turn-keys, who sometimes complained that these old prisoners had more power than themselves. It was said that the prisoner had " more fear of the power of the wardsman to injure him than confidence in the Governor's power to protect him." This must have been so when the Governor was as incompetent a rogue as Cope seems to have been. The wardsmen had every sort of privilege in comforts, bedding, etc., and they even made money out of drawing briefs and petitions for their fellow-prisoners.

Not the least glaring instance of corruption in gaol was the sale of immunity from irons. Although the gaoler on his appointment swore before the Lord Mayor and Aldermen that " neither he nor any of them shall take fines or extortionate charge from any prisoner by putting on or taking off his irons," the practice was chronic. Until a short while before the closing of the gaol irons were placed on new arrivals and removed only on payment of fees. They were of course re-fettered preparatory to their appearance in the Old Bailey.

The imposition of fees left prisoners destitute on their discharge, without funds to support them in their first struggle to recommence life with character ruined, and bad habits and health contracted in gaol. But fees and extortion pursued them even on discharge. As early as 1732 the Corporation of London had promulgated an order that all prisoners acquitted at the Old Bailey should be released without fees. In 1774 a law abolishing fees was passed. But the law was openly evaded by the clerks of assize and clerks of the peace, who declared that their fees were not cancelled by the Act. In one case at Durham Assizes in 1775 the keeper was fined £50 for detaining an acquitted prisoner, but the fine was remitted on explanation. In another, regulations were evaded on the pretence that the prisoner could not be released until Judges left town, as there might be other indictments, or, if this plea was too specious, it was held necessary that they should be taken back to prison to have their irons knocked off.

The broad general principle upon which the day-to-day administration of Newgate was conducted was that all criminals of whatever age or sex were alike and must, subject of course to their ability to pay fees, have the same treatment and be associated together. To our own generation, which conducts the prison system on the basis of the most comprehensive scheme of classification, it is almost inconceivable that for centuries in the principal gaol in the City of London there was no attempt to introduce the three most elementary forms of classification—that of age, of sex, or degree of crime.

It is safe to say that in Newgate before 1812 there was no classification so far as crime was concerned. The middle yard within its limits was supposed to be appropriated to felons and transports. Each ward was calculated to accommodate twenty-four, but owing to the number of those awaiting transportation it often rose to forty, the balance sleeping on the floor. Associated with these convicted felons were often to be found numbers of juveniles and even infants of tender years. Boys were often kept here three to four weeks awaiting trial for quite trifling offences, tossing in the streets, etc. Buxton found seven or eight children, the youngest barely nine, the oldest only twelve or thirteen, exposed to all the contaminating influences that surrounded them night and day.

The Select Committee that reported on the Metropolitan Police in 1812 included in its summary the following indictment :

It is scarcely possible to devise a system better calculated to vitiate and corrupt than the mode in which juvenile offenders are thus confined—the number of boys are mixed indiscriminately together from the ages of 8 to 16 or 18, exhibiting a great variety of character and differing in degrees of guilt, the tried and the untried, and the first offender with the hardened convict.

Some of them were only nine, ten or eleven years of age.

No one but those who have witnessed such painful exhibitions can be aware of the pleasure which the older thieves take in corrupting those who have just entered vicious courses, by the detail of their exploits, the narrative of hair-breadth escapes, the teaching of technical phrases ; all of which are great allurements of the idle and the resource of the desperate, and serving to enliven and dispel the solitude of the prison.

Even after the publication of the report of 1814–15 the boys, although kept as far as possible apart from the men, were not classified as between themselves. Hence, in one long room which they occupied and used for all purposes, the older and more vitiated boys were still able to exercise a baneful influence upon the young and innocent. From the Inspector's report on Newgate in 1835 we still have evidence of a reprehensible want of classification. Although the prison population had fallen, the authorities, doubtless for their own convenience, closed one portion of the gaol and crowded up the other. The same indiscriminate association therefore continued, the convicted and the untried, the felon and misdemeanant, the sane and the insane, the old and the young. Perhaps the most flagrant example of this complete neglect of the morals of those under the control of prison authority was the fact that men charged with and convicted of unnatural offences were shut up with lads of tender years. On the master's side, which had only one washing place, seventy-eight prisoners of every variety of age, habit and delinquency were incarcerated together without employment, oversight or control.

If there was little classification amongst the male population of the prison, there seemed to be still less amongst the women, even apart from the fact that there was not sufficient classification to segregate them completely from the men. Early in the nineteenth century on the female side it was no uncommon condition of things for 300 women, with their innocent children up to the age of sixteen, quite contrary to regulations, all together, felon and misdemeanant, tried and untried, to be confined in four rooms comprising about 190 superficial yards, the whole under the superintendence of an old man and his son, who had charge of them by night and day. In the same rooms, in rags and dirt, destitute of sufficient clothing, for which there was no provision, sleeping without bedding on the floor, the boards of which were in part raised to supply a pillow, they lived, cooked and washed. The female prisoners were exposed to the full view of the men, the netting in front of their gallery being useless as a screen. There was no glass in the windows except in the infirmary.

The evidence given by Mrs. Fry and two of her associates, Mary Sanderson and Elizabeth Pryor, divulges the abject condition of these unfortunate women:

It was on visits to the school where some of us attended almost every day that we were witnesses to the dreadful proceedings that went forward on the female side of the prison, the begging, swearing, gaming, fighting, singing, dancing, dressing up in men's clothes, scenes too bad to be described, so that we did not think it suitable to admit young persons with us.

The railing was crowded with half-naked women, struggling together for the front situations with the most boisterous violence, and begging with the utmost vociferation. I felt as if I was going into a den of wild beasts and well recollect quite shuddering when the door closed upon me and I was locked in with such a herd of novel and desperate companions . . . With the proceeds of their clamourous begging, when any stranger appeared amongst them the prisoners purchased liquors from a regular tap in the prison. Spirits were openly drunk and the ear was assailed by the most terrible language. Beyond that necessary for safe custody there was little restraint over their communication with the world outside.

Although military sentinels were posted on the leads of the prison, such was the lawlessness prevailing that Mr. Newman, the Governor, entered this portion of it with reluctance. Fearful that their watches should be snatched from their sides he advised the ladies (though without avail) to leave them in his house, surely a confession of weakness on his part.

There was a master's side for females who could pay the fees, but they were associated with the rest in the one narrow yard common to all. Girls of twelve or thirteen were seen among a herd of depraved adults. Griffiths mentions a case of a woman who had been convicted thirty times residing in Newgate generally nine months out of every twelve, being the wardswoman, with nearly unlimited power. There was no separation for the women under sentence of death, who lived in the crowded common ward. Only when the order of execution came down were those about to suffer placed apart in one of the rooms in the arcade of the middle ward.

Finally, there survived all too long one of the worst

abuses due to lack of classification of every kind. When the first Inspector visited Newgate there were eight lunatics living with the sane, " the sport of the idle and depraved," an expression which connotes everything most degenerate. As late as 1814 it was found that a lunatic, incurable and sometimes dangerous, had been confined in Newgate for six years.

This deplorable want of classification led, of course, to those who had been convicted for the mildest offences and whose dispositions were absolutely normal becoming contaminated by evil communications with the vilest of humanity. There is an account of Mr. Bennett, quoted by every writer and historian on Newgate but which bears repetition, of a notable example of the consequent moral and physical deterioration—it is the case of a man of respectable family, a lawyer by profession, being for some offence committed to Newgate. The first fortnight he slept in the same bed with a highwayman on one side and a man charged with murder on the other. Spirits were freely introduced to the ill-assorted company he was obliged to affect, and although he first abstained from partaking of his share he discovered that abstinence resulted in his having to endure a persecution which was pompously termed " putting him out of protection of their internal law." In other words, he would be subjected to a mock trial with very real punishments, which could only be evaded by the payment of a bribe. The unfortunate man was ultimately compelled to adopt the habits of his associates,

by insensible degrees he began to lose his repugnance to their society, caught their flash terms and sang their songs, was admitted to their revels and acquired, in place of habits of perfect sobriety a taste for spirits.

His wife visited him in Newgate and wrote a pitiable

account of the state in which she found her husband. He had become intimate with those whose language and manners, whose female associates, prevented her from going inside, and she used to communicate with him through the bars from the passage. One day she was obliged to enter the ward as he was too ill to come to her. She found him " pale as death, very ill and in a dreadfully dirty state, the wretches making game of him " and enjoying her distress. She discovered he had been up all night with the others. Though they could not force him to gamble he was compelled to drink, and she was obliged to let him have five shillings to pay his share or otherwise he would have been stripped of his clothes.

It has already been made clear that the security of the prisoner being the sole preoccupation of authority, all other considerations for his material or moral welfare were entirely left out of account. So long as a prisoner remained in durance it did not matter how vile that durance might be. This principle connoted, of course, that, so long as the rule that a prisoner should not escape was observed, all other rules might be broken, more especially if the official and unofficial staff of the prison obtained higher fees for their breach than for their observance. The turn-keys never entered the wards from the time they locked up at night until they unlocked again in the morning, leaving the convenience and the morals of the prisoners to the wardsmen, themselves convicted felons, with results better imagined than described. Escapes, of course, were not unknown. These were no doubt partly due to the drunkenness or the cupidity or the slackness of the turn-keys. Jack Sheppard was left all day long alone on the occasion of his most wonderful escape.

Nothing in all the horrors of Newgate appears to the

student of its history more reprehensible than the laxity of prison discipline within the prison walls. Committee after committee reported that Newgate prisoners before and after trial were under no efficient superintendence. "There was no restraint or attempt at restraint." Spirits, smuggled in or more usually introduced by the usual process of bribing authority, were consumed in amazing quantities. Drunkenness was rampant, especially as there was no penalty for such excess unless, as the author of the *History of the Press Yard* tells us, that on the following morning all who had exceeded the previous night had to pay the usual forfeit in alcoholic currency to the turn-keys, who read out each morning a list of these lucrative offenders. Beer, with the full approval of the sheriff, but with no sort of supervision as to its quantity, was sold in the gaol by the potman.

A wife was allowed to spend the night with her husband in Newgate if she offered sufficient remuneration to the turn-key. The custom of husbands cohabiting with their wives in captivity was an ancient one. In the course of centuries a considerable number of children were born in the gaol. No allusion can be made to this subject without reference to the celebrated case of Bernhardi, an adventurer who sided with James II in exile, after his abdication. His imprisonment lasted until the reign of Queen Anne. In his sixty-eighth year he married in Newgate a second wife who, incredible as it may seem, bore him as many as ten children in wedlock. Evidence was given before the Parliamentary inquiry in 1814 to the effect that female criminals were often delivered of children in rooms crowded with their fellow-inmates.

The custom of allowing cohabitation between husband and wife in Newgate, as might be expected, engendered another even less desirable. Prostitutes passing themselves off as the wives of prisoners were, on payment, probably of a much larger fee than that extracted from a genuine wife, allowed the same privilege. As there was no privacy, and as the young had to pass the night in the same cell as adults, it can be imagined what effect this produced upon the general moral tone of the prison community. A complaint being made to the Keeper of Newgate, he replied that admitting it to be true, it might prevent even worse vice, not a very edifying commentary on the management of their chief prison by an official in the service of the Corporation of London.

The following is an extract from the Inspector's report referring to the corruption of the average youth in Newgate :

He is allowed intercourse with prostitutes who, in nine cases out of ten, have originally conduced to his ruin, and his connection with them is confirmed by that devotion and generosity towards their paramours in adversity for which these otherwise degraded women are remarkable.

It will be remembered that Jack Sheppard effected one of his spectacular escapes from Newgate with the assistance of the two notorious ladies with whom he habitually consorted.

Besides opportunities for indulging in every form of vice at night facilities of another kind were afforded by day to complete the corruption of the young. Visitors of every variety, mostly undesirable, as many as three hundred at a time, were allowed into the prison yards without any questions being asked as to the object of their visit. Boys were allowed to hold communication with their sweethearts. Those under the name of husbands, brothers and sons had access to the female side on Sundays and Wednesdays to visit their supposed relatives. Numbers of the criminal type still at large came to hatch plots with their less fortunate or less adroit accomplices. It is said that so little supervision was exercised that forged notes had been fabricated there. Mr. Bennett said : " I believe there is no place in the Metropolis where more crimes are projected or where stolen property is more secreted than in Newgate."

It must be remembered that throughout the eighteenth century in Newgate, and likewise in previous centuries, there was no system of prison labour. There was no provision for the delinquent to occupy his time save every conceivable opportunity for his indulgence in vice and debauchery. The first two Inspectors wrote :

Forced and constant intercourse with the most depraved individuals of his own class, the employment of those means and agents by which the lowest passions and the most vulgar propensities of man are perpetually kept in the highest state of excitement, drink, gaming, obscene and blasphemous language, utter idleness, the almost unrestricted admission of money and luxuries, uncontrolled conversation with visitors of the worst description—prostitutes, thieves, receivers of stolen goods ; all the tumultuous and diversified passions and emotions which circumstances like these must necessarily generate, forbid the faintest shadow of a hope that in a gaol so unfavourable for moral culture, any awakening truth, salutary exhortation or resolutions of amendment can take root or grow.

Under a bad governor, and there were more bad than good, there was no vestige of supervision. The report on Governor Cope is probably typical. Although he was under the obligation of visiting the prison every twenty-four hours, for days he would not enter the wards—sometimes only once during a whole fortnight, and even so his inspection was merely perfunctory. He was ignorant of the abuses. He kept no records. The Aldermen, as much to blame as he was for his culpable negligence, never called upon him to report, and left him practically with a free hand. His discipline was utterly lax and he made favourites of particular prisoners, retaining some felons who should have been sent overseas. Idleness, gambling, drinking, debauchery, went on unchecked. The newspaper men who had access to the gaol were never required to be searched, and brought in forbidden articles, not the least pernicious being literature of a pornographic character, which in their state of degradation appealed to the victims of Newgate more than anything of an intellectual character. It is interesting to remember that one of the most famous lawsuits in our history, that of Stockdale *v.* Hansard, arose out of this hawking of obscene literature.

The weekly introduction of food and drink, we are told, was the occasion for carousals enlivened by flash songs and thrilling descriptions of robberies. The language was always appalling. New arrivals, especially the innocent, were tormented with rude horse-play. Fighting was constant. The prisoners picked the pockets of visitors or robbed one another. One of the prisoners had a hot poker run into his eye. The only reason to doubt the story is that it is difficult to understand how the hot poker was heated. On one occasion when a young man who was being teased seized a knife and stabbed his tormentor in the back, it was to the wardsman and not to the officer to whom the report was made, and no official inquiry or punishment followed. Riots were not uncommon. The act of locking up was the signal for the commencement of obscene revelry and violence.

It will be gathered from the above that the spiritual welfare of the prisoners was not considered by the Corporation of London to be a principle upon which a well-conducted gaol should be run. The Chaplains, or

Ordinaries, as they were somewhat appropriately desig-nated, although records show one or two bright excep-tions, were very indifferent specimens of their calling, and seemed to be more concerned with their own material welfare than the spiritual needs of the prisoners. As an example, the Rev. Brownlow Forde, LL.D., who gave evidence before the Committee of 1814, was not only perfectly incompetent for any purpose for which he was employed but was not afraid to say so. He casually observed in the course of his evidence that had a prisoner sent for him he might have gone, but as no one ever did except they were sick unto death, he confined his minis-trations to the condemned, whom he visited twice a week in the day room of the Press Yard, and daily after the order for execution had arrived. He repudiated the notion that he had anything to do with the state of the morals of the gaol. In his view prisoners were only harassed and worried by philanthropists and ministers. It was not to be expected of them with their habits that they should be crammed with preaching and prayer. He felt no obligation to instruct youthful prisoners or attend to the spiritual needs of the mere children so often thrown into Newgate. He saw boys of tender age in chapel, but their instruction, he considered, was not at all part of his duties—" their time there is so exceed-ingly short. If it was a house calculated for reformation it might be different, but they are here to-day and gone to-morrow." He never went to the infirmary, and often knew nothing of a prisoner's illness until warned to attend the funeral. While admitting that the hideous scenes of debauchery, violence and gambling was the normal condition in which the Corporation of London and its underlings permitted Newgate to continue were sufficiently loathsome to turn the stomach of the chaplain and to make him despair of the effectualness of any efforts of his, it must be remembered that lay men and lay women ultimately succeeded where he failed.

There was no compulsion to attend chapel except upon condemned prisoners of the established church—

When weather is severe [explained the Ordinary before the Committee of Inquiry] and they are very badly clothed and shivering with cold, they will not come in, perhaps it is snowing, perhaps it is raining, and there is no fire in the chapel.

There were often disgraceful scenes within the sacred precincts. As the prisoners trooped into the galleries they shouted and hallooed to their friends in the body of the church. Since the Ordinary was rarely a person who inspired any respect let alone admiration, it was not to be expected that he would be able to control the behaviour of his wretched congregation. Unrestricted noise continued during the service. The Governor never attended. The turn-keys who were compelled to be on duty were completely indifferent to the behaviour of their wards provided they were in security. On " curiosity days," that is to say the days upon which the condemned sermon was preached in the presence of those about to die on Tyburn Tree, a large congregation attended, more, it need hardly be doubted, from morbid curiosity than any solicitude to intercede for the condemned. The chapel was sometimes used as an overflow bedroom for debtors, when services had to be discontinued.

The physical and moral conditions in any gaol are so interdependent as to warrant simultaneous treatment. The factors which made more than anything else for the immorality of Newgate " a hell above ground " were the laxity of the rules and the want of classification, and the nature of the prisoners' accommodation. Under these conditions there was no chance for the depraved ever being anything else, and there was little enough chance for anyone not already so failing to become depraved.

The gaol was throughout its history chronically over-crowded, a condition which was all the worse for the physical and moral health of its inhabitants. Sleeping accommodation consisted of a " barrack bed," which was a wooden flooring on a slightly inclined plane, with a beam running across the top to serve as a pillow. When the sleeper had the full lateral space on this filthy contraption allotted to him, it amounted to no more than one foot and a half, but when the ward was obliged to accommodate double the ordinary number, as it fre-quently was, the sleepers covered the entire floor with the exception of a passage in the middle. Under Cope they still slept on rope mats on the floor, herded together in companies of half-a-dozen to keep themselves warm and under a couple of stable rugs which were never washed. These rugs were supplied by the City of London, but there was always a shortage, as prisoners would steal them, tear them up to make mops with, and women would carry them out of the prison con-cealed under their clothing. There was no regular medical attendant. The prisoners in the daytime were ragged and filthy, many without stockings or shoes to their feet in the depth of winter.

The condition of mind and body to which even the strongest were reduced by this complete lack of all attention to health and morals was deplorable. It is recorded that when the Gordon rioters set fire to Newgate Gaol and released the prisoners some of the latter had been so repressed in body and spirit that, like the prisoners of the Bastile in history and the pupils of Dotheboys Hall in fiction, they had no heart to go elsewhere. Some returned a few days later and gave themselves up to their tormentors. It is said that many others were drawn back by an irresistible perverted inclination, and were actually found loitering about the open wards of the prison. Fifty were thus retaken within the walls the day after the fire, and others kept dropping in by twos and threes impelled by the same crazy fascination.

All the misdemeanants (and the most heinous criminals in those days came under that head) were lodged together in the Chapel ward. But even in these latter days this attempted classification does not seem to have been scrupulously carried out. In 1817 the Hon. H. G. Bennett saw in one yard thirty-five tried and thirty-seven untried together. Two of the untried were there for murder. Persons convicted of publishing libels were still immured in the same room with transports and felons.

There is yet one subject to complete this picture of horror—that of the condemned cell. There is nothing perhaps more terrible even to-day than the condemned cell in a prison where executions are carried out, but the old condemned cells of Newgate were infinitely more so than their modern equivalent. It was said that when Colonel Turner was executed in 1712 on the scaffold, in the course of a discursive speech he described the condemned cell in Newgate as " more terrible to me than this death." In the days when no less than 166 different crimes incurred the death penalty a large number were reprieved, but it was seldom less than six months before the felon was acquainted with his ultimate fate. The interval depended upon the frequency or the reverse of the meeting of the Privy Council. When this august body had reached its conclusion the news was conveyed to Newgate by the Recorder, who there made his " report." It was generally received at night. The whole of the condemned were assembled together in one ward and made to kneel down. To them entered the chaplain, who in solemn tones communicated to each in turn his fate. At the conclusion of the proceedings a thanksgiving was offered up for those pardoned. Until the final decision was communicated the condemned passed his time with those who were not under sentence of death. When his fate was inevitable he was segregated in the condemned cell. The new press yard was the receptacle of the male condemned, and this was generally crowded. On a certain occasion there were as many as one hundred, one of whom had been under sentence for two years awaiting the " report." Except in murder cases, where the execution was prompt, the delay was inconceivable. This unwarrantable postponement bred callousness, and the unfortunate victims of it spent their time in roystering and gambling : " Corrupt conversation obliterated from the mind of him who is doomed every serious feeling and valuable impression." The old condemned cells were incorporated in the newer building. John Howard records :

I was told by those who attended them that criminals who had affected an air of boldness during their trial and appeared quite unconcerned at the pronouncing sentence upon them, were struck with horror and shed tears when brought to these darksome solitary abodes.

Mrs. Fry's colleagues thus describe the condemned cell :

Those certain to suffer and those unlikely to are herded together, as many as 50 or 60 crowded into the press yard. One man declared that the language of the condemned rooms was disgusting, that he was dying a death every day in being compelled to associate with such characters. Anyone who tried to pray became the sport of his associates. They took exercise in the common airing yard so that those who knew they were to be hanged were with those who knew they would be reprieved. The latter, light-hearted, conducted themselves recklessly, playing every sort of game, oblivious to or careless of what fate held in store. Those condemned complained bitterly of an association so disturbing, and craved to be segregated from the mockery and insults of their more fortunate fellows. The chaplain had become lax because he was so much interfered with and laughed at from seeing that no success attended his efforts.

Small wonder that the report of the first two Inspectors' made to Lord John Russell contained the following strictures :

We cannot close these remarks without an expression of the painful feelings with which we submit to your Lordship this picture of the existing state of Newgate. That in this vast Metropolis, the centre of wealth, civilization and information, distinguished as the seat of religion, worth and philanthropy, where is to be found in operation every expedient by which ignorance may be superseded by knowledge, idleness by industry, and suffering by benevolence, that in the Metropolis of this highly favoured country to which the eyes of other lands turn for example, a system of prison discipline such as that enforced in Newgate should be for a number of years in undisturbed operation, not only in contempt of religion and humanity but in opposition to the recorded denunciations of authority and in defiance of the express enactments of the law, is indeed a subject which cannot but impress every considerate mind with humiliation and sorrow. We trust, however, that the day is at hand when this stain will be removed from the charters of the City of London, and when the first municipal authority of our land will no longer be subjected to the reproach of fostering an institution which outrages the rights and feelings of humanity, defeats the ends of justice, and disgraces the profession of a Christian country.

But the Corporation was more solicitous to remove the stain from its own reputation than to remedy the cause thereof. They produced a lengthy blue book denying some of the charges and excusing themselves for others. The Inspectors very properly retorted by merely reiterating their indictment, and with such effect that in the following year they were able to express satisfaction that their censures had had some perceptible influence even upon the Corporation of London : " It has aroused the attention of those upon whom parliamentary reports and grand jury presentments have hitherto failed to make the slightest impression."

As a matter of fact few reforms were ever at any time instituted at Newgate, although the Prison Discipline Society succeeded in achieving some measure of progress in spite of the opposition it met from those who might have known better. It is quite true that Committee after Committee sat and reported. It is quite true that upon their reports legislation was promulgated, too much of it merely permissive, but the laws were flagrantly violated. It is also true that the gaol was reconstructed in 1770, but it fell as far short of the demands made upon it as did the old. When the House of Commons Committee reported in 1815 immediate effect was given to those of the recommendations which could be carried out with any degree of facility. Before 1812 there was, as we have seen, little or no classification. After that date an attempt was made to divide the prisoners into separate categories—those awaiting trial, those under sentence for a fixed period or until they had paid fines, transportees awaiting removal to the colonies, who often had to wait a considerable time to the detriment of the prison accommodation, and finally convicts awaiting execution. After 1812 a yard was set apart for the untried, who were often supplemented by Class 2 misdemeanants. This was the Chapel yard, with its five wards which were calculated to hold seventy prisoners, but which often were constrained to hold more. Some attempt was made at night to separate misdemeanants from felons, but all freely mingled during the day. The state side ceased to exist and the female prisoners regained some of the space of which they had been so unjustifiably deprived. The privileges of the master's side disappeared. " Garnish " was prohibited. A certain number of beds and more bread were provided, but the City, it was said, could not afford extending the limits of the prison by which means alone classification and separation, the most essential reform of all, could be effected. A school was established for juveniles over which the chaplain, who was now in communication with the Philanthropic and other institutions, presided. Promising cases were removed to the care of these societies. But in spite of these minor reforms we read that Newgate as late as 1823 was still a byword. " Defective construction must always bar the way to any radical improvement." No rules or regulations were printed. Justices failed to inspect. Idleness still prevailed and by 1827 visitors were again allowed to infest the purlieus. In endeavouring to obviate contamination prisoners were more closely confined and associated in smaller numbers, but this had the effect of throwing them into closer contact with each other and making them more intimately acquainted.

In that same year the Prison Discipline Society reported that

the gaols attached to corporate jurisdictions continue to be the fruitful sources of vice and misery, debasing all who are confined within their walls and disseminating through their respective communities the knowledge and practice of every species of criminality.

We have the evidence of the Inspectors from the

inception of their labours over a period of years, to prove that in Newgate the worst evils persisted.

The mischief of gaol associations which has been demonstrably proved to be the fruitful source of all the abuses and irregularities which have so long disgraced Newgate is not only permitted still to exist in the prison but is rendered more powerful than before.

In 1837 the Inspectors report a retrograde movement. For nearly twenty-two hours the prisoners are locked up, during which time no officer is stationed with them. The reports continue in the same vein. The Corporation displayed a certain measure of irritation. But even the prison officials appear to have ranged themselves on the side of the Inspectors. In a resolution passed by the Court of Aldermen in 1842 it is ordered

that the Ordinary of Newgate be restricted from making any communications to the Home Office or the Inspector of Prisons, and that he be required wholly to confine himself to the performance of his duty as prescribed by Act of Parliament.

In their tenth report they find that they are compelled by an imperative sense of duty to advert in terms of decided condemnation to the lamentable condition of the prisons of the City of London. " Their duties gave them no choice but to report matters as we found them and again and again to protest against Newgate as it at present exists."

In 1840 the Government decided to erect a model prison at Pentonville at a cost of £90,000. During the next six years fifty-four prisons were built on that model, but unfortunately various jurisdictions adopted various methods of internal administration and this want of uniformity hindered progress in the right direction.

Newgate, as usual, lagged behind. Not much had been done by 1850 to remedy old defects, but the evil of overcrowding had at least been eliminated, due to the frequent sessions of the Central Criminal Court and the use of other gaols. The population seldom rose above 250, and even fell as low as fifty, although transports and misdemeanants were still accommodated in its precincts. But there was as yet no effective control over the prisoners after locking-up time, which in winter was as early as five o'clock. They were still left to themselves during fourteen or fifteen hours without check or hindrance. It is true that later iron cages were constructed on the landings in which warders spent the night alert to watch the sleepers below, and when gas was invented it was introduced into the prison. The wards had open fires, but the separate cells were not heated at all.

A year after the opening of the new model at Pentonville a serious effort was made to reconstruct Newgate, but the Home Secretary had laid it down that at least five acres would be indispensable for this purpose, and such an area it was impossible to obtain within the boundaries of the City. The Tufnell estate in Holloway, where the City owned twenty acres, was therefore decided upon as the site for the new City gaol. After its completion the uses of Newgate were narrowed down almost entirely to those of a detention prison. It was intended that, except those awaiting trial, no one should be sent there. With the consequent reduction of numbers the more crying evils, the more habitual malpractices, fell into desuetude. But it was too late for amendment. Newgate, like a venerable invalid racked with disease from which there was no hope of any recovery, was dying a natural death.

At length in 1877 under the premiership of Lord Beaconsfield, one of the first Prime Ministers to take any heed of domestic affairs, the entire prison system passed under the control of the State. Three years after the appointment of the first Prison Commissioners it was decided by Sir William Harcourt to discontinue further use of Newgate, as Clerkenwell was now sufficient to accommodate whatever prisoners still remained there.

In the year 1903 Newgate fell beneath the stroke of the housebreaker's hammer. Never was that ruthless implement wielded to so good a purpose. No language however lurid, no rhetoric however sensational, could distort the horror of its age-old abuses. Newgate—the very name is septic with its corrupt and covetous officials, its grinding extortions, its reeking cells, its physical and moral pestilence, its dissolute associations, and its human anguish of soul and body. And the more amazing its long continuance must seem when it is taken into consideration that the description set out in the foregoing pages, hardly to be believed were it not founded upon incontrovertible evidence, applies to Newgate as it was in an age when England was supposed to be a civilized country, its destinies controlled by illustrious and far-sighted statesmen, its armed forces victorious by land and sea, and its commerce placing the nation's credit in an unrivalled position of security and wealth amongst all her foreign rivals.

But day after day, year after year, while clergy and congregations committed to their charge prayed mechanically for pity upon prisoners and captives beneath the great dome which cast its shadow upon Newgate, while prisoners and captives—men, women and children—languished in mind and body, the victims of the vilest of human institutions, the City Fathers who were directly responsible for its conduct and its continuance solaced themselves with the assurance given to them by Mr. Pitt himself that England would save Europe by her example.

CHAPTER V

THE DISSEMINATION

CENTURIES of experience were needed to convince Authority that public display of the retribution which overtakes the criminal, far from serving as a warning or a deterrent to potential enemies of society, produced in the aggregate exactly the opposite effect to what was originally intended by this device. In the eighteenth century the more savage was the exhibition of the death penalty the more capital offences increased. And yet until the later part of the nineteenth century publicity continued to be an essential feature of this general scheme of maladministration.

In order the better to account for an apparent paradox, some descriptions drawn mainly from the direct evidence by eye-witnesses of public executions at Tyburn are reproduced below in detail.

It will be instructive in the first instance to trace the course of the criminal from the condemned cell to the place of execution. Publicity commenced in the prison itself. The condemned man was allowed to receive as many visitors as he desired, or perhaps it would be more accurate to say that he was allowed to receive as many who cared to pay a substantial fee to the gaoler for that purpose. It is recorded that crowds of infatuated females congregated at Newgate to offer their condolences to that prince of lady-killers Claude Duval in his last hours of life. The number of visitors that flocked to interview Jack Sheppard included Sir James Thorn-

hill, who seized the occasion to paint his portrait.
James Maclean, the famous twenty-six-year-old gentleman highwayman, who lodged in St. James's Street
and frequented masquerades, was paid the compliment
of being visited by 3,000 people, who rendered the
atmosphere so oppressive that he fainted twice as
a consequence. Horace Walpole commented severely
on " this ridiculous rage there is for going to Newgate
and the prints that are published of the malefactors
and the memoirs of their lives set forth with as much
parade as Marshal Turenne's." But this undesirable
publicity was even fostered by the chaplains of the
gaol, who from contemporary accounts were more
solicitous to extract information from the condemned
man as to the intimate details of his career with the
purpose of selling the same to the public, than of attending to the needs of his soul. While the encouragement
and gratification of morbid curiosity of this kind was all
to the bad, the effect of elevating a common murderer
to the status of a popular hero was still more detrimental
to public morals.

Within the precincts of the gaol it was not only
in his cell where the unfortunate victim was paraded
before the public gaze. Upon the Sunday antecedent
to the execution visitors were admitted to the chapel
so that they might satisfy an unwholesome curiosity to witness the behaviour of the condemned in
so awful a predicament. This demoralizing ordeal,
savouring rather of *polichinelle* than of divine service, was
so much dreaded by the more decent-minded amongst
the condemned that they preferred abjuring their faith
rather than have recourse to so flagrant a mockery of
religious consolation.

The unfortunate objects of these unedifying demon-
strations occupied an open pew in the centre of the

chapel, which was draped with black cloth for the occasion. Upon a table was placed a coffin in full view of those whom it was intended to impress. Every available space was filled with a crowd of spectators composed partly of morbid-minded sightseers, partly of friends or relations who with ribald gestures and cries endeavoured to keep up the spirits of the doomed men and women.

Dr. Bernard Mandeville, who lived during the earlier part of the eighteenth century, has left us a vivid description of the scene in Newgate Gaol on the morning of an execution.

The horrid aspect of turn-keys and gaolers in discontent and hurry, the dreadful looks of rogues in irons, the scolding and grumbling and drinking . . . but what is most shocking is the behaviour of the condemned, who for the greatest part you will find drinking madly or uttering the vilest ribaldry and jeering at others that are less impenitent, whilst the Ordinary bustles amongst them and shifting from one to another distributes scraps of good counsel to inattentive hearers, and near him the hangman, impatient to be gone, swears at their delays and as fast as he can does his part in preparing them for the journey.

On the morning of an execution, which usually took place once a month, the condemned, if neither of rank nor wealth, was ensconced in a wretched wagon along with a coffin so soon to receive the lifeless body, always provided his relations could afford this last attention to his needs. A condemned man, if of any social consequence, for example Lord Ferrers, who was executed in 1760 for the murder of his steward, was allowed to proceed in an elaborate mourning coach with all the paraphernalia of funeral furnishings. Edward Bird, an old Etonian, went to Tyburn in a mourning coach accompanied by his mother.

Sometimes a clergyman accompanied the victims on the long journey to Tyburn. This concession to the spiritual needs of the victim on one occasion invested the proceedings with an element of farce. It is recorded that a Jacobite, condemned to death for his part in the rebellion of 1715, was accommodated with two divines of different persuasions, who together came to fisticuffs over his soul. The non-juror, superior in physical force if not in moral suasion, kicked the Rev. Paul Lorraine neck and crop out of the cart as they neared Tyburn Tree, and gave the lad absolution for his crime.

The distance from Newgate to Tyburn is three miles. As the drab procession emerged from the gloomy gateway a motley crowd joined with it composed of the idlest of the working classes, the most honourable, as Mandeville observes, being prentices and journeymen to the meanest tradesmen. All the rest were of an even lower order in the social scale. The publication of the dates of executions served as an invitation to all thieves and pickpockets to make carnival. Old offenders who would not have dared to show their faces to the light of day upon any other occasion found safety in numbers upon this. The route from one end to the other was invariably lined with a vast crowd of spectators. The execution of the brothers Perreau in 1776 was witnessed by a crowd estimated at 30,000 persons. In the case of the execution of a famous criminal such as Jack Sheppard, the number is placed at 200,000. When Lord Ferrers was executed in 1760 the crowd was so great that the procession took three hours to travel from Newgate to Tyburn. This unfortunate peer confided to the sheriffs that passing through a multitude of such a size and character was an ordeal worse than death itself. One wretched woman, a Mrs. Meteyard, was carried senseless in the cart from the prison to the gallows. Fielding, who has described the scene, was struck by the size of the mob in virtue of the frequency of these executions in London.

So great, as a rule, was the throng as to interrupt every 20 or 30 yards the progress of the melancholy procession. Let us turn to the pages of Dr. Mandeville once more for an account from an eye-witness :

All the way from Newgate to Tyburn is one continued Fair for whores and rogues of the meaner sort. Here the most abandoned rakehells may light on women as shameless. . . . Where the crowd is least, which, among the itinerants, is nowhere very thin, the mob is rudest. No modern rabble can long subsist without their darling cordial " geneva." The intelligible sounds that are heard among them are oaths and vile expressions. As these undisciplined armies have no particular enemies to encounter but cleanliness and good manners, so nothing is more entertaining to them than the dead carcases of dogs and cats, or for want of them, rags flung as high and as far as a strong arm can carry them, and commonly directed where the throng is thickest.

The attitude adopted in this gruesome parade by the main actors of the drama varied, of course, with their temperaments. But it is to be feared that if the experience was intended to inspire the victims with awe or to make them reflect the deeper upon their situation, far from exercising even a wholesome restraint it egregiously failed in any kind of salutary effect. Contemporary accounts suggest that in the case of the impenitent they affected an air of composure or indifference. Fielding records that three of those he accompanied on their last journey

at first seemed not enough concerned, grew most shamefully daring and wanton, behaving themselves in a manner that would have been ridiculous in men in any circumstances whatever. They swore, laughed and talked obscenely, and wished their wicked companions good luck with as much assurance as if their employment had been the most lawful.

It is recorded of Dick Turpin that he purchased a new suit of fustian and a pair of pumps to wear at the gallows. In the case of those who would have preferred to adopt a reverent attitude, such was rendered impossible by the behaviour of the crowd. This complete inversion of the influence the ordeal was intended to exercise on the mind of the accused inspired one Richard Dow to devise an expedient by which he hoped to counteract the evil effects produced upon the condemned by the obscene behaviour of the crowd. By will he bequeathed £50 a year, which was to be expended in the following manner. A gratuity was to be given to the bell-man or sexton of St. Sepulchre's Church (where it had been the former custom for the condemned to be presented by their paramours or friends with bouquets, which they stuck in their breasts) in order that he should toll the bell and at the same time pronounce an exhortation to this effect :

All good people pray heartily to God for these poor sinners, who are now going to their deaths, for whom this great bell doth toll. You that are condemned to die repent with lamentable tears. Ask mercy of the Lord for the salvation of your own souls, through the merits, death and Passion of Jesus Christ, who now sits at the right hand of God to make intercession for as many of you as persistently return unto him. Lord have mercy upon you ! Christ have mercy upon you !

Which last words the bell-man repeats three times.

Whether Richard Dow's bequest fulfilled the purpose of the testator in any appreciable degree it is impossible to estimate. Our only information on this head comes from the pen of Fielding, who rode on a horse beside the wagon which drove some wretches to execution.

The exhortation [he tells us] spoken by the bell-man from the wall of St. Sepulchre's Churchyard is well intended, but the noise of the officers and the mob was so great, and the silly curiosity of people climbing into the cart to take leave of the criminals made such a confused noise, I could not hear the words of the exhortation when spoken.

Too often, no doubt, the prisoners had taken effective precautions even before setting out from Newgate to quell their fears by artificial means, so that their condition of mind was not susceptible to such influences. The cart stopped at frequent intervals along the route. These halts invariably increased the numbers that surrounded the procession. The former comrades of the condemned, especially the younger men, more eager than the rest of the throng, broke through all obstacles to take a final leave, struggling through the crowd for a shake of the hand, " not to lose before so much company the credit there is in having had such a valuable acquaintance." At the hospital of St. Giles in the Fields there was observed a very questionable custom, abolished in 1750, of presenting to the condemned a great bowl of ale " thereof to drink at their pleasure, as to be their last refreshment in life." It is to be presumed that one description partook of it with avidity bred of custom, and the remainder welcomed any restorative to aid their composure. Not only at St. Giles but at other convenient places the procession stopped for this purpose before it came to the journey's end.

The attitude of the mob towards the occupants of the cart depended much upon whether the nature of his crime qualified the criminal as a martyr or an object of execration. Highwaymen were invariably accepted as romantic heroes. Thief-takers came in for a well-merited share of opprobrium from those who were their potential victims. In the case of the infamous Mrs.

Brownrigg the mob called out to the Ordinary to " pray for her damnation, as such a fiend ought not to be saved," and of Williamson (hanged in Moorfields for starving his wife to death) it is recorded that, apprehensive of being torn to pieces by the mob, he hastened the executioner in the performance of his office. It might be said that in the case of a public enemy the spectators were prepared to anticipate, in the case of a public idol were prepared to obviate the work of the executioner. But all accounts agree in the ribaldry and indifference to human suffering displayed by the vast concourse of persons that came to witness it in its most poignant form.

The face of everyone [writes Fielding] spoke a kind of mirth, as if the spectacle they beheld had afforded pleasure instead of pain . . . here all was hurry and confusion, racket and noise, praying and oaths, swearing and singing psalms . . . Every street and lane I passed through bearing rather the face of a holiday than that of sorrow which I expected to see, for the untimely deaths of five members of the community.

The scene at the place of execution was usually something in the nature of a riot. The "tree" itself, triangular with crossbeams capable of hanging twenty-four at a time (a test it was occasionally put to) was, until the movable gallows took its place in 1759, situated at the junction of the Edgware and Bayswater Roads, where it had stood since the twelfth century, accounting for the public execution of at least 50,000 criminals. According to contemporary prints there were grandstands of the sort that are erected in our own times for the accommodation of crowds at football matches, where seats could be reserved and for which, no doubt, large sums were exacted. The cart came to a standsill immediately beneath the gallows. Mandeville describes the scene at this stage of the proceedings :

Execution at Tyburn

William Hogarth del.

The violent efforts of the most sturdy and resolute of the mob on one side and the potent endeavours of rugged gaolers and others to beat them off on the other, the terrible blows that are struck, the heads that are broke, the pieces of swinging sticks and blood that fly about, the men that are knocked down and trampled upon are beyond imagination, while the dissonance of voices and the variety of outcries that are heard there make up a discord not to be paralleled.   If we consider besides all this the mean equipages of the sheriffs' officers and the scrubby horses that compose the cavalcade, the irregularity of the march, and the want of order among all the attendants, we shall be forced to confess that these proceedings are very void of that decent solemnity that would be required to make them awful.   At the very place of execution the most remarkable scene is a vast multitude on foot intermixed with many horsemen and hackney coaches, all very dirty or else covered with dust, that are either abusing one another or else staring at the prisoners, among whom there is commonly very little devotion.   But to require this exercise or to expect it of every wretch that comes to be hanged is as wild and as extravagant as the performance of it is commonly frightful and impertinent.

What the feelings of the victims must have been at the moment of halting, when not only their fate was upon them but their situation was being rendered a thousand times worse by the ghastly scenes enacted in their neighbourhood, beggars the imagination.

At the place of execution [writes Fielding in 1741] the scene grew still more shocking, and the clergyman who attended was more the subject of ridicule than of their serious attention. The psalm was sung amidst the curses and quarrelling of hundreds of the most abandoned and profligate of mankind, upon whom, so dead are they to every sense of decency, all the preparation of the unhappy wretches seems to serve only for subject of a barbarous kind of mirth, altogether inconsistent with humanity.

It is not, therefore, surprising to learn that " the

Ordinary and Executioner, having performed their different duties with small and equal concern, seem to be tired and glad it is over." This description is fully borne out by other observers of these rites. Silas Told, one of the few lay visitors to Newgate Gaol, who was in the habit of contributing what he could to the redemption of the prisoners, describes a scene of which he himself was witness. When attending one May Edmonson, who had been convicted of murder and condemned to death on the flimsiest of evidence, he addressed some words of spiritual comfort to her.

This produced a pleasant smile on her countenance, which when the sons of violence perceived they d——d her in a shameful manner; this was accompanied with a vengeful shout, " see how bold she is, see how the —— laughs."

The following is another description of similar proceedings taken from a contemporary pamphlet written with the purpose of abolishing the outrageous practice of public executions :

On reaching the fatal tree it becomes a riotous mob, and their wantonness of speech broke forth in profane jokes, swearing and blasphemy. The officers of the law were powerless. No attention was paid to the convict's dying speech, an exhortation, for example, to shun a vicious life addressed to thieves actually engaged in picking pockets. The culprit's prayers were interrupted. His demeanour, if resigned, was sneered at and only applauded when he went with a brazen effrontery to his death. Thus are all the ends of public justice defeated, all the effects of example, the terrors of death, the shame of punishment, are all lost.

Colquhoun pointedly confirms this verdict :

Since even the dread of this punishment in the manner it is now conducted has so little effect upon guilty associates attending executions, that it is no uncommon thing for these hardened offenders to be engaged in new acts of theft at the very moment their companions in iniquity are launching, in their presence, into eternity.

The hangman of those times was usually a reprieved criminal, such as John Price, who was ultimately hanged himself, being, it is said, actually arrested in the process of performing his revolting duty. Dennis was sentenced for complicity in the Gordon riots, but was pardoned on condition he would hang his fellow-conspirators. It must be inferred that the profession of executioner was not held in very high esteem, and that there was no very severe competition to obtain the appointment. From various gruesome details which have been handed down to us we must conclude that not only were their characters questionable, but their professional skill left much to be desired. Many are the tales that confirm this estimate of their proficiency. At the execution of the famous pirate, Captain Kidd, the rope broke at the critical moment, with the result that he was again submitted to the process of hanging, conscious the while. That the performance was often ineffective is witnessed by the fact that the crowd was always prepared to break through to put the wretched victim out of his misery, a proceeding which in one case at least led to a deplorable result. Thus the friends of another famous pirate, John Gow, added their weight to his with such force that the rope broke before he had expired, necessitating a repetition of the ordeal of execution.

That the gallows was occasionally cheated by the mismanagement of the executioner is proved by a number of authentic cases of resuscitation after cutting down, a result achieved by immersing the victim in hot water and massaging the limbs, a circumstance which incidentally gives us surprise that there should have been no official certificate of death.

The system of fees and gratuities which seemed to be the very essence of the whole treatment of criminals in those days found an ultimate illustration in the claim of the hangman to the clothes in which the criminal was executed. This claim was occasionally disputed. An account has survived of the vigorous protest made by Hannah Dagoe, a herculean Covent Garden porter. When the cart was drawn in under the gallows she managed to loosen her arms. Seizing the executioner she struggled with him and dealt him so violent a blow on the chest that she nearly knocked him down. Tearing off her hat, cloak, and other garments which he had claimed as his proper perquisites, she distributed them amongst the crowd. After a long struggle he adjusted the rope around her neck, but she threw herself out of the cart with such violence that she anticipated the operation of the gallows.

A particularly revolting practice is mentioned by one writer. Children were taken upon the scaffold after an execution, to have the hand of the corpse applied to them, the " death sweat " of a man who had been hanged being held to be a cure for scrofulous disease. This superstition was indulged in as late as the year 1760.

If the proceedings before and during the execution were demoralizing, they were the more so after their completion. As soon as the bodies were cut down extraordinary scenes were witnessed due to the fact that by an Act of George II it was provided that " for the better prevention of murder some further terror and peculiar mark of infamy be added to the punishment of death—the bodies to be given to the Surgeons Company for dissection," carried out in the case of Newgate prisoners in the Surgeons Hall adjoining the prison. That this was regarded by both the convicted and the convicteds' friends with disapprobation is amply attested.

William Smith, executed in 1750, had in an advertisement entreated contributions for his decent interment, so that " his poor body might not fall into the hands of surgeons and perpetuate the disgrace of his family." The murderer would beg his friends to rescue his body if any attempt were made by the surgeons to procure it, a request which was usually respected amid scenes of riot and disorder, which did nothing to make the spectacle less degrading. Such a scene occurred on the day that Fielding witnessed an execution.

As soon as the poor creatures were half dead I was much surprised before such a number of peace officers to see the populace fall to hauling and pulling the carcasses with so much earnestness as to occasion several warm encounters and broken heads. These, I was told, were the friends of the persons executed, or such as, for the sake of tumult, chose to appear so, and some persons sent by private surgeons to obtain bodies for dissection. The contests between these were fierce and bloody and frightful to look at, so that I made the best of my way out of the crowd, and with some difficulty rode back among a large number of people who had been upon the same errand as myself.

He also records that one of the bodies was carried to the lodging of his wife, who not being in the way to receive it, they immediately hawked it about to every surgeon they could think of, and when no one would buy it they besmeared it with tar and left it in a field hardly covered with earth. Another contemporary account details a curious scene and describes a

movement at the gallows where a vast body of sailors, some of whom armed with cutlasses and all with bludgeons, began to be very clamourous . . . which Mr. Sheriff perceiving he rode up to them and inquired in the mildest terms the reason of their tumult. Being answered that they only wanted to save the bodies of their brethren from the surgeons, and the Sheriff promising that the latter should not have them, the sailors thanked the magistrate, wished every blessing to attend him, and assured him they had no design to interrupt him in the execution of his office.

If the dissecting table was not the ultimate destination of the body of the hanged, his relatives and friends either had permission or took it to remove the corpse for burial to a churchyard.   The body of Jack Sheppard met with an entirely different and less romantic fate than that described in Harrison Ainsworth's highly fictitious narrative, but mainly typical.   When the body had hung the appointed time an undertaker ventured to appear with a hearse, but being taken for a surgeon's agent he was obstructed by a crowd of roughs who demolished the hearse and fell upon the undertaker, who escaped with some difficulty.   They thereupon seized the body, and passed it from hand to hand until it was covered with bruises and dirt.   It was taken as far as the Barley Mow in Long Acre, where it lay for some hours.   On its being discovered that a trick had been devised by a bailiff in the pay of the surgeons and that the body had been forcibly taken from a person who really intended to bury it, the mob was excited to frenzy, and a serious riot followed.   The military were called in, and with the aid of several detachments of guards the ringleaders were secured.   The body was given to a friend of Jack Sheppard's.   The mob attended it to St. Martin's-in-the-Fields where it was deposited under a guard of soldiers and eventually buried in the old churchyard, where the National Gallery now stands, and not, as Harrison Ainsworth states, in Willesden churchyard by his mother's side.   In 1866 his coffin was discovered by some workmen next to that of the philantropist, George Heriot.   In all likelihood his remains found a final resting-place in the Rookwood cemetery, for it was there that all the bodies that were not claimed by descendants were sent for final interment on the closing of old St. Martin's churchyard. It is not to be supposed that poor Jack had any relict who was likely to be concerned with the ultimate fate of his ashes.

The *Annual Register* for 1764 refers to a curious method by which sometimes the criminal retaliated upon witnesses who had furnished evidence of his guilt. An illustration given is the case of a condemned man who addressed the mob round the scaffold at Tyburn, and asked them to carry his body after execution and lay it at the door of one Parker, a butcher in the Minories, who was the principal witness against him, which request being complied with, the mob behaved so riotously before the unfortunate man's house that it was no easy matter to disperse them. The same source relates another case of the body of the criminal, Cornelius Sanders, being carried to the home of a Mrs. White in Spitalfields, from whom he had stolen £50, and laid before the door. Her house was completely wrecked by the mob before the guards could be called to the scene of action.

It is recorded that Claude Duval, after hanging, lay in state in the Tangier Tavern in St. Giles, in a room draped in black adorned with escutcheons—eight wax tapers surrounded the catafalque, and as many chief mourners in long cloaks, doubtless visited by a multitude of female admirers, who, we are told, witnessed the execution in masks.

Hanging was not the only form of execution which took place in public during the eighteenth century. Women were burnt at the stake at Tyburn, but the procedure by that time was to strangle the victim before the faggots were lighted. Blackstone accounts for this custom with the following commentary: " As the decency due to the sex forbids the exposing and public mangling their bodies the sentence is to be drawn to the gallows and there burnt alive," a curious concession to the proprieties one would have thought. In July, 1721, Barbara Spencer was thus burnt for coining. Her last wish was that she might say a prayer in peace, but the mob would have none of it and threw stones and missiles at her while engaged in her devotions. In 1726 there was the terrible case of Mrs. Hayes. The flames scorching the hands of the executioner he prematurely released the rope with which he was proceeding to strangle her. In an agony of pain she thrust the blazing faggots from her, rending the air with piercing shrieks until she was consumed.

As recently as the year 1788 a woman, by name Phœbe Harris, was burnt for coining before the door of Newgate. She was made to walk to a stake fixed in the road half-way between the scaffold and Newgate Street. She was then tied by the neck to an iron bolt fixed near to the top of the stake. The stool upon which she stood was drawn away and her lifeless body was left suspended for half an hour. Finally a chain fastened by nails to the stake was secured to her waist by the executioner, who piled up faggots around her, which when kindled burnt the halter so that the body fell a short distance into the flames. This horrible scene was witnessed by a vast concourse of people.

At length even the Sheriffs themselves had to acknowledge that these infamous public debaucheries, far from discouraging crime, had favoured its increase. It was decided therefore that executions in future should take place immediately in front of the gaol. This decision called forth from Dr. Johnson some observations which have probably been taken much too seriously by the many authors who have quoted them. " The age is running mad after innovation," so Boswell records the

sage to have said, " all the business of the world is to
be done in a new way. Tyburn itself is not safe from
the fury of innovation ! " In response to the argument
that it was an improvement he replied :

No, sir, it is not an improvement. They object that the old
method drew together a number of spectators. Sir, executions
are intended to draw spectators. If they do not draw spectators they don't answer the purpose. The old method was
most satisfactory for all parties. The public was gratified by a
procession, the criminal was supported by it. Why is all this
to be swept away ?

That such observations were egregious nonsense not
even the most idolatrous of Dr. Johnson's admirers
could deny, but it must be remembered that not only
had Dr. Johnson a heavy sense of humour, but he also
had the spirit of opposition most highly developed, and
it is therefore more than probable that he adopted this
attitude " with his tongue in his cheek." Be this as it
may, mercifully no remonstrance from Dr. Johnson or
from anyone else availed in checking the decision of the
Corporation of London to make a different experiment.
But the transference of the place of execution to
greater seclusion only effected one reform. Although
the new site being within a few yards of the condemned
cell the *via dolorosa* was thus shortened from three miles to
a few yards, the publicity of the execution still remained
a public scandal. Instead of carting criminals through
the streets to Tyburn, the sentence of death was carried
out in front of Newgate, where it is true 5,000 persons
only instead of 300,000 could be accommodated. Here
upon a temporary scaffold hung with black, no other
persons but those authorized were allowed to stand.
During the execution a funeral bell was tolled, which
formality it was hoped, quite mistakenly, would have
the desired effect of impressing both the prisoner and

the spectators with the solemnity of the occasion, but
it would have required something even more impressive
than the tolling of a bell to counteract other influences
which such spectacles exercised upon those who witnessed them.

For the best part of another century the same demoralizing scenes around the scaffold were destined to be re-
enacted. The criminals were not exposed to view until
they actually mounted the scaffold. That part of the
stage which adjoined the prison was enclosed by a temporary roof, under which were placed two seats for the
reception of the Sheriff, one on each side of the stairs
leading to the scaffold. Round the north, west and
south sides were erected galleries for the reception of
officers, attendants, etc., and at a short distance was fixed
a strong railing all round the scaffold to enclose a space
for the constables. In the middle was placed a movable
platform, in the form of a trap-door 10 feet long by
8 feet wide, in the middle of which was placed the
gibbet, extending from the gaol across the Old Bailey.
This movable platform was raised 6 inches higher than
the rest of the scaffold, and upon it the convicted were
placed. The contrivance was supported by two beams,
which were held by bolts. The movement of the lever
withdrew the bolts and the platform was thus made to
subside.

How far these new arrangements produced a sobering
effect upon those who witnessed them can be gathered
from a description in *The Times* dated as late as November, 1864, of Müller's execution. According to this
testimony there were more men than women, the latter
being the most degraded variety, with a very great
preponderance of younger men,

sharpers, thieves, gamblers, betting men, the outsiders of the
boxing-ring, bricklayers, labourers, dock workmen, with the

rakings of cheap singing halls and billiard rooms, the fast young men of London . . . Before the slight slow vibrations of the body had well ended, robbery and violence, loud laughing, oaths, fighting, obscene conduct and still more filthy language reigned round the gallows far and near. Such too the scene remained with little change or respite till the old hangman (Calcraft) slunk again along the drop amid hisses and sneering inquiries of what he had had to drink that morning. After failing once to cut the rope he made a second attempt more successfully, and the body of Müller disappeared from view.

It is recorded that at the particular execution above described as much as £25 was paid for a window which commanded a good view of the proceedings.

At the execution of Courvoisier, the murderer of Lord William Russell, Sir William Watkins Wynn hired a room for the night at the George public house in order that the next morning he and his friends should watch the execution in comfort. In an adjoining house Lord Alfred Paget watched the proceedings. Ladies of rank and fashion were also present. In 1807 so great and unruly was the crowd at the execution of Holloway and Haggerty that nearly 100 dead and dying were discovered lying in the street when the crowd began to thin.

After the executions at Newgate the Governor was in the habit of giving breakfast to any persons of distinction who had watched the proceedings, and if there were no more than six or seven of them his guests would return grumbling and disappointed home to breakfast, complaining that " there were hardly any fellows hanged this morning." His good-looking daughter, who did the honours at the table, admitted, however, that few did much justice to the fare. The first call of the inexperienced was for brandy, and the only person with a good appetite for the broiled kidneys, a celebrated dish of hers, was the chaplain. After breakfast was over the whole party adjourned to see the " cutting down."

George Selwyn was one of the many distinguished persons who habitually attended executions. He witnessed the execution of Lord Lovat, justifying himself by saying he made amends by going to the undertaker's to see the head sewn on again.

Read what accounts we may, there is nothing to prove that these exhibitions, even under the altered circumstances at Newgate, had the smallest deterrent value— on the contrary it is painfully obvious that they produced the most demoralizing effect upon those who witnessed them.

Many years before the processions to Tyburn were abolished Beccaria had given his verdict that

The death of a criminal is a terrible but momentary spectacle, and therefore a less efficacious method of deterring others than the continued example of a man deprived of his liberty and condemned to repair by his labour the injury done to society— a condition so miserable is a much more powerful preventative than the fear of death, which men always behold in distant obscurity.

But the British Government allowed these public exhibitions to continue until 1864, when a Royal Commission was set up to make recommendations on the subject. In spite, however, of all the evidence furnished by this means opinion was still much divided. The Commission recommended that executions should for the future take place inside the gaol " under such regulations as might be considered necessary to prevent abuse and satisfy the public that the law had been complied with." It is curious to note that among other eminent persons John Bright was a dissentient from its findings. Mr. Hibbert's Bill became law in 1868, the last public execution being that of the Fenian, Michael Barrett, who was convicted of complicity in the Clerkenwell explosion intended to release Burke and Casey from that prison.

The hangings at Tyburn Tree and in front of Newgate Gaol were not the only forms of publicity that the Government encouraged in order to deter the populace from crime during the eighteenth and nineteenth centuries, although they unquestionably were the worst influence. For centuries hanging the corpses of the executed in chains for the public gaze, on gallows by the roadside or in conspicuous places in towns, as a gamekeeper hangs up dead vermin by the covert-side, had been the usual custom. After it was abolished an attempt to revive it in 1832 in Leicester created a tumult, a fair being held and cards being played immediately under the gruesome trophy. So great was the public scandal created that any repetition of a spectacle which at last had revolted public opinion was doomed to extinction.

Another brutal practice of publicly exhibiting the body took the form of a parade through the streets. An example of this was provided in 1811. The body of a murderer, Williams by name, was made the centre of attraction in a regular procession with police escort marching alongside. It was extended on an inclined platform erected upon a cart, with the instruments he had used for the murder arranged around him as an object-lesson. The procession halted for a quarter of an hour in front of his own dwelling, presumably without the smallest consideration for the feelings of his kith and kin.

Temple Bar itself will always be associated with the public exposure of the remains of the executed.

I have been this morning [writes Horace Walpole] at the Tower, and passed under the new heads at Temple Bar, where people made a trade of letting spy-glasses at a half-penny a look.

The pillory and the stocks were often used as milder methods for holding criminals up to public execration, the former not being abolished until the year 1816. Public flogging was not abolished until 1817. The ducking of scolds obtained until 1809.

There are numerous examples of the flagrant cruelty inseparable from the punishment of placing transgressors in the pillory. The following description is all too typical. One Japhet Cook, convicted of forgery, stood in the pillory at Charing Cross from twelve to one o'clock. He was set on a chair when the hangman, dressed like a butcher, with an implement like a gardener's pruning knife, cut off his ears and with a pair of scissors split both his nostrils, all of which the victim bore with fortitude, but at the searing with a hot iron of his right nostril the pain was so violent that he rose from his chair.

As to the flogging of females, as late as 1764 a woman was conveyed in a wagon from Clerkenwell Bridewell to Enfield, and publicly whipped at the cart's tail by the common hangman for cutting down and destroying wood in Enfield Chase. She was constrained to undergo the same ordeal on two subsequent occasions. There is on record a bill for a nurse to ascertain whether the woman was with child before she was whipped. This form of punishment was often inflicted within the precincts of the gaols.

It is perhaps unnecessary to harrow the feelings of the reader with any further examples of the abominable practice of exposing to the public gaze those things which if they must obtain should be altogether concealed from view. Like the ferocity of the sentences passed upon the criminal, the publicity of his punishment seems to have produced nothing but the most disastrous effect both upon the victim and upon the crowds who congregated to witness the law's retribution. To a more enlightened generation, better versed in human psychology, there is no great difficulty in accounting for what appears at first sight to be a paradox. There is a complex by no means rare in human nature which induces a craving for publicity whatever form that publicity may take and under whatever circumstances it occurs. A certain perverted vanity is a very common characteristic of the nature that yields easily to temptation. To make a public occasion of the carrying into effect of the sentence passed upon the convicted criminal is to give this curious craving satisfaction. A large proportion of those who appear in our courts to-day derive considerable consolation from what they feel to be the importance of their situation, and if, added to this, they are aware of a certain amount of hero worship from the motley audience that fills the public gallery, the frame of mind in which they face their ordeal is anything but appropriate.

As to the effect which public executions, public floggings, and other exhibitions in the street of a like nature produced upon the crowd, it is surely patent enough to the most casual student of human nature. There can be no baser instinct in mankind than the fascination of seeing others suffer. It is one of those instincts which seem to assimilate human beings to the level of the brute creation. Freud and his school would probably trace it to some perverted sex instinct. Be its origin what it may, for government to conduct the operation of the criminal administration so as to give such an instinct free rein is in the last degree reprehensible.

It is true that in our own times there is no punishment *coram populo* or any of those disgusting exhibitions calculated to satisfy the morbid curiosity of the lewd or the vanity of the criminal, but there is still far too much publicity of another kind which invests him with a quite undue degree of importance. The spirit of adventure has few outlets in these unromantic days, and when a young man of an exuberant nature discovers that the committing of a crime invests him with an importance he would be unlikely to acquire by any other means, not only does this compensate him for much inconvenience but his associates are encouraged to go and do likewise.

A young man should be taught that crime is sordid, selfish and mean, something to be ashamed of and to be dismissed from the mind when the penalty has been paid and reformation in him has been effected. The proceedings which it is necessary to institute to exact the due penalty in the case of the young cannot be too much hidden from public gaze. If there is to be any publicity in connection with crime let it be the publication of the reforms which have been achieved by the new methods and let the only influence upon the public mind be a willing co-operation in the efforts of those who undertake the strengthening of the weakest link in the life of the community and the salvation of those who without these beneficent activities would become a reproach to government and a liability to their fellow-men.

CHAPTER VI

FRESH FIELDS

IT is not the purpose of the present chapter to examine the economic problem occasioned by the initial attempt to colonize virgin soil with convict labour. Experts holding various views will probably debate about its merits or defects to the end of time with no more satisfaction than to cancel out each other's arguments. The subject is here dealt with as part of a consecutive investigation into the methods of the treatment of crime in the eighteenth and the opening years of the nineteenth century.

The motive which first inspired the home authorities to devise some expedient for relieving the mother country of her surplus criminal population was a physical rather than a moral one. The gaols were egregiously overcrowded. Crime, thanks to an inability on the part of statesmen to link up cause and effect with any measure of success, was notably on the increase. Something had to be done to relieve the congestion of the prisons.

It is quite true that in the official announcement as to the intentions of government there are to be found certain pious aspirations, novel as they are suspect, as to the reformation of felons. The object of transportation, it is protested, is

the restriction of the number of capital offences as far as is consistent with the security of society and the employment of every method that can be devised for rendering the guilty persons serviceable to the public and just to themselves, for correcting their moral depravity, inducing habits of industry, and arming them in future against the temptations by which they have once been ensnared.

So far so good, but a careful study of the methods by which this solution of the problem was carried into effect must leave us somewhat sceptical of the sincerity of these Pecksniffian sentiments, and induces us to suspect that the main consideration in official circles was that as, according to an accepted but erroneous theory, criminals form a definite class, every reduction of their number would be so much gain to the mother country, whatever it might be to the land of their destination. It had been anticipated that the great distance, the vast expanse of waters between England and Australia, would not only prevent the return of those who had been transported, but would add to the deterrent value of the punishment, a hope that was to be falsified by the considerable number of those who by hook or by crook contrived their return. If indeed reformation was the object in view little was done to give any effect to such a purpose. But at least it must be conceded that one step forward had been taken from the previous crude method of reducing the so-called criminal population.

The idea of transportation was not a novel one. It may be traced back to the law according to which persons who had taken sanctuary might abjure the realm. Those who took advantage of this custom were not, it is true, sent to a penal colony or to any particular destination, but were cast adrift to live as best they might wherever they could. In all probability the majority selected the pirate vessel as most congenial to their temperaments and circumstances. The Stuart monarchs and Oliver Cromwell found the system of depatriating inconvenient subjects was not without its advantages, but the actual sale of criminals for terms of years to American planters, although the process originated during the Restoration, was first introduced by Act of Parliament in the year 1718. Shippers received the transportees in return for authority to dispose of them at £20 each. In this way it was taken for granted that there would be less loss of life among their unfortunate charges, it being to the interest of the contractor to keep this human cattle not only alive but in good condition, although they did not always find it easy to fulfil their obligations in virtue of the fact that so many of the convicts came on board with scorbutic diseases contracted in gaol. Mortification of the feet was so prevalent and so deadly that death from this cause alone almost destroyed the profits of the journey. On the whole, however, the trade was a lucrative one and went gaily on at the very time when our statesmen, quick to discern and reprobate the faults of other nations, were asserting the freedom of the black slaves, with whom our English slaves incidentally shared the lash on the American plantations.

The Act of Parliament above referred to allowed the Court a discretionary power to order felons who were by law entitled to " benefit of clergy " to be transported to the American colonies for seven years. This system continued in force until the American Civil War in 1775 during which period a great number of felons were sent to Maryland, where the rigid discipline which the colonial laws authorized the master to exercise over servants, joined with the prospects which agricultural pursuits after some experience was acquired by these outcasts, tended, it is said, to reform them.

Possessed in general as every adroit thief must be [says Colquhoun in his somewhat ungainly style] of good natural abilities, they availed themselves of the habits of industry acquired in the years of their servitude, became farmers and planters on their own account and many of them, succeeding in these pursuits, acquired not only that degree of respectability which is attached to property and industry, but also in their turn became masters and purchased the servitude of future transports sent out for sale.

According to the same authority, the person contracting for the transportation of convicts to the colonies or their assigns had an interest in the service of each for seven or fourteen years according to their term of transportation. Ultimately the services of convicts were considered so valuable in Maryland that contracts were made to convey them without expense whatever to Government.

The temptation must again be resisted to examine the problem from its economic aspect, and our attention must be exclusively focussed upon the methods by which transportation was carried into effect.

When the American Civil War broke out, America ceased automatically to be a dumping ground for English ne'er-do-wells. The Government had to discover some other solution for the overcrowding of our prisons. Accordingly a project was formed for transporting convicts to an island in the Gambia, but it was soon abandoned as impracticable. Mr. Eden's fantastic proposal that the surplus convicts should be given to the Mohammedan pirates of Algiers and Tunis in exchange for more honest Christian captives was also rejected, and, until some better expedient could be discovered, an Act was passed for the establishment of hulks in home waters. In 1776, as the gaols were insufficient to contain all the convicts who would previously have been transported, the hulks were resorted to as a temporary expedient for their accommodation, but in origin they served as the first primitive model of the establishments at Portland and elsewhere in which convicts were employed upon works of more or less public utility. Although far from ideal for the purpose, not until the penitentiaries were established had they any rival in such respect. In the space of nineteen years, during which this form of detention existed, about 8,000 convicts were relegated to an old ship, with the inappropriate name of *Justicia*, which was moored at Woolwich, and to two others in Langston and Portsmouth Harbours. Howard in the first instance seems to have favoured the hulks as useful places of confinement for convicts sentenced to hard labour, but probably only as a *pis aller* and because, if only to a limited extent, one of his favourite reforms, that of convict labour, was thus given effect to.

The punishment in the hulks usually consisted of enforced labour in the dockyard during working hours and confinement in the vessel after dark. Whatever chance there might have been of reformation being effected in the daytime was offset by the vicious conditions under which the convicts spent the night. Colquhoun was far from complimentary about the system.

The hulks vomit forth at stated times upon the public a certain amount of convicts who have no asylum, no home, no character, and no means of subsistence. Polluted and depraved by every human vice being rendered familiar to their minds in those seminaries of profligacy and wickedness from whence they have come, they employ themselves constantly in planning and executing acts of violence and depredation upon the public.

Howard himself could have been under no illusions. His personal investigations revealed an atrocious state of affairs in these floating prisons. He records that out of 632 prisoners on board the *Justicia*, 116 died within nineteen months. In one room 70 feet by 18 feet and

6 feet high were situated nearly seventy convicts, all in total idleness except six or seven who were building a boat for the captain. Five hundred and fifty in all were herded together without classification of age or character. There was no chaplain. Three miserable objects, for attempting to abscond, had been confined in a dark cell at the bottom of the vessel, where they lay nearly naked upon a little straw. At Gosport he found nearly 300 confined in the hulks, and among them were boys not more than ten years old. He describes the convicts on the *Justicia* as of wretched appearance. Many had no shirts, some no waistcoats, some no stockings, others no shoes. Several of them required medical attention, but none was available. The broken biscuit given to them was green and mouldy. The sick, who were only separated from the healthy, if any such there could be in this loathsome prison, by a few boards roughly nailed together, had nothing to sleep on but the bare decks. The water they drank was much tainted. A fœtid smell permeated the decks. The sabbath day was observed by a cessation of labour, for which Howard says was substituted profanity. On his telling a surgeon in a Naples galley that in England part of the hulks was a hospital, the latter replied " this must soon make the whole a hospital." It is not then very astonishing to learn from Archbishop Whateley that, were it not for the risk of the hulks, the Irish peasantry would have regarded the sentence of transportation as an easy method of emigration.

Thanks to Howard's representations the hulks were much improved, but they obviously could not continue to be the sole solution to the overcrowding of the gaols.

Now it happened that the eastern seaboard of New Holland, the original designation of the Australian continent, recently discovered by Captain Cook and called by him New South Wales, had been pronounced by this pioneer of empire to be " beautiful for scenery, delicious for climate, and rich in soil." It remained only for man to make it vile. The coincidence of such a discovery and the necessity of doing something to rid England of the incubus of overcrowded gaols suggested to the Government that this new El Dorado would suit its purpose. Accordingly an official letter dated 18th August, 1786, was addressed to the Lords Commissioners of the Treasury suggesting Botany Bay,

a series of beautiful meadows abounding in the richest pastures and only inhabited by a few savages might be an admirable destination for the savages at present a heavy charge upon their Lordships at home.

In a contemporary pamphlet it is protested that

the heavy expense Government is annually put to for transporting and otherwise punishing felons together with the facility for their return are evils long and much lamented. *There* is an asylum open and it will considerably reduce the first and wholly prevent the latter.

Under the existing circumstances and so long as the administration of justice and prisons went unremedied it cannot be questioned that there was some merit in the proposal. It must be remembered that the alternatives for the hardened criminal were Newgate, the hulks, and for a selected number Tyburn Tree. It is not surprising therefore to find recorded in contemporary writings that some of the felons

embraced this rigorous alternative even with a degree of cheerfulness and, strange to tell, there have not been wanting voluntary candidates for banishment to that remote shore.

But so long as brutal methods of treatment of felons obtained the system of transportation was from the point of view of reformation foredoomed to failure and great suffering was certain to follow in its operation. The methods adopted transgressed all those wise precepts set out by Francis Bacon in his Essay on Plantations. Abuses commenced before the convict embarked. As Archbishop Whateley observed,

sentence of transportation does not, as a stranger might suppose, imply some one description of punishment, but several different ones such as (besides actual removal to New South Wales) imprisonment in a house of correction, confinement on board the hulks, etc., with the greatest uncertainty as to what description of punishment really does await each criminal.

Thus there grew up the abominable abuse that in many cases the term of their transportation did not begin until three or four years after the convicts had received sentence, languishing in Newgate in the meanwhile.

Welcoming any expedient which was calculated to get these undesirables out of sight and out of mind, Parliament readily approved and set about making the necessary dispositions.

There was to be a Governor, Lieutenant-Governor, a Commissary and a Chaplain. Captain Arthur Phillip, described, probably correctly, as "intelligent, active, firm in making his authority respected, combined with mildness to render it pleasing," was selected for the post of Governor. Lord Sydney, First Lord of the Admiralty, gave him some discretion as to the choice of locality. He received his commission on 27th April, 1787.

It is fair to Captain Phillip to explain that his original ambition had been to build up a community consisting of free settlers sprinkled over a convict base. But such an ideal solution of the problem set him was easier to conceive than to carry into effect. The vast distance from home, with such inadequate communication and ignorance of the potentialities of the land were sufficient at first to deter any free men from undertaking the risk and hardship of blazing the trail until those who were compelled to go had effected the essential pioneering work and had made some of the rough places smooth for their successors.

In May, 1787, the first fleet collected at Spithead, containing exclusively officials, troops and convicts. There were six convict ships accommodating 558 men, 192 women, of whom twenty-eight were wives, and twenty-eight children. The experiences of that first journey have been but meagrely recorded. For two months the ships delayed, swinging at anchor in the Solent. Ultimately they set out by a circuitous route via Rio de Janeiro in order to avoid the great areas of calm atmosphere near the African coast.

Many of the convicts were embarked in a sickly state, some of them were too elderly for such an enterprise. Before the journey was over the death-roll had risen to seventy-two. There is one reference to an attempted mutiny, which was suppressed. Beyond the above meagre details we can learn little of the experiences endured by the victims on that infernal journey.

If only Governor Phillip had been given any encouragement instead of being met with blank negatives at every turn he might have proved by his humanity and ingenuity a great pioneer of the new treatment of the delinquent. Before starting he had asked for such officers as would, when they saw the convicts diligent, say a few words of encouragement to them. Those who were selected, however, both civil and military, refused to respond to such an appeal. " They declared against what they called interference with convicts, and I found myself obliged to give up the little plan I had formed on the passage for the government of these people." It was a great opportunity missed for breaking away from the old tradition that the convict was a brute and that nothing but brutal treatment was appropriate, but the opportunity was lost. If some reforming genius of the type now in charge of our boys' prisons, with no idea influencing him but to raise the fallen, had been in command of that first expedition, a very different story might have been told of this first venture in the colonization of our dominions overseas.

Captain Phillip arrived at Botany Bay on 18th January, 1788, but he found Port Jackson "the finest harbour in the world" and more suitable for his ships. He called the cove "Sydney." A crude ceremony took place on the 21st January, the date of the settlement, when all officials paraded, guns were fired from the ships, and convicts were given a ration of rum. The occasion seemed almost auspicious. The Governor read the Act of Parliament creating the colony and addressed the convicts, telling them it was to their interest to forget the habits of idleness in which hitherto too many of them had lived. He exhorted them to be honest among themselves, obedient to their overseers, and attentive to the works upon which they were about to be employed. He told them that he had noticed illegal intercourse between the sexes, which encouraged general profligacy, and he strongly recommended them to marry. His advice on this subject was readily accepted, and fourteen couples were married in the following week. We are told, however, that some of the convicts wished to marry in the belief that marriage would entitle them to more comforts and privileges, a novel and intriguing form of "marriage of convenience." When they were disillusioned some of them asked to have their marriages annulled. Marriage of those who had partners forsaken in England was of course refused, although convicts so situated thought bigamy under such circumstances would be legal. It is said that the Governor was constrained to give warning that marriages contracted in New South Wales would be regarded as binding, despite the contrary belief amongst the convicts.

His exhortations in other directions were not quite so successful. Nine convicts deserted soon after their arrival, purloining the implements they had been served out with. Two fair shop-lifters hearkened to the blandishments of some French sailors on a discovery ship, which had entered the bay almost simultaneously with the English expedition, and were missed when the French ship had sailed. The absconding of even predatory females must have been, under the peculiar circumstances, an appreciable deprivation to this infant colony.

Men who had been of good behaviour on the journey out were appointed as overseers. Thatched huts for the temporary accommodation of the convicts were built until the brick gangs were able to improve their output sufficiently to supply material for more substantial dwellings. Ground was cleared for storehouses.

But the high hopes which were at first entertained for the success of the scheme soon evaporated. The Lieutenant-Governor, writing home a few months after the landing, passed the following strictures upon the experiment :

I think it will be cheaper to feed convicts on turtles and venison at the London Tower than to be at the expense of sending men here. In the whole world there is not a worse country than what we have seen. All that is contiguous to us is so very barren and forbidding . . . almost all the seeds we have put in the ground have rotted. . . . If the Secretary of State sends out more convicts I shall not scruple to say that he will bring misery on all that are sent.

Successive Secretaries of State were evidently of a

different mind or were of a cast of mind that was indifferent to human suffering. Between 1787 and 1857 no less than 108,715 convicts were transported to the Australian colonies.

The account given by the Lieutenant-Governor is corroborated by the French discoverers who, as described, had abused Captain Phillip's hospitality. "The country is poor," they said, "the people are miserable."

At first it was reported that the prisoners conducted themselves with more propriety than could have been expected from their antecedents. But Phillip had soon occasion to revise such an estimate. It became necessary for him to threaten execution for robbery from huts or stores, so scarce and valuable was the food supply. The seamen from the transports gave trouble by bringing spirits ashore with which to tempt the convicts.

The Governor suffered little delay in setting up a criminal and a civil court, the former being badly needed. Although for those days a humane man it is on record that he hanged a youth of seventeen years of age for stealing stores from a tent, and gave another 150 lashes for some similar offence. The lash has been too closely identified with early British colonization to suffer us to believe that the original settlement was conducted upon any other method but that of brutality.

Amid various discouragements, including famine and illness—there was much scurvy and dysentery—the convicts did not prove themselves industrious. They only worked sufficiently hard to avoid punishment. But when it is said that the labour of these convicts was of little value it must be remembered that they often set forth to their work in a half-starved and ill-clad condition. The food supply was always a problem. Careful rationing was indispensable and often exiguous. Fishing, as a method of increasing the scant food supply, was not a great success. Two years' provisions had been brought from England, and these had been supplemented with stores taken on board *en route*. But little could be done to augment the supply except for seed, wheat and flour procured from the Cape. Under such circumstances the convicts suffered much from want of proper nourishment. Owing to reduced rations there was even pilfering of the ripening wheat. Convicts would eat their weekly supply of rations in a day or two, and then rob to supply the necessaries for the remaining days. The convict overseers proved useless as an adjunct to authority.

One undesirable diversion was the intercourse of the convicts with the natives, who Phillip describes as "noisy but friendly, curious, but tractable when not insulted or injured." Friendliness, however, was soon at an end. With so small a female population in their own settlement doubtless the main attraction of the kraals of the aborigines were their womenfolk. Bonwick records that the convicts stole and ill-treated the native children, seized upon the young women to subject them to their brutal passions, and wounded or slew complaining husbands or fathers. So serious did the tension between white and black become that on one occasion after a fight the Governor ordered 150 lashes for each of his unwounded subjects, who were compelled to wear fetters for twelve subsequent months, the same punishment being enacted for the wounded on recovery.

The soldiers were a constant cause of annoyance to Governor Phillip. Writing in 1794 he says, "They were observed to be very intimate with the convicts, living in their huts, eating, drinking, and gambling with them, and perpetually enticing the women to leave the men." Hunter in 1796 makes even stronger complaint of them :

They are sent here to guard and to keep in obedience to the laws when force may be requisite a set of the worst, the most atrocious characters, and yet we find amongst those safeguards men capable of corrupting the hearts of the best disposed and often superior, in every species of infamy to the most expert in wickedness amongst the convicts.

Exemplary punishment was growing daily more necessary in this quaint microcosm of the outside world. Much disorder arose in early times from the want of night accommodation for the convicts, who had to perform extra work after Government hours to earn the means for a lodging. Prowling, drinking, debauchery and robbery ensued. To obviate perpetual thieving an order was given that those found guilty would be clothed in a canvas frock and trousers. Those who failed to do a fair day's work were to receive only two-thirds of the normal ration. A woman caught as a receiver was ordered to have her head shaven and was clothed in a canvas frock with a threat of further punishment if she discarded it. It was found necessary to make regulations that boats should not be built exceeding a certain size in order to deter attempts to escape by sea. Rigours of the country inland and the hostility of the natives prevented escape in any other direction, but even so it became necessary for the Governor to warn convicts that any trying to escape into the woods were to be shot at sight.

In 1788 a small colony was established on Norfolk Island owing to the lack of fertility on the mainland. For this purpose seventeen acres of land were cleared, a night watch was set at Rose Hill (afterwards Parramatta) to prevent offences at night. A system of patrols drawn from the more trustworthy convicts was devised. They detained stragglers found abroad after dark, tracked gamblers and those who stole their clothes and provisions. Greater fertility decided the Governor to increase this miniature colony, which existed for some years until for various reasons the place was evacuated.

As time went on more transports arrived bearing more convicts. There were constant reports from the Governor of these transportees arriving in a deplorable condition, "so emaciated, so worn away by long confinement or from want of food or from both these causes." Many died as they were being landed. "All this was to be attributed to confinement in a small space and in irons, not put on singly but many of them chained together." The convicts slept in long prisons below deck in bunks and hammocks, five in a berth. In these quarters they worked, ate their food and spent the greater part of the day. They came on board in double irons, which were sometimes struck off after the voyage had begun, but were resumed in cases of convicts proving troublesome. Corporal punishment was frequent. Although they were allowed on deck only very few at a time several had died in irons, their deaths being concealed by their fellows so that the latter could obtain for as long as possible the rations of their dead companions.

In July, 1790, Surgeon White compiled a report in which occurs this passage :

Of the 939 males sent out by the last ships 261 died on board and 50 have died since landing. The number of sick this day is 450, and many who are not reckoned as sick have barely strength to attend to themselves. Such is our present state.

He further records that, having placed these wrecks of humanity under tents, he did his best for their relief, but though accustomed to the sight of human suffering he broke down in his grief at the recital of their tales of misery. The bodies of those who had died after the ships had weighed anchor, before they could be taken on shore, were thrown into the harbour. Their dead bodies could be seen cast up naked upon the rocks.

The blame for the atrocious conditions under which convicts were deported must attach to the Home Government. Incredible as it may appear, the authorities responsible entered into a contract with a firm of London merchants for transporting a thousand convicts at £17 a head, embarked, including feeding them, without any stipulation whatever for their well-being or indeed for their preservation. To the owners of these vessels the dead were as profitable as the living, " if profit alone was consulted by them and the credit of their house was not at stake." James Bonwick, in his *First 25 Years in Australia*, observes :

The worst system ever adopted was that in which the Ministry fancied they relieved themselves of all responsibility. By paying shippers so much a head for the voyage they made no provision for the due performance of the contract. The voyages were often much more tedious from the miserable vessels engaged. The food was scanty and bad ventilation was ignored. Discipline was lax or brutal. It was to the interest of merchants that the number of rations be reduced. Every death on the voyage was a gain of so many pounds. The officers on board were often parties in the traffic, personally interested in landing as few as possible. . . . It is calculated that during the first eight years at least one-tenth died on the way. A much larger proportion suffered in health and died after landing. . . . By the regulations the convicts were allowed ten at a time to take exercise upon deck, and yet on one plea or another days and even weeks passed without their deliverance from the hold. . . .

The real or pretended attempts at mutiny intensified the misery of the passage. The poor wretches might well have complained of hard fare and hard usage— stowed below in fœtid quarters, half-clad, lying in wet

The Prison Ship

places with insufficient covering or absolutely destitute of it, stripped of the few comforts which had been provided by friends, bullied by brutal officers, beaten without cause, conscious of exposure to disease and death, helpless and hopeless in their half-starved condition. Did they complain, the remonstrance was made the ground for inflicting fresh tortures. Chains and floggings added to their horrors.

Phillip, in his dispatches, indicates a terrible negligence on the part of the home government in relation to the circumstances of transportation.

No kind of necessaries for the sick after landing were sent out. Most of the tools were bad. Of 30 pipes of wine ordered for the hospital only 15 were purchased. Not a wooden bowl that would hold a quart. The clothes of the convicts are in general bad and there is no possibility of mending them for want of thread. It is the same with the shoes, which do not last a month.

There is extant an interesting account given by Captain Hogan of a mutiny of convicts aboard H.M.S. *Marquess of Cornwallis*, outward bound in 1796 for New South Wales. Most of the convicts were Irish. One of their number revealed to the Captain a plot on the part of his fellows to kill the officers and take the ship to America. The Captain thereupon held a council of war with the soldiers and crew.

They were [he said] unanimously of the opinion that the ringleaders should be punished, and it was not without much difficulty I was able to get their lives spared, by promising the seamen and the honest part of the soldiers that each man should take his part in flogging them at the gangway . . . at eleven o'clock we commenced flogging these villains and continued engaged on that disagreeable service till 42 men and 8 women received their punishment. . . . On the 22nd at 9 p.m. I heard dreadful cries in the prison and found those who had not been punished were murdering those that gave any information, which were now above twenty—too many to keep on deck. To rescue these from the vengeance of the others I was obliged to fire amongst them with blunderbusses and pistols, and on appeasing their rage, I hauled out some of the fellows they were destroying almost speechless. None of the convicts were killed on this occasion, but many of them dangerously wounded.

Small wonder that Governor Phillip found cause to complain of the poor condition in which his settlers arrived at their destination!

Although it must be admitted there is a brighter side to the history of transport ships, and on occasions the human cargo would arrive healthy and speaking well of their treatment, there can be no doubt that brutal hardship, and unnecessary suffering and degradation characterized this abominable abuse in the service of the State. It was some while before the Government repented it of these evils and had recourse to the simple expedient of paying a premium to the officers in charge for the number landed in health.

For several years after the first settlement reports are constant of increasing famine. In fact it was even said that the dreadful mortality on board the convict ships was a blessing in disguise, as there was thereby a lessened demand upon the stores.

Eventually the day dawned when the Governor was faced with the problem of the time-expired convict settler. It was within the power of the Governor to permit remission of part or the whole of the term for which convicts had been transported. These were informed they would be given every encouragement to settle in the colony. Those not wishing to settle would have to work for their keep from 12 to 18 months, and then if any wished to return to England they would do so at their own expense. Although most of them wished to return home no assistance was given to them by Government. They were made to declare how they wished to live in the future. Those wishing to provide for themselves received a certificate stating they were free men and were thereupon struck off the provision and clothing list. They were to report weekly how they were employed and by whom. If they were willing to work for the public they were to give their names to the Commissary in order that they might be clothed and fed as far as the food and clothing in his department sufficed. It was a very difficult matter to get away from the colony as the ship masters had a clause in their contracts which forbade them to enship ex-convicts without permission of the Government. Many of the convicts made indifferent settlers. On Norfolk Island they were only industrious to raise money sufficient for their journey to England.

In 1792 the Governor in a dispatch wrote home :

A few intelligent farmers as settlers would do more for the colony than 500 settlers from soldiers or convicts, very few of whom are calculated for the life they must necessarily lead in this country, where they are so entirely cut off from those gratifications in which most of them have placed their happiness.

In 1795 the Governor, in addition to the chronic complaints of shortage of food, made representations as to the need for material for clothing. He writes to the Prime Minister : " Your Grace's own private feelings will suggest what I must experience by continual petitions for a people nearly naked, expressive of wants which it is not in my power to relieve."

Apart from economic difficulties, another problem due to the negligence or indifference of the home authorities presented itself to the Governor of this early settlement. There were apparently no records relating to the convicts transmitted to the Governor on their arrival, in some cases not even any information as to the term of their service. It was obviously wrong that, when first disposed of on shore, convicts were not classified according to their offences. Under the circumstances the most ferocious murderer and the comparatively innocent man transported for some political or military offence were classed together, and worse still, assigned into the same private service. The plan of employing them as domestic servants was detrimental. Felons under the care of a good master could be seen working unconcerned as if they had arrived with the most unblemished characters or highest recommendations. Yet another fault of the system was allowing men to be assigned to their own wives. Nothing was more common than for the husband to be transported leaving the wife to follow with the plunder, and, on her arrival, by this subterfuge living comfortably in conjugal felicity on the profit of their former depredations.

Assignment of prisoners to private individuals first commenced in the case of the civil and military officers. They usually made better masters than those who had themselves emerged from bondage. The assignment system continued in force in New South Wales and Van Dieman's Land till the matter was brought up at home chiefly through Archbishop Whately.

No account of the earlier settlement of New South Wales would be complete without detailed reference to the treatment of women convicts. For a government which did not care whether they were redeemed or not the chances of any kind of reformation in the case of females from this novel experiment were obviously remote.

Licentiousness [as Bonwick remarks] could not but follow the evil arrangements made by the Home Government that sent out so few females, even of convicts, and that provided no means for the emigration of free women of a better character, many of whom were then sadly in want of a decent home in Britain.

It was a practice amongst the female transportees to riot previous to their departure from Newgate, breaking windows, furniture or whatever came within their reach. They were generally conveyed from the prison to the waterside in open wagons and went off in anything but a chastened mood in full view of a crowd of loafers, whose behaviour was not calculated to make the scene any the more edifying. The mode in which they were brought on board is thus described—they arrived from the country in small parties at irregular intervals, having been conveyed on the outside of stage coaches or any other available conveyance under the care of a turn-key. Some were accompanied by their children as destitute as themselves, with insufficient clothing, others were destined to be separated for ever from their families. They were almost invariably ironed. On one occasion eleven from Lancaster boarded the ship with a metal hoop round their legs and arms, and chained to each other. Until as recently as the year 1842 there were no female officers to receive the convicts on board or to remain in charge of them from the time of their embarkation until they reached the land of exile.

Women and sailors lived promiscuously together on the ships going out to the colony. In spite of complaints made to Governor Macquarie no effort had been made to remedy this scandal.

Lieutenant Bond, of the Marines, records what he alleges he saw on the arrival at the port of Sydney:

The commissioned officers then come on board, and as they

stand upon deck select such females as are most agreeable to their persons. . . . In this state some have been known to live for years and to have borne children. The non-commissioned officers were then permitted to select for themselves, the privates next, and lastly those convicts, who having been in the country a considerable time and having realized some property are enabled to procure the Governor's permission to take to themselves a female convict. The remainder, who are not thus chosen, are brought on shore, and have small huts assigned them, but through the want of some regular employment are generally concerned in every artifice and villainy which is committed.

This evidence is corroborated more or less by other witnesses. Men claimed female convicts, newly arrived, as the wives they had left in England, while it was useless to contest the point if the woman was a willing accessory to the fraud. "No objection was offered by the authorities unless they were desired by a more influential applicant."

Small wonder that an adverse report was made in 1800 of these unfortunates "who to the disgrace of their sex," according to this account, "are far worse than the men and are generally found at the bottom of every infamous transaction that is committed in the colony." But surely it would have been more to the point had a Member of Parliament protested that it was to the disgrace of the Government and administration responsible that conditions should exist which ensured the prostitution of women who might otherwise have become a credit to their sex.

Writing home in 1819 the Rev. Samuel Marsden, Chaplain in New South Wales, makes reference to the plight of these unfortunate exiles :

I have been striving for more than twenty years to obtain for them some relief, but hitherto have done them little good. It has not been in my power to move those in authority to pay much attention to their wants and miseries.

In the year 1807 I returned to Europe. Shortly after my arrival in London I started a memorial to His Grace the Archbishop of Canterbury relating to the miserable condition of the female convicts, to His Majesty's Government at the Colonial Office, and to several members of the House of Commons. On my return to the Colony in 1810 I found things in the same state I left them in . . . no instructions had been communicated to His Excellency by His Majesty's Government. Nothing has been done to remedy the evils of which I complain. For the last five and twenty years many of the convict women have been driven to vice to obtain a loaf of bread or a bed to lie upon. To this day there has never been a place to put the female convicts in when they land from the ships. Many of these women have told me with tears their distress of mind on this account, some would have been glad to return to the paths of virtue if they could have found a hut to live in, without forming improper connections. Some of these women when they have been brought before me as a magistrate, and I have remonstrated with them for their crimes, have replied, " I have no other means of living. I am compelled to give my weekly allowance of provisions for my lodging, and I must starve or live in vice." I was well aware that this statement was correct, and was often at a loss what to answer. It is not only the calamities that these wretched women and their children suffer, that is to be regretted, but the general corruption of morals that such a system establishes in this rising colony and the ruin their example spreads through all the settlements. The male convicts in the service of the Crown or in that of individuals are tempted to rob and plunder continually to supply the urgent necessities of these women. All the female convicts have not run the same lengths in vice. All are not equally hardened in crime. It is most dreadful that all should alike, on their arrival here, have to be liable and exposed to the same dangerous temptations without any remedy.

What was known as the Cascade Factory was a receiving house for the women on their first arrival, is not already assigned from the ship or on their transition from one place to another, and also a house of correction for faults committed in domestic service, but with no pretensions to being a place of reformation or discipline, and seldom failing to turn out women worse than when they entered it. Religious instruction there was none except that occasionally on the sabbath day the superintendent or the chaplain, who had also an extensive parish to attend to, read prayers. The officers of the establishment consisted of only five persons. The number of prisoners in the factory was 550. It followed as a consequence that nothing resembling prison discipline could be enforced or even attempted. In short, so congenial to the taste of the majority of the inmates was this place of custody that they returned to it again and again when they wished to change their situation in service, and they were known to commit offences on purpose to be sent into it preparatory to their being assigned elsewhere.

In July, 1812, a House of Commons Committee reported on the affairs of New South Wales. In 1810 the population consisted of 5,513 men, 2,220 women, and 2,721 children. A considerable proportion of these were convicts. There were in addition 1,100 troops. In good years the colony had proved itself to be self-sufficient in corn, but it was still necessary to continue to import a certain amount of salted provisions. Attempts to regulate the supply of spirits had met with considerable difficulties. Such system of licensing as there was could not be expected to compete with illicit stills. The jurisdiction of the magistrates was the only resource available to the inhabitants for their protection against offenders.

The Committee found that the manner in which the Government's extensive powers had been used was not always such as to give satisfaction to the colony. A suggestion was made for a Governor's council.

If the prosperity of the colony be chained to unwholesome restrictions the exertions and industry of the convicts cannot be advantageously called into action during their servitude, and but little inducement will be held out to them to become settlers after their emancipation.

The Committee proceeded to describe the method of transportation from England. When the hulks were full up a vessel was employed to take part of the convicts to New South Wales. A selection was in the first instance made of the males under the age of fifty, if sentenced to transportation for life or for fourteen years, and the number was filled up with such of those sentenced to transportation for seven years as were the most unruly in the hulks or had been convicted of the most atrocious crimes. With respect to female convicts, it had been customary to send, without any exception, all those whose state of health would permit and whose age did not exceed forty-five years. The Irish were sent with less discrimination than the English as the hulks had not been instituted in any part of Ireland. Transport ships were advertised for and the lowest tender was accepted. Clothing, provisions and a doctor were supplied during the voyage, but no arrangement had been made for the convicts' spiritual welfare. There were approximately 200 carried in each vessel, with a guard of thirty men and one officer.

" However bad the treatment of the convicts on board the vessels formerly may have been," runs the report, " the present system appears to your Committee to be unobjectionable." This expression of view must surely apply to the setting up at this time of a Transport Board under the orders of the Treasury and Home Office, which engaged the vessels and victualled them through a Victualling Board, a distinct improvement upon the previous procedure. The master of the ship was now liable under heavy penalties if he did not hand convicts over safely at the end of the voyage. The Governor gave a certificate if he was satisfied that orders had been complied with. But without such a certificate the master might be prosecuted in England or lose part payment for his services. Subsequently naval surgeons were appointed by the Transport Board to which and not to the master of the ship they were responsible. It was certainly high time that a more systematic control of the convict ships was exercised by Government.

The Committee records that, between 1795 and 1801, 3,833 convicts were embarked, of which 385 died on the voyage, a death-roll of one in ten. After 1801, 2,398 were embarked, of whom one in forty-five had died.

Upon arrival of a transport returns were asked for the number of men wanted by the settlers, the skilled labour being reserved to Government.

Prisoners who have been in a higher station of life have tickets of leave given them and are exempt from compulsory labour. Similar tickets are given to men not used to active employment such as goldsmiths, the rest being distributed amongst settlers as servants and labourers. The convicts in Government service are divided into gangs with superintendents chosen from those of good behaviour. The working hours are from 6 a.m. to 3 p.m., with the rest of the day to themselves. They are clothed, fed decently, and mainly lodged by Government.

The Committee animadverts on the subject of flogging, which from certain contemporary accounts had become a scandal, although the settlers had no authority to inflict this punishment, which could only be carried out by the order of a magistrate. As many as 300 lashes had been administered. The following account, given by a witness, the reliability of which is vouched for, is not an attractive picture of the methods of discipline employed.

I have seen men, for mere venial offences, scourged until the blood has dripped into their shoes, and I have seen the flesh tainted and smelling on a living human body from the effects of severe flagellation . . . upon a charge of an overseer that the prisoner neglected his allotted task. After being flogged he must again instantly to the fields . . . for him there is no compassion.

This and similar testimony induced the Committee to suggest that extra labour should be given as an alternative to flogging.

The Committee, however, reported that it had heard nothing but good of the treatment of male convicts by the settlers. Where two or three convicts were domiciled in a family they were forced into industrious habits and their chances of reformation were consequently greater than if they were working in gangs with every inducement to vice of all kinds. Distribution of convicts as servants and labourers of individuals was therefore recommended. Freedom had been given to convicts whose time had expired and were at liberty to return to England. Grants of land, however, were made to them according to their needs, and they were fed from Government stores for eighteen months after their release. Many were reported to be doing well.

But however much the Committee viewed with favour the treatment of the men, no words could be trenchant enough to describe the situation of the women convicts. It is a terrible indictment of the system.

Received rather as prostitutes than as servants, and so far from being induced to reform themselves, the disgraceful manner in which they were disposed of operated as an encouragement to general depravity of manners.

When Governor Bligh arrived two-thirds of the children born in the colony were illegitimate. Governor Macquarie took measures to encourage marriage and to ensure a proper distribution of female convicts. The already great disproportion of the sexes made this desirable.

Presumably this is the most authoritative account of the colony as it presented itself after the first twenty-four years of its existence. It is obvious that many abuses had been redressed, but there is little either in this account or any other to justify from the moral point of view, however successful it may have been from the economic, the experiment of colonization with convict personnel.

An editorial of the *Sydney Gazette* dated 20th November, 1820, the historical value of which it is difficult to determine, hardly bears out the findings of the House of Commons Committee :

The prisoners of all classes in Government service are fed with the coarsest food, governed with the most rigid discipline, subjected to the stern and frequently capricious and tyrannical will of an overseer ; for the slightest offence (sometimes for none at all, the victim of false accusation) brought before a magistrate whom the Government has armed with the tremendous powers of a summary jurisdiction, and either flogged or sentenced to solitary confinement or re-transported to an iron-gang, where he must work in heavy irons, or to a penal settlement, where he will be ruled with a rod of iron. If assigned to a private individual he becomes the creature of chance. He may fall into the hands of a kind and indulgent master, who will reward his vitality with suitable acknowledgment, but in 99 cases out of 100 he will find his employer suspicious or whimsical, or a blockhead, not knowing good conduct from bad, or a despot who treats him like a slave, cursing and abusing and getting him flogged for any reasonable cause. He may be harassed to the very death, he may be worked like a horse. The master, though not invested by law with uncontrolled power, has yet great authority, which may be abused in a thousand ways precluding redress. Even his legal power is sufficiently formidable. A single act of disobedience, a single syllable of insolence, is a legitimate ground of complaint before a magistrate, and is always severely dealt with. But besides the master's power, the prisoners are in some measure under the domination of the free population at large, any man can give him in charge without ceremony. If seen drunk, if seen tippling, in the public-house, if met after hours in the street, if unable to pay his trifling debt, if impertinent, the free man has nothing more to do than to send him to the watch house, and get him punished. The poor prisoner is at the mercy of all men. . . . Submission from convict servants is not only expected but enforced, and yet the treatment they generally receive nourishes all the elements of disobedience and rebellion. Reformation is forgotten.

Charles Darwin, in his *Voyage of the " Beagle "* in 1836, is equally at variance with official findings :

There is much jealousy between the children of the rich emancipists and the free settlers, the former being pleased to consider honest men as interlopers. There are many serious drawbacks to the comforts of a family, the chief of which is being surrounded by convict servants. How thoroughly odious to every feeling, to be waited on by a man who the day before, perhaps, was flogged from your representation for some trifling misdemeanour. The female servants are of course much worse. Hence children learn the vilest experiences and it is fortunate if not equally vile ideas. . . .

The corporeal wants of the convicts are tolerably well supplied, their prospect of future liberty and comfort is not distant, and after good conduct certain . . . yet with all this, and overlooking the previous imprisonment and wretched passage out, I believe the years of assignment are passed away with discontent and unhappiness . . . the convicts know no pleasure beyond sensuality, and in this they are not gratified. . . . The character of the convict population is one of arrant cowardice . . . the worst feature in the whole case is, that although there exists what may be called a legal reform, yet that any moral reform should take place appears to be quite out of the question . . . a man who should try to improve could not while living with other assigned servants, his life would be one of intolerable misery and persecution.

Herman Merivale, in his *Lectures on Colonization*, is of much the same view :

The state of public morals in New South Wales and Van Dieman's Land is but too plainly evinced by the criminal returns from those countries. Severe and constant watchfulness alone restrains the commission of crime. Almost every wickedness of luxurious and corrupt societies is practised there amidst a scanty, laborious and unrefined population. This vicious class exercises an extensive influence on the remainder of the community. Convict servants introduced crime and recklessness into families of respectable emigrants. Freed convicts either became low and brutal or else able and dextrous, amassing fortunes by iniquitous means.

Until the arrival of General Darling there was no classification of prisoners attempted. An article in a newspaper of 1832 states that the Governor depended for the success of his administration upon the maxim that " where education has been implanted morality may slumber but never die." Those who had had the advantage of a decent upbringing were placed in the distant settlement of Wellington Valley, and the result of their segregation from the lower type of criminal was extremely favourable. During former governments they had been subjected to the most degrading punishments and privations without adequate cause, sometimes exceeding that to which the most abandoned ruffians were subjected, placed as they were under brutal overseers, themselves criminals, who obtained their brief authority by means of bribery, fraud and subserviency.

In 1831 a Select Committee on Secondary Punishment revealed some further interesting details on the whole question of transportation, but the evidence as to the circumstances and welfare of the convict settlers was still somewhat conflicting. It is possible, however, from this and other reliable sources to form a composite picture of the general average conditions prevailing during the last phases before transportation finally ceased. The fate of the convict when he arrived now depended upon his classification. There is no question that the actual penal settlements both in Australia and Tasmania, with their insufficiency of food rations, the filthy quarters the victims were compelled to inhabit, with their chain gangs, floggings, and other attendant horrors, condemned them to the most atrocious conditions of life. But the lot of the assignees who went up-country and were allocated as domestic servants or labourers to a free settler was not invariably so rigorous or so degrading. This contingency, of course, depended much upon the character of the employers, the majority of whom being in those days pioneers themselves, opening up a new country, were likely to exact the uttermost effort from workmen whom they could utilize for the purpose at a much lower wage than that offered to a free labourer. Accounts were given in evidence of many of these assignees undergoing severity of treatment, working from morning until night, being deprived of what few trivial comforts that fell to their lot, such as tea and tobacco, for the slightest offence. Convicts running away from their masters received 50 to 100 lashes.

It is not surprising to learn that agricultural labourers in England, who received accounts from overseas, should have regarded the prospect of transportation with terror. The London thief, especially the married man with a family, preferred to remain in England, and to endure the rigours of Newgate in the hope of returning to his relations when free again. Although it is true that it was ultimately found necessary to send wives and children of transportees out to them at public expense, provided the husband could support them, the conditions of this concession being a minimum of three years' convict service with good conduct, as a matter of fact few families went from England, and not a third of the wives.

The general impression was that ticket-of-leave men or emancipated convicts had not been reformed. Male and female convicts were permitted to intermarry during their bondage with the sanction of the Governor and on the recommendation of their masters. The state of morals in the towns, especially Sydney, was bad. Emancipists who from a state of degradation and restraint at once arrived at all the privileges of free subjects, could not be punished summarily, and were held to be mainly responsible for the low standard of general conduct. The morals amongst the women left much to be desired. The Factory at Parramatta, where they were sent for punishment, had an ill name and was badly administered.

It remains to give some description of the convict settlement in Van Dieman's Land, the original name given to the Island which is now Tasmania. The novel-readers of the nineties were much intrigued with a story by Marcus Clarke—*For the Term of his Natural Life*—which through the medium of fiction conveyed an impression which, discounting the romantic element, was hardly in excess of the terrible truth.

The convict settlement in Tasmania had its origin in an expedition sent by Governor King of New South Wales, under the supervision of Lieutenant Bowen in the year 1803, consisting of two ships carrying three officers, a lance-corporal and seven privates in charge of twenty-five convicts and six free men. In the same year a Colonel Collins brought more soldiers, convicts and officials, and gradually the convict settlement increased and continued until its abolition in 1853. The voyage of the convicts to Van Dieman's Land seems almost to have excelled in hardship and suffering similar voyages to the Australian Continent. There was no employment on board, and the convicts spent their leisure in conversation which was the reverse of edifying for the younger section of the transportees, and in thieving from each other. Boys were huddled below in a separate compartment, exposed, as could only be expected, to considerable moral pollution, made the worse by their association with the older men on deck. There was no close superintendence to counteract these evils. On disembarkation the convicts were transferred to the barracks, where they were kept until they were assigned. Boys were allowed to mix with the men in this place of reception during the day, with ill effects. The language, pilfering and sexual vice were attested by witnesses before the Committee. But it was not until 1838 that the full detail of the horrors that disgraced the convict settlements of Tasmania was revealed to the world.

It was the Secretary of State who arranged as to which particular colony the convicts should be sent, but his selection does not seem to have been determined by the particular nature of the crime. In a colony the convicts were classified into seven classes, ticket-of-leave men, convicts assigned as servants, convicts employed on public works, those in road parties not in chains, the same in chains, convicts ordered to the penal settlements and those in the penal settlements in chains. It was the last two categories that met with such vile and brutal treatment at the hands of those set in authority over them. The ticket-of-leave man had a comparatively pleasant life and commanded better wages, owing to his experience of the colony, than the free emigrant. About two-thirds of the convicts became assigned servants. The assignees were distributed to their respective destinations by a Board convened for that purpose. If one of these misbehaved he was liable to be taken before a magistrate and sentenced to be flogged. His contentment depended upon the caprice of the master to whom he was assigned, but whatever his circumstances he was much in the position of a slave. There were two small hulks kept for punishment.

By the year 1838 there were about 3,000 transportees in Van Dieman's Land. Unfortunately the number of males far exceeded the females, a condition of affairs which not only made temptation far greater for the women but was responsible according to various witnesses for a prevalence of unnatural vice. It was said that the females were " too often returned on the hands of the Government in the family way."

In 1843 a report reached England of the condition of female prisoners in Van Dieman's Land, the only colony to which at that time they were sent. The assignment of men had all but ceased, but female convicts were still disposed of in the manner to which the term " domestic slavery " was so appropriately applied. When a convict ship arrived from England, as many or more persons than there were prisoners on board were immediate petitioners for their services. These applicants were not bound to show any qualifications of their fitness to be the employers of convicts. Publicans or ticket-of-leave

holders were not permitted to take them into their
employ, but with these exceptions they might, immediately on landing from the ship, be located in the
families of the colonists. Those selected as the most
suitable were assigned to the best masters and mistresses,
whilst the refuse fell to the lot of the lower ranks of
society. As a great proportion of the tradesmen were at
that period emancipated convicts the chances the prisoner
servant stood of any reformation in character or behaviour
were remote.

For some reason the system of punishment in Van
Dieman's Land was infinitely more rigorous than in New
South Wales. As late as the year 1835 a quarter of the
male convicts and one-fifth of the women were undergoing punishment for new crimes committed in the
settlement. The number of executions appears to have
been excessive. Prisoners, it was said, grown desperate
from the severity of their punishment, determined at
whatever cost to release themselves from this thraldom.
After escaping they would purloin what provisions they
chanced upon and then took to the wilderness, where
more often than not they died of exhaustion and
starvation.

The worst of the atrocities are associated with the ill-
famed Macquarie Harbour, situated on the west coast of
the island, the setting of the most lurid passages in
Marcus Clarke's novel. It consists of a large bay with
several small islands, two of which were used as penal
settlements. During the early days of colonization the
convicts were sent to this place of ill repute for drunkenness, disobedience, neglecting duties, petty thefts, and
other transgressions. The food was bad. There was
no classification. Refractory convicts were marooned
on a small rock in the harbour and left there all night,
often wet through.

In the convict barracks they slept in wet clothes or stark naked, nine-tenths of them in heavy irons. Their work was felling timber on the mainland. Men under punishment were deprived of meat rations and were ironed in the " chain gangs." The most dreaded labour was that which necessitated the men operating in the water, building small piers on the island. Flogging with the cat-o'-nine-tails was almost a daily punishment. During five years 167 out of 245 prisoners annually were flogged, the total number of lashes inflicted being 33,723, an annual average of 6,744. The type of cat used was much larger and heavier than the normal pattern. It had the customary number of " tails," but each was a double twist of cord, and each tail contained nine knots. Flogging produced nothing but the worst moral and physical effect upon the victims. It was said that convicts would threaten to commit a crime which would lead to their execution rather than continue a life of such degradation. In five years 116 absconded from Macquarie Harbour, seventy-five of whom were believed to have perished in the woods, two were shot at sight, twenty-four escaped, thirteen hanged for bushranging, two for murder, but the most horrible fate was experienced by five of a party of seven on their wanderings through the trackless deserts of the interior of the island.

On 20th September, 1822, a convict, Alexander Pierce by name, was, according to his own subsequent statement, working in a gang with six companions, John Mather, Alexander Dalton, Edward Brown, William Kennelly, Thomas Bodenham and Matthew Travers. They together planned to procure a boat and by this means to reach Hobart Town. One Robert Greenhill was called for at the mines as he was known to be a good navigator. The latter broke open some of the miners' chests in a hut containing provisions. The absconders thought they had evaded detection, but they had reckoned without the miners who, resenting the robbery, lit fires all along the beach to give the alarm. Fearing pursuit by water they landed and destroyed the boat. They concealed themselves from observation until the sun was low and then spent the night on the hills. Travelling during the two subsequent days in difficult country they became weak from want of food, having run out of provisions for two days. On this laborious march they disputed amongst themselves about the merest trivialities, as men do in such dire straits. Kennelly said he was so hungry that he could eat a piece of a man. This was an unfortunate remark, and seems to have given Greenhill furiously to think, as on the following morning he reopened the subject and observed that he had " seen the like done before and that it ate much like pork." From hints he passed to definite suggestions. One of his companions objected that it would be murder to do such a thing, to which Greenhill replied, finding a certain diffidence among the rest, " I will do it first myself and eat first of it, but you must all lend a hand so that you may all be equal in the crime." Greenhill then proposed that Dalton should be the first victim, as he had volunteered at the convict station to act as a flogger. Accordingly, in the early hours of the morning, when Dalton was asleep, Greenhill struck him on the head with an axe, " and he never spoke a word after." One of the gang thereupon cut Dalton's throat with a knife and bled him as if he had been cattle. The body was dragged to a distance, the head cut off and the trunk eviscerated. Greenhill fried the heart and ate it, but none of the others would join him that night in this ghoulish feast. The following day two of the company were missing. Edward Brown and William Kennelly, apprehensive of a similar fate, effected their escape from the party. They succeeded in returning to the settlement in a state of complete exhaustion, but both died in hospital a few days later.

Four days more through difficult country brought the party to a large river, which they crossed with much delay and hindrance. The next few days were spent in traversing a bleak and barren wilderness. At length Greenhill and two of his companions consulted together as to who should be the next victim. Having sent two of his companions to gather wood Greenhill attacked and killed Bodenham. The heart and liver were eaten that night. The choice for those that remained was between cannibalism or death by starvation. Treated like animals when in captivity they now found no alternative to starvation but behaviour as such. Mather had been eating some of the flesh of his companion, Bodenham, when Greenhill suddenly struck him in the forehead with an axe. Mather, being of abnormal strength, recovered from the blow and secured the axe from Greenhill. Later in the day Greenhill, with the assistance of Travers seized Mather and gave him half an hour to pray and prepare for death. Mather, probably by this time not much caring whether he lived or died, gave his prayer book to Pierce, lay down as if for execution, while Greenhill took up the axe and killed him. The rest shared the body, and after two days' rest the party resumed its march, all except Travers who, getting a thorn in his foot, was compelled to lag behind. Returning to look for him they found him asleep. Whereupon Greenhill killed him with his axe. Greenhill and Pierce were now the only survivors of this ghastly journey. Both naturally became suspicious one of the other. Greenhill never would part from his axe, keeping it strapped to his body, but one morning Pierce found it under him as he lay asleep and, upon the principle of self-preservation, seized the opportunity to dispatch his one surviving companion. He took part of the thigh and arm from the corpse and travelled on for one or two days. At length he came to country where he was able to obtain food of a different kind. He fortunately came upon a flock of sheep, caught a lamb and ate it raw. The shepherd, on observing his plight, had mercy upon him, took him to his hut and gave him food and shelter. Pierce spent the next few weeks travelling from one shepherd's hut to another, living by depredation, but ultimately he was recognized and informed about by a woman convict. The shepherd with whom he was sojourning, enlightened as to his visitor, showed him the door. Once again he became a fugitive upon the face of the earth, living by his depredations until he was ultimately seized by soldiers who suspected his identity. When he was taken by the military there was no proof against him except his own statement, which was not relied upon. His confession was made while he was ill in hospital and expecting to die. On his recovery he was returned again to the penal settlement of Macquarie Harbour.

Pierce absconded a second time on 16th November, 1823, with a fellow prisoner named Cox, who could hardly have been aware of his previous exploits. A few days later he gave himself up, in all probability demented as the result of his cruel treatment in the convict station and his subsequent experiences. He was seen making smoke signals from the beach near Macquarie Harbour by a passing vessel, which reported the circumstance. A boat was sent to the spot manned with troops, who found him wearing the clothes of his murdered companion. The wretched fugitive confessed to having murdered his fellow-prisoner, Thomas Cox, two days before, and that he had "lived upon his body ever since." About half a pound of human flesh was found

upon him. Pierce told an officer the details of the
murder and indicated where the remains were to be
found. A boat was sent to King's River next morning,
and the body was discovered, dreadfully mangled, with
all the fleshy muscles torn off, also the thick part of the
arms missing, which the depraved man declared was
" delicious food." He had roasted and devoured part
of the heart and liver, although " he was in no want of
food at this time, as he had been only three days from the
settlement and had some flour in his possession when he
absconded, and when he was taken he had some pork
with him, some bread and a few fish," which he had not
tasted, explaining that " human flesh was by far preferable." He had apparently quarrelled with Cox about
their route, and as Cox was the stronger Pierce took up
his axe, with which he killed his companion. The
reason he adduced for giving himself up was that he had
despaired of ultimately effecting his escape, and that he
was so horror-struck at his own inhuman conduct that
he was beside himself when he made the smoke signal.
Whether or not his confession was in the nature of a
desperate attempt on his part to obtain an *ad misericordiam*
reprieve, he was taken to Hobart Town, where he was
tried and executed.

It is perhaps not possible to vouch for every detail of
this ghastly story narrated by men beside themselves with
misery and privation, in desperate flight from the most
degrading treatment of the convict settlements, but there
is little doubt that in the main it is true. The feelings of
the reader have not been spared these nauseating details,
for the sufficient reason that no account of the treatment of
criminals during the eighteenth and nineteenth centuries
could be complete without them. This episode, more
than any other evidence, gives the measure of the evils of
transportation. An analysis of the circumstances induces

certain definite conclusions. The first that we arrive at must be that if no less than seven men could have been guilty simultaneously of such atrocities we must look further for some more convincing reason than their own innate depravity. We must on these facts institute an inquiry as to whether transportation should ever have been employed as a method of obviating crime and punishing the criminal. The reason that the home authorities decided upon it as an expedient for dealing with convicted men and women was primarily that the gaols in England were overcrowded. But the very reason that the gaols were overcrowded was that the system of dealing with crime was so senseless, so calculated to defeat its own ends, that the consequent increase could no longer be coped with from within the four corners of the British Isles. Had modern methods been employed at home there would have been no need to have recourse to transportation.

But let us examine transportation on its own merits. It has already been shown in this chapter that the transportees were of all degrees of criminality, and that those who had committed only minor offences stood every chance both in the hulks and upon the voyage of assimilating themselves to the most depraved. Transportation could only have effected reform under certain favourable conditions. The first was that those in charge should have been humane and intelligent persons who took a real and lively interest in the reform of the convict settlers. The second condition was that the circumstances under which they started their new life, so many thousand leagues distant from home, should have been such as to induce them to retrieve their lost reputations. But these conditions were completely absent. The lives that these poor exiles led, both in the settlement at Macquarie Harbour and at Port Arthur, far removed from any kindly influence, were such to turn men into animals, to drive them demented into committing crimes which make us shudder to contemplate.

The circumstances in which they found themselves were so demoralizing that cases of murder or assault occurred not infrequently as the result of convicts hoping to be removed thereby from Macquarie Harbour to the mainland. Their confederates would confess to be witnesses with the same end in view. The Governor in 1822 had three men executed there for murdering other convicts. According to the evidence of the Surgeon who witnessed the proceedings,

their execution produced a feeling of the most disgusting description. The convicts were on that occasion all assembled around the gallows for the purpose of witnessing the execution, and so buoyant were the feelings of the men who were about to be executed, and so little did they seem to care about it, that they absolutely kicked their shoes off among the crowd as they were about to be executed in order, as a term expressed by them was, that they might die game. It seemed, as the Sheriff described it, more like a party of friends who were going on a distant journey.

Boys sent to Macquarie Harbour became, if it was possible, even more depraved as a result of associating with the older felons. They were taught to take part in thefts from other convicts and to commit sexual offences. It was found that Sunday, far from being a sacred day for the convicts, was more productive of crime and disturbance than any other day of the week.

In 1830 the convict settlement of Port Arthur on the Tasman Island had been founded. Men who were sent there were the twice convicted, some from Macquarie Harbour and also the worst characters transported from England—desperate housebreakers, murderers. There was also included a number of boys who had been convicted for minor offences such as pick-pocketing in the streets of London. The worst criminals were passed on to Port Arthur from Hobart Town as soon as they arrived, where, as elsewhere, very little classification had been effected. Although the men were not quite so desperate as at Macquarie Harbour, and the punishments were not quite so severe, the whole system was unsatisfactory in the last degree. One of the usual punishments was that of working men in irons under direct surveillance, with solitary confinement during all intervals from labour, meals and rest-time. The system, far from producing any good effect, hardened them, made them dead to all sense of shame and careless of trifling punishment. Their main work was timber-felling and leather-working. The older and more experienced convicts exercised a complete tyranny over new-comers, and quickly rendered them as bad as themselves. They were not allowed tobacco and spirits, and they never came in contact with women. It is true that the boys were taught to read and write and were instructed in work which would be useful to them in after life—but they learned other lessons less desirable, and it was said by the Surgeon in his evidence that Port Arthur was a school for eliciting and perfecting immoral propensities and depraved habits. There were no free settlers at Port Arthur. It was exclusively a penal establishment. Even the soldiers were discouraged from associating with the convicts.

The 1837 Committee provided the historian with a fresh budget of information on first-hand evidence which does nothing to correct the impression of the failure of transportation to effect what was originally intended. It is a melancholy and monotonous story of the evil consequences of a system, however valuable in itself, which is ill directed from above and badly administered below.

One witness declared that juvenile prostitution was

very common, especially with children of tender age, who more often than not were corrupted by their parents. Unnatural crime was very general, especially in the up-country farms amongst the stockmen and in the penal settlements, owing largely to the disproportion of the sexes. Prostitution was generally common among convict women. Concubinage was allowed among convicts. Magistrates refused to interfere in cases where convicts lived in concubinage, but merely in cases where they were living in adultery.

Punishments were of a most degrading character, especially the scourging, and relegation to the chain gangs locked up in prisons resembling dog-kennels.

On looking into these boxes [observed one witness] I found that there was a ledge on each side, and that the men were piled upon the ledges and others were below upon the floor, and I believe from the bringing together of such numbers of men, heated as they are and excited, the consequences are of a very immoral character.

Once again it was asserted that the conduct of the women was even worse than the men. Older ones would debauch the others and teach them every form of vice. When assigned, they were addicted to drinking, debauchery and pilfering. They were noisy and quarrelsome in the factory at Parramatta, and sometimes vicious. There had been free female emigrants as domestics, but their bad conduct had caused abandonment of the scheme as they increased the amount of vice to a very great extent. Children in families where they were assigned as servants lost their reverence for authority, acquired bad language and often became dissolute at an early age. Drunkenness was very prevalent.

Some attempt was made in 1837 to send out boys in a separate ship with a full complement of educational instructors and monitors with a view to starting a juvenile establishment at Port Puer, well conducted on humane and sensible lines, and where they might be taught trades.   If such an experiment had been started on a large scale many years before, the history of transportation might have been very different.   As it was, it was observed that the boys under sentence of transportation for life had generally conducted themselves in a very reckless manner, under the impression that their situation could not be worse.   It was suggested that some prospect might be held out for them beyond that of adults under similar sentence in order to correct this impression.

A magistrate, James Mudie, who had lived in New South Wales, gave the Committee a curious picture of the colony as it existed in 1837.   He had left as he did not consider it safe to remain.   He had employed a large number of convicts, including shepherds, cattlemen, ploughmen, who spent their spare time in plaiting straw hats for sale and in gambling whenever they could lay their hands on playing-cards.   After dark the greater proportion of them would slip out to indulge their taste for pilfering in the neighbourhood.   This happened on most estates.   The witness declared that he himself lost annually some two or three hundred pounds from plunder by the convicts.   Part of the contents of sacks of wheat would be taken on the way to Sydney and the proceeds exchanged for drink.   In this manner he would sometimes experience a loss of twenty out of 120 bushels at a time.   Small squatters, usually free men or ticket-of-leave men, took up their quarters near large estates and opened business as receivers of stolen goods.   The police were corrupt ex-convicts for the most part, so that these thefts were not often brought home to the thief.

There was a Government order, generally evaded, against unmarried men having female servants assigned

to them.   One witness, being a married man, had some
female convict servants in his employ.

You can have no conception [he observed before the Com-
mittee] of their depravity of character.   If you apply, for
instance, for a dairywoman or housemaid, perhaps you will
have a lady sent to you that has been walking the lobby of the
theatres.   This is your dairymaid.

One woman who was assigned to him refused to work
and after a day or two absconded with nine of his men.
Practically all the available women were of loose morals.

As to marriage among the convicts, if one of them was
well behaved and his master wished to retain his services
he was given permission to get a wife from the factory.
The master had to undertake to feed and support the
woman in addition to providing for any children there
might be, to obviate them becoming a burden on the
Government.   When the convict wished to marry he
obtained an order upon the matron of the factory, where
a number of women were paraded before him like cattle
in the show-ring or slaves in an Eastern market-place.
Subject to her consent he could appropriate the woman of
his choice.   Those convicts who had already married in
England would sometimes send a letter to friends at home
to be re-posted there alleging that their wives had died.
This spurious evidence was produced in Australia and the
men were free to re-marry with impunity.

It remains to say something of the assignment of
certain convicts as domestic servants in families.   Whatever benefit this system may have conferred on master or
a man was considerably outweighed by the disadvantages
of the system.   Owing, however, to the great expense
and the scarcity of free labour the settlers had little choice
in the matter.   It was especially difficult to get free
female servants of respectable character.   The Assistant

Surgeon at Port Arthur, giving evidence before the Committee on the subject observed :

I think they did a great deal of mischief, particularly to the rising generation, in corrupting them, both boys and girls, It is natural for them to associate with the convict servants about the house, and I think they have been frequently very much corrupted by them, and, with the free settlers, the effect has been such as to make the lower order of free men just as bad as the convicts. The number of women who became reformed was much smaller than that of the men . . . being generally most mischievous in attempting to contaminate the daughters of the settlers.

In one case three girls of thirteen or fourteen were left in charge of a female convict maid. She made them accomplices and even witnesses of her intrigues, and all three afterwards became mothers as the result of affairs of their own. Some settlers preferred male convicts for domestic work to females " because of the evil conduct and habits of the women." A very large proportion of the women sent out from England to Tasmania appear to have been prostitutes of the most abandoned type.

The assignment system blunted the master's feelings, so that he came to look upon his servants merely as slaves. The servants on their part looked upon him as their task-master and nothing else. There were, of course, good masters and considerate employers, and as is the usual experience of such, they were well served and their households were the only ones in which reformation ever occurred. Free men and convicts associated together to the detriment of both parties. There were places in the colony called " sly grog shops," where spirits were illicitly sold, and these disreputable taverns were the common resort of the depraved, free and bond.

It was perhaps evil reputation which, thanks to the mismanagement of the penal settlements by those responsible, deterred many decent people from emigrating over-seas. The result was, that except in private houses in towns, there were no households staffed entirely with free labour. The disproportion between the sexes among the convicts, roughly three men to one woman, made the problem worse, as it was responsible for a great prevalence of unnatural offences in the colony.

Such being the conditions it is not a matter for surprise that in 1836 an address was sent to the King from the free settlers of Hobart Town, asserting

that the evil character of the penal settlement has lately increased and is increasing to a frightful extent, thereby violating the feelings of the adult and barbarizing the habits and demoralizing the principles of the rising generation; [praying] that His Majesty will be pleased to remove from the colony of Van Dieman's Land the degradation and other unspeakable evils to which it is subjected, in consequence of its present penal character.

But His Majesty's advisers were much too far removed from the unspeakable evils from which the free settlers suffered. There were evils just as bad in London itself to which His Majesty's advisers were equally blind. It was not until 1853 that the home government put an end to the vile abuses of the Tasmanian convict settlement.

The verdict of the Commission in 1838 was that the system of transportation was unequal and that it was cor-rupting to convict and colonist, besides being a great burden on national resources. Punishment in peni-tentiaries was recommended as a substitute.

Under the Penal Servitude Act of 1853 sentence of transportation could not be passed upon any man who had been sentenced for less than fourteen years. For the rest a sentence of penal servitude was enforced. Trans-portation to New South Wales had ceased in 1840.

During the Home Secretaryship of Sir George Grey a

scheme was suggested by which released convicts who were supposed to be regenerated were to be transported. But no colony would accept those convicts discharged on licence, known as ticket-of-leave men. Only Western Australia accepted the scheme, but even so it was found that the requisite number could not be absorbed.

By the year 1867 transportation ceased altogether. It was anticipated that one of the results would be an increase of the criminal population at home, but by this time the new methods were in a fair way to justifying themselves and exactly the reverse process was witnessed, proving conclusively, if indeed by this time any proof were needed, that all the efforts hitherto made to decrease crime in England had been founded upon a total misconception.

CHAPTER VII

THE GOOD HUSBANDMEN

IT is a favourite diversion of biographers to indicate occasions which, trivial in themselves, conceivably determined the course of history and the fate of mankind. So often has it happened that some incident in the life of an individual, which by itself appeared at the time it occurred to be of no very outstanding significance, provided the opportunity for great and enduring achievement.

The influences which in all likelihood were most conducive to determine the beneficent activities of John Howard, one of the most celebrated of all English reformers, who but for these incentives might have confined his philanthropic activities within the limits of a parish, were various in character. After the death of his first wife, who, it is said, he married in recognition of the services she rendered to him as his landlady, he set off upon the first of a series of protracted journeys upon the Continent. Taking ship for Portugal, the packet he selected to travel by, owing to untoward circumstances, was captured by a French privateer. The crew and the passengers were taken prisoners bodily to France, where they were incarcerated in a particularly noisome dungeon. There can be no doubt whatever that a fellow-feeling with all prisoners that such an experience must have engendered in so sympathetic a nature as his, made an indelible impression upon John Howard's mind. Returning to England on parole he was fortunately able to effect an exchange for himself and to resume those tranquil domestic duties which for the present claimed his exclusive attention.

Having been left an adequate competence by his father, he settled down upon his small estate at Cardington in Bedfordshire. After a few years of widowhood he married one Henrietta Leeds, a lady of good looks and considerable charm, but once again Fate remorselessly intervened. She died in giving birth to a son, whose misdeeds and misfortunes together were to provide a further incentive for John Howard to employ his energies unremittingly upon the work which was to make his name famous for all time. This second conjugal bereavement was to prove irreparable. From the moment that the grave closed over the remains of his beloved wife all chance of being able to pursue the even tenor of his way or to find solace in comparative obscurity upon that small estate, where he had planned model cottages, elementary education and village industries for his tenants, was at an end. A restlessness of mind and body seized upon him, from which distemper he was to experience no relief until he found a last resting-place in a distant foreign field. But all his biographers are agreed that the immediate occasion for addressing himself to the reform of the prisons was a discovery he made soon after his appointment as High Sheriff of Bedfordshire. In this particular capacity it came to his notice that some of those declared not guilty were detained for months in gaol until the payment of the customary fees. His suggested cure for this glaring abuse was that salaries should be paid in lieu of these extortions, but the Bench, made oblivious no doubt by long usage to such malpractice, was reluctant to adopt the proposal unless a precedent could be found for charging such expenses as might be incurred thereby upon the county.   Nothing daunted, John Howard went forth on his own account to provide one, if it was any-where to be revealed.   Incidentally, on this first philan-thropic venture he made two further discoveries which started new lines of thought in that restless brain of his. On inquiry he learned that the most miserable prisoners came from the so-called " bridewells," and that gaol fever had become so grave a menace as to require the im-mediate attention of those responsible for the proper conduct of the prisons.

The term " bridewell " is used by Howard as a synonym for a particular type of reformatory, which in the eighteenth century seems to have been as defective in every respect as Newgate itself.   The original Bride-well, the name probably being derived from St. Bridget's Well, was a royal castle situated by the Fleet ditch, dating from Norman times.   Henry VIII restored it and took up his residence there during his divorce proceedings at Blackfriars.   Edward VI made it over to the Lord Mayor and Corporation as a penitentiary for vagabonds and loose women and as a depository for the incorrigibly lazy.   With these objects in view it was intended to set up plant to provide work for the inmates, but for various reasons the scheme miscarried.   At first these penal institutions answered the purpose for which they were intended, but they soon degenerated into " no other than schools of vice, seminaries of idleness and common sewers of nastiness and disease."   In some there was insufficient provision for work.   Though nominally distinct they were for all practical purposes ordinary gaols even where the same building did not serve as both gaol and bridewell.   The normal population consisted of labourers and apprentices guilty of insubordination to their masters, boys and girls who had committed petty theft, in addition to drunkards who had repented when

sober of the acts they had done when drunk, and some
offenders under the Bastardy Acts, a curious selection to
classify with boys and girls. In spite of good intentions,
it was a system which strictly limited any scope for
reforming the criminal. Of these Bridewells Fielding
has some rough comments to make. He speaks of

the wretches brought before me, the most impudent and
flagitious of whom have always been before acquainted with
the discipline of Bridewell . . . a very severe punishment this,
of being confirmed in habits of idleness, and in every other
vicious habit may be esteemed so.

The voyage of discovery upon which John Howard
had now embarked was to be the first of a long series of
investigations into the various prison systems personally
undertaken by him, not only in England, but throughout
the length and breadth of the Continent, even as far as
Russia and Turkey. Any temptation to relax for one
moment this lifelong devotion to a cause and to confine
his efforts to narrower preoccupations was completely
frustrated by the severing of the one link which might
have bound him to his home. The behaviour and
ultimate destiny of the only son, upon whose education
he had lavished so much misdirected effort, and upon
whose future he had set so much store, was the final
stroke of fate that shaped John Howard's ends. " I
could not," he said on one occasion, " enjoy any ease and
leisure in the neglect of an opportunity offered me by
Providence of attempting the relief of the miserable."
It is a lamentable circumstance that one whose career
was so teeming with adventure and incident and whose
character was worthy of a more judicious analysis, should
have been commemorated by two of surely the stupidest
biographies in the English language. It is difficult to
appreciate why, after James Baldwin Brown had given

the world his pages of vapid and unalloyed panegyric, the Rev. T. Field should have thought fit to publish another biography so exactly similar both in material, in expression of view, and in failure to do proper justice to the theme. Biographers for the most part are either idolators or iconoclasts. As a rule there is no compelling necessity for them to indulge either in idolatry or iconoclasm, as few of the men worthy of the biographer's attention are wholly good or wholly bad. But these works above mentioned, together with Dr. Aiken's memoirs, are the most authoritative biographies on the subject in hand, and from their perusal it is difficult to arrive at a just estimate of John Howard's character.

Although there was nothing in him of the bigot, he was certainly of an austere disposition. In private life he combined with a tendency to intolerance a quiet modesty. On one occasion when a lady expressed surprise that he should interest himself so much on behalf of what she described as characters so depraved and vicious, he meekly replied, " I do so because I consider that, had it not been for Divine grace, my conduct might have been as profligate and vile as theirs."

It was in the same spirit of humility that in later years he wrote the following passage :

Those gentlemen who, when they are told of the misery which our prisoners suffer, content themselves with saying " Let them take care to keep out," prefaced perhaps with an angry prayer, seem not duly sensible of the favour of Providence which distinguishes them from the sufferers . . . they also forget the vicissitudes of human affairs, the unexpected changes to which all men are liable, and that those whose circumstances are affluent may in time be reduced to indigence and become debtors and prisoners. As to criminality, it is possible, that a man who has often shuddered at hearing the account of a murder, may on a sudden temptation commit that

very crime.   Let him that thinks he standeth take heed lest he
fall and commiserate those that are fallen.

In the great work of his life he proved himself to be
broadminded, tolerant and of wide vision, but like so
many other reformers he was less successful in his own
domestic circle than in that of his neighbours.   While
discarding as pure fiction the ill-treatment of his son,
which Lamb and other writers have laid to his charge, we
can be in little doubt that he was a trying parent.   His
son from all accounts was very unlike his father in
appearance or disposition.   He was extremely handsome
and fond of the good things of this life, but John Howard
was of the type of parent who endeavours to run counter
to Nature herself rather than adjust his precepts to the
inclinations of his offspring.   He laid down the most
rigid rules of deportment and discipline which might
have proved disastrous in any less high-spirited and
worldly minded than his son.   The result was only what
could have been expected.   At home the boy's one
associate besides his father was a youth who, for some
reason not recorded, had been absorbed into the household and appears to have occupied the status of the old-
time apprentice.   Thomasson was a very good-looking
and likely young man.   There existed between himself
and his master a sincere affection which remained proof
against all circumstances and vicissitudes of fortune.
He not only acted as body-servant to his employer but
also as companion to the son.   It is not surprising that
the two lads whose tastes and dispositions were so
similar were drawn together into a close association and
that they devised, in spite of the rigid discipline imposed
upon them, opportunities for giving their natural inclinations an outlet.   This intercourse led to their indulgence
in dissipations, probably no more and no less than what

most attractive and high-spirited youths are addicted to.
It was certainly no justification for James Baldwin
Brown to stigmatize Thomasson as Judas Iscariot, or to
attribute young Howard's subsequent madness to a few
youthful peccadilloes. In any case it must be assumed
that John Howard himself did not share this view, as he
left Thomasson an annuity when he died. Whatever the
physical causes may have been, young Howard's reason
forsook him. The distress which this last domestic
affliction caused his father prevented him from ever
looking to the domestic circle again for solace or occupation. He henceforth devoted his life exclusively to that
work of high endeavour to which Edmund Burke
referred in such glowing terms in a speech delivered
before the electors of Bristol. Oft-quoted as it has been
it well bears repetition :

I cannot name this gentleman without remarking that his
labours and writings have done much to open the eyes and
hearts of mankind. He has visited all Europe—not to survey
the sumptuousness of palaces or the stateliness of temples, not
to make accurate measurements of the remains of ancient
grandeur, nor to form a scale of the curiosity of modern art,
not to collect medals or collate manuscripts—but to dive into
the depths of dungeons, to plunge into the infection of
hospitals, to survey the mansions of sorrow and pain, to take
the gauge and dimensions of misery, depression and contempt, to remember the forgotten, to attend to the neglected,
to visit the forsaken, and to compare and collate the distresses
of all men in all countries. His plan is original and it is as full
of genius as it is of humanity. It was a voyage of discovery,
a circumnavigation of charity. Already the benefit of his
labour is felt more or less in every country ; I hope he will
anticipate his final reward by seeing all its effects fully realized
in his own. He will receive not by detail but in gross the
reward of those who visit the prisoner ; and he has so fore-
stalled and monopolized this branch of charity that there will

be, I trust, little room to merit by such acts of benevolence hereafter.

The misgivings expressed in the last sentence Edmund Burke might have spared himself. More scope than enough was there to be provided for many years to come, after this immortal panegyric had been uttered, for the benevolent efforts of Howard's successors upon work so consistently neglected by the Parliament of which Edmund Burke was a member.

After his first tour of inspection John Howard quietly and deliberately set to work upon a survey of the existing evils which was to suggest recommendations that are at the basis of our existing treatment of crime and the criminal to-day.

From now onwards until his death he occupied most of his time in universal travels of investigation, both in England and in Europe, journeying altogether 60,000 miles, a truly remarkable achievement when the inconvenience, tardiness, discomfort and even danger of such a performance is taken into consideration, and expending incidentally no less than £30,000, equivalent to at least double that amount to-day, on these beneficent activities. The result of his journeys is recorded in voluminous reports which, although they have little merit in style or composition, were instrumental in effecting reforms the importance of which it is impossible to exaggerate.

His visits of inspection were conducted upon the principle that surprise was the essence of their success. For this purpose he would often pay a second visit if upon his first he was suspicious that something had escaped his notice either by accident or by design.

In his earlier tours he found the experience revolting to his senses. He records :

Air which has been breathed is made poisonous to a more

intense degree by the effluvia from the sick and whatever else in prisons is offensive. My readers will judge of its malignity when I assure them that my clothes were in my first journeys rendered so offensive that in a post-chaise I could not bear the windows drawn up, and was therefore obliged to travel commonly on horseback. The leaves of my memorandum book were often so tainted that I could not use it till after spreading it an hour or two before the fire, and even my antidote, a vial of vinegar, has after using it in a few prisons become intolerably disgusting. I did not wonder that in those journeys many gaolers made excuses and did not go with me into the felons' ward.

By degrees custom frayed his susceptibilities and he ceased to care. Later he writes :

I have frequently been asked by friends what precautions I use to preserve myself from infection in the prisons and hospitals which I visit. Next to the free goodness and mercy of the Author of my being, temperance and cleanliness are my preservatives. Trusting in Divine Providence and believing myself in the way of my duty . . . I fear no evil. I never enter into a hospital or prison before breakfast, and in an offensive room I seldom draw my breath deeply.

A curious passage which suggests that John Howard relied upon the principle that "God helps those who help themselves."

To follow John Howard upon all his tours of investigation in Great Britain, Ireland, and on the Continent would not be convenient to the reader. An epitome of his discoveries upon his provincial tours is all that the limits of the present work permits.

He found the "bridewells" particularly defective. At some there was no official allowance of food at all, and in others the keeper often "farmed out" what exiguous fare was provided. Howard on many occasions saw the prisoners eating bread boiled in water—their staple diet. Although the inmates were condemned to hard labour there were neither accessories nor machinery of any kind to give effect to the sentence. They were not allowed to be issued with tools for fear they should employ them for less desirable ends than merely keeping their hands in for their respective trades. The result was inevitable. Sloth, profanity and debauchery were the common characteristic of these so-called reformatories. There was no provision made for the sick, and it is therefore legitimate to infer that illness came to be regarded by authority as an effective instrument for decreasing the surplus population. Starvation both in the bridewells and the county gaols was so rife that those who did not sicken and perish in confinement were so weak on their release that they were incapable of performing labour and of rendering services which might have enabled them to reinstate themselves as useful members of society. Water was always deficient; it often happened that not more than three pints a day was allowed for all purposes. Many of the bridewells were overcrowded because the accommodation designed for ordinary prisoners was occupied by the insane. No special care whatever was taken of these poor mental deficients, who disturbed and often terrified their fellow-prisoners. So much for the bridewells.

The following strictures apply to most of the county gaols which John Howard visited. There were seldom bedsteads of even a primitive variety supplied. In some cells he observed an inch or two of water, and the straw or rude bedding laid upon the floor in this condition.

There was no allowance of bedding or even litter. If prisoners obtained such modest luxuries in the first instance they were never renewed. The majority lay upon filthy rugs on the bare floor. Where prisoners were not incarcerated in underground cells they were confined to their rooms because either there was no courtyard whatsoever or the walls were so low as to be insufficient to restrain the prisoners from attempts to escape, or the gaoler desired extra accommodation for his own personal use. Some gaols had no sewers. Others, Howard remarked, would be better off without the sewers which existed.

The confinement of all sorts of prisoners together was the common practice—debtors, felons, men and women, the young beginner, the old offender and those who should have been sent to houses of correction. Howard found instances where the gaol also served as the bride-well; in others they were contiguous and shared a common courtyard. There the petty offender found opportunity for further instruction in crime by the most profligate. He saw boys of twelve or fourteen years of age eagerly listening to the stories told by practised and experienced criminals, of their adventures, successes, strategems and escapes.

Owing to the complete absence of any system of prison labour the time of the inhabitants was occupied with gaming, cards, dice, billiards, and other diversions of such a nature.

I am not an enemy to diverting exercise [John Howard protested], yet the riot, brawling and profaneness that are the usual consequences of their play, the circumstances of debtors gaming away the property of their creditors, accomplishing themselves in the frauds of gamblers, who if they be not themselves prisoners are sure to haunt where gaming is practised, these seem to be cogent reasons for prohibiting all kinds of gaming.

In county gaols the abuse of ironing was even more pernicious than in Newgate itself, particularly in view of the circumstance that the locality of the Assizes varied from year to year, so that sometimes prisoners were forced to walk ten or fifteen miles in irons to their trial. Gaol deliveries took place at rare intervals, sometimes but once a year. It is said that one reason for this delay was the exorbitant cost of entertaining judges and their retinue in the towns they visited on circuit. At Hull the Assizes were held but once in seven years. Peacock, a murderer, was in prison before his trial for nearly three years, during which the principal witness died—it is not recorded whether of old age or otherwise—and the murderer was acquitted. The fact that the latter at any rate had little ultimately to complain of in view of the extraordinary circumstances does not exculpate those responsible for such a dilatory system of dispensing justice.

Debtors crowded many of the gaols with their wives and children—often ten or twelve in a middle-sized room —thus increasing the danger of moral and physical infection. Prostitutes were admitted under the name of wives.

A few illustrations of particular cases drawn from the great mass of material collected on these tours by John Howard may not be without interest to the student of prison history. In the county gaol of Southwark he found no separation of the sexes, debtors, assize felons, quarter-sessions prisoners, and those awaiting transportation were all herded together indiscriminately. Some of the latter had been sentenced for four years and had not yet been dispatched to their destination. They were all in a wretched condition, with worn-out shoes and stockings and hardly any clothes to cover themselves with.

In Glasgow, as the prison building was insecure, the prisoners were chained by the neck and feet. The tolbooth had no courtyard. There being no whitewash used, the walls were in a filthy condition. The gaoler, who lived away from the gaol, was permitted to sell spirituous liquors to his charges. In the house of correction, which seemed calculated to correct nothing but virtue, there were three men and forty-seven women, many of them sick, in three closed rooms. No magistrate or clergy ever visited these infernal regions. Howard complained to the Provost, who replied that the inmates were so hardened it was useless to make the attempt to reclaim them. This counsel of despair drew from Howard an angry retort:

That, allow me to say, is by no means the case, for on talking seriously with them only for a few minutes I saw tears start from their eyes, a convincing proof that they were not wholly insusceptible of good feeling. I am apprehensive that the splendid improvements in your places of entertainment, your streets, squares, bridges and the like occupy all the attention of the gentleman in office to the entire neglect of his essential branch of police.

At Morpeth he found a woman heavily ironed for stealing a handkerchief of trifling value, although it was known she had been recently confined. At Exeter at the period of his visit there were three sick females in the infirmary of the gaol, and with them a shoemaker, the husband of one of them, busily employed upon his trade in these incongruous surroundings. His wife had been committed for a theft and was sentenced to be transported for seven years. She had been condemned to the hulks at Plymouth, but on account of some disablement as the result of a fever caught in gaol she could not be removed. She had given birth to a number of children while in prison, and such was the attachment of her husband that he declared he would never leave her.

At Chester he saw convicts and prisoners for trial severely ironed by the neck, hands, waist and feet, chained to the floor in the day-time and at night to their beds in that vile dungeon. There was, as usual, no proper separation of the sexes. At Appleby the gaoler had recently expired from hard drinking. At Gloucester the gaol for debtors was disgracefully conducted by a publican, who made a veritable inn of the prison. In the Staffordshire county gaol only one small day-room was allowed for all the prisoners, men and women. In the dungeon for male felons fifty-two victims were chained down to the floor, a space of only 14 inches being allowed for each to occupy. The moisture from their breath dripped from the walls. The stench, the heat and the livid colour of their countenances appalled even John Howard, who might have become accustomed to such nightmares. In another dungeon, scarcely less offensive, were the women, also in irons. Seven of the felons had died within the previous year. The carelessness and inattention of the keeper were not calculated to improve the situation.

In the Warwick gaol Howard discovered in a dungeon of only 22 feet in diameter, down a flight of thirty steps, more than thirty convicts all in irons. There were three others suffering from disease, in a room by themselves, but their irons had not been removed. In two small rooms with only apertures in the doors for air were fourteen women, all of them on the point of suffocation. Previous to the removal of convicts to Plymouth these dens were so overcrowded that their unhappy occupants were compelled to stand erect while others slept, and the steam from their breath issued from the opening like the smoke of a chimney in winter.

At Montgomery gaol the chaplain told him that on execution day, while he was endeavouring to prepare the unhappy criminals for the awful change they were about to undergo, his ears were frequently assailed by oaths and blasphemies uttered by individuals in the taproom, a scene of noise and confusion occasioned by the numbers who often came to the gaol that day out of curiosity, many of whom were in a state of intoxication. At Devizes " bridewell " Howard was informed that no fuel was granted, and so scanty was the allowance of bread that a prisoner in one of the solitary cells had recently died. The coroner's verdict on this unfortunate victim of official incompetence was that he had died of hunger and cold. At Rochester he was told by the governor of the gaol that the windows of the prison being on the street it was impossible to keep the prisoners sober. So great was the liberality of the public in supplying them with alcohol that individuals had been known to solicit confinement to have the benefit of the " begging grate."

In the Dublin Newgate his investigations revealed that prisoners would sell their bread at any price to secure whisky, with which they were so plentifully supplied that a " puncheon " of this beverage had been consumed in a week. Prisoners frequently died of intoxication and the fighting to which it led. Indeed one lay dead of this cause at the time of Howard's visit. In the debtors' prison of the same city whisky was sold by the debtors, and as a means of procuring it one of the rooms was converted into a pawnbroker's shop. The Marshal assured his visitor that when his prison was full a hogshead of whisky had been disposed of in a clandestine manner in a week, besides what was sold at his own tap. The night before Howard's visit so serious a drunken riot had broken out within the walls of the gaol that the Sheriff and city guard had turned out. The " garnish " here was two bottles of whisky supplied by the wives of debtors, who brought spirits with them and converted most of the lower rooms into a gin-shop. The physician told Howard that he had just lost three men out of four incapacitated in a drunken carousal, where they drank twelve shillings' worth of brandy (in those days a considerable quantity) in punch, besides porter and other liquors. Limerick gaol was so crowded that between sixty and seventy individuals were thrust into a room a little more than 20 feet square.

Some of the privately owned gaols in England were the worst, and of these Ely, the property of the bishopric, which Howard quotes in particular, was quite out of repair and positively unsafe. Felons and debtors were herded together. There was no clean water to drink, no straw to lie upon, and no infirmary for restoring to health the victims of this neglect. The method of securing the prisoners was by chaining them down on their backs upon the floor, across which were several iron bars, with a spiked iron collar about their necks.

At Macclesfield the " bridewell " consisted merely of a ruinous room where men and women were confined together night and day. At Nottingham he found a man who had received the King's pardon and yet was detained in custody to pay the gaoler's fees. At Knaresborough, in the debtors' prison, there was one room difficult of access with an earth floor and no fireplace, percolated by an uncovered sewer from the town. Howard was told that a few years before his visit to this dungeon an inmate had taken his dog with him to defend himself from the vermin, but that his face had been disfigured by their attacks. In the " bridewell " of Wymondham a prisoner complained to him of being obliged to lie in one of the pent-up closets used for night-rooms with two boys afflicted with a cutaneous disease.

As to the Metropolitan prisons, enough has perhaps already been recorded of the condition of Newgate in the eighteenth century to convince the reader of their atrocious character, but Howard has much to say on the subject. He found the Savoy, Wood Street, Whitechapel and Westminster were in a filthy condition, the inmates being nearly naked, the sick utterly neglected and left in some cases to lie in close offensive quarters on the bare boards. The refractory were punished with the greatest severity. In the Horsemonger Lane gaol he found fifty transportees, who had not been delivered in execution of their sentence, in a direful state, scantily clothed, and almost perishing from want of proper nourishment. At the Marshalsea, on making inquiries of a turn-key as to the drinking habits of the inhabitants, his informant replied: "The chief vice among the prisoners is drunkenness. It is that which often brings them here—and while they drink and riot in prison they will disregard confinement." On the night of his visit many had been gambling, drinking and fighting. In the Fleet prison he noticed that the prisoners played at games in the courtyard, not a reprehensible circumstance in itself, but it was not only prisoners who congregated within the precincts for this purpose. He saw in their company all sorts and conditions of riff-raff from the market. Besides the inconvenience of this practice he adjudged that the frequenting of a prison by the free, lessened in them the wholesome dread of being confined. On Monday nights there was a wine club, on Thursdays a beer club, each lasting usually until the small hours of the morning to the annoyance of the sober and the invalids.

The above are but a few extracts taken at random from Howard's reports, telling with a monotonous consistency a long tale of utter reproach to those who governed England in the eighteenth century. Reading gaol was one of the few bright exceptions, which only goes to prove that had the majority of those in authority been prompted by humanity and common decency the social history of England at that period would have been far different.   At Reading gaol Lord Craven and his fellow-magistrates made a point of frequently visiting the prison, with the result that it was maintained in excellent order.

The accumulated knowledge from the experience gained in John Howard's successive peregrinations up and down the country was to bear fruit in a series of recommendations and the draft of a Bill to be introduced into Parliament.   In the first instance he drew up a list of remedies.   As far as the plan of the prison was concerned he suggested better facilities for securing fresh air and pure water, separate cells with some privacy for the prisoners at night, that women should be kept in a different section of the gaol from the men, and the young from the hardened, debtors from felons, with separate conveniences for each category.   As to the better personal comfort of the prisoners, there should be a proper furnishing of the cells, particularly in the infirmary, and that there should be no contracts for these with the gaol officers.   The wards and the bedding and clothes should be kept clean.   Food should be improved and no gaoler should be interested in the amount given.   An experienced surgeon or apothecary should be allotted to each gaol for the health of the prisoners.   There was to be no close confinement except for the recalcitrant.   As to the conduct of the prisoners, there should be a prohibition of intoxicating liquor in gaol.   Workshops should be provided to save them from idleness.   There was to be a chapel and a competent chaplain in each prison. Visitors were to be limited.

No prisoner was to be subject to any demand for fees, and the gaoler should have salary in lieu thereof.   Debtors should have a free ward and not be subject to demand for rent.   Gaolers should be men of good character; no prisoner should be a turn-key.

For the rest, a list of regulations was to be placed in a conspicuous place. There should be a proper inspectorate. There should be immediate discharge of those acquitted, and no detention on account of fees or so-called debts claimed by gaolers. Employment should be proportioned to the strength and the degree of criminality. There should be a system of rewards, such as shortening term of confinement as recompense for good behaviour, or perhaps a system of grades with work more agreeable as the prisoner advances into a higher class. Money and clothes, and a character if deserved, should be given on discharge. A good infirmary was essential. If a prisoner died there should be a coroner's inquest and funeral, the expenses of which should be allowed for, outside the precincts of the gaol.

In his revolutionary suggestions for the " bridewells " which he urged should be entirely separate establishments more of the nature of a reformatory, he displayed foresight uncharacteristic of his time—in fact, some of his suggestions conform to the most up-to-date views only recently put into practice. " Let the sober and the diligent be distinguished by some preference in their diet or lodging, or by shortening the term of their confinement, and giving them when discharged a good character." The profit of the work done in gaol might, he suggested, be applied to benefit the institution, and those who would employ themselves in extra hours should have the profit to themselves, and also it would be an encouragement to diligence to give them some portion of the profit made during the stated hours. He argued that if complaint was made of the increased cost to the public thus incurred, that cost would be light weighed in the balance with the benefit which would thereby accrue to the public. Money to the amount of thousands, he argued, is not withheld when town halls are wanted;

why should it be spared when the morals and lives of thousands are at stake.

Howard realized that it would be objected that the dread of prison might be removed if these receptacles for the wrongdoer were made as comfortable as their own homes.

I have proposed nothing [he said] to give them an air of pleasantness. With respect to the more humane treatment of the prisoners in the articles of food, lodging and the like, I venture to assert that if to it be joined such strict regulations in preventing all dissipation and riotous amusement, confinement in a prison, though it may cease to be destructive to health and morals, will not fail to be sufficiently irksome and disagreeable, especially to the idle and the profligate.

Taking what he had seen in Holland as his model, he suggested Penitentiary Houses which should not only have incarceration as their object but also reformation and amendment. In 1780 Parliament passed an Act to facilitate their erection. Howard was to have been the first supervisor, but as the authorities would not accept his suggestion for a site in Islington he resigned and resumed his Continental journeys. In his appendix he gives his views as to how they should be conducted:

To these houses I should wish that none but old hardened offenders and those who have, as the law now stands, forfeited their lives by robbery, housebreaking and similar crimes, should be committed. I wish that no persons might suffer capitally but for murder, setting houses on fire, and for housebreaking attended with acts of cruelty. Our present laws are certainly too sanguinary and are therefore ill executed, which last circumstance, by encouraging offenders to hope they may escape punishment even after conviction, greatly tends to increase the number of crimes. Yet many are brought to a premature end who might have been made useful to the State. Indeed I the more earnestly embarked in the scheme of erecting

Penitentiary Houses from seeing cartloads of our fellow-creatures carried to execution when at the same time I was fully persuaded that many of those unhappy wretches by regular discipline in a Penitentiary House would have been rendered useful members of society, and above all, from the pleasing hope that such a plan might be the means of promoting the salvation of some individuals of which every instance is, according to the unerring word of truth, a more important object than the gaining of the whole world.

He then proceeds with a sketch of his Penitentiary House which is to be built by convicts themselves.

After many comprehensive tours of investigation, Howard in 1784 published an appendix to his larger work in which he gives his impression as to how far any reform had been effected as the result of his previous representations. He drew the conclusion therein that as far as the health of prisoners was concerned there had been a great improvement since he first raised the matter.

With satisfaction I have also observed the liberal and humane spirit which engages the public to alleviate the sufferings of prisoners in general, and particularly to release many industrious though unfortunate debtors. But at this point the spirit of improvement unhappily seems to stop, scarcely touching upon the still more important object—the reformation of morals in our prisons. Yet it is obvious that if this be neglected, besides the evil consequences that must result from such a source of wickedness, a suspicion will arise that what has been already done has proceeded chiefly from the selfish motive of avoiding the danger to our own health in attending courts of judicature.

On the completion of his third journey on the Continent where he had travelled a distance of 4,630 miles, visiting the gaols of Holland, Flanders, Germany, Italy, Switzerland and France, he had made another general survey of English, Irish and Scottish gaols, hoping to find some amelioration. In this, with the exception of certain minor reforms which had been effected since his first visit, he was destined to be disappointed. In Exeter, women were still herded with the men during the day-time, being obliged to associate with them and to witness if not to share in every iniquity. At Oxford the gaol in the castle was still the same as the prisoners occupied at the time of the Black Assize in 1577. In the "bridewell" at St. Albans he found two soldiers and a girl sentenced to a year's imprisonment locked up all day together. At the Castle of Gloucester eight prisoners had recently died of smallpox, but there was no infirmary. In the same gaol there was a want of proper separation of the sexes, and of the bridewell prisoners from the rest. From the gross inattention of the magistrates to this point the most licentious intercourse prevailed, so that all the efforts of the chaplain to promote reformation amongst its abandoned inmates were defeated by the encouragement of vice, which the less hardened offenders were receiving from the more accomplished. Five or six children had lately been born in this hotbed of iniquity. At Pembroke there were 113 French and American prisoners of war, most of them with bare feet and some with no shirts. There was no systematic victualling. They lay on straw which had not been changed for weeks. In a so-called hospital they were lying upon straw without anything but a mere coverlet.

In Dublin the bad custom of fees continued, so that even boys under the age of twelve years, almost naked, would be kept in prison for two years with the aggravated cruelty of losing their allowance of bread the while. Howard incidentally paid their fees for them, but as they had been associated with the most profligate felons for many months he was not surprised to learn that some of them returned to gaol after a few days. In another

Dublin prison he found eleven young creatures who for trifling offences were confined with outrageous lunatics of both sexes in spite of laws to the contrary. At Clerkenwell prison those who had turned King's evidence, to secure them from the resentment of their fellow-prisoners, were improperly put into the women's ward. The keeper of the gaol at Carnarvon regularly stopped sixpence from the meagre allowance of each prisoner. In Chester, prisoners were still confined in a dungeon aired by two leaden pipes about an inch in diameter. At the Taunton bridewell men remained in irons. At Thetford twenty-seven persons were being confined for four nights in a suffocating dungeon.

The above is a selection typical of the disappointments which met John Howard at every turn on his final survey, and proved to him that not even the publication of the ghastly condition of English gaols could move authority to pity the plight of his wretched fellow-countrymen.

John Howard is not an attractive writer nor was he a master of English prose. His reports are ill-arrayed, but they teem with material which furnishes information that would never have been made available but for the heroic self-sacrifice of this great reformer. Rarely does he break away from a matter-of-fact detailing of his experiences, but at the conclusion of his appendix occurs a passage which reveals to us the motive force of his enthusiasm.

To my country I commit the result of my past labours. It is my intention again to quit it for the purpose of re-visiting Russia, Turkey, and some other countries, and extending my tour in the East. Trusting, however, in the protection of that kind Providence which has hitherto preserved me I calmly and cheerfully commit myself to the disposal of unerring wisdom. Should it please God to cut off my life in the prosecution of this design let not my conduct be uncandidly imputed to rashness or enthusiasm but to a serious deliberate conviction that I am pursuing the path of duty and to a sincere desire of being made an instrument of more extensive usefulness to my fellow-creatures than could be expected in the narrow circle of a retired life.

In the year 1790 John Howard, somewhat disillusioned, set out upon his last journey. During a visit to South Russia, he, who had so often risked and escaped the contagion of poor invalid prisoners in gaols all over Europe, fell a victim to what was known as camp fever at Kherson, where he lies buried in a walled field north of the town. Thus passed away one of the noblest of Englishmen who spent his whole energy

> In deeds of daring rectitude, in scorn
> For miserable aims that end with self,
> In thought sublime that pierce the night like stars
> And with their vast persistence urge men's search
> To vaster issues.

As a prison reformer John Howard was perhaps not absolutely the original pioneer in this field of endeavour, although no other can compare with him in the lifelong devotion and indefatigable zeal which signalized his service to humanity. James Oglethorpe, who sat as Member for Haslemere for thirty-two years, may be said to be the first individual holding a public and responsible position to bring to the notice of Parliament the grave abuses of the prison system. His interest and sympathy were enlisted by the circumstance that a friend of his, one Castell, who had incurred liabilities he was unable to meet, had been thrown into the Fleet prison, and there being unable to pay the fees, was confined in a house where smallpox was raging and caught the disease of which he died. From that moment Oglethorpe interested himself and others in the reform of the debtors' prisons.

A still greater reformer than Oglethorpe arose in the person of James Neild, subsequent to John Howard's activities. He started life as a skilled jeweller, eventually setting up in the jewel business in St. James's Street, by which means he amassed a competent fortune. Like Oglethorpe his interest was first aroused in the need for reform in our prisons by a visit paid to a friend of his who had incurred the usual penalty of running into debt. Following in the footsteps of John Howard he made extensive tours of inspection of the prisons both at home and abroad. The result of his investigations is contained in various of his published writings which produced the desired effect upon public opinion. He died in 1814 after a career of conspicuous service to his fellow-men.

It was while Neild was carrying out his investigations and making his report that there appeared upon the scenes one of the most remarkable women in English history. It was in the year 1813 that for the first time a turn-key of Newgate unlocked the door to admit Mrs. Fry. Just as Florence Nightingale moved through the wards of the hospital at Scutari amongst the soldiers wounded in body, so Elizabeth Fry, bearing the lamp of kindliness in her hand, brought solace and refreshment to her wretched fellow-beings wounded sore in spirit. The ministration of Mrs. Fry is the most epoch-making incident in the history of our prisons.

Mrs. Fry has suffered almost as much as John Howard from her biographers. The authoritative edition of her journals was published almost *in extenso* by her two daughters. It is inconceivable that anyone save an historical research student could plough through those ill-edited volumes to-day, and even for his purpose he would only meet with disappointment. It is equally inconceivable that Mrs. Fry herself would have permitted their publication had she been consulted. True there is a day-to-day entry from her diary which, considering her experiences, should have been replete with interest and incident for the benefit of the general reader, but the major portion of each day's record consists of prayer and supplication, more appropriate to the silent closet than to the bookseller's counter. Moreover, Mrs. Fry was, of course, a Quaker, and presumably a modesty of expression is part of a Quaker's make-up. From one end of these diaries to the other she indulges in a perfect orgy of self-depreciation which conveys to the reader's mind what must be a quite misleading impression of her true character. When she was sixty-two years of age, the mother of eleven children and with more than treble that number of grandchildren, she writes in her journal :

I have not enough dwelt upon the extraordinary kindness of our dear brother and sister Buxton to us at this time, truly humbling to me, a poor unworthy worm of the dust.

Surely this must have been a *façon de parler*. There was not much " unworthy worm of the dust " about Mrs. Fry when she was importuning monarchs, prime ministers, and others in authority, both compatriot and foreign, to procure redress for the victims of our prison system. Both Florence Nightingale and Mrs. Fry have acquired a reputation for gentleness and meekness which it is very difficult to believe is, in the case of either of them, altogether appropriate.

To-morrow [writes Mrs. Fry in 1840] the King of Prussia has appointed me to meet him at luncheon at the Mansion House. I have rather felt its being the Sabbath, but as all is to be conducted in a quiet, suitable and most orderly manner consistent with the day I am quite easy to go.

This extract suggests that she must have made some stipulation that there should be no roystering or any of that scandalous behaviour which, for all her misgivings, is not usually associated with the austere residence of London's first citizen. " I entreated the Lord Mayor to have no toasts, to which he acceded and the King approved, but it was no easy matter. I rejoice to believe my efforts were right." The "unworthy worm of the dust " evidently turned when it came to a suggestion of toasts on Sundays at the Mansion House.

" I have fears for myself in visiting palaces rather than prisons." But it may be justifiably inferred that Queen Charlotte and others of her royal hosts and hostesses suffered as much trepidation in her presence as she did in theirs.

It is hoped that the following brief appreciation of a long and valuable career may serve to dispel some of the illusions which might possess the minds of those who take her diaries too literally.

At the time when Mrs. Fry, accompanied by a sister of Sir Thomas Buxton, first visited Newgate, the torch which John Howard had hoped to hand on brightly burning to his successors in charity, was wellnigh extinguished. " Howard and his humane exertions appear to have been forgotten and Acts of Parliament to become a dead letter and openly violated," she bitterly complains in describing the result of her first acquaintance with the existing conditions of the chief Metropolitan prison. This discovery of hers is borne out by the testimony of Neild, who in 1812 writes :

The great reformation produced by Howard was in several places merely temporary ; some prisons that had been ameliorated under the persuasive influence of his kind advice were relapsing into their horrid state of privation, filthiness, severity or neglect ; many new dungeons had aggravated the evils against which his sagacity could not but remonstrate, the motives for a transient amendment were becoming paralysed, and the effect that had ceased with the cause.

As an illustration of how valueless her own journals are to the historian, there is no explanation to be found in these voluminous pages as to what interval elapsed between her first and second visits to Newgate or the reason for this discrepancy. It is surmised that a protracted illness and family afflictions were the cause. In any case her daughters date the resumption of her beneficent work from the year 1816.

Mrs. Fry's eulogists rightly divide her work for the English prisons into two categories : first, her personal ministration amongst the prisoners themselves within the walls of the prison, and second, the successful effort she made in suggesting the reform of its administration. There can be no two opinions about her administrative ability, which far exceeded that of the statesmen she set out to influence. As to her methods, both the character and the result thereof may be more open to certain doubts and criticisms. It would be well, then, to explain in the first instance how Mrs. Fry and her noble band of coadjutors set about reforming the female side of Newgate.

The ladies arrived at the hour of unlocking and spent the whole day in the prison. They found Newgate in much the same condition as is described in a previous chapter. It is hardly to be supposed that the reader requires nauseating any further with details of the atrocious circumstances of those who became the object of their administrations.

Having explained their purpose to constituted authority they were met, be it said to the credit of those concerned, with a warm welcome, although with complete scepticism. " This, like many other useful and benevolent designs for the improvement of Newgate," said one official, " would inevitably fail." It is difficult to appreciate what Mrs. Fry's conductor meant by " many other designs." There are none known to the historian up to this date save those suggested by Howard and Neild, and even these were neglected by the authorities. Another official bade Mrs. Fry not despair, but—in her own words—" he has since confessed when he came to reflect on the subject and especially upon the character of the prisoners, he could not see even the possibility of success." The Sheriff, Mr. Bridges, who was only too willing to be of assistance, told her that the concurrence of the women was indispensable, and he warned her that it was vain to expect such untamed and turbulent spirits would submit to the regulations of women armed with no proper authority and unable to inflict any punishment.

The two sheriffs met Mrs. Fry in Newgate and explained to the women the purpose and implications of her visit, investing it with their official sanction and support. To their surprise the women readily acquiesced in the schemes which were proposed. One of the two sheriffs thereupon turned to Mrs. Fry with the exclamation, " Well, ladies, you see your material."

At first acquaintance the material to which they were thus introduced could not have seemed very promising, but the ladies, nothing daunted, set to work. The essence of their teaching was to impart to the prisoners a nobler ideal of life and conduct based upon the gospels.

If anyone wants a confirmation of the truth of Christianity [wrote Mrs. Fry after having put her methods to the test] let him go and read the scriptures in prisons to poor prisoners. You there see how the gospel is exactly adapted to the fuller condition of man. It has strongly confirmed my faith.

Convinced therefore of the efficacy of this method Mrs. Fry and her ladies instituted a regular reading of scriptures which was open to any of the inmates to attend. The effect produced, according to the ladies' own account, surpassed any expectations, but eulogistic biographers are apt in their enthusiasm to go far beyond what is capable of proof. In view of the picture which John Howard and others have given to us of Newgate it is difficult to conclude that the result of their system was as far-reaching as their own testimony would lead us to believe. It must be borne in mind that in terms of human beings there were many mansions in Newgate, and the success of the method must be measured by the quality and character of those upon whom these experiments were tested.

There are two letters written by female prisoners which have been invariably quoted by every writer on Newgate. As far as the theme of this work is concerned the material for the student is not inexhaustible, and each writer reproduces with a tiresome reiteration all that there is available. The two letters in question are included in every previous work dealing with the subject, presumably with the object of demonstrating the effect of Mrs. Fry's methods upon the wild viragoes of Newgate. They are reproduced here for the purpose of demonstrating that previous historians have left out of account two essential considerations, and have therefore been drawn to somewhat doubtful conclusions with regard to those who composed them. The first is a letter written by a woman condemned to death for forgery on the morning of her execution, and reads as follows :

HONOURED MADAM,

As the only way of expressing my gratitude to you for your very great attention to the care of my poor soul I fear I may have appeared more silent than perhaps some would have been on so melancholy an event, but believe me my dear madam I have felt most acutely the awful situation I have been in. The mercies of God are boundless and I trust through His grace this affliction is sanctified to me, and through the Saviour's blood my sins will be washed away. I have much to be thankful for. I feel such serenity of mind and fortitude. God, of His infinite mercy grant I may feel as I do now in the last moments. It was a feeling I had of my own unworthiness made me more diffident of speaking so brief as was perhaps looked for. I once more return you my most grateful thanks. It is now past six o'clock. I have not one moment to spare. I must devote the remainder to the service of my offended God.

The other, written to some fellow-prisoners, was as follows :

Impressed with the deepest sense of your feelings for me under my awful situation I am sure was I to ask anything of you it would be granted . . . I would wish to impress on your minds the true light of the Gospel. . . . In the first place God gave me the spirit of humility, you must feel a love and affection for those that so kindly visit this prison. Then pray to the Lord to give you the grace of His Holy Spirit, and I am sure our dear beloved friends (Mrs. Fry and her ladies) will acquaint you by what way that is to be found . . . then pray, I entreat you, do not neglect the great work. Go upstairs rejoicing as if to a bridal feast. Oh ! should the Lord deliver you from these walls think on me, and remember the end of sin is death. You all have my prayers . . . may the Lord be with you and keep you all.

Now it is quite obvious that neither of these letters was written by one of the hoydens that are so graphically described by all contemporary visitors to Newgate. They are the letters not only of well-educated but of intellectual women. It must be remembered that only a very small proportion of the women prisoners was able to read or write. Therefore in quoting them as an example of the miraculous cure which Mrs. Fry's readings of the scriptures effected with the wild and dissolute inhabitants of this " hell above ground " her biographers are hardly doing justice to the intelligence either of Mrs. Fry or their readers. The fact probably was that any women who were well educated and of decent upbringing found in Mrs. Fry's Bible classes a welcome haven from the stormy atmosphere of the yards and cells of Newgate. Others who were probably incapable of appreciating the true bearing of her teaching found a solace in that beauteous and heavenly presence. There were also, it must be remembered, Quakers in Newgate whose worst crime in the eyes of the law was that they were Quakers, and were unable to take the oaths of Allegiance and Supremacy. On her second visit when she was for the first time left alone for several hours with the women, Mrs. Fry records that " some asked who Christ was." We can well believe that many of her audience were entirely unversed in things spiritual. And yet even discounting the enthusiasm of her biographers it must be admitted that all those, and there were many, who witnessed the remarkable scene of Mrs. Fry's Bible reading were amazed at the transformation she seemed to have effected, and the number of miracles she effected in cases which seemed incurable. There is the example which has been quoted by every writer who has written on the subject, or any remotely connected with it, of the woman that the ladies saw yelling like a wild beast, rushing round the yard with her arm extended, tearing the caps off her fellow-prisoners' heads, who under their influence afterwards became humanized, and on regaining her liberty married and settled down to a respectable life.

There is no question that remarkable cures were effected. One witness thus describes the transformation :

The courtyard into which I was admitted instead of being peopled with beings scarcely human, blaspheming, fighting, tearing each other's hair or gaming with a filthy pack of cards for the very clothes they wore, which often did not suffice for decency, presented a scene where stillness and propriety reigned. I was conducted by a decently dressed person, the newly appointed yardswoman, to the door of a ward, where at the head of a long table sat a lady belonging to the Society of Friends. She was reading aloud to about sixteen women prisoners, who were engaged in needle-work around it. Each wore a clean-looking blue apron and bib. They all rose on my entrance, curtsied respectfully, and then at a signal given resumed their seats and employments. Instead of a scowl, leer, or ill-suppressed laugh, I observed upon their countenances an air of self-respect and gravity, a sort of consciousness of their improved character and the altered position in which they were placed.

Much to her distaste almost a public exhibition was made of these readings. Mrs. Fry only consented to the presence of genuinely interested onlookers because she realized it was essential that the work she was doing should be emulated by other philanthropists elsewhere in England and abroad. Persons in the highest stations of life were induced to attend by the report of the miraculous cures which Mrs. Fry had effected. Among these was the King of Prussia, who had taken the liveliest interest in her work. In his presence she read to the female convicts the twelfth chapter of the Romans, after expressing the hope that the attention of none, particularly the poor prisoners, might be diverted from the reading by the company there, however interesting, but rather that they should remember that the King of Kings

Mrs. Fry in Newgate

Richard Dighton del.

234]

was there, in whose fear all should abide. In her usual humble vein Mrs. Fry records in her journal " our Newgate visiting could no longer be kept secret, which I endeavoured that it should be, and therefore I am exposed to praise that I do not the least deserve." Her visits became the theme of conversation in all circles of society. Lady Mackintosh refers to a dinner-party at Devonshire House—where the principal subject of conversation was Mrs. Fry's ministrations in Newgate—amongst a brilliant company which included the Duke of Norfolk, Lords Lansdowne, Lauderdale, Albemarle, Cowper, Hardwicke, Carnarvon, Sefton, Milton, Ossulton and others.

Mrs. Fry's activities often brought her into close communication with the condemned criminals in that prison. Invariably were to be seen at the Bible readings some females under sentence of death from the Old Bailey, who were awaiting the news of their final doom from the decision of the Privy Council.

However effective her methods of visiting may have been upon those who sat at her feet, there is no doubt that she proved that she had administrative qualities of the highest order, and that for creative ability few could compare with her. It was the experience which she gained in immediate contact with the prisoners themselves which started the train of her reflections. For instance, one woman the day before her execution said to Mrs. Fry, " I feel life so strong within me, that I cannot believe that this time to-morrow I am to be dead." This close association with the real tragedy of life gave her the opportunity she needed to reinforce her ideas with experience. No doubt such a cry of the heart made her rebel against the ferocity of a law by which the most trivial of offences forfeited the life of many a decent citizen. After her death some rough notes on the subject in her handwriting were found amongst her effects.

Does capital punishment tend to the security of the people? By no means. It hardens the hearts of men, and makes the loss of life appear light for them and it renders life insecure in so much as the law holds out that property is of greater value than life. The wicked are consequently more often disposed to sacrifice life to obtain property. It also lessens the security of the subject because so many are so conscientious, that they had rather suffer loss and sustain much injury, than be instrumental in taking the life of a fellow-creature. The result is, the innocent suffer loss and the guilty escape with impunity. Does it tend to the reformation of any party? No, because in those who suffer it leads to unbelief, hypocrisy and fatalism, in those who remain to discontent, dissatisfaction with the laws and the powers which carry them into execution, to hardness of heart and deceit. Does it deter others from crime? No, because the crimes subject to capital punishment are gradually increasing. Punishment is not for revenge, but to lessen crime and to reform the criminal.

Mrs. Fry's work for the criminal was twofold; she was largely responsible for the reform of the domestic arrangements of the gaols, but she was equally responsible for the ultimate reform of the administration of the criminal law.

In the prison itself she found children almost naked and pining for want of food, fresh air and exercise. She therefore proposed to the women to start a school, to which suggestion they acceded with tears of joy in their eyes. She selected from their own number a governess who proved thoroughly well qualified for the task, a circumstance which indicates that there were women of intellect and education within the precincts. An unoccupied cell was provided for this purpose. So successful was the venture that for want of sufficient accommodation Mrs. Fry was compelled to refuse admission to many who wished to profit by it.

These and other of her reforms were welcomed with the cordial approbation of, if with some scepticism by, the Sheriffs, the Governor of the gaol, and the Ordinary.

The next step was to obtain work which could usefully employ the women's time, which now hung heavy upon their hands. It had occurred to Mrs. Fry that the manufacture of cloth for the penal settlements overseas would be an appropriate enterprise. She therefore called upon the firm of Mann, Richmond, Dixon & Co., of Fenchurch Street, who hitherto had held the contract. She explained her project, warning the manager that she was in this venture seeking to deprive him of this business. Finding her arguments irresistible the firm magnanimously waived their rights in favour of her project to help those who they willingly recognized were not appropriate subjects for commercial exploitation.

At Mrs. Fry's request the Sheriffs sent carpenters into Newgate. The old prison laundry, having been cleaned and whitewashed, was transformed into a workroom. Mrs. Fry then assembled the prisoners, acquainted them with her scheme and read a list of rules which she put to the vote. Although they were stringent the women readily subscribed to them all. Begging, swearing, gambling, quarrelling and immoral conversation were forbidden. All were required to submit themselves to the yard-keeper, monitors and matron, who were to be elected to these posts by themselves. These rules were religiously kept. Mrs. Fry in the course of one month was able to report to the Corporation the progress she had made. In response, the Lord Mayor, Sheriffs and Aldermen visited the prison. Amazed at the transformation she had effected in manners, dress and conversation they accepted her scheme of reform with alacrity. Mrs. Fry's rules were thereupon adopted into the prison system, power was conferred upon the ladies to punish the refractory, and the salary of the matron was incorporated with the regular expenses of the prison.

Another cognate problem upon which Mrs. Fry devoted her very particular attention was the atrocious circumstances of the female transports. Ever since the *Maria* was first visited in 1818, Mrs. Fry, accompanied by her devoted companion in charity, Mrs. Pryor, visited with only one exception every transport ship which sailed from England with female convicts, until prevented by the sickness which terminated in her death in 1845.

One K. B. Martin, captain of a merchant vessel, who on a certain occasion came to the rescue of these two ladies when their small boat was caught by a squall, has left us his impressions of Mrs. Fry :

I was then a dashing high-spirited sailor, but I had always a secret admiration of the quiet demeanour of that Society (Quakers). I had some dislike to sects then . . . but who could resist this beautiful, persuasive, and heavenly minded woman. To see her was to love her, was to feel as if a guardian angel had bid you follow that teaching which could alone subdue the temptations and evils of this life and secure our Redeemer's love in eternity. . . . I feel assured that much of the success which attended her missions of mercy was based upon that awe which such a presence inspired. It was something to possess a countenance which portrayed in every look the overflowings of such a heart, and thus as a humble instrument in the hands of Divine Providence she was indeed highly favoured among women. . . . It was an honour to know her in this world.

Being made aware of the disgraceful scenes that the departure of these poor women occasioned, she promised them if they would behave decently she and the other ladies would accompany them to Deptford. When they first started upon this work of compassion they were distressed to see so many women and children herded together below deck. Mrs. Fry arranged that they should be divided and classified under monitors according to ages and criminality. In order to provide them with healthy occupation she started the industry of patchwork, which was so successful that the proceeds of the sale enabled them on arrival overseas to obtain shelter which was not provided by a beneficent government until engaged in service. Hitherto neither factory nor barrack of any description existed for the reception of the women when landed in the colony, not so much as a hut in which they could take refuge, so that they were driven to vice or mendicancy, in some cases even against their inclination. A small space towards the after part of the ship was set apart for the children where they could learn reading, knitting and sewing, one of the convicts undertaking to be mistress. During the five weeks that the ship lay in the river Mrs. Fry's ladies devoted much of their time to making these arrangements for the welfare of the transported women and their families.

In her evidence before the House of Commons Committee Mrs. Fry said :

In no instance have I more clearly seen the beneficial effects of ladies visiting and superintending prisoners than on board the convict ships. I have witnessed the alteration since ladies have visited them constantly in the river. I heard formerly of the most dreadful iniquity, confusion and frequently distress ; latterly I have seen a very wonderful improvement in their conduct, and on the voyage I have the most valuable certificates to show the difference of their condition on arrival in the colony. Samuel Marsden, who has been chaplain there a good many years, says it is quite a different thing, that they used to come in the most filthy, abominable state, hardly fit for anything, now they arrive in good order and a totally different situation.

There is a picturesque description in the pages of Mrs. Fry's biography of her work in the docks :

The last time that Mrs. Fry was on board the *Maria* whilst she lay at Deptford . . . there was a great uncertainty whether the poor convicts would see their benefactress again. She stood at the door of her cabin attended by her friends and the captain, the women on the quarter-deck facing them. The sailors, anxious to see what was going on, clambered into the rigging, upon the capstan or mingled in the outskirts of the group. The silence was profound when Mrs. Fry opened her Bible, and in a clear audible voice read a portion of it. The crews of the other vessels, attracted by the novelty of the scene, leant over the ships on either side and listened apparently with great attention. She closed the Bible and after a short pause knelt down on the deck and implored a blessing on this work of Christian charity from that God who, though one may sow and another water, can alone give the increase. Many of the women wept bitterly, all seemed touched. When she left the ship they followed her with their eyes and their blessings, until her boat having passed within another tier of vessels they could see her no more.

Mrs. Young, wife of the Admiral of the Dockyard, recorded her impression of a similar experience :

I could scarcely look upon her as any other than an angel of mercy calmly passing from one to another of the poor wretched beings around her with the word of counsel, comfort or reproof that seemed suited to each individual case.

Miss Young, her daughter, was present when Mrs. Fry and Wilberforce on one occasion addressed the convicts off Woolwich, and has left us an account of it :

On board one of them between two and three hundred

women were assembled in order to listen to the exhortation and prayers of perhaps the two brightest personifications of Christian philanthropy which the age could boast. Scarcely could two voices ever so distinguished for beauty and power be imagined, as indeed was testified by the breathless attention, the tears and the suppressed sobs of the gathered listeners. . . . No lapse of time can ever efface the impression of the 107th Psalm as read by Mrs. Fry with such extraordinary emphasis and intonation that it seemed to make the simple reading a commentary.

It was not only by the Word that she helped and cheered these wretched outcasts. She made application that matrons should be carried on these transport ships. Hitherto the convict women had been placed under the care, or perhaps it would be more appropriate to say at the mercy of, the sailors. The masters of these vessels as well as their crews had free communication with the women, not only during the voyage but whilst they were at anchor in the Thames, which was frequently the case for weeks at a time. Putting temptation thus in the way of rough sailors and still rougher women, the majority of both accustomed to the loosest manner of living, was hardly fair upon those in whose way it was placed.

Mrs. Fry fully realized that all her efforts on behalf of the female transportees at the port of embarkation would be rendered futile so long as the victims were without shelter, resource or protection when they arrived at their destination and commenced their life of exile. Rations sufficient only to maintain life were allowed them, but no place in which to reside, no clothing for themselves or for the children. Existence under these circumstances could only be maintained at the price of virtue. Much of these pitiable details she learned from the prisoners themselves.

It was Mrs. Fry who was mainly instrumental in improving the organization of reception in the colonies for these women. In 1819 she received from the Rev. Samuel Marsden, Chaplain in New South Wales, the following appreciation of her work:

It may be gratifying to you, madam, to hear that I meet with these wretched exiles who have shared your attentions and who mention your maternal care with gratitude and affection.

Other tributes were not lacking. The surgeon of a ship called *The Brothers* writes in 1824 from Port Jackson: "The force of example and the moral discipline have been admirably shown on this voyage." A missionary sailing in the same vessel wrote to her:

I beg leave to report to you the good conduct and decent behaviour of the Newgate women. That the kind instructions you have given them were not in vain was very evident on the voyage.

Both Admiral Young of the Dockyard at Deptford and Admiral Sir Byam Martin, Comptroller of the Navy, fully appreciated her splendid work.

Mrs. Fry was herself under no illusions as to the comparative merits of individual effort and the control of government in these matters.

I am anxious [she writes] that a few things which would greatly tend to the order and reformation of these poor women and protect their little remaining virtue should become established practices authorized by Government and not dependent upon a few individuals whose life and health and everything else are so uncertain.

But it required all her persistency to arouse officialdom to any sense of its responsibility in this direction. Particularly did she encounter the obstructive attitude of Sidmouth, better known as Addington, and not too well known as either Sidmouth or Addington, a thorough-paced Tory who opposed Catholic emancipation, the great Reform Bill, and by the same token Mrs. Fry and all her works. It seemed to him that Mrs. Fry's sympathy with brutal felons was as misplaced as it was inconvenient to himself. Nothing daunted she sought from Lady Harcourt an interview with the Home Office. Although it was accorded to her she left the premises "wounded and grieved" to attend a ceremony at the Mansion House, by command of Queen Charlotte, connected with schools for poor children.

Yesterday I had a day of ups and downs [she writes of this occasion] as far as the opinions of man are concerned in a remarkable degree. I found that there was a grievous misunderstanding between Lord Sidmouth and myself and that some things I had done had tried him exceedingly. . . . When under great humiliation in consequence of this Lady Harcourt took me to the Mansion House. . . . Among the rest the Queen was there. Much public respect was paid me and except the Royal Family themselves I think that no one received the same attention. There was quite a buzz when I went into the Egyptian Hall, where one to two thousand people were collected, and when the Queen came to speak to me, which she did very kindly, there was I am told a general clap. I think I may say this hardly raised me at all. I was so very low from what had occurred before.

The incident proves that although Ministers had no appreciation of her work the great public, even in those unregenerate times, was more susceptible to her reforming zeal.

Mrs. Fry did not confine her beneficent activities to the Metropolis. Like John Howard she devoted much of her activity to tours of inspection in the provinces and on the Continent. In October, 1818, she and her brother made a tour under the ægis of the Society of

Friends of various towns—Durham, Haddington, Aberdeen, Glasgow, Carlisle, etc. At the penitentiary at Portsea two of the inmates were pointed out as being particularly intractable. When she was about to go away she went up to these two and extending her hand to each of them said in a tone and manner quite indescribable, but so touching, " I trust I shall hear better things of thee." The hearts which had been proof against the words of reproach and exhortation softened at the words of hope and kindness, and both burst into tears.

Of the Haddington gaol Mrs. Fry writes :

It is difficult to conceive anything more entirely miserable—very dark, excessively dirty—clay fireplaces, straw in one corner for a bed with perhaps a single rug—a tub in each of them, the receptacle of all filth. No clothing was allowed. No medical man and no chaplain were in attendance. The inmates never left their cells, for there was no change of rooms and no airing ground, nor could they be under anyone's constant care, for the gaoler lived away from the prison. The debtors, whether they were healthy or sick, were confined night and day without change to a closet measuring not quite nine feet square and containing one small bed.

These conditions were fairly characteristic of all the similar penal institutions they visited in Scotland. Lunatics confined in association with the sane left a deep impression on the minds of the reformers.

It is safe to say that Mrs. Fry was the first, not only to treat prisoners as human beings but also to establish relations of sympathy with them. There is a letter published when she was ill in 1819 which, although obviously composed by an inmate superior to those she spoke for in intellect and address, no doubt expressed in more elaborate language than they could have commanded the true sentiments of the subscribers, a number of transportees :

It is with sorrow we say that we had not the pleasure of seeing you at the accustomed time which we have been always taught to look for ; we mean Friday last.   We are fearful that your health was the cause of our being deprived of that heart-felt joy which your presence always diffuses through the prison, but we hope we shall be able personally to return you the grate-ful acknowledgment of our hearts before we leave our country for ever, for all the past and present favours so benevolently bestowed upon what has been termed the most unfortunate of society until cheered by your benevolence, kindness, and charity, and hoping that your health which is so dear to such a number of unfortunates will be fully re-established before we go, so that after our departure from our native land they who are so unfortunate as to fall into the same situation as those who now address you may enjoy the same blessings spiritually and temporally that we have done before them . . .

Signed, The Prisoners of Newgate.

At about the same date Mrs. Fry received a letter from eleven women who had made a disturbance in Newgate, which together with its reply reveals to what extent she had established mutual relations of sympathy.   It is to this effect :

With shame and sorrow we once more humbly beg leave to address you in duty and respect to you and in justice to the greater number of our fellow-prisoners who through miscon-duct have fallen in general disgrace which our behaviour has brought upon us all, for which we are sincerely sorry, and entreating our sorrow may be accepted and forgiveness granted by her who we look up to as our most respected friend and benevolent benefactress.   We are not only called by justice for this submission and acknowledgment of our fault but by gratitude to you, honoured madam, and the rest of the worthy ladies who have interested themselves in our behalf. . . . Entreating you to impute it to our being led away by the passion of the moment and humbly hoping this acknowledgment may prove successful in restoring us to your good opinion and contradicting the bad one impressed on the public mind.

To these letters Mrs. Fry replied in the following terms :

You have often been in my affectionate remembrance, accompanied with anxious desires for your good. I am fully sensible that many of you claim our pity and most tender compassion, that many have been your temptations, many your afflictions. But mournful as your state is yet you may have hope, and that abundantly. . . . Do you not remember in the parable of the Prodigal Son that when he was yet afar off, the Father saw him, had compassion on him and even went out to meet him. So I doubt not, you would find it, even some of you who are now afar off from what is good. If you are only willing to return, you would find yourselves met by your Lord ever with great compassion, and He would do more for you than you would ask or think. I feel much love for you and much desire for your own sakes, for the sake of others and for our own sakes, who are willing to do what we can to serve you that you would thus in heart seek the Lord and prove your love to Him, and your repentance by your good works and by your orderly conduct. I was much grieved at the little disturbance amongst you the other day, but I was pleased with the letter written me by those who were engaged in it and I quite forgive them. Let me entreat you whatever trying or even provoking things may happen, to do so no more, for you sadly hurt the cause of poor prisoners by doing so, I may say, all over the kingdom, and thus enable your enemies to say, that our plans of kindness do not answer, and therefore they will not let others be treated kindly. Before I bid you farewell I will tell you that I am not without hope of seeing you before long, even before the poor women go to the Bay, but if I do not may the blessing of the Lord go with you when on the mighty deeps and in a strange land. What comfort would a good account of you give us, who are so much interested for you, and in case I should not see you I have two things especially to mention to you and guard you against, things which I believe have brought most of you to this prison. The one is giving way to drinking too much, the other is freedom with men. I find I can most frequently trace the fall of women to these two things, therefore let me beseech you to watch in these respects and let your modesty and sobriety appear before all and that you may grow in these and every other Christian virtue and grace is the sincere desire and prayer of your affectionate friend and sincere well-wisher.

Mrs. Fry was perhaps the first affectionate friend and sincere well-wisher these unfortunate prisoners had ever experienced.

We continue to have much satisfaction [she writes at this period] in the results of our efforts in Newgate. Good order appears increasingly established, there is much cleanliness amongst our poor women, and some very encouraging proofs of reformation in habit and what is much more in heart. . . . I am of opinion from what I have observed that there are hardly any amongst them so hard but that they may be subdued by kindness, gentleness and love so as very materially to alter their general conduct. Some of the worst prisoners have, after liberation, done great credit to the care taken of them.

But she knew that nothing short of a complete change in administration and a change of heart in government could effect permanent and general good. The main points upon which she insisted in her evidence given before the House of Commons were that matrons and only female officers should function on the female side, that prisoners should be employed, that there should be separation between the sexes, especially at night, that there should be compulsory instruction in the case of illiterate prisoners, that there should be careful superintendence of intercourse during the day, solitude at night and finally that there should be lady superintendents of the gaol.

At the time when Mrs. Fry reached the meridian of her activities the Newgate Association was established as the result of a three-years' probationary test, and a committee was formed to answer inquiries and communicate information elsewhere. Ladies' associations were formed in the provinces, but for the present some degree of classification, employment and moral influence were all that could be effected without further assistance from above. Mrs. Fry with her two elder daughters made another tour encouraging the function of these associations.

No description of the activities of the reformers is complete without allusion to the Prison Discipline Society founded in 1818, with whose admirable work the name of Sir Thomas Fowell Buxton will always be associated. Coming of Norfolk stock he combined with his philanthropic ventures a love of sport and nature which the Eastern counties seem to engender in the sons of their soil and an aptitude for business which so often reveals itself in Quaker stock. He had married the sister of Elizabeth Fry and found in the latter a congenial spirit for the noble work upon which they together laboured unremittingly. He was the author of a pamphlet entitled *Whether crime and misery are produced or prevented by our present system of Prison Discipline*, which occasioned the establishment of the Society. In the preface of this pamphlet he observes :

It is evident, I conceive, that where the law condemns a man to jail and is silent as to his treatment there, it intends merely that he should be amerced of his freedom, not that he should be subjected to any useless severities. . . . Prisons must contain masses of offenders with different shades and distinctions of guilt, and we must either make imprisonment as bitter as possible and thus involve the comparatively innocent in those hardships which were imposed upon delinquency of the deepest hue, confounding all notions of equity, or we must come to the conclusion that imprisonment is nothing more than deprivation of liberty and ought therefore to be attended with as little of what is vexatious and as little of what is hurtful as possible. . . . Prison is a place of retention not of punishment.

As to the prisoner,

You have no right to abridge him of pure air, wholesome and sufficient food and opportunities of exercise. You have no right to debar him from the craft on which his family depends, if it can be exercised in prison. You have no right to subject him to suffering from cold by want of bed-clothing by night or firing by day, and the reason is plain, you have turned him from his home, and have deprived him of the means of providing himself with the necessaries of life, and therefore you are bound to furnish him with moderate but suitable accommodation.

You have no right to ruin his habits, by compelling him to be idle, his morals by compelling him to mix with a promiscuous assemblage of hardened and convicted criminals, or his health by forcing him at night into a damp unventilated cell . . . or to make him sleep in contact with the victims of contagious and loathsome disease. . . . Whoever heard of a criminal being sentenced to catch the rheumatism or typhus fever. . . .

The convicted delinquent has his rights. All measures and practises in prison which may injure him in any way are illegal because they are not specified in his sentence. He is therefore entitled to a wholesome atmosphere, decent clothing, bedding, and a diet sufficient to support him.

The Prison Discipline Society made a report in the year 1820 indicating the flagrant violation of the Acts of George IV. Although it was incumbent upon two or more justices to visit prisons three times a quarter and to report in writing to Quarter Sessions this regulation had been neglected, as justices feared the fever which their visits might have obviated. Whereas it was enacted that the personnel of the prisons should be classified into prisoners convicted of felony, prisoners convicted on charge or suspicion of felony, prisoners guilty of misdemeanours, prisoners charged with misdemeanours, and debtors, it was revealed that in 1818 out of 518 prisons to which 100,000 prisoners had been committed, in one year only twenty-three prisons were divided according to the law.   Whereas it was enacted that male and female prisoners should be kept separate only twenty-three prisons observed the regulations strictly and fifty-nine had no division whatever.   Whereas work was to be provided, in 445 prisons there was no work done at all.   As to overcrowding, in 100 gaols capable of accommodating 8,500 there were as many as 13,000 inmates.

It is quite true that the penitentiary system suggested by Howard and revived by Jeremy Bentham had been carried into effect to the extent that land was bought for building thereon Millbank Penitentiary at a cost of half a million, but owing mainly to the unworthy personnel of the prison, the scheme failed to do itself justice.   The Prison Discipline Society, however, persevered in spite of all disappointment and the inveterate hindrance which came both from expected and unexpected quarters.   The celebrated wit, Sidney Smith, be it said, was one of its most persistent foes.   Amongst other of its achievements were the establishment of refuges in Hoxton for males and in the Hackney Road for deserving cases of females discharged from prison.   In these institutions training in habits of industry and morals was the main objective.

An Act was passed in 1824 which greatly strengthened the hands of the Prison Discipline Society.   Its provisions included those for the better moral and physical health of the prisoners.   It provided for convict labour, the separation of sexes, classification, female warders for the female side, proper religious equipment, instruction in reading and writing and the prohibition of ironing except in urgent cases. But in spite of this beneficent legislation progress was slow. One of the difficulties to be met was the lack of uniformity in the enforcement of penalties, exercise, employment and general administration noticeable in various prisons, which was destined to continue for another half-century until the Prison Act of 1877 corrected this abuse.

The law had defined general principles of prison government but hitherto left it too much to the discretion of the magistracy to fill in details. The Legislature only recommended when it should have compelled. Moreover, numerous prisons under local jurisdiction which were exempted from the operation of the law were so defective that reform seemed hopeless, and it was thought wiser not to bring them within provisions which under the circumstances would be inoperative. One hundred and seventy local authorities possessed the right of trying criminals. One hundred and sixty had gaols of their own withdrawn from central authority where rules were ignored.

Members of the Society in their tours of inspection still found the old abuses all too prevalent. In one typical instance the hospital was filled with infectious cases, and in a room 7 feet by 9, with closed windows, a lad lay ill with fever with three healthy prisoners. Mr. Buxton counted eleven children hardly old enough to be released from the nursery at Bristol. It was

a scene of infernal passions and distresses which few have imagination sufficient to picture and of which fewer still would believe that the original is to be found in this enlightened and happy country.

Furnished with a candle he descended eighteen long

steps into a vault. At the bottom was a circular space through which ran a narrow passage, and the sides of which were fitted with barrack bedsteads. The floor was on a level with the river and very damp. The smell was excruciating. On a dirty bedstead lay a wretched being in the throes of sickness. The place was only ventilated by a kind of chimney which prisoners kept hermetically sealed and which had never been opened in the memory of the turn-key. Untried persons were often lodged here, and sometimes were loaded with heavy irons for a whole year awaiting gaol delivery.

Mrs. Fry had by now become a recognized authority on prison management. Even magistrates sought her advice, and from foreign capitals came frequent requests for her views. In June, 1821, she had occasion to rejoice when she witnessed the Freemasons' Hall filled with persons of rank and influence on the occasion of the meeting of the Society for the Improvement of Prison Discipline. The Duke of Gloucester presided, supported by Lord John Russell, Lord Stanley, Lord Belgrave, Lord Calthorpe, Sir James Mackintosh, Sir Thomas Baring, and other men of light and leading. She was loudly applauded on leaving the hall.

In her later years appear characteristic entries in her journal, from which the following selection is made. In 1823 she writes :

I dined at the Mansion House—a change of atmosphere spiritually. . . . Generally speaking I believe it is best to avoid such occasions for they take up time and are apt to dissipate the mind, although occasionally it may be the right and proper calling of Christians, thus to enter life.

On the 5th day of March I went to meet the Secretary of State (Sir Robert Peel) and the Speaker of the House of Commons at Newgate with my brother Fowell Buxton and my husband. Sixth day in town again to Newgate, one of the Bishops and many others there.

12*th April*: We have been engaged in various ways particularly in the sale of work done by the poor prisoners in Newgate. This has been a considerable public exposure, but I trust not without profit. I deeply felt upon entering it the danger of the pollutions of the world.

January, 1831. My interest in the cause of prisons remains strong and my zeal unabated, though it is curious to observe how much less is felt about it by the public generally.

In 1832 she writes:

I rather feel having to go before the Committee of the House of Commons on the subject of prisons. May any good to this important cause be done by it and may I be helped to do my part with simplicity as unto God and not unto man.

The object of this Committee was to ascertain the best modes of secondary punishment with a view to the suppression of crime. Mrs. Fry's considered opinions were expressed both on this occasion and on others as the result of personal experience derived from tours of inspection and also from mature consideration.

Her views on solitary confinement, a subject at that time exercising the minds of the reformers, were that very many hours might be passed alone with advantage and the night always, but she recognized a considerable difference between useful and improving reflection and the imagination dwelling upon past guilt or prospective guilt. Her conviction was that with the greater number of criminals left to feed upon their own mental resources the latter state of mind was highly probable, the former very unlikely. Confinement that secluded them from the vicious but allowed of frequent intercourse with the sober and well-conducted persons would have been in her view the ideal to be aimed at. Some years later in France she discussed these matters with M. de Béranger.

She explained to him the above views, which experience had taught her, but warned him of the difficulty of obtaining a sufficiency of officers of good character. If of bad character the prisoners are subject to the moral contamination of the officers.

On that visit she incidentally discovered that by the laws of the country a boy was not held responsible for his actions under sixteen years of age, and if he committed a crime he was detained but not sentenced. Fathers had the power of confining their sons under age.

In 1832 she received a letter from the Home Office assuring her that even Lord Melbourne was fully sensible of the good which had been done by herself and the ladies connected with her in many of the prisons, and of the great benefit derived from their exertions by the female transportees, and that His Lordship was anxious as far as it could be that the visiting magistrates should favourably entertain and second her benovolent intentions.

In the year 1833 we find her visiting the Island of Jersey and giving to the authorities there a piece of her mind.

Our protracted residence in this beautiful and interesting island has afforded me a full opportunity of observing the manner in which the defective system pursued in the management of the Prison appears to operate upon its inmates, and I feel it to be my duty to represent to you the effects which my experience has taught me must necessarily result from its operation as being nothing less than a gradual but certain demoralization of the lower and some of the middle classes of society and the increase rather than the diminution of crime.

Twice again she crossed to Jersey to see that her recommendations had been given effect to.

In the year 1835 she was ordered to attend the Select Committee of the House of Lords appointed to inquire into the state of the gaols. An eye-witness writes a vivid account of her on this occasion.

Never, I should think, was the calm dignity of her character more conspicuous. Whatever her inward feelings might have been, nothing like excitement was visible in her manner, nothing hurried in her language. Perfectly self-possessed her speech flowed melodiously, her ideas were clearly expressed, and if another thought possessed her besides that of delivering her opinions faithfully and judiciously on the subjects brought before her it was that she might speak a word for her Lord and Master in that company.

In 1840 she recorded the fact in her journal that she visited Parkhurst,

an interesting new prison for boys which gave me much satisfaction. It was curious to see some of the very things that in early life I in part began carried out in practice. I have lived to see much more than I expected of real improvement in prisons.

In 1842 she sat between the Prince Consort and Sir Robert Peel at a Mansion House banquet, to which she makes a quaint but characteristic reference:

I find that the newspaper report of the dinner has excited some anxiety at my being there for the toasts, music, etc., it is thought I set a bad example by it and it may induce others to go to such dinners, and that my being present appeared like approving the toasts. At the same time I felt so much quietness and peace when there and afterwards that I fear being now too much cast down or tried by these remarks.

In the same year she is still pursuing her endeavours on behalf of the female transportees.

By the year 1845, when she attended for the last time the meeting of the British Ladies' Society, she had the happiness of knowing that Newgate, Bridewell, the Millbank Prison, the Giltspur Street Compter, White

Cross Street Prison, Tothill Fields Prison and Cold Bath
Fields Prison were all in a state of comparative order,
some exceedingly well administered, and the female
convicts in all visited and cared for by the ladies.
Although the initial interest of the public occasioned
by her visits to Newgate had by now subsided, everywhere a steady resolute improvement was perceptible.

Well might she say toward the end of her days :

My life has been a remarkable one, much have I had to go
through, more than mortal knows or ever can know. My
sorrows at times have been bitter, my consolations sweet.

She died on 12th October, 1845.

Although before her death she had much consolation
and satisfaction in the apparent results of her work, many
years were to pass ere the full measure of reform
which she had advocated was achieved. Most authorities agree that the present system of prison administration can be dated from 1840, five years before the death
of Mrs. Fry, when Pentonville Prison, with its system
of separate cellular confinement, was built, although
the Prison Act of 1778 incorporated that system in its
provisions. Within half a dozen years no less than
fifty-four prisons were erected by local authorities
upon this model, but prison reform could be but
slowly effected so long as a complete lack of homo-
geneity amongst local authorities obtained. In 1849
Mr. Charles Pearson moved for a Select Committee to
report upon the best means of securing a uniform
system. Apart from the convict prisons being placed
under a Board of Directors, nothing was done for
thirteen more years, when in 1863 another Committee,
set up with the same terms of reference, reiterated the
same views. Even the Prison Act of 1865 failed to
secure complete uniformity. Crime, however, gradually

came to be regarded not only as of local but of national concern. Prison charges, it was argued, should be borne by the Exchequer and not by local rates. Once this principle was acknowledged the whole question of prison reform took on a different aspect. By the Prison Bill of 1877 the control of all gaols was vested in a body of Prison Commissioners appointed by and responsible to the Home Secretary. What followed justified Lord John Russell's prophecy at the time of the first prison reformers' activities :

I believe our country is about to become distinguished for triumphs, the effect of which should be to save and not to destroy. . . . Instead of laying waste the provinces of our enemies we might begin now to reap a more solid glory in the reform of abuses at home and in spreading happiness through millions of our own population.

CHAPTER VIII

THE PURGING OF THE SOIL

FAR-REACHING and enduring as were the results of the efforts of those intrepid reformers, who justifiably usurped the functions proper to and yet abdicated by Government in the manner described in previous chapters, it is doubtful if the most enlightened of them either in the eighteenth or the early years of the nineteenth century probed deep enough down to fundamentals. As we have seen, there were three stages in the development of the treatment of crime, the first influenced by the principle, singularly futile as it proved, that the punishment should suit the crime. The second stage witnessed application of another principle in almost direct abnegation of the former of suiting the punishment to the criminal. In the third stage the more enlightened view was adopted that both the first and the second principle were abortive unless the reformation of the criminal was to be the paramount consideration.

But that which differentiates modern methods from obsolete is recognition that more effective still than the process of either punishing or reforming the transgressor is the removal of the causes that create in him criminal tendencies, although it is only fair to the memory of Jeremy Bentham to credit him with an effort to discover and to combat the causes of crime, a more valuable contribution towards its eradication than his famous " Panopticon." It is expedient therefore to inquire what are the most potent causes of crime apart from what might be termed accidents which may occur in any class of society or under any circumstances of human existence. There are perhaps three causes more accountable for the manufacture of crime than any other of the numerous occasions pleaded in extenuation of guilt. These are defective education, bad housing and poverty. The first concerns the moral aspect of the question, the second and third the physical.

Various authorities who have written upon the subject of crime and its origin have discussed its interaction with education. It has even been seriously advanced by at least one investigator that education, far from serving as an antidote to criminal tendencies merely aggravates them. One author sums up against education on the ground that it brings new crimes in its train. We might surely just as fittingly despair of the human race because the procreation of children under certain circumstances leads to bastardy. It may be arguable that education has actually engendered a particular type of crime, and that the development of banking, commerce and industry has been favourable to the operation of a more intellectual type of malefactor. It is conceivable that forgery, coining and variations of commercial fraud require a comparatively high standard of education in the perpetrator, but this is a very specious argument. We have not to go much deeper to expose its fallacy. Let us take for the purposes of our investigation the man with no erudition whatsoever, one who knows nothing of the sublimation of animal instincts with intellectual pursuits, it is certain enough that his refraining from anti-social conduct is exclusively due to fear of the consequences if there are any detrimental to his own interests, and indeed, if he be sufficiently intelligent to appreciate what such consequences may be. It is very difficult to understand how any higher ideal could be inculcated into one who is so ignorant that he is unable either to read the thoughts and opinions of others or to put his own with coherent sequence into writing. There may be a few who have that instinctive discrimination between right and wrong that we perceive even in certain domesticated animals, but it is only when man learns to read and write that he can acquire any true knowledge of good and evil and the faculty for regulating his elementary passions and impulses.

The initial difficulty we are confronted with is that argument on this subject is almost impossible of demonstration or of proof. A method which might be suggested would be to compare the statistics of crime to-day with those at a period of history when only a negligible proportion of the community were well educated. Not only is such information lacking to us, but once we take a plunge into the swirling pool of criminal statistics we are caught by so many cross-currents that the chances of reaching *terra firma* again are remote. There is nothing more misleading or more illusive than statistics of crime. While new varieties have been added in comparatively recent years to the list of crimes committed, some would say through the medium of education or through certain reactions of civilization, there has been a very decided improvement in police organization, which makes the apprehension and the conviction of criminals more infallible. Statistics are more meticulously kept than of old. Under a more lenient code there is less reluctance to prosecute. And many other reasons can be adduced to demonstrate the futility of instituting a comparison between the records of to-day and those of a century ago.

The only conclusive method of proving the case would be if by a miracle the whole community could be made to forget all that it had learned and were to return to the jungle from whence it came, left with animal instinct as its only guide. There can be little doubt that if this supernatural process could be put into operation proof positive would be forthcoming to establish that education is one of the supreme influences in obviating crime.

After all, the mere fact that a man can read opens up to him, if he takes advantage of his opportunities, not only a wide range of intellectual accomplishments which keep in abeyance his lower instincts, but assist him to form a right judgment in all things. The philanthropists who cleansed our gaols, who re-fashioned our administration of justice and taught the best methods of prevention of crime and the amelioration of the criminal, owed their benevolent predispositions to education. It is all to the good that our judges no longer are so ill educated as to believe in witchcraft. The whole police organisation in this country could not be the efficient instrument it is were it not for the fact that its personnel is composed of men the majority of whom have received a competent education and include a number who have been educated up to a very high standard.

But perhaps the most conclusive proof of all that education and crime are antipathetic, is that the present-day inhabitants of our gaols, with the fewest possible exceptions, are the least well educated of the general community either in erudition or in conduct.

Finally it must be remembered that if it is to be accepted as a definite constitutional axiom that ignorance of the law does not excuse a breach of the law, it is incumbent upon the State to ensure that every individual coming within its jurisdiction is sufficiently well educated to be able to acquire a competent knowledge of the laws he will be penalized for breaking.

The miscellaneous physical causes of crime are no

less important than the moral, because the two categories are absolutely interdependent. Such physical conditions as bad housing, malnutrition and uncleanliness of every variety have a detrimental effect not only upon the bodies but upon the minds of those who suffer from them. The impoverishment of the mind and body are inseparable concomitants.

It often happens for the very reason that physical weakness is produced by the evil circumstances of the victim that moral weakness also ensues. Although this may be a platitude of the first order of precedence, it is only during the last fifty years that there has been any indication that Government has awakened to the importance of improving the housing conditions of our people, and even to-day a great deal of headway in this direction will have to be made up before the ideal standard is attained.

Perhaps the reader will be indulgent enough to allow me at this point to obtrude my own personal observations. Hitherto I have relied for my material upon the experience and the writings of others, but in the remaining paragraphs of this work I should prefer as far as possible to depend for my conclusions upon what I have heard with my ears and seen with my eyes, not because I wish to assert the opinions I have formed to the exclusion of or in preference to those of others more expert than myself, but because I agree with Fielding when he writes :

If any gentleman who hath had more experience, hath more duly considered the matter, or whose superior abilities enable him to form a better judgment shall think proper to improve my endeavours he hath my ready consent. Provided the end be effected I shall be contented with the honour of my share how inconsiderable is the means.

There has recently been brought to my notice a number

of disturbing examples of present-day overcrowding in the industrial districts of London, of which I will provide the reader with a sufficient selection to open his eyes if they need opening to the dimensions of this particular social evil in its relation to the root cause of crime. In M—— Street a man, his wife, two sons of thirteen and four years of age, are living and eating in one squalid basement room. In a second example we find the ground-floor back room has three beds placed close together with barely sufficient room for the door to open. In this room sleep five boys, aged twenty-two, twenty-one, eighteen, six and five years of age, respectively, together with two girls aged twelve and nine years. In the third example the tenant sleeps in the first-floor back room with her husband and a boy of seventeen years of age, the ante-room being occupied by four grown-up girls, while the front room is inhabited by her married daughter and her husband together with boys aged fourteen, thirteen, ten, seven, six and two years of age, in which room the family meals are taken.

While it may not be possible to doubt that such a want of segregation of the sexes or any kind of domestic seclusion has a deteriorating effect upon the very young mind, it is equally impossible to withhold a tribute of admiration from many of those of our unfortunate fellow-countrymen who are compelled to live in such vile conditions and yet are able to conduct themselves as decently and respectably as those who in youth are sheltered from the realities of life. Apart, however, from these considerations, no one can deny that such domestic conditions as I have described in the preceding paragraphs must affect adversely the physical health of parents and children alike, and that in bodies so weakened the resisting power to evil moral influences must be the less. Healthy, decent housing conditions cannot fail to contribute to the decrease of criminal tendencies. Furthermore, the absence of home life which we cherish so much in England—and there can be no home life in such habitations—is another serious aspect of the question. It does not require a very considerable experience of the slums to appreciate that, there being no available space in the home in which to spend his spare time, there can be no alternative for the youth but the street, which leads the young wayfarer too often in a direction that ends in disaster. Incidentally it is in making provision against such contingencies that the voluntary organizations have been instrumental in supplying a national need of inestimable value serving to keep in abeyance tastes and inclinations which are the reverse of wholesome.

The effect of poverty due to unemployment or to employment with so low a rate of remuneration as to deny to the worker a decent standard of life, upon the increase of crime is too obvious to need elaboration, but poverty is without any doubt one of the main contributory causes.

It is extremely difficult to disentangle one cause of crime from various others. For instance, at more than one period of English history drunkenness was a menace to the health of the nation, but one of the causes of drunkenness was the poverty, misery and lack of wholesome amenities that characterized the lives of the workers during those periods. This most insidious of all vices has been so much on the decrease during the last two or three decades that it has ceased to rank high as a cause of crime. That the State should interfere to check its prevalence was recognized as long ago as the reign of James the First, when the sovereign himself issued licences for bowling alleys and other places for indoor pastimes with the express purpose of providing a counter-attraction to drink. With the same object in view he even wrote a treatise in favour of permitting sports and recreation on Sundays after the hours of Divine Service, and required the clergy to read it in their churches. Unfortunately, the entertainment to which the English people of that period were most partial consisted of bull and bear baiting and brawling, so that the good intentions of this enlightened monarch were not fulfilled. But from this time onwards we find at recurring periods the State taking cognizance of the drink evil with more or less satisfactory result. There can be no question that the present decline in drunkenness, while it is to be attributed to a variety of causes, has been due in part to legislation. But it is not only legislation that has caused this noticeable decrease in drunkenness. It is difficult to resist the conclusion that the insobriety of the masses in the eighteenth century and the prevalence of crime due directly or indirectly to that vice owed its origin to the fact that there were so few wholesome amenities in the lives of the working classes. No greater change has taken place in the habits and customs of those who dwell in the industrial districts of great towns than that which is derived from the increased opportunities for recreation and healthy amusement. However much Local Government may be taken to task by the ratepayer for what he considers culpable extravagance there is no question that money has been well spent, if lavishly, in providing interesting and diverting occupation in their leisure hours for workers of all ages, who with better wages can now afford the fees necessary for indulging in them. The provision of swimming baths and pools, dance halls, public libraries, gymnasia, recreation grounds, and numerous other facilities for amusement has been of great moral value in inducing men, women and children to utilize their spare time well and to correct tendencies that lead to vice and crime. But it is not only local authorities that have provided such valuable amenities. In the last twenty or thirty years many voluntary associations have sprung into existence to meet the needs of adolescence in this respect. The result they have achieved is of inestimable importance to the State.

Another factor sometimes ignored by writers on this subject, which has indirectly served to decrease crime by raising the standard of living is the redistribution of wealth. Until recently it can be said that most of the wealth of the country was in the hands of a very small, governing class, of which the great landowners formed the predominant section. The vast majority of English men and women were situated very little, if at all above the subsistence level. Wealth has been redistributed in various ways, but mainly by the steepening of the Income Tax grade and the imposition of estate duties, and also by the increase of wage and salary standards by which the capitalist ceases to claim so great a share of the profits of industry. A more equitable distribution of wealth, whether or not successive Chancellors of the Exchequer intended it to produce this result, has certainly been of incalculable advantage in decreasing crime by providing the majority with more decent standards of living and more opportunities for healthful recreation. No one who has had any acquaintance with the so-called slums can fail to appreciate the remarkable change for the better, with the possible exception of housing, that has taken place within the last twenty-five years. Those who are reluctant to acknowledge the validity of this argument will no doubt adduce in their favour the evidence of a considerable increase of juvenile crime in recent years. It must be acknowledged that while most of the factors which were mainly responsible for juvenile crime in the eighteenth century have been removed, others, some of them equally detrimental, have come into play. While some of the tares have been weeded away it is certainly true enough that others have grown in their place. The problem of the recent increase in juvenile crime is discussed in later paragraphs, but no one can gainsay that the notable improvement in the standard of living has reduced crime in a remarkable degree.

We are drawn, then, to the first conclusion that the rooting out of those conditions which make human beings criminal contrary to their better natures and inclinations is the first step in the elimination of law-breaking. This process must, of course, be a question of time. The evils are too deep-seated to be easily eradicated, and we can be sure that human nature being, and likely to remain, what it is the problem of crime will always be with us, and therefore we shall never be relieved of the obligation to study its incidence and to discover appropriate methods of treatment and of reformation.

With regard to the first guiding principles of treatment there are two considerations which at a certain point seem to conflict : the first is the security of the general public, in other words the protection of decent law-abiding citizens from violence and depredation ; the second, equally important, is the reformation of the malefactor. In the case of the first offender his reformation is a consideration of supreme importance for his own and the public's sake, but, in proportion as the offender persists in breaking the law so the consideration of the protection of the public from his law-breaking must in proportion become increasingly predominant. How, therefore, to obviate the first offender developing into a persistent and incorrigible offender should be the main consideration of government in dealing with crime, and as the majority of first offenders are youths it is around youth that the problem centres.

If it is established, and clearly it must be, that the first essential of dealing with the whole problem of the criminal is to negotiate it at the right end, the proper scientific treatment of youthful delinquency is the next most important consideration. Recognition of this fundamental axiom has been conceded in recent times by the State itself. During the years 1907 and 1908 there was placed upon the Statute Book a trinity of measures which have effected the most beneficial revolution in the treatment of crime, namely, the Acts that sanctioned the Probation System, the Borstal Institutions and the Juvenile Courts.

We start to-day with the immeasurable advantage of having made in quite recent years some all-important discoveries in this direction. We have discovered, for instance, that to treat boys who have committed different offences in the same way, as was the procedure in the eighteenth century, would be as absurd as to administer the same treatment for measles as for rheumatism. Again, we now realize that to treat boys the same just because they have committed identically the same crime would in many cases be as inappropriate as to give the same medical treatment to persons of weak and strong constitutions. Having rejected the idea, firmly rooted in human prejudices, that there is a definite criminal type innate and indelible, and even perhaps to a large extent having discarded the theory of heredity, we have discovered that it is just as important to make meticulous inquiry into the circumstances, antecedents and environment of the delinquent as it is to make investigation into the nature of his crime. In this connection, and particularly with regard to the adolescent, for proper diagnosis and prognosis of each

The Raw Material of to-day   *From a drawing by the Author*

case it is impossible to ignore the all-important question of sex. Again, our standards of value as regards crime in their application to its treatment have been radically altered for the better, although in my own opinion, they yet need considerable modification. It is now realized that punishment, although essential, is worse than useless unless the reforming of the criminal is an integral part of the method to be employed for that purpose. Not by any means the least important discovery we have made is that, however scientific your treatment may be, one vital consideration is the suitability of the personnel that administers the process of regeneration. We have discovered that treatment will fail in the vast majority of cases unless the after care is regarded as important as the treatment within the institution. We have discovered that prison is always a hazardous expedient for curing criminal tendencies, and that it should be postponed until through the persistency in crime of the subject of your treatment the safety of the public becomes again the predominant consideration.

Finally we have made discoveries too numerous to be catalogued as to the conduct of institutions which deal with juvenile delinquency that have resulted in those institutions recording a very high percentage of success. These discoveries are so important, and, in spite of being so obvious, so difficult to be appreciated in all their bearings by those who have not made a special study of the subject that perhaps the reader will permit an attempt on my part to elaborate them. A personal association in both an official and an unofficial capacity for a number of years with the problem of the young delinquent has taught me that although there may be certain denominators common to the majority, and, although for reasons I have already enumerated, they are mostly drawn from the indigent section of the community, there is an infinite variety of character and type demanding an infinite variety of treatment. It would therefore obviously be impossible to lay down any rules of general application as, for instance, how many times a youth should be placed on probation, or as to what particular type of institutional treatment is the most suitable, or how long that treatment should last. Individual prescription in each separate case is essential. This principle has been recognized now in our Courts of Law, and although there is still a certain degree of misdirection from the Bench as to the proper destination of the culprit, it may fairly be said that every provision has been made in recent years for dealing with each case on its merits.

As to the precaution which is now invariably taken to make the most meticulous inquiries into the history, physical and moral, and circumstances of erring youth, nothing has contributed more to ameliorate methods of the treatment of crime. Mrs. le Mesurier, who herself for many years has taken a leading part in this all-important work, has provided for our instruction, in her admirable treatise on boys in trouble, some vivid pictures illustrating this essential aspect of the treatment of young delinquents. The analogy of a doctor and a patient is a perfect one. No doctor would attempt to prescribe for one under medical treatment without making similar inquiries. If he neglected to do so he would risk making the same blunders with the invalid as the State through its negligence has, in less enlightened days, made with the criminal.

The problem of adolescence, that discordant prelude to maturity, is perhaps one of the most complex and difficult of all to negotiate. Until quite recent times the problems associated with sex were for various reasons, but more especially because the Victorians regarded the whole subject as distasteful and prurient, completely ignored and left to solve themselves, if indeed solution were thought possible. The fatal misconception that the withholding from youth essential instruction in its complexities served the interests of morality, the refusal of authority to recognize the importance of the study of the problem in all its aspects wrought immeasurable harm and postponed those discoveries indispensable to the successful treatment of youthful delinquency. Discoveries contributed by duly qualified practitioners working within the prisons and institutions have been of inestimable value in this connection. Moreover, to whatever extent some of us may differ from them in particulars we must all acknowledge that in broad general principles we owe a great debt to Freud and the psychoanalysts, who have not only revealed much of value that before their researches lay hidden, but suggested for those disorders of the mind traceable to adolescence, remedies the merit of which has been definitely proven.

There is no doubt that there still remains buried a vast store of knowledge on the subject waiting to be mined. New seams stretching far and wide are perpetually being opened up by the perseverance of the investigator. Material is constantly being brought to the surface of utility to the framers of the new systems.

As an example of how the phenomenon operates in a disguise too impenetrable to have been suspected by previous generations it has been discovered that certain criminal tendencies and actions which superficially appear to have no connection whatever with sex can be traced to that cause. Certain attitudes of mind, call them perverted if you will, can be explained as manifestations of adolescence. Although it is easy for the amateur student of psychology to find himself out of his depth if he pursues the subject to such lengths as this, there are various aspects of the question which hardly need an expert to appreciate.

Adolescence reacts unfavourably in varying degrees upon different individuals. It exercises different influences upon what appear to be two youths of the same type. It may be said as a general rule that it produces a certain instability which rarely leaves the subject without some modification of temperament, although it is very easy to exaggerate its mischievous effects in the majority of cases. In many instances any evil result is hardly noticeable. But contrary to some preconceived views on this subject the storm often breaks with greater havoc upon the weak than upon the robust. Strong sex instincts frequently reside in the most miserable of human frames while those of normal or superior physical health and strength are often singularly immune from the distresses and anxieties associated with them. Adolescence is, of course, with all a period of physical change, and in certain cases under certain conditions the change may produce dangerous results upon the mentality of the victim. But it is all to the good that these discoveries have been made and that its reactions are now definitely taken into account in the treatment of the young offender.

Imprisonment, with its frustration of natural desires, of necessity involves the operation of inhibitions which may in some produce deplorable consequences. A youth incarcerated during the most exuberant period of human existence, without any outlet for his physical energy beyond what is distasteful to him, is obviously called upon to exercise a very considerable measure of moral self-restraint. When the Borstal system was first adopted the broad general principle upon which it was based was that it was preferable for a boy who showed signs of persistent offending to undergo a long period of detention in an institution resembling a school, with reform rather than punishment as its objective, than to serve a short term in prison which, while essentially punitive in character, would not be sufficient to effect any other result than an undesirable familiarity with its contaminating influences. But the conditions of a school cannot be faithfully reproduced in a Borstal institution. It is true that the boy at a public school who approximates to the Borstal boy in age has three or more years under strict discipline and control, and while at school is segregated from the opposite sex, but at any rate in his case he spends a considerable portion of the year in comparative freedom under perfectly natural and normal conditions, while the Borstal boy has no vacation and is living throughout the term of his sentence under circumstances which cannot be described as either normal or natural. Moreover, from the nature of his case his standards of virtue and morality are not very exacting, his sex inclinations when he was at large were probably not under any very strict control. Even before the Borstal age was raised many of them were in the Institutions at a period of life when under normal circumstances they would have married. Some are married. Yet those who serve the full sentence are for three years segregated entirely from the opposite sex. On the other hand it is quite true that with a large number of young men any period of institutional training less than three years is not sufficient to produce the desired improvement, and it is also true that for a certain proportion of them the dangers alluded to above are not considerable. One solution of this complex problem is to prescribe a more intensified training in a shorter period of time. Such an experiment is in process of being tested, but only for a carefully selected type of youth that is capable of reacting favourably to its vigorous standards, both physical and moral, a type which may prove to be a very limited one indeed. Admittedly exaggeration in these matters of sex must be avoided. There is, of course, an appreciable number of youths who are capable of exercising self-restraint and for whom grave danger need not be feared in this respect—but the problem still stands.

Few considerations are more important in determining the treatment of juvenile or indeed any kind of delinquency than the fixing of a proper standard of values in crime. But by the same token there are few matters more highly controversial or upon which those best qualified to express a considered view are more in disagreement. I was privileged in my youth to act in the capacity of Judge's Marshal to the late Lord Mersey— then Mr. Justice Bigham—during Assizes on the North-Eastern Circuit. I suppose that rarely has a more fair-minded or tender-hearted man dispensed justice in a criminal court. On one occasion, entering his private room at Newcastle, I found him in earnest conversation with a man whom he had that morning sentenced. He explained to me afterwards that there seemed to be something in the demeanour of this individual which called for such a proceeding on his part. With a Judge so sympathetic I was surprised therefore when, on a subsequent occasion, he expressed the view that he considered crimes of violence the most reprehensible breaches of the law. It seemed to me that this wise and humane Judge had established for himself an unaccountable standard of values. I ventured to suggest that a crime of violence, committed probably in the majority of cases at a time when the criminal was hardly conscious of his action, in the heat of passion, of jealousy or of hate, without any premeditation whatsoever, was hardly comparable with the deliberate corruption of youth, the training of young men in crime over a long period of years which is part of the stock-in-trade of the receiver of stolen goods, or with the vile arts of the blackmailer, who for his own profit sets out to destroy the career and character of an innocent and virtuous fellow-citizen, or with one of those devastating City frauds ingeniously planned with the full knowledge and intention that the risk shall be taken by those who are ignorant of the wiles of the company promoter and who cannot afford to run the risk involved. No doubt in old days the physical safety of the public was a consideration of more importance than its moral welfare, and therefore crimes of violence, murder and assault were adjudged the most detrimental to the community. But our forbears failed to appreciate that even the murder of an individual cannot do so much harm to the community as the corruption of one of its members by another. Broadly speaking, I am disposed to believe that our standard of values in the matter of crime should be established not so much by the particular nature of the crime as by whether it was carefully premeditated and whether the criminal is persistent in his criminal actions or merely the victim of a sudden overwhelming obsession. In the first place such a standard would be of far more value in determining the nature of the treatment of the criminal, and in the second place it would be a much more effective safeguard for the security and safety of the general public. Although in a measure this is the recognized criterion, I believe that the standard of values indicated by the code of our laws and the sentences passed in recent cases leaves room for considerable revision. Many still endure long terms of imprisonment whose transgressions are not so reprehensible or so detrimental to the community as those committed by criminals with whom the law has dealt much more leniently. In the boys' prisons perhaps the standard of values is more nearly allied to common sense than elsewhere.

That reformation is the most essential feature of our prison system is perhaps the most important discovery of all. Reformation, it goes without saying, is much easier to effect in the first offender than in one habituated to crime. It is for that reason that the process is more successful in the boys' institutions than in convict prisons. From all that has preceded in these pages dealing with the prison system both in the eighteenth century and most of the nineteenth century it is obvious that reformation was not only left out of account but rendered impossible by an unscientific and neglectful administration. This discovery is closely allied to another I have mentioned in a previous paragraph, namely, that the personnel of the staff in whose hands the process of regeneration is conducted must be appropriate for the task. Not so long ago governorships of prisons and posts of a lower grade in the prison service were regarded as honourable retirement for those who had acquitted themselves well in professions which were not even remotely connected with the treatment of offenders, instead of being regarded as posts of a highly specialized and onerous character. If this consideration is important in the case of convict prisons it is infinitely more so in the case of every kind of institution which deals with the young offender. Provided that it is possible to secure the individual who combines in himself all the essential qualities that are needed, it is obvious that the success of your reforming system is thereby rendered the more certain. In Borstal Institutions it is all to the good to man your staff if possible with those who have not forgotten the days of their youth, and are still mindful of the dangers of a dangerous period of human existence and who can readily sympathize with and assist those who have yielded to them. Nevertheless, a knowledge of the world is one of the essential qualifications, and that is not always in the possession of a young man. That there are now many directing the Institutions who combine the essential attributes is a gratifying fact. It is a noble calling, the reformation of erring youth, and the value to the community of the results so achieved is beyond estimate.

There comes, then, the question of after care, equally important as treatment during the period of detention. Until the Borstal system became part of the general administration, after care was left to such voluntary associations as the Discharged Prisoners' Aid Society and others which have rendered such signal service to mankind within the limits set to them, but now, after care is on a more regular footing. When a boy is discharged, he is out on licence to the Borstal Association for a year after the full term of his sentence has expired, liable to have his licence revoked and sent to the Boys' Section at Wandsworth Prison in the event of his not fulfilling the conditions imposed upon him. During this first period of his freedom he is rendered assistance in a variety of ways by the local Associate. It is a system which certainly has a remarkable record of success to its credit. It yet has its failures, which are carefully studied by those who are interested in reducing them. The causes of failure, after we have discounted those who would fail, whatever system was employed on their behalf, are various, but it may well be that the sudden transition from detention to freedom is one of the most potent. The change from institutional life to ordinary conditions outside is indeed an abrupt one. This circumstance has, of course, been taken into consideration by the authorities concerned, and experiments are now being tried out with those who are due to be discharged in a few weeks' time by endeavouring to approximate as far as possible conditions inside the Institution during the final stages of his training, to conditions outside. But

277

here we are met with an insoluble difficulty. There are certain conditions inside the Institution which are completely dissimilar to those outside, and which, try as you may, cannot be eliminated. The first is the boy's constant association with a large number of cheerful companions in not altogether unpleasant surroundings. Many ex-Borstal boys complain of loneliness and even of nostalgia on regaining their freedom. The second is the perpetual and careful supervision exercised over him by those responsible for his reclamation. The Associate cannot possibly maintain the same superintendence over his goings in and his comings out which he experienced while he was in the Institution. The third is regular employment, with no danger of unemployment, which cannot be guaranteed to him when he goes out into the great world. The fourth is his complete immunity from all gambling, prostitutes, and a variety of the temptations which he encounters the moment that he leaves. The new-found freedom to indulge in amenities, whether wholesome or unwholesome, certainly all of them expensive, often induces the boy to steal in order to afford their enjoyment. We cannot then resist the conclusion that it is not possible inside the Institution to prepare boys adequately for the disconcerting contrast which their enlargement will present. Would it not be legitimate to canvass the idea of making some better provision against this abrupt change of circumstances which he experiences when he leaves the Institution? Would it not be possible to establish for these boys a buffer state in between prison and freedom? I have already spoken of one of the dangers of the three years' sentence. Could not this alone be obviated by assigning for them in the first instance a shorter period of more intensified training in the Institution? The "buffer state" might be made in some fashion to resemble camp life, always a wholesome influence with boys ; their employment would be principally upon works of public utility, not necessarily in juxtaposition to the camp, and they would be brought as much as possible into contact with other of their fellow creatures and with normal conditions outside, with all the paraphernalia of wages, insurance and other incidents of an ordinary citizen's life. Home leave might be liberally conceded.

I have also mentioned the discovery that prison for the young is the worst of all expedients and the most unlikely to effect a cure, and that the boys' acquaintance with it should be postponed until all the other numerous devices have been tried. The preferable alternatives now in operation are the Home Office schools, which are the modern development of the old reformatories, the system of probation, the Borstal Institutions already mentioned, the age limit of which has been raised three years, and the appropriate homes which are to-day provided for those on remand. But it does not always happen that a persistent young offender necessarily goes through all or any of these processes. Youths under twenty-one are still sent to prison, and it yet remains in the discretion of the Court to decide upon the destination which is considered most appropriate to each individual case.

While everyone is agreed that prison should be the last resource, it must be understood that the alternatives are still in an experimental stage, and that statistics regarding them are not in every case encouraging. It cannot be denied that all these new experiments have not succeeded, or that they have succeeded with some individuals and failed with others. But, as in scientific experiments so with these—you have to persevere by trial and error until a satisfactory result is obtained. I am inclined to think that progress is being unnecessarily delayed by a reluctance to discard or modify any of the new expedients which have failed for fear of incurring the reproach that such a step would appear to be reactionary. There can be no greater misconception. To demolish what is defective or unsuccessful is not a reactionary process. If, for instance, we have come to the conclusion that raising the age of the children's court has not decreased crime and that boys of between sixteen and seventeen merely hold its procedure in contempt, there is nothing reactionary in rescinding such a provision. I see no merit in failure even if your system that fails is in its nature progressive. Because an advance in one direction fails to lead to the desired objective that does not mean that we need retreat back to where we started and remain there disconsolate. We may still advance, although to another point of the compass, and that we shall probably discover to be our most prudent course.

Finally there are the numerous discoveries as to the conduct of the institutions which deal with juvenile delinquency. Fresh discoveries of this description are constantly being made. The systems are not static. By long experience and patient investigation definite guiding principles are being evolved. The crude and ill-informed criticisms which are still levelled at the Borstal system from various quarters are for the most part either manifestly out of date and refer to errors made perhaps twenty-five years ago and which have long since been rectified, or are devoid of any connection with established facts. No one who has not had a constant association with these Institutions can perhaps fully appreciate how silly and obsolete these criticisms are.

Before quitting the subject of juvenile deliquency some reference must be made to the controversy which has recently arisen in the Press and elsewhere on its apparent increase. There may be some justification for a

suspicion in the minds of those who have but a superficial knowledge of the working of the new systems that
this increase may be traced to their operation. But due
reflection, I think, will dispel these misgivings. While
no one claims that all the new experiments have yet
justified themselves or that they are infallible, and while
it may be true that a very small proportion of this
increase is in some measure attributable to certain experiments which have failed, there can be little doubt that if
we discarded all the new methods and reverted to that
age of moral obliquity treated of in the second chapter,
juvenile crime would increase by leaps and bounds. No
one could with reason maintain that all the latest develop-
ments in our social life accrue exclusively to the benefit of
the race. We must investigate them with impartiality
to determine if they have contributed to the increase of
crime among youthful citizens.

While in the second chapter I invited the reader to
examine the causes which operated to increase crime in
the eighteenth century, many of which have now been
eliminated, I would equally invite the reader to examine
a new set of causes which operate to increase crime in the
twentieth. One of these new causes is undoubtedly the
fact that the amenities of life have prodigiously increased,
and a much larger section of the community with indeed
some degree of justification regards it as a right to share
in those amenities. But they are expensive, and while
wages have not increased in the same proportion the
wage-earner nevertheless demands an increasing partici-
pation in their enjoyment. If the wherewithal to pay for
their share cannot be met entirely out of honestly earned
wages there is a great temptation to increase purchasing
power by less legitimate means. A youth steals a bicycle
and sells it for a few shillings. He does not steal for the
sake of stealing ; he does not steal the bicycle for its use

as a bicycle. He is in need of a few shillings to indulge his taste in amusements, either legitimate or illegitimate. While there is nothing new in such a crime or such an object for a crime the temptation is far more potent to-day than when there were fewer occasions to spend money in the pursuit of pleasures. Although this consideration might appear to conflict with an earlier statement I have made to the effect that the increase of amenities should save youth from crime, I believe that fairer wages should readjust the balance of my argument.

Let us adduce the analogy of Jack Sheppard once again. Had he and Edgeworth Bess lived in the twentieth century instead of the eighteenth the temptations presented to both would have been infinitely more expensive although no doubt infinitely more respectable. The " flash-house " in all probability supplied quite sufficient needs for their entertainment. There are no " flash-houses " to-day, and if there were they would merely form one item in the daily round of social amenities. Edgeworth Bess, had she lived in our own times, would have required her lover to take her to the cinema or to a dance hall several times a week, and in the holidays to Southend. If Jack Sheppard failed to-day to take advantage of the many opportunities for reform and had remained an idle apprentice, which I still reserve to myself the right to doubt, there would have been even more pressing necessity than there was of old for him to rob his employer's till.

I believe this to be a very widespread cause of the present increase of crime among adolescents. Another tributary flowing into the main stream of causes is a noticeable decrease of parental control and parental responsibility. In this connection there is reason to suppose the new methods of treatment have not acted favourably. They certainly tend to relieve the parent of responsibility, but that is not the whole story. In all ranks of society, even in those where the State's interference is negligible, there is a very appreciable decline of parental control and a consequent increase of independence in the young of both sexes. It is a matter of controversy as to what this phenomenon is due. Some will contend that it is one of the aftermaths of the Great War, during which the younger generation, having had more responsibility thrown on its shoulders than ever before and less control at home, shook itself free from the shackles of convention and claimed the right to think and to act on its own initiative, and to take nothing for granted. Whatever the reason, the younger generation is more independent than ever before, and this freedom has its detrimental aspect in being one of the contributory factors to the increase of juvenile crime. I would add that, in this connection, I have, for many years, been afforded the opportunity of examining the officially compiled histories of Borstal boys. As a result of these researches I am impressed with the high percentage of these boys whose parentage is defective—either the marriage tie does not exist at all or is so loose as to demoralize the household, a severe commentary on a growing social evil.

Unemployment, which has never appeared in so devastating a form or upon so extensive a scale as during the last decade of our domestic history, must be held in part accountable for the same phenomenon. While its share in the responsibility is unquestionable it has exercised a detrimental influence in various ways, some obvious and some insidious. Unemployment rarely fails to produce in a young man who genuinely wants to work an anti-social complex. Disillusioned, he protests that there must be something defective in a system which deprives him of one of the most elementary rights of citizenship, the right to labour for his own living and for the good of the community. As a result he ceases to regard himself as under any obligation to society in general or to the laws imposed by it. He may not think the matter out in so logical or so definite a form, but these are his subconscious promptings which move him to disregard those restrictions to which under normal conditions he would willingly submit.

Then there is the disastrous and sometimes permanent effect of unemployment that is produced upon those youths who from the time they leave school have never been in work, or who have been so infrequently employed that they have had neither sufficient occasion nor opportunity to acquire habits of industry and self-discipline. They are perhaps the most vulnerable when assailed by the overwhelming temptations of an aimless existence.

Not the least deleterious effect is the general depression of spirits and even in some cases the detriment to health produced by enforced idleness, which leaves the sufferer with none too much strength to resist temptations which under healthier conditions he would have no difficulty in subduing.

Finally there is the mechanical contrivance which seems to have become almost part and parcel of human existence and to which has been attributed a share of the malignant influences operating upon the behaviour of our youth to-day. Its intrusion upon our daily lives is almost universal. There is hardly a by-street in any city of the world where it fails to hold a very distorting mirror up to nature. It is true that a number of reformers whose enthusiasm outruns their discretion, indict the cinema as responsible for the recent disturbing increase of depravity in the adolescent. But the probabilities are that its influence either for good or for ill is unconscionably exaggerated. Although I may be ranging myself against the experts in psychology I remain sceptical of its power. I am well aware, from personal experience, that many young men who find themselves in the police court are only too ready, when given any encouragement, to impute the blame for their predicament to the Hollywood hierarchy, but they are usually of the type that is prepared to trace it to anyone, or to anything rather than to the true source and origin, namely, their own innate selfishness. I would certainly always favour a most sedulous supervision being exercised by a censoring authority over the abominations that reach us from American film studios, so that it may be assured that any corrupting constituents should be completely eliminated, but I am still of the opinion that it is not reasonable to contend that the cinema has occasioned any very considerable decline of moral standards in the young.

I have endeavoured to enumerate and to analyse the various causes, some potent and others less so, to account for a phenomenon which must give those who have the future welfare of the nation at heart, grave concern. We observe that as we eliminate one cause of crime too often another appears in its stead from an unsuspected source, but at least to-day we have an alert and vigilant administration ever watchful against these spiritual enemies of youth, and alert to devise expedients by which their evil influence may be counteracted.

But there is a broader side to the question, one so highly controversial that it needs considerable temerity even to refer to it in the vaguest terms. The education of youth in this country is tending to become increasingly materialistic. The influence of religion in schools is daily declining. I am well aware that to make sweeping generalizations to the effect that the Churches have lost their hold upon the community is to challenge the question as to what precisely is meant by such an expression of view. In this country there are many religious denominations. The various churches exercise influence in various ways and in varying degrees in various parts of the British Isles. A generalization that might accurately apply to the home counties would be totally inappropriate for Wales or the North of England. Equally, where one religious sect has failed another has succeeded.

I suppose, that in the aggregate the religious-minded members of the community can be divided between those who accept authority and tradition unquestioned, and whose institutions cannot be modified or changed, and those who have much wider latitude in their choice of what they will accept and what they will not, and whose religious views have become so broad, so abstract and so unorthodox, they are scarcely intelligible views at all. It is the children of the latter who form the large majority of the school population, but taking all sides of the problem into due consideration there can be no doubt whatever that spiritual influences have failed to keep pace with the exigencies of a rapid industrial development, and that the religious side of the education of youth in this country is swiftly being superseded by a purely utilitarian and mundane training. A very large percentage of teachers in the state-aided schools no doubt console themselves with the reflection that it is possible to inculcate a high ethical standard in the young without the aid or the basis of any dogmatic religious teaching, although statistics, whatever their value may be to anyone else, are certainly not conspicuously on their side. Twenty-six per cent. of the indictable offences in the year 1935 were committed by persons under seventeen years of age. A percentage of these doubtless passed through the Church Schools, but this distressing evidence of juvenile depravity hardly goes to prove that the youth of to-day is absorbing high ethical standards through the medium of rationalistic teaching. Others will assure us that it is quite fallacious to imagine that adequate religious instruction is not given in Council Schools. In reply I range myself on the side of those who hold that a perfunctory Bible reading conducted by those who but for an inadequate course at a normal college or elsewhere have no specific qualification to teach religion, or by those definitely hostile to religion, is at its best a waste of time and at its worst merely a source of bewilderment to the pupil. In any case, the ignorance about all matters religious displayed by the average youth educated at any of the elementary Council Schools of the Metropolis is truly remarkable and authorizes us to question the conviction of those who persuade themselves that there is any religious instruction given to them which is of efficacy or value.

Some well-intentioned persons are under what I regard as an illusion that the voluntary associations can take the place of or can at any rate supplement the Churches and the Schools in the function of religious instruction, and advocate that services should be habitually held in clubs, community centres, and other headquarters of social or athletic activities. But this leaves out of account the fact that voluntary associations cannot undertake the essential religious instruction. Moreover, many of them are undenominational, and many of them are exclusively recreative and athletic, and their staffs and daily activities are inappropriate for the purpose. I should have thought that the Churches are the proper places for religious services, the clergy of all denominations the proper teachers of religion, and, failing facilities for instruction in the home, admittedly the most desirable seminary for that purpose, the class-room the proper place for its instruction. Unless a youth has been properly grounded in religion by those best qualified to instruct, a religious service will not have very much significance for him, and the fact that it is held in his club instead of, more appropriately, in a Church, will not aid him to understand what he is doing and saying. The most that the voluntary associations can do on the spiritual side, always agreed that " stunts " and hysterical revivals are valueless, is to set a high ideal before youth to which youth will inevitably respond if some spiritual training has been previously inculcated, but the majority of the youth of this country are being brought up without religion of any kind. Whatever else the effect may be of this prevalent indifference to things spiritual, I say without scruple or hesitation that I believe this to be one of the causes of the increase of juvenile crime.

The Churches are for ever animadverting upon the want of religious zeal in the youth of the country to-day. How far this estimate can be substantiated it is not easy to determine. It is fair to suggest, however, that the average youth of to-day takes nothing for granted, refuses to submit to any restraint which he feels is of no concrete value to himself, and that he finds religious practices for the most part unattractive, anachronistic and monotonous. There is in fact a general insurgence amongst the new generation against customs and practices that are considered inappropriate to the exigences of the modern fashion of living. But is the matter just to rest there ? Is it really the case that youth to-day is exclusively material in his make-up. Does this frigid latitudinarianism provide for all his spiritual necessities ? Is it religion or is it certain institutions of religion that he discards ? Not long since there was a sufficiently strong recognition in the Established Church of the failure of institutionalism to meet modern needs for the promotion of legislation to revise its 300-year-old prayer book. It may well be that if some anxiety were evinced to adjust religious practices rather more to contemporary needs and predilections a ready response would be evoked. It is a significant fact that in the fold of the Established Church recent statistics demonstrate that while there has been a considerable decrease in attendance at Matins there has been a considerable increase in the number of communicants.

I refuse to believe that youth to-day is purely materialistic in its outlook. But is there no alternative for the rising generation than the religious teaching of our fathers and the bleak materialism of Herbert Spencer and John Stuart Mill? Surely somewhere between these two extremes stretches a golden road for youth to tread.

There remains to be discussed the most baffling of the whole range of problems relating to the treatment of the criminal, one which was not seriously negotiated with until recent years and which to a large extent even now frustrates the ingenuity of the expert—that of the persistent and hardened offender. To remove as far as possible the main causes of crime and to save the novice from developing into a systematic criminal both serve to reduce the problem to reasonable proportions, but we may be sure that we shall never eliminate it altogether. The persistent offender will always be with us, a burden to himself and the community which must be protected from his anti-social conduct.

In the first instance there is, apart from the young men who are still sent to prison who ought not to go there, an intermediate type between the young offender and the hardened criminal—one whose case is inappropriate for a Borstal sentence but who are sufficiently malleable for a modified Borstal treatment in the prison for which they are sent. The Commissioners have exercised a considerable amount of ingenuity with a considerable degree of success in their case, but compared with that of the persistent *old* offender it is one which presents no very formidable difficulty.

As to the treatment of the persistent old offender, for a proper investigation we must retrace our steps to the commencement of the previous century. The failure of Sir George Grey's scheme of the enforced emigration of released convicts in whom a cure was presumed to have been effected has been noted in a previous chapter. It has also been recorded how his ticket-of-leave system failed owing to the fact that there was not sufficient supervision exercised over these enlarged convicts. We have also noted how Committee after Committee on prison discipline sat and deliberated with little success in securing general uniformity in the conduct of British prisons. But it must not be inferred that Sir George Grey's long administration at the Home Office produced no tangible results. That would be doing less than justice to this quiet, unassuming individual who had no other ambition than to leave his country better than he found it and in particular to improve the prison administration. He belongs to that long line of modest public men who sacrificed so much for their fellow-citizens without recognition or recompense and who surely deserve to be commemorated in more generous measure by posterity than a certain meretricious order of individual which seems to establish a stronger hold upon the imagination of mankind.

Until Lord John Russell, one of the few Prime Ministers who had hitherto concerned himself with the problems of crime and its cure, appointed Sir George Grey as Home Secretary it was hardly to be supposed that Government which had failed quite completely to appreciate the claims of youth upon its solicitude would be likely to find a specific which would cure the old offender of his persistent transgression. But when Sir George Grey entered upon office the executive was at length aroused to some sense of its responsibility. To his credit, among other salutary amendments of the criminal code, stands the Convict Discipline Bill, which substituted for transportation abroad the employment of convicts upon public works at home.

It would be a tedious process to follow the gradual, the very gradual, development of those methods which have improved the convict prisons in this country and have opened up some prospect of amendment to the hardened criminal, but a few general words in summary may be set before the reader.

When the control of all the prisons of this country passed into the hands of the Commissioners there was initiated that long series of administrative reforms which continues to be supplemented to this day. Difficult as the problem of the persistent offender always has been, and still remains, gradually methods are being evolved which although they cannot be expected to provide an infallible solution have certainly done much to break the spell of despondency and resignation which holds him in its thrall.

The first edition of penal servitude was probably not sufficiently deterrent. That was the official view at the time of its adoption. Accordingly sentences were lengthened, dietaries were diminished and the mark system, the outcome of Sir Joshua Jebb's progressive stage principle, was introduced, by which every convict was enabled to earn remission by his individual industry. It was not, however, until the year 1880, after Lord Kimberley's Commission had reported, that there was any real attempt to segregate from each other those versed in crime, first offenders and those yet presumed innocent. At that date was introduced the formation of a special class dissociated from the hardened veteran in crime. Apprehension, however, existed in the mind of the public that individual attention to the prisoner was being prejudiced by the over-emphasis upon uniformity. A Committee of Inquiry reported that prisoners were treated as worthless and hopeless. The result was the Prison Act of 1898 by which the Secretary of State was empowered to make rules for the administration of the prisons and a triple division of offenders was instituted.

Although the Act of 1898 laid greater stress upon the necessity of segregation there was still far too much imprisonment for misconduct which cannot be categorized as criminal, for example breaches of municipal by-laws and regulations. In the nineties as a result there were fifty-six local prisons.

In 1904 there was a new classification instituted, the Star Class, the intermediate who had not necessarily offended before but who were considered for various reasons unsatisfactory, and the recidivist.

But it is perhaps in the last twenty-five years that the most important changes have taken place. Apart from the supremely important remedial measures dealing with the young offender already alluded to, that period was responsible for the introduction of the Prevention of Crime Act 1908 which created the system of preventive detention and the Criminal Justice Act of 1914 which has more than any other act solved the problem of the habitual offender.

An extract from the Commissioners' annual report for 1922–3 best describes the new spirit actuating those who administer our prison system:

It is not to make prison pleasant, but to construct a system of training such as will fit the prisoner to re-enter the world as a citizen. To this end the first requisite is greater activity of mind and body and the creation of habits of sustained industry. Longer hours of work are therefore the first item in our programme. Next comes the removal of any features of unnecessary degradation in prison life and the promotion of self-respect and education on broad lines calculated to arouse some intelligent interest and to raise the mind out of a sordid circle of selfish broodings. Finally we endeavour to awaken some sense of personal responsibility by the gradual and cautious introduction of methods of limited trust. Each separate measure is a part of the whole scheme.

Owing to these enlightened methods, together with the probation system, the new Act dealing with the payment of fines, the raising of the age of committal to prison, the decrease of drunkenness and the riddance from the prisons of the feeble-minded, the prison population has so much decreased that the number of local prisons has fallen from fifty-six in 1910 to twenty-six to-day, and the annual receptions during the same period have decreased to a third of the original number.

Classification, the most important consideration of all, is now carried out on the most rational principle. The establishment of the Borstal Institutions is the most conspicuous example of successful classification. Not only does the Borstal system connote the segregation of young offenders from the hardened, but each of the seven institutions for boys is classified for different types of lad. Difficult as classification is in prison itself, Wormwood Scrubbs on the adult side has been reserved since 1925 for star class prisoners from the Metropolitan area, Wakefield since 1923 for selected prisoners from the Midlands and North, and Chelmsford since 1931 for younger convicts up to the age of thirty. Young recidivists between the ages of twenty-one and twenty-five now form a special class at all local prisons. All male prisoners from sixteen to twenty-one with sentences over one month are now collected and treated at six collecting centres, but it is to be hoped that the time is not far distant when no youth under 21 will see the inside of a prison wall.

In taking a survey of this long and painful history of the treatment of the criminal in England, which I have epitomized all too inadequately, certain of its features stand out clear cut and conspicuous. It is abundantly evident that until comparatively recent times the State failed to regard it as a primary obligation of government to interfere either with the conditions that made the criminal or to exercise any vigilance over the administration of institutions which provided for the criminal when he was made. It is also obvious that until comparatively recent times public interest failed to be aroused in those measures of social improvement which now form the staple ingredients of our domestic legislation.

This callous indifference of government to so essential a service can be attributed to the fact that during the period of which this work treats its personnel was recruited from what used not inaptly to be termed the governing classes, who were completely out of touch with and ignorant of the conditions in which the so-called lower orders lived and had their being. The " governing classes " monopolized the wealth of the nation and consequently the amenities of life. Patrician and plebeian lived a completely separate existence. The contrast presented between the two was so striking, the difference of circumstances between the opulent and the indigent was so much to the advantage of the former and so little to the profit of the latter that it is difficult to appreciate why those who toiled did not take the initiative earlier than they did and assail a system by which the fruits of their labour were almost a complete monopoly of those who employed them.

This phenomenon can only be accounted for by the fact that the abject condition of ignorance in which they were retained rendered them incapable of developing their critical faculties. Nor was it the statesmen and the politicians who were instrumental in inaugurating any change for the better or in breaking down the barriers which concealed from their view the execrable conditions which the great mass of the people were compelled to endure. We scan in vain the official reports for evidence that Parliament exhibited any symptoms of taking a lively interest in the welfare of the working population. The statesmen of the eighteenth century were serenely established upon Olympian heights above the clouds that obscured the struggling world beneath them. In the Senate the palm, as it often does to-day, went to the dialectician and the orator who, for all their elaborate periods and skill in the tourney of debate, achieved far less of benefit to their fellow-beings than those who unostentatiously went about the work of human regeneration. The whole scheme of government in those days was based upon a narrow and inadequate conception of the requirements of a rapidly developing industrial people.

While we have seen that the reformers, most of whom were drawn from the upper classes, did much to draw the attention of government to the need for drastic action, it is doubtful if they could have effected any abiding reform unless public resentment had been aroused. The Churches during the eighteenth century were for the most part too stagnant, too barren in resource or, where enthusiastic, too much occupied with theological controversy to take a leading part in social reform. They misread the signs in the heavens. Even in the nineteenth century a famous divine confessed that he regarded the poor as fit objects for compassion and benevolence. Presumably he conceived that they had been brought into this world for the express purpose of giving to the rich the satisfaction of salving their consciences with the dispensing of charity to the poor. It never seemed to have occurred for one moment to disciples of this particular school of thought that the objects of their misplaced and futile benevolence were citizens claiming equal rights with their wealthier fellows, that their dependence upon the patronage and condescension of others was no solution but rather an aggravation of their miserable lot in life. To be merely the recipients of charitable distribution and the commiseration of the well to do was not the rôle the average decent working man had any wish to affect. Until better relations could be established between capital and labour, until there was co-operation between class and class, until there was some assurance given to the worker that he would be entitled to claim his proper share of the profits of his labour, until it could be realized that independence of eleemosynary effort was the goal to be aimed at no fundamental reform could be effected.

While it is difficult to assess the comparative value of contributions made towards reform, it was unquestionably the novelists of the Victorian era that first made the well-to-do public familiar with the conditions in which the poor lived, and who roused both governors and governed to a sense of their respective responsibilities and mutual obligations.

Then the Press emerged into the field, and by those somewhat sensational methods which may not have proved edifying to the fastidious, at least achieved the desirable result of bringing into focus and riveting public attention upon those social evils that were rapidly making us a reproach to the whole world. Reform by this means became the main preoccupation of the philanthropist and the dominant issue in Parliament. The survey undertaken by Charles Booth and his collaborators made a very wide public familiar with circumstances which had hitherto been hidden under a bushel. The immediate effect was an outbreak of charity, a great deal of it indiscriminate, most of it detrimental, on the part of ignorant but well-meaning persons whose nerves had been played upon and whose emotions had been excited by these disturbing revelations. This unbalancing of popular judgment was redressed by the liberalizing study and excellent leadership of the universities which, although the tangible results of their schemes may not have been commensurate with the enthusiasm which they inspired, certainly directed men's minds into the right and proper channels. The conclusions to which they were drawn were in the first place that charity was not the cure for these organic social evils, and that regeneration could only be accomplished by altering the conditions of living and by the enrichment of the drab lives of the working classes. By degrees the greatest discovery of all was made, namely, that the vast majority of those who had hitherto been classified as criminals were nothing of the sort, and that many who had lived evil lives were not so guilty as those responsible for the terrible conditions in which they lived, and with this discovery there was revealed the all-important fact that the needs and necessities of the youth of the nation must be the first responsibility of government.

Reform followed reform in prison administration as the new ideas possessed the imaginations and directed the energies of those charged with the responsibility. We witness to-day a revolution so complete in the treatment of the young offender that misgivings have arisen as to the effect of experiments which in the view of some critics err on the side of leniency. A very plausible argument is often advanced that so much effort and attention is being bestowed upon the malefactor as to place him in a position of advantage over those " just persons that need no repentance." Very little reflection will serve to dispel such an illusion. What is the alternative? Is it suggested we should return to the old unregenerate methods described in the earlier chapters of this work? Are the refining and restoring influences of the new system to be denied to the young offender in order that those who have been better endowed physically and intellectually should have a monopoly of human assets? If it is valid to take exception to the solicitude which is now being exercised in strengthening the weakest link in the chain then the whole system of education must come under review. An exact analogy can be adduced from every description of educational establishment. Surely it is a mere waste of time for a teacher to devote attention to a pupil who sails up to the head place in the school without effort on his part or assistance from any other human agency. The instructor would be better advised to confine his ministrations to those who need them, and the community will be the richer for his discretion. By the same token it is of supreme importance to the community itself that no effort should be spared upon the reclamation of the young offender. There can be no more dominant concern of government in the sphere of domestic administration than the eradication of crime. How egregiously our forbears failed to appreciate its significance it has been the purpose of these pages to demonstrate. How vital it is that the new methods should continue to be discriminately exercised and developed by those in whose hands authority is wielded, it has been the intention of the author to suggest.

The conditions are eminently favourable. The young man's way has been cleansed of much that made his journey through the world hazardous and insecure. His life has been enriched with opportunities designed to assist him in appreciating whatever is lovely and of good report and of discarding what is evil. His moral sense has been quickened and his spiritual necessities relieved by beneficent influences brought to bear upon him from his earliest hours. There is a finer adjustment of the balance of interests between class and class, employer and employed, governors and subjects, which effects a closer co-operation among all men for the common weal. There is far less hypocrisy and cant in the attitude of society towards its erring members who no longer are regarded as pariahs outside the pale of human sympathy, but rather as fit subjects for the regenerating process to which so many favourably react.

THE END

INDEX